Photography

Photography: A Critical Introduction was the first introductory textbook to examine key debates in photographic theory and place them in their social and political contexts, and is now established as one of the leading textbooks in its field. Written especially for students in further and higher education and for introductory college courses, this fully revised edition provides a coherent introduction to the nature of photographic seeing.

Individual chapters cover:
- Key debates in photographic theory and history
- Documentary photography and photojournalism
- Personal and popular photography
- Photography and the human body
- Photography and commodity culture
- Photography as art.

This revised and updated fifth edition includes:

- New case studies on topics such as: materialism and embodiment, the commodification of human experience, and an extended discussion of landscape as genre.
- 99 photographs and images, featuring work from: Bill Brandt, Susan Derges, Rineke Dijkstra, Fran Herbello, Hannah Höch, Karen Knorr, Dorothea Lange, Chrystel Lebas, Susan Meiselas, Lee Miller, Martin Parr, Ingrid Pollard, Jacob Riis, Alexander Rodchenko, Andres Serrano, Cindy Sherman and Jeff Wall.
- Fully updated resource information, including guides to public archives and useful websites.
- A full glossary of terms and a comprehensive bibliography.

Liz Wells is Professor in Photographic Culture in the Faculty of Arts, Plymouth University.

Contributors: Michelle Henning, Patricia Holland, Derrick Price, Anandi Ramamurthy and Liz Wells.

Praise for previous editions:

'A brilliantly designed book. It provides a much-needed conceptual perspective, so lacking in other histories of photography, and with the new material on photojournalism [the book] is even stronger.

Ulrich Keller, University of California at Santa Barbara

'Bravo to Liz Wells for putting together such a comprehensive critical introduction. Lucid, smart and well illustrated, this will be a "must read" for every serious student of the medium.'

Deborah Bright, Professor of Photography and Art History, Rhode Island School of Design

'An essential purchase. It raises awareness of the main contemporary issues related to photographic practice.'

Howard Riley, Swansea Institute of Higher Education

'A timely revision of a great book. It is invaluable in setting the stage for critical research in photography. . . . A substantial contribution to the critical study of photography.'

Professor Lynne Bentley-Kemp, Rochester Institute of Technology

'Precisely the kind of book I have been yearning to see appear for a long time. Carefully structured, it fulfils the need for a critical theory text for FE, HE and introductory college courses.'

Nicky West, University of Northumbria at Newcastle

'Ideal for stimulating discussions on the critical use of photographic images and their evaluation. It is ideal for teaching this part of my BTEC Media and BTEC Art and Design courses.'

Ken Absalom, Gwent Tertiary College

'Well structured – each chapter is thorough and relevant. The quality of the finish is superb – lovely photos and good use of margin notes.'

Richard Swales, Roade School, Northampton

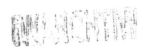

Photography
A Critical Introduction

Fifth Edition

EDITED BY LIZ WELLS

Routledge
Taylor & Francis Group

LONDON AND NEW YORK

This fifth edition published 2015
by Routledge
2 Park Square, Milton Park, Abingdon, Oxon OX14 4RN

and by Routledge
711 Third Avenue, New York, NY 10017

*Routledge is an imprint of the Taylor & Francis Group,
an informa business*

First edition published by Routledge 1996

Fourth edition published by Routledge 2009

Trademark notice: Product or corporate names may be
trademarks or registered trademarks, and are used only for
identification and explanation without intent to infringe.

British Library Cataloguing in Publication Data
A catalogue record for this book is available from the British
Library

Library of Congress Cataloging in Publication Data
Photography : a critical introduction / edited by Liz Wells. –
    Fifth edition.
    pages cm
    Includes bibliographical references and index.
    1. Photography. I. Wells, Liz, 1948–
    TR145.P48 2015
    770–dc23
    2014031957

ISBN: (hbk) 978–0–415–85428–3
ISBN: (pbk) 978–0–415–85429–0
ISBN: (ebk) 978–1–315–72737–0

Typeset in Bembo and Frutiger by
Florence Production Ltd, Stoodleigh, Devon, UK
Printed by Bell & Bain Ltd, Glasgow

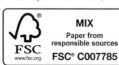

FSC
www.fsc.org

MIX
Paper from
responsible sources
FSC® C007785

Contents

Contributors

Michelle Henning is Senior Lecturer in Media Studies, specialising in Photography and Visual Culture in the School of Art, Design and Media at the University of Brighton (since 2013). She also holds the post of Senior Visiting Research Fellow in the Digital Cultures Research Centre at the University of the West of England, where she was Associate Professor in Media and Culture until 2013. She is the author of *Museums, Media and Cultural Theory* (Routledge 2006) *Museum Media* (Blackwell 2014) and numerous essays on photography, museums, digital culture, media history and cultural theory. She also works as an artist and photographer.

Patricia Holland is a writer, lecturer and researcher specialising in television, photography and popular imagery. Her interest in domestic photography and popular imagery goes back to the 1980s, when she collaborated with photographer Jo Spence to produce *Family Snaps: The Meanings of Domestic Photography* (Virago 1991). She is also the author of *Picturing Childhood* (I.B. Tauris 2006). She has contributed to several Readers on photography, television and cultural studies and is the author of *The Angry Buzz: 'This Week' and Current Affairs Television* (I.B.Tauris 2006) and *Broadcasting and the NHS in the Thatcherite 1980s: The Challenge to Public Service* (Palgrave Macmillan 2013).

Derrick Price is a writer who has published extensively on photography, landscape and visual culture. He worked for many years in arts education, most recently as Associate Dean of the Faculty of Art, Media and Design at the University of the West of England. An active participant in cultural projects he is a member of the Board of Management of Ffotogallery, Cardiff, and Chair of the Council of Management, Watershed Media Centre, Bristol. He is currently writing a book on the landscape and culture of industrial South Wales.

Anandi Ramamurthy is Senior Lecturer in Media and Cultural Studies, University of Central Lancashire where she teaches on BA Film and Media and MA Photography in the School of Journalism and Media. She is the author of *Imperial Persuaders: Images of Africa and Asian in British Advertising* (Manchester University Press 2003) and *Black Star: Britain's Asian Youth Movements* (Pluto 2013). She is co-editor of *Visual Culture in Britain at the End of Empire* (Ashgate 2006) and *Colonial Advertising and Commodity Racism* (Lit Verlag 2013). She is the founder of www.tandana.org, a web-based archive of visual ephemera relating to the Asian Youth Movements in Britain.

Liz Wells is Professor in Photographic Culture, Faculty of Arts and Humanities, Plymouth University, UK. Publications on landscape include *Land Matters, Landscape Photography, Culture and Identity* (2011). She edited *The Photography Reader* (2003), and is a co-editor for *photographies*, Routledge journals. She has contributed numerous essays on people and place to photographers' monographs and exhibition catalogues. Recent exhibitions as curator include *Light Touch* (Maryland Arts Place for Baltimore Washington International Airport, Feb–June 2014); *FUTURELAND NOW* (Laing Gallery, Newcastle, Sept 2012–Jan 2013); *Sense of Place, European Landscape Photography* (BOZAR, Brussels, June–Sept 2012); *Landscapes of Exploration*, recent British art from Antarctica (UK venues: Plymouth, Feb–Mar 2012; Cambridge, Oct–Nov 2013; Bournemouth, Jan–Feb 2015).

Editor's preface

This book aimed to remedy the absence of a good, coherent introduction to issues in photography theory, and resulted from the frustrations of teaching without the benefit of a succinct introductory textbook. There were a number of published histories of photography which defined the field according to various agendas, although almost invariably with an emphasis upon great photographers, historically and now. Fewer publications critically engaged with debates about the nature of photographic seeing. Most were collections of essays pitched at a level that assumed familiarity with contemporary cultural issues and debates which students new to this field of enquiry may not yet have had.

The genesis of this book was complex. The first edition resulted initially from a discussion between myself and Rebecca Barden, then Media editor at Routledge, in which she solicited suggestions for publications which would support the current curriculum. Responding subsequently to her invitation to put forward a developed book proposal, two factors were immediately clear: first, that the attempt to be relatively comprehensive could best be tackled through a collective approach. Thus, a team of writers was assembled right from the start of the project. Second, it quickly became apparent that the project was, in effect, impossible. Photography is ubiquitous. As a result, there are no clear boundaries. It follows that there cannot be precise agreement as to what a 'comprehensive' introduction and overview should encompass, prioritise or exclude. After much consideration, we focused on issues and areas of practice that, given our experience as lecturers in a number of different UK university institutions, we knew feature frequently. That we worked to a large extent in relation to an established curriculum did not mean that the project has been either straightforward or easy. On the contrary, the intention to introduce and explore issues reasonably fully, taking account of what critics have had to say on various aspects of photographic practices, involved investigating and drawing upon a wide and diverse range of resources.

The overall response to the first edition was positive. Comments included some useful suggestions, many of which we incorporated within the second, revised edition which, in response to feedback, included a new chapter on the body in photography. This chapter, taken as a whole, stands as an example of the range of debates that may become engaged when the content or subject matter of images is taken as a starting point. In this respect it contrasts in particular with chapters 2 and 6, in which the focus is on a specific genre, or an arena, of practice. The third edition was updated and included colour plates. It was translated and published in Greek in 2008. The fourth edition was further amended and incorporated colour illustrations throughout. A Chinese version was published in 2012.

More radically, in this fifth edition we have dropped the final chapter. When we first planned the book there were key debates raging as to the import, impact and likely future developments for the digital in photography. These debates questioned some of what had previously been taken for granted in photographic documentation. Previous editions have included a final chapter, titled 'Photography in the age of electronic imaging' (intended as a reference to Walter Benjamin's famous article on 'The Work of Art in an Era of Mechanical Reproduction' and, indeed, to debates of the early twentieth century on the social implications of the mass reproduction and circulation of photographic imagery. At the time of our first edition, there were discussions as to the implications of a shift from analogue to digital imaging – for reference, two of the diagrams that illustrated this discussion follow the Glossary in this edition. Now this is past history, the digital is completely integrated within photographic procedures and, more particularly, is no longer a matter of theoretical challenge or debate, although aspects of the virtual, of the centrality of online space continue to pre-occupy. For these reasons – the transcendence of questioning the import of the advent of the digital, along with the realisation that there are many questions to be asked about the social implications of visual media within virtual (global) space – led us to decide to integrate all discussion of the digital within the other chapters with which, at least in editions 3 and 4 of the publication, a considerable degree of overlap had developed.

As editor, further researching this book over the twenty years since the first edition has led to further questions, as well as to engaging discoveries. The tension between looking, thinking, investigation and discovery is one of the pleasures of academic research. Repeatedly revising the book has offered opportunities to revisit and further clarify various points as well as to reflect on recent critical developments in historical research and theoretical engagements. Given the number of publications on photography that have appeared in the last two decades, we have enhanced discussion of further references.

This book aims to be relevant, and of interest, to students of photography, graphics, fine art, art and design history, journalism, media studies, communication and cultural studies. We hope that it proves both useful and enjoyable.

Acknowledgements

This book could not have been produced without the support of a number of people. First and foremost I should like to thank Michelle Henning, Patricia Holland, Derrick Price and Anandi Ramamurthy, without whom the book would not have been possible. I would also like to thank Martin Lister for his key contribution to earlier editions of the book. The project has been a difficult one but nonetheless a happy one, due to the quality of the team which I have had the good fortune to be in a position to assemble. I should like to thank Rebecca Barden for first commissioning this book: in addition, Natalie Foster, Sheni Kruger, Emma Hudson and others at Routledge for their support.

I should like to thank colleagues, especially Kate Isherwood, and students who, over the years and in some instances without realising, have contributed to shaping and developing the project. Needless to state, the book could not have been further developed without this extensive feedback for which we are all very grateful. We would also like to thank staff at various archives for their help in introducing us to their study collections, and, in particular, the many photographers and archivists who have given permission for use of their images as illustrations.

Liz Wells
May 2014

Illustration acknowledgements

We are indebted to the people and archives below for permission to reproduce photographs.

Disclaimer

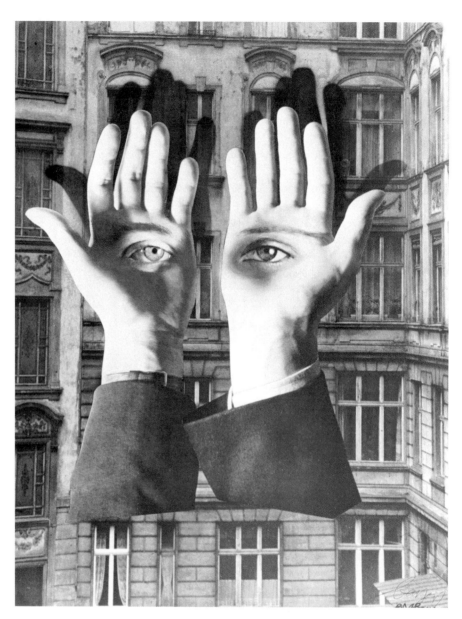

Herbert Bayer, *Lonely Metropolitan*, 1932

Introduction

LIZ WELLS

Introduction

THE PURPOSE OF THIS BOOK

This book introduces and offers an overview of conceptual issues relating to photography and to ways of thinking about photographs. It considers the photograph as an artefact used in a range of different ways and circumstances, and photography as a set of practices that take place in particular contexts. Thus it is essentially about *reading* photographic images rather than about their making. The principal purpose is to introduce key debates, and to indicate sources and resources so students (and other readers) can further develop lines of enquiry relevant to them. The book primarily examines debates and developments in Britain, other parts of Europe and in North America. The perspective is informed by the British base of the team of writers, particularly showing the influence of cultural studies within British academia in the 1990s when the book was first planned. Our writing thus reflects a specific point of departure and context for debates. There is no chronological history. Rather, we discuss past attitudes and understandings, technological limitations and developments, and socio-political contexts through focus on issues pertinent to contemporary practices. In other words, we consider how ideas about photography have developed in relation to the specific focus, or field of practice that forms the theme of each chapter. We cannot render theory easy, but we can contribute to clarifying key issues by pointing to ways in which debates have been framed.

Why study theory? As will become clear, theory informs practice. Essentially there are two choices. You can disregard theoretical debates, taking no account of ways in which images become meaningful, thereby limiting critical understanding and, if you are a photographer, restricting the depth of understanding supporting your own work. The alternative is to engage consciously with questions of photographic meaning in order to develop critical perceptions which can be brought to bear upon photographic practices, historically and now, or upon your own photography.

HOW TO USE THIS BOOK

This book introduces a range of debates pertaining to specific fields of photographic practice. We identify key reading and other resources, in order to illuminate critical debates about photography itself, and to place such debates in relation to broader theoretical and critical discussions. Our aim is to mediate such discussions, indicating key intellectual influences within the debates and alerting you to core reading and other resources. In some instances, our recommendations are highly directive. Thus, we summarise and appraise different critical positions, and point to books and articles in which these positions have been outlined. In most cases the literature which we discuss offers clear priorities and quite explicit points of view in relation to photographic cultures. One part of our task is to draw attention to implicit, underlying assumptions which inform the theoretical stances adopted.

Since the purpose of the book is to introduce issues and ideas that may not yet be familiar, design elements have been incorporated to help. Some chapters include specific case studies that are separated from the main flow of text. This is so that they can be seen in relation to the main argument, but also considered relatively autonomously. Likewise, photographs are sometimes used to illustrate points of discussion. However, images may also be viewed as a specific line of development. In order to facilitate visual connections we have limited the range of topics or genres in each chapter. Thus, for instance, Chapter 2, on documentary practices, concentrates primarily upon street photography. Comparison of images of similar content should help you to see some of the ways in which forms and styles of documentary and photojournalism have changed over time. It should be added that, in order to keep the size (and price) of the book reasonably manageable, we have used fewer photographs than is really desirable in a book about photography. You will need to use other visual sources, books and archives, alongside this book, in order to pursue visual analysis in proper detail.

There is a margin for notes throughout the book. Key references to core reading, and also to archive sources, appear in the margin so you can follow up the issues and ideas which have been introduced. References are repeated in a consolidated bibliography at the end. The margins are also used for technical definitions and for mini-biographies of key theorists. Terms which may be new to you are printed in bold on their first occurrence in each chapter, and there is a glossary at the end of the book. We also list principal magazines and journals published in English, and some key archives.

The book is in six chapters, each of which may be read separately, although there are points of connection between them. We have indicated some of these links between chapters, but it is up to you to think them through in detail. A summary of the principal content of each chapter follows at the end of this introduction. This will help you to map your route through the book.

Over the course of the twenty years of this textbook photography has changed in various respects, with a number of issues slipping off the agenda or reformulated to take into account new socio-political concerns and circumstances, and, indeed, the responses of new generations of photographers, historians and theorists to ways in which previous academic generations framed debates and prioritised particular questions. Shifts have been particularly manifest in ways of thinking about the import and impact of electronic imaging and of virtual space. How the nature of photography has changed remains a matter of research and debate, as does the impact of digitalisation on the whole field of media and communications (Lister *et al.*, 2013) However, over the course of the five editions of this publication, digital technology has become thoroughly assimilated to photography in all areas of practice and online space has become a primary public interface for institutions and individuals. Previous editions included a chapter specifically detailing and addressing developments in electronic imaging as they impacted on photography. Given the integration of the digital across all aspects of photographic practices, such separate address is no longer appropriate or relevant.

Discussion cannot be fully comprehensive. Photographic practices are diverse, and it is not possible to focus upon every possible issue and field of activity that might be of interest, historically and now. Furthermore, since the book is reliant on the existence of other source material to which it acts as a guide, it is largely restricted to issues and debates which have been already documented and discussed. Some areas of practice have not had the full focus they might be deemed to deserve. For example, there are many collections of fashion photographs, and there have been numerous articles and books written in recent years on questions of gender, representation, fashion, style and popular culture. But, aside from a couple of recent publications, there remains relatively little *critical* writing on fashion photography. This is an omission which we could not rectify here. Thus, fashion photography forms one section of the more general chapter on commodity culture rather than attracting a chapter to itself. Likewise, a number of more technical practices within medical and scientific imaging fall beyond the scope of this book as, until recently, these areas of photography did not attract the specific philosophic and analytic focus that is now emerging; current interest in the history of uses of photography within science and in contemporary photographic practices within inter-disciplinary environmental research means that there has been an increase in critical writing in this arena.

In some respects the chapters seem quite different from one another. There are a number of reasons for this, of which the first – and most obvious – is that each is written by a different author, and writers have their own individual style. The specific tasks allotted to each chapter, and the material included, also lead to different approaches. The chapter on photography in relation to commodity culture concentrates on the contemporary. The chapter on the body in photography takes image content as the starting point for discussion. Three chapters, in appraising the specific fields of documentary and photojournalism, photography as art, and personal photography, are more obviously historical in their approach. Each takes it as axiomatic that exploration of the history of debates and practices is a means to better understanding how we have arrived at present ways of thinking and operating.

Finally, of course, writing is not interest-free. You should not take the discussion in any of the chapters as representing everything that could be said on its subject. Aside from the limitations of length, authors have their own priorities. Each chapter is written from a considered viewpoint, and each of the authors has studied their subject in depth over many years. As a result of their expertise, and their broader political and social affiliations, they have arrived at particular conclusions. These contribute to determining which issues and examples they have selected for central focus and, indeed, the way they have structured the exposition and argument in their chapter. Whilst each offers you the opportunity to consider key issues and debates, you should not view them as either comprehensive or somehow objectively 'true'. Rather, you should see the book as a guide to what is at stake within particular debates, bearing in mind that the writer, too, has something at stake. You should also remember that this is essentially only an introduction to issues and ideas.

CHAPTER BY CHAPTER

● In Chapter 1 we introduce key issues relating to photography and, most particularly, identify some of the positions elaborated by established theorists. The chapter focuses initially on a number of debates which have characterised theoretical and critical discussions of the photograph and of photographic practices starting with the interrelation between aesthetics and technologies. We then summarise and discuss historical accounts of photography. Finally we consider sites of practice, institutions and the audience for photography. Central to the chapter is a case study of ways in which one single image, Dorothea Lange's *Migrant Mother*, has been discussed. It acts as a model of how particular attitudes and assumptions can be illuminated through considering a specific example. The chapter is designed as a foundation for discussions, many of which will be picked up again for more detailed examination later in the book.

● Chapter 2 focuses upon the documentary role of the camera, especially in relation to recording everyday life. There is also some discussion of travel photography and of photojournalism, especially the expanding journalistic role for photography in the early twentieth century. Claims have been made for the authenticity or 'truth' of photography used within social surveys or viewed as evidence. The chapter considers disputes that have arisen in relation to such claims in the nineteenth century, in the early twentieth century – especially in the 1920s and 1930s when the term 'documentary' was coined – and in relation to contemporary practices in documentary and reportage.

The chapter is concerned throughout with the multiple discourses through which the nature of photography and its social project has been constructed and understood. By concentrating on particular periods it offers a critical history of documentary which problematises and clarifies the relationship of a specific form of representation to other debates and movements.

● Chapter 3 focuses upon the popular and the personal, developing an historical overview of leisure and domestic uses of photography as a medium of everyday immediate communication as well as one through which individual lives and fantasies have been recorded. Particular attention is paid to the family album, which both documents social histories and stands as a talisman of personal experience. The chapter also considers the strategies by which a mass market for photography was constructed, in particular by Kodak, and notes contemporary developments in digital imaging for domestic use. Finally the chapter comments upon recent research on the family photograph, considering what is concealed, as much as what is revealed, in family relationships, gender and sexuality. Attention throughout is drawn to the role of women as photographers and keepers of the photograph album.

In keeping with the style of this book, this chapter signals key texts and further reading. However, the history of popular photography to date has attracted less critical attention than has been directed to other fields of photographic practice; for instance, documentary. In contrast to other parts of the book, this chapter draws upon original research and materials that, being personal, are little known.

● Chapter 4 focuses upon the body photographed, discussing the extent to which the body image came under scrutiny especially at the end of the twentieth century. Here a history of attitudes to photography and the body is traced, noting ways in which the photograph has been taken to embody social difference. Taking as its starting point the proposal that there is a crisis of confidence in the body consequent upon new technological developments, along with a crisis of representation of the body, the chapter explores questions of desire, pornography, the grotesque and images of the dead, in relation to different modes of representing the body familiar from media imagery as well as within art history.

● Chapter 5 continues the focus upon everyday uses of photography through considering commodity culture, spectacle and advertising. Photography is a cultural tool which is itself a commodity as well as a key expressive medium used to promote commercial interests. These links are examined through a series of case studies on global brand identity, and on tourism, fashion and the exotic; sample analyses of single images are also included. Within commodity culture, that which is specific to photography interacts extensively with broader political and cultural issues. Thus we note references both to commercial photography and, more generally, to questions of the politics of representation, paying particular attention to gender and ethnicity. The chapter employs semiotics within the context of socioeconomic analysis to point to ways in which photography is implicated in the concealing of international social and economic relations.

● Chapter 6 considers photographic practices in relation to art and art institutions, discussing claims made for the status of photography as a fine art practice, historically and now. The chapter is organised chronologically in three sections: the nineteenth century; modern art movements; postmodern and contemporary practices. This historical division is intended not as a sort of chart of progress so much as a method of identifying different moments and shifting terms of reference relating to photography as an art practice. Attention is paid to forms of work and to themes which feature frequently in contemporary practice, including questions of gender, ethnicity and identity. Illustrations particularly relate to land, landscape and environment. This chapter is principally concerned to trace shifts in the parameters of debate as to the status of the photograph as art, to map historical changes in the situation of art photography within the museum and gallery, and to comment on photography as contemporary art practice.

CHAPTER 1

Thinking about photography

Debates, historically and now

DERRICK PRICE
LIZ WELLS

A knowledge of photography is just as
important as that of the alphabet. The illiterate
of the future will be ignorant of the use
of camera and pen alike.

László Moholy-Nagy 1923

Thinking about photography

Debates, historically and now

INTRODUCTION

In his Preface to *Photography, A Very Short Introduction*, historian Steve Edwards asks us to imagine a world without photography (Edwards 2006). His point, of course, is that it is almost impossible for us to do so; photography permeates all aspects of our life, acting as a principal source and repository of information about our world of experience. It follows that historical, theoretical and philosophical explorations of photographs as images and objects, and of photography as a range of types of practice operating in varying contexts, are necessarily wide-ranging. There is no single history of photography.

As E.H. Carr has observed, history is a construct consequent upon the questions asked by the historian (Carr 1964). Thus, he suggests, histories tell us as much about the historian as about the period or subject under interrogation. Stories told reflect what the historian hopes to find, and where information is sought. He was writing in an era when libraries and archives were the primary research locations. Nowadays we may start by researching online. But his note of caution remains relevant: fact gathering may be influenced by many factors, not least the particular networks used by web-based search engines. It is up to us to evaluate the status of our sources and the significance of our findings.

Furthermore, the historian's selection and organisation of material is to some extent predetermined by the purpose and intellectual parameters of any particular project. Such parameters reflect particular institutional constraints as well as the interests of the historian (for instance, academics may be expected to complete research within a set period of time). Projects are also framed by underpinning ideological and political assumptions and priorities.

Such observations are obviously pertinent when considering the history of photography. They are also relevant to investigating ways in which photography has been implicated in the construction of history. As the French cultural critic, Roland Barthes, has pointed out, the nineteenth century gave us both history and photography. He distinguishes between history which he describes as 'memory fabricated according to positive formulas', and the photograph defined as 'but fugitive testimony' (Barthes 1984: 93).

Attitudes to photography, its contexts, usages, and critiques of its nature are explored here through brief discussion of key writings on photography. The chapter is in four sections: Aesthetics and technologies, Contemporary debates, Histories of photography, and Photography and social history. The principal aim is to locate writings about photography both in terms of its own history, as a specific medium and set of practices, and in relation to broader historical, theoretical and political considerations. Thus we introduce and consider some of the different approaches – and difficulties – which emerge in relation to the project of theorising photography. The references are to relatively recent publications, and to current debates about photography; however, these books often refer back to earlier writings, so a history of changing ideas can be discerned. This history focuses on photography itself as well as considering photography alongside art history and theory, and cultural history and theory more generally.

As with any abbreviated history, this chapter can only offer brief summaries of some of the historical turning points and theoretical concerns that have informed and characterised debates about photography from its inception. Our aim is to identify some key questions and offer starting points for further research and discussion which are taken up in the following chapters and also through the references to further reading (in margins and notes). Photography is ubiquitous and it penetrates culture in very diverse ways. Nowadays, it plays a central role within social media on the one hand, while being a major factor within the art market on the other. These activities go on alongside longer standing fields of operation (including but not restricted to: documentary and photojournalism; people and places; personal, domestic and family photography; travel, exploration and representation of cultures other than our own; commerce and advertising). The questions that we might ask, then, shift according to the type of practice being considered, but whatever the field of operation analysis of the role of photographic images is always pertinent to critical interrogations.

AESTHETICS AND TECHNOLOGIES

The impact of new technologies

In the 1920s, when Moholy-Nagy commented on the future importance of camera literacy, he could hardly have anticipated the extent to which photographic imagery would come to permeate contemporary communication. Indeed, the late twentieth-century convergence of audio-visual technologies with computing led to a profound and ongoing transformation in the ways in which we record, interpret and interact with the world.

In recent years this has been marked both by the astonishing speed of innovation and by a rapid extension and incorporation of technologies within new social, cultural, political and economic domains. As Martin Lister remarked in 2009, we have 'witnessed a number of convergences: between photography and computer-generated imaging (CGI), between photographic archives and electronic databases, and between the camera, the internet and personal mobile media, notably the mobile telephone' (Lister in Wells 2009). Indeed, nowadays the mobile (cell) phone is also the camera.

We often see this ferment of activity as a defining feature of the twenty-first century and, perhaps, think of it as a unique moment in human history. But, in the 1850s, many people also thought of themselves as living in the forefront of a technological revolution. From this historical distance, it is hard to recapture the extraordinary excitement that was generated in the middle of the nineteenth century by a cluster of emerging technologies. These included inventions in the electrical industries and discoveries in optics and in chemistry, which led to the development of the new means of communication that was to become so important to so many spheres of life – photography. Hailed as a great technological invention, photography immediately became the subject of debates concerning its **aesthetic** status and social uses.

The excitement generated by the announcement, or marketing, of innovations tends to distract us from the fact that technologies are researched and developed in human societies. New machinery is normally presented as the agent of social change, not as the outcome of a desire for such change, i.e. as a cause rather than a consequence of culture. However, it can be argued that particular cultures invest in and develop new machines and technologies in order to satisfy previously foreseen social needs. Photography is one such example. A number of theorists have identified precursors of photography in the late eighteenth century. For instance, an expanding middle-class demand for portraiture which outstripped available (painted) means led to the development of the mechanical physiognotrace[1] and to the practice of silhouette cutting (Freund 1980). Geoffrey Batchen also points out that photography had been a 'widespread social imperative' long before Daguerre and Fox Talbot's official announcements in 1839. He lists 24 names of people who had 'felt the hitherto strange and unfamiliar desire to have images formed by light

1 For definitions see Gordon Baldwin and Martin Jürgens (2009) *Looking at Photographs: A Guide to Technical Terms.* Revised ed. Los Angeles: Getty Publications.

spontaneously fix themselves' from as early as 1782 (Batchen 1990: 9). Since most of the necessary elements of technological knowledge were in place well before 1839, the significant question is not so much who invented photography but rather why it became an active field of research and discovery at that particular point in time (Punt 1995).

Once a technology exists, it may become adapted and introduced into social use in a variety of both foreseen and unforeseen ways. As cultural theorist Raymond Williams has argued, there is nothing in a technology itself which determines its cultural location or usage (Williams 1974). If technology is viewed as determining cultural uses, much remains to be explained. Not the least of this is the extent to which people subvert technologies or invent new uses which had never originally been intended or envisaged. In addition, new technologies become incorporated within established relations of production and consumption, contributing to articulating – but not causing – shifts and changes in such relations and patterns of behaviour.

Art and technology

Central to the nineteenth-century debate about the nature of photography as a new technology was the question as to how far it could be considered to be **art**. Given the contemporary ubiquity of photography, including the extent to which artists use photographic media, to posit art and technology as binary opposites now seems quite odd. But in its early years photography was celebrated for its putative ability to produce accurate images of what was in front of its lens; images that were seen as being mechanically produced and thus free from the selective discriminations of the human eye and hand. On precisely the same grounds, the medium was often regarded as falling outside the realm of art, as its assumed power of accurate, dispassionate recording appeared to displace the artist's compositional creativity. Debates concerning the status of photography as art took place in periodicals throughout the nineteenth century. The French journal *La Lumière* published writings on photography both as a science and as an art.[2] **Baudelaire** linked 'the invasion of photography and the great industrial madness of today' and asserted that 'if photography is allowed to deputize for art in some of art's activities, it will not be long before it has supplanted or corrupted art altogether' (Baudelaire 1859: 297). In his view photography's only function was to support intellectual enquiry:

> Photography must, therefore, return to its true duty which is that of handmaid of the arts and sciences, but their very humble handmaid, like printing and shorthand, which have neither created nor supplemented literature. Let photography quickly enrich the traveller's album and restore to his eyes the precision his memory may lack; let it

2 Lemagny and Rouille (1987: 44) point out that the subtitle for the journal was 'Review of photography: fine arts-heliography-sciences, non-political magazine published every Saturday'.

CHARLES BAUDELAIRE
(1821–1867) Paris-based poet and critic whose writings on French art and literature embraced modernity; he stressed the fluidity of modern life, especially in the metropolitan city, and extolled painting for its ability to express – through style as well as subject-matter – the constant change central to the experience of modernity. In keeping with attitudes of the era, he dismissed photography as technical transcription, perhaps oddly so given that photography was a product of the era which so fascinated him.

adorn the library of the naturalist, magnify microscopic insects, even strengthen, with a few facts, the hypotheses of the astronomer; let it, in short, be the secretary and record-keeper of whomsoever needs absolute material accuracy for professional reasons.

(Baudelaire 1859: 297)

'Absolute material accuracy' was seen as the hallmark of photography because most people at the time accepted the idea that the medium rendered a complete and faithful image of its subjects. Moreover, the nineteenth-century desire to explore, record and catalogue human experience, both at home and abroad, encouraged people to emphasise photography as a method of naturalistic documentation. Baudelaire, who was among the more prominent French critics of the time, not only accepts its veracity but adds: 'if once it be allowed to impinge on the sphere of the intangible and the imaginary, on anything that has value solely because man adds something to it from his soul, then woe betide us!' (1859: 297). Here he is opposing industry (seen as mechanical, soulless and repetitive) with art, which he considered to be the most important sphere of existential life. Thus Baudelaire is evoking the irrational, the spiritual and the imaginary as an antidote to the positivist interest in measurement and statistical accuracy which, as we have noted, characterised much nineteenth-century investigation. From this point of view, for many nineteenth century critics in Western culture, steeped as they were in empiricist methods of enquiry, the mechanical nature of the camera militated against its use for anything other than mundane purposes.

Nineteenth-century photographers responded to such critical debates in two main ways: either they accepted that photography was something different from art and sought to discover what the intrinsic properties of the medium were; or they pointed out that photography was more than a mechanical form of image-making, that it could be worked on and contrived so as to produce pictures which in some ways resembled paintings. 'Pictorial' photography, from the 1850s onwards, sought to overcome the problems of photography by careful arrangement of all the elements of the composition and by reducing the signifiers of technological production within the photograph. For example, they ensured that the image was out of focus, slightly blurred and fuzzy; they made pictures of allegorical subjects, including religious scenes; and those who worked with the gum bichromate process scratched and marked their prints in an effort to imitate something of the appearance of a canvas.

In the other camp were those photographers who celebrated the qualities of **straight photography** and did not want to treat the medium as a kind of monochrome painting. They were interested in photography's ability to provide apparently accurate records of the visual world and tried to give their images the formal status and finish of paintings while concentrating their attention on its intrinsic qualities.

See ch. 6 for discussion of Pictorialism as a specific photographic movement.

straight photography
Emphasis upon direct documentary typical of the Modern period in American photography.

Most of these photographs were displayed on gallery walls – this was a world of exhibition salons, juries, competitions and medals. In the journals of the time (which already included the *British Journal of Photography*), tips about technique coexisted with articles on the rules of composition. If the photographs aspired to be art, their makers aspired to be artists, and they emulated the characteristic institutions of the art world. However, away from the salon, in the high streets of most towns, jobbing photographers earned a living by making simple photographic portraits of people, many of whom could not have afforded any other record of their own appearance. This did not please the painters:

> The cheap portrait painter, whose efforts were principally devoted to giving a strongly marked diagram of the face, in the shortest possible time and at the lowest possible price, has been to a great extent superseded. Even those who are better entitled to take the rank of artists have been greatly interfered with. The rapidity of execution, dispensing with the fatigue and trouble of rigorous sittings, together with the supposed certainty of accuracy in likeness in photography, incline many persons to try their luck in Daguerreotype, a Talbotype, Heliotype, or some method of sun or light-painting, instead of trusting to what is considered the greater uncertainty of artistic skill.
>
> (Howard 1853: 154)

The industrial process, so despised by Baudelaire and other like-minded critics, is here seen as offering mechanical accuracy combined with a degree of quality control. Photography thus begins to emerge as the most commonly used and important means of communication for the industrial age.[3]

Writing at about the same time as Baudelaire, Lady Elizabeth Eastlake agreed that photography was not an art but emphasised this as its strength.[4] She argued that:

> She is made for the present age, in which the desire for art resides in a small minority, but the craving, or rather the necessity for cheap, prompt, and correct facts in the public at large. Photography is the purveyor of such knowledge to the world. She is the sworn witness of everything presented to her view . . . (her studies are 'facts') . . . facts which are neither the province of art nor of description, but of that new form of communication between man and man – neither letter, message, nor picture – which now happily fills the space between them.
>
> (Eastlake 1857: 93)

In this account, photography is not so much concerned with the development of a new aesthetic as with the construction of new kinds of knowledge as the carrier of 'facts'. These facts are connected to new forms of communica-

3 For an interesting account of debates and discourses on realism and photography in the nineteenth century see Jennifer Green-Lewis (1996) *Framing the Victorians, Photography and the Culture of Realism*, Ithaca and London: Cornell University Press.

4 Lady Eastlake, a photographer in her own right, was married to Sir Charles Eastlake, first President of the London Photographic Society (later the Royal Photographic Society).

tion for which there is a demand among all social groups; they are neither arcane nor specialist, but belong in the sphere of everyday life. In this respect, Eastlake was one of the first writers to argue that photography is a democratic means of representation and that the new facts will be available to everyone. Photography does not merely transmit these facts, it creates them, but Eastlake characterised photography as the 'sworn witness' of the appearance of things. This juridical phrase strikingly captures what, for many years, was considered to be the inevitable function of photography – that it showed the world without contrivance or prejudice. For Eastlake, such facts came from the recording without selection of whatever was before the lens. It is photography's inability to choose and select the objects within the frame that locates it in a factual world and prevents it from becoming art:

> Every form which is traced by light is the impress of one great moment, or one hour, or one age in the great passage of time. Though the faces of our children may not be modelled and rounded with that truth and beauty which art attains, yet *minor* things – the very shoes of the one, the inseparable toy of the other – are given with a strength of identity which art does not even seek.
>
> (Eastlake 1857: 94; emphasis in original)

The old hierarchies of art have broken down. Photography bears witness to the passage of time, but it cannot make statements as to the importance of things at any time, nor is it concerned with 'truth and beauty' or with teasing out what underlies appearances. Rather, it voraciously records anything in view; in other words the image captures information beyond that which concerned the photographer.

Photography, then, is concerned with facts that are 'necessary', but may also be contingent, drawing our attention to what formerly went unnoticed or ignored. Writing within 15 years of its invention Eastlake points to the many social uses to which photography had already been put:

> photography has become a household word and a household want; it is used alike by art and science, by love, business and justice; is found in the most sumptuous saloon and the dingiest attic – in the solitude of the Highland cottage, and in the glare of the London gin palace – in the pocket of the detective, in the cell of the convict, in the folio of the painter and architect, among the papers and patterns of the mill owner and manufacturer and on the cold breast of the battle field.
>
> (Eastlake 1857: 81)

For Eastlake, photography is ubiquitous and classless; it is a popular means of communication. Of course, it was not true that people of all classes and conditions could commission photographs as a necessary 'household want' –

she anticipates that state by several decades, during which time the use of photography was also spreading from its original practitioners (relatively affluent people who saw themselves as experimenters or hobbyists) to those who undertook it as a business and began to extend the repertoire of conventions of the 'correct' way to photograph people and scenes.

Eastlake's facts are produced, she claims, by a new form of communication, which she is unable to define very clearly. But for all her vagueness, she does identify an important constituent in the making of modernity: the rise of previously unknown forms of communication which had a dislocating effect on traditional technologies and practices. She was writing at an historical moment marked by a cluster of technical inventions and changes and she places photography at the centre of them. The notion that the camera should aspire to the status of the printing press – a mechanical tool which exercises no effect upon the medium which it supports – is here seriously challenged. For Eastlake calmly accepts that photography is not art, but hints at the displacing effect the medium will have on the old structures of art; photography, she says, bears witness to the passage of time, but it cannot select or order the relative importance of things at any time. It does not tease out what underlies appearances, but records voraciously whatever is in its view. By the first decade of the twentieth century the Pictorialists had all but retreated from the field and it was the qualities of straight photography that were subsequently prized. Moreover, modernism argued for a photography that was in opposition to the traditional claims of art.

The photograph as document

In Britain, as elsewhere, the idea of documentary has underpinned most photographic practices since the 1930s. The terminology is indicative: the *Oxford English Dictionary* definition of 'documentary' is 'to document or record'.

In the days of chemical photography, and prior to the possibilities afforded by internet tools such as Google Earth, the simultaneous 'it was there' effect of photographs recording people and circumstances contributed to the authority of the photographic image and, arguably still does so. However, nowadays, in according authority to pictures, we are more likely to question the circumstances under which photographs have been made, their source, the status of the photographer and the purpose for which an image was made. For example, we might view pictures uploaded by local people documenting an incident or set of circumstances as *more* authentic than images authorised by a company or political organisation. Accepting that digital photography and digital imaging are now major industries contributing within print and online media, when assessing the significance of particular pictures we take into account image-making contexts and purposes. If documentary as a genre involves visual records for future reference, now we are very likely to ask from whose point of view such documents were made.

WALTER BENJAMIN
(1892–1940) Born in Berlin, Benjamin studied philosophy and literature in a number of German universities. In the 1920s he met the playwright, Bertolt Brecht, who exercised a decisive influence on his work. Fleeing the Nazis in 1940, Benjamin found himself trapped in occupied France and committed suicide on the Spanish border. During the 1970s his work began to be translated into English and exercised a great critical influence. His critical essays on Brecht were published in English under the title *Understanding Brecht* in 1973. Benjamin was an influential figure in the

The simultaneous 'it was there' (the pro-photographic event) and 'I was there' (the photographer) effect of the photographic record of people and circumstances contributes to the authority of photographs. Photographic aesthetics commonly accord with the dominant modes and traditions of Western two-dimensional art, including perspective and the idea of a vanishing point. Indeed, as a number of critics have suggested, photography not only echoes post-Renaissance painterly conventions, but also achieves visual renderings of scenes and situations with what seems to be a higher degree of accuracy than was possible in painting. Photography can, in this respect, be seen as effectively substituting for the **representational** task previously accorded to painting. In addition, as **Walter Benjamin** argued in 1936, changes brought about by the introduction of mechanical means of reproduction which produced and circulated multiple copies of an image shifted attitudes to art (Benjamin 1936). Formerly unique objects, located in a particular place, lost their singularity as they became accessible to many people in diverse places. Lost too was the 'aura' that was attached to a work of art which was now open to many different readings and interpretations. For Benjamin, whether operating to allow more people to view likenesses of persons, places or existing objects (for instance, reproductions of paintings or sculptures) or facilitating novel forms of visual communication that might not otherwise have occurred, photography was inherently more democratic than previous forms of image-making. Yet established attitudes persist. In Western art the artist is accorded the status of someone endowed with particular sensitivities and vision. That the photographer as artist, viewed as a special kind of seer, chose to make a particular photograph lends extra authority and credibility to the picture.

In the twentieth century, photography continued to be ascribed the task of 'realistically' reproducing impressions of actuality. Writing after the Second World War in Europe, German critic **Siegfried Kracauer** and French critic André Bazin both stressed the ontological relation of the photograph to reality (Bazin 1967; Kracauer 1960). Walter Benjamin was among those who had disputed the efficacy of the photograph in this respect, arguing that the reproduction of the surface appearance of places tells us little about the sociopolitical circumstances which influence and circumscribe actual human experience (**Benjamin 1931**).

The photograph, technically and aesthetically, has a unique and distinctive relation with that which is/was in front of the camera. Analogical theories of the photograph have been abandoned; we no longer believe that the photograph directly replicates circumstances.

Yet, technologically, the photographic image is an indexical effect based on observable reality. The chemically produced image brought together a range of considerations – including subject-matter, framing, light, characteristics of the lens, chemical properties of the film used and the paper on which a picture was printed, and creative decisions taken both when shooting and in the darkroom. The digital image differs in certain respects, including the greater

exploration of the nature of modernity through essays such as his study of Baudelaire, published as *Charles Baudelaire: A Lyric Poet in the Era of High Capitalism* (London: Verso, 1973). He is acclaimed as one of the major thinkers of the twentieth century, particularly for his historically situated interrogations of modern culture. Two highly important essays for the student of photography are 'A Short History of Photography' (1931) and 'The Work of Art in the Age of Mechanical Reproduction' (1936). The latter essay and 'Theses on the Philosophy of History' are frequently drawn upon in discussion of the cultural implications of new technological developments.

SIEGFRIED KRACAUER
(1889–1966) German critic, emigrated to America in 1941. His first major essay on photography was published in 1927 in the *Frankfurter Zeitung*. The subtitle of his best-known work *Theory of Film: The Redemption of Physical Reality* indicates his focus on images as sources of historical information. Benjamin's renowned 'Short History of Photography' (1931), along with his 'artworks' essay (1936), was, in effect, a response to Kracauer's 1927 essay.

WALTER BENJAMIN (1931) 'A Short History of Photography' in (1979) **One Way Street**, London: New Left Books.

diversity of image manipulation possibilities, and the visual effect of the surface of the computer screen when compositing, editing and viewing. None the less, the basis in the observable fuels realist notions associated with photography, despite our familiarity with digital manipulation possibilities. Paradoxically, perhaps, we want to believe what we see, even though at the same time we know that photographic images are selective, and may be significantly changed from that originally seen through the viewfinder.

Italian **semiotician** Umberto Eco has commented that the photograph reproduces the conditions of optical perception, but only some of them (see Eco in Burgin 1982). That the photograph appears iconic not only contributes an aura of authenticity, it also seems reassuringly familiar. The articulation of familiar-looking subjects through established aesthetic conventions further fuels realist notions associated with photography.

Related to this are the interests and motivations that impel photographers towards particular subjects and ways of working. Very many biographies have been written purporting to explain photographs through the investigation of photographers' personal experiences and political engagements; all too often tribute to the photographer and a particular way of seeing outweighs more critical analysis of the affects and import of a particular body of work. Yet questions of motivation and the contexts and constraints within which photographers operate clearly influence picture-making. Whilst not writing biographically, questions of motivation are woven within Geoff Dyer's reflections on the nature of photographs (Dyer 2005). Why might a particular subject be chosen, and why do some types of object, pose or place seem to be repeated so often? As a cultural critic he comments that in trying to construct a taxonomy of photographs he found endless slippages and overlaps. This led him towards appraisal of photography via what can be known, or speculated, about the motivations of photographers. His examples are largely restricted to well-known American practitioners, and to documentary modes, yet his musings have wider pertinence as he provokes us to reflect upon the historical emergence of certain themes and subject-matter, and the evolving attitudes towards decorum or explicitness of image-content. Questioning why a photographer might have made and published a particular image is one starting point for thinking about the significance of particular photographs or types of photography.

Thus philosophical, technical and aesthetic issues – along with the role accorded to the artist – all feature within **ontological** debates relating to the photograph. But in recent years, developments in computer-based image production and the possibilities of digitisation and reworking of the photographic image have increasingly called into question the idea of documentary realism. The authority attributed to the photograph is at stake. That this has led to a reopening of debates about 'photographic truth' in itself shows that, in everyday parlance, photographs are still viewed as directly referencing actual observable circumstances.

See ch. 2 for further discussion.

20

Photography and the modern

Photography was born into a critical age, and much of the discussion of the medium has been concerned to define it and to distinguish it from other practices. There has never, at any one time, been a single object, practice or form that is photography; rather, it has always consisted of different kinds of work and types of image which in turn served different material and social uses. Yet discussion of the nature of the medium has often been either reductionist — looking for an essence which transcends its social or aesthetic forms — or highly descriptive and not theorised.

Photography was a major carrier and shaper of **modernism**. Not only did it *dislocate* time and space, but it also undermined the linear structure of conventional narrative in a number of respects. These included access to visual information about the past carried by the photograph, and detail over and above that normally noted by the human eye. Writing in 1931, Walter Benjamin proposed that the photograph records the 'optical unconscious':

> It is indeed a different nature that speaks to the camera from the one which addresses the eye; different above all in the sense that instead of a space worked through by a human consciousness there appears one which is affected unconsciously. It is possible, for example, however roughly, to describe the way somebody walks, but it is impossible to say anything about that fraction of a second when a person starts to walk. Photography with its various aids (lenses, enlargement) can reveal this moment. Photography makes aware for the first time the optical unconscious, just as psychoanalysis discloses the instinctual unconscious.
>
> (Benjamin 1972: 7)

Benjamin was writing at a time when the idea that photography offered a particular way of seeing took on particular emphasis; in the 1920s and 1930s both the putative political power of photography and its status as the most important modern form of communication were at their height. Modernism aimed to produce a new kind of world and new kinds of human beings to people it. The old world would be put under the spotlight of modern technology and the old evasions and concealments revealed. The photo-eye was seen as revelatory, dragging 'facts', however distasteful or deleterious to those in power, into the light of day. As a number of photographers in Europe and North America stressed, albeit somewhat differently, another of its functions was to show us the world as it had never been seen before. Photographers sought to offer new perceptions founded in an emphasis upon the formal 'geometry' of the image, both literally and metaphorically offering new angles of vision. The stress on form in photographic seeing typical of American modern photography parallels the stress on photography, and on cinematography (kino-eye), as a particular kind of vision in European art movements of the 1920s. Our ways of seeing will be changed because we can observe the world from unfamiliar viewpoints, for instance, through a microscope, from the top of high buildings, from under the sea. Moreover, photography validated our experience of 'being there', which is not merely one of visiting an unfamiliar place, but of capturing the authentic experience of a strange place. Photographs are records and documents which pin down the changing world of appearance. In this respect the close kinship between the still image and the movie is relevant; photography and film were both implicated in the modern stress on seeing as revelation. Indeed, artists and documentarians frequently used both media.

In addition, photography was centrally implicated in the burgeoning of print media that dated from the early years of the twentieth century. It was precisely this mass circulation of images that allowed Benjamin to conceptualise photography as a democratic medium. Arguably it was what was happening on the printed page that excited imagination at the beginning of the twentieth century. Posters, photomontage, and – later – photographic magazines such as *Time, Life, Picture Post, Vue* offered opportunities for experimentation with image juxtapositions and modes of visual story-telling. However, as David Campany notes in an account of the work of American photographer, Walker Evans, by their very nature, magazines are transient. He suggests that,

> The photobook form always has at least half an eye on posterity but the illustrated magazine has a very different temporality and culture significance. It is not made to last, but lives and dies, succeed or fails in the space of its short shelf life.
>
> (Campany in di Bello *et al.*, 2012: 73)

He goes on to argue that the reproduction of documentary and photo-journalistic images made for publication that were 'essentially ephemeral' but later singled out for exhibition in museums or inclusion in monographs 'does little to capture the contingent complexity of their initial page presentation' (*loc cit*) remarking that it is only in the beginning of the twenty-first century that researchers have started to consider the history of photo-magazines along with that of the photobook. In some respects this is accurate. But we might also note the influence of photomontage and poster campaigns typical of early Soviet photography on uses of photography within 1970s and 1980s political activism in Britain, Germany, USA and elsewhere.

Indeed, European modernism, with its contempt for the aesthetic forms of the past and its celebration of the machine, endorsed photography's claim to be the most important form of representation. Moholy-Nagy, writing in the 1920s, argued that now our vision will be corrected and the weight of the old cultural forms removed from our shoulders:

> Everyone will be compelled to see that which is optically true, is explicable in its own terms, is objective, before he can arrive at any

halftone By the mid-1890s 'halftone', based on tiny dots of various sizes, could facilitate the tracing of tones of photographs into ink ready for mechanical reproduction alongside written text. Previously engravers were employed in the laborious process of tracing and gouging out images on wooden blocks that were then inked to enable printing. The halftone allowed newspapers and magazines to use up-to-date photo illustrations, enabling mass circulation of imagery, in effect contributing a basis for photojournalism.

possible subjective position. This will abolish that pictorial and imaginative association pattern which has remained unsuperseded for centuries and which has been stamped upon our vision by great individual painters.

(Moholy-Nagy 1967: 28)

Modernist photography was grounded in the sweeping away of pictorialism and the rejection of all attempts to simulate 'artistic' forms. As with the radical shift that modernism brought about in music, literature, architecture and art, the photographic image was to be a reflexive, self-conscious medium which revealed its own, particular properties to the viewer. This way of working spread around the world, so that (for example) modernist photography in Europe, the USA, Latin America and India can all be studied. But modernism was not a simple blueprint that all societies copied; its particular forms in specific places emerged in response to already existing cultures and histories. The aspiration that a world cleansed of traditional forms and hierarchies of values would be established, one in which we would be free to see clearly without the distorting aesthetics of the past, had to contend with the pressures and embodied histories of existing societies. However, the transformative power of modernism did seem to many to be heralding a new world as exemplified by Paul Strand when he described American photographic practice, which he saw as indigenous and viewed as being as revolutionary as the skyscraper. As he put it in a famous article in the last issue of *Camera Work*:

America has been expressed in terms of America without the outside influence of Paris art schools or their dilute offspring here . . . [photography] found its highest esthetic achievement in America, where a small group of men and women worked with honest and sincere purpose, some instinctively and a few consciously, but without any background of photographic or graphic formulae much less any cut and dried ideas of what is Art and what isn't: this innocence was their real strength. Everything they wanted to say had to be worked out by their own experiments: it was born of actual living. In the same way the creators of our skyscrapers had to face the similar circumstances of no precedent and it was through that very necessity of evolving a new form, both in architecture and photography that the resulting expression was vitalised.

(Strand 1917: 220)

Here, then, in a distinctively American formulation, photography is seen as having been developed outside history. Strand is claiming that a new frontier of vision was established by hard work and a kind of innocence, that it was a product of human experience rather than of cultural inheritance.

The postmodern

Postmodernism was an important, and much contested philosophical term, which emerged in the mid-1980s. It remains difficult to define, not least because it was applied to very many spheres of activity and disciplines. Briefly, writers on postmodernism postulated the idea that modernity had run its course, and was being replaced by new forms of social organisation with a transforming influence on many aspects of existence. Central to the growth of this kind of social formation was the development of information networks on a global scale which allowed capital, ideas, information and images to flow freely around the world, weakening national boundaries and profoundly changing the ways in which we experience the world.

Among the key concepts of postmodernism were the claims that we are at the 'end of history' and that, as Jean-François Lyotard suggested, we are no longer governed by so-called 'grand' or 'master' narratives – the underpinning framework of ideas by means of which we had formerly made sense of our existence. For instance, Marxism in emphasising class conflict as the dialectical motor of history, provides a material philosophical position which can be drawn upon to account for any number of sociopolitical phenomena or circumstances (Lyotard 1985). This critique was accompanied by the assertion that there has been a major shift in the nature of our identity. Eighteenth-century 'Enlighten-ment' philosophy saw humans as stable, rational subjects. Postmodernism shares with modernism the idea that we are, on the contrary, 'decentred' subjects. The word 'subjects', here, is not really concerned with us as individuals, but refers to the ways in which we embody and act out the practices of our culture. Some postmodernist critics argued that we are cut loose from the grand narratives provided by history, philosophy or science; so that we live in fragmented and volatile cultures. This view was supported by the postmodern idea that we inhabit a world of dislocated signs, a world in which the appear-ance of things has been separated from authentic originals.

Writing over a century earlier in 1859, the American jurist and writer Oliver Wendell Holmes had considered the power of photography to change our relationship to original, single and remarkable works:

> There is only one Coliseum or Pantheon; but how many millions
> of potential negatives have they shed – representatives of billions of
> pictures – since they were erected! Matter in large masses must always
> be fixed and dear; form is cheap and transportable. We have got the
> fruit of creation now and need not trouble ourselves with the core.
> Every conceivable object of Nature and Art will soon scale off its
> surface for us. We will hunt all curious, beautiful grand objects, as they
> hunt the cattle in South America, for their skins, and leave the carcasses
> as of little worth.
>
> (Holmes 1859: 60)

Holmes did conceive of some essential difference between originals and copies. Nevertheless, he realised that the mass trade in images would change our relationship to originals; making them, indeed, little more than the source of representation.

The postmodern was not concerned with the aura of authenticity. For example, in Las Vegas hotels are designed to reference places such as New York or Venice, featuring 'Coney Island' or 'The Grand Canal'. Superficially the resemblance is impressive in its grasp of iconography and semiotics, specifically, in understanding that, say, Paris, can be conjured up in a condensed way through copying traditional (kitsch) characteristics, for example, of Montmartre. Actual histories, geographies and human experiences are not only obscured, they are irrelevant, as these reconstructions are essentially décor for commercialism: gambling, shopping, eating and drinking. Indeed, communications increasingly featured what the French philosopher **Jean Baudrillard** called 'simulacra': copies for which there was no original.

In a world overwhelmed by signs, what status is there for photography's celebrated ability to reproduce the real appearance of things? Fredric Jameson argues that photography is:

> renouncing reference as such in order to elaborate an autonomous vision which has no external equivalent. Internal differentiation now stands as the mark and moment of a decisive displacement in which the older relationship of image to reference is superseded by an inner or interiorized one . . . the attention of the viewer is now engaged by a differential opposition within the image itself, so that he or she has little energy left for intentness to that older 'likeness' or 'matching' operation which compared the image to some putative thing outside.
>
> (Jameson 1991: 179)

He was among a number of contemporary critics who argue that photography has given up attempting to provide depictions of things which have an autonomous existence outside the image and that we as spectators no longer possess the psychic energy needed to compare the photograph with objects, persons or events in the world external to the frame of the camera. If a simulacrum is a copy for which there is no original; it is, as it were, a copy in its own right. Thus, in postmodernity, the photograph had no necessary referent in the wider world and could be understood or critiqued only in terms of its own internal aesthetic organisation.

Aesthetics in an era of digital imaging

This separation of the image from its referent crucially underpins the way in which we can think about the digital image. In analogue photography a

JEAN BAUDRILLARD
(b.1929) French philosopher, Jean Baudrillard, has theorised across a very wide terrain of political, social and cultural life. In his early work he attempted to move Marxist thought away from a preoccupation with production and labour to a concern with consumption and culture. His later work looks at the production and exchange of signs in a spectacular society. His notions of the hyperreal and of the simulacrum are of great interest to those interested in theorising photography, and were among the core concepts of postmodernism.

picture was formed through transcription, in principle tracing or witnessing actual people, places and circumstances (although, of course, selection, cropping, image retouching and other processes could be used to adjust the image content and qualities). Digital photography operates through a conversion whereby physical properties are symbolised through numerical coding (see pp. 367–8). Furthermore, digital 'photographs' can be constructed with no reference to external phenomena. In practice, photography has become hybrid in that we continue to compose pictures in documentary idiom, but can amend and adjust – not to mention, delete – with great ease. The photographs that we see nowadays are normally digital. Yet we continue to ascribe authenticity to photographic images (whether our own personal photographs, photo-journalism, forensic photography, travel and tourism, and so on). As Roland Barthes argued, the photograph is always and necessarily of something (Barthes 1984: 28). But arguably the *basis* of our belief in photographs has shifted (see discussion in the next section of this chapter).

The advent of the digital has led to a greater integration of industries and practices. As Martin Lister pointed out in relation to professional spheres of photography,

> In the period since the 1990s, 'digital photography' and 'digital imaging' have developed as major creative industries, and have become a taken-for-granted part of the media landscape. The once firm separations between older twentieth-century specialist divisions of skill and labour have become permeable, especially between photography, typographic and graphic design, project management, editorial work, and still and moving image production. Even for those professional photographers who continue to use film for some of its distinctive properties, digital technologies and processes are now an essential part of their post-production practices.
>
> For many others, digital technologies have replaced analogue processes: traditional cameras are replaced by digital and even virtual kinds, films by memory cards and hard drives, 'wet' physical darkrooms and optical enlargers by computers and software.
>
> (Lister 2013: 313)

More generally, digital cameras, mobile phones and computer photo applications have become ubiquitous, and the use of data storage facilities for and social media modes of communication are normal, certainly in parts of the world with ready access to electricity and internet connections. As Lister also remarked,

> The snapshots once pasted into the traditional family photo-album are now stored in electronic 'shoe-boxes', the majority never taking a

'hard-copy' form, to be displayed instead on the screens of televisions, personal computers, or the LCD screens of the very cameras with which they are taken.

(Lister 2013: 315)

Here again, the inter-relation of aesthetics and technologies is evident. For instance, an image viewed on a computer screen acquires a translucence that rarely characterizes a traditional printed version, and the scale of images tends to become uniform as the same appliance is used for viewing images of very different types, from those constructed as online commercial advertisements to panoramic landscapes reflecting the environmental concerns that preoccupy several contemporary artist-photographers.

Some photography does not traffic in multiple images but, rather, is constructed for the gallery. Cultural theorist Rosalind Krauss has described photography's relationship to the world of aesthetic distinction and judgement in the following terms:

Within the aesthetic universe of differentiation – which is to say; 'this is good, this is bad, this, in its absolute originality, is different from that' – within this universe photography raises the specter of nondifferentiation at the level of qualitative difference and introduces instead the condition of a merely quantitative array of difference, as in series. The possibility of aesthetic difference is collapsed from within and the originality that is dependent on this idea of difference collapses with it.

(Krauss 1981: 21)

Like Benjamin she noted the loss of aura introduced by the mass repro-ducability of photographs, but here she draws attention to the impact of this inherent characteristic within the gallery and the art market. The 'collapse of difference' has had an enormous effect on painting and sculpture, for photography's failure of singularity undermined the very ground on which the aesthetic rules that validated originality was established. Multiple, repro-ducible, repetitive images destabilised the very notion of 'originality' and blurred the difference between original and copy. The 'great masters' approach to the analysis of images becomes increasingly irrelevant, for in the world of the simulacrum what is called into question is the originality of authorship, the uniqueness of the art object and the nature of self-expression.

Indeed, in a world wherein images, which appear increasingly mutable, circulate electronically, such issues may seem irrelevant. Most of us now experience some of the effects of the ongoing digital revolution. Many of us receive photographs on e-mail, send them via mobile phones, store them in electronic archives, combine them with text to create brochures, or manipulate them to enhance their quality. Photography has always been caught up in new technologies and played a central part in the making of the modern world. However, one feature of the digitisation of many parts of our life is that potential new technologies are discussed in detail long before they become an everyday reality. In terms of photography many people anticipated a loss of confidence in the medium because of the ease with which images could be seamlessly altered and presented as accurate records. That this does not appear to have happened is testimony to the complex ways in which we use and interpret photographs. Nevertheless, these technologies are having a decided impact on the nature of the medium and are changing the ways in which it is used in all spheres of life. These changes continue to be made as the complex mix of technologies leads to the production of new products, stimulates new desires and evolves new forms of communication.

Writing about the problem of attention, Jonathan Crary makes it clear that each new technological form is not simply an extension of a stable, unchanging, quality of human vision. Instead, he argues that:

> If vision can be said to have any enduring characteristic within the twentieth century, it is that it has no enduring features. Rather it is embedded in a pattern of adaptability to new technological relations, social configurations, and economic imperatives. What we familiarly refer to, for example, as film, photography and television are transient elements within an accelerating sequence of displacements and obsolescences, part of the delirious operations of modernization.
>
> (Crary 1999: 13)

In this account the old notion of particular ways of seeing (of a 'photo-eye', for example) gives way to the idea of vision as a mutable faculty that is constantly adapting to a cluster of social and technical forces, while apparently stable forms such as photography or television are themselves being continuously transformed.

CONTEMPORARY DEBATES

What is theory?

> The first myth to dispel about 'theory' is the idea that we can do without it. There is no untheoretical way to see photography. While some people may think of theory as the work of reading difficult essays by European intellectuals, all practices *presuppose* a theory.
>
> (Bate 2009: 25)

The purpose of theory is to explain. All discussions of photographs rest upon some notion of the nature of the photographic and how images acquire meaning. Theory offers a system or set of tools whereby we can understand objects, processes and the implications of imagery. The issue is not whether theory is in play but, rather, whether theory is acknowledged. Two strands of theoretical discussion particularly featured in debates about photography towards the end of the twentieth century: first, theoretical approaches premised on the relationship of the image to reality; second, those which stress the importance of the interpretation of the image by focusing upon the reading, rather than the making, of photographic representations. In so far as there has been crossover between these two strands, this is found in the recent interest in the contexts and uses of images.

'Theory' refers to a coherent set of understandings about a particular issue that have been, or potentially can be, appropriately verified. It emerges from the quest for explanation and reflects specific intellectual and cultural circumstances. Theoretical developments occur within established paradigms, or manners of thinking, which frame and structure the academic imagination. On the whole, modern Western philosophy, from the eighteenth century onwards, has stressed rational thought and posited a distinction between subjective experience and the objective, observable or external. One conse-quence of this has been positivist approaches to research both in the sciences and the social sciences; indeed, photography as a recording tool has been centrally implicated within notions of the empirical. (See ch. 2.) Positivism has not only influenced uses of photography; it has also framed attitudes towards the status of the photograph.

Academic interrogation of photography employs a range of different types of theoretical understandings: scientific, social scientific and aesthetic. Historically, there has been a marked difference between scientific expectations of theory, and the role of theory within the humanities. Debates within the social sciences have occupied an intellectual space which has drawn upon both scientific models *and* the humanities. In the early/mid-twentieth century literary criticism centred upon a canon of key texts deemed worthy of study. Similarly, art history was devoted to a core line of works of 'great' artists, and much time was given to discussion of their subject-matter, techniques, and the provenance of the image. The academic framework was one of sus-taining a particular set of critical standards and, perhaps, extending the canon by advocating the inclusion of new or newly rediscovered works. A number of major exhibitions and publications on photography have taken this as their model, offering exposition of the work of selected photographers as 'masters' in the field. This approach, in literature, art history and aesthetic philosophy, has been critiqued for its esoteric basis. It has also been criticised for reflecting white, male interests and, indeed, for blinkering the academic from a range of potential alternative visual and other pleasures. For instance, within pho-tography the fascination of domestic or popular imagery, in its own right as well as within social history, was long overlooked, largely because such images do not necessarily accord with the aesthetic expectations of the medium and because they tend to be anonymous.

A more systematic critical approach, associated with mainland European intellectual debates, penetrated the Anglo-American tradition in some areas of the humanities, especially philosophy and literary studies, in the 1970s. The parallel influence on visual studies came slightly later. This impact was most pronounced in the relatively new – and therefore receptive – discipline of film studies. But there was also a significant displacement of older, established preoccupations and methods within art history and criticism. Increasingly, methodologically more eclectic visual cultural studies have superseded the more limited focus of traditional art history and aesthetic philosophy although, as has been argued in particular by Geoffrey Batchen, art-historical methods and presumptions have to some extent dominated photo-analysis, leading to an emphasis on photographs as images and thereby displacing critical engagement with photographs as material objects (Batchen 2007, 2008; di Bello 2007). Batchen's exhibition, *Forget Me Not – Photography and Remembrance* paid specific attention to various forms in which photography may be physically manifest, from ornate framing, family albums and images in lockets, to lampshades or cushions (Batchen 2004).

Indeed, within visual studies there has been an increased interest in the **phenomenological**, in ways in which other senses, particularly touch and the tactile, interact with the sight contributing to how photographs, as objects as well as images, affect us. As Elizabeth Edwards succinctly suggests:

> Photographs are the focus of intense emotional engagement. In premising photographic effect on the visual and the forensic alone, we limit our understanding of the modes through which photographs have historical effect because photographs both focus and extend the verbal articulation of histories and the sound world they inhabit.
>
> (Edwards 2008: 241)

Photography theory

DAVID BATE (2009)
Photography, The Key Concepts. Oxford and New York: Berg. An introductory guide to conceptual issues that includes sections on history, theory, documentary and story-telling and globalization, as well as overviewing selected genres in photography.

In *Photography: The Key Concepts* **David Bate** defines three periods in the development of theory relating to photographic practices and the significance of photographic imagery: Victorian aesthetics, mass reproduction in the early twentieth century and critical debates of the 1960s and 1970s that, as he phrases it, 'rippled over' into discussions of the postmodern in the 1980s. We might also add a fourth period of theoretical debates wherein the photographic became implicated within ways of thinking about digital imaging and virtual space. His use of the term 'rippled' is significant; it reminds us that the framing of particular debates, and of positions argued, is not neatly contained within any one period of history or, indeed, in specific places and contexts. Ideas and positions maybe re-inflected, threading their way into subsequent debates. Here the Hegelian notion of **dialectics** is useful in suggesting that a thesis and antithesis (anti-thesis) may become synthesised into a position that itself becomes a new starting point or thesis for further critical reflections. Singular dialectical thinking offers too linear a notion of philosophical processes given the cultural complexities of cultural circumstances including spillages between the local and the global, the virtual and the real. Jae Emerling utilises the metaphor of a game of chess as a means of conveying the complexity of the inter-relations of discourses pertinent to critical reflections on photography; each piece moves according to specific allocated rules and each move changes the overall pattern of relations (Emerling 2012). The analogy is pertinent although perhaps fails to indicate the sense of speed and fluidity of change that characterises contemporary digital environments within the global context. Arguably for dialectics to remain intellectually useful we need to think of reflective processes as analogous to a continuously spinning web of inter-secting lines of dialectical reflections and developments.

One of the central difficulties in the establishment of photography theory, and of priorities within debates relating to the photographic image, is that photography lies at the cusp of the scientific, the social scientific and the humanities. Thus, contemporary ontological debates relating to the photo-graph are divergent. One approach centres on analysis of the rhetoric of the image in relation to looking, and the desire to look. This is premised on models of visual communication which draw upon linguistics and, in particular, **psychoanalysis**. This approach locates photographic imagery within broader **poststructuralist** concerns to understand meaning-producing processes.

Up until the 1980s 'photography theory' within education had been taken to refer to technologies and techniques as in optics, colour temperature, optimum developer heat, etc. 'Theory' related to the craft base of photography. In introducing the collection of essays *Thinking Photography*, artist/critic Victor Burgin argued that photography theory must be interdisciplinary and must engage not only with techniques but, more particularly, with processes of signification (**Burgin 1982**). Writing in the context of the 1970s and 1980s, and drawing on work from a range of disciplines, he commented that photography theory does not exist in any adequately developed form. Rather, we have photography criticism which, as currently practised, was evaluative and normative, authoritative and opinionated, reflecting what he terms an 'uneasy and contradictory amalgam' of Romantic, Realist and Modernist aesthetic theories and traditions. We might ask to what extent this is different now, a quarter of a century later. He also suggested that photography history, as written up until the 1980s, reflects the same ideological positions and assumptions; that is to say, it uncritically accepts the dominant paradigms of aesthetic theory. Burgin warns against confusing photography theory with a general theory of culture, arguing for the specificity of the still, photographic image.

In relation to this, as we have already seen, a number of critics have focused on the realist properties of the image. Film critic André Bazin in the

VICTOR BURGIN (ed.) (1982) **Thinking Photography**, London: Macmillan. A collection of eight essays, including three by Burgin himself, which, although varying in theoretical stance and focus, all aim to contribute to developing a materially grounded analysis of photographic practices.

SUSAN SONTAG (2002)
On Photography,
Harmondsworth: Penguin, new
edition with introduction by
John Berger. A collection of six
essays on various aspects of
photography which, despite
seeming slightly out of date in
its concern with realism, still
offers many key insights. Her
programme on photography, *It's
Stolen Your Face*, produced for
the BBC in 1978, was based on
this collection.

ROLAND BARTHES (1984)
Camera Lucida, London:
Fontana. First published in
French in 1980 as *La Chambre
Claire*. In this, his final book,
Barthes offers a quite complex,
rhetorical, but nonetheless
interesting and significant set of
comments on how we respond
to photographs.

1950s, in his key essay on the subject, emphasised the truth-to-appearances characteristics of the photographic (Bazin 1967). Albeit within wider-ranging terms, **Susan Sontag**, in her 1970s series of essays collected as *On Photography*, also discussed photographs as traces of reality and interrogated photography in terms of the extent to which the image reproduces reality. Similarly, Roland Barthes emphasised the referential characteristics of the photograph in his final book *Camera Lucida* (**Barthes 1984**).

Critical reflections on realism

Photographing is essentially an act of non-intervention.

(Sontag 1979: 11)

Because of the disjunction between the thinking, seeing photographer and the camera that is the instrument of recording, the viewer finds it more difficult than with other visual artifacts to attribute creativity to any photographer.

(Price 1994: 4)

In philosophical terms, any concern with truth-to-appearances or traces of reality presupposes 'reality' as a given, external entity. Notions of the photograph as empirical proof, or the photograph as witness offering descriptive testimony, ultimately rest upon the view of reality as external to the human individual and objectively appraisable. If reality is somehow there, present, external, and available for objective recording, then the extent to which the photograph offers accurate reference, and the significance of the desire to take photographs or to look at images of particular places or events, become pertinent.

Despite the broader promise of its title, *Photography Theory*, edited by James Elkins, centres primarily on the photograph as image and on the **indexical**, that is, ways in which the image stands as a reference to or trace of actual phenomena (Elkins 2007). His focus is on photography as art; everyday photographic phenomena and practices are not core considerations, although, as many photography theorists have argued, contexts in which we view photographs, what we want of particular images (for instance, of family, friends, places, or celebrities), and how they relate to broader contemporary debates and currencies (for example, political concerns, or new phenomena within popular culture) are equally as significant as the image in itself. But the publication offers an example of ways in which the relation between the image and its referent continues to pre-occupy photo theorists

Susan Sontag defined the photograph as a 'trace' directly stencilled off reality, like a footprint or a death mask. *On Photography* offered a series of interconnected essays, essentially based on a realist view of photography. Her concern was with the extent to which the image adequately represents

32

the moment of actuality from which it is taken. She emphasised the idea of the photograph as a means of freezing a moment in time. If the photograph misleads the viewer, she argued this is because the photographer has not found an adequate means of conveying what he or she wishes to communicate about a particular set of circumstances. Her focus was on the photograph as document, as a report, or as evidence of activities such as tourism. She commented that the use of a camera satisfies the work ethic and stands in when we are unsure of our responses to unfamiliar circumstances, but can also reduce travel and other experiences to a search for the photogenic. Sontag also discussed the ethics of the relationship between the photographer as reporter and the person, place or circumstances recorded. The photographer, especially the photojournalist, is relatively powerful within this relationship, and thus may be seen as predatory. She pointed out that the language of military manoeuvre – 'load', 'shoot' – is central to photographic practices. Given this relative power, in her view it is even more important to emphasise the necessity of accurate reporting or relating of events. Photographs are not necessarily sentimental, or candid; they may be used for a variety of purposes including policing or incrimination.

Sontag's discussion veers between the reasons for taking photographs and the uses to which they are put. It is marked by a sense of the elusiveness of the photo-image itself. She noted our reluctance to tear up photos of relatives, and the rejection of politicians through symbolically burning images. She describes photographs as relics of people as they once were, suggesting that the still camera embalms (by contrast with the movie camera, which savours mobility). Thus she drew attention to the fascination of looking at photographs in terms of what we think they may reveal of that which we cannot otherwise have any sense of knowing, characterising photographs as a catalogue of acquired images which stand in for memories. Photographs can also, she suggests, give us an unearned sense of understanding things, past and present, having both the potential to move us emotionally, but also the possibility of holding us at a distance through aestheticising images of events. Photographs can also exhaust experiences, using up the beautiful through rendering it into cliché. For instance, she notes that sunsets may now look corny; too much like photographs of sunsets. The overall impact of her essays is rhetorical in that she makes grand claims for photography as a route to seeing, and, by extension, understanding more about the world of experience. Throughout, we have the sense that meaning may be sought within the photograph, providing it has been well composed and therefore accurately traces a relic of a person, place or event. Yet the collection does not include examples of actual photographs and there is no detailed analysis and discussion of specific images.

In her book *The Photograph: A Strange, Confined Space* (1994), American critic, Mary Price, argued that the meaning of the photographic image is primarily determined through associated verbal description and the context in which the photograph is *used*. By contrast with Sontag's emphasis on the relation between the image and its source in the actual historical world, Price starts from questions of viewing and the context of reception. Thus, she suggests, in principle there is no single meaning for a photograph, but rather an emergent meaning, within which the subject-matter of the image is but one element. Her analysis is practical in its approach. She takes a number of specific examples, aiming to demonstrate the extent to which usage and contextualisation determine meaning. Related to this, in *No Caption Needed,* **Robert Hariman** and **John Louis Lucaites** discuss iconicity and photographs as public art through focusing on nine examples of pictures, with documentary or photojournalistic origins, that have become iconic; photographs for which meaning now transcends the specific circumstances of their making as they have come to represent particular ideologies or political attitudes (Hariman and Lucaites 2007). Whilst meaning may once have been anchored through context and caption, as we shall demonstrate in the case study of Dorothea Lange's 'Migrant Mother' 1936 (see below), many further references become woven into what such an image has subsequently come to connote. This study is significant for its analysis of ways in which photographs may acquire political significance through reference to collective memory.

Realist theories of photography, then, can take a number of different starting points: first, the photograph itself as an aesthetic artefact; second, the institutions of photography and the position and behaviour of photographers; third, the viewer or audience and the context in which the image is used, encountered, consumed. The particular starting point organises investigative priorities. For instance, ethical questions relating to who has the right to represent whom are central when considering the photographer and institutions such as the press.

Sontag takes a particular position within debates about realism, stressing the referential nature of the photographic image both in terms of its iconic properties and in terms of its indexical nature. For Sontag, the fact that a photograph exists testifies to the actuality of how something, someone or somewhere once appeared. Max Kozloff challenged Sontag's conceptual model, criticising her proposition that the photograph 'traces' reality, and arguing instead for a view of the photograph as 'witness' with all the possibilities of misunderstanding, partial information or false testament that the term 'witness' may be taken to imply (Kozloff 1987: 237). In his earlier collection of essays, *Photography and Fascination,* Kozloff starts from the question of the enticement of the photograph. He concludes that:

> Though infested with many bewildering anomalies, photographs are considered our best arbiters between our visual perceptions and the memory of them. It is not only their apparent 'objectivity' that grants photographs their high status in this regard, but our belief that in them, fugitive sensation has been laid to rest. The presence of photographs

ROBERT HARIMAN AND JOHN LOUIS LUCAITES (2007)
No Caption Needed, Iconic Photographs, Public Culture, and Liberal Democracy, Chicago: University of Chicago Press.

reveals how circumscribed we are in the throes of sensing. We perceive and interpret the outer world through a set of incredibly fine internal receptors. But we are incapable, by ourselves, of grasping or tweezing out any permanent, sharable figment of it. Practically speaking, we ritually verify what is there, and are disposed to call it reality. But, with photographs, we have concrete proof that we have not been hallucinating all our lives.

(Kozloff 1979: 101)

However the relation between the image and the social world is conceptualised, it is worth noting that the authority that emanates from the sense of authenticity or 'truth to actuality' conferred by photography was a fundamental element within photographic language and aesthetics. This authority, founded in realism, came to be taken for granted in the interpretation of images made through the lens.

It is precisely this that sets lens-based imagery apart from other media of visual communication. Again, to quote Kozloff, 'A main distinction between a painting and a photograph is that the painting alludes to its content, whereas the photograph summons it, from wherever and whenever, to us' (1987: 236). Chemical photography is distinct from the **autographic**, or from the digital, in that it seems to emanate directly from the external. Inherent within the photographic is the particular requirement for the physical presence of the referent. This has led to photographs (along with film and video) being viewed as realist in ways that, say, technical drawing or portrait painting are not (although they are also based upon observation).

That this was the case needs to be clearly acknowledged and addressed in order to understand theoretical debates as they were engaged historically as well as the legacies of this for contemporary debates. It is no coincidence that indexicality has become a contemporary focus of enquiry (for example, Elkins 2007). Perhaps one of the most curious facets of contemporary imaging is that, despite knowing the extent to which pictures can be and are manipulated and the ease with which this can be achieved through various software, we suspend disbelief and continue to ascribe authenticity to photographic images. What was – and remains – at stake in terms of provenance and authenticity in relation to the evidential authority of the photographic image continue to preoccupy many historians and theorists.

Reading images

It is seeing which establishes our place in the surrounding world, we explain that world with words, but words can never undo the fact that we are surrounded by it. The relationship between what we see and what we know is never settled.

(Berger 1972a: 7)

In the late twentieth century two key theoretical developments, semiotics and psychoanalysis, significantly contributed to changes within the humanities and both figured in debates relating to the constitution of photographic meaning. Semiotics (or **semiology**), the idea of a science of signs, originated from comments in Ferdinand de Saussure's *General Theory of Linguistics* (1916) but was not further developed until after the Second World War. Essentially, semiotics proposed the systematic analysis of cultural behaviour. At its extremes it aimed at establishing an empirically verifiable method of analysis of human communication systems. Thus, **codes** of dress, music, advertising – and other forms of communication – are conceptualised as logical systems. The focus is upon clues which together constitute a *text* ready for reading and interpretation. American semiotician C.S. Peirce further distinguished between iconic, indexical and symbolic codes. Iconic codes are based upon resemblance, for instance, a picture of someone or something; indexical codes are effects with specific causes, for example, footprints indicate human presence; symbolic codes are arbitrary, for instance, there is no necessary link between the sound of a word and that to which it refers.

The key limitation of semiotics as first proposed, with its focus upon systems of signification, was that it failed to address how particular *readers* of signs interpreted communications, made them meaningful to themselves within their specific context of experience. It became common to use the term 'semiology' to refer to the earlier, relatively inflexible approach based upon structuralist linguistics, and to use 'semiotics' to indicate later, more fluid models, incorporating psychoanalysis, wherein the focus is more upon meaning-producing processes than upon textual systems. Social semiotics, taking account of questions of interpretation and context, inflects the emphasis specifically towards cultural artefacts and social behaviour.

Roland Barthes was known for his contribution to the semiological analysis of visual culture, in particular from his early work, *Mythologies*. Working inductively from his observations of differing cultural phenomena, he proposed that everyday culture could be analysed in terms of language of communication (visual and verbal) and integrally associated myths or culturally specific discourses. The central objective of this early work was the development of all-encompassing models of analysis of meaning-production processes. Later works, including *The Pleasure of the Text* (1973) and *Camera Lucida* (1984), were no longer focussed on sentences or images as texts so much as on ways in which meaning might be deciphered. These works take more account of the individual reader, of processes of interpretation, of psychoanalytic factors, and of what we might term cultural 'slippages' – thereby implicitly accepting a degree of unpredictability in human agency or response.

Camera Lucida was motivated by an ontological desire to understand the nature of the photograph 'in itself'. In semiotic terms, the photograph is disorderly because its ubiquity renders it unclassifiable: 'photography evades us' (Barthes 1984: 4). The style of writing is narrative and rhetorical, the tone

ROLAND BARTHES
(1915–1980) Studied French Literature and Classics at the University of Paris, and taught French abroad in Romania and Egypt before returning to Paris for a research post in sociology and semiotics. He taught a course on the sociology of signs, symbols and collective representations at the École Pratique des Hautes Études, and became known for his contribution to the development of semiology, the science of signs, first proposed by linguist Ferdinand de Saussure in 1916 but not fully explored until after the Second World War. Barthes' publications include *Mythologies* (1957), *Elements of Semiology* (1964), *The Empire of Signs* (1970) and *Image, Music, Text* (1977), which includes his well-known essay on 'The Rhetoric of the Image'. *Camera Lucida*, originally titled *La Chambre Claire* (1980), was his last work, and the only publication devoted entirely to photography.

is personal: he starts from discussion of himself as reader of the photographic image, asking why photos move him emotionally. In Part One he develops a commentary upon the nature and impact of the photograph using examples from documentary and photojournalism. In Part Two he focuses on his own family photographs, particularly images of his mother – some of which date from 'history', that is, a time before his birth – in order to contemplate more subjective meanings (this discussion is not illustrated). However, the objective is not to do with specific genres. For instance, there is no discussion of commercial imagery, nor of fine art uses of the medium. His purpose is essentialist in that he seeks to define that which is specific to the photograph as a means of representation. He is not concerned with the taker of a photograph (the photographer or, as he terms it, 'operator') and the act of taking but, rather, with the act of looking (the spectator) and with the 'target' of the photograph, that is, the object or person represented within the 'spectrum' of the photograph. Thus he observes that the knowing portraitee adopts a pose which anticipates the representational image, and takes account of the fact that this piece of paper will outlast the actual person who is the subject of the portrait becoming the 'flat death', which both exposes that which has been and precedes actual death.

Barthes concludes that it is 'reference' rather than art, or communication, which is fundamental to photography. Central to his exploration is the contention that, unlike in any other medium, in photography the referent uniquely sticks to the image. In painting, for instance, it is not necessary for the referent to be present. Painting can be achieved from memory, (chemical) photography cannot. From this emerges the time-specific characteristic of the photograph. It deals with *what was*, regardless of whether the terms or conditions continue to obtain. For Barthes, photography is never about the present, although the act of looking occurs in the present. In addition, the photograph is indescribable: words cannot substitute for the weight or impact of the resemblance of the image. The photograph is always about looking, and seeing. Furthermore, the photograph itself – that is, the chemically treated and processed paper – is invisible. It is not *it* that we see. Rather, through it we see that which is represented. (This, he suggests, is one source of the difficulty in analysing photography ontologically.) Likewise, the characteristics of the screen on which we may be viewing – mobile phone, computer – are disregarded, even though the screen size and surface affects visual qualities that are in turn influencing our responses.

What, then, is the attraction of certain (but never all) photographs for the spectator? As writer-lecturer Philip Stokes has pointed out in relation to the potentially boring experience of looking at other people's family albums, 'in every dreary litany there is an instant when a window opens onto a scene of fascination that stops the eye and seizes the mind, filling it with questions or simply joy' (Stokes 1992: 194). Why do some images arrest attention, animating the viewer, while others fail to 'speak' to the particular spectator?

Barthes proposes that photographs arrest attention when they encompass a duality of elements – two (or more) discontinuous, and not logically connected, elements which form the 'puzzle' (our term, not his) of the image. Here he distinguishes between *studium*, general enthusiasm for images and, indeed, the polite interest which may be expressed when confronted with any particular photograph, and the *punctum* (prick, sting or wound) which arrests attention. Previously, in an essay entitled 'The Third Meaning', he had suggested that photographs encompass the obvious and the obtuse, implying play of meaning within the photograph as text (Barthes 1977c). This leads him to explore why, when so many images are noted as a matter of routine, only some images make an impact on us. Here, again, he makes a detailed distinction between the photograph which captures attention through 'shouting' or because of the *shock* of revelation of subject-matter (for instance, a particularly startling photojournalistic image), and the punctum of recognition which transcends mere surprise, or rarity value, to inflict a poignancy of recognition for the particular spectator. This, he proposes, emanates more often from some detail within the image which stands out, rather than from the unity of the content as a whole. He sees this effect as essentially a product of the photograph itself. This, we would suggest, limits his discussion. The noticing of detail is also a consequence of the particular spectator's history and interests – even a relatively insignificant detail might offer a key point of focus for a person. Indeed, as Margaret Olin observes, in his discussion of punctum Barthes describes a ribbon of braided gold that is not actually in the James Van Der Zee image that he is analysing, but appears worn by his aunt in one of his family photographs reproduced elsewhere (Olin 2009). As Olin suggests, this displacement, a Freudian slip, a trick of memory, reflects the centrality of Barthes' own family pictures and memories as well as his quest for his mother as the motivator for *Camera Lucida*. But it also illustrates the point that the poignancy or joy of recognition is founded in the relation between the spectator and the photograph.

Barthes goes on to suggest that the photograph in itself, through being contingent upon its referent, is outside meaning. In this sense he views it as 'a message without a code' (to use a phrase drawn from his earlier essay on the rhetoric of the image). Thus he suggests that it is the fact of social observation which is immediate rather than the photograph. For Barthes, photography is at its most powerful not because of what it can reveal, but because it is, as he terms it, 'pensive'. It thinks. Of course Barthes does know that a photograph is not a thinking subject: the photograph itself is an inanimate piece of paper. The photographer thinks, the portraitee poses, and the spectator may respond reflectively. Animation occurs only through the act of looking.

Barthes' precise use of words (which, in the French, offers careful nuancing but, in translation, may seem over-precious), and the personal tone, to some extent obscure the general argument which is more phenomenological than semiotic in its method. His discussion is useful in reminding us of the essential contingency of the photograph. Like Sontag, he draws attention to its referential characteristics; unlike Sontag, who relates this to a range of practices, he defines this as that which characterises the medium, but it does not necessarily follow that this is a representation without a code. On the contrary, it is impossible to contemplate the image without operationalising a range of aesthetic and cultural codes. Ultimately, he also takes relatively little account of the specificity of the spectator and reasons and contexts of viewing. Despite his emphasis upon looking, and seeing, he focuses centrally on the image as text rather than upon the relation between image and spectatorship. This does limit his ontological conclusions.

Photography reconsidered

The individual as spectator, the reception and usage of photographs, and the nature of processes whereby photographs become meaningful subjectively and collectively have remained central to contemporary debates. Here the influence of psychoanalysis has to be taken into account alongside semiotics, together with the concerns of **social history**.

Psychoanalysis, founded in **Freud**'s investigations of the human psyche (from the 1880s onwards), centres upon the individual in ways which are now taken for granted but which, at the time, reflected certain revolutionary strands of political and philosophical thought. For political theorists the individual became viewed as the basic social unit; also, as someone expected to take personal responsibility for social and economic survival. Philosophers such as Nietzsche, regarded by many as the father figure of individualism, emphasised personal moral responsibility, engaging, in particular, with what he conceptualised as the enslaving influence of Christianity. Individualism is a taken-for-granted feature of twentieth-century Western experience. We talk of the individual consumer, individual professional responsibilities, individual responsibilities within the family, and so on. Yet this emphasis is relatively new. Psychoanalytic understandings of individual subjective responses to social experience have offered new models of insight into human behaviour in ways which have been challenging academically (as well as offering therapeutic means of coming to terms with personal trauma).

As already noted, Victor Burgin's *Thinking Photography* (1982) focused on debates within the theory, practice and criticism of photography. The book's authors set out to challenge the notion of the autonomous creative artist, to question the idea of documentary 'truth' and to interrogate the notion of purely visual languages. The intention was to situate photography within broader theoretical debates and understandings pertaining to meaning and communication, visual culture and the politics of representation.[5] The history of theories of art as they relate to – or 'position' – photography is also a key theme. The eight essays (including three by Burgin himself), while they vary in their theoretical stance and critical style, share 'the project of developing a materialist analysis of photography'. What Burgin is concerned with is

SIGMUND FREUD
(1856–1939) Freud's copious writings and his work with patients form the basis of the discipline of psychoanalysis, used both as a therapeutic method and as a tool to understand interpersonal relations and cultural activities. Psychoanalysis has irrevocably changed the way we understand the world and ourselves. Possibly Freud's most important contribution to modern thought is the concept of the unconscious, which insists that human action always derives from mental processes of which we cannot be aware. Many photographers have used the ideas of Freud as the basis of their work.

5 At this time Burgin lectured in photography at the Polytechnic of Central London (now the University of Westminster). His other publications include *Between* (1986), *The End of Art Theory* (1986), and *Formations of Fantasy* (co-edited 1989). He was based at the University of California throughout the 1990s, and subsequently at Goldsmiths College, University of London.

photography 'considered as a practice of *signification*'; that is, specific materials worked on for specified purposes within a particular social and historical context. Semiotics is one starting point for this theoretical project, but, as Burgin states, semiotics is not sufficient to account for 'the complex articulations of the moments of institution, text, distribution and consumption of photography' (Burgin 1982: 2).

In effect, this collection of essays traced a particular trajectory through Left debates of the 1970s, centring on questions of class, revolutionary struggle and the role of the artist, through semiotics, to questions of realism, psychoanalysis and spectatorship. (Questions of gender are addressed, although, notably, no essays by women theorists are included.) The book posits two key theoretical starting points: materialist analysis, as represented in the reprinting of Frankfurt School theorist Walter Benjamin's essay on 'The Author as Producer' (first published in German in 1966) and the semiotic, represented in Italian semiotician Umberto Eco's essay, 'Critique of the Image'. The other central historical reference is that of Russian Futurism and the **formalist–constructivist** theoretical debates which followed.

Classic Marxist models of artistic production are addressed, critically, in the penultimate essay of the book, 'Making Strange: The Shattered Mirror', by Simon Watney. Focusing on seeing, vision and the social nature of perception, Watney discusses various 1920s/1930s manifestations – in Russian aesthetic debates and in Brecht – of the proposal that through alienation, or 'making strange', new ways of 'seeing', politically and aesthetically, may be forged. The subtitle, 'The Shattered Mirror', refers to the rupturing of any notion of the photograph as a mirror or transparent recorder of reality. (It does not carry the psychoanalytic implications which, as we shall see, characterise Burgin's contributions.) The essay situates ideas of defamiliarisation in relation to past practices in order to reflect upon modern European and American work which he exemplifies, briefly, through reference to French photographer Atget; Bauhaus theorist-photographer Moholy-Nagy; and American documentarian Berenice Abbott. He argues that the project of defamiliarisation in photography rested upon acceptance of the fallacy of the transparency of the photograph. In other words, if we relinquish realist theories of the photograph, the problem of employing effective techniques for defamiliarisation dissolves.

Semiotics, in conjunction with psychoanalysis, informs Burgin's own three essays which, respectively, develop a series of related points about: the nature of the photograph as conceptualised in the context of new art theory; the experience of 'looking at photographs' from the point of view of the spectator; and exploring the psychological nature of the pleasurable response to the image. Thus he was concerned to trace links between the image, interpretation and ideological discourses. The model is most fully developed in 'Photography, Phantasy, Function', wherein the main part of the essay draws upon Freud to discuss psychological aspects of the act of looking, noting that looking is not indifferent. Thus he draws our attention to the voyeuristic and fetishistic investment in looking, arguing that to look is to become sutured within ideological discourse(s). He further argues that the photograph, like the fetish, is the result of an isolated fragment or frozen moment, and describes the fetishistic nature of the photograph as one source of its fascination.

Theory, criticism, practice

What has all this got to do with making photographs? Visual methods of communication are, of course, embedded in particular cultural circumstances and therefore reflect specific assumptions and expectations. For instance, as has been argued, given the nineteenth-century desire for empirical evidence, photography was hailed for its apparent ability to represent events accurately. This desire or expectation persists in fields such as photojournalism. Further-more, theoretical concepts interact. For instance, criteria based upon established visual aesthetics inform the assessment of what makes a 'good' photograph, photojournalistic or otherwise. Similarly, questions of representation pertaining to, for example, gender or race, which have contributed to the challenge to the canon within literary studies and art history, are relevant to photography.

The key point is that theoretical assumptions founded in varying academic fields, from the scientific to the philosophic and the aesthetic, intersect to inform both the making and the interpretation of visual imagery. One consequence of the postmodern debates of the second half of the twentieth century was a broadening of theoretical concerns. Similarly, debates concerning the import of digital imaging and online space at the turn of the twenty-first century. New developments not only impact on practices but also on ways in which theoretical concerns are framed. As Martin Lister remarks,

> Most discussions of 'digital photography' fail to remember that there is no single thing called photography, but there are many 'photographies' (Tagg 1988: 14–15). As a technology, photography has given rise to many different practices, uses and genres. However, many assessments about the 'impact' of digital technology have been flawed by a tendency to generalise about 'photography' as a whole.
>
> (Lister in Wells 2009: 328)

As he notes, one of the initial responses to the import of the digital was a concern with photographic 'truth', a notion that, as we have seen, is founded in empirical ideas that suggest that the relation between an image and its referent is its the crucial constituent. He adds,

> Although this claim or belief was only ever true of some kinds of photography (documentary, photojournalism, the biographical snapshot, and related forms of 'straight' photography where photographic realism and its use as evidence and testimony, were once particularly high) it was rapidly generalised to be a threat to 'photography' *per se*. It became a

question about the very ontology of all photography. However, the new ability to manipulate and synthesise diverse photographic image elements could hardly be experienced as a threat to advertising, art or fashion photography. These are kinds of photography where an enhanced ability to manipulate the 'real' is sought after and welcomed; cases where celebration rather than regret would be more appropriate.

(loc cit)

In other words, photography/photodigital is not a singular field; it encompasses a range of genres, practices and, indeed, differing moral considerations (touching up a fashion plate is of an entirely different ethical order to, say, photo-montaging a gun into the hand of a criminal suspect). That there may be differences in principle between chemical and digital processes may be relevant but not necessarily significant in particular genres or circumstances. Preoccupation with realist debates risks distracting from questions of reception and social uses of photographic imagery within which the indexicality of the image is only one consideration amongst many others.

If we take the context and interpretation as crucial components within meaning-production processes, then questions of authenticity in the sense of the relation of the image to the circumstances pictured become less important than the story-telling aspects of photography. As Lister also points out,

While it is perfectly possible to consider the difference between the photo-mechanical process of traditional photography and the electro-mathematical processes of digital imaging as an ontological issue (that is, as a matter of fundamental differences in their mode of being) it is also necessary to deal with their use in social practice where such differences do not always have meaning. In fact, where 'new' digital media are concerned, the widespread transformations that they have brought about in traditional media are matched by an enormous range of uses. While they may do so in radically different ways, digital media can, and are, used to perform most of the functions of old media. It follows then that in investigating their relationships, different kinds of photography, and different affordances of digital image technology move in and out of the foreground of our attention.

(loc cit)

Yet, in common with other fields of the arts, photography criticism still tends to be normative, evaluating work in relation to established traditions and practices. At its worst, criticism masks personal opinion, dressed up as objective or authoritative with the aim of impressing, for example, the readers of review articles in order to generate respect and support for the reviewer. At its best, criticism helps to locate particular work in relation to specific debates about practice through elucidating appreciation of the effect, meaning, context and import of the imagery under question.

So, in order to think about photographic communication, we need to take account of communication theory in broad terms as well as focusing specifically on photographs as a particular type of visual sign, produced and used in specific, but differing, contexts. The photograph, therefore, might be conceptualised as a site of intersection of various orders of theoretical understanding relating to its production, publication and consumption or reading. Central to the project of theorising photography is the issue of the relation between that which particularly characterises the photographic (which, as we have seen, is its referential qualities), and theoretical discourses which pertain to the making and reading of the image but whose purchase is broader, for instance, aesthetic theory or sexual politics. What is crucially at stake is how we think about the tension between the referential characteristics of the photograph and the contexts of usage and interpretation.

Given the ubiquity of photographic practices, a twofold problem emerges: first, to analyse ways in which clusters of theoretical discourses intersect, or acquire priority, in particular fields of practice; and second, to define and analyse that which is peculiar to photography. If we take Barthes' final words on the subject, it is primarily its referential characteristic which variously lends it particular credibility, force or significance. If we start from the greater diversity of positions – semiotic, psychoanalytic and social-historical – outlined in Burgin's edited collection, then the focus must be upon the political and **ideological**. Within contemporary developments ideas about the fluidity of virtual space and globalization have also become central to theoretical concerns, not least because of the extent to which photographic media have become integral within international border agency controls and other surveillance systems. The project of theorising photography thus relies upon the development of complex models of analysis that can take account of these rather different starting points.

Within this conceptual approach it is not the objective presence of the image which is at stake, but rather the force-field within which it generates meaning. This contrasts with semiological stress on systems of signification. In effect we are invited to consider not only the text, its production and its reading, but also to take account of the social relations within which meaning is produced and operates.[6] Here, the semblance of the real underpins processes of interpretation. Photography is reassuringly familiar, not least because it seems to reproduce that which we see, or might see. In so far as visual representations contribute to constructing and reaffirming our sense of identity, this familiarity, and the apparent realism of the photographic image, render it a particularly powerful discursive force.

Nowadays, many people think about photography only within the wider world of image-making, and reflect on the dominance that 'the visual' has in a global, post-industrial society. It is a truism that we are saturated with images, but it is arguable that the more images we make and receive, the more 'natural' and unexceptional they appear. Vilém Flusser once put this in a rather dismissive way:

6 For a good general discussion of questions of representation, semiotics and discursive practices see Stuart Hall (1997) 'The Work of Representation', Chapter 1 in Stuart Hall (ed.) (1997) *Representation, Cultural Representations and Signifying Practices*, London: Sage/Open University.

JAE EMERLING (2012) **Photography, History and Theory**. Focussing on photography as art, this publication argues that histories of photography are inextricably inter-related with theoretical discourses. This is pursued through reference to 'Frame', questions of documentary 'truth', the archive, and 'Time-images', with particular reference to writings by Walter Benjamin, Roland Barthes, Susan Sontag, Michel Foucault and Vilém Flusser. The discussion is complexly woven, so might be taken as a further, more advanced, step towards immersion in questions of the ontology of the photographic.

people taking snaps are unable to decode photographs: They think photographs are an automatic reflection of the world. This leads to the paradoxical result that the more people take snaps, the more difficult it becomes to decode photographs: Everyone thinks there is no need to decode photographs, since they know how photographs are made and what they mean.

(Flusser 1983: 59)

Thirty years on from Flusser's observation, we swim in a world of images that was unimaginable at the time. But if photographs are 'coded' there are no simple rules to 'decode' them. To do this we need to try to understand not only the ways in which an information system structured around images functions, but also the nature of the medium of photography itself. This inevitably leads us to undertake the study of the history of photography; of its social and cultural functions; of its particular aesthetic; its distinctive genres, and its relationship to other media. We need to consider, amongst other things, the ways in which we receive and are affected by photographs and how they illuminate aspects of human existence. The way we set about these tasks, the way we interrogate the nature of photographs over time, will be determined by the organized and structured sets of questions that we bring to bear on them – that is, by the theories we employ.

CASE STUDY: IMAGE ANALYSIS: THE EXAMPLE OF *MIGRANT MOTHER*

In 1936 the documentary photographer Dorothea Lange was working for a government-run project known as the Farm Security Administration (FSA). Lange has recounted the story of how she stopped one night on the road – although she was already exhausted by the work of the day – to investigate a group of people who were employed to pick peas. In less than a quarter of an hour she was back on the road having taken several shots of the woman with her children. One of these photographs, *Migrant Mother* (Figure 1.1), became the most reproduced image in the history of photography, appearing on covers of publications not only about Lange herself (Durden 2006) but also about 1930s documentary photography (Hurley 1972), iconic photographs (Hariman and Lucaites 2007) or – significantly given the range of available possibilities – about American photography (Orvell 2003). It is known to many people who could not name its author.

In subsequent years this photograph has been used and contextualised in a number of ways. This, not only as a photograph; it has appeared on a USA postage stamp (illustrating the decade of the 1930s) and has acted as a source for cartoons. The picture has had a history beyond its original context within the FSA and it is regularly referred to as one of the world's greatest news

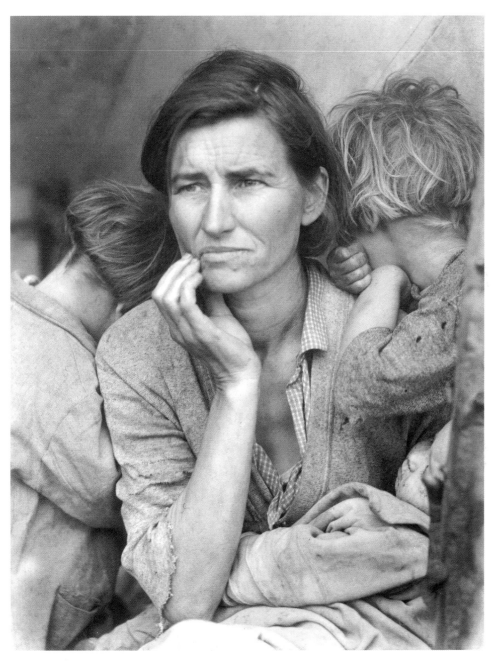

1.1 Dorothea Lange, *Migrant Mother,* **1936**

See, for instance, Martha Rosler's celebrated essay 'In, Around, and Afterthoughts (on Documentary Photography)' (reprinted variously), or the opening section of Judith Fryer Davidov (1998) *Women's Camera Work*, Durham and London: Duke University Press.

Commonly, discussion of images draws upon two or three analytic approaches. For instance, those concerned with the status of a photograph as evidence may also be interested in the intentions of the photographer and the context of making; semiotic analysis makes reference to aesthetic coding and to cultural contexts.

In order to avoid emphasising artificial boundaries between academic disciplines, and to demonstrate the extent to which we operate in an interdisciplinary manner, this case study is organised under a series of headings which allow us to indicate the range of concerns that may be implicated simultaneously in writing about a photograph.

Looking at the picture alongside the others allows us to explore the criteria by which photographers select, shape and organise images, and to consider why none of the other images could have acquired the same status in terms of documentary aesthetics and its iconic status.

Clarke does not discuss the specific history and context of the making of the image, or of its immediate use. By excluding detail, Lange made it possible for the picture to be seen as a universal symbol of motherhood, poverty and survival. Clarke seems to go along with this. His approach emphasises the notion of the good photograph, but the criteria whereby an image might be considered 'good' are taken for granted. Emotional empathy is clearly one element, but this is assumed rather than treated as something for critical discussion.

photographs. Many critics have commented on this, noting various moments of appropriation of the image.

A number of differing approaches may be used to analyse photographs. Each model reflects its own particular concerns and priorities. For instance, any single photograph might be:

● viewed primarily as social or historical evidence
● investigated in relation to the intentions of the photographer and the particular context of its making
● related to politics and ideology
● assessed through reference to process and technique
● considered in terms of aesthetics and traditions of representation in art
● discussed in relation to class, race and gender
● analysed through reference to psychoanalysis
● decoded as a semiotic text.

Here we take the example of Dorothea Lange's *Migrant Mother* in order to illustrate and comment upon some of the ways in which this photograph has been discussed, and to draw attention to assumptions which underpin particular remarks about it.

The photograph as testament

Given that Lange took a number of shots of the woman and children, why is it this image which has become so famous? A number of critics have commented upon this:

> The woman is used purely as subject. She is appropriated within a symbolic framework of significance as declared and determined by Lange. Indeed, the other images taken by Lange at this 'session' add to the sense of construction and direction. They remain distant, though, and lack the compelling presence which Lange achieves in the Migrant Mother image. In this Lange creates a highly charged emotional text dependent upon her use of children and the mother. The central position of the mother, the absence of the father, the direction of the mother's 'look', all add to the emotional and sentimental register through which the image works. The woman is viewed as a symbol larger than the actuality in which she exists. As Lange admitted, she wasn't interested in 'her name or her history'.
>
> (Clarke 1997: 153)

Lange made five exposures of the woman and children in a tent (see figures 1.2–1.5). One image was selected for publication and this became one of the most famous photographs of the twentieth century. We can see that this image excludes literal detail (reference to the whole tent and the woodlands beyond, or to domestic objects) which might anchor the image to a particular place and time.

46

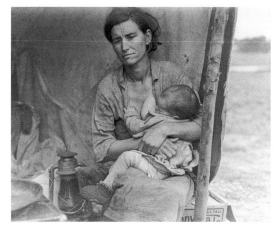
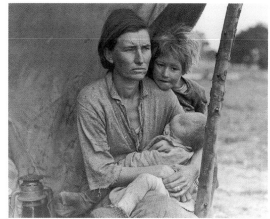
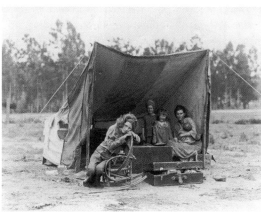
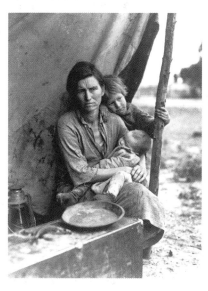

1.2–1.5 *Migrant Mother*, alternative versions

That the image was in accordance with the intentions of the photographer, and, indeed, of the FSA project, is confirmed by Roy Stryker, director of the project, in an interview:

STRYKER: I still think it's a great picture. I think it's one of America's great pictures . . .

INTERVIEWER: Would you want to say anything about what that picture means to you personally?

STRYKER: I can, in two words. Mother and child. What more do I need to say? A great, great, great picture of the mother and child. She happens

Stryker's emphasis on the drama of the photograph reflects his drive to use pictures for emotional impact.

47

to be badly dressed. It was bad conditions. But she's still a mother and she had children. We'd found a wonderful family.

(Doherty *et al.* 1972: 154)

Here Tucker is taking a critical stance, discussing the impact of the picture in terms both of culture and ideology and of the reception of the image, acknowledging differences between now and then.

Note also that she credits her source. This allows us to find the original context of the Heyman quote to check whether we agree with Tucker's interpretation. Crediting sources is a part of good academic practice, as it acknowledges previous critical contributions and helps the reader to find further information.

Clearly the potential for the image to transcend its particular location and socioeconomic context was recognised by those involved in this project. In this sense, the image reflects a humanitarian notion of universal similarities in the condition of humankind. Many critics have noted this, for instance:

For Lange, a compelling photograph presented an engaging human drama that addressed questions larger than the immediate subject. Her subjects gained importance from external value systems. . . . 'We were after the truth', she wrote, 'not just making effective pictures'. She was concerned with the human condition, and the value of a fact was measured in terms of its own consequences. . . . Today, the subjects of Lange's picture are, as Therese Heyman has observed, 'figures in history whose hardship the present viewer is incapable of healing – symbols of timeless sorrow'.

(Tucker 1984: 50–1)

7 *Family of Man*, facsimile catalogue, p. 151.

This essay by Barthes is included in his early collection, *Mythologies*. He draws our attention to, and questions, the fundamental premise of the exhibition. See general discussion of Barthes (pp. 31–3).

Indeed, this picture was included in the exhibition, 'Family of Man' (organised by the American curator, Edward Steichen, in 1955 as a sort of indirect response to the Second World War).[7] The exhibition set out to emphasise all that humanity has in common. Roland Barthes commented on the 'ambiguous myth' of community whereby diversity between peoples and cultures was brought into focus in order to forge a sense of unity from this pluralism (Barthes 1973).

The photographer's account

In an essay written almost 30 years after the event, entitled 'The Assignment I'll Never Forget', Dorothea Lange gave us her story of how she made the photograph.

The fact that Lange's story was reprinted in a major collection suggests that a photographer's account is of particular interest in considering the image. The intention of the photographer and her memory of the occasion are in some way assumed to add to our appreciation of the image and our understanding of its significance. We have to ask ourselves, 60 years on, why this should be relevant to our reading of the image now, in different circumstances.

I saw and approached the hungry and desperate mother, as if drawn by a magnet. I do not remember how I explained my presence or my camera to her, but I do remember she asked me no questions. I made five exposures, working closer and closer from the same direction. I did not ask her name or her history. She told me her age, that she was thirty-two. She said that they had been living on frozen vegetables from the surrounding fields, and birds that the children killed. She had just sold the tires from her car to buy food. There she sat in that lean-to tent with her children huddled around her, and seemed to know that my pictures might help her, and so she helped me. There was a sort of equality about it.

(Lange 1960: 264)

48

In relation to the alleged 'equality' between the photographer and her subject it is worth noting that in 1978, the 'Migrant Mother' herself, Florence Thompson, was tracked down to her trailer home in Modesto, California. One of the twentieth century's most familiar and telling images was recuperated as an ordinary, aged woman who was poor in a humdrum way and no longer able to function as an icon of nobility and sadness in the face of destitution.

Her image has appeared in many forms and in many settings, and has been multiply copied millions of times. She was a most familiar figure, but not until 50 years after the event did she get to comment on it publicly. She told United Press that she was proud to be the subject of the photograph, but that she had never made a penny out of it and that it had done her no good (Rosler 1989).

Genre and usage

The FSA project was essentially documentary. However, control of the reproduction of images did not lie in the hands of the photographers. As photohistorian, Naomi Rosenblum notes, the FSA in effect acted as a photo agency supplying pictures for photojournalistic use:

> In common with other government agencies that embraced photographic
> projects, the F.S.A. supplied prints for reproduction in the daily and
> periodical press. In that project photographers were given shooting scripts
> from which to work, did not own their negatives, and had no control
> over how the pictures might be cropped, arranged, and captioned.
> Their position was similar to that of photojournalists working for the
> commercial press – a situation that both Evans and Lange found
> particularly distasteful.
>
> (Rosenblum 1997: 366–9)

One of the central principles of the documentary aesthetic was that a photograph should be untouched, so that its veracity, its genuineness, might be maintained. Even minor violations of this principle were frowned upon:

> Lange's great *Migrant Mother* photograph had always bothered her a
> little. Just at the instant that she had taken the picture, a hand had
> reached out to draw the tent flap back a bit further and the photograph
> had caught a disembodied thumb in the foreground. That thumb had
> worried Lange. So, when she prepared the picture for *American Exodus*,
> the thumb was retouched out of the negative.
>
> This was a simple technique that she had employed hundreds of times
> during her career as a portrait photographer. For Stryker it was a lapse of
> taste. He was quite bitter over the incident.
>
> (Hurley 1972: 142)

In this account, the significance of the question of who retains control of the image rests upon an unspoken notion of the integrity of the image in terms of its original composition. For those concerned with a notion of documentary authenticity, there are ethical implications relating to the use of images. These ideas are not brought into question here. If, however, we take the more contemporary view that photographic meaning shifts according to usage or, indeed, that the photograph, once in circulation, stands apart from its maker, this is less a matter of concern.

For discussion of the concept of documentary see ch. 1, pp. 18–19 and ch. 2, pp. 79–81.

This quote reminds us of rules that functioned as indicators of authenticity. It seems to be concerned with realism. However, implicit within this is a very literal notion of realism viewed as pictures true to appearance. A number of critics, among whom Brecht and Benjamin were prominent, have argued that realism goes beyond a mere matter of appearances and, indeed, that the photograph, in its apparent literal veracity, is limited in its ability to convey information about socioeconomic and political relations.

Image in context

The FSA project was a response to the economic crisis of 1929 and the ensuing economic depression of the 1930s together with the collapse of sharecropping agriculture in a number of the south-west states of the USA. It aimed to document and record statistically the position of the rural poor, but the photographers it employed eschewed a mere photography of record in favour of works that stressed the depiction of human destitution and distress. Such images had a clear political purpose, but one that has been criticised for individualising what were collective problems with potentially collective solutions. Abigail Solomon-Godeau:

> Commenting on the works of Dorothea Lange, the film maker Pare Lorentz noted the following: 'She has selected with an unerring eye. You do not find in her portrait gallery the bindle-stiffs, the drifters, the tramps, the unfortunate, the aimless dregs of a country.' In other words, the appeal made to the viewer was premised on the assertion that the victims of the Depression were to be judged as the deserving poor, and thus the claim for redress hinged on individual misfortune rather than on systematic failure in the political, economic, and social spheres.
>
> (Solomon-Godeau 1991a: 179)

Here Solomon-Godeau is concerned with the political implications of that to which the image testifies.

Image-text

The image is titled *Migrant Mother*. This caption, together with the formal organisation of the photograph, are key elements of its appeal. Yet in *A Concise History of Photography* by Helmut and Alison Gernsheim, published in 1965, the same picture is captioned *Seasonal Farm Labourer's Family*, a title which seems less potent since it implies the presence of a working father. The original title and date are given by Andrea Fisher as 'Destitute pea pickers in California, a 32 year old mother of seven children. February 1936'.

Aesthetics and art history

Western aesthetic philosophy is concerned to examine principles of taste and systems for the appreciation of that which is deemed beautiful. Thus the aesthetics of photography have been concerned with formal matters such as composition, subject-matter, and the organisation of pictorial elements within the frame. It has also encompassed questions of technique – sharpness of image, exposure values, print quality, etc. Karin Becker Ohrn tells us that:

> Many of Lange's prints were poor. She made them according to no formula, and they varied widely in density, making it a challenge to print them.
>
> (Ohrn 1980: 228)

In analysing this quote, we want to ask whether Lorentz is accurate in his comment – are there examples of photographs by Lange which might contradict his view? (Several other photographs by Lange are included in Andrea Fisher (1987) *Let Us Now Praise Famous Women*, London: Pandora). Furthermore, do we agree with Solomon-Godeau's interpretation of his comment? Finally, what distinction is being made here between 'individual misfortune' and 'systematic failure' and what political positions underpin each of these phrases? (Pare Lorentz was head of the short-lived US Film Service, formed by Roosevelt, and director of documentary films including *The Plow That Broke the Plains*, 1936 and *The River*, 1937.)

Titles contribute to holding the meaning of pictures, to limiting the potential range of interpretations or responses on the part of the audience or reader. Examining – or imagining – alternative titles for an image can help us understand how the title lends resonance to the picture.

50

These failures of technique were unimportant when the photographs were reproduced in books and journals, but towards the end of her life, Lange presented her work in a number of major exhibitions, and this required careful technical work to take place:

> The prints were processed to archival standards and placed on white mounts. The final result was superb; the print quality was commended by several reviewers of the exhibition.
>
> (ibid.)

The context of viewing is also influential. Naomi Rosenblum comments:

> The images were transformed into photographic works of art when they were exhibited under the auspices of the Museum of Modern Art. For the first time, photographs made to document social conditions were accorded the kind of recognition formerly reserved for aesthetically conceived camera images.
>
> (Rosenblum 1997: 369)

If the photograph is in a book or magazine concerned with social conditions, its status as evidence is foregrounded. Lange's photographs were published by the FSA in 1939 as a book titled *An American Exodus: A Record of Human Erosion*. The title directs the reader to consider the group of photographs sociologically; the focus is upon the implications of the content. By contrast, when exhibited in the art gallery the context invites us to look at the picture in aesthetic and symbolic terms. For instance, art historians have observed that Lange's photograph is related – in terms of both subject-matter and framing – to the many paintings of the Madonna and Child in Western art.

As gendered image

A number of feminist photohistorians have looked at the FSA in terms of the participation of women photographers and the gendering of the image. Lange has been cast as 'mother' of documentary. Thus, for instance, Andrea Fisher in *Let us Now Praise Famous Women* discusses her contribution:

> Dorothea Lange became a key figure in securing the humanism of documentary. She was repeatedly represented in popular journals as the 'mother' of documentary: the little woman who would cut through ideas by evoking personal feeling. Through her pathos for destitute rural migrants, the New Deal's programs of rural reform might be legitimized, not as power, but as the exercise of care. Her place in the construction of documentary rhetoric was thus crucially different but every bit as important as Walker Evans', more widely recognized as the paradigmatic figure of documentary. Where Evans was thought of as the guarantor of

This concern with print quality is often seen as excessively formal, privileging matters of technique at the expense of content, meaning and context. However, different contexts require differing levels of attention to print quality. While a mediocre print may be adequate for newspapers given their low-quality reproduction, gallery exhibition demands high-quality visual resolution. Shift in usage of the image required a different degree of precision.

In traditional art history, questions of genre, form and technique, as well as subject-matter deemed appropriate for artistic expression, are central. When photographs are re-appropriated within the gallery context, specific art-historical traditions associated with them come into play, becoming, as it were, laid over the picture.

honest observation, with his flat-lit frontal shots, Lange was lauded as the keeper of documentary's compassion.

(Fisher 1987: 131)

Fisher argues that Stryker over-edited the FSA work and in so doing obscured the work and the role played by women in the project. She particularly argues that representations of femininity played a crucial role in the rhetoric of the FSA photographs, both in terms of the gender of the photographer and subject-matter.

In hailing Lange as the 'Mother', Stryker placed her as the mirror of immutable motherhood that many of her photographs would subsequently suggest. Her consuming empathy for her subjects became synonymous with her subjects' caring for their children. Though only a fraction of her images conformed to the transcendent ideal of mother and child, it was the image of the Migrant Mother which soared to the status of icon, and became the hallmark of Lange herself:

> The naming of Lange as 'Mother' folded across the reading of her images. It not only prioritized certain images, but became intimately embedded in the sense that could be made of them.

(Fisher 1987: 140–1)

Photography critic John Roberts has summarised her argument thus:

> Fisher argues that one of the principal ideological props of the way FSA photographs were used to construct an American community under threat was the image of the maternal. She cites Dorothea Lange's *Migrant Mother* (1937) as a primary example of this, one of the most reproduced photographs of the period, so much so in fact that it could be said to stand in iconically *for* the Depression. For Fisher the way the image was cropped and contextualised reveals how much the image of a damaged femininity came to symbolise the crisis of community for the American public. Anxious and in obvious poverty, the woman holds on to her two children, suggesting the power of maternal values to overcome the most dire of circumstances. Here is a woman who has lost everything, yet heroically, stoically keeps her family together. Here in essence was what the magazine editors were waiting for: an image of tragedy AND resistance. That this image became so successful reflects how great a part gender played in the symbolic management of the Depression.

(Roberts 1998: 85)

Fisher herself offers a slightly different account:

> The incessant picturing of women with their children was never prioritized by Stryker for his photographers; *it was not a conscious political device*.

Here Fisher draws attention to the centrality of 'motherhood', a concept which was brought under scrutiny in feminist critiques of the 1970s.

But perhaps it arose, like the whole of Stryker's enterprise, as part of that widely felt nostalgia for a mythic American past: an American essence as natural as the land, and so located in an immutable rural family. But only for an urban audience could the land achieve this mythic status, and the rural mother the status of universal touchstone. Perhaps, too, that desire for lost plenitude found in the image of the Mother its most appropriate analogue.

(Fisher 1987: 138; our emphasis)

Here, questions of gender are seen as interrelating with other sets of ideas about Americanness. Fisher points to the power of this interaction.

Semiotics focuses on the formal components of the image, emphasising the centrality of sign systems. Sign systems are viewed as largely conventional; that is, primarily consequent not upon 'natural' relations between images and that to which they refer but upon cultural understandings. As noted (p. 31), for American semiotician C.S. Peirce, signs may be iconic (based upon resemblance to that represented), indexical (based upon a trace or indicator, for instance, smoke indicates fire) or symbolic (based upon conventional associations). Chemically produced photographs incorporate all three constituents: images resemble the person or place or object re-presented; they are indexical in that the subject had to be present for the photograph to be made, which means that the image is essentially a 'trace'; and images circulate in specific cultural contexts within which differing symbolic meanings and values may adhere.

Reading the photograph

As we have noted, the 1960s and 1970s witnessed a shift in photography theory whereby images became viewed as complexly coded artefacts to be read as cultural, psychoanalytic and ideological signs. For Barthes, in his later writings, specifically *Camera Lucida*, the photograph signifies reality, rather than reflecting or representing it. The emphasis is upon what the viewer as 'reader' of the image takes as the principal cues and clues for use as the basis of interpretation.

In reading photographs we may choose to concentrate on the formal qualities of the image; for example, its arrangement within the frame, or the dispositions, stances and gestures of its subjects. Alternatively, or additionally, we may seek to locate the work within the history of image-making, noting similarities and differences from other works of the same kind. Or we may want to explore the way in which the image may be examined from the standpoint of a number of disciplines or discourses which exist outside the photographic.

John Pultz begins his analysis of *Migrant Mother* by referring to these ideas in the context of a reading of the gestural system at work within the image. He then moves to consider the woman's body within the tradition of painting; and concludes by commenting on the gendered nature of the space within which the image is set:

Questions of gender have been discussed both in relation to the photographer and to the content of the image as a particular representation of, in this instance, maternity. But Roberts takes this up in terms which contain overtones of conspiracy, seeing the gendering in terms of political rhetoric. When we look back to Fisher herself we find a different emphasis. This illustrates, once again, the importance of checking original sources. As we see, Roberts has imposed a specific inflection on Fisher's original research.

Freudian theory has been acknowledged in Western academia, especially in the latter part of the twentieth century. Within photography criticism, two influential ideas derived from psychoanalytic theory have been that of the function of the gaze, and of analysis of the way in which what might be thought of as 'abstractions' may be inscribed upon the body – literally embodied. These ideas form the background to Pultz's discussion of how we look at this image. Note that in this instance it is the interrelation of gender and of aesthetics which is woven into his analysis. However, we might ask whether Pultz believes Lange's reference to the virgin and child was conscious on her part.

Migrant Mother . . . centers on the female body, the body that is socially constructed through the gaze, and has the quality 'to be looked at'. In *Migrant Mother*, Lange builds a narrative around a woman and her three children, centered on the single gesture of an upraised arm. As the two older children turn their heads away from the photographer (out of shame or shyness?) and an infant child sleeps, the mother alone remains awake and vigilant. Her arm is upraised, not to support her head but to finger her chin in tentative thought. The picture is created around certain notions of the female body, including the idea of the nurturing mother. Lange drew on traditional, such as Renaissance depictions of the Virgin and Child and the secularised versions of these that began to appear in the mid nineteenth century with the rise of the Victorian cult of domesticity. Moreover, even though *Migrant Mother* was made in a public space, the close cropping of the image creates within the frame itself a protected, interior, feminised space.

(Pultz 1995a: 93)

Image as icon

Halla Beloff wants to grant the image an iconic status that takes it out of the realm of representation altogether:

Such is the power of the camera that we can easily think of photographs as having a kind of independent reality. Dorothea Lange's *Migrant Mother* is a picture that has entered Western consciousness. She is not a mere representation.

(Beloff 1985: 15)

'Icon' here refers not so much to the verisimilitude of the image but to the symbolic value invested in it.

Here, there is a notion of photographs as containing 'reality' – a commodity that, as it were, leaches out over time, so that the initial complexity gives way to the merely iconic. Do we agree with this? Or does the image continue to be 'troubling'?

It is, indeed, one of the key examples selected by Hariman and Lucaites in their useful discussion of the political ramifications of images, iconicity and public culture (Hariman and Lucaites 2007). Part of the iconic power of the work derives from its multiple appearances over the years, in many contexts and forms. For instance, in 1964 it appeared on the cover of the Hispanic magazine, *Bohemia Venezolana*, and in 1973 was referenced in *Black Panther* magazine (figures 1.6 and 1.7). Paula Rabinowitz comments on this aspect of the photograph in the following terms:

I do not need to remind my readers of the power of images – a power that includes their ability to exceed the original impulse of their creation. For instance, the troubling story of Lange's 'Migrant Mother', told and retold, offers with acute poignancy an example of discourse as repository of meaning – the photograph as much as its checkered history includes a woman and her children, a photographer, a government bureau, popular magazines, museums, scholars, and a changing public – an image and tale composed, revised, circulated, and reissued in various venues until

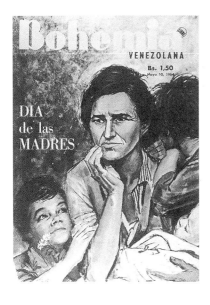

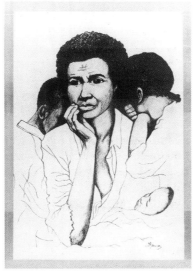

1.6 Reference to 'Migrant Mother', *Bohemia Venezolana*, **1964**

1.7 Reference to 'Migrant Mother', *Black Panther* **magazine, 1972**

whatever reality its subject first possessed has been drained away and the image becomes icon.

(Rabinowitz 1994: 86)

In summary, critical writings appropriate and 're-frame' images in relation to particular sets of concerns. This image has attracted extensive discussion from a range of perspectives, reflecting many differing concerns. Our procedure here was to seek out, select and analyse specific quotes as examples of different 'takes' on the picture.

See ch. 4 for further examples of analysis of specific images.

HISTORIES OF PHOTOGRAPHY

Inventions – the name by which we call devices that seem fundamentally new – are almost always born out of a process that is more like farming than magic. From a complex ecology of ideas and circumstance that includes the condition of the intellectual soil, the political climate, the state of technical competence, and the sophistication of the seed, the suggestion of new possibilities arises.

(Szarkowski 1989: 11)

From its inception photography spread to every continent and most countries, but we now live in a globalised world that is increasingly connected. It is one in which billions of messages and images are exchanged every hour. The invention of photography was a pre-condition for the existence of such a world, but photographs also comment on and critique globalisation. In these conditions it is hard to imagine anyone setting out to write a synoptic and encyclopaedic history of world photography. In the last century histories of photography were produced that helped to structure the way in which the medium was understood and appreciated. Today, useful and informative histories of photography continue to appear, often organised around the material available in particular archives.

Typically, histories of photography offer a series of histories of photographers illustrated with examples from their work. In the twentieth century, in common with other areas of the arts, such as painting or the novel, there was a tendency to conflate the history of the subject with the work of particular practitioners. The central purpose of this opening section is to compare key books, published in English, most of which are variously titled *The History . . .* or *A Concise History . . . .*

What is the story of photography? It was invented in 1839, or so we have commonly been led to believe, but this apparently simple statement masks a complex set of factors. It is true that it was in 1839 that both Fox Talbot in England and Daguerre in France announced the processes whereby they had succeeded in making and fixing a photographic image. But the idea of photography long precedes that date.

To a large extent the history of photography prior to 1938, when **Beaumont Newhall** first published his commentary, then entitled *Photography, A Short Critical History*, has been represented as a history of techniques. The focus was not on what sorts of images were made, but on how they were made. This approach is to some extent reflected in museum collections wherein it is the instruments of photography which are prioritised for display, with photographs acting as examples of particular printing methods, detailed in accompanying descriptions. The subject-matter of such photographs (and associated aesthetic and social implications), if acknowledged at all, is presented as being of secondary importance.

So, was the story of photography always an account of changing technologies? Martin Gasser suggests that this history is more complicated (Gasser 1992). Considering German, French, British and American publications written between 1839 and 1939, he identifies three emphases: first, what is termed 'the priority debate'; second, histories of the development of photography written primarily as handbooks detailing methods and techniques and also potential uses for photography; third, histories of the photograph as image. It is worth noting that it is the proliferation of material in the second of these categories which has led to the false assumption that the first hundred years of publication were largely devoted to technologies and techniques. Aside

BEAUMONT NEWHALL (1982) **The History of Photography**, New York: MOMA, fifth edition, revised and enlarged. This remains a key text, although, as a number of critics have commented, it is limited in its compass by its foundations in the MOMA collection which is primarily American in orientation and idiosyncratic in its holdings, having been built up over the years according to the interests and tastes of its particular curators.

Key archives in Britain for equipment and techniques:
- The National Museum of Media, Bradford
- The Fox Talbot Museum, Lacock, Wiltshire (National Trust)

from any other consideration, a number of the papers published in the early years of photography made assertions about the intrinsic nature of the medium and speculated on its potential uses.

Which founding father?

Before considering histories of the photograph as image, the priority debate deserves brief comment. This debate is concerned with who first achieved the fixing of the photographic image. A number of historical accounts exist whose primary purpose is to argue – usually through a combination of biography and discussion of photographic techniques – that someone other than Fox Talbot in Britain or Daguerre in France 'invented' photography. These two men were the first to announce their findings publicly (in the appropriate scientific journals of the time, in Britain and France) in 1839. But it is also clear, from contemporary correspondence, that Fox Talbot was not alone in Britain in his experimentation. Similarly, in France, Nicephore Nièpce was responsible in the early 1820s for key discoveries leading up to the **daguerreotype**. As every history of early photography emphasises, the challenge did not lie with the development of camera and lens technology. The principle of concentrating light through a small hole in order to create reflection on the wall of a dark chamber was known to Aristotle (384–322 BC). The photographic camera was based on the camera obscura, described as early as the tenth century AD, of which the first illustration was published in 1545. The problem which preoccupied experimentation in the late eighteenth and early nineteenth centuries was how to fix the image once it had been obtained.

The credit for discovering practical chemical processes lies with no single person, nor, indeed, with any particular nation, although the ascription of credit has always had nationalistic overtones with, for example, the French, keen to downgrade British claims (1839 was within a generation of the Battle of Trafalgar). Likewise, strenuous rewritings of history allowed the German photohistorian, Stenger, writing in the 1930s during the ascendance of Hitler, to claim German experiments of the eighteenth century as fundamental for photography. Re-examining the prehistory, Mary Warner Marien urges caution in two respects: first, she warns against too uncritical an acceptance of the work of early photohistorians. She notes the extent to which the burgeoning of research in the field since the Second World War has both uncovered new findings and suggested new ways of thinking about previously known facts within the history of photography; recent research represents only the beginning of a much needed archaeology of early photography. In addition, she emphasises the broader historical context of political, technological and cultural change within which photography developed. The overall point is that, in considering the origins of photography, a stance which is both cautious and critical should be adopted (Warner Marien 1991). Geoffrey Batchen offers a more detailed discussion which points to the complexities involved in

daguerreotype Photographic image made by the process launched by Louis-Jacques-Mandé Daguerre in France in 1839. It is a positive image on a metal plate with a mirror-like silvered surface, characterised by very fine detail. Each one is unique and fragile and needs to be protected by a padded case. It became the dominant portrait mode for the first decades of photography, especially in the United States.

reappraising early photography in terms of who founded it, where, and for what purposes (Batchen 1997).

The photograph as image

While earlier writing on photography had not exclusively focused on technology and techniques, since the Second World War art-historical concerns have become more central, together with a new stress on connoisseurship of the photograph as a privileged object analogous to a painting. A number of the books which we now take as key texts on the history of photography were first written as exhibition catalogues for works collected and shown in institutions. For instance, Beaumont Newhall's *The History of Photography* stems from a catalogue written to accompany 'Photography 1839–1937' at the Museum of Modern Art (MOMA) in New York in 1937. The broader context for the introduction of art-historical methods and concerns into photography collection and exhibition includes the development of art history as an academic discipline and, more particularly, the increasing influence of art criticism within modern art in the first half of the twentieth century. Here it is relevant to remember the emphasis upon art as a set of special practices which informed modernist thinking. A central feature of modernist criticism was that of maintaining a clear distinction between high and low culture, a differentiation which was equally evident in the writings of some Marxist critics as it was among conservative critics. If photographs were to take their place in the gallery, they inevitably became caught up within more general intellectual trends and discourses.

Since the Second World War, then, the predominant approach to writing the history of photography has been to focus on the photograph as image. Two classic histories, still consulted, are Beaumont Newhall's *The History of Photography* (now in its fifth, revised edition); and **Helmut and Alison Gernsheim**'s *History of Photography*, which, as we have seen, was organised in its earliest form in relation to developing technologies but has subsequently been rewritten to take fuller account of photographs as specific types of image. It is worth pausing to consider and compare these two publications; together they established a specific canon for the history of photography which has been the basis for further development – or taken as a starting point for challenge – ever since.

Educated as an art historian, and appointed onto the library staff at New York's Museum of Modern Art, Newhall was invited to research its first major photography exhibition. His historical overview, which formed the principal essay in the exhibition catalogue, described changing techniques, but also included comments on specific photographers and particular periods of aesthetic development. Newhall was one of the first to introduce aesthetic judgements into the discussion of photographs, but, at this stage, as he has noted himself, he avoided the identification of artists, thereby refusing MOMA's expectations of what an exhibition catalogue should be. It was only

HELMUT AND ALISON GERNSHEIM (1969) **The History of Photography from the Earliest Use of the Camera Obscura in the Eleventh Century up to 1914**, 2 vols, London and New York: McGraw-Hill (first edition, 1955). One of the two classic histories. It is interesting to compare later editions with the first edition in order to see how their interests and research developed.

in the third edition of his *History of Photography* that emphasis on photographers and an account of the work of practitioners emerges. In this edition he also, for the first time, introduced chapters on straight photography, documentary and 'instant vision', thereby acknowledging characteristics specific to photography. The third edition thus represents the beginning of an engagement with the idea of photography theory as distinct from art theory.[8]

Similarly, it is only in later editions that Helmut Gernsheim refocuses the history to comment more extensively upon particular practitioners. His contribution to the history, developed in collaboration with Alison Gernsheim, was founded in the study of their collection of nineteenth-century photographs.[9] The full title of their research, first published in 1955 and dedicated to Beaumont Newhall, is *The History of Photography from the Earliest Use of the Camera Obscura in the Eleventh Century up to 1914*. The second edition, in 1969, was divided into two volumes, with considerably more emphasis on illustration than previously. The third, revised edition appeared in the 1980s, by then under the single authorship of Helmut Gernsheim (since the death of his wife). The first volume of *The History of Photography* focuses on the origins of photography in France, America, Great Britain and Germany.[10] A chapter on Italy was added later, in the third edition, which was published in 1982. A summary version of the research was published in 1965 as *A Concise History of Photography*, offering a shorter, and thus easier entry into his work. This version includes a brief, and highly selective, discussion of modern photography up to the 1950s. (For purposes of studying the nineteenth century, the two-volume edition, which is in large format, with good-quality picture reproduction, is recommended for the detail of observation and the range of imagery.)

Both Newhall and Gernsheim focus upon Western Europe and the United States (with no comment, for instance, on Soviet Russia or South America). The key difference between Newhall and Gernsheim lies in Gernsheim's relative concentration on the nineteenth century, and his greater emphasis on technical aspects of photography. His study is more lengthy and less literary in approach than Newhall's. This may reflect the origins of Newhall's essay as an exhibition catalogue, which meant that he had to take account of the problem of succinct communication to a diverse audience. Further differences may stem from nationality: Newhall was American; Gernsheim was born in Germany but was naturalised British. As has already been noted, they were working in relation to particular archive collections, the former drawing upon the collection at MOMA with, inevitably, a central focus upon developments in America, as well as upon the research in Europe conducted prior to the 1937 exhibition. The Gernsheim collection focused on the nineteenth century, and was centred upon British photography.

Both publications proceed to a greater or lesser extent by way of discussion of great photographers. Gernsheim notes that their collection was organised not only in files about photographic processes, apparatus, exhibitions, but also

8 All editions are credited to Newhall, but a number of commentators have noted the research contribution of his wife, Nancy Newhall.

9 The Gernsheim collection is now at the University of Texas in Austin.

10 The chapter is in fact entitled 'The Daguerreotype in German-Speaking Countries'. He refers to what is now Germany and Austria.

PAUL HILL AND THOMAS COOPER (1992) **Dialogue with Photography**, Manchester: Cornerhouse Publications.

Also see:
VICKI GOLDBERG (ed.) (1981) **Photography in Print**, Albuquerque: University of New Mexico Press.

NATHAN LYONS (1966) **Photographers on Photography**, Englewood Cliffs: Prentice-Hall.

CHRISTOPHER PHILLIPS (ed.) (1989) **Photography in the Modern Era**, New York: Metropolitan Museum/Aperture.

folders on important photographers (see **Hill and Cooper 1992**). Newhall, as an art historian, was accustomed to emphasis on the contribution of the individual artist, and by the fifth edition of his work, the contribution of individual photographers and the authority of their work is clearly a priority. This has the effect of raising the profile of certain 'masters' of photography, thereby defining a canon, or authoritative list, of great practitioners. It also renders history as a relatively simple chronological account, devoid of broader social context. The canonisation of photographers as artists, in line with the emphasis on individual practitioners in other art fields in the Modern period, characterises many contemporary publications. For instance, Photo Poche publish a three-part 'history' organised as brief biographies with comments on photographers, accompanied by one image selected from their lifetime's work. Similarly, *The Photography Book*, published by Phaidon, includes 500 photographs by 500 different photographers (presented alphabetically by surname). Such collections offer useful starting points for identifying the style of particular photographers, but the socio-historical contextualisation is strictly limited. By selecting known practitioners, rather than sets of ideas or types of practice, such books have the effect of reinforcing the canon of acclaimed photographers and marginalising practices which cannot be illustrated through reference to specific names.

History in focus

There are several consequences of canonisation: first, changing attitudes to photography as a set of practices have tended to become obscured behind the eulogisation of particular photographers, their photographs and their contribution. Second, the focus (led by male historians) has been upon male photographers, with the consequence that the participation of women has been overlooked or obscured. Third, there has been relatively extensive discussion of professional and serious commercial practices, but relatively few accounts of popular photography or of more specialist areas of practice, such as architecture or medicine. Fourth, as has already been mentioned, photography history has tended to prioritise aesthetic concerns over broader and more diverse forms of involvement of photography in all aspects of social experience, including personal photography, publishing and everyday portraiture.

MARY WARNER MARIEN (2014) **Photography, A Cultural History**, London: Laurence King Publishing Ltd.

More recent histories published in English have offered broader perspectives. Of these, the most comprehensive is **Mary Warner Marien**'s *Photography, A Cultural History* which considers a range of amateur and professional uses of photography, from art and travel, to fashion and the mass media. Although organised broadly chronologically, it is structured primarily in terms of discussion of particular practices rather than technologies or practitioners, although both the latter are acknowledged in mini case studies which feature throughout; the book is clearly written and amply illustrated. The central focus is upon developments in Europe and North America, but it also takes advantage of recent research into non-Western photography. **Gerry Badger**'s *The Genius* *of Photography* (published to coincide with a BBC television series under the same title) weaves together the thematic and the chronological (and includes a useful historical timeline). The subtitle, 'How photography has changed our lives' indicates his focus on the import and impact of photographs on human experience. **Naomi Rosenblum**'s *A World History of Photography* likewise offers an excellent, well-written account which is thorough and markedly international in its compass. The device of including three separate sections on technical history allows her to focus on images and movements in the main body of the text, which is extensively illustrated.

Mark Haworth-Booth's discussion of *Photography: An Independent Art* offers an eminently readable account of the development of the photography archive at the Victoria and Albert Museum in London. While focusing upon images in that particular collection, his discussion is informed and informative about more general developments in photography as both art and technology. Likewise, **Ian Jeffrey**'s account *Photography, A Concise History* is purposeful and generally clearly written. This book set out to be a radical reappraisal of the history of photography as written to date, although Stevie Bezencenet has argued that it was less than successful in its re-evaluation on the grounds that to produce a history of photography now requires a diversity of academic approaches (Bezencenet 1982b). She also notes that Jeffrey offers another history overwhelmingly concerned with male practitioners, making the point that, however radical his declared intentions, his work mirrors the established formula of a chronological account of changes and focuses on dominant modes of photography and particular practitioners.

Lemagny and Rouille's account is of interest to the English reader, for its central starting point is within French culture which, in effect, recentres France within photography history. While discussion of photography in Britain is more limited than in some of the other accounts, the references to Europe as a whole are more comprehensive. This book is an edited collection. Despite the editors' stated intention of holding a balance between discussion of photography as a field in itself, and discussion of the broader context within which it functions, some chapters succeed in being more analytic than others. While expressing strong criticisms, in reviewing the book Warner Marien suggests that its strengths lie in two chapters on photography as art, and she adds that in general this collection takes more account of contemporary theoretical ideas than do most works of this kind (Warner Marien 1988). Likewise, **Michel Frizot**'s *A New History of Photography* is written from a French perspective, as indicated, for instance, in its emphasis in early chapters on the spread of the daguerreotype. Organised chronologically, it offers groups of images juxtaposed with specific thematic discussions which range from the technical to particular fields of practice. In a similar vein, **Graham Clarke** explores how we understand a photograph through a brief introductory historical overview of practices in terms of genres: landscape, the city, the portrait, the body, documentary, fine art, and photographic manipulations.

GERRY BADGER (2007)
The Genius of Photography – How Photography has Changed our Lives, London: Quadrille.

NAOMI ROSENBLUM (2007)
A World History of Photography, New York, London, and Paris: Abbeville Press. Previous editions, 1984, 1989, 1997.

MARK HAWORTH-BOOTH (1997) **Photography: An Independent Art**, London: V&A Publications. Haworth-Booth was Curator of Photography at the V&A. This book was published to coincide with the establishment, in May 1998, of a permanent photography gallery at the V&A for showing works from the museum's collection.

IAN JEFFREY (1981) **Photography, A Concise History**, London: Thames and Hudson.

JEAN-CLAUDE LEMAGNY AND ANDRÉ ROUILLE (1987) **A History of Photography**, Cambridge: Cambridge University Press.

MICHEL FRIZOT (ed.) (1998) **A New History of Photography**, Cologne: Könemann.

GRAHAM CLARKE (1997) **The Photograph**, Oxford: Oxford University Press.

The year 1989 saw the publication of two major historical overviews, both designed to accompany retrospective exhibitions celebrating 150 years of photography. The title of Mike Weaver's *The Art of Photography* (1989) reflects the location of this exhibition at the Royal Academy in Piccadilly, London. This was the first ever exhibition of photographs to be held there and, as such, both the show and the accompanying publication emphasise the image as art and the status of the photographer as artist. Similarly, **John Szarkowski**'s *Photography Until Now* (1989) – which accompanied the MOMA celebration of 150 years of photography – in relying primarily on the MOMA collection reinforces the American canon (which includes a number of European photographers). Szarkowski trained both as an art historian and as a photographer before working in the MOMA collection for 30 years. His interests centred upon the formal and technical properties which distinguish photographs from other visual media, and in the status of the unauthored or vernacular photograph. However, the production values of both of these publications are high, which makes each a useful source for visual reference and research.

If you are coming to the story of photography for the first time, Rosenblum offers a good, clearly written starting point for engaging with this history. Alternatively, Szarkowski and Jeffrey complement one another in taking America, or Europe, as central starting points. Indeed, Szarkowski specifically comments on the difference in the situation of photography in the US, as opposed to Europe, at the turn of the century. He suggests that American (he specifies 'Yankee') photographers were more inclined towards reportage than their European counterparts, having invested less in claims for the status of the photograph as art, since America lacked the depth of artistic tradition that was central to post-Renaissance Europe.

Each of the histories reviewed above reflects, to a greater or lesser degree, an established selection of photographers and their images. Similarly, histories of photography specific to a particular country or region tend to draw upon established sources and archives, thereby in effect re-affirming orthodoxies in terms of the canon of well-known photographers. The 'great masters' approach has been challenged variously. Anne Tucker, in *The Woman's Eye* (1973) was among the first to draw attention to the considerable participation of women as photographers historically. As the title implies, she suggests that what we see photographically – that is, subject-matter and treatment – to some extent reflects gender. This question of gender has been pursued by **Val Williams** in her discussion of British women's participation in a range of practices, including the local (studio) and the domestic (the family album), and, like Mary Warner Marien, her historical account takes stock of commercial practices. A more recent collection of essays on European women photographers includes individual critical studies of the contribution of specific women photographers particularly in Sweden but also in Denmark, Germany, Italy, Poland and France. The essays, which make extensive use of archive

JOHN SZARKOWSKI (1989) **Photography Until Now**, New York: MOMA. Published to coincide with the exhibition of the same name on the occasion of the 150 years' celebration.

VAL WILLIAMS (1986) **Women Photographers: The Other Observers, 1900 to the Present**, London: Virago. Revised edition (1991) **The Other Observers: Women Photographers from 1900 to the Present.**

materials, are simultaneously biographical in introducing the work of photographers not necessarily familiar to us and analytical in appraising the context
and import of their work within a range of personal and professional spheres
of practice. By contrast, **Naomi Rosenbaum**, in reappraising photo-histories,
focuses primarily upon work by American women photographers. Likewise,
Jeanne Montoussamy-Ashe (1985) reinstates black women into the history of
American photography, noting, for instance, documentation for the 1866
Houston city directory which lists 'col' against the name of a female photographic printer. (Some women are also listed in D. Willis Thomas' *Black
Photographers* bio-bibliography (1985), again American.) In all instances, what
is at stake is to note the presence of women within a particular field and
to consider ways in which gender, positively or negatively, contributed to
constructing or limiting the roles played. By contrast, Constance Sullivan's
Woman Photographers (1990), considering European (including British) and
American examples, has stressed women's participation as artists, arguing that
women's work historically has demonstrated equivalent aesthetic values to those
which characterise the work of their better-known male contemporaries,
while often bringing different subject-matter into focus. This book is particularly useful for its quality reproduction of images. But the fundamental point
is that each author focuses on putting women back into the picture even if,
ultimately, they challenge the canon rather than canonisation.

Van Gelder and Westgeest (2011) examine the particular nature of
photography as a visual medium through a series of case studies including
comparison of photography with painting, virtual places and time-based art.
They also explore the way in which it has functioned as a documentary form
and has been used to delineate and critique social and cultural issues.

LENA JOHANNESSON AND
GUNNILLA KNAPE (eds) (2003)
**Women Photographers –
European Experience**,
Gothenburg: Acta Universitatis
Gothoburgensis.

NAOMI ROSENBLUM (2010)
**A History of Women
Photographers**, New York,
London and Paris: Abbeville
Press.

Also see:
LIZ HERON AND VAL WILLIAMS
(1996) **Illuminations,
Women Writing on
Photography from the
1850s to the Present**,
London and New York:
I B Tauris.

HILDE VAN GELDER AND
HELEN WESTGEEST (2011)
**Photography Theory in
Historical Perspective**,
Oxford: Wiley-Blackwell.

PHOTOGRAPHY AND SOCIAL HISTORY

Social history and photography

There has been a further challenge to the dominance of the 'great masters'
history of photography from those who have re-examined the status and
significance of popular photography. By 'popular' we refer to personal
photography, or to photographs which may have been commissioned from
professional photographers, but were intended for personal use (see chapter
3). The term also extends to include postcards exchanged between individuals,
and pictures made to record events or membership of clubs and societies. The
high street portrait studio is also a legacy of Victorian photography, and was
by no means confined to major cities. Such studios were often family
enterprises, or were run by women photographers.

The contribution of particular photographers, and the economic circumstances within which Victorian and Edwardian photography was pursued, has
become a focus of much recent research. But one of the points about reviewing

popular photography and rethinking its significance is that concern with the authoring of images is related to questions of provenance (establishing where and when a photograph was taken) rather than to questions of artistic significance. This is because popular photography is increasingly used as social-historical evidence. Personal albums, and other materials, are viewed as a form of visual anthropology and are catalogued within a number of archives, of differing scale and thematic concern. Public museums and libraries may have photographic collections within their local or regional archive; and there are many independent collections.[11] Such rich collections offer myriad research possibilities. They also contribute to the 'Heritage' industry wherein photographs play a high profile as 'evidence' from the past. As such, they are displayed, or used as reference for the design of reconstructions of buildings or machinery, or republished as postcards.

11 See the Royal Photographic Society (1977) *Directory of British Photographic Collections*, London: Heinemann.

The photograph as testament

Photographs are commonly used as evidence. They are among the material marshalled by the historian in order to investigate the past. They have become a major source of information by which we picture, understand or imagine the nineteenth century. Historians have for the most part had an uneasy relationship with the medium, as their professional training did not introduce them to an analysis of visual images. It was television that first raided the many photographic archives for images of historical interest; this necessarily led to some difficulties, not least of which was that of an archive used in a general way to illustrate commentary, with scant regard for the purposes for which the photographs were made. The social historian may be interested in changing modes of dress, or agricultural and industrial machinery. Photographs are used as evidence of such changes, which means that the detailing of the source and date of the photograph – that is, its *provenance* – becomes especially important. Hence we come across titles of publications such as 'The Camera as Historian' or 'The Camera as Witness'.[12]

12 Tagg (1988) remarks on the publication in London as early as 1916 of a handbook entitled *The Camera as Historian* aimed at those who used the camera for survey and record societies.

Social history has also become a form of popular entertainment. For example, around the world *Heritage Trails* are undertaken with portable digital devices which download appropriate talks, photographs or moving images at key points. These trails locate historical events within the landscape in which they originally took place, so that civil wars, industrial unrest, royal ceremonies or great engineering feats can all be celebrated. Photographs are often key documents here as they validate the accuracy of the narrative that, in fact, has often been constructed in relation to them.

Popular education also led to a growth in the use of photographs for the analysis of local or community history.[13] There are a number of reasons why people are interested in using old photographs: some have an ethnographic curiosity about the kinds of clothes or tools that were common at a particular period, while others are fascinated by the characteristic stance and gait of workers in particular trades. Social and labour historians who wanted to gain

13 See 'The Pencil of History' in Patrice Petro (ed.) (1995) *Fugitive Images*, Bloomington: Indiana University Press.

some idea of ordinary life and work in the Victorian era have also been drawn to the examination of visual material; not merely for the information provided by photographs, but also to begin to recognise in the faces and stances of the subjects something of the real people in the scenes that have been the subject of so many accounts and narratives.

Photography was used throughout the nineteenth century in the service of political and industrial change. One reason for landscape photography was governmental employment of photographers for civil and military mapping purposes. For instance, the British government used photographers for a military survey of the Highlands of Scotland in order to help quell anti-English rebellion (Christian 1990). Similarly, in America, early landscape photography in the West was often commercial in origin: Carleton Watkins' employers included the California State Geological Survey and the Pacific Railroad Company (Snyder 1994). These photographs, along with others made for less systematic purposes, are used as a form of social-historical evidence. Examples range widely: for instance, Alison Gernsheim used photographs as a basis for a survey of changing fashions (Gernsheim 1981). The status of the photograph as evidence is not questioned. Likewise, books based on past photojournalism are common.[14] Such books purport to present the past 'as it was', taking for granted that this is what photographs do. As is asserted on the inside cover of one such book presenting pictures of Britain and Ireland, 'More than words, more than paintings or prints, old photographs convey an immediate, undistorted impression of the past' (Minto 1970).

Such use of photographs reflects a broader set of academic assumptions. Traditionally, British historical, scientific and social scientific method was characterised by empiricism. The nineteenth century was a period of extensive technological and social change, typified by faith in progress and 'modernity'. Modernity has to be distinguished from modernism. Historians have argued constantly about when 'modernity' begins, but it much pre-dates the twentieth-century art movements – aesthetic and philosophical developments in art and design – that are called modernism. Modernity is usually dated from the middle of the eighteenth century. Important changes included the transformation of the economy through new techniques of production; the development of new materials and commodities; the growth of industrialisation and, related to this, the expansion of towns and cities as people moved to live in centres of employment; the creation of new kinds of communication systems and forms of display. In Britain, France and elsewhere, such changes were underpinned economically through imperialism (which made available raw materials and cheap labour from other parts of the world) and through the low pay and poor working conditions experienced by industrial and agrarian labour at home. All these factors contributed to the increasingly public and urban nature of modern life, and to emphasising the separation of the aristocracy (in Britain), the professional and entrepreneurial middle classes, and the workers.

14 There are too many examples to enumerate, but many draw upon pictures from the *Illustrated London News* or *Picture Post*.

Photography not only developed in the Victorian era but was also implicitly caught up in nineteenth-century interests and attitudes. The Victorians invested considerable faith in the power of the camera to record, classify and witness. This meant that the camera was also entrusted with delineating social appearance, classifying the face of criminality and lunacy, offering racial and social stereotypes. In one of few histories to investigate the photograph neither primarily as image nor as technology, **Alan Thomas** in *The Expanding Eye* considers ways in which early uses of photography reflect and reinforce nineteenth-century concerns. Centred upon Victorian Britain, his account focuses on the popularisation of photography both in terms of uses of photographs (it is one of the first accounts to give a whole chapter to photography as family chronicler) and in terms of representation of the everyday. Thus he includes discussion of personal uses of photography in, for instance, the family album; portraiture (including theatre portraits); and photographs which investigate rural and urban working and living conditions. Likewise, **Mary Warner Marien**, in the publication which preceded her comprehensive cultural history, critically considers the history of the idea of photography, its cultural impact and implications in the nineteenth and early twentieth century, including discussion of the photograph within mass culture.

One of the consequences of extensive social change was a series of social surveys, which were designed to try to understand further how different social groups responded to the changing times and sought explanation through the quantitative assembly of information. In 1851 the Great Exhibition celebrated industrial and technological achievement. In that same year, the British Census recorded differences in work status and living circumstances.[15] The motivation for the Victorian survey was not simply academic. Also in 1851 Henry Mayhew published his *London Labour and London Poor*. This first survey of living conditions was illustrated with wood engravings based upon photographs, and therefore stands as an early example of the photograph being used as documentation. It became common for authenticity to be stressed through using such phrases as 'drawn from an original photograph'. The photographic image was already being mobilised as witness.

Categorical photography

In the 1970s and 1980s a number of academics and critics became centrally interested in the institutional structures through which photography functioned. They replaced a primary concern with the immanent image with the study of the ways in which photography was caught up in the social articulation of power and control.

John Tagg has written extensively on the uses of photography within power relations, noting that photographs became implicated in surveillance very early on. He employs the genealogical method typical of the work of French philosopher, **Michel Foucault**. In *The Burden of Representation* Tagg traces intersecting ways in which photography was involved in maintaining social

ALAN THOMAS (1978)
The Expanding Eye: Photography and the Nineteenth-Century Mind, London: Croom Helm.

MARY WARNER MARIEN (1997)
Photography and Its Critics, A Cultural History, 1839–1900, Cambridge: Cambridge University Press.

15 It is interesting to note that in 1851 51 people recorded themselves by occupation as photographers, and in 1961 there were 2,879 (Gernsheim and Gernsheim 1969: 234).

JOHN TAGG (1988) **The Burden of Representation: Essays on Photographies and Histories**, London: Macmillan.

class hierarchies through delineation of, for instance, prisoners or the poor. He insists on the need to trace the complex relations between representation, knowledge and ideology in terms that take account of fundamental class interests at stake. In his essay 'The Currency of the Photograph' (Burgin 1982) Tagg focuses on what he terms 'the prerequisites of realism'. His title metaphorically references the notion of the photograph as symbolic exchange, while simultaneously referring to the values implicated in such an exchange. Thus he discusses the relationship of the photograph to reality, the constitution of photographic meaning, the social utility of photographs, and the institutional frameworks within which they are produced and consumed. This work has been criticised by writers who argue that, in teasing out the structures through which photography creates and sustains meaning, these critics neglected the primary object of study – the photograph itself. Ian Jeffrey puts it this way:

> Historians in the 1970s tried to take account of the new persuasiveness of photography by drawing on the work of the French theorists, Foucault and Lacan in particular. Foucault, with his interests in management and surveillance, stimulated attention to photographic recording, with respect to prisoners and marginal. Unfortunately, the new historians were more devoted to their theory sources than they were to the material in question. The result was a macaronic writing, splintered by attention to an excess of sanctified theoretical texts. All the same, the determination to broaden the scope of photographic studies was admirable.
>
> (Jeffrey 2001)

However, reappraisals of the uses of photography within social anthropology, and within the records of colonial travellers implicated in European imperialism, have drawn attention to the political and ideological implications of using photography to define social types viewed as different or **Other**. As a number of critics have variously observed, such definitional uses of the image contribute to legitimating colonial rule (**Edwards 1992**). Furthermore, as Sarah Graham-Brown has argued, there is a complex interplay between imperialism and patriarchy, within which women become particular sorts of exoticised victims of the stereotyping of the colonial Other (Graham-Brown 1988).

In his 'The Body and the Archive' (1986), photographer and critic Allan Sekula traces the attempts of Victorian men of science to delineate, record and classify particular 'types' of human being (Sekula 1986). They used physiognomy and phrenology to show that it was possible to read from the surface of the body the inner delineation and moral character of the subject being studied. They employed the developing science of statistics in order to demonstrate that science – aided by one of its new tools, the seemingly impartial eye of the camera – would reveal and systematically record the varieties of criminal faces.

MICHEL FOUCAULT
(1926–1984) One of the most influential of French philosophers of recent times. He enjoyed a distinguished career as a scholar and academic which culminated in his appointment as Professor in the History of Systems of Thought at the Collège de France. In the 1960s Foucault rejected humanism and philosophies of consciousness and set about the construction of a new kind of critical theory. His concerns were with the way in which specific social institutions and practices construct the objects and forms of knowledge and help to determine our human subjectivity. Some key works in this project are, in English translation: *The Order of Things: An Archeology of the Human Sciences* (1970); *The Archeology of Knowledge* (1972); *The Birth of the Clinic* (1973); *Discipline and Punish* (1977); *The History of Sexuality* (1978).

ELIZABETH EDWARDS (ed.) (1992) **Photography and Anthropology 1860–1920**, New Haven: Yale University Press. An impressive collection of essays on the subject which takes advantage of access to key archives including the Pitt Rivers Museum, Oxford, where Edwards was Curator of Photography.

See ch. 4, pp.196–201.

In this complex article Sekula is particularly interested in photography's relation to police procedures, but mad people and native peoples from other cultures were similarly subjected to processes of measurement and scentific appraisal. In 1869 T.H. Huxley was asked to make a photographic record of people from a number of races:

> Huxley . . . was asked . . . by the Colonial Office to devise instructions for the 'formation of a series of photographs of the various races of men comprehended within the British Empire'. The system he conceived called for unclothed subjects to be photographed full- and half-length, frontally and in profile, standing in each exposure beside a clearly marked measuring stick. Such photographs reproduced the hierarchical structures of domination and subordination inherent in the institutions of colonialism.
>
> (Pultz 1995b: 24–5)

But a number of further issues beg attention in considering surveillance, social survey and other 'mapping' usages of photography. In referring to the photograph as 'fugitive testimony', Barthes draws our attention to the fleeting nature of the moment captured in the photograph and the extent to which contemporary experience (we are looking back with eyes informed by circum-stances and ways of thinking of the 1990s when this book was first conceived), along with limited knowledge of the specific context within which – and the purpose for which – the photograph was taken, make the image an unreliable witness. Photography is involved in the construction of history. But when photographs are presented as 'evidence' of past events and circumstances, a set of assumptions about their accuracy as documents is being made. Such assumptions are usually acknowledged through statements of provenance: dates, sources, and so on. But this is to ignore wider questions relating to visual communication and ways in which we interpret photographs.

Not all accounts of history are of a formal kind and over several decades photography has been used by those who want to construct history around the notion of 'popular memory'. Here the photographs are often of a personal nature, through which communities might begin the process of establishing their own non-formal history; accounts which might well challenge or be oppositional to more official versions. One problem with this is that photo-graphs have often been treated as though they really were a source of dis-interested facts, rather than as densely coded cultural objects:

> Ultimately, then, when photographs are uncritically presented as historical documents, they are transformed into aesthetic objects. Accordingly, the pretence to historical understanding remains although that understanding has been replaced by aesthetic experience.
>
> (Sekula 1991: 123)

We should note that the ability of photographs to inform us about the processes and narratives of history is challenged by the fact that they are, in themselves, constructed objects. Debates about the loss of facticity in the manipulated digital world are only the latest iteration of a debate about the photography's relationship to the real. Sarah Kember asked:

> Computer manipulated and simulated imagery appears to threaten the truth status of photography even though that has already been undermined by decades of semiotic analysis. How can this be? How can we panic about the loss of the real when we know (tacitly or otherwise) that the real is always already lost in the act of representation?
>
> (Kember 1998: 17)

One answer to this question is that human beings have, over a long time, invested a great deal of psychic energy in the notion of photography's 'realism'.

This requires us to recognise that photography is part of a scopic regime that is far wider and has a much longer history. We must consider the cultural identity of the 'viewer' who sees with the centred, focused eye of the camera, a way of seeing shaped over centuries.

At the centre of this history of Western visuality stands the humanist self. This is a conception of the human subject who is understood to be the rational centre of the world and the prime agent in seeking its meaning and establishing its order. The humanist subject searches for certain and objective knowledge.

In her own reflection on the question, Kember stresses that this subject and this scopic regime are part of a larger scientific system and mode of enquiry, 'fashioned in Enlightenment philosophy and by Cartesian dualism and perpectivalism' (1998: 23). It is a system in which the viewer is understood as a centred, knowing subject coaxing information from a passive supine nature. She reminds us that however dominant this rational-scientific system and the centred humanist subject became over a period of some 500 years, this position was always unstable and gendered. It was gendered because typically the 'knowing subject' was figured as male and 'supine nature' as female.

It was unstable, because it was a system that depended upon (and was simultaneously troubled by) a desire to exercise power and control over nature and over others. Seen in this context we can understand that our 'panic' about the computer's threat to photography's realism does not actually take place at the level of the image itself. It is cultural panic over the potential loss of our centred, humanist selves, with our 'dominant and as yet unsuccessfully challenged investments in the photographic real' (op cit. 18). The perceived threat is to our subjectivity, where a more fundamental fear is triggered which concerns 'the status of the self or the subject of photography, and . . . the way in which the subject uses photography to understand the world and intervene in it' (loc cit).

Photography, accordingly, depends not only on its technology or the way it 'looks' but also upon our historical, cultural and psychic investment in it as a way of seeing and knowing. It affords us a position, an identity, a sense of power, and it promises to fulfil a desire for security.

If our psychic responses to images, formed within particular regimes of the visual, have been important in determining how we understand photographs, so have the social and institutional forms that have structured them.

The history of photography is to a large extent shaped by the characteristic ways in which photographs have been collected, stored, used and displayed. With the passage of time the original motive for the making of a photograph may disappear, leaving it accessible to being 're-framed' within new contexts.

The extraordinary growth in the use of cameras in mobile phones means that both personal memories and political events are being directly inscribed as images, and almost instantly published on social networks and websites. The ways in which this will change the manner in which history is recorded and understood can, at the moment, only be guessed at, but it is clear that that the photographic visual will be of primary interest.

Institutions and contexts

Let us assume that a photograph of a homeless, unemployed man, published in a 1930s magazine to advance some philanthropic cause, is shown, massively enlarged, on the walls of a gallery decades after it was first made. Originally tied to the page with a caption and an explanatory text, it now stands alone as some kind of art object. How are we to read such an image? As an example of a genre? For its technical qualities? As part of the oeuvre of a distinguished practitioner? As a work of art, or as an historical object which conveys specific information or exemplifies 'pastness'? Do we try to make sense of it in terms of its distance from our own lives, or because there are many similarities to prevailing conditions? Do we try to read through the image some notion of human nature, of how, regardless of political context or the specificity of time, it would feel to be destitute and suffering? Or do we see it merely as a photograph, one among many and to be distinguished in terms of its formal, aesthetic qualities rather than its relationship to a world outside itself?

The very ubiquity of the medium has meant that photographs have always circulated in contexts for which they were not made. It is also important to remember that there is no single, intrinsic, aboriginal meaning locked up within them. Rather, there are many ways in which photographs can be read and understood, but in 'reading' photographs we rely on many contextual clues which lie outside the photography itself. We rarely encounter photographs in their original state, for we normally see them on hoardings, in magazines and newspapers, as book covers, on the walls of galleries or on the sides of buses. Their social meanings are already indicated to us and they are designed into a space, often accompanied by a text that gives us the preferred readings of their producers and allows us to make sense of what might otherwise be puzzling or ambiguous images. Indeed, commercial uses of photography, especially in advertising, often play on the multiple possible connotations that are provoked by the image.

Increasingly, our access to photographs is online, and new kinds of contextual format are being created. In these hybrid forms there is little sense of an image that is carefully framed and contextualised. Photographic images are hauled in from many sources; they are cropped, altered, distorted or enhanced with little respect for the original. Here, we need to look at the unceasing flow of images as an interesting new form.

Nevertheless, it remains the case that a major determinant of the way in which we understand photographs is the context within which we view them, and key institutions shape the nature of photography by the way they provide this context. This approach to understanding photography was particularly influential in Britain in the 1970s and 1980s and was central to the concerns of a number of magazines at that time, pre-eminently *Ten/8* and *Camerawork* (**Evans 1997**). As was argued, photographs are weak at the level of imminent meaning and depend for their decoding on text, surrounding, organisation, and so on. Although collections of photographs have always been assembled, photography's ambiguous status with regard to Art has often meant that they were not displayed in museums as objects in themselves, but rather, used as a source of supplementary information to some more valued objects.

Museums and archives

Around the world there are now moves to bring together museums, libraries and archives. This is, in part, a response to the development of digital technologies and the implied promise of online access to every artefact. Any study of the use of photographs within conventional museums will tell us much about their status and function over time. From the earliest days they were used to record and illustrate other objects, but found no place in major collections in their own right. This status was gradually accorded to them during the twentieth century.

Not all critics have unequivocally celebrated this change. Most notably **Douglas Crimp** has argued that the entry of photographs into the privileged space of the museum stripped them of the multiple potential meanings with which they are invested. They were removed from the many realms within which they made sense, in order to stress their status as separate objects – as photographs. Crimp is particularly interested in the work of the Museum of Modern Art, New York, in transforming photographs into objects of merely aesthetic attention. He is not alone in drawing attention to the way in which MOMA embraced photographs as art objects, brought them into the privileged space of the gallery and surrounded them with the apparatus of scholarship, appreciation and connoisseurship formerly reserved for paintings and sculptures.

JESSICA EVANS (ed.) (1997)
The Camerawork Essays,
London: Rivers Oram. Includes
15 essays originally printed in
Camerawork between 1976 and
1985.

DOUGLAS CRIMP (1995)
On the Museum's Ruins,
Cambridge, MA: MIT Press.
A collection of key essays
originally published in *October*
and other journals.

But Crimp also examined the practice of the New York Public Library which, becoming aware of the number of photographs it possessed and of their historic and financial value, created a Department of Photography. They scoured all sections of the huge library for a trawl of photographs, which were removed from multitudinous subject areas and reclassified as photographs, often under the individual photographer.[16] Crimp comments of photography that:

16 Likewise, the collection of photographs at the V&A, London, was established through bringing together photographs from a number of different sections of the museum.

> Thus ghettoized it will no longer primarily be useful within other discursive practices; it will no longer serve the purposes of information, documentation, evidence, illustration, reportage. The formerly plural field of photography will henceforth be reduced to the single, all-encompassing *aesthetic*.
>
> (Crimp 1995: 75)

What is lost in this process is the ability of photography to create information and knowledge through its interaction with other discourses. Photographs, doomed to the visual solitude of the art object, lose their plurality and their ability to traverse fields of meaning. They are treated as though they are unique and singular, rather than as the kind of industrial object – capable of being multiply reproduced – that constitutes their real existence.

The idea that the defining feature of photography is to be found in photographs' ability to be endlessly reproduced derives from Walter Benjamin's important essay 'The Work of Art in the Age of Mechanical Reproduction' (1936). More recently there has been an increased interest in the materiality of the photograph. Its physical existence and the kinds of questions that can be asked about the material on which it has been reproduced, and the nature of the processes through which it came into existence. **Elizabeth Edwards and Janice Hart** have drawn attention to the fact that while scholars have analysed the taxonomic meaning and functions of archives within the museum the *material objects* themselves that make up 'the archive' have been largely invisible, naturalised within institutional structure, their own social biographies as objects obscured and denied precise critical attention (Edwards and Hart 2004: 48).

ELIZABETH EDWARDS and JANICE HART "Mixed Box" in ELIZABETH EDWARDS and JANICE HART Eds) (2004) **Photographs Objects Histories: On the Materiality of Images**, London: Routledge.

In addition to photographs that can be found alongside other exhibits in museums, there are also, of course, specialist photographic archives. These, too, now function digitally with only specialist researchers examining the material photograph itself. These often have a particular resonance as an archive of representation is consulted both for the things it shows and for the way in which it shows them. Describing the now digitised Magnum archive Geoff Dyer pertinently says:

In STEVEN HOELSCHER (ed.) (2013) **Reading Magnum: A Visual Archive of the Modern World**, Austin: University of Texas Press, vii.

> The Magnum archive presents a constantly shifting, mutually illuminating relationship between what is depicted and how it is

depicted. It records a world history of events while simultaneously enacting and demonstrating an incomplete history of photography, of the way the medium and the uses to which it has been put have developed over time: the aesthetic imperatives and choices that have shaped our ideas of what constitutes news, a story, a photograph.

One of the advantages of access to archives is that many people have found this an easy way to research their own and family history, which has made many more people familiar with the working of at least some archives. At the same time, many artists have a new interest in making work that draws on or responds to archives of older images. Jane Connarty comments on the importance of the archive for art practice in the following terms:

> The themes of history and memory have been central to cultural production and discourse through much of the 20th and into the 21st centuries. Photography, film and the archive are associated with the concept of memory, functioning as surrogate, or virtual sites of remembrance, or as metaphors for the processes of recalling the past. The experience of viewing archival photographic prints or film can have a seductive, even spellbinding effect on the viewer; their material and aesthetic qualities acting as a trigger to memory, evoking a sense of time and nostalgia, or conjuring fantasies of history.
>
> (Connarty and Lanyon 2006: 7)

The power of the photographic archive was central to Allan Sekula's article 'Reading an Archive' (1991). There are, of course, many different kinds of archive, from those held in museums to commercial or historical collections or family albums. They are found in libraries, commercial firms, museums and private collections. What they have in common is the fact that they heap together images of very different kinds and impose upon them a homogeneity that is a product of their very existence within an archive. The unity of an archive, he argues, is imposed by ownership of the objects themselves and of the principles of classification and organisation by which they are structured.[17]

Photographs of many kinds, which may have been taken for different – perhaps even antagonistic – purposes, are brought together: 'in an archive, the possibility of meaning is "liberated" from the actual contingencies of use. But this liberation is also a loss, an *abstraction* from the complexity and richness of use, a loss of context' (Sekula 1991: 116). But archives play an important function in the creation of knowledge. Characteristically, an archive seeks to grow; it aspires to completeness and through this process of mass acquisition a kind of knowledge emerges:

> And so archives are contradictory in character. Within their confines meaning is liberated from use, and yet at a more general level an

This contrast between the material form of the photograph and that of the digital image is one of the challenges that face those people who are constructing museums that will archive and display digital works alongside more conventional artefacts.

For a critical account of these processes, see: FIONA CAMERON AND SARAH KENDERDINE (eds) (2007) **Theorizing Digital Cultural Heritage**, Massachusetts: MIT Press

Of course, artists have also explored the importance of materiality in photography in interesting ways. For example, Mohini Chandra's interesting collection shows the backs of her family photographs with studio stamps, handwritten notes and explanatory glosses, but does not reveal the photographs themselves. MOHINI CHANDRA (2001) **Album Pacifica**, London: Autograph

17 See Chrissie Iles and Russell Roberts (eds) (1997) *In Visible Light*, Oxford: Museum of Modern Art. This exhibition catalogue includes four key essays on photography and classification in art, science and the everyday.

empiricist model of truth prevails. Pictures are atomized, isolated in one way and homogenized in another.

(Sekula 1991: 118)

But if serious historians have sometimes neglected to read photographs in the complex way they deserve, the heritage industry has used photography as a central tool in its attempt to reconstruct the past as a site of tourist pleasure. Here, photography becomes a direct way through which our experience of the past is structured.

Many critics have been worried by, or contemptuous of, the touristic use of historical materials and of the function of the visual. For example, Donald Horne claims that photography is an essential part of the tourist experience because it allows us to convert the places we visit into signs which we can then possess. Photography, he suggests:

> offers us the joys of possession: by taking photographs of famous sites and then, at home, putting them into albums or showing them as slides, we gain some kind of possession of them. For some of us this can be the main reason for our tourism. Between them, the camera and tourism are two of the uniquely modern ways of defining reality.
>
> (Horne 1984: 12)

Similarly, Robert Hewison argues:

> Heritage is gradually effacing history, by substituting an image of the past for its reality. At a time when Britain is obsessed by the past, we have a fading sense of continuity and change, which is being replaced by a fragmented and piecemeal idea of the past constructed out of costume drama on television, re-enactments of civil war battles and mendacious celebrations of events such as the Glorious Revolution, which was neither glorious nor a revolution.
>
> (Hewison in Corner and Harvey 1990: 175)

JOHN TAYLOR (1994)
A Dream of England: Landscape, Photography and the Tourist's Imagination, Manchester: Manchester University Press.

This is brought into particular focus in ch. 2, on documentary, and ch. 3, on personal photography.

Now the archive is raided not for photographs as aesthetic objects, but for photographs as signifiers of past times. Blown up from their original proportions, sepia-toned and hung on gallery walls, or recycled as advertising imagery, photographs retain their implicit claim to authenticity. This kind of commodification of the image continues to raise complex questions about how history is constructed and photographs employed to visualise the past.

CHAPTER 2

Surveyors and surveyed

Photography out and about

DERRICK PRICE

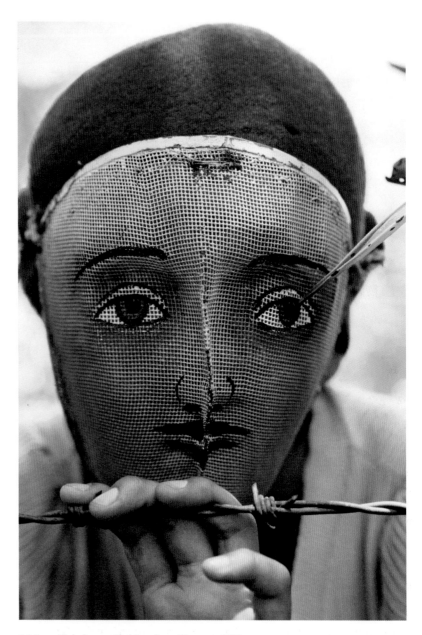

2.1 Susan Meiselas, mask picture from *Nicaragua*, 1978
Susan Mieselas's 1970s book, Nicaragua, documented the armed struggle in that country in striking colour images. It has become a central work which has influenced many other photographers. These elegant masks were used to conceal the identity of the wearer.

Surveyors and surveyed
Photography out and about

INTRODUCTION

Within a decade or two of its invention, photography was used to chronicle wars, to survey remote regions of the world and to make scientific observations. Life on the streets of great cities was recorded, but so were the monuments of Egypt and Syria, the vast ranges of the Himalayas, the USA railroad as it moved West, the fishing village of Whitby and the architecture of Paris. Pornographic images were soon in circulation, as were charity shots of the poor and homeless. **Montage** techniques were used to produce pictures of fairies, ghosts and elves. Less sensationally, the dead were recorded as they lay in their coffins (photography was hailed as an excellent substitute for the death mask), while all the living seemed appropriate subjects for the camera's **gaze**.

In this chapter we examine some of the ways photography has been used in order to bring us images of the wider world. We are essentially concerned with documentary photographs and with the history through which they were shaped and developed, but documentary is closely associated with other kinds of photography, especially those of war, travel, and photojournalism. There are often no clear lines of demarcation between these genres, nor is it possible to find exclusive descriptions of them. They cannot be defined simply by studying the intrinsic characteristics of the photographs themselves, but have to be

montage or **photomontage**
The use of two or more originals, perhaps also including written text, to make a combined image. A montaged image may be imaginative, artistic, comic or deliberately satirical.

understood through an examination of the history of their practices and social uses in particular places at determinate times. In this sense the chapter is centrally concerned with questions of history, but it does not aspire to provide a chronicle of events around the world, or a register of great practitioners over the last 150 years. Indeed, so all-pervasive has been documentary, and its associated forms, that such a chronicle would need to include many of the major figures in the history of photography. We discuss particular photographers in order to illustrate some aspect of the documentary project, rather than to provide a description or evaluation of their work.

As elsewhere in the book, our concern is with *critical* questions about the nature of documentary realism and the way in which debates about its form, status and characteristic practices change over time in response to social, political, economic and technological pressures and opportunities. Our approach has been to explore the connections between documentary, social investigation, modes of **representation** and forms of reportage at particular times.

In the first section we look at the relationship of documentary to photo-journalism and explore the ways in which both may be said to offer authentic images of life. This question was made particularly pertinent by the development of increasingly sophisticated forms of digital imaging. We then examine the ways in which nineteenth-century debates and preoccupations often prefigure our contemporary concerns and we look at the archetypal subjects of documentary – workers, the poor, the colonised and victims of war.

The following section focuses on the 1930s as the decade in which most of our ideas about documentary, together with its characteristic social and political objectives, were formed. To illustrate this we discuss the work of the US Farm Security Administration Project.

Next, we consider the way documentary loses its stable identity and is dispersed through a variety of other, related, practices, for example, American street photography, French humanism, and new kinds of work in Britain.

We then examine how documentary has been critiqued and consider its ability to reveal significant features of everyday life before, finally, looking briefly at what the future may hold for documentary and photojournalism.

We begin by noting photography's inexhaustible ability to provide us with pictures of the world; images which we are asked to accept as faithful to the real appearance of things. We want to examine the medium's putative capability to furnish us with accurate transcriptions of reality, an ability once thought to be guaranteed by the technology itself. Later this naive view was challenged and, as we shall see, the relationship of photography to reality was problematised and contested.

DOCUMENTARY AND PHOTOJOURNALISM: ISSUES AND DEFINITIONS

Documentary photography

Documentary has been described as a form, a genre, a tradition, a style, a movement and a practice; it is not useful to try to offer a single definition of the word. John Grierson coined it in 1926 to describe the kind of cinema that he wanted to replace what he saw as the dream factory of Hollywood, and it quickly gained currency within photography. The word had an imperialist tendency, and rather different kinds of photography were soon being subsumed within it. Some nineteenth-century photographers had regarded their work as 'documents', but many more were innocent of the fact that they were documentary photographers. Indeed, **Abigail Solomon-Godeau** (1991a) has pointed out that in the nineteenth century almost all photography was what would later be described as 'documentary'.

But, if most photographs were a *kind* of documentary, how can we make distinctions between them? Historians and critics have frequently drawn attention to the difficulty of defining documentary that cannot be recognised as possessing a unique style, method or body of techniques. One answer to the question is to define documentary in terms of its connection with particular kinds of social investigation. Karin Becker Ohrn argues:

> The cluster of characteristics defining the documentary style
> incorporates all aspects of the making and use of photographs.
> Although not rigid, these characteristics serve as referents for comparing
> photographers working within . . . the documentary tradition – a
> tradition that includes aspects of journalism, art, education, sociology and
> history. Primarily, documentary was thought of as having a goal beyond
> the production of a fine print. The photographer's goal was to bring the
> attention of an audience to the subject of his or her work and, in many
> cases, to pave the way for social change.
>
> (Ohrn 1980: 36)

Our concern in this chapter will be to unpick some of the components of this tradition and examine ways in which we can distinguish documentary from other kinds of **straight photography**. Certainly the nature of an image itself is not enough to classify a particular photograph as in some essential way 'documentary'; rather we need to look at the contexts, practices and institutional forms within which the work is set. Documentary work may be seen to belong to the history of a particular kind of social investigation, although it employed its own forms, conventions and tropes. **Martha Rosler** (1989) tells us that to understand it we need to look to history, and she characterises documentary as 'a practice with a past'. A past, we might add, which, despite changing technologies, practices and fashions, was always

ABIGAIL SOLOMON-GODEAU (1991) **Photography at the Dock**, Minneapolis: University of Minnesota Press.

straight photography Emphasis upon direct documentary typical of the Modern period in American photography.

MARTHA ROSLER (1989) 'In, Around and Afterthoughts (on Documentary Photography)' in R. Bolton (ed.) **The Contest of Meaning: Critical Histories of Photography**, Cambridge, MA: The MIT Press.

concerned to claim for documentary a special relationship to real life and a singular status with regard to notions of truth and authenticity.

Photojournalism

Documentary and photojournalism are intimately linked, and many practitioners of straight photography are interchangeably described as either photojournalists or documentary photographers. However, photojournalism does, as the name indicates, have a special relationship to other texts and is seen, in its classic form, as a way of narrating current events or illustrating written news stories. While announcements of the news have existed since antiquity, and newspapers have been around for hundreds of years, the word 'journalism' entered the language only in the 1830s, so we may say that journalism as a modern profession grew up at the same time as photography. A modern press catering to the needs of a newly literate, urban population sought easy, graphic ways of spelling out the news while, at the same time, seeking to validate the truth and objectivity of their publications. Photographs seemed able to satisfy both of these demands – although print technology made it impossible to reproduce them until the 1880s. Nevertheless, magazines that told stories with the help of pictures were extremely popular. The *Illustrated London News* sold 26,000 copies of its first issue in 1842, and by 1863 had a weekly print run of 310,000. The illustrations were in the form of wood engravings that were produced with machine-like speed and precision through the use of a complex division of technical and artistic labour.

The spread and new excitement of photojournalism from the 1930s also owed much to the fact that there were many outlets through which such work could be shown and for which it could be commissioned. These magazines, which were based on the extensive use of photographs to tell stories, constitute the start of the modern movement of photojournalism. They include *Look* and *Life* in the USA, *Vu* in France, and *Illustrated* and *Picture Post* in Britain. There was also a host of new or revitalised publications in Germany where the movement began and most of the rhetorical devices of presentation were established – devices that allowed picture editors and designers to create powerful stories through the juxtaposition of image and text. Many of the German *Illustrierte* disappeared after Hitler came to power in 1933 and the editors and photographers who had worked for them went into exile, taking their skills with them to their adopted countries. Within a few years photojournalism became a worldwide phenomenon and attracted very large readerships; however, the spread of television, and changes in the patterns of newspaper ownership and financing put pressure on the illustrated magazines. By the 1960s readerships had fallen and several well-known magazines had ceased to exist. At the same time, new kinds of newspaper supplements appeared. These were full colour productions and contained many photographs, but they were advertising-led and their primary purpose was to sell

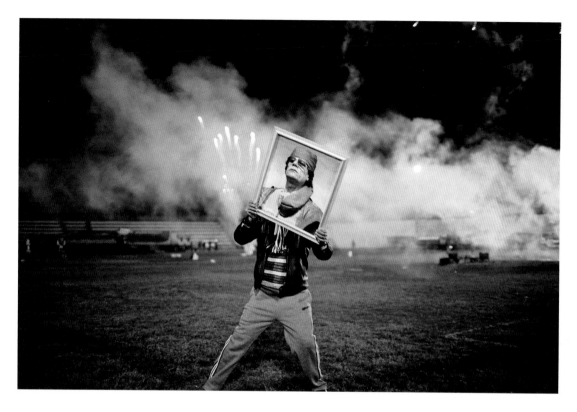

goods rather than to report the news. Photojournalists had to find new outlets for their work and new strategies in order to continue their practice.

Almost every aspect of social, political and personal life has been told through photojournalism and, despite the fact that television and video have become the dominant means of reportage, it is still an important source of news. However, the lack of photo magazines, the development of online reporting and the decline of photo stories in newspapers (in favour of single shots to illustrate the news) together with a new interest in personality based stories, have all led to a growing crisis in photojournalism, which can only flourish where there are editors to commission work and outlets in which to publish them.

Photography and war

One major factor in the development of photography around the world was the desire to record wars. Even today most people's understanding of the nature of war comes from photographic images rather than literary accounts. It was, however, the highly critical reports of the London *Times* reporter William Russell on the progress of the Crimean War that led to Roger Fenton being sent to take photographs that would reassure the public. Fenton used the newly

2.2 Moises Saman, *Libya*, 2011
In the 'Arab Spring' of 2011 a Libyan supporter of Quaddafi holds up a photograph of him while fireworks light up the sky. An example of a new kind of photojournalism, this image can be read as comment, reportage or art – a potent mixture that informs modern photojournalist practice.

collodion This process, known as wet collodion (or Ambrotype), invented by English photographer Frederick Scott Archer in 1851, increased the speed of photography as the glass plate was treated and exposed while still 'wet' (i.e. gummy) but it had the drawback of involving bulky equipment. It became one of the major processes until the invention in the 1870s of gelatin-coated plates known as dry plates.

invented wet **collodion** process to produce more than 350 photographs which did, indeed, show scenes of calm and disciplined order. He produced a number of handsome albums with original photographs 'tipped in', but his images were also used as the basis of illustrations in the *Illustrated London News*. Illustrated newspapers produced hundreds of woodcuts, often laid out to create a narrative of events. It seems that an added sense of realism was given to the piece if it was 'based on photographs' rather than being the work of an artist or illustrator, even though the engraver would omit or add material in order to make a visual point or a more pleasing aesthetic effect.

Fenton spent only a short time in the Crimea and his work did little to reveal the hardships or horrors of war. The American Civil War (1861–5) was the first to be photographed extensively throughout its duration, and in which photography was seen not only as providing realistic images of the struggle, but also as 'news'. In this sense, it also provided one of the foundation stones for the development of photojournalism. Michael L. Carlebach comments that:

> Two weekly newspapers that were established in America in the years just preceding the Civil War made photographs and other visual materials equal partners of the printed word in the reporting of news. These new publications would provide the public, or at least the northern public, with accurate and timely illustrations of the war. The pictures they published, many based on photographs, offered vivid, graphic and reliable glimpses into all aspects of the conflict. For the first time, Americans would see through the eyes of a score of photographers, exactly what was going on at the front.
>
> (Carlebach 1992: 63)

But, as Carlebach makes plain, these significant images were not the most numerous of the photographs produced in the war. A boom was experienced by photographic studios trying to deal with the demand for portraits of those who were going into battle. In addition, photographs of the commanders of the Federal army were turned out by the hundred; purchased by people anxious to support the cause and made the subject of a special tax.

The most important photographer of the Civil War was Matthew Brady. Already celebrated for his portraits, 'Brady of Broadway' produced photographs that showed scenes of action, together with shots of the dead on the battlefield, and more tranquil views of soldiers relaxing at their camps. Brady put teams of photographers into the field of battle, including Alexander Gardner, Timothy O'Sullivan and George Barnard, and published this work under his own imprint. Alan Trachtenberg describes his function in the following terms:

> 'Brady's pictures' did not mean pictures made by Brady himself but those he displayed or published. . . . Organiser of one of several corps of private photographers, collector of images made by others, a kind of

archivist or curator of the entire photographic campaign of the war,
Brady played many roles, swarmed with ambiguities, in the war.

(Trachtenberg 1989: 72)

Since Brady's time, no war or violent conflict has lacked its photographic record
and interpreters. For example, hundreds of thousands of images of the First
World War were made, most of which have been rendered anonymous by the
system of classification and archiving that was subsequently employed. Despite
the sheer number of photographs of that conflict, there is little work that really
gives us a sense of the nature of trench warfare, and the poetry, films and
paintings of the time are often more moving and revealing.

Photography was considerably more important as a means of depicting the
Spanish Civil War (1936–9). The many illustrated journals of the day carried
photographs and these images were influential in shaping people's view of the
war. The single most famous photograph was Robert Capa's *Death of a Loyalist
Soldier* which later became the subject of speculation as to its authenticity.
Capa was also one of the photographers of the Second World War whose
work became very familiar to the public, along with that of Bert Hardy, W.
Eugene Smith, Carl Mydans and *Life* photographer David Douglas Duncan,
who went on to produce heroic images of American soldiers in Korea and
Vietnam. After the Spanish Civil War, Capa was one of the founders of the
photo agency Magnum, which has enrolled many distinguished photographers
over the years.[1] Many histories of documentary and photojournalism in the
last half century are written essentially around the work of members of the
agency. Photo agencies are vital to the work of independent photographers
and the archives they establish and support are a most important resource.

The Second World War (1939–45) blurred the distinction between
combatant and civilian and, thereafter, war photographers concentrated as
much attention on those caught up in conflict as on the soldiers themselves.
This is, of course, also true for violent conflict which is not defined as a 'war',
as in Cyprus or Northern Ireland.

Jorge Lewinski has commented that:

It is only in the post-war period, starting with the Korean war, that the
immediacy of war photographs begins to have a significant effect. Since
then, a stream of authentic images has overwhelmed us with cumulative
power. The images from Korea, Cyprus, Israel, the Congo, Biafra and
Vietnam have left their indelible mark on our imaginations.

(Lewinski 1978: 12)

Certainly, it is often said that the stream of images revealing the death, injury
and sorrows of the people of Vietnam was a major factor in the public's
eventual repugnance for that war. In the sophisticated photographic work of
the time the themes of martial conflict and civilian anguish are inter-

1 Magnum Photos is one of
the world's most prestigious
photographic agencies. It
was founded in 1947 by
four photographers: Robert
Capa, Henri Cartier-
Bresson, George Rodger
and David (Chim) Seymour.
Its membership now reflects
a range of different styles
and practices and includes in
its distinguished list:
Eve Arnold, David Hurn,
Josef Koudelka, Susan
Meiselas, and Martin Parr.

twined. An excellent example is given in the work of Philip Jones Griffiths, who produced one of the most important photographic records of the war (Griffiths 1971).

War has been seen as an important subject for photography for a number of reasons: the photographer might reveal scenes and actions which would not otherwise come to the attention of the public; war inevitably throws up scenes of great emotional force which can best be captured by the camera; it has a dark psychic fascination for us, which coexists with our feelings of revulsion. The person who has most mused on this ambivalence is the English photographer Don McCullin, who has documented many wars and violent uprisings since the early 1960s (McCullin 2003).

We might ask why we particularly remember some photographs of war and what social function they might serve. It has been suggested that certain images are given iconic status within a society because they evoke and structure ideas about the culture of that place and are congruent with how its citizens feel about themselves.

Michael Griffin puts it succinctly:

> The enduring images of war are not those that exhibit the most raw and genuine depictions of life and death on the battlefield, nor those that illustrate historically specific information about people, places and things, but rather those that most readily present themselves as symbols of cultural and national myth.
>
> (Griffin 1999: 123)

On this reading, there are no unequivocally great photographs of war, only those that structure or re-enforce feelings already extant within a particular culture.

We should remember that war reporting, like other kinds of reportage, has depended historically on the ability of the photographer to bear witness to the action taking place. But, so powerful has been the influence of war reporting that military authorities make every effort to control journalists and photographers working in scenes of conflict. The unattached freelance reporter has all but disappeared and photographers increasingly find themselves forced to work at a distance from violent action. For some photojournalists, war reporting has, in consequence, taken on new forms that are more akin to meditations on the nature of war than direct reportage. For example, the French photographer Luc Delahaye (who is a member of Magnum and worked for *Newsweek*) became famous for his close-up pictures of war and scenes of violence. However, he abandoned this photojournalistic approach in favour of working with large-scale or panoramic cameras to produce big images that were designed to be shown in galleries. Instead of the vibrant confusion of struggle we are given a more distanced, considered and detached view of conflict.

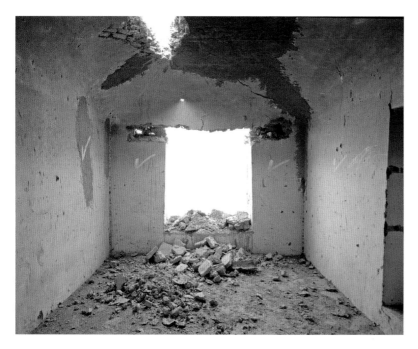

2.3 Paul Seawright, *Room 1*, 2003
The Irish photographer was commissioned by the Imperial War Museum to photograph the aftermath of conflict in Afghanistan. This haunting image is from the collection *Hidden*.

This new kind of retrospective work, which has been called 'aftermath photography', may be seen in the pictures of a number of photographers, including those the Irish photographer Paul Seawright took in Afghanistan for the Imperial War Museum, London. These are large, colour works, that have no images of direct conflict, but show the traces of war, the scarred buildings and furrowed earth, together with the characteristic debris of battle. They have none of the busy activity of war photography, but are carefully composed works through which we can explore the nature of violent conflict.

Sarah James has described work in this kind in the following terms:

> Surveying sites ruined by war and catastrophe – Bosnia, Iraq, Afghanistan, Kuwait, Beirut, Baghdad, Lebanon, Palestine, or Manhattan's Ground Zero – photographers such as Simon Norfolk, Paul Seawright, Joel Meyerowitz and Sophie Ristelhueber have developed this strange new genre. Each works in saturated or subdued colour, often on a monumental scale and with thrilling precision . . . The surreal landscapes and alien environments charted by these photographers are as abstract, inhuman and incomprehensible as the wars that caused them.
>
> (James 2013: 115)

Describing the work of Anne Ferran, Geoffrey Batchen points out that:

> Refusing to tell us anything about what we are seeing, to give us the explanatory information we crave, these photographs challenge us to bring our own knowledge and desires to them. They might be said to represent the ground of history itself, waiting to be inscribed with meaning.
>
> (Batchen *et al.* 2012: 228)

This strategy raises a number of questions: the old assertion based on authenticity ('I saw it; I was there') no longer holds good, but is replaced by a new implicit claim to respect the suffering of others by producing more structured and complex works that function as objects of critical contemplation. This moves the photographer out of the world of the media with its insatiable demand for immediate images and into the world of art. These pictures are no longer to be found in newspapers and magazines, but are to be seen on the walls of galleries. An apparent opposition is sometimes seen to exist between the world of concerned photography and the realm of art. **Susan Sontag** has argued that this is an exaggerated distinction:

SUSAN SONTAG (2003)
Regarding the Pain of Others, London: Hamish Hamilton.

> Transforming is what art does, but photography that bears witness to the calamitous and the reprehensible is much criticised if it seems 'aesthetic'; that is, too much like art.
>
> (Sontag 2003: 68)

To escape the voyeuristic position of photojournalism, then, one may be accused of making elegant art objects out of the victims of disaster. But photojournalism is also under attack from quite different kinds of image-making. Commenting on the images of tortured Iraqi prisoners in Abu Ghraib, **Andy Grundberg** laments the fact that the old disciplines of photojournalism have all but disappeared:

ANDY GRUNDBERG (2005)
'Point and Shoot: How the Abu Ghraib Images Redefine Photography', **American Scholar**, 74(1), Winter 2005: 108. Quoted in ERINA DUGANNE (2007) 'Photography After the Fact' in MARK REINHARDT, HOLLY EDWARDS and ERINA DUGANNE (eds) **Beautiful Suffering: Photography and the Traffic in Pain**, Chicago: University of Chicago Press, p. 73.

> These photographs tell us that the codes of objectivity, professional ethics and journalistic accountability we have all relied on to ensure the accuracy of the news – at least in rough draft form – are now relics. In their place is a swirling mass of information, written as well as visual, journalistic as well as vernacular, competing to be taken as fact.
>
> (Grundberg 2005: 108)

The Abu Ghraib photographs, then, were seen all over the world, and their shocking claim to authenticity resided in part in the fact that they were not presented as objective documents. Taken with cheap digital cameras and on mobile phones they were a species of personal photograph, of snapshots, made for the amusement of the photographers and their putative audience of

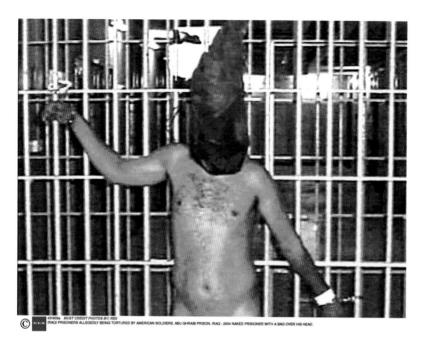

2.4 Abu Ghraib, 2004
The photographs from Abu Ghraib were shocking and were seen all over the world. They also drew attention to the ways in which informal snapshots might be more potent than carefully composed images.

colleagues and friends. Freed from any of the codes that govern the practice of photojournalism, they had a rawness and immediacy that contributed to their appalling power. We should observe, however, that carrying on the old task of 'bearing witness' while working outside the structures of professional photography has become quite common. Many of the photographs of the destruction of the Twin Towers in New York or the effects of Hurricane Katrina in New Orleans were similarly made by amateurs using very simple devices. In both cases they were exhibited together with work by artists and photojournalists. This new promiscuous heaping together of work made for different reasons and from different professional standpoints makes it very difficult to be clear about the current state of photojournalism.

Certainly, in recent years the relationship between photographer and suffering subject has become increasingly the subject of debate. The argument that photography gives an aesthetic gloss to anguish is a very old one, but is far from being resolved. **David Levi Strauss** has argued that:

The idea that the more transformed or 'aestheticized' an image is, the less 'authentic' or politically valuable it becomes, is one that needs to be seriously questioned. . . . To represent is to aestheticize: that is, to transform. It presents a vast field of choices but it does not include

D.L. STRAUSS (2003) **Between the Eyes: Essays on Photography and Politics,** New York: Aperture Books.

87

the choice *not* to transform, not to change or alter whatever is being represented. It cannot be a pure process in practice. This goes for photography as well as for any other means of representation.

(Strauss 2003: 9)

Susie Linfield argues that photojournalists now find themselves in a Catch 22 situation:

Some are criticized for taking too-beautiful pictures, while others are chided for images that are too ugly to bear; some are criticized for a gruesome realism, while others are accused of being overly romantic in their approach.

(Linfield 2010: 44)

She argues that these dichotomies are inevitable when trying to 'show the unshowable' and suggests that:

These critics seek something that does not exist: an uncorrupted, unblemished photographic gaze that will result in images flawlessly poised between hope and despair, resistance and defeat, intimacy and distance.

(ibid.: 44)

Photographers and editors still have to make crucial choices about the technical means of production; the intended audience, the medium through which photographs are displayed and the relationship of any particular images to the vast number already in circulation.

Reviewing the prestigious World Press Photo awards, the artists Adam Broomberg and Olivier Chanarin described photojournalism as 'a photographic genre in crisis' and went on to list the dominant themes of the 81,000 photographs submitted for consideration:

Again and again similar images are repeated with only the actors and settings changing. Grieving mothers, charred human remains, sunsets, women giving birth, children playing with toy guns, cock fights, bull fights, . . . [etc]

(Broomberg and Chanarin 2008: 99)

In their own work Broomberg and Chanarin combine photographs and texts in order to unpick the nature of documentary photography. In 2013 they won the Deutsche Börse photography prize and were praised for their book *War Primer 2*, which uses internet screengrabs and photographs taken on mobile phones to rework Berolt Brecht's *War Primer* of 1955. The piece is a sustained exploration of the role of photography in what the Americans called 'the war on terror'.

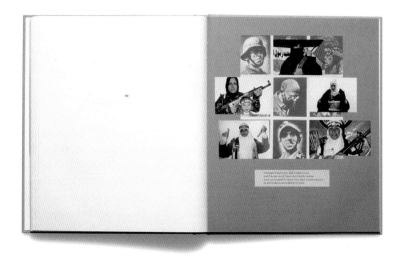

2.5 Adam Broomberg and Oliver Chanarin, Plate 80 from *War Primer 2*, 2011

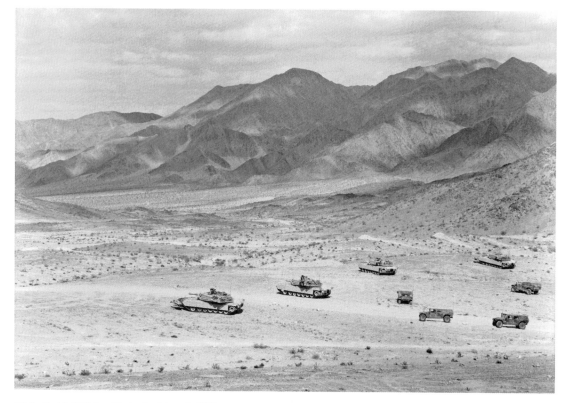

2.6 An-My Lê, *29 Palms: Mechanized Assault*, 2003–4
Here An-My Lê has photographed US military exercises as troops prepare for war in Iraq and Afghanistan. Well removed from the field of battle, these staged photographs evoke the destructive power of the military machine.

89

Documentary and authenticity

Photojournalism and documentary are linked by the fact that they claim to have a special relationship to the real; that they give us an accurate and authentic view of the world. This claim has often been challenged on a number of grounds. Perhaps the simplest and most obvious test of authenticity is to ask whether what is in front of the lens to be photographed has been tampered with, set up, or altered by the photographer.

Early in its history photography had been presented with many cases of fraud, as, for example, when the French photographer E. Appert published his book *Les Crimes de la Commune* in 1871. This purported to be a record of the vile behaviour of those who took part in the rising of the Paris Commune and was received with relish by many bourgeois commentators of the time. It consists, for the most part, of crudely montaged and retouched photographs, but was convincing enough for a public who were confident that the camera could not lie. It would, however, be incorrect to deduce that in the nineteenth century only outright deception was commented upon. Many sophisticated arguments about the ability of photographs to be true to appearances were rehearsed at that time. Indeed the Victorians were to stage a dramatic debate on the relationship between truth and representation in the public trial of Dr Barnardo.

In 1876 the philanthropist Dr T. J. Barnardo appeared at a hearing, having been charged with deceiving the public. His detractors claimed, and Barnardo finally conceded, that he had misled the public in his use of 'before and after' photographs of the orphans in his care. He had produced a series of cards which purported to reveal the transformative power of his project: one card was of dirty, ragged children lounging about against a background of urban decay; a second card showed one of these children cleaned up and neatly dressed, undertaking some useful task. Dr Barnardo used child models for these cards and one, Katie Smith, is pictured in several of them, posing as a crossing-sweeper or a match-seller. At the hearing Barnardo agreed that Katie had never sold matches, but he pointed out that she was a child of the streets who might well have ended up as a beggar and that, in any case, she represented the appearance and state of a match-girl in an honest manner. Moreover, Katie could easily have stumbled into that kind of life had she not been saved by his mission.

As a result of the public hearing Barnardo gave up using photographs in this way, but his case raises questions that were to recur throughout the next century. Why should we trust the camera to be true to appearances? What is the relationship between the accurate portrayal of a single case and a general truth about the nature of things? Cannot something arranged or set up offer us an authentic insight into reality? It was questions of this kind that were rehearsed, long after Barnardo, in the furore that broke out over a photograph made in the USA.

In 1936 the American photographer Arthur Rothstein photographed a steer's skull that had been bleached by the sun and left lying on the earth. This was a simple still life, then, but one that was clearly intended to exemplify the contemporary crisis in agriculture. Rothstein took two photographs of this object, the most famous of which shows it lying on cracked, baked, waterless earth. The second, however, revealed it as resting on the less symbolically charged ground of a stretch of grass. The photographer acknowledged that he had moved the skull a few metres in order to obtain a more dramatic pictorial effect. When the presence of these two rather different images was discovered there was an outcry from Republican politicians, who claimed that the public had a right to see photographs that were objectively true rather than those that had been manipulated in order to make a rhetorical point. Two kinds of truth were in play; for, while the right-wing politicians demanded a truth at the denotative level, the photographer, like Dr Barnardo, laid claim to a greater truth at the connotative level. Nevertheless, Rothstein was at pains to draw attention to the smallness of his intervention in the 'real' state of things and would certainly have subscribed to the view that the authentic could only be guaranteed by a relatively unmediated representation of things as they are.

So, the practice of documentary was and is problematic and, over time, a number of conventions and practices evolved to mark 'authentic documentary' from other kinds of work. These included, for example, printing the whole of the image with a black border around it to demonstrate that everything the camera recorded was shown to the viewer. At another time, scenes lit by flash were deemed illegitimate, as only the natural light that fell on the scene should be used. A kind of rudimentary technical ethic of documentary work emerged which 'guaranteed' the authenticity of the photograph. We may note that studio-based photography, whether for commercial purposes or as art, was made by suppressing what was contingent within the photographic frame. The scene was designed in such a way that all aspects of the image were controlled and carefully placed. We have already observed that any attempt to arrange and structure the location by a documentary photographer would be regarded as illegitimate behaviour, yet the aesthetic demand for well-composed shots remained.

Documentary photographers, too, took considerable pains to control the nature of a scene without making any obvious change to it. Thus, the celebrated French photographer Henri Cartier-Bresson lay in wait for all the messy contingency of the world to compose itself into an image that he judged to be both productive of visual information and aesthetically pleasing. This he called 'the decisive moment', a formal flash of time when all the right elements were in place before the scene fell back into its quotidian disorder. Increasingly, documentary turned away from attempting to record what would formerly have been seen as its major subjects. Instead, it began to concentrate on exploring cultural life and popular experience, and this often led to representations that celebrated the transitory or the fragmentary. The endeavour to make great statements gave way to the recording of little, dislocated moments which merely insinuated that some greater meaning might be at stake (Cartier-Bresson 1952). Cartier-Bresson's humanist work is often regarded as documentary or as photojournalism but he is also seen as working outside the constraints of labels of this kind. As photographer and theorist **Allan Sekula** has pointed out,

ALLAN SEKULA (1978) 'Dismantling Modernism, Reinventing Documentary (Notes on the Politics of Representation)' in J. Liebling (ed.) **Photography: Current Perspectives**, Rochester, NY: Light Impressions Co.

> Documentary is thought to be art when it transcends its reference to the world, when the work can be regarded, first and foremost, as an act of self-expression on the part of the artist.
>
> (Sekula 1978: 236)

The problem, then, becomes how we define 'reference to the world' and how documentary photographers can demonstrate their fidelity to the social world. To have to engage with particular conventions, technical processes and rhetorical forms in order to authenticate documentary undermines the notion of the objective camera and with it, one might imagine, any claim of documentary to be any more truthful to appearances than other forms of representation.

Defining the real in the digital age

We are now so used to the dominance of digital media in photography that we scarcely need reminding that the convergence between computing and audio-visual technologies has produced new technologies which have transformed the means of image-making together with its social, commercial and aesthetic practices. Digital media are marked by more than simply radical changes in photographic technologies. Their ability to create, manipulate and edit images has given new prominence to arguments about the nature of photography and taken them into the popular domain. These may briefly be summarised as questions about the nature of the photographic image and about new ways of defining and understanding 'the real'. At first digital technologies simply copied those of traditional photography and there is still a sense in which a world of pixels and bytes has simply replaced that of chemicals and paper. However, all profound changes in technology begin by aping the past before going on to offer novel ways of using a medium. Fred Ritchin notes that:

> Digital media . . . will not merely simulate an older style of photography, but strategies will emerge that are more capable of depicting an evolving universe. Rather than attempting simply to imitate previous media while offering an increase in efficiency, digital media, including their visual aspects, will eventually involve a more flexible, integrative, 'hyperphotography' that takes advantage of the many potentials of digital platforms, including links, layers, hybridization, asynchronicity,

nonlinearity, nonlocality, malleability, and the multivocal. The results may at first resemble gimmickry, but eventually they will be transformative.

(Ritchin 2013: 57)

It is commonplace now to note that images with all the appearance of 'real' photographs may have been created from scratch on a computer, montaged from many sources, altered in some respects, or radically transformed. Figures may be added or removed and the main constituents of the picture rearranged to suggest new relationships or bizarre conjunctions. Does all this not destroy the claim of photography to have a special ability to show things as they are and raise serious doubts about those genres with a particular investment in the 'real' – documentary and photojournalism?

We can, of course, observe that, as we have already seen, the manipulation of images is nothing new and that photographs have been changed, touched-up or distorted since the earliest days. But we are not looking here merely at a technically sophisticated way of altering images, but at much more profound changes that challenge the ontological status of the photograph itself. If a photograph is not *of something* already existing in the world, how can we regard it as an accurate record of how things are? Roland Barthes' influential conception of the nature of the photograph is that it is the result of an event in the world, evidence of the passing of a moment of time that once was and is no more, which left a kind of trace of the event on the photograph. It is this trace which has been considered to give photographs their special relationship to the real. That is that they function, in the typology of signs offered by the American semiotician C.S. Peirce, as **indexical** signs.

The nature of the sign within semiological systems is important, but it is interesting to note that we have always known that photographs are malleable, contrived and slippery, but have, simultaneously, been prepared to believe them to be evidential and more 'real' than other kinds of images. It is possible to argue that the authenticity of the photograph was validated less by the nature of the image itself than through the structure of discursive, social and professional practices which constituted *photography*. Any radical transformation in this structure makes us uneasy about the status of the photograph. Not only do we know that individual photographs could have been manipulated, but our reception and understanding of the world of signs may have been transformed.

Writing in the French newspaper *Liberation* in 1991, the social theorist, Jean Baudrillard famously remarked that 'the Gulf war did not take place' (Baudrillard 1995). He was commenting on the nature of the real and the authentic in our time and suggesting that in the world of the spectacle, it is pointless to posit an external reality that is then pictured, described and represented. In his view everything is constructed and our sense of the world is mediated by complex technologies that are themselves a major constituent of our reality. What took place, then, was not the first Gulf War but a whole sequence of political, social and military actions that were acted out in a new kind of social and technical space. While this may be an extreme way of formulating the argument, it is clear that a complex of technical, political, social and cultural changes has transformed not just photography, but the whole of visual culture. For example, David Campany points out that 'almost a third of all news "photographs" are frame grabs from video or digital sources' and comments that:

> The definition of a medium, particularly photography, is not autonomous or self-governing, but heteronymous, dependent on other media. It derives less from what it is *technologically* than what it is *culturally*. Photography is what we do with it. And what we do with it depends on what we do with other image technologies.
>
> (Campany 2003: 130; emphasis in original)

One significant consequence of this has been a new merging and lack of definition between photographic genres. It is increasingly difficult to distinguish one kind of photographic practice from another. As we shall see later, titles such as 'documentary' are of little use as labels for the new kind of work that is being produced. Indeed, all descriptive titles have been freely appropriated and find themselves used in curious couplings, for example one sub-genre of photography now well established in the USA is that of 'wedding photojournalism'.

In more recent years there has been a huge increase in the number of news story photographs taken by amateurs. A new figure has come onto the stage: that of the citizen photographer. These are people who may have no particular training in photography, who are answerable to no editor, and do not necessarily subscribe to any journalistic ethic. Sometimes these are individuals who happen to record some exciting event on a single occasion, but a growing number are people who set out in a systematic way to record the scenes around them using a mobile phone or small digital camera. Where they are caught up in dramatic events their work may be seen around the world and may help shape the dominant perceptions of these events. Elsewhere, the pictures may simply be shared with family and friends.

For decades documentary and photojournalism depended on a system that had a clear separation, but interdependence, between its various parts. Between photographers and the subjects of photographs, between the publishers of these photographs (with a staff of people who influenced the nature of the final image – editors, picture editors, layout artists, printers) and the consumers of the photographs – the readers of the newspapers or illustrated magazines in which they appeared. Editors could commission photographs or draw on specialist agencies or picture libraries for them. It is this system that has gradually disappeared. The illustrated magazines gave way to the influence of television and newspaper colour supplements. These were, at first, a rich site for serious photojournalism, but were primarily vehicles for advertising and came to specialize in fashion, lifestyle and celebrity stories. This system is now largely a thing of the past. The citizen journalist can upload images to a number of sites without intervention from editors or other gatekeepers and the consumers of these pictures are usually also producers. Not only are social networks acting as publishers of photographs and news stories, but, increasingly, the mainstream media are accessing and referencing them to follow events as they unfold.

Newspaper and magazine editors, then, can commission work of this kind or draw on online sites as a source of images. The presence of citizen photographers is changing the nature of reportage, a process that is also driven by the economic imperatives of modern journalism. Noting that the profession of photojournalism has been in decline since the fall of the illustrated magazines, Julian Stallabrass comments that:

> Economically pressed news organisations often prefer to provide c
> ameras (but little training) to willing locals rather than fly out
> professionals to a scene of conflict. Rates paid for the publication of
> newspaper photographs have been in steep decline. Foreign news – and
> indeed all hard news – has been squeezed for resources and space by
> cheaper and more advertising-friendly features on lifestyle, products and
> celebrity.
>
> (Stallabrass 2013: 44)

If we add to these economic forces the fact that some governments and participants make it increasingly difficult for photographers to work in scenes of conflict, the rise of the on-the-spot amateur would seem to be irresistible. They might be seen to be carrying on the old task of 'bearing witness' while working outside the structures of professional photography. Indeed, it is possible that the pictures of conflict returned from a simple camera or a mobile phone may imprint the notion of the authentic more securely than the sophisticated images presented by a professional photographer.

Of course, professional and highly developed photo agencies are still a source of images for editors. Even here, though, the world is changing. Many major agencies are now storing only digital images. Magnum, for example, has given up sending paper-based photographs to those who wish to use them. Digitized and stored online, it is now quick and easy to download images, but some people regret the passing of material objects and the ability to handle an actual print. The Magnum archive has passed to the Harry Ransom Center at the University of Texas where it will be available to scholars who want to explore the nature of photography in the twentieth century.

STEVEN HOELSCHER (ed.) (2013) **Reading Magnum: A Visual Archive of the Modern World**, Austin: University of Texas Press.

SURVEYS AND SOCIAL FACTS

Victorian surveys and investigations

Photography has always had to take its place within a range of discourses and visual practices. One reason why the veracity of the camera was readily accepted in the nineteenth century was that photographs appeared to confirm ideas about the world that had been the subject of other artistic and cultural forms. The camera reinforced journalistic and literary accounts of aspects of social life that had rarely been seen or experienced by middle-class people. Moreover, we may argue that Victorian actuality photographs were regarded as 'authentic' precisely because they were images of the poor and the dispossessed; people whose lives had about them (to the middle-class spectator) an air of being simple, real and untrammelled by the overt complexity of middle-class existence. Photography's subjects were those that had already been the topic of examination in reports, surveys, philanthropy and literature. It established itself as part of a tradition of enquiry into the health, housing, education, economic condition and moral state of the poor. Enquiries emanated from government departments, newspapers, independent scholars, medical practitioners, religious leaders and philanthropic bodies.

Photography also became a mode of surveying the unknown, and apparently mysterious and threatening city streets were being visually inspected and hauled into the light of day. Describing the anonymous photographers of the time, the historian **Alan Thomas** comments that:

ALAN THOMAS (1978)
**The Expanding Eye:
Photography and the
Nineteenth-Century Mind**,
London: Croom Helm.

> They entered the back streets, it appears, in the same spirit as
> expeditionary cameramen journeying in strange lands, for one of the
> commonest documentary photographs of the century shows a line of
> back street dwellers, generally women and children, with perhaps a man
> lurking in the rear, who are ranged across the middle of the
> composition, gazing expectantly into the camera. From the 1860s to the
> end of the century, and from every great city comes this photograph;
> it always seems worth looking at because of the candid directness with
> which the subjects give themselves to the camera – like those foreign
> aboriginals photographed for the first time by expeditionary
> photographers.
>
> (Thomas 1978: 136)

If the professional reporter journeyed to the dark places of the city, an army of amateur photographers snapped away in the more salubrious areas, but here the presence of photographers was considered to be undesirable, and by the 1880s they had been defined as a public nuisance. In London, licences were required to film in many places, while the photographic press carried articles deploring the activities of those who photographed respectable people without their specific consent.

Codes of conduct were beginning to emerge and a range of permissible and impermissible subjects was being informally drawn up. If the photographers were middle class, the posed *anonymous* subjects were likely to be poor or working class. What distinguished documentary photographers within this ferment of picture-making was that they worked with some notion of improving or ameliorating the lot of their subjects. But this, in turn, led to some curious social interactions. To illustrate this point it is worth looking at the work of the photographer who is generally taken to be the first of the American documentary photographers, Jacob Riis.

Danish-born Riis emigrated to the USA in the 1860s. He worked as a police reporter firstly for *Tribune* and later for the *Evening Sun* and began to concentrate on reporting the conditions of life in the East Side slums of New York City. Like many philanthropists and reporters before him, Riis was frustrated by his inability to convince people of the nature of the poverty, overcrowding, sweated labour and sheer misery that existed at the heart of a prosperous city.

He produced a picture of social conditions that is of considerable interest, despite the lack of formal aesthetic qualities in his images. In a typical Riis picture a crude flash of light in an otherwise dark room illuminates a scene of woeful overcrowding, with ragged people huddled on wooden benches or asleep on the floor. Others show garment-workers at their trade and, of course, children sleeping in doorways or labouring alongside their parents in tiny rooms. Riis worked at a time when the conventions of documentary photography had yet to be established, and he certainly wasted no time by seeking the cooperation of his subjects. Perhaps inevitably, his photographs provide us with ethnographic detail of material life and social conditions rather than more complex subjective readings of the nature of poverty and destitution. Work of that kind was left to his successors, but Riis is important as a forerunner, and as a figure who directly connected photography to the journalistic enterprise. He was in no doubt of the power of photography to be a witness to the true nature of things. Describing a case of gross overcrowding, he writes:

> When the report was submitted to the Health Board the next day, it did not make much of an impression – these things rarely do, put in mere words – until my negatives, still dripping from the dark-room, came to re-enforce them. From them there was no appeal. It was not the only instance of the kind by a good many. Neither the landlord's protests nor the tenant's plea 'went' in the face of the camera's evidence, and I was satisfied.
>
> (Riis 1918: 273)

'Mere words' were to give way, in Riis' opinion, to the irrefutable veracity of the camera, and he saw his contribution as being that of bringing evidence to bear on what might otherwise be problematic. But he would not have seen his own personal vision as being of importance: the facts would speak for themselves and the people of the slums had, through the power and authority of the camera, been converted into 'facts' whose function was to exemplify and embody social problems. If complex and difficult lives are simplified into iconic statements of social deprivation, this is a problem not merely for Riis, but for the documentary project itself. Riis captured his photographs as if he were shooting game; he inscribed 'objectivity' into his images by refusing to allow his subjects to negotiate in any way the manner in which they might be recorded. Sally Stein has commented perceptively on this:

> We can indeed marvel at the consistency of Riis's photography in which so few of the exposures presented a subject sufficiently composed to return the glance of the photographer. That he rejected those rare photographs in which the subject did happen to look back suggests how premeditated the effect was. . . . The averted gaze, the appearance of unconsciousness or stupefaction, were only a few of the recurring features which gave Riis's pictorial documents stylistic unity and ideological coherence in relation to the text.
>
> (Stein 1983: 14)

A history of documentary could be structured around an account of the association between photographer and subject, and of the power relationships that are mediated between them. In the ostensible interest of revealing (and subsequently ameliorating) harsh conditions of life, photographers often rendered those they recorded into passive sufferers of poverty, rather than active agents in their own lives.

Photographing workers

Documentary photographers were always keen to represent the life of the poor. Constituted as 'the **Other**', workers, the poor, lumpen-proletariat or criminals, were often ill-distinguished in the middle-class mind, despite the efforts of people such as the social observer and writer Henry Mayhew to provide detailed typologies of the 'labouring poor'. Mayhew's approach to his investigations – a mixture of interview, statistics and descriptive writing – was to be one of the dominant modes through which working people were surveyed. Nor is it any accident that his monumental study of London life was illustrated with engravings that were based on photographs (Mayhew 1861).

In the last decades of the nineteenth century a number of significant British photographers recorded the life of the poor in great cities: John Thomson and Paul Martin in London, and Thomas Annan in Glasgow are three examples. Working several decades before Jacob Riis, they were influenced by the studies

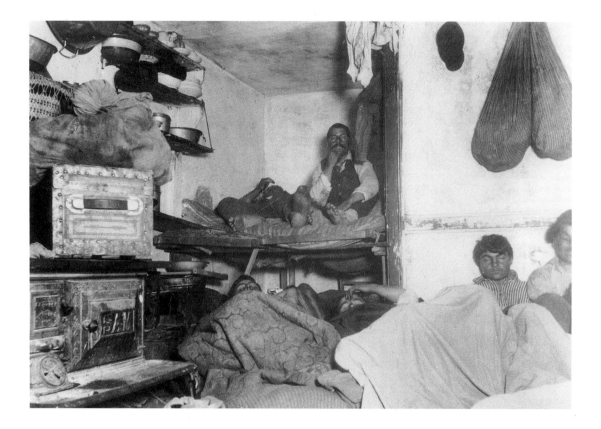

of the poor being carried out in literature and by philanthropists and social investigators. John Thomson directly cites the work of James Greenwood, the journalist, and Mayhew's monumental study, *London Labour and the London Poor*. Thomson is anxious to demonstrate that photography was a guarantor of authenticity and that his studies transcended the casual illustration of idiosyncratic types. He asserts that he is:

> bringing to bear the precision of photography in the illustration of our subject. The unquestionable accuracy of this testimony will enable us to present true types of the London Poor and shield us from the accusation of either underrating or exaggerating individual peculiarities of appearance.
>
> (Thomson 1877: n.p.)

2.7 Jacob August Riis, *Lodgers in a Crowded Tenement* – 'five cents a spot', 1880s
A typical scene of poverty and overcrowding is revealed in the harsh light of Riis' flash gun.

Thomson may also have been attempting to distinguish his work from the staged productions of other photographers. In the 1860s and 1870s the poor were seen as suitable subjects for art. Notable photographers, such as Oscar

Gustav Rejlander, produced picturesque studies of ragged street children that were much admired and, indeed, were used by Dr Barnardo to justify his own practices.

This preoccupation with the poor was not matched by a similar concern with capturing images of the world of work. Photography came into existence at a dynamic period in the development of capitalism, a time of technical innovation and of major engineering feats. Little of this energy is represented in the photographic archives; nor is the sheer drudgery of work and the army of labourers who carried it out made visible. Where there are shots of workers they tend to be inadvertently caught in a corner of the frame, or deliberately placed so as to give a sense of scale to some major building scheme.

There are many reasons for the absence of portraits of workers, not least that photographers tended not to live in the sites where industrial work was carried out. Moreover, notions of what made a good subject for a photograph were determined by convention, and also by such factors as the subjects set by the juries of photographic competitions. In the 1890s many clubs established 'street characters' or 'city trades' as subjects for competition, but they would have been very unlikely to establish categories based on industrial labour or domestic work.

Photographers were deeply influenced by conventional subjects and ways of treating the poor, and there are some examples of sustained and careful recording of working life. For example, Frank Meadow Sutcliffe diligently documented the village of Whitby as both a fishing village and a holiday resort over a long period of time. This work drew on the picturesque qualities of much of the labour involved, but also added new qualities of directness and close observation.

But such detailed, long studies were rare, and confined to one or two trades. Other workers passed without any great notice; of the vast army of clerks and domestic workers there is scarcely a sign, and those photographs of workers that do exist are usually of male labourers engaged in heavy, manual tasks. There are few images of women carrying out any kind of work and they are absent from the ranks of manual labourers. Indeed, if it were not for the curious obsession of **Arthur Munby**, women manual workers would have disappeared with scarcely a trace (Hudson 1972).[2]

Of course, some documentary photographers were able to undertake sustained studies of labour, as did Lewis Hine in the United States from the turn of the nineteenth century. Hine was a most committed and subtle photographer of people at work and was dedicated to the cause of using his images in the service of social reform. His output spans the time from Jacob Riis to the Farm Security Administration project of the 1930s. An excellent account of the work of Lewis Hine is given in **Trachtenberg**'s *Reading American Photographs* (1989).[3]

2 Arthur Joseph Munby (1828–1910) Munby was a barrister and minor poet who is now best known for his diaries and notebooks which tell us something about the fashionable and artistic life of the time, and also reveal his obsession with working women. In journeying round England and Wales, he sought out women working in coalmining, fishing and farming and commissioned local photographers to make portraits of them. A collection of these photographs at Trinity College, Cambridge provides an invaluable historical resource for anyone exploring the way in which labour has been depicted. Munby did not confine his passion to organising these pictures; he also secretly married his maidservant, Hannah Cullwick, and they lived together for many years. A useful book on Munby is Derek Hudson (1972) *Munby: Man of Two Worlds*, London: John Murray.

ALAN TRACHTENBERG (1989) **Reading American Photographs**, New York: Hill and Wang.

3 For an account of the connections between photography and other kinds of social investigation in the nineteenth and twentieth centuries see Derrick Price (1983), 'Photographing the Poor and the Working Class', *Framework* 22(22), Autumn.

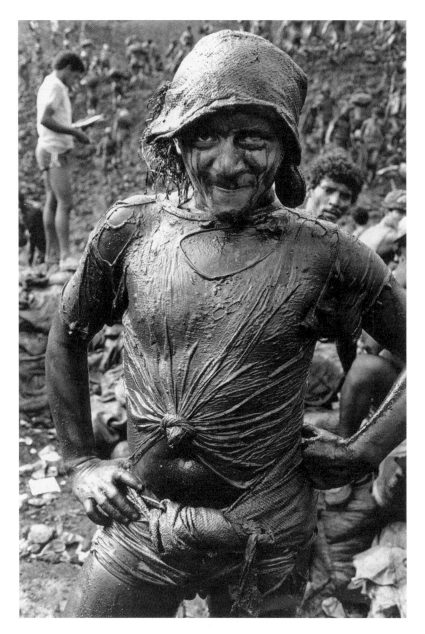

2.8 Sabastião Salgado, *Serra Pelada (Workers in Mud)*, 1986.
Salgado's study of landless Brazilian families struggling to make a living was published in his book, *Terra: Struggle of the Landless*, in 1997. The powerful images of poverty and work connect with the themes of earlier documentary practitioners.

For a good account of Salgado's work, see PARVATI NAIR (2011), **A Different Light: The Photography of Sebastiāno Salgado**, Durham, NC: Duke University Press.

Photography and colonialism

Despite the physical difficulties of transporting large, unwieldy cameras and portable darkrooms, photographers covered the world in search of images of historic sites, sacred places and curious people. Photography developed in Europe at the height of the British Empire and amongst the first subjects of the lens were colonised peoples around the world. There has been a great deal of scholarly and critical work that explores the way in which the camera was used as an instrument of symbolic control. Indeed, Thomas Richards has pointed out that the British ruled huge parts of the world with little military presence and that its control was exercised through its extraordinary grasp of systems of information – its passion for inventories, lists, maps and pictures.

> From all over the globe the British collected information about the countries they were adding to their map. They surveyed and they mapped. They took censuses, produced statistics. They made vast lists of birds. Then they shoved the data they had collected into a shifting series of classifications. In fact they often could do little other than collect and collate information, for any exact civil control, of the kind possible in England, was out of the question. The Empire was too far away, and the bureaucrats of Empire had to be content to shuffle papers.
>
> (Richards 1993: 3)

While photographs are an important part of these archives, they derive their importance from their relationship to other kinds of material and from the body of scientific ideas by which they were validated. So great was this passion that some critics have argued that it was the driving force behind the collection of a diverse range of material:

> Colonial exploitation opened up vast new populations as much to scientific study as to economic exploitation, and although the need to organize and control was clearly important to the task of classification of racial and other types, the 'taxonomic imperative' of Victorian science appears to have been sufficient motivation in itself to promote anthropological photography.
>
> (Hamilton and Hargreaves 2001: 87)

The Victorian fervour for classification, then, extended to whole peoples, who were categorised and ranked according to 'anthropological type'. Supported by theories of physiognomy, these sought to demonstrate the 'objective' differences between peoples, races, castes and social categories. Those who were subjected to the coloniser's gaze were often seen as merely representative of racial or social groups, and were usually posed so as to embody particular kinds of dress, social roles and material cultures. Peter Quartermaine, in his discussion of the photographs of Johannes Lindt of the native peoples of Australia and New Guinea, comments that:

> These people were photographed as 'other': the white settler population was interested in learning *about* them, a quasi-scientific attitude, which presupposed a controlling, position. The photographic images produced by Australian photographers sold to a metropolitan and international consumer market. Such prints doubly privileged the purchasers since, although reflecting their own aesthetic (natives clothed and posed with decorative artefacts), they also supposedly granted direct access to the culture depicted; their use as raw evidence by anthropologists and ethnographers certainly assumed this.
>
> (Quartermaine 1992: 85)

The concept of the Other is of central importance to this argument. The phrase has been used in feminist, **psychoanalytic** theory to indicate that men construct women as 'the Other'; that is, as an opposite, in reaction to which their own maleness can be defined. Similarly, European culture was defined *against* 'the Other' of colonised peoples:

> Photography is here no mere handmaid of empire, but a shaping dimension of it: formal imperial power structures institutionalised the attitudes and assumptions necessarily entailed in viewing another individual as a subject for photography.
>
> (Quartermaine 1992: 85)

We must remember that, unlike the body of painting and engravings of 'exotic' peoples that had been popular Victorian subjects, photography claimed to be able to create objective, 'scientific' records that were free from the bias of human imagination. Carefully contrived and constructed photographs were consumed as though they were unmediated and offered a neutral reflection of the world. They were, however, far from being transparent and dispassionate images, for, as Jill Lloyd puts it: 'both photography as a medium and anthropology as a discipline masked their ideological standpoints and connotative potential with the appearance of scientific objectivity' (Lloyd 1985: 13). What were returned to the Western spectator were images of native peoples that established them as primitive, bizarre, barbaric or simply picturesque. In the service of these images, people were photographed in what appeared to be archetypal ways. While 'primitive' dress was sometimes stressed, there was also a great emphasis on nudity:

> Throughout the colonial and postcolonial periods, photography was a major tool in the framing of a confrontation between local and external cultural styles. In this confrontation, nudity was used as a visual marker

of specific, but contradictory, local characteristics. It stood variously for primitivity, underdevelopment, indecency and indigeneity.

(Van Schendel 2002: 34)

While nudity was employed as an indicator of particular kinds of subjectivity, this quotation from Van Schendel also reminds us that control of the body is central to colonial modes of power, including the processes of representation. Much of the critical work in the study of colonialism and postcolonialism has been concerned with the body, and, at the symbolic level, photography was, as we have noted, of central importance in mediating the relationship between the colonised and coloniser. John Urry tells us that:

To photograph is in some ways to appropriate the object being photographed. It is a power/knowledge relationship. To have visual knowledge of an object is in part to have power, even if only momentarily over it. Photography tames the object of the gaze, the most striking examples being of exotic cultures. In the USA the railway companies did much to create 'Indian' attractions to be photographed, carefully selecting those tribes with a particularly 'picturesque and ancient' appearance.

(Urry 1990: 139)

Victorian notions of progress allowed colonised people to be seen as occupying a lower scale of human existence than Europeans, but it was a stage from which, it was imagined, they would evolve in the long march to civilisation. A cluster of ideas such as these underpin the colonial enterprise, so that James R. Ryan has argued that:

Despite claims for its accuracy and trustworthiness, however, photography did not so much record the real as signify and construct it. Through various rhetorical and pictorial devices, from ideas of the picturesque to schemes of scientific classification, and different visual themes, from landscapes to 'racial types', photographers represented the imaginative geographies of Empire. Indeed, as a practice of representation, photography did more than merely familiarise Victorians with foreign views: it enabled them symbolically to travel through, explore and even possess those spaces.

(Ryan 1997: 214)

It is this 'imaginative geography of empire' with which we are concerned and which has absorbed the attention of critics working on questions of postcolonialism. We need to remember here the scale of modern empire and understand that the structures of power established by colonialism are still active

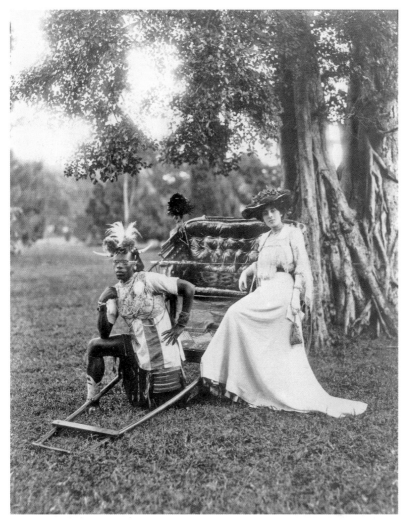

2.9 William Thomas, *Mrs Lewis Waller with a Kaffir Boy*, 1903
The relationship between coloniser and colonised is sharply focused in this portrait of Mrs Waller and her African servant.

in our globalised world, albeit often disguised in a variety of social and cultural practices. We can, to take just one example, see many of the tropes through which colonised peoples were pictured, drawn on in modern tourist photography. Like colonial photographers they stress the indigenous nature of people, their settled lives, picturesque or exotic appearance and timeless existence. In contrast to this, postcolonial commentators draw attention to the vast diasporic movement of peoples around the globe; examine the sets of appropriations and relations of hybridity between coloniser and colonised, and problematise questions of identity and subjectivity. Work of this kind is being made in many places by very different kinds of artists and photographers.

While a number of important critical and analytical concepts have emerged from postcolonial work, we need to remember that each society was very different in terms of its history, its indigenous forms of image-making and its cultural practices. Critically informed photography often works across the terrain of the local, as that has been constructed, reflected, transformed or employed in the imaginative geography of Empire. Ryan investigates the range of work which collectively produced the geography of imperialism and he looks at a number of individuals, places and activities – from African explorers, travellers in India, commercial photographers, military campaigns and the study of racial types – all of which helped to construct an archive of the achievements of the Victorian colonial and imperial project.

The public appetite for images of native peoples was accompanied by a demand for photographs of historic sites, many of which were familiar from paintings and engravings, but which were given a new authenticity by the camera. It is difficult now to gain any idea of just how many travel photographs were made and sold, but the market for them was certainly vast. In addition to the beautifully mounted and bound albums that are now preserved in archives and museums, the new commercial photography firms that were established in the years after 1850 sold thousands of cheap postcards and single prints. For example, in 1865 the London Stereoscopic Company sold half a million pictures, many of them scenes from foreign places. At the same time we see the emergence of the professional travel photographer of whom Francis Frith is probably the best known. In addition to his own work, he established a company bearing his name that was to become the largest publisher of photographs in its time. The camera and travel became linked together and, as tourism slowly developed into a mass industry, photography functioned both to set the scene in advance of a trip and to provide a record of the journey when it was over. Soon there were few places in the world that had not been surveyed by the camera and few people who had not been subjected to the photo-eye; wildernesses gave up their seclusion as surely as cities yielded their secret places to the new image-makers.

For a series of stimulating essays on this subject see: ALI BEHDAD AND LUKE GARTLAN (eds) (2013) **Photography's Orientalism: New Essays on Colonial Representation**, Los Angeles: Getty Research Institute.

THE CONSTRUCTION OF DOCUMENTARY

During the 1930s the paradigmatic form of documentary was produced: one which cast its subjects within a 'social problem' framework, and which argued for a politics of reform, and social education. Describing photographs produced much earlier as 'documentary' was not a simple act of labelling, but meant that we were invited to reconsider this work within the framework of the 1930s documentary project.

Photography in the 1930s was influenced by a number of factors. Technically the development of new, lightweight 35mm cameras made the act of
photographing people less obtrusive and increased the range of possible camera
angles. There was a growth in the number of illustrated magazines and, within
these, an increasingly sophisticated approach to the role of photo editors and
the construction of photo-essays. Not least, there was a new and vast public
with a hunger to see images drawn from real life. Following Grierson,
documentary was regarded as a tool of education that would militate against
foolish distractions and anchor people in a rational world of work and social
obligation.[4] It would offer, in an exciting form, facts about the social order
that everyone would need in order to play a part in modern society. But how
would documentary function in order to achieve these objectives? In an
influential book on documentary, **William Stott** (1973) writes:

> This is how documentary works. . . . It defies comment; it imposes its
> meaning. It confronts us, the audience, with empirical evidence of such
> nature as to render dispute impossible and interpretation superfluous.
> All emphasis is on the evidence; the facts themselves speak . . . since just
> the fact matters, it can be transmitted in any plausible medium. . . .
> The heart of documentary is not form or style or medium, but always
> content.
>
> (Stott 1973: 14)

On this reading the documentary genre is held to be able to transcend the
discursive structures of any particular form: imposing rather than creating
meaning; disempowering the reader or spectator from any acts of interpretation
vis-à-vis the text. Documentary, on this definition, becomes a kind of
ideologically charged common sense that is inaccessible to critical engagement.
It is a fascinating definition because it spells out, 40 years after the time, what
lies at the heart of 1930s notions of documentary. There was an assumption
that the world was productive of facts and that those facts could be communicated to others in a transparent way, free of the complex codes through
which narratives are structured.

Picturing ourselves

In the 1930s a plethora of conventional and novel means of investigation
were employed by a variety of people. In addition to formal reports based on
statistical investigation, there were varieties of journalistic reportage, travel books,
diaries, films, photographs and newsreels. The study of the exotic was now
accompanied by an attempt to look at ordinary life through objective eyes.

The best-known organisation that set out to make an anthropological survey
of British life in the 1930s is *Mass Observation* which was founded early in
1937 by Tom Harrison and Charles Madge. Harrison was an anthropologist
newly returned from Borneo, and Madge a poet. What their project has in

4 John Grierson
(1898–1972) was one of
the founders of the British
documentary film
movement. He stressed the
educative function of film,
which he saw as one means
of creating an informed
public able to play an active
part in running a
democratic society.
Grierson's philosophy and
ideas influenced the way in
which 'documentary' was
understood in film and also
in other media such as
literature and photography.
See Ian Aitken (1990) *Film
and Reform*, London:
Routledge.

WILLIAM STOTT (1973)
**Documentary Expression
and Thirties America**,
London: Oxford University
Press.

common with the documentary movement is the sense that the world could no longer be taken for granted and understood; that ordinary day-to-day lives needed to be made strange by being examined with the supposedly 'impartial' eye of the social scientist. *Mass Observation* recruited many respondents who, through the use of diaries and formal reports, would scrutinise and record their own day-to-day actions and behaviour, together with that of other people. The organisation was particularly interested in examining what happened on buses, in pubs, at the seaside and other areas where collective behaviour in public places could be observed.

Mass Observation used respondents, editors, painters and photographers in its attempt to build up an accurate picture of everyday life. Photographers adopted a range of techniques in order to capture their subjects; while some sought cooperation, most were concerned not to be observed and to work without the knowledge of the photographed. One characteristic response of photographers to the political and moral debates of the time was to see themselves as part of the camera, merely recording what was in front of them. Bert Hardy, who worked his way up from being a delivery boy to becoming a major photographer on *Picture Post*, described his practice in *Camerawork*:

> I didn't think of it politically. I was never a political animal. I mean the journalists had that sort of job to do. I think I just photographed what I saw. I never angled anything.
>
> (Hardy 1977: 9)

However, Humphrey Spender (in a later issue of the same journal) comments on the work he did in Bolton for *Mass Observation* and makes clear his desire to work voyeuristically:

> My main anxiety, purpose, was to become invisible and to make my equipment invisible, which is one of the reasons I carried around an absolute minimum of equipment. . . . Summing up the relics of feelings toward *Mass Observation* I think I can remember the main enemy being boredom and tedium and embarrassment.
>
> (Spender 1978: 7)

Working for a number of magazines and newspapers as well as for *Mass Observation*, Humphrey Spender made many of the pictures of working-class life which were later thought to be exemplary images of the time. In one account of this work he described his procedure as allowing 'things to speak for themselves and not to impose any kind of theory'. However, many people have noted the admixture of realism and Surrealism within his work (see Walker 2007). Spender described the difficulty of his journey as the fact that:

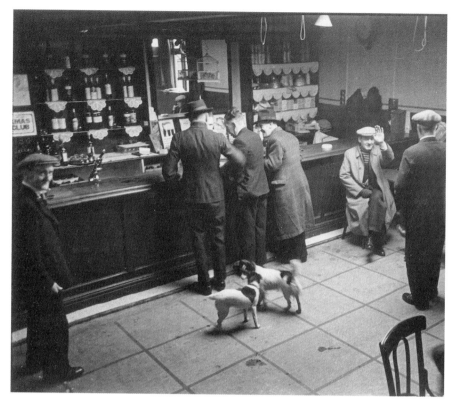

2.10 Humphrey Spender, *Men Greeting in a Pub*, Worktown Series, 1937
This carefully composed, gentle and humorous photograph reveals the influence of both realist photography and
Surrealism on Spender's work.

> I had to be an invisible spy – an impossibility which I didn't particularly
> enjoy trying to achieve . . . I was somebody from another planet
> intruding on another way of life. . . . A constant feature of taking the
> kind of photograph we're talking about even when people were unaware
> that they were actually being photographed – was a feeling that I was
> exploiting the people I was photographing, even when . . . the aim
> explicitly was to help them.
>
> (Spender 1978: 16)

Spender's description of himself as an alien and a spy is a dramatic way of
emphasising social distance, and in his account of his own feelings he points
up the fact that 'our way of life' might also be seen as distinct and separate
'ways of life'. The notion of the workers as productive of useful facts gives
way to a consideration of the subjects of representation as potentially exploited
by the encounter. Spender worked for *Mass Observation*, but his photographs

also appeared in the *Daily Mirror* and in *Picture Post*, and by the 1930s the market for actuality photographs had grown to very large proportions. While the styles and approaches of photographers differed one from another, it is also possible to see continuities and influences from the past as well as gender differences in the way in which documentary photographers carried out their work. Val Williams has argued that women photographers did not adopt

> candid photography as exemplified in the discreet, detached observation of photographers like Frank Meadow Sutcliffe and Paul Martin. Both Sutcliffe and Martin had pictured the world as full of vitality, as a kaleidoscopic spectacle of trades and crafts and distinguishing costume. . . . The style which they evolved affected the production of British documentary photography enormously, and reverberated through to *Picture Post* and beyond. For many of those who later took up photojournalism – a hybrid of press, candid and documentary photography – the stance became obligatory, particularly for war photographers working from the late thirties onwards. It indicated not only a kind of political detachment, allowing photographers to see themselves as reporters rather than participants, but also a particular machismo.
>
> (Williams 1986: 25)

Williams describes women photographers as using the medium for 'diverse and often very personal reasons' while 'women documentarists usually set out to record rather than to captivate and the avoidance of the dramatic and the candid was a primary influence upon each of them' (Williams 1986: 26).

Together with these gender differences in the approach to photography, we might also consider uses of the medium that were influenced by considerations of social class. We have seen that the documentary movement was part of a reformist political project and we should remember that, politically, it was concerned with the promulgation of liberal social values rather than with the revolutionary politics to which so many people in the 1930s subscribed. Closely associated with this is the charge that the political project implicit in much documentary work was unlikely to succeed given that documentary can, at best, show suffering, degradation, despair, but can do nothing to illuminate the causes of these woes. Power and causality are difficult to express through photographic images, as are collective struggle and resistance. Martha Rosler has critiqued this political stance in the following terms:

> In contrast to the pure sensationalism of much of the journalistic attention to working-class, immigrant and slum life, the meliorism of Riis, Lewis Hine, and others involved in social work propagandizing argued, through the presentation of images combined with other forms of discourse, for the rectification of wrongs. It did not perceive those

wrongs as fundamental to the social system that tolerated them – the assumption that they were tolerated rather than *bred* marks a basic fallacy of social work.

(Rosler 1989: 304)

Of course, many people in the 1930s did see poverty and dispossession as consequences of the prevailing social system and this belief gave rise to a vibrant left oppositional practice of radical theatre, film and photography. Workers' film and photo leagues were established in both Britain and the USA and opened up the medium of photography so that workers could make their own records of their lives and struggles. This was an important principle, but there is little evidence that the results challenged the nature of documentary reportage or established new kinds of image-making. Perhaps more interesting were those groups who maintained that questions of representation were a central part of political struggle, and developed an alternative photographic practice to exemplify those ideas. Their intention was not to reveal how things looked in the 'real world', but to disrupt the surface appearance of the image in order to construct new meanings out of the old pictorial elements. The painter, sculptor and photographer Alexander Rodchenko in the USSR and the German Dadaists at the end of the First World War elaborated this practice. Working against the central tenets of documentary, these artists argued that, in order to arrive at the meaning that lies below the surface of a photograph, it was necessary to contrive and manipulate the image. John Heartfield's incisive, politically charged photomontages, which developed from his work with the Berlin Dadaists, are the best-known constructions of this kind.

The Farm Security Administration (FSA)

The function of documentary in the service of radical politics was affected not only by the beliefs of individual photographers, but also by the uses for which pictures were commissioned; the professional practices through which they were produced, and the source of the finance that made them possible. In this respect the Farm Security Administration project is of considerable interest.

This was a government agency established in 1935 as part of the Roosevelt administration's attempt to rebuild the economy of the United States. A young social scientist, Roy Stryker, was appointed to head the photography section of the FSA. His main responsibility was to provide contemporary images to illustrate and support the written accounts of conditions in agriculture that were published in official reports.

The enterprise became the most important example of a major state-funded documentary project in the world and many of its participants have entered into the pantheon of 'great photographers': Walker Evans, Dorothea Lange, Russell Lee, Arthur Rothstein, Ben Shahn, Marion Post Walcott. We saw in Chapter 1 how Dorothea Lange's *Migrant Mother* became an iconic work, but many other photographs from the project have been reproduced extensively on book jackets, as illustrations, on gallery walls, even in advertisements. They are often described in histories of photography as having revealed the human face of Depression Day America.

Their initial task, however, was to show America at work and to provide images of workers rather than the displaced poor. Once on the road, though, the photographers were free from the constraints of Washington and often returned very different kinds of photographs to those that were expected. Some critics claim that their genius as visual artists allowed them to go beyond the mundane business of recording labour to penetrate to the secret heart of things. In fact, among the many thousands of negatives of the project there are very many which concern themselves with human toil.

But the huge archive has been used as a resource from which some photographs have been selected more often than others, so that our social and political sense of the project is constructed from the editing that has taken place over the years. In some ways this body of work does present us with an apparently coherent critique of American life. The most famous photographs are those of the sharecroppers of the southwest and their migration west out of the 'dustbowl' to the orange groves and fruit farms of California in search of work as itinerant labourers. This is a familiar story and was the subject of one of the most celebrated 'social' novels and movies of the time, John Steinbeck's *The Grapes of Wrath*.

Through the interest shown in them by photographers, writers and painters, these people were to become emblematic of the US Depression. What we remember about them is that the winds eroded their fields, destroying their livelihood, and that they were forced, though desperately poor, to travel long distances to try to find work in the low-wage fruit and cotton fields. The FSA photographs are almost always of individuals and families, and often show them as weary and defenceless. They evoke images of strain, of mental fatigue, but they also tease out the bonds of affection and connection between people, especially between mothers and children. And, of course, they show people on the road, moving out; their possessions packed away, their furniture roped to the tops of cars or heaped on to a rickety truck. In these images the solid elements of domestic life are often dissolved and relocated in strange, outdoor spaces. Objects do service as carriers of emotion; objects that are stranded, dislocated, treasured though cheap. For instance, Russell Lee shows us a harmonium upright, ready to be played, out in a field, all by itself, surrounded by mud. Walker Evans records a roughly piled grave of loose earth topped with the impermanent and unstable memorial of a dinner plate. Nothing appears to be anchored or solid, instead dust is everywhere; a friable earth is heaped against the walls of houses, has shawled over the gas pumps and the Coca-Cola signs, and is etched into the lines of faces and hands.

These documentary photographs, like all others, are densely constructed works which use certain techniques and forms to produce a desired response

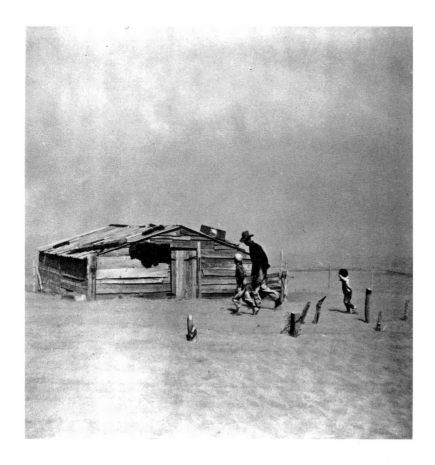

2.11 Arthur Rothstein,
Dust Storm, Cimarron
County, Oklahoma, **1936**
One of the original FSA
photographers, Rothstein
contributed many striking
images to the archive.

in the spectator. They do contain 'facts' in a simple sense: a woman wears a dress made from a flour sack, a family lives under a hastily constructed tent of twigs and tarpaulin. There is, in other words, plenty of evidence of poverty indicated by the traditional markers of lack of material prosperity. But, in their more complex versions, they are photographs of the (literally) dispossessed, carefully constructed to produce a meaning that transcends what is shown.

These people were not chosen merely for their 'representative' qualities: they are not simple icons of dispossession. Although they are anonymous subjects of the camera, their singularity is often stressed and their individual gestures carefully recorded. This is emphasised by the closeness of the camera and the informal stances people are allowed to take up in front of it. We feel that we are not in the presence of representatives of a class, but of ordinary people, much like us, who have fallen on hard times and are doing the best they can in the circumstances. Poverty and misery thus cease to be possessions of particular social groups living at a particular time in determinate conditions, and become a kind of dislocation or breakdown into which any one of us might stumble. In other words, we are asked to accept that we can make immediate connections between this body of work and our own life and condition; but also that these are photographs which sum up the specific experience of the migrant workers in the USA. We are invited to accept that these are 'honest' images drawn from life, but are also the product of extraordinarily gifted photographers. Some of the central contradictions of the social project of documentary photography are revealed here, for these photographs are treated as historical, but timeless; densely coded, but transparent; highly specific, but universal. And these various readings militated against the idea that the photographs should have been immediately accessible as evidence against the social and political system.

DISCUSSION: *DRUM*

In 2004 Zola Maseko directed *Drum*, a feature film which explored life in South Africa in the 1950s and depicted the forced clearance of Sophiatown and other violent acts carried out by the apartheid regime. It was widely distributed and won an award at the Durban Film Festival. The film was based on the life of the South African journalist Henry Nxumalo who worked for the illustrated magazine *Drum*. Founded in South Africa in 1951 *Drum* has been described as Africa's first lifestyle magazine. It was launched at the beginning of a decade that was to see an extension of the powers of the apartheid state. At the same time, the African National Congress launched its *Defiance Campaign* and the anti-racist *Freedom Charter* was produced. This political ferment was encouraged by the growth of a sophisticated, urban black population that formed the core of *Drum*'s readership.

Despite its justly deserved reputation for investigative journalism, *Drum* was not an overtly political magazine. Rather it embraced popular culture and was a heady mix of sport, jazz, fiction, gangsters and glamour. It also ran a famous Lonely Hearts column and, of course, told stories in pictures as well as words. Soon after it grew out of a short-lived magazine, *African Drum*, it was selling close to 200,000 copies a month and it was to spread, through the energy and ambition of its most important founder, Jim Bailey, the son of a mining millionaire, to many other African countries, including Nigeria, Ghana, Sierra Leone, Kenya, Uganda, Tanzania, Zambia and Zimbabwe. Produced and circulated with great difficulty, it was often banned, but is now remembered as one of the most influential of illustrated magazines.

It was important because of the writers it found and encouraged, several of whom have become well-known journalists, novelists and critics. In addition to Henry Nxumalo there were Lewis Nkosi, Bloke Modisane, Can Themba, Arthur Maimane and Todd Matshikiza. It was influential, too, because of its ability to train and nurture excellent photographers: people such as Bob Gosani, Peter

ALL NAMES MENTIONED IN THIS ARTICLE ARE NECESSARILY FICTITIOUS, BUT MR. DRUM KNOWS, AND CAN PROVIDE, THE ACTUAL NAME AND ADDRESS IN EACH INSTANCE.

THE STORY OF BETHAL

USUALLY *in South Africa a farm labourer's life, poor and simple though it is, has the same pleasant easy-going nature as is found in the countryside throughout much of the rest of the world. His is a skilled job and he has much of the natural independence of the skilled worker. If he grew up on the farm, he quite possibly became the playmate of the farmer's son and a happy association might well start that way which will last for the rest of their lives. On top of that, the rapid industrialisation of South Africa, by drawing off labour from the countryside with the offer of higher wages and a more gaudy life in the towns, puts increasing pressure on the farmer to improve working conditions if he wishes to keep his labour.*
BUT BETHAL IS DIFFERENT.

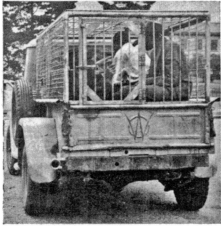

CAGED AFRICANS being taken to a farm from the Johannesburg Fort. Farmers drive into Johannesburg in lorries to collect convicts to serve their sentences on farms. This picture was taken by the photographer of a Johannesburg daily paper, while the farmer was away on business in the city. The convict labour system accounts for a good deal of labour in the Bethal Area.

EVIL RECORD

FOR MANY YEARS BETHAL HAS BEEN NOTORIOUS for the ill-treatment of the African labourers on the farms. As far back as April 12, 1929, there was a case (Rex v. Nafte, at the Circuit Court at Bethal) of a farmer who was found guilty of tying a labourer by his feet from a tree and flogging him to death, pouring scalding water into his mouth when he cried for water. In January, 1944 (Rex v. Johannes Mahlangu), a labourer, Philipp Lebovo, was found to have been beaten to death for attempting to escape, and a few months later (Rex v. Isaac Sotetshi), another labourer, Franz Marie, was beaten to death. On June 3, 1947 (see De Echo, Bethal, of 6.6.47) there was a case of a farmer assaulting two labourers, setting his dog on them, flogging them and chaining them together for the night; and only a week later, on June 11 (De Echo, 13.6.47), a farm foreman was found guilty of striking a labourer with sjambok and setting his dog on him. A month later (Rand Daily Mail, 16.7.47) another foreman was found guilty of ill-treating labourers, and a similar case appeared in Witbank two days later (Rand Daily Mail, 18.7.47). These cases all came up in court and were strongly condemned by the magistrates: in one of them the magistrate, Mr. R. H. Wooler, described the incident as being sordid, despicable and reminiscent of slavery, and the local European paper, De Echo, described the conditions disclosed as being "tantamount to slave-driving." And it seems clear that for every case that came before a magistrate there were many more that were never found out.

WE *publish this important and revealing story in order to protect our readers, and all Africans, from the hardships and dangers they may suffer as a result of signing a contract they do not fully understand. It is our intention to assist the authorities by making clear to would-be recruits the workings of the contract system, and by presenting the true facts of the case. We are all too aware of the damage to good relations between the races that the conditions at Bethal have brought about, and we wish to do all we can to prevent such happenings in the future.*

SYSTEM 'A GREAT SCANDAL'

SINCE the publicity given to Bethal by these and other court cases and by private investigations, some action has been taken to prevent similar cases, and the Government, particularly the Department of Native Labour, has shown itself anxious to remove the injustices and abuses of the contract system. It seems clear, however, that it is impossible to prevent abuses of the employment of contract labour with the accompanying compound system, and this has been emphasised by many authorities. In 1944 Mr. JUSTICE MARITZ (in Rex v. Isaac Sotetshi) pointed out that the compound labour system was "something quite new in agricultural economy," and condemned the whole system as responsible for cruelty and injustice. In October, 1944, the DIOCESAN SYNOD OF THE ANGLICAN CHURCH issued a memorandum stating that "it must be clear that the extension of the mine compound system to farms without any of the safeguards against the exploitation of the labourer is leading in the country to the kind of exploitation of the labourer characteristic of the worst periods of the Industrial Revolution in Europe." And as recently as June, 1951, Mr. JUSTICE LUCAS, sentencing a farmer in Delmas to five years' hard labour for assault, condemned the system as "a great scandal and one which may still have a very serious result on racial relations in this country."

The following is a typical account of the workings of the contract system, as told by a relative of Mr. DRUM's who was sent to Bethal early in 1949:

Continued on page 7

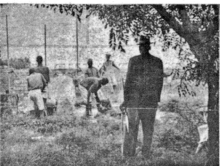

PRISONERS FROM BETHAL PRISON at work on building. In the foreground is the boss-boy, and the man with the cap is a prison supervisor running towards Mr. Drum to prevent the picture being taken. Officials describe the farm prison system as the "ideal rehabilitation scheme," but when farmers can use prison labour, there is obviously less incentive to attract voluntary labour by better conditions and pay.

2.12 *Drum*, March 1952

Drum, Africa's most famous illustrated magazine, offered a unique blend of investigative journalism, sport and crime to a new, urban readership.

Magubane, and the German photographer, Jürgen Schadeberg who was for many years the senior figure in the group. Also working for the magazine were Ernest Cole, whose photographic book *House of Bondage* became essential reading for anyone interested in life in South Africa, and the white photographer Ian Berry who later joined *Magnum* and whose photographs for *Drum* of the Sharpeville massacre (21 March 1960) circulated around the world.

This extraordinary array of talented individuals was led in the first years by an English editor, Anthony Sampson, who had no experience of magazine editing, but was a friend of Jim Bailey's from their time together at Oxford. Sampson established the characteristic content of the magazine, its relaxed way of working and its central concerns. His book *Drum*, published in 1956 and updated in the 1980s, gives a fascinating account of the early years of the magazine (Sampson 1983). Sampson was succeeded as editor first by Sylvester Stein then by Tom Hopkinson who had developed and inspired the famous British illustrated magazine *Picture Post*. Hopkinson has also given an account of his years with the magazine as it developed in a number of African countries (Hopkinson 1962).

Although *Drum* found a ready readership for its social and entertainment content, it is as a crusading magazine that its early years will be remembered. It is not too extravagant to claim that a single story established *Drum* on its first anniversary. The story was an exposé of the brutal conditions of life and work suffered by black people arrested for failing to carry a pass and sentenced to work on a white-owned potato farm. In the persona of Mr Drum, Henry Nxamalo infiltrated the farm together with the writer Arthur Maimane and photographer Jürgen Schadeberg. The success of the piece meant that exposés became the order of the day and over the years Mr Drum went, with great success, on trips to many sites of oppression and injustice.

Despite this investigative work, *Drum* could only exist because it did not directly challenge the government of the day, or overtly proselytise for any political party. This lack of direct political struggle was criticised by some people on the Left in Africa. Graeme Addison sums up the position in the following terms:

> The Magazine remains a problem for the critic because it sprang from a matrix of white entrepreneurship, editorial opportunism, and non-militant black talents, none of whom had a prime interest in the liberation of the masses. *Drum* did not aim to mobilise these masses, but it did educate and inform them, perhaps better than any other medium.
>
> (Addison 1984)

We might add that *Drum* was witty, caustic, brash and knowing. It provided its early readers with an irreplaceable mix of ideas, fashions, insights and information that was conveyed through a mix of pictures and text. The magazine continued with varied journalistic success through the 1960s and 1970s until in 1984, to everyone's surprise, Jim Bailey sold it to the pro-government Afrikaaner group, Nasionale Pers. It became a weekly in 1996 and now describes itself, with its mix of fashion, advertising and leisure interest features as 'a vibrant magazine for the young, upwardly socially mobile South African'. Although it has lost its political edge its archives are increasingly seen as a vital resource for people researching the nature of political and social life in the country during the apartheid years.

DOCUMENTARY: NEW CULTURES, NEW SPACES

The archetypal documentary project was concerned to draw the attention of an audience to particular subjects, often with a view to changing the existing social, cultural, or political situation. To achieve this goal, documentary photographs were rarely seen as single, independent images. They were usually accompanied by or incorporated into written texts. Within this context the images functioned both to provide information about the nature of things and to confirm the authenticity of a written account. Individual photographers were rarely credited for their work in magazines, and photographs were treated as though they were anonymous productions. The postwar consumer boom, exemplified in the introduction of television and the growth of car ownership, produced a very different society to that of the 1930s. In commenting on this new social scene some photographers produced work that was to transform the nature of documentary photography. Especially in the USA, documentary began to be concerned with new kinds of cultural spaces, in particular those that were encountered in everyday life, rather than places that were exemplary of grinding poverty or social injustice.

Photography on the streets

Documentary and photo-journalism are two closely related genres of photography, but there are other kinds of work that connect closely with them, not least that of street photography. This is difficult to define precisely for, as Clive Scott puts it:

> Street photography certainly puts us in a taxonomic quandary, not only because it stands at the crossroads between the tourist snap, the documentary photograph, the photojournalism of the *fait divers* (news in brief) but also because it asks to be treated as much as a vernacular photography as a high art one.

> (Scott 2007: 15)

**2.13 Melanie Einzig,
*Spring Corner, New York
City*, 2000.**

This picture is characteristic of
contemporary street
photography that explores the
bizarre, random and diverse
nature of modern cities.

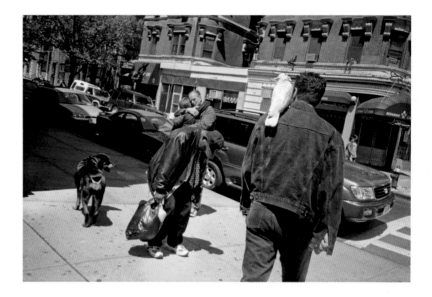

So, we find street photography difficult to define precisely because it cuts
across a number of genres and practices. As we have seen, what were once
thought to be fixed and immutable practices have more recently become fluid
in response to technological, social and cultural changes. However, in recent
years there has been an increased interest in the activity of street photography
as people capture life in public places or record unexpected events on their
mobile phones. It seems that every moment of urban life can be recorded and,
via social networking sites, distributed to family, friends or thousands of
followers.

We should remember, though, that throughout its history images from
the street have been a mainstay of photographic practice, so that there might
already be said to be a tradition of street photography, which is defined
by Westerbeck and Mayerowitz as 'candid pictures of everyday life in the street'
although they also add that by 'the street' is meant any public space, including
bars, cafés, parks, dance halls, etc. (Westerbeck and Meyerowitz 1994: 34–5).

This was a tradition that produced a number of great practitioners, but many
of the photographs that now seem so evocative of a particular place at a
particular time were taken by anonymous photographers and often for reasons
that we can only guess at.

Although difficult to distinguish precisely from documentary or casual
tourist snaps, we can explore street photography in terms of its predominant
styles and subject matter. These are often pictures that have a casual air, but
prize the representation of a moment sealed in time from the everyday confusion of the street. They are of ordinary people, although they may be pictured
at an extraordinary moment in their lives.

In the nineteenth century photographs of people working, lounging or playing in the streets were posed, and photographers often worked with the intention of creating a typology of trades or games or practices. With the rise of the documentary movement photographs in the street were frequently made in order to illuminate a social point – one thinks of the unemployed man lounging on a street corner so often used to illustrate the wastefulness of unemployment or the shoeless child that became an icon of poverty. These were often commissioned together with articles on social or political topics. Even when the coming of lightweight cameras freed photographers to wander the streets with ease and make images in every milieu, there was always a particular interest in the people who occupied the marginal, dangerous or neglected parts of the city.

Paris is regarded as the predominant site of modern street photography not least because street photography has been seen as a component of, and deeply influenced by, the development of modernity. It is, for example, coeval with the birth of department stores, of tabloid newspapers and other forms of the press. Certainly by the 1920s and 1930s there was an extraordinary outpouring of work made on the city's streets by photographers who are now regarded as great photographers, for example Robert Doisneau, Willy Ronis, Cartier-Bresson, Brassaï, and Robert Capa.

French humanism and a particular kind of populism helped to sustain an interest in the appearance of ordinary people. These people were not seen as exemplary subjects of some social cause, as they might be by documentary photographers. Rather, the fascination of street photography was with the infinite ways of being that were acted out in little moments in public spaces. By the 1950s this mood was changing in France and the dominant practice of street photography moved to the USA, which, of course, already had a developed tradition of such work. Amongst the distinguished US street photographers we may name Robert Frank, Roy de Caverra, William Klein, Helen Levitt, Joel Meyerowitz and Diane Arbus. The streets of the United States were very different to those of European cities and the world seen from an automobile becomes a central feature of some of this work.

In his collection *The Americans*, Robert Frank offered his own version of American life in which he eschewed the usual subjects of documentary investigation and presented us instead with cool and ironic images of the fleeting moments of ordinary life. Significantly enough, the introduction to the book was written by the Beat writer Jack Kerouac, who said: 'After seeing these pictures you end up finally not knowing any more whether a juke box is sadder than a coffin' (Frank 1959: 5).

Born in Switzerland, Robert Frank brought an outsider's eye to bear on the USA of the 1950s. He went on the road with a camera, an old car and a Guggenheim scholarship and photographed not only juke boxes and coffins, but cowboys, long empty roads, tract houses on lonely fields, flags and bikers, drive-in movies and barbers' chairs. Frank caught America at the point where commonplace life was about to be turned into myth; where even the banal and the prosaic were soon to be commodified into spectacle. People in these photographs are not constituted as 'poor' or 'workers' or, indeed, as any particular kind of social being. They exist as spectators, gazing out at some invisible scene: other people, the road ahead, a movie screen, a parade going by. In these closed, watchful faces we can read no significant facts, and if we have a sense of 'being there', it is as a witness to nothing of any great importance. Frank refused a documentary project that saw life as productive of weighty events that the photographer might chronicle and analyse. He seems to be saying that none of the many scenes that happen in the world are invested with any special meaning, although some may be made distinctive by the very act of being photographed. It is important to notice that coffins are no sadder than juke boxes precisely because an old hierarchy of importance has been abolished; hereafter the subject matter of documentary is both dispersed and

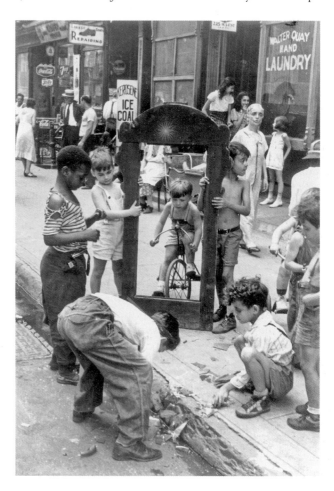

2.14 Helen Levitt, *New York* (broken mirror), c. 1942
Levitt photographed New York as a place of community and neighbourhood as in this wartime shot of children playing cheerfully in a lively street.

expanded to include whatever engages or fascinates the photographer. Facts now matter less than appearances. The old documentary project is fractured into work that explores the world in terms of particular subjectivities, identities and pleasures.

Frank was not alone in offering new, less monumental images of America in the 1950s. Around the same time William Klein was photographing New York in a manner that stressed the disorder and randomness of life in great cities. Halla Beloff comments on them in the following terms:

> It is the truth value of American street photographs . . . that gives them their special artistic and psychological interest. Their style and their subject matter in a state of consonance, they randomly sample their subject matter. They show fragments, *randomly* set out, *arbitrarily* cut off, with *bizarre* juxtapositions, and these epithets invite us to move from the photographs to the culture and people in them.
>
> (Beloff 1985: 99)

In Klein's crowded streets the point of photographic interest may lie in a half-concealed detail somewhere in the background of a shot. His city is restless, crowded, neurotic and alienating, and was to become one dominant version of how cities were perceived and represented by later commentators. A different version of urban life was created by some French or British photographers; for example, Roger Mayne's photographs of street life in West London provided a portrait of the lives of people in a particular place that was relaxed, incisive, intimate and very different from earlier British documentary work (Mayne 1986).

Work from the streets was changing the nature of 'realist' photography both by presenting new subject-matter and by treating old themes in novel ways. Sometimes called 'subjective' documentary, this work was very influential in both the USA and Britain. It liberated documentary from the political project with which it had formerly been associated, and allowed photographers to move away from both the traditional subjects of documentary and the conventions of documentary representation. Now, Lee Friedlander could make a series of photographs full of visual ambiguity and allow his own silhouette to fall across his subjects to celebrate his shadowy presence on the scene. Gradually, there was an extension of the subjects that were deemed suitable for documentary. For example, Tony Ray-Jones' *A Day Off: An English Journal* (1974) attempted to cover a spectrum of social class in looking at the English at play, from Glyndebourne and Eton to Butlins and Brighton's Palace Pier. In the 1930s, perhaps the most famous photographer of British life, Bill Brandt, had compared photographs of rich and poor; for example, putting maids and mistresses into a double-page spread so that we could observe difference and privilege. By the 1960s, however, photographers were concerned to offer more personal versions of the nature of social existence.

Street photographers depended on their work being published in illustrated magazines and in monographs, although they were also included in exhibitions. The decline of these outlets and the rise of televised pictures of streets and public spaces led to a lack of interest in the movement for some decades. Now, however, street photography is back as more and more people want to capture curious or poetic moments on the street and share them with others. Indeed, few street scenes would be complete without someone using a phone as a camera. The Brooklyn-based photographer Gus Powell puts it like this:

> It's harder and harder to take a picture without somebody in the picture who's also taking a picture. We all take pictures now, that's just what we do.
>
> (Powell in Howarth and McLaren 2010: 9)

Most of these photographs remain as personal documents or may be shared on social networks, but there are many committed photographers working regularly in public spaces. How the presence of so many images of our ordinary existence will change our social and cultural life remains to be seen. And we should remember that there have often been times when cities seemed to be overwhelmed by amateur photographers, to the considerable annoyance of many of their citizens. Jennifer Tucker has noted that:

> As cameras became smaller, cheaper, and easier to use in the late nineteenth and early twentieth century, thousands of amateurs armed with cameras joined professional photographers in recording pictures of urban public spaces not only in the United States, France and Britain but also in cities across India, Russia, Japan and many other nations, raising a new set of issues around the appropriation of public spaces for private purposes.
>
> (Tucker 2012: 11)

If many of these people were seen as a social nuisance, the present position is made more complex by the fact that, in addition to thousands of casual recorders of our actions, we are all the photographic subjects of a stream of images made by the dispassionate eye of surveillance cameras. Millions of these now exist in urban spaces around the world. Owned by government bodies and private commercial organisations they constantly survey public spaces by day and night and many have the sophisticated 'face recognition' technology, so that particular individuals or types can be picked out from the urban mass. Many people welcome these cameras as offering a potential deterrent to crime, but others see them as voyeuristic and intrusive.

Some people seek to oppose the power of this kind of systematic observation. One of the key weapons of those who engage in performances designed to challenge street surveillance systems is that of wearable technologies

– small computers that are attached to the body and record the world without the direct intervention of the wearer. Wearable computer technologies are being developed by commercial and business organisations, who see their power to increase sales, as well as by those who want to challenge or disrupt the existing systems. Increasingly, small and relatively cheap cameras that will take a stream of photographs based on changes in light, direction, colour and temperature are coming onto the market. Using very wide-angle lens they produce up to 2,000 pictures a day that can be uploaded to a computer in order to be edited.

It seems, then, that we may be drawing close to a time when every moment of our lives is capable of being recorded, not by street photographers or happy snappers, but by ourselves.

Theory and the critique of documentary

From the 1970s, a stream of critical work began to reject the notion that acts of looking and recording can ever be neutral, disinterested or innocent, and described them instead as containing and expressing relations of power and control. Perhaps the single most important influence on British documentary after 1970 came from the new ways in which photography was theorised and the functions it was considered to be able to play in cultural politics. **Semiological** analysis treated films and photographs as *texts* in order to investigate the components of sign systems through which meaning is structured and encoded within a work. The point of concern was not whether the work adequately revealed or reflected a pre-existing reality, but the way particular signifying systems imposed order and created particular sets of meaning. Inscribed within the photograph, then, was not some little likeness to reality, but a complex set of technical and cultural forms that needed to be decoded. Far from being innocent transcriptions of the real, photographs were treated as complex material objects with the ability to create, articulate and sustain meaning. Using theoretical tools that often derived from Film Studies or Literary Studies, critics began to explore the way in which photography functioned as a signifying system. One of the characteristics of photography is, as we have seen, the fact that it appears to have a special relationship to reality. We speak of *taking* photographs rather than *making* them, because the marks of their **construction** are not immediately visible; they have the appearance of having come about as traces from the scene itself, rather than as carefully fabricated cultural objects. As spectators we are positioned as the eye of the camera and we gaze upon an apparently natural and unmediated scene. Our acts of looking were no longer considered to be disinterestedly innocent, but were analysed in order to distinguish the kinds of psychic pleasure and relations of power that are invested in the process. The concept of power that is being used in this analysis owes much to the work of the French philosopher **Michel Foucault**. (See note p. 67.)

Power is not seen by Foucault as a force held by a particular social group that enables it to coerce another, but is located within all parts of the social system. Power resides in all aspects of a knowledge system including the construction of archives, the codification of information and the communication chains through which it is disseminated. Nor is 'truth' a special kind of knowledge that allows us to escape the pervasive reach of power: truth and power are also intertwined. Each society has constructed its own 'regime of truth', elaborating frameworks, institutions and discourses which validate particular procedures and permit us to distinguish true from false statements.

Power, on this account, flows through the processes of science; through discourses and the apparently trivial encounters of everyday life. Nor is power an abstract force that is only occasionally employed in order to enforce obedience, but, within a disciplinary society, it is inscribed on the body through the processes whereby the body is objectified as a source of knowledge. Photography's obsessive concern to record, catalogue, explore, reveal, compare and measure the human body was one way in which it could be seen to be an important form within the disciplinary process (see ch. 4, pp. 196–201).

JOHN TAGG (1988) **The Burden of Representation: Essays on Photographies and Histories**, London: Macmillan.

In his collection of essays *The Burden of Representation* (1988), **John Tagg** analyses the vast increase in the *power* of photography in the latter half of the nineteenth century and traces the 'complicity' of photography in the articulation of particular kinds of surveillance and observation. Documentary is seen as part of the process of examination described by Foucault as 'a procedure of objectification and subjection', in which ordinary lives are turned into accounts – into writing or, for that matter, into photographs. Such an analysis of the function of documentary clearly casts considerable doubts on the reformist social and political project with which it had been identified for so long. Its overt or implicit use as a means of surveillance and control was now being stressed, rather than its ability to reveal the nature of suffering or destitution in the service of social reform. Photography is seen as being complicit in the discourses which function to exert social control. 'Documentation' cannot act to reveal inequalities in social life, for there can be no document that is merely a transcription of reality. Rather, as part of a discursive system, it constructs the reality that it purports to reveal. But this is not a random creation, for it is made within the ideological positions framed by the discourses which are themselves part of the system of power. Cultural critic Julian Stallabrass has commented on Tagg's analysis in the following terms:

> Tagg presents 'documentary' – which includes documentary photography
> – as 'a liberal, corporatist plan to negotiate economic, political and
> cultural crises through a linked programme of structural reforms, relief
> measures, and a cultural intervention aimed at restructuring the order
> of discourse, appropriating dissent, and rescuing the threatened bonds of
> social consent'. In this retrospective view which entirely discounts the

beliefs of those individuals involved – including some who were committed to overthrowing capitalism – the complex and diverse currents of documentary photography serve the conspiracy by which the system survives.

(Stallabrass 1997: 136)

Cultural politics and everyday life

Documentary was grounded in the recording and delineation of commonplace life, but the idea of 'ordinary, everyday life' was itself now understood to be a problematic concept. Rather than being seen simply as a method of recording, photography begins to be regarded as a means through which we can express and articulate our own particularity and difference. We can move, as Don Slater has put it, from being consumers of images to becoming active producers:

> The camera as an *active* mass tool of representation is a vehicle for documenting one's conditions (of living, working and sociality; for creating alternative representations of oneself and one's sex, class, age-group, race, etc; of gaining power of analysis and visual literacy) over one's image; of presenting arguments and demands; of stimulating action; of experiencing visual pleasure as a producer, not consumer of images; of relating to, by objectifying, one's personal and political environment.
>
> (Slater 1983: 246)

If we can actively work on 'representations of ourselves', it seems that documentary, with its historic weight of practice and ostensible claim to transparency, might not be the perfect photographic form by which this could be achieved. Documentary began to be deserted in favour of contrivance and artifice. Work of this kind came from community groups and feminist collectives, and was to be found in certain kinds of gallery practice. For example, the East London community group Hackney Flashers used their photographic project to politicise activities and concepts such as motherhood, housework and child-care. They used a variety of montage techniques, together with text and slogans, to overcome the perceived limitations of documentary photography, a limitation that was outlined by Angela Kelly when making her 1979 selection of feminist photographs:

> The 'analytical' approach sees conventional documentary as problematic in the sense that the medium itself is a complex signifying process. Photographic images are presented as constructs and the viewer is forced to read the system of signs and to become aware of being actively involved in the process of the creation of meaning. This approach stands in opposition to the notion of the photograph as a transparent 'window on the world'.
>
> (Kelly 1979: 42)

Kelly makes it clear that she does not endorse the documentary project, which she considers to confirm, at least implicitly, photography's claim to be 'true to appearances'. Similarly, more than a decade later, Tessa Boffin and Jean Fraser introduced their book of lesbian photography with an explanation that, since sexuality is socially constructed, documentary realism might be an inappropriate form for its representation:

> Lesbianism exists in a complex relation to many other identities;
> concerns with sexuality intersect with those of race, class and the body
> . . . we looked for work which concentrated on constructed, staged or
> self-consciously manipulated imagery which might mirror the socially
> constructed nature of sexuality. We have not included much
> documentary work as the realism of documentary has often been used
> ideologically to reinforce notions of naturalness. We do not want this
> book to claim a natural status for lesbianism but rather to celebrate that
> there is no natural sexuality at all.
>
> (Boffin and Fraser 1991: 10)

Photography has been used in projects of this kind in order to explore subjectivity, but, while working-class life has been surveyed through documentary, it seems that gender, race and sexuality have been analysed in terms of other kinds of photographic discourses and practices – those which stress a Brechtian concern with construction and fabrication in photography. Called into question was the ability of realist practices adequately to unmask the nature of the prevailing social conditions or to explore the social and political nature of our subjective lives. John Roberts has suggested that the movement away from documentary is associated with the 'downgrading of class within cultural politics' and a retreat from class politics itself. Rather than simply endorse the documentary movement, however, he argues:

> There can be no representation of class subjectivities without the
> photographer intervening *in* the process of the production of meaning.
> Whether you are studio-based or working with conventional
> documentary images then, work on the representation of class cannot
> proceed without a recognition of those symbolic processes that shape
> and determine the construction of class identity.
>
> (Roberts 1993: 13)

Throughout the twentieth century, there were documentary photographers who were still concerned to represent the nature of work and the lives of working people in a style that owed a great deal to classic forms of documentary photography. Today, work and class relationships are less important subjects for practicing photographers. Perhaps more interest lies in an examination of the ecological consequences of industrialisation on a global scale as exemplified in the works of Edward Burtynsky. These show the dereliction brought about by huge land projects – strip mining, dams, quarrying, etc. In this work the woeful destruction of the earth is counterpoised by the aesthetic beauty of the large, colour images. Burtynsky's work is discussed in detail in Chapter 6.

The real world in colour

In the 1960s, not only were themes changing, but the very technical and aesthetic basis on which documentary photography was founded was being challenged. Colour photography was largely confined to advertising and the publicity industry until the American William Eggleston started to use it in his work. With the support of John Szarkowski he mounted a now famous exhibition at the Museum of Modern Art in New York. The colour photographs had been made using the dye-transfer process, which gave them intense colour saturation, and became the subject of great debate as to their validity and artistic merit. His subjects were mundane, everyday, often trivial, so that the real subject was often seen to be colour itself. Thomas Weski describes it in the following way:

> Eggleston's particular interpretation of pictorial colour is largely responsible for the fact that his photographs often induce the feeling that we have never before consciously seen the situations and objects depicted, or that we are discovering a side of them that has hitherto been hidden from us. This was the first time that colour had been used in art-photography not simply to replicate reality but to express and induce feelings.
>
> (Weski 2003: 25)

Important as Eggleston is in making colour an acceptable part of art and documentary photography, he was not, of course, alone in employing it. Paul Outerbridge, Stephen Shore, John Divola and Alex Harris all worked in different ways with colour. This American-led innovation spread to Britain where, in very different ways, a number of photographers moved from monochrome work to the expressive use of colour photography. Writing in *Creative Camera,* Susan Butler saw the use of colour by British photographers as a way of making visible aspects of life that had been largely ignored in the struggle to reveal class positions and social problems:

> But one can shift the perspective yet again to make the case that in the area of new colour work in Britain, many 'straight' photographers are expanding documentary concerns to include a broader range of social and, in effect, anthropological readings as opposed to a more overtly political but rather confined range of social issues based mostly in class and work, although these concerns as well have begun to figure in colour work, and are being revitalised by it.
>
> (Butler 1985: 122)

Indeed, many British-based photographers were being influenced by the demands and possibilities of colour at the time. They include Paul Graham, Anita Corbin, Jem Southam, Martin Parr, John Podpadec and Peter Fraser, and many others who clearly did not share a common practice or approach to photography in other respects. An example of Martin Parr's work is reproduced in this book (Figure 2.15). It is important to realise that the use of black and white film and, in the case of documentary, a particular kind of subject-matter, were considered to be the necessary markers of a serious photographer. Colour not only belonged to the world of commerce, but was regarded as lacking the technical control and aesthetic order of black and white photography. Moreover, in earlier years people were nervous about the possibility of using what seemed to be the unstable medium of colour. In 1952 the famous French humanist photographer **Henri Cartier-Bresson** said:

2:15 Sanjeev Saith, *Between Houses, Ranikhet*, 1992
Here Saith uses colour and the pattern of shadows to charge an ordinary street scene with emotion.

> Colour photography brings with it a number of problems which are hard to resolve today, and some of which are difficult even to foresee, owing to its complexity and its relative immaturity. . . . Personally, I am

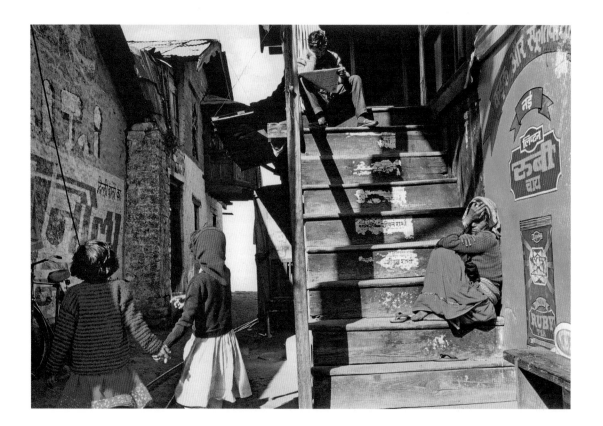

half afraid that this complex new element may tend to prejudice the achievement of the life and movement which is often caught by black and white.

(Cartier-Bresson 1952: 48)

Today, the victory of colour over black and white is complete in documentary, street photography and photojournalism. To work in black and white now is to make a deliberate aesthetic statement or to reference work from the past in a particular way. The effect of the coming of colour has been to introduce new subjects (drawn from the whole range of everyday life) and to create new expressive approaches to those subjects from many photographers.

Documentary and photojournalism in the global age

We have seen that all over the world people continue to make documentary photographs, which are shown in journals, books and newspapers, exchanged on social media sites and flashed around the world by mobile phones. But we should notice that much of this work has become largely dislocated from any social or political project. Moreover, much documentary work is now to be seen on gallery walls and the archetypal small, monochrome print has frequently given way to large colour images. As we have noted, even that most rigorous practitioner Sebastião Salgado exhibits his photographs in gallery settings before reproducing them as books, while photographers increasingly seek out new kinds of commercial and cultural spaces in which to show their work. The conditions of reception, then, have changed dramatically and the gallery has become an important space not only for documentary, but also for photojournalism. It may seem strange that works created to comment on current events are shown, divorced from any serious text, in the contemplative space of the gallery. Certainly, this has been partly a response to the decline in outlets for print-based photojournalists, but it is also a consequence of a change in intention on the part of photographers in response to the pressures of the structure of contemporary communications. The globalisation of news and the demand for information around the clock has changed the organisational structure of magazines and newspapers and brought about a new division of labour. For example, it has been noted that the growth of digital photography means that photographers tend to select images and edit in camera. Not only are potential archives (formerly built around retaining negatives) lost, but fewer photographers are employed on the staff, and the availability of digital cameras has made it possible for print journalists to send images directly to the picture desk (Burgess 2001). David Bate has pointed out that manipulation of press images by the computer has transferred power away from the photographer and to the picture editor who, increasingly, controls the nature of what is seen (Bate 2001). In response to this apparent lack of either immediate relevancy or control of their own work, some

H. CARTIER-BRESSON (1952)
The Decisive Moment,
New York: Simon & Schuster.
Quoted in Clive Scott (2007)
Street Photography from Atget to Cartier-Bresson, London: I.B. Tauris.

photographers have chosen to adopt (at least in some respects) the condition of the artist: to organise their images in a gallery setting, and to sell them in the growing commercial market for photographs. Inevitably, this has led to an abandonment of the well-worn tropes of photojournalism in favour of work that is allusive rather than direct and that cannot be seen and understood in an instant.

This blending of genres is leading to new kinds of extremely interesting work, but we ought to remember that there are still many photojournalists working in a more traditional way and contributing to newspapers and magazines around the world, and that long-established debates on the ethics, efficacy, political bias, or objectivity of realist photography are still vigorously conducted.

The development of a consumer culture displaced photography from its more traditional functions and sent out images in vast numbers to sell goods. In the 1980s and 1990s, postmodernists questioned the nature of 'originals' and 'copies', and regarded images as transmutable objects that are involved in endless, complex acts of circulation and exchange. Such objects have no necessary context, so that documentary photographs of the 1930s unemployed might be massively enlarged and used as part of the decor of restaurants; images of the dispossessed could be used to sell jeans, while the homeless of earlier generations might find themselves presented as picturesque urban characters on gallery walls. The growth of the heritage industry has led to a great demand for pictures that show us something of the world as it was. Indeed, in many of the new sites that celebrate older forms of life and labour, it is the 'original' black and white photographs that act as guarantors of authenticity. These multiple uses of documentary photography, and the lack of demarcating boundaries between them, were explored by theorists of postmodernity. Postmodernist movements existed at many levels, from serious philosophical reflection to particular kinds of surface style and fashions. Linking them all was a concern with the nature of images and their circulation; an elision between high and popular culture; a scepticism about the nature of 'the real' or 'the authentic' (for the 'simulacrum' was held to have taken over from the original); and a suggestion that the discourses which once bounded and structured knowledge (such as history or science) had broken down.

Under these conditions, what future might there be for documentary; is it a practice that has run out of history? In this context it is useful to look at the output of practising photographers whose work is of a kind that would formerly have been labelled 'documentary'. A good example is the 1990s exhibition and book by Martin Parr, *Small World*, which has a commentary by Simon Winchester (Parr 1995). Parr returns us to the world of travel photography, for his images were taken in several places around the world. Like any good Victorian photographer, he visits Egypt and the Far East, Switzerland and Rome. What he returned with, however, are not carefully composed shots of temples and pyramids, nor artfully posed portraits of

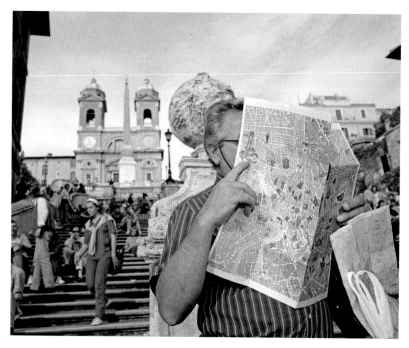

2.16 Martin Parr, *The Spanish Steps, Rome*, 1993
Parr's photograph of tourists in Rome is illustrative of the way in which, photography and tourism are linked in a modern way of experiencing the world as spectacle.

picturesque native peoples, but images of other tourists; those who form part of the movement of mass tourism. Photographed in rich colour, the tourists struggle with maps, follow the raised umbrellas of guides, buy beads in Goa, take photographs and pose for photographs. What connects the world in this exhibition is the multiple presence of the camera. Images are intertwined with what would once have been called the 'original' object; signs have broken loose from their former anchorages and float freely around a world that has been constituted as a site of spectacle. Can we consider work of this kind, with its multiple references to other images and its unwillingness to make authoritative statements, to be documentary? Certainly it fulfils a minimal condition of documentary: that it provide an account of events that have their own existence outside the frame of the photograph or the confines of the studio walls. We are no longer asked to accept that such images are impartial or disinterested; instead we inhabit a space between scepticism, pleasure and trust, from which we can read documentary images in more complex ways.

It would be unwise, however, to assume that documentary was once an easily understood practice, which has only lately been made more complex. Regis Durand reminds us that:

... the question is and will remain: in documentary photography, what is it that is really documented? Not only is it not usually what is supposed to be the document's obvious object ... but that object can be shifted and reconstituted again and again during the course of our historical perception of it. And this still leaves the essential question of the subject (what the photograph is about, what is recorded and done when it is taken) and even more the problem of reception.

(Durand 1999: 38)

These are central questions that have been at the heart of enquiries into documentary throughout its history and ones that, in a world of constantly changing technologies and photographic practices, will become increasingly pertinent.

CHAPTER 3

'Sweet it is to scan ...'

Personal photographs and popular photography

PATRICIA HOLLAND

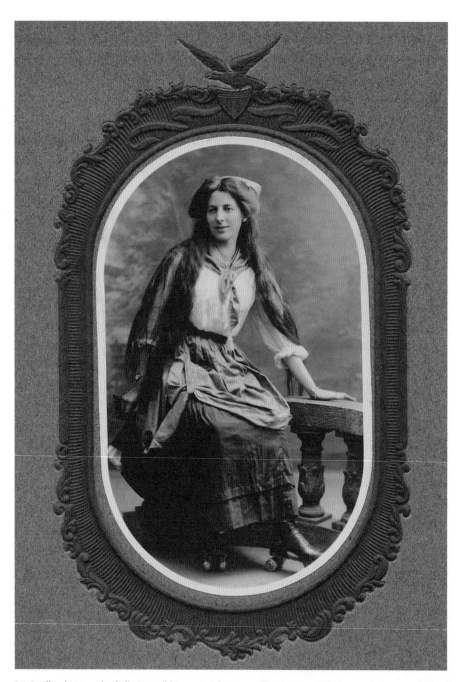

3.1 Studio photograph of Lily Peapell in peasant dress on roller skates, c. 1912

'Sweet it is to scan ...'

Personal photographs and popular photography

'When amid life's surging battle
Reverie its solace lends
Sweet it is to scan the faces –
Picture faces – of old friends
. . .
Some have passed the mystic portals
Where the usher Death presides
Some to distant climes have wandered
Borne on Time's relentless tides;
Some, perchance, to paths unholy;
Some to deeds without a name
But the faces in the album
Are for aye and aye the same.
. . .
Picture faces! Oh what volumes
Of unwritten life ye hold:
Youthful faces! pure, sweet faces!
Dearly prized as we grow old'

M.C. DUNCAN
Frontispiece to Richard Penlake
*Home Portraits for Amateur
Photographers* (1899)

INTRODUCTION

The doggerel, couched in the language of late Victorian sentiment, with its yearning for purity and sense of the closeness of death, fronted a book of advice for 'amateur photographers' just at the time when home photography was undergoing a dramatic transformation. The crafted work of the 'gentleman amateur' or hobbyist, whose proliferating equipment involved tripods, black cloths, glass plate negatives, special backdrops, darkrooms and a cocktail of chemicals, was giving way to an instant push-button affair, in which the film could be sent off for processing and no special skills were required. In 1888 George Eastman marketed his revolutionary hand-held Kodak with the cheery slogan 'You press the button, we do the rest' and was about to launch the 'Box Brownie' – the camera he claimed that everyone could afford and was easy enough for children to use. 'Kodak's advertising purged domestic photography of all traces of sorrow and death' writes **Nancy Martha West** (2000: 1). This was the beginning of an era when the 'amateur' photographer was likely to be a woman, interested in 'home portraits', records of family life and much else besides. The new technology of the day was bringing a revolution in ways of perceiving the immediate domestic world, and in redefining who had the right to record that world. Photography was being democratised.

NANCY MARTHA WEST (2000)
**Kodak and the Lens of
Nostalgia**, Virginia: University
of Virginia Press.

RISTO SARVAS AND DAVID
FROHLICH (2011) **From
Snapshots to Social
Media: The Changing
Picture of Domestic
Photography**, London:
Springer.

JONAS LARSEN AND METTE
SANDBYE (eds) (2013) **Digital
Snaps: The New Face of
Photography**, London:
I.B.Tauris.

1 Flickr is an image and
video hosting website,
launched in 2004, used to
share personal photographs,
and also by bloggers and
professional journalists. It
invites viewers' comments
and discussion. Facebook is
a social networking site,
launched in 2004 as a
Harvard student network,
where participants exchange
messages and images with
online 'friends'.

2 A *Guardian* website on
family history, launched in
2007, includes numerous
links, as well as information
on photographs, artefacts
and specialist archives (April
2007). See http://lifeand
health.theguardian.com/
guides/familyhistory/
0,,2053687,00.html
(accessed 20 December
2013).

A century later, digital technology was creating a new revolution in personal imagery. By the early 2000s 'domestic' photography was flowing far beyond the limits of the home. It was becoming more interactive, more interventionist, and more inclusive (**Sarvas and Frohlich 2011**; Lister (ed.) 2012: **Larsen and Sandbye (eds) 2013**). It was linking friends and relatives through social media and camera phones, and displaying itself proudly to the public at large on websites, such as Flickr.[1] 'Doing the rest' is now as easy as 'pressing the button', and an even wider range of controls is in the hands of the home photographer. Huge numbers of domestic scenes are now recorded with unparalleled ease, and the images shared across the globe at the touch of a key. Sophisticated procedures that had been the preserve of the professional or the dedicated amateur are now available to a broad swathe of the population, and are taught to primary school children. There is an infinity of playful ways of manipulating and organising (and rearranging) personal pictures using simple computer programs, and of distributing them instantaneously. Pictures are less likely to be precious one-offs. They are more malleable, more disposable. In addition, digital technology has broadened perception both beyond the immediate and beyond the contemporary. History has been popularised, and family history has been re-framed and made more public. An explosion of interest in tracing ancestors and rediscovering pictures from the past has been fuelled by television programmes, numerous publications and specialist websites.[2] And the past, too, can be reconstituted, too. Dead relatives can be scanned into contemporary pictures; family groups can be constructed which never existed in real life. When M.C. Duncan wrote 'sweet it is to scan . . .' he was thinking of the poignant experience of gazing at the present image of those who have 'passed the mystic portals' or 'wandered to distant climes'. Little did he imagine the unique pleasure of digitally scanning such images to construct a more fluid perception of the gap between present and past. In sum, the twenty-first century has seen changes at every point in the creation, circulation and use of personal photographs.

Reviewing the development of domestic photography in the light of these changes, Risto Sarvas and David Frohlich have outlined a history of technological evolution in which an established 'technological path' is disrupted by a radical invention. This launches an 'era of ferment' and experimentation, but eventually settles to a new stable technological path. The invention of the hand-held Kodak was the disruption which moved domestic photography from what Sarvas and Frohlich describe as the 'portrait path' when personal pictures were largely taken in studios by professionals, to the 'Kodak' path, when anyone could press the button, because 'we do the rest'. The era of ferment was brief, and 'Kodak culture' came to dominate photography for almost a century. However, in contrast to the 1890s, the radical inventions which launched the digital path in the 1990s initiated an extended period of ferment which still shows no sign of settling down (Sarvas and Frohlich 2011:13–21). The uncertainty and confusion which accompany attempts to describe and account for the personal uses of photography in the twenty-first century are to a large extent a result of this continuing ferment, and have been frequently accompanied by a sense of loss, as the immaterial digital image replaces a material and valued object. Yet judgements can only be provisional, as practices continue to change with staggering rapidity.

In this chapter we will outline this complex history in which taking pictures is both a leisure pursuit and an increasingly flexible medium for the construction of ordinary people's accounts of their lives and **fantasies**. In order to trace the interplay of change and continuity, the chapter will be looking at some key *moments* in the practice of personal photography. These include the moments of taking, organising, viewing and sharing an image, as well as searching and re-viewing – looking back at a single picture or across a collection of images. We will also consider how the history of such practices, together with the interpretive meanings we bring to the pictures, are inevitably intertwined with social, cultural and economic changes. The meanings gathered in personal collections both meet up with, and part company from, the external realities of the historical world, particularly when pictures are associated with major trauma or historical displacement.[3]

Private lives and personal pictures: users and readers

We have chosen to speak here of 'private' or 'personal' pictures rather than the more usual 'family' or 'domestic' pictures, because our private lives cover so much more than our family lives. The equation between 'the family' and private experience is too easily made and excludes too much.[4] The evolution of private photography has indeed been family based but that link is historically contingent, not, as is often assumed, the consequence of 'natural' necessity. The story of personal photography is interwoven with a constant re-creation and subversion of what it means to be a family including single parent families, same sex partnerships and reconstituted families. In 1899 it was the picture faces of 'old friends' that were apostrophised in M.C. Duncan's verse, and in the twenty-first century, camera phones are as likely to capture a night out on the town with work colleagues as baby's first steps. The point has been made by writers such as Terry Dennett, who compare family albums to other sorts of albums that record the lives of clubs, political groups and other networks of support and obligation (**Spence and Holland 1991**: 72).

That private photography has become *family* photography is itself an indication of the domestication of everyday life and the expansion of 'the family' as the pivot of a century-long shift to a consumer-led, home-based economy. Personal photography has evolved as part of the interleaving of leisure and the domestic, whose development runs parallel to the history of photography itself.

In Britain and the West, the gradual expansion of domesticity from the respectable middle classes through to all but the very poorest has drawn

3 Literary theorist Shoshanna Felman and psychoanalyst Dori Laub discuss the significance of certain family photographs for survivors of the Holocaust in *Testimony* (1992), which deals with memory and the possibility of witness. See also Janina Struck (2004) *Photographing the Holocaust: Interpretations of the Evidence* London I.B. Tauris.

4 See Michèle Barrett and Mary McIntosh (1982) *The Anti-Social Family*, London Verso for a development of this argument.

JO SPENCE AND PATRICIA HOLLAND (eds) (1991) **Family Snaps: The Meanings of Domestic Photography**, London: Virago.

5 For an account of the
evolution of 'domesticity' as
a concept and a way of
living, see Hall (1979) and
Davidoff and Hall (1976).
For an exploration of the
cultural rituals which have
sustained family life, see
Gillis (1997).

6 Nancy Van House has
distinguished helpfully
between functions of
vernacular photography,
memory building, identity
formation, communication,
entertainment (2011).

7 The distinction between
users and readers derives
from Basil Bernstein's
analysis of elaborated and
restricted codes. A restricted
code is one that depends on
its context to be understood
(see Bernstein 1971: 76–7).
See also Eco (1979).

women, children and finally even men into the 'charmed circle of home'.[5] By the twentieth century such activities as child-care, the preparation of meals and work on improving the house and garden came to be seen as pleasures rather than duties, and the nuclear family became the main resource for close relationships and expressive emotion. Taking snapshots joined a plethora of leisure pursuits which underpinned that specific form of family life. However, photography occupies a peculiar place among those activities, since pictures are themselves carriers of meanings and interpretations. They record and reflect on daily activities, delicately holding within the innocent-seeming image much that is intimate and might otherwise be hidden. Here are M.C. Duncan's 'volumes of unwritten life' for which we must scan beyond the edges of the frame.

Personal photographs are embedded in the lives of those who own or make use of them. Even when they are professionally taken, there is a contract between photographer and subject quite different from other types of photography. The photographs we make for ourselves are treasured less for their quality than for their *context*, and for the part they play in confirming and challenging the identity and history of their users.[6] Personal pictures have been made specifically to portray the individual or the group to which they belong *as they would wish to be seen* and as they have chosen to show themselves to one another. Even so, the conventions of the group inevitably overrule the preferences of individual members. Children, especially, have very little say over how they are pictured, and this discrepancy is the source of many of the conflicting emotions analysed by writers on family photography (Kuhn 1991; Watney 1991; Walkerdine 1991). Perhaps this accounts for the excesses of some contemporary young people's self-representations, as the more flexible technologies of the digital era appear to offer an escape from family constraints.

In this discussion it will be useful to distinguish between users and readers of personal pictures, whether family snaps, school photos or the transitory image on the camera phone.[7] *Users* bring to the images a wealth of surrounding knowledge. Their own private pictures are part of the complex network of memories and meanings with which they make sense of their daily lives. For *readers*, on the other hand, a hazy snapshot or a smiling portrait from the 1950s is a mysterious text whose meanings must be teased out in an act of decoding or historical detective work. Users of personal pictures have access to the world in which they make sense; readers must translate those private meanings into a more public realm. Private photographs, taken alone, are a 'restricted code' in the sense described by Basil Bernstein, dependent for their specific meanings on knowledge of the rich soil of meanings that holds them in place (Bernstein 1971). Wrenched from that context, they appear thin and ephemeral, offering little in the way of either aesthetic pleasure or historical documentation. But, although such ghostly hints of other lives may tempt the reader to engage in the detective project and to construct stories from these tentative clues, the empirical historian would do well to treat them with extreme caution. The

138

peculiar fascination of personal photographs comes from this contrast between an almost unbearable richness of potential meaning and the inconsequentiality and triviality of the medium. The theorist Roland Barthes, writing on photography and memory, could not bear to reproduce the snapshot of his recently deceased mother, even though it gave rise to his essay (**Barthes 1984**).

For many years, private pictures which offer up so little to the critic and art historian, have tended to feature in histories of photography chiefly as examples of technological improvement. Historians have noted the increasing lightness of cameras, the invention of colour film and similar developments (**Coe and Gates 1977; Ford 1989**). Twentieth-century snapshots tended to be seen as slight and unimportant, of poor quality and of value only to those who make use of them. In recent years the arrival of the camera phone and digital media has led to a new surge of interest (see p. 179 below) but, from around the 1980s, the study of history itself began to change, and personal pictures were already being taken more seriously. A concern with local and family histories, women's history, the history of everyday life and 'history from below' gave a new significance to personal pictures (**Linkman and Warhurst 1982; Linkman 1993**; Drake and Finnegan 1994). When scrutinised under the detective's magnifying glass, it seems that private pictures offer up many public meanings, some superficial, some historically illuminating. They tell us about the style of crinoline fashionable in the 1860s and about the donkeys used by beach photographers in the 1910s. They express private emotions, and they also display public **ideologies** – stories and ideas about how things are and how they ought to be (Isherwood 1988).

Historically, personal pictures may be deeply unreliable, yet for many it is in this very unreliability that their interest lies. It has led to a new set of questions – for whom are these pictures? who sees them? to whom do they communicate? In making an effort to *reread* private pictures, there has been a move to revalue the undervalued and to bring into public discourse meanings which have hitherto been concealed in the most secret parts of the private sphere. The practices of personal photography have led writers, photographers and curators (Jo Spence, Val Williams and Marianne Hirsch among them) to interpret history through private lives and autobiography. While drawing attention to the importance of this most popular of photographic practices, they have insisted that the *privacy* of its meanings should not be dispersed (Spence and Holland 1991; **Spence 1987, 1995; Williams 1986; Hirsch 1997**).

In a parallel development, personal photography has played a different but equally important role in the **modernisation** of Western culture. It has developed as a medium through which individuals confirm and explore their **identity**, that sense of selfhood which is an indispensable feature of a modern sensibility – for in Western urban culture it is as *individuals* that people have come to experience themselves, independently of their role as family members or as occupying a recognised social position. The consumer-led economy of

ROLAND BARTHES (1984) **Camera Lucida**, London: Fontana.

BRIAN COE AND PAUL GATES (1977) **The Snapshot Photograph: The Rise of Popular Photography 1888–1939**, London: Ash and Grant.

COLIN FORD (1989) **The Story of Popular Photography**, Bradford: Century Hutchinson Ltd/National Museum of Photography, Film and Television.

AUDREY LINKMAN AND CAROLINE WARHURST (1982) **Family Albums**, Manchester: Manchester Polytechnic. A fully illustrated exhibition catalogue with an introduction.

AUDREY LINKMAN (1993) **The Victorians: Photographic Portraits**, London: Tauris Parke Books.

JO SPENCE (1987) **Putting Myself in the Picture**, London: Camden Press; (1995) **Cultural Sniping**, London: Routledge.

VAL WILLIAMS (1986) **Women Photographers: The Other Observers 1900 to the Present**, London: Virago.

MARIANNE HIRSCH (1997) **Family Frames: Photography, Narrative and Postmemory**, Cambridge, MA: Harvard University Press.

the twentieth-century shifted these new individuals away from a culture based on work and self-discipline to one based on libidinous gratification which encourages us all to *identify* our pleasures in order to develop and refine them. At the same time, the century of Freud became an age of inwardness and self-scrutiny. These changes are reflected in the images we produce of ourselves, the uses we make of them, and our scrutiny of the Internet for material relevant to ourselves. Scanning personal pictures has become part of that act of self-contemplation (Martin and Spence 2003; Spence 1987, 1995; Slater 1995b).

Despite the intensity of such a project, in one of those many paradoxes that makes its study so fascinating, private photography has insisted on being a *non-serious* practice. Cuthbert Bede, writing in 1855 in the facetiously punning style enjoyed by the mid-nineteenth century, reminded his readers that photography was 'essentially a *light* subject and should be treated in a light manner' (Bede 1855; **di Bello 2007**). And so it has continued over its history, seeking the playful and celebrating the trivial. Personal photography sets out to be photography without pretensions, and that is how we intend to approach it. As we trace the development of personal photography, in the spirit of other work by feminist writers on women's culture we will not be arguing that these forms of photography should be valued as they have been used and interpreted in the galleries and by artists, but that what is needed is to understand them on their own terms.

IN AND BEYOND THE CHARMED CIRCLE OF HOME

The public and the private in personal photography

A blurring of the boundaries between public and private contexts has recently been attributed to digital practices. However, from its earliest days, personal photography has looked outwards as well as being domestically based. During the nineteenth century, images of the strange and exotic were marvels which enhanced the comfortable home and became as much part of home entertainment as television is today. In some family albums, preserved by prosperous patriarchs before the turn of the twentieth century, we can see how the middle-class home, even as it became increasingly separated from political and economic activity, depended on the world outside. Although the keeping of photographic – and other – albums was largely an activity for the women (di Bello 2007), the feminine domesticity of the extended family was visibly sustained by masculine adventure, both military and entrepreneurial.[8] The copious albums preserved by Sir Arnold Wilson dramatically illustrate the point. Sir Arnold was a well-connected army officer serving in India and Persia in the early years of the twentieth century. He worked with the Anglo-Persian Oil Company in the 1920s and became a Conservative MP in the

PATRIZIA DI BELLO (2007)
Women's Albums and Photography in Victorian England: Ladies, Mothers and Flirts London: Ashgate

8 I am using mainly British (or rather British-based) examples here. For a discussion of the US experience see Hirsch (1997) and Langford (2001).

140

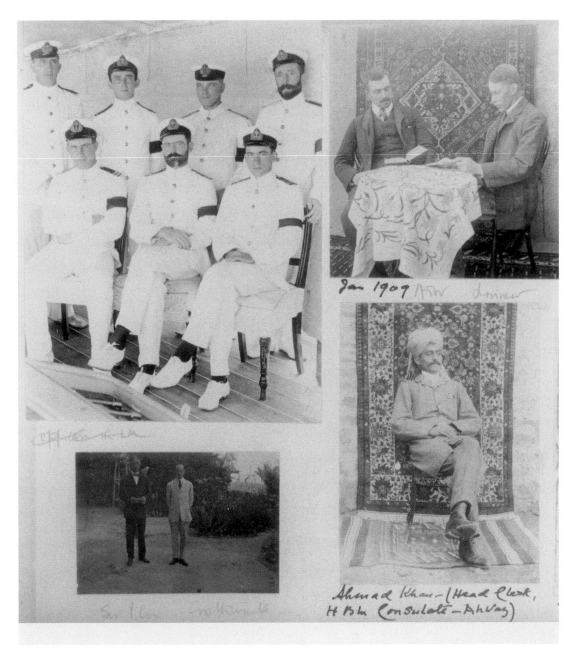

3.2a From the album of Sir Arnold Wilson (No. 3 Persian scenes), 1909

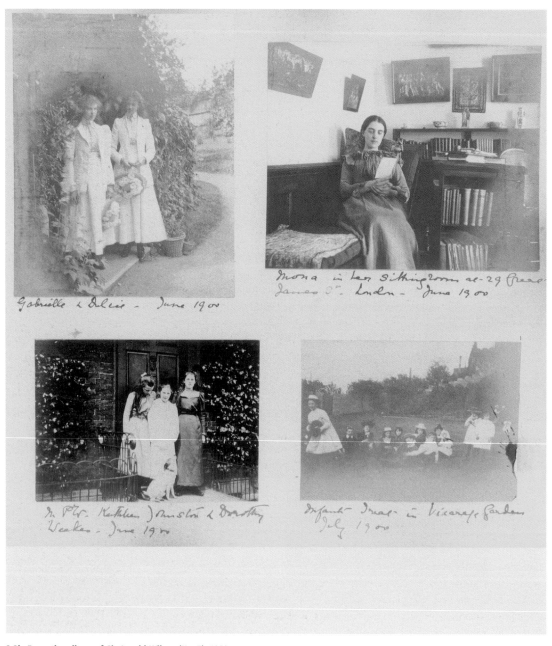

3.2b From the album of Sir Arnold Wilson (No. 7), 1900

1930s. His family albums cover a period from 1870 to 1920, recording holiday trips, afternoons in the vicarage garden and regimental postings. Set-piece photographs of India and the Middle East are juxtaposed with gentle family groups and intimate portraits in the gardens and drawing-rooms of the family's homes at Leighton Park Estate and in the countryside near Rochdale. In India the regimental tug-of-war team and the local Gurkha regiment present themselves proudly to the camera. In the Middle East, British officers pose one by one with local sheikhs. Tourism overlaps with colonial rule as spectacular views of the Himalayan hill station at Muree are followed by annotated pages showing the complex decoration of local mosques. In the Persian album, alongside the purchased images of silversmiths and weavers at work, Sir Arnold included pictures which claimed to be of executioners and torturers demonstrating their craft.

Discussing the colonialist imagery of advertising at the turn of the century, Anne McClintock argues that 'the cult of domesticity became indispensable to the consolidation of British imperial identity' (McClintock 1995: 207). The starkness of the contrast in Sir Arnold Wilson's albums makes visible the tensions on which domestic photography has continued to be based. They look inwards at an increasingly privatised and protected domestic haven and outwards at a world of political violence, re-presented as spectacular and exotic. The pictures in Sir Arnold's albums present this outside world with great confidence, gazing with the eyes of those who would control it and claim to civilise it. As the twentieth century progressed, and as photography became available to the ruled as well as the rulers, the politics of the world beyond the family group came to be **repressed** in the domestic image. The *consequences* of colonial domination and the ever possible presence of violence must be read beyond the limits of the frame (Hall 1991: 152). The two sides of popular photography remained, and can be traced in colonialist and postcolonialist photography (Holland and Sandon 2006; Gilroy 2007), and in the frequently shocking pictures taken by soldiers on active service (Struk 2011). However the imperial aspiration of this vision, and the celebration of commerce and military adventure of the Victorian era have long since been replaced by a tamer record of travel and tourism.

Beyond the domestic

From the very early days through to the unflagging popularity of posters and postcards in the twenty-first century, popular photography has continued to include purchased pictures of unknown people and places. William Henry Fox Talbot, who first developed a negative/positive **calotype** process in Britain in 1839, hastened to patent his invention and turn it to financial advantage. In 1843 he set up the first printing workshop to reproduce photographs for sale. His book *The Pencil of Nature* was amongst the earliest to be photographically illustrated.

calotype Photographic print made by the process launched by William Henry Fox Talbot in England in 1840. It involved the exposure of sensitised paper in the camera from which, after processing, positive paper prints could be made. Not much used in England in the early days because it was protected by Fox Talbot's own patents, but its use was developed in Scotland, especially by David Octavius Hill and Robert Adamson.

Within 20 years there was a thriving industry in photographic prints, which included impressive landscapes, views and still lifes. If Sir Arnold Wilson's turn-of-the-century collection carries the confidence of those who seek to control what they see, these pictures marketed from the 1850s onwards had the more modest aim of entertainment. However, what John Urry described as 'the tourist **gaze**' (Urry 1990) itself ensures a separation between the one who does the looking, assumed to be familiar and like 'us', and that which is looked at, assumed to be different and strange. A taste for the exotic was already well established in the mid-nineteenth century and photography gave it a new boost. Francis Frith set up a highly profitable company which produced saleable photographs of parts of the world which up until that time had only been seen through the eyes of artists or the imaginative descriptions of travellers. From 1856 he made three expeditions to the Bible lands of the Middle East and *The Times* called his resulting photographs 'the most important ever published' (Macdonald 1979). His photographers travelled the length of the British Isles and at the height of his business his firm claimed to have one million available prints, including photographs of every city, town and beauty spot in Britain. By the later years of the nineteenth century, photographs of parts of the world, impressive because of their distance, their strangeness or the difficulty experienced in reaching them – from the high Alps to remote areas of China and Japan – were published as prints, lantern slides and stereoscopic views.

The coming of photography gave rise to a new set of dilemmas around the production of the exotic. On the one hand it displayed images of hitherto unknown and remarkable places and people, but at the same time it had to be recognised that these were *real* places and people. The veneer of exoticism

THE PHOTOGRAPHIC CRAZE: A VILLAGE BESIEGED.*

3.3 'The photographic craze', *Amateur Photographer*, 10 June 1887

may be confirmed or challenged by the photograph itself. We should not forget that photography was also developing in those very places that seemed exotic to the untravelled British. By the end of the nineteenth century in China, Japan and India, local photographers were making pictures for local use (Falconer 2001). Pictures which would be seen as exotica in the metropolitan West are someone else's family photos (Kalogeraki 1991).

Popular photography has rarely been a medium of record. Foreign views exaggerated the exotic and the strange, and a fashion developed for the quaint and the traditional (for example, George Washington Wilson's pictures of gnarled old Scottish fishermen and other local types). With hindsight this fashion can be seen as the beginnings of a heritage industry in which the imagery was threaded through with nostalgia partly brought about by photography itself, already capturing a disappearing past. Groups such as the Society for Photographing Relics of Old London set up in 1875 contributed to an archive of the past which helped to construct a tourist view of the world (**Taylor 1994**).

JOHN TAYLOR (1994)
A Dream of England: Landscape, Photography and the Tourist's Imagination, Manchester: Manchester University Press.

Middle-class artistic travellers came to deplore 'vulgar' sightseers, who, they claimed, ruined the very views they had come to discover. But from the turn of the century, a new generation of tourists took their cameras in search of scenic beauties previously seen only on postcards and in travelogues. At first they went by train or bicycle, but by the 1920s many were travelling by car. In the United States the publicity-conscious Kodak company pointed out scenic views with road signs reading 'Picture ahead! Kodak as you go!' (West 2000: 65). With each wave of visitors the possibility of an undiscovered rural scene or an unspoilt village seemed ever more elusive. A photograph was a nostalgic compensation for the loss of a world that appeared to be uncorrupted by industry and urbanisation. The heritage industry and the tourist trade between them had provided renovated antique buildings and tidied up picturesque views to create ready-made photo opportunities. Taking a picture is an intrinsic part of the tourist experience and 'places of interest' dominate the albums of many a modest traveller just as they did those of Sir Arnold Wilson – although today millions of pictures are captured on digital cameras and camera phones and instantly e-mailed to friends or posted on Facebook or Flickr for a wider audience (Urry and Larsen 2011).

Fiction and fantasy

Fiction and fantasy have long been more attractive than the mundanities of everyday life, and this was certainly true of one of the most popular of nineteenth-century domestic media, the stereoscopic view. From 1854 the London Stereoscopic Company produced double pictures which gave a 3D effect when peered at through a binocular viewer. This could be a small hand-held affair or a grand piece of drawing-room furniture. By 1858 there were 100,000 different views on offer and the company's slogan was 'No home without a stereoscope'.

**3.4 Stereoscopic slide
from the late nineteenth
century**

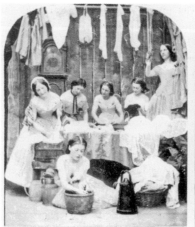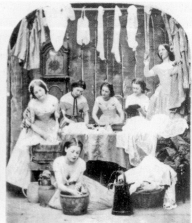

Many stereoscopic scenes exploited the Victorians' love of theatrical tableaux and aimed for a style and subject-matter suited to the taste of their middle-brow purchasers. Such 'stereoscopic trash' outraged the proponents of photography as art (see ch. 6, pp. 268–71). The Photographic Society (later to become Royal), founded in 1853 to protect artistic standards, deplored the debasement of the medium. In 1858 its journal fumed,

> To see that noble instrument prostituted as it is by those sentimental 'Weddings', 'Christenings', 'Distressed Seamstresses', 'Crinolines' and 'Ghosts' is enough to disgust anyone of refined taste. We are sorry to say that recently some slides have been published which are, to say the least, questionable in point of view of delicacy.
>
> (Macdonald 1979)

Sentiment, jokes, horror, melodrama and material which verged on pornography – this was the stuff of nineteenth-century photographic entertainment. Some stereoscopes even came with a locked drawer for a gentleman to keep his risqué pictures away from his family (see ch. 4, p. 177 on the reputation of laundresses as sexually loose women). In those days before the cinema, magic lantern shows were also popular. Impressive views could be watched in a darkened room, enhanced by exciting optical effects – from a sunset over the Alps to lifelike thunderstorms (Chanan 1996). The making of personal portraits was part of this popular aesthetic, firmly embedded in commercial practices.

Portraits and albums

Louis-Jacques-Mandé Daguerre's invention of positive images on silvered metal, each one unique, was, from the 1840s, the dominant format for personal portraits. Enterprising **daguerreotypists** learned the new skills and tried to

daguerreotype Photographic image made by the process launched by Louis-Jacques-Mandé Daguerre in France in 1839. It is a positive image on a metal plate with a mirror-like silvered surface, characterised by very fine detail. Each one is unique and fragile and needs to be protected by a padded case. It became the dominant portrait mode for the first decades of photography, especially in the United States.

interest customers in towns across Europe and the New World. In those very early days, sittings for 15–20 minutes in as bright a sunlight as possible led to extreme discomfort for the sitter and some fairly unflattering pictures which could be difficult to discern on the highly reflective surface. Even so, within a few years, huge numbers of people of middling income wanted their portraits taken, and 'daguerreomania' had taken hold. Photographic 'glasshouses' – so called because of the wide expanse of window needed to maximise daylight – were established in urban centres across Europe and the United States. In Britain, Antoine Claudet had a 'temple of photography' designed by Sir Charles Barry, who built the Houses of Parliament. In Leicester Square in London there was a 'Panopticon of science and art' with a room 54 feet long (approximately 16.5 metres) 'enabling family groups of 18 persons to be taken at once', which also offered lessons in daguerreotyping and studios for hire. Studio portraitists introduced painted backdrops so that the customers, what- ever their social standing, could choose to place themselves within dignified parklands, seascapes, conservatories or palm houses. Many were extremely successful: Richard Beard was said to be photography's first millionaire (Macdonald 1979; Tagg 1988; Ford 1989; **Kenyon 1992**: 11–12).

DAVE KENYON (1992) **Inside Amateur Photography**, London: Batsford.

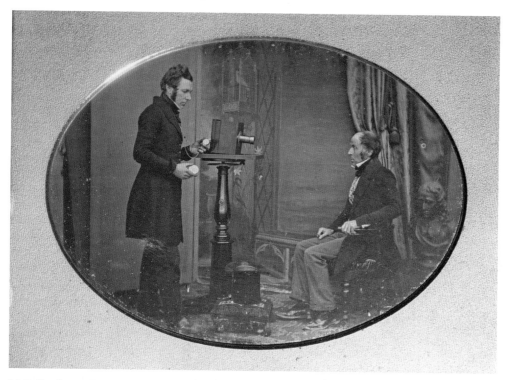

3.5 Earliest known daguerrotype of a photographer at work. Jabez Hogg photographs Mr Johnson, c. 1843

147

The 'cheap and common establishments' in the less fashionable parts of town got a bad name for aggressive touting for trade. Someone stood outside shouting, 'Have your picture taken', and virtually 'dragging customers in by the collar' (Werge 1890: 202). Most of these early portraits were carefully posed and touched up so as to produce as flattering an image as possible under difficult circumstances. A head brace could keep that most important feature, the face, static for the lengthy exposures needed. Alternatively the posing individual was asked to lean on a table or a mock-classical pillar which also served decorative and symbolic functions. The head resting on the hand achieved the popular Victorian soulful look, as well as helping the sitter to keep still. Smiles were difficult to sustain under such circumstances: the modern ubiquitous snapshot smile should be seen as a technological achievement as well as a change in social mores.

Every innovation was hailed as spreading photography more widely across the classes. 'Such portraits are to be found in everybody's hands', wrote André-Adolphe Disdéri, who invented the '**carte-de-visite**' in 1854 (Lemagny and Rouille 1987: 38). Named after the leisured classes' 'visiting cards', these were small paper prints mounted on the photographer's own decorated card. Several poses could be produced on a single negative so that the process was speeded up and multiple copies were easily available. This was the first attempt at a form of mass production of popular photographs, and certainly class differences were far less visible in such pictures than they were in everyday life. Shopkeepers, minor officials and small traders all took themselves and their children to pose stiffly in their best clothes in front of one of these early cameras.

A craze for collecting *cartes-de-visite* of the famous developed. Some of the earliest photographic albums were not 'family albums' at all, but handsomely bound volumes filled with pictures of royalty, celebrities and politicians. As pressure increased on middle-class women to make their lives within the confines of the home environment, useless but suitably decorative hobbies such as collecting *cartes-de-visite* fitted in well with other genteel activities such as sketching and pressing flowers (Davidoff and Hall 1976; Warner 1990; Swingler 2000; di Bello 2007).

Queen Victoria's family was presented as a model of the new respectable domesticity, but published photographs of the Royal Family remained strictly formal. When the celebrated photographer Roger Fenton was invited to photograph the Queen's children dressing up and presenting tableaux, the pictures were felt to lack dignity and were never released to the public (Hannavy 1975). Even so, it was the more relaxed picture of Princess Alexandra giving her daughter Louise a piggyback that became the best-selling *carte-de-visite*. Among their many hobbies and pastimes, women members of the Royal Family took up photography themselves, and Queen Victoria's and later Queen Alexandra's own copious albums were filled with views of family picnics and hunting parties (Williams 1986: 75).

carte-de-visite A small paper print (2½–4½″) mounted on a card with the photographer's details on the reverse. This way of producing photographs for sale was developed by André-Adolphe Disdéri in France in 1854. Eight or more images were made on the same glass negative by a special camera with several lenses and a moving plate-holder. The prints were then cut up to size. Such prints could be produced in very large numbers.

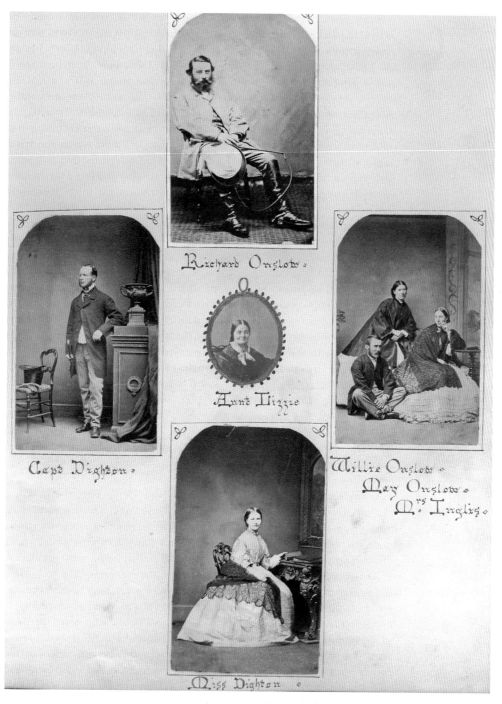

3.6 A page from the album of R. Foley Onslow, *c.* **1860**

149

Home photography was not for public display, but for fun with friends. In 1855 Cuthbert Bede described, for the benefit of 'all the light-hearted friends of light painting', many such social activities, including 'visiting country houses and calotyping all the eligible daughters' (Bede 1855: 44). The light-hearted uses of photographs, part of the Victorian fascination for fads and fancies, included mounting dainty miniatures into brooches and lockets, decorating jewel cases, or even setting them into the spines of a fan (di Bello 2007). A Victorian album was itself a series of visual novelties, with the portraits often cut up and arranged in decorative shapes and incorporating drawings and other scrapbook items. Mary Queen of Scots going to her execution was a favourite. And there were the mottoes: 'Love me, love my dog' heads a page of pets squatting smugly on their cushions. The interest is not just in the individual pictures but in the arrangement as a decorative collection (Smith 1998: 57).[9]

The family-based albums of the nineteenth century are those of prosperous dynasties whose members had both the leisure and the money to take up photography, as well as to buy commercially produced pictures. The life of the Helm family, in their spacious mansion in Walthamstow, elegantly photographed by James Helm and preserved in a set of albums put together in the early 1860s, demonstrates not so much the luxury and overt enjoyment of a free-spending leisure class, but the decency and quiet respectability of the middle-class suburb (Cunningham in Thompson 1990). The group is large and diverse, with aunts and other relatives and friends as regular members, in striking contrast to today's pictures of tight-knit families in which parents and young children predominate. The leisurely lifestyle included croquet on the lawn, amateur dramatics, young men posing with their musical instruments and dignified ladies in layered crinolines taking tea. These are scenes from everyday life, carefully organised and staged in the tableau manner. In the 1840s, Fox Talbot had written, 'when a group of persons has been artistically arranged and trained by a little practice to maintain an absolute immobility for a few seconds of time, many delightful pictures are easily obtained. I have observed that family groups are especial favourites' (Ford 1989). The tableau was a pleasing artistic picture as much as a family record. Pictures such as these were marking out the evolving domestic sensibility of the nineteenth century, which made the home environment the centre of decent living. It was a model which the lower-middle and working classes were to emulate in the coming century.

If the home was becoming a site of leisure, the creation of the 'hobbyist', and its more elevated relative the 'amateur', meant that leisure time could be used both for scientific experiment and the creation of works of art. Although one aspect of the evolution of domesticity meant that 'the feminine ideal was to be weak and childlike' (Davidoff in Thompson 1990: 84), women could become home-based hobbyists. 'Photography is the science for amateurs, equally adapted for ladies and gentlemen, which cannot be said of the generality of sciences', wrote Bede. Among the most celebrated photographers of the nineteenth century were comfortably off women with plenty of leisure and

9 It is relatively new for photographic historians to recognise the album's importance as a complete entity. Collectors have frequently purchased an album simply to remove one or two remarkable prints. Curator Pam Roberts of the Royal Photographic Society began preserving and cataloguing albums in their own right. She made the point that the way photographs have been selected and put together is an important part of the personal meaning of the pictures in an album (personal communication).

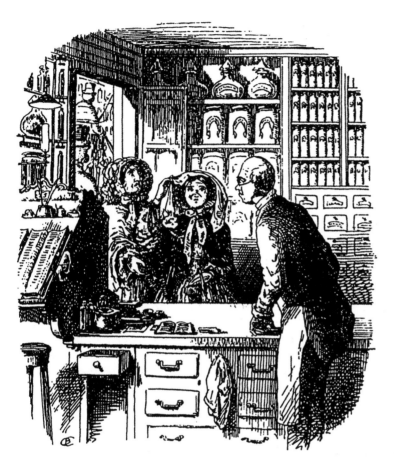

A PHOTOGRAPHIC POSITIVE.

LADY MOTHER (loquitur) "I SHALL FEEL OBLIGED TO YOU, MR. SQUILLS, IF YOU WOULD REMOVE THESE STAINS FROM MY DAUGHTER'S FACE. I CANNOT PERSUADE HER TO BE SUFFICIENTLY CAREFUL WITH HER PHOTOGRAPHIC CHEMICALS AND SHE HAS HAD A MISFOR: -TUNE WITH HER NITRATE OF SILVER. UNLESS YOU CAN DO SOMETHING FOR HER, SHE WILL NOT BE FIT TO BE SEEN AT LADY MAYFAIR'S TO-NIGHT. "

LONDON, PUBLISHED BY T. MC·LEAN.

3.7 Illustration from Cuthbert Bede, *Photographic Pleasures*, 1855

151

domestic help, who made use of their family and immediate surroundings as raw material for their photographic works, rather than as family record. Julia Margaret Cameron's misty portraits and visions of cupids and angels embraced and transcended Victorian sentimentality (ch. 6, pp. 298–9). Working-class women were needed as servants and helpers to service the middle-class domestic haven. Indeed, Julia Margaret Cameron's own favourite model was her assistant and maid, Mary Hillier (Mavor 1996). There were women working as portraitists, too. John Werge remembers a 'Miss Wigley from London' who came to his home town in the North of England to practise daguerreotyping as early as the mid-1840s (Werge 1890).

Informality and intimacy

The repertoire of personal imagery was changing. There had been an elegiac tone to much Victorian personal photography, evoked by the solemnity of middle-class portraiture and by the awareness that so many died young. Death was a central part of family life, and memorial pictures of the dead and dying were common. Babies who had died were dressed in their best and photo-graphed in their mother's arms (Williams 1994; West 2000; ch. 4, p. 191). But by the end of the century the emphasis was changing to a more present celebration of life and a taste for informality.

Photographic portraits had long been valued not only for their likeness to the sitter but also for the apparent escape from convention and the greater naturalness offered by the mechanical process. Bede had written that a calotype is a step beyond a painted portrait, for a painting has 'the artist's conventional face, his conventional attitude, his conventional background' (Bede 1855: 45). In 1899 Richard Penlake advised amateur photographers how to avoid 'perfect' pictures like those of a celebrity, who is so carefully made up and posed as to seem like a wax model, or of royalty, in which the very best pose is selected from many exposures and even then 'so worked up that scarcely a single part of the original negative prints at all' (Penlake 1899: 16).

Penlake also offered advice on tricks and optical effects, such as making double images – so that the sitter magically appears twice in the same picture – and **montaging** photographed heads on to caricatured bodies: techniques which would come back into fashion a century later with the easy manipul-ability of digital photography. However, in the late 1800s, with the coming of hand-held cameras such conceits were on the way out. Albums of the 1880s, compared with those of the 1860s, show a much more relaxed style and closeness to the subjects. The movement and visual interest was now in the picture itself rather than in the decoration and arrangement of the pictures on the page. On one page in Sir Arnold Wilson's album, girls and boys in sailor suits and boaters are trying out a bicycle. They are 'captured' with their backs to the viewer, in mid-conversation with each other, pointing their own hand-held cameras and playing up to the photographer, in a sequence of images which have much in common with the new 'candid' work by professional

montage or **photomontage**
The use of two or more originals, perhaps also including written text, to make a combined image. A montaged image may be imaginative, artistic, comic or deliberately satirical.

photographers such as Paul Martin and Frank Meadow Sutcliffe. At the time 'detective cameras' were all the rage. They were tiny, unobtrusive or concealed so that pictures could be taken without the knowledge of the subject. There was a growing taste for a different sort of personal picture, one where the contract between photographer and subject is brought into question. Secret observation was not always welcome to the observed. One local paper wrote in 1893:

> Several decent young men are forming themselves into a Vigilance Association with the purpose of thrashing cads with cameras who go around seaside places taking pictures of ladies emerging from the deep in the mournful garments peculiar to the British female bather . . . I wish the new society stout cudgels and much success.
>
> (Coe and Gates 1977: 18)

The working classes picture themselves

From the mid-nineteenth century in Britain and the USA the middle classes began to move away from the city centres to the newly built suburbs. Behind their privet hedges they were able to protect themselves from the grime of industry and the potential immorality of the streets. But the working classes remained confined to the inner cities, in areas that were filthy and unhygienic. Their homes were not places of pleasurable relaxation and they could rarely afford the cost of representing themselves through photography. We twenty-first-century seekers for the past may look at the family of Sir Arnold Wilson and see its members as they would like to be seen, but the image of the working classes which we have inherited has been produced either by those, like Oscar Rejlander, who aestheticised and sentimentalised it, or those, like Thomas Annan, who documented it for the benefit of various official projects. A sense of working-class identity is largely absent. Middle-class concern frequently took the form of outrage at the state of the less salubrious areas, often describing the people who lived there as distasteful, smelly and unhealthy like their dwellings. Photographer Willie Swift, who published *Leeds Slumdom* in 1897, turned his pictures into lantern slides and 'with the help of my daughters who sang suitable solos for us, we went up and down showing the dark places of the city, helping to create that healthy public opinion which eventually demanded clearance of the places shown' (Tagg 1988: 225). In New York city, the photographer Jacob Riis was spectacularly successful, both with his dramatic photographs of slum dwellings, and his successful campaign for the demolition of 'these sewers'. The area that was Mulberry Bend is now Jacob Riis Park (Tagg 1988: 152; see ch. 2, pp. 96–7).

Against this background, middle-class intervention became the context for another kind of personal photograph, often valued by those it represents although not necessarily made for their sake. Following the Education Acts of 1870 and 1893, which introduced universal schooling in England and

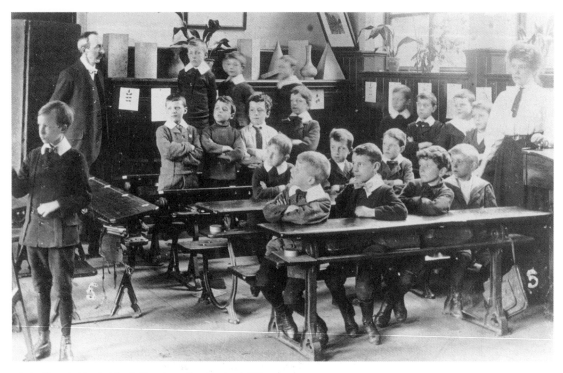

3.8 Pupils at St Mary's School, Moss Lane, Manchester, c. 1910

polaroid The Polaroid Land camera, producing instant black and white positives, was first marketed in 1947, but produced poor-quality images. Polaroid instant colour prints and slides were launched in 1963, and production was terminated in 2008.

tintype or **ferrotype** Tintypes, instant positive images on enamelled iron plates, were produced from 1852 to around 1946. As one of the cheapest methods, they were especially favoured by seaside photographers.

Wales, some of the earliest photographs kept by working-class families are those depicting their children ranked behind wooden desks. In 1891 and 1893 respectively, the Church Lads' Brigade and the Boys' Brigade were launched to tidy up disorderly youngsters and get them off the streets. Photographs of clubs and bands present a disciplined image, modelled on those produced by the likes of Arnold Wilson and his regiment out in the hill stations of Muree.

However, the shortening of the working week and the coming of the Saturday day off led to new sporting and leisure activities, which working-class people could organise for themselves and which they were beginning to record for their own pleasure (West 2000: ch. 2, on the links between Kodak marketing and leisure, especially in the USA). Modest photographs from the 1890s onwards show the cycling group, the football supporters and, above all, the trip to the seaside, made possible by the expanding railway network. Opportunist photographers were now on hand for trippers who wanted their picture taken. Long before the **polaroid**, the **tintype** (or **ferrotype**) could produce an instant metal positive showing little boys with buckets and spades, toddlers perched on the photographer's donkey, and young women holding up their voluminous skirts as they paddle in the shallows. Photographers

154

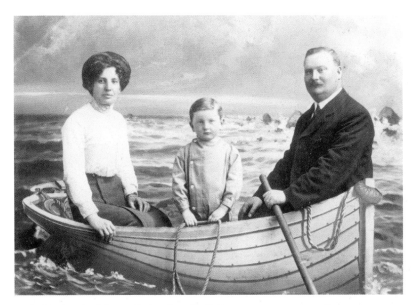

3.9 Holiday postcard from a Blackpool studio, 1910

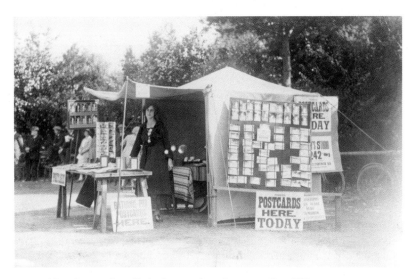

3.10 Mobile sales tent for Bailey's photographers, Bournemouth, c. 1910

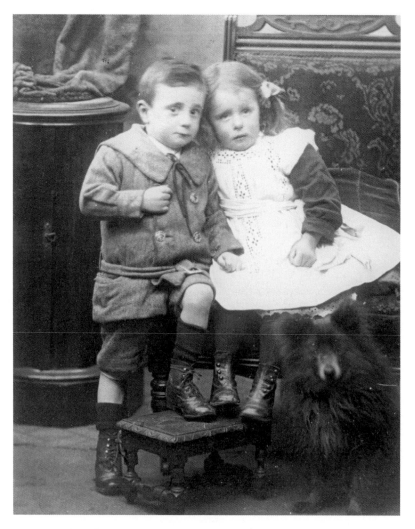

3.11 Studio photograph of Edward and May Bond, c. 1910

working in the new postcard format were ready with cheeky devices: 'The subject's head would join a monstrously fat body holding countless bottles of beer, or he would sit in a wooden aeroplane among painted stars' (Parr and Stasiak 1986: 13).

Not surprisingly, many of the poorer people continued to choose studio portraits where dignified or exotic backdrops would remove them from their poky homes. However, when the travelling photographer came by to set up his equipment in a local street, all the children of the neighbourhood ran after him to get in the picture. 'Do not take too much notice of how they are

156

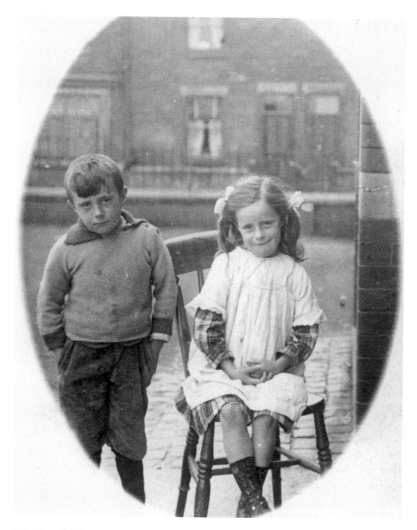

3.12 Edward and May Bond taken by a street photographer outside their home in Manchester, c. 1912

taken', wrote Edward and May Bond's mother when she sent such a picture to her eldest son, 'for they look a bit untidy but I did not know they were having their likenesses taken, but I thought I would buy one to let you have a look at their dear little faces' (Figures 3.11 and 3.12).

By 1910 postcard sales were averaging 860 million per year (Pryce 1994: 143). As well as the usual repertoire of views, royalty, celebrities and tableaux, travelling photographers would set up their stall at a fair or a local beauty spot and offer to put *your* picture on a postcard. When people couldn't afford the threepence (1.5p) or so for a picture, clubs were set up to pay in instalments.

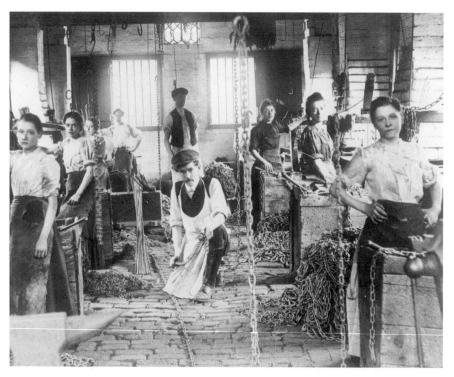

3.13 Black Country chain-makers, postcard, 7 August 1911

These jobbing photographers came from a class background similar to those whom they served. Photography was fast becoming a medium in which working-class people could present themselves to each other, creating a confident working-class identity.

Enterprising postcard photographers would visit local collieries, docks or mills, often producing the only photographic record of such workplaces that exist. Others specialised in local events, such as strikes, lockouts or disasters. In 1910, John Leach, a Whitehaven photographer, put together a montage of 124 of those killed in an appalling explosion and fire in the Wellington pit, as a memorial for the traumatised local community (Hiley 1983). Pictures of festivities were especially important to local people. At the Manchester Whit Walks, 'the working class was on display and they knew it' (Linkman and Warhurst 1982). Children who were untidy or had no clean clothes were kept well out of sight by their parents, and such pictures gave a very different impression of life in the inner city from the documentarist's view of picturesque misery. Photographs made for the benefit of the photographer, whether as artist or concerned reporter, stand in striking contrast to those made for the eyes of the people whom they represent.

Kodak and the mass market: the Kodak path

It was not until George Eastman, an American photographic plate manufacturer, successfully produced sensitised paper in 1884, and followed it up with his hand-held camera in 1888, that the paraphernalia of tripods and glass plates could finally be put aside and home photography for all became a possibility. The Kodak path was launched. Eastman was an entrepreneur with a flair for publicity, who sought to dominate the world market with a camera simple enough to be used by anyone. His crucial move was the separation of the *taking* of an image from the other stages involved in making a photograph. The smelly and difficult business of processing and printing was placed, conveniently out of sight, in a factory. This leisure activity for the home was supported by mass production and an army of employees – mostly women. Hence, in a single gesture, photography was both domesticated and industrialised. The first celebrated Kodak camera was a lumpish wooden box with a hole at one end for the lens. When all the exposures had been made, and they amounted to about a hundred on a single film, the whole thing was sent back to the Eastman factory for processing and reloading. The slogan 'You press the button, we do the rest' was to form the basis of personal photography for the following century (West 2000).

Don Slater has argued that this drastic simplification amounted to depriving the new users of photography both of skills they might have put to more radical effect and a practical understanding of how photography creates meanings: 'Being separated from a knowledge of process, we have no sense of photography as manipulation, as a form of action, as a making sense through the manipulation of tools of representation and meaning' (Slater 1991: 54). However, looking back with the hindsight of the twenty-first century, it is clear that such an analysis underestimates the scale in which a *new* skill was introduced at the end of the nineteenth. Selecting, framing and achieving the content of a photographic image was now a possibility for those who did not have the time, the money nor the inclination to engage in the complex processes of amateur photography. Don Slater's arguments also disregard Cuthbert Bede's reminder that personal photography is a *light* art. Photographic manipulation had long been part of the games people played with their cameras. Producing joke pictures and clowning in front of the lens are activities which have turned taking pictures into a pastime that secures friendship and insists on interaction between photographer and subject. This *is* collaboration in 'manipulating the tools of representation and meaning', even when it's just for fun.

The more individualist activities that the full photographic process demanded became part of a separate movement known as 'amateur photography'. The population in general, with little distinction of sex or even age, had become regular snapshooters, whereas amateur photography remained a more masculine pastime, scornful of the snapshot's cheery refusal to concern itself with the complexities of the medium. Serious amateur practice retained its fascination with established technology and its striving for aesthetic control. It launched its own magazines, established competitions and standards. Today these have been replaced by numerous websites, open to all comers, in which the specialist status previously claimed by the serious amateur can be challenged by those happy to compete for the award for the best 'urban wildlife', 'vanishing culture' or any number of other categories.

Meanwhile, George Eastman's commercial operations rapidly reached from Rochester, New York State to Harrow in Middlesex, and across the world. Developments followed each other in quick succession. Daylight loading, where the celluloid film came in light-tight cartons, was an advance that meant there was no longer a need to send the whole camera back to the factory. 'Anybody can use it. Everybody will use it' ran the publicity, listing some of those possible users:

> *Travellers and tourists*: Use it to obtain a picturesque diary of their travels. . . . *Bicyclists and boating men*: Can carry it where a larger camera would be too burdensome. . . . *Ocean travellers*: Use it to photograph their fellow passengers on the steamship deck. . . . *Sportsmen and camping parties:* Use it to recall pleasant times spent in camp and wilderness . . . and *Lovers of fine animals*: use it to photograph their pets.
>
> (Coe and Gates 1977: 18)

Contrary to many accounts, the first theme was looking outwards. Novice photographers were encouraged to make the most of expanding facilities for travelling – whether by ocean liner or bicycle – and point their cameras at the picturesque and the unusual. Kodak even encouraged soldiers to take their cameras to the front when war was declared in 1914 –even though this was strictly forbidden by the authorities (Struck 2011: ch. 2).

By contrast, looking inwards towards the domestic and creating an exclusive record of your family became an increasingly important message, directed largely at the women of the middle classes. This new technology was *gendered*. The advertising implied that its simplicity of operation meant that the woman of the house could use it, while the chemicals and other technical paraphernalia could be left to the men. And what activity could be more suitable for a woman than to photograph her children. 'Do you think baby will be quiet long enough to take her picture mama?' asks a cartoon-style advertisement from 1889, as a mother lines up her camera on her toddler and replies, 'The Kodak will catch her whether she moves or not. It is as quick as a wink.' The prosperity of those late decades of the nineteenth century had brought women a new sense of independence. The passive 'angel in the house' was being superseded by the 'new woman', and those who took up their cameras were not just housebound mothers. 'Thousands of Birmingham girls are scattered about the holiday resorts of Britain this month, and a very large percentage of them are armed with cameras', wrote *Photographic News* in September 1905. 'It is as

much a feminine as a masculine hobby these days, perhaps more so' (Coe and
Gates 1977: 28).

Kodak advertisements overwhelmingly showed women carrying the camera,
very often out together with other women (West 2000: 53). The 'Kodak girl'
was introduced in 1893 – as an independent, stylish and youthful amateur who
would typify the new brand. In 1910 she gained her smart but comfortable
blue and white striped dress, easily adapted to changing fashions in skirt length

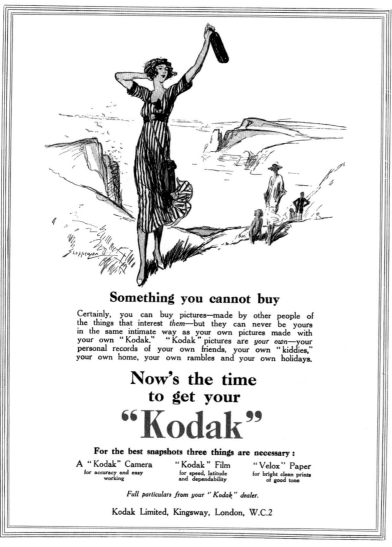

3.14 Kodak advertisement, 1926

and outline, which always seemed to be blowing in some breeze or other. Variously drawn by a number of well-known artists, she balanced her camera casually in her hand in Kodak advertisements for nearly 80 years. Always out of doors, she may be perched on a rock pointing out to sea, leaning on a jetty watching the yachts come in, or celebrating the Paris World Fair in 1934. She may be picturing children romping on the beach, or a rustic cottage, or a modern young woman in a car, while urging purchasers to 'Make Kodak snapshots of every happy scene' (Figure 3.14). As time went on, even the cameras were feminised. In the late 1920s, Kodaks were produced in fashion colours – pinks, blues and greens – and 'Vanity Kodaks' came with a matching lipstick, mirror and compact holder.

The 'Box Brownie', launched in 1900, cost five shillings, a quarter of an average week's wages, which brought it into the reach of all but the poorest.[10] Now the advertisements were directed at children, too. The Brownie was a camera for little folk and could, the advertisements claimed, 'be operated by any school boy or girl'. Like the other Kodaks, it was not only easy to use but was guaranteed to be successful. However inept the operator, its pictures will always come out. Brownie albums were provided, with spaces ready prepared for slotting in a sequence of the snapshots (Figure 3.15).

Photography was not the only medium to shift from small-scale craft production to industrial production for a mass market in the last decades of the nineteenth century. Universal literacy, new printing techniques and the entrepreneurial ambitions of such men as Northcliffe and Rothermere meant that popular newspapers were launched for an unprecedentedly large readership. The advertising industry was rapidly expanding, and the mass production of all sorts of goods for domestic consumption required wider and more innovative marketing. Photography was at the centre of these developments and was to become the heart of the intensely visual popular culture of the twentieth century (see ch. 5 on photography and commodity culture). After the *Daily Illustrated Mirror* (today's *Daily Mirror*) was launched in 1903 as the first British newspaper to use photographic illustrations, the popular press came to depend on photography as an indispensable part of *news* reporting, and even more importantly, as central to its *entertainment* role (Holland 1997). Pictures of celebrities and royalty, which in the mid-nineteenth century had found their way into *carte-de-visite* albums, were now to be found in newspapers and later in the burgeoning consumer magazines. Val Williams has described the relaxed pictures of the little Princesses, Margaret and Elizabeth, taken in the 1930s, as a studied model to which the whole nation could aspire (Williams 1986: 72). From the latter half of the twentieth century, the coming of high-quality full-colour printing, first in magazines, then in newspapers, meant that a huge range of topics – fashion, gardening, cookery, travel and tourism, entertainment, celebrities and music – became part of a light-hearted and pleasurable lifestyle created by high-quality photographic imagery. Over the years, this commercial and popular photography would exert a significant

10 Kenyon (1992) has a detailed discussion of income relative to price of cameras and film.

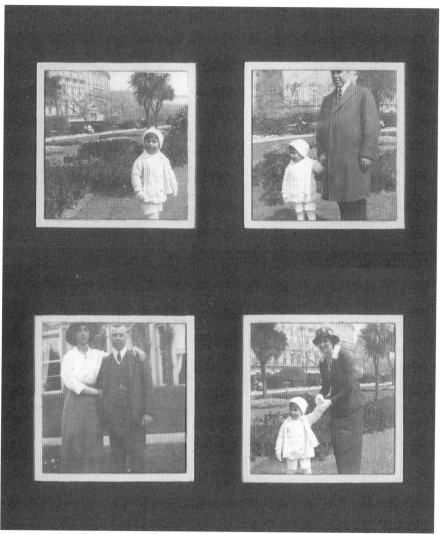

3.15 A page from a Kodak 'Brownie' album, c. 1900

influence on personal photographic styles, promoting ideas and aspirations as well as commodities.

In the early years of the twentieth century the new domestic photographers had fewer models to imitate. But, as life improved for the less well-off, the working classes were beginning to follow the familial ideal established – and indeed enforced – by the Victorian middle classes (Davidoff in Thompson 1990: 106). As the lifestyles of the different classes grew closer together, the

163

snapshot came to influence a casual and informal mode which gave a democratic veneer to social divisions. Yet, the poorer the community, the less directly their daily activities are reflected in the pictures they keep. Those who lived in the inner city tenements remained anxious to record the formality and dignity of their life, not its more distressing moments.

With the coming of the First World War there was a boom in camera sales, which reached its peak in 1917 as families bought cameras to record soldiers leaving for the war (Coe and Gates 1977: 34). Portraits of young men in uniform, many of whom never returned, made a poignant moment in most twentieth-century family collections. However, the increase in working-class incomes paradoxically brought about by the war meant that, by 1916, the *Kodak Trade Circular* could advise retailers that:

> the people of the working class could be looked on as a likely buyer . . .
> it may even be said that they are better able to appreciate the Kodak
> than some of the people who usually buy it. The craftsman who works a
> high speed tool and who has to work to very fine measurements is just
> the right type of man to admire the mechanical excellence of the
> Kodak. . . . If your shop is near a working class neighbourhood, think
> this over.
>
> (Coe 1989: 69)

The supersnap in Kodaland

Following the two major wars of the twentieth century, each of which created unprecedented social upheavals, 'the family' was reasserted as a force for reconstruction and social cohesion. During the Second World War, for a brief period, popular photography had included high-quality photojournalism developed by *Picture Post*, which concerned itself with the 'home front', public life and communal responsibility, as well as with military campaigns; but in the postwar period, just as in the years following the First World War, a reconstructed economy was based on domestic consumption and the domestic ideal. This required, in particular, women's willing return to the home to become the pivot of family life, relinquishing their public presence in the workplace and revaluing the ideal of a private sphere where political forces appear irrelevant. Twentieth-century family photography, with its resolute insistence on the creation of *happy* memories, determinedly reflected this mood, in which politics and world affairs, even the most disruptive, are pushed to the background of public consciousness (Taylor 1994: 141).

Despite the Depression, it was during the inter-war years of the 1920s and 1930s that a home-based family idyll took hold in the mock Tudor, semi-detached suburbs of English towns. Here the rising working class found for the first time 'such homes of which thousands have only dreamed' (Holland 1991). The stiff front parlour became a living room designed for leisure use and rigid gender and age divisions gave way to companionate marriage and

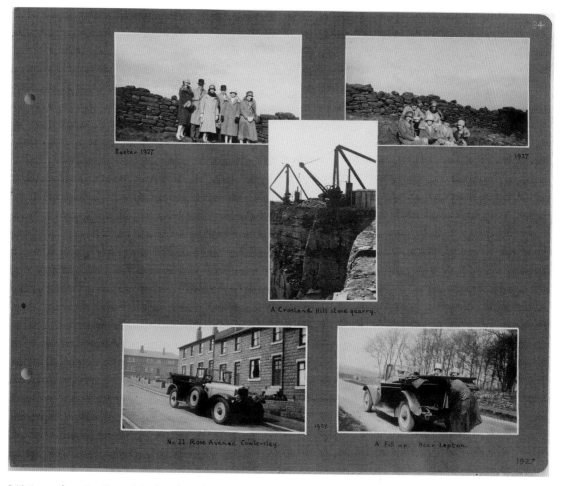

Easter 1927

1927

A Crosland Hill stone quarry.

No. 11 Rose Avenue. Cowlersley.

1927

A Fill up. Near Lepton.

1927

3.16 A page from the album of Frank Lockwood, 1927
Frank Lockwood was a Birmingham watercolourist and designer for Cadbury Brothers.

demonstrative parenting (Davidoff in Thompson 1990: 116). The domestic ideal, built up over the nineteenth century as a space that would be calmer and morally superior to the turbulent world outside, was being narrowed down to a much smaller family, made up of two parents and their younger children, who aimed to lead a pleasurable rather than dutiful life. A state of mind was coming about in which the satisfaction of each *individual's* desire for comfort and satisfaction would not seem incompatible with the mutual obligations demanded by family groups. The increasing relaxation and informality appearing in family snapshots echoed that change.

The image of the child became the central icon of family life. By the 1930s the two- or three-child family was the norm, which meant that individual attention could be given to each child and there was more time for birthday celebrations, Christmas trees and the snapshots which accompany these ceremonies. The domestic camera was confirmed as a ritualised element in joint celebrations (Musello 1979). As well as the visible markers for home-centred values, children signified the aspirational optimism of a century dominated by the newly prosperous working and lower-middle classes, whose horizons seemed to be ever widening. The modest pictures of the period between the wars give off a sense of hope, a belief in progress and in the possibility of a comfortable life for all.

Despite the ideology of 'home' as a warm, familial centre, most collections of personal pictures are, in fact, dominated by time spent *away* from the home. As well as becoming closer and more inward-looking, the family was also becoming *mobile* (Slater 1995b: 132). The gradual spread of motor-car ownership meant that holidays and days out could be more private, enjoyed by the couple or the young family instead of the noisy, gregarious group. The domestication of the *un*familiar, by capturing it on film, has remained one of the most important uses of snapshot cameras since Kodak's first appeal to tourists and travellers. A site is not a sight until we've snapped it and made it ours, often by placing a familiar face – whether travelling companion or family member – in an unfamiliar place. Many of Kodak's early advertisements addressed themselves to those who set out in search of the impressive and the educational, but these adult activities take second place to trips and holidays which have become an indispensable element of family pleasures. The centre of Kodak's advertising, from the Kodak girl on the windswept British beach to the sun-saturated images from the Costa del Sol, has been the child-centred family holiday.

In the second half of the twentieth century, increasing prosperity, together with the introduction of package tours and the establishment of an energetic tourist industry, meant that overseas holidays were to become the norm. But, while personal collections became filled with photos of Mum, Dad and the kids in ever more distant locations, pictures of *home*-based daily life emerged in *commercial* imagery. The expansion of packaged foods and branded goods brought new outlets for visual images which showed what a happily consuming family *should* be like. Commercial photographers studied how to create ever more convincing pictures of appetising food consumed by ecstatic and grateful youngsters and of well-groomed mothers delighting in their newly technologised kitchens. Such images, perfected for advertisements and promotional design, were routinely delivered to the breakfast table on cornflakes packages and baby food jars, and greeted shoppers with their serried ranks on the shelves of the early supermarkets. The 1960s burst into commercial colour as the burgeoning products for domestic use were promoted by advertising-based supplements to the Sunday papers and an expanding range of consumer magazines which drew on the new, high-quality colour printing techniques (Crawley 1989). The lush photography on their feature pages came to cover every aspect of domestic life – from *Home and Garden* to *Mother and Baby* (Holland 1992). Snapshots and consumer imagery were fast becoming two sides of the same coin.

In 1963 Kodak produced 'a complete new system of snapshot photography' when it brought out its 'Instamatic' series of small reliable cameras (Ford 1989: 141). It was the result of ten years of research which sought to make snap-shooting even easier. Cheap colour printing and faster film stocks made it increasingly possible for home photographers to emulate the sophisticated images they were seeing all around them. Snapshot photographs now came in 'bright, beautiful colours and subtle shades – like life', in the words of a Kodak advertisement from 1969. Once more, women were the target purchasers. Unlike the 'male jewellery' of massive lenses and proliferating accessories, the 'Instamatic' removed the technological mystique. Cartridge loading and fixed focus made it so simple that 'even Mum could use it'.

Advertisements encouraged a wider range of subject-matter and ever more casual and informal pictures, catching 'the moment as it happens'. Automatic built-in flash meant that colour pictures could be taken indoors, in dull weather or in the rain. 'Memories are made of this', was the slogan. Through hundreds of glowing, full-colour pictures, a couple could now confidently record every precious moment, from the birth of their first baby to their grandchildren and beyond. The last quarter of the twentieth century became the age of the 'supersnap in Kodaland'.

Those are the words of Jennifer Ransom Carter, advertising photographer for Kodak Ltd from 1970 to 1984. She produced many of those joyful images which offer themselves in advertisements and on print wallets for snapshooters to emulate. She 'tried to get pictures which were as close as possible to those that people would have liked to take for themselves'. In Majorca she photographed holiday-makers as well as models. Promotional pictures 'had to have a universal appeal, so that people would say "*I* want to take a picture like that . . .". We aimed to tread a line between reality and unreality as we produced a professional interpretation of the family snap.'[11] And, of course, the pictures people want to keep are those that record the 'happy memories', not the messy reality. It is hardly surprising that family collections include annual pictures of Christmas dinners and birthday teas, but hardly any of the daily meal or the act of peeling the potatoes or washing up. No children's party is complete without snapshots, but crying, bullying or sulky children are definitely not for posterity.

As Leonore Davidoff has pointed out, as the family became more inward-looking, it came to contain 'the most immediate experience of love and hate, power and dependence, interpersonal attention and interpersonal violence that most people would experience in their lifetime' (Davidoff in Thompson 1990: 129). It was that gap between the enrichment and proliferation of ideal images of family life and the complexity of its lived reality which led to the damning critiques of the 1970s, particularly from the youthful and energetic women's movement. Unhappy childhoods, broken families, child abuse, disgruntled

11 Information from conversations with Jennifer Ransom Carter.

teenagers and the persistence of poverty are only a few of the all too common experiences *not* recorded in domestic pictures. The family image came to be seen as riven with fractures and contradictions. Divided, individualised, hypo-critical, it was argued that 'the family' itself was coming up against its limits.

Many commentators have stressed the cohesive function of family photo-graphy, but the use of snapshots to celebrate time out and time off has long meant that fun in Kodaland, seeking individual pleasures, may well be at odds with family obligations. A hint of disruption hovers nervously just below the surface of so many personal pictures – a tendency which has increased with the coming of camera phones and instant imaging. Holidays are a time for throwing off constraints, a time of sexual adventure and illicit indulgence, and in the snapshots many such moments are for ever preserved. Pictures of leisure activities increasingly included the **carnivalesque** – cross-dressing for the last-night party, sidling up to the Greek waiter, the work outing when everyone was impossibly drunk, the risqué nude image, the scantily clad teenage clubbers. Just as Mediterranean food and street cafés spilled back on to previously drab British streets, the holiday mood of these snapshots offered a reproach to dutiful lifestyles. Local pubs began to cover their walls with beery pictures which verged on the lewd, where skirts are raised, the wrong husbands kiss the wrong wives, and family values are playfully – and sometimes really – put to the test. With the increasing informality and emotional expressiveness of social behaviour, a hedonistic culture of clubbing and binge drinking took over the night-time streets in the 2000s. Young people using their camera phones to capture each other drunk, vomiting, taunting and even attacking each other became a new, and darker, phenomenon in the history of personal photography. Newspaper reports began to include headlines such as 'Wine Women and photos':

> Women are posting pics of their drunken antics on Facebook. . . . Nearly 150,000 people have joined Facebook's group '30 Reasons Girls Should Call It A Night', which shows pictures of women caught with their pants down, collapsed on the dance floor and arm in arm with the sick bucket.
>
> (*The London Paper*, 12 November 2007)

PATHS UNHOLY AND DEEDS WITHOUT A NAME?

Re-viewing the archive

Giving an account of recent personal photography is a complex task. Nineteenth-century pictures are beyond living memory. They can be treated on their own terms – as documents, as aesthetic creations or as someone else's story.[12] Late twentieth- and twenty-first-century pictures are part of lived experience and hint at meanings which are tantalisingly within our grasp. Almost everyone has their own collection of pictures – the earlier ones may be organised in packets or drawers, some may be in albums, others scattered around in a disorderly fashion but impossible to throw away. Ever increasing

12 Marianne Hirsch refers to our relationship with pictures of our ancestors as 'postmemory': 'postmemory is distinguished from memory by generational distance, and from history by deep personal connection' (Hirsch 1997: 22).

168

numbers are digitally stored on a computer, a tablet or a camera phone. Every collection is different, every example unique. It is no longer sufficient to outline a social history of such images, since any history must include interpretations and contextual information brought by their owners and users.[13] These pictures do not stand alone but are enriched by memory, conversation, anecdote and whispered scandal. They are truly personal because they are part of the accumulated history of people currently alive, who know all too well that memories are not exclusively happy ones. Above all, they include pictures of oneself as a child and at earlier periods of one's life, pictures which carry a burden of significance that only their subjects can comprehend. It is hardly surprising that collections of such photographs hold great personal importance. In an American study of people's 'most cherished objects', many respondents broke down when describing those pictures they felt they could never part with (Csikszentmihalyi and Rochberg-Halton 1992: 68). Yet for writer Teshome Gabriel, a snapshot of himself as a young man, given to him by his mother when he returned to his birthplace in Ethiopia after an absence of 32 years, proved to be an 'intolerable gift' (Gabriel 1995). Because photography in all its forms holds the past before our eyes with unprecedented verisimilitude, a sense of the recent past, including one's own, is more vividly present to those now living than to any previous generation. Yet no photograph can give a clear and straightforward insight into the past. Personal photography, as we have seen, has a history of its own which meets up with and overlaps with social history but needs to be explored on its own terms. While many individuals bring to their personal collection the sort of emotional investment shown by those elderly Americans in the 'cherished objects' study, these are their responses as *users* of the images. To make sense of pictures which are not our own, we must change gear to become *readers* of the pictures and engage in a textual and **semiotic** exploration, paying attention to cultural as well as photographic **codes**. As we will see, many writers have argued that one may become a reader of one's own pictures, too; teasing out meanings that go beyond questions of factual memory and emotional response, giving a different sort of understanding to the history they represent.

Possibly the most frequent – and most important – image in anyone's snapshot collection is the simple shot of a subject presenting themselves to the camera, standing, perhaps in front of a famous monument or beside a car or house, but basically just *being there*. Yet this is the least readable of images, depending heavily on knowledge of the subject, on why the picture was taken and on its context. As Stuart Hall pointed out in relation to portraits of black Britons from the 1950s – dressed in their best and presenting themselves with great dignity – such innocence will always be deceptive, subject as it is to pressures from outside the frame (Hall 1991). The calmest portrait may offer evidence of recovery from illness or survival against the odds, and the most conventional of snaps may conceal dreadful abuse (Williams 1994: 31). Discrimination, persecution and social injustice are rarely explicit. 'How will

13 When she was curator of the Documentary Photography Archive, Manchester, Audrey Linkman created a context for the collection of about 70,000 photographs copied from local family albums by supporting them with detailed information about the subject and the photographer.

you understand your past when all you have is photographs?' asks Ilan Ziv in his film about memories of the Holocaust.[14]

As we have seen a rereading and re-viewing of family pictures was promoted by the radical history movements of the 1970s. This brought different ways of understanding history, more sensitive to the type of information carried by everyday documents, including personal snaps. Not only academic historians, but also reminiscence groups, women's groups and local historians, set out to challenge the politics of traditional history writing by looking at the past from a different perspective. There was a desire to write history from below, to listen to ordinary people's accounts and to recapture the texture of ordinary lives. Those who had been hidden from history – women, black people, working-class people and many minorities – insisted on writing their own histories that ran counter to the dominant view of events, and they used personal photographs as part of the process. Arguing that women's stories have been concealed by the conventional ways of recording history, women writers drew on personal pictures to fill those absences. Projects included getting elderly women to recall their times at work, and tracing female ancestors (Stanley 1991; Grey 1991). Radical photographic movements – Camerawork, Hackney Flashers and others – joined in a campaigning attack which took on convention, capitalism and the ideology of the family.

To look back at personal pictures and tease out their meanings has meant that various different approaches to history have been brought into play. First, *community* histories have been recognised; histories of specific groups of many different kinds, say, the working class from the North-east of England; recent immigrants from Afghanistan; those with an Oxbridge education; second generation British Asians. Personal photographs expect to be understood within an interpretive community, a group of users who share the same understandings of pictures which record and confirm valued rites of passage and culturally significant moments (Bhabha 1990: 17). Pictures of events such as anniversaries, religious holidays and weddings are symbols of social integration. They have different significations for different cultural groups, who bring an instant recognition to the details by which the meaning of the event 'subtly overwhelms the personal aspect of the picture and fills it with allusions to tribe and ritual' (**Hirsch 1981: 59**).

Even while acknowledging such visible community cues, *family* stories may cut across communal meanings. Julia Hirsch discusses wedding photographs of mixed marriages which must find a way of dealing with two sets of cultural conventions. Family histories often tell of conflict with a community or marginality to it, of migration and mobility across the generations, so that the photographs which accompany family members shift in and out of different contexts of understanding (Solanke 1991). On investigation, many people find that their stories tell of hybridity and cultural mixing, of postcolonial guilt or resentment. Ursula Kocharian put together an album to show the complex ancestry of her sons, born in Bradford because 'so many families were uprooted

14 *Tango of Slaves* written and directed by Ilan Ziv, TX, 31 January 1994, Channel Four Television.

JULIA HIRSCH (1981) **Family Photography: Context, Meaning and Effect**, New York: Oxford University Press.

from their countries of origin due to political events'.[15] By 'reading' the pictures, and referring to influences from popular culture, she produced a document in which cultural, political and family changes are displayed. Ursula's husband, Serge, comes from Iran, where his Armenian family fled from the Turkish massacres of 1915. Her own father came from Poland to fight alongside the British during the Second World War; his album, which he had published at his own cost, was a record of the Polish regiment's campaigns across Germany. The long pressure of political history, invisible in the simplicity of the family photographs of the two boys, has shaped the family's movements, through wars, revolutions and enforced migration (Figures 3.17a and b).

15 Information from conversations with Ursula Kocharian.

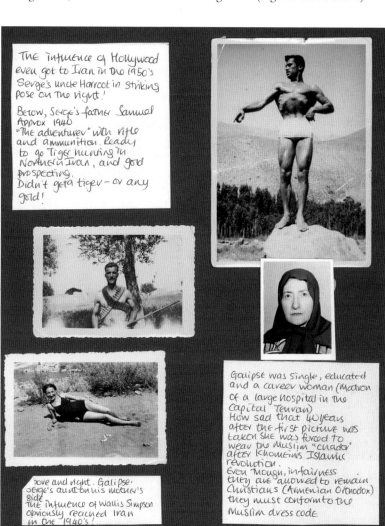

3.17a From the album of Ursula Kocharian

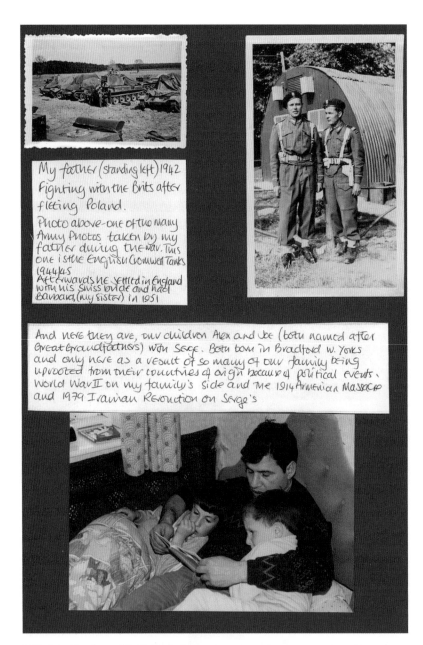

My father (standing left) 1942
Fighting with the Brits after
fleeing Poland.

Photo above - one of the many
Army Photos taken by my
father during the war. This
one is the English Cromwell Tanks
1944/45
Afterwards he settled in England
with his Swiss bride and had
Barbara, (my sister) in 1951

And here they are, our children Alex and Joe (both named after
Great Grandfathers) with Serge. Both born in Bradford W. Yorks
and only here as a result of so many of our family being
uprooted from their countries of origin because of political events.
World War II on my family's side and the 1914 Armenian Massacre
and 1979 Iranian Revolution on Serge's

3.17b From the album of Ursula Kocharian

172

Just as family histories fit uneasily with histories of communities, *personal* histories remain part of, yet often at odds with, the histories of families. These three overlapping modes, community, family and personal, rub up against each other. Each one important in its own right, but questioned and often invalidated by the others in a recurring dissonance that frequently underlies discussions of personal photographs.

The more ceremonial the occasion, confirming familial and communal rituals, the more important it is that certain rules are followed in the production of the photographs that mark the event. Weddings must provide pictures of the bride and groom together, dressed in the clothes that make the occasion special. 'We do not care whether it was taken, like so many other ceremonial photographs, the day before the wedding or three hours later; we care only that the man and woman look like bride and groom and uphold the decorum of formal weddings' writes Julia Hirsch (1981: 62). This is one occasion for which a professional photographer (who knows the photographic rules and will abide by them) is usually engaged, for the power of such photographs is precisely in their embrace of convention. However, in recent years, alongside the official photographer, more and more participants bring out their digital cameras or use their camera phones to capture a stream of images which are more informal, and sometimes subversive.

Recognising their role in creating cohesion often goes along with resisting that cohesion at a personal level. Family photographs tend to be constructed with the aid of what Marianne Hirsch describes as a '*screen* made up of dominant mythologies and preconceptions'; nevertheless, she adds, they 'can more easily show us what we wish our family to be, and therefore what, most frequently, it is not' (Hirsch 1997: 7–8). Pictures which live up to expectations give enormous pleasure precisely *because* their familiar structure is able to contain the tension between an ideal image and the ambivalence of lived experience. They can offer a framework within which understandings of the various realities we inhabit may come into play. While the historian is seeking out the truths of the past, the *user* of a personal collection is engaging in acts of recognition, reconstructing their private histories and setting a personal narrative against more public accounts (Walkerdine 1991; Watney 1991; Kuhn 2002).

While family pictures may, on the surface, act as social documents, a closer examination reveals the complex of interrelations and scandals that weave through the soap opera of personal life (Isherwood 1988; Martin 1991; Spence 1991). The placing of divorced spouses, children from a previous marriage, disgraced relatives, gay relationships, even awkward and sulky teenagers, poses problems for those who want their pictures to abide by the conventions. The very hints and puzzles they contain have enticed both detectives of family history and those who want to explore the ways in which their present identity carries the weight of the past. Personal pictures may act as an emotional centre for individual self-exploration. Autobiography, 'memory work' and forms of self-expression based on settling accounts with the past have become central to feminist approaches. The disjunction between image and remembered experience, the uncertain borderline between fantasy and memory, the tracing of identity and a sense of self back through one's parents and their sense of *them*selves, the opportunity to relive or re-enact the past – these have all been ways in which family photographs have been used to recapture personal history and make sense of individual lives (Spence 1987; Hirsch 1997; Langford 2001; Kuhn 2002).

During the 1980s, photographer and writer Jo Spence pioneered this movement and shed new light on the construction of complex identities, drawing on domestic photographs and family albums for her own, intensely personal work. She began by using the snapshots of her childhood to draw attention to the codes of domestic photography. At the age of five, her mother photographed her with her bubble curls and coy smile to look just like Shirley Temple. When she became a teenager she instinctively took up the pose of the glamorous pin-ups of 1950s cinema. In the exhibition *Beyond the Family Album* at the Hayward Gallery in London in 1979, she offered her awareness of the sickness, shame and struggles of everyday life as a commentary on the conventional smiles of the snapshots themselves. Annette Kuhn has written that they seemed 'conspicuous by their ordinariness . . . but in aggregate the work felt utterly out of the ordinary' (Spence 1995: 20). It contributed to a revaluation of photographic genres, so that snapshots could no longer be ignored as trivial and irrelevant.

Jo Spence went on to explore her childhood experience within her own photographic work (Figure 3.18). In collaboration with Rosy Martin she staged possible family pictures in a dramatic performance of concealed relationships and submerged emotion. The work developed into a form of therapy, working through traumatic moments and reliving the intensities of childhood usually accessible only through **psychoanalysis** (Spence 1987; Martin and Spence 2003). Her work was embattled and engaged, determined to explore the taboos and hidden truths which bedevil family histories. She dealt with class, as she reflected on her working-class upbringing and the half-articulated exclusions that implied; she dealt with gender, approaching the world from an uncompromising feminist perspective with a campaigning edge; and she dealt with subjectivity, always 'putting myself in the picture' in a form of 'politicised exhibitionism' (Spence 1987; 1995: 94). Her most striking images represent her struggles with illness as she faced an operation for breast cancer in 1981. In a series of pictures that were also an ironic commentary on the process of photography itself, she asserted her right to define her own body. Ten years later she faced the ultimate taboo with her approaching death from leukaemia, but the project of photography remained with her until the last. In one of the few pictures which show her in the hospice where she died, taken by her long-standing collaborator Terry Dennett, she is lying to one side of the bed,

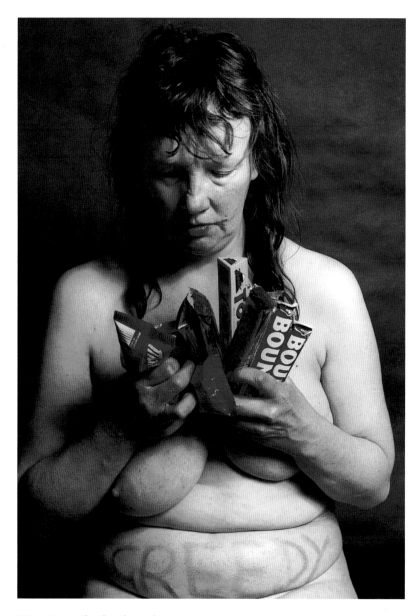

3.18 Jo Spence/Tim Sheard, *Greedy – I recreate my journey into emotional eating, a rebellion against parental disapproval*, 1989

almost pushed off its edge by the dozens of photographic prints spread across it. Her revelation of inner pain and her dialogue with her own body proved an inspiration for many and gave an impetus to a new generation of women photographers.

Other writers, including Annette Kuhn and Valerie Walkerdine, have also used the snapshots of their childhood to tease out the ways in which personal memory and childhood fantasy overlap, and how both interleave with the social and with popular culture. Such memories are rarely comfortable. Looking at pictures of oneself as a child can be a disturbing experience, recognising in the calm exterior of an image the traces of a turbulent inner world. In a series of articles using the insights of psychoanalysis, Valerie Walkerdine writes of an obsession with sickness, death and incestuous sexuality as she repeatedly re-contextualises a snapshot of herself in carnival dress as the 'Bluebell Fairy': 'Even when the images of myself present me as the feminised object of the male gaze, as a pretty little girl who smiles for the camera, there is a terrible rage underneath' (Walkerdine 1991: 40). Critical work like that of Jo Spence and Valerie Walkerdine lays bare the trauma of an ordinary childhood. Revelations about child abuse and family discord indicate that worse horrors may underlie the aspirational surface of the innocent family snapshot. Family secrecy can give way to family horror story.

Yet late twentieth-century traumas did not only come from within. With the persistence of poverty and the decay of inner city neighbourhoods, the happy memories promised by the Kodak snapshot remained a remote possibility for the disaffected youngsters and struggling single parents living on desolate estates that seemed to have been abandoned by a shrinking welfare state (Hanley 2007). Family images which came to epitomise 1990s Britain were the school photos of the 11-year-old boys who murdered toddler James Bulger, and the fuzzy image from a surveillance camera which failed to prevent that dreadful act (Kember 1995b; Holland 2004: 114).

Despite the privacy of family discourse, the public narratives of community, religion, ethnicity and nation cannot be put aside. As the twentieth century ended and the second millennium began, the public media themselves began to look back on personal upheavals. It has become common for hitherto unspoken memories to be given public expression, be they of childhood distress or of global traumas, like those undergone by survivors of the Holocaust or Hiroshima. Often, such traumatic memories can only be given voice many years after the event. The pictures treasured by those who tell their story have been used not to remember but to forget.

As Ursula Kocharian's snapshots illustrate, for huge numbers of people migration and dispossession are part of recent history. Journeys always disrupt borders, and more journeys are made from economic pressure or are enforced by war or political rupture than are made purely for pleasure. Increasing disparity between the rich and the poor nations has given rise to increasing

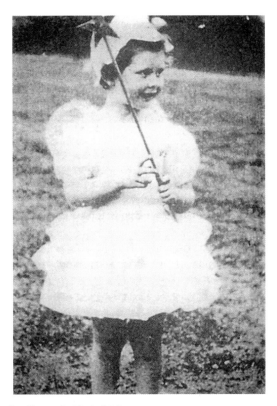

3.19 Valerie Walkerdine as the Bluebell Fairy

numbers of asylum seekers in the prosperous West. Where do family albums record such present distress and memories of atrocities past? Only in sudden disappearances and truncated lives. Violence is only hinted at in the pictures of 'the old country' kept by immigrants and refugees. Whether from former Czechoslovakia, Hungary and Poland, or from Somalia, Sri Lanka, Colombia or Libya, the previous generations who seem so composed in their portraits have so often perished in violent conflict, famines or concentration camps (Struk 2003). And yet the second generation of immigrants is often ashamed of its parents: they speak with an accent, their clothes are different, they cling to the past and their memories are a burden to their children. Their parents look like other people's postcards (Kalogeraki 1991: 40).

Yet, snapshots can be objects which enable the ego to 'bear the difference between now and then',[16] and more distant generations are able for the first time to look back at traumas suffered by their relatives, such as the sole survivor from a cultured Jewish family in Slovakia, who set about making a 'family album' which attempted to piece together obliterated family histories.[17]

16 Quoted from a lecture given by Mark Cousins at the Architectural Association, London 1994.

17 See also Serge Klarsfeld's meticulous collection of photographs of thousands of Jewish children deported from France, mostly to Auschwitz between 27 March 1942 and 22 August 1944, in *French Children of the Holocaust: A Memorial*, New York: New York University Press, 1997.

Andrew Dewdney launched an investigation into hybridity and mixing with a group of teachers and students in Sydney. They were the children of immigrants to Australia from Greece (driven by economic necessity) and Vietnam (driven by war). He himself is from the English port of Bristol, made rich by the slave trade. In the resulting 'extended and shared family albums', the experiences of the indigenous Australians proved more distressing than those of the first generation white immigrants (Dewdney 1991).

Post-family and post-photography? The digital world and the end of privacy

By the beginning of the twenty-first century, there was a public acceptance that the Western two-parent, two-child family which the snapshot tradition had yearned to reflect was no longer the dominant family form – if it ever had been. Second marriages, step-children, re-constructed families, single parents, same-sex couples – infinite variations on the family form are now visible as never before. Arguably this is partly due to the popular exploitation of domestic imagery in some very public contexts, both in print and online. The popular press and celebrity magazines such as *Hello!* and *OK* reveal the indiscretions and private moments of the well known and not so well known with an appealing gloss, using photographic styles which range from the captured paparazzi shot to the formal portrait, as well as the constructed hyperrealism of contemporary fashion photography. Something of this luscious, colourful imagery can be seen reflected in family pictures of the 'post-photography' era. Digital photographic culture has created a fluidity and malleability of the image. Colours may be digitally heightened, imperfections erased and juxtapositions carefully arranged between the casual and the formal. Nick Saunders's richly detailed, digitally generated montage celebrates such a 'post-family' as it charts the progress of his daughter, Eve (Figure 3.20). Both Eve and her mother, Karen are disabled. Karen and Nick are separated and Karen has support from the local authority to help look after Eve. Nick is also disabled and remains a devoted and supportive father. Yet, despite its *visual* complexity, the image barely hints at the complexity of the lives it reflects. Instead it focuses on Eve and her world of colourful toys and nursery food. Despite a contemporary mood in which the mobility and irregularities of family life are taken for granted, in this context, even post-photography does not necessarily challenge the traditional values of family imagery.

However, for the digital generation, the *experience* of personal and family photography has radically changed and it is that experience we will focus on here. As the extended 'era of ferment' described by Frolich and Sarvas continues, new possibilities continue to open up with startling rapidity, constantly offering new types of image and new relationships between those who take and those who look at the pictures. As different and ever more accessible and easy-to-use forms of technology become available, new practices of personal photography continue to develop. While post-families may create good-humoured images to sustain complex relationships, there are fewer constraints on bypassing traditional values, contacting strangers rather than relatives, and exploring the darker fantasies through the exchange of images on the screen.

As writers on photography attempt to come to grips with this new situation in all its fluidity, personal photography has gained a new prominence. Martin Lister notes that evolving practices pose significant problems for the main traditions of photographic studies, which have focussed on the image rather than exploring its context and use. But now 'problems which have stalked the margins of photographic theory . . . begin to move to centre stage' (Lister 2012; 2013: 3). As we have pointed out in this chapter, personal photography derives its power from its role as a social practice, embedded in its context. Consequently, when once snapshots and vernacular use were dismissed as largely irrelevant to photographic history, they have now become central to understanding the digital era. The modes and practices of personal photography are exerting influence across the genres. At the same time, changes in technology are affecting personal photography to a greater extent than other photographic practices. Post-family and post-photography, the distinction between public and private, professional and vernacular are becoming less clear cut. As we move to a situation which Joanne Garde-Hansen describes as 'the public domain of networked intimacy' (2013: 88), personal photography itself continues to maintain an ever-shifting balance between change and continuity.

Changes

When Frolich and Sarvas identified three 'pathways' in the history of photographic technology, they pointed out that it is only this last one, the digital pathway, which is immaterial. A picture is no longer a physical object, but a digital code which may be accessed on any number of screens of different sizes and capacities. The twenty-first century experience of a personal photograph is of a communication which can be called up on a luminous screen. In the words of Mette Sandbye, it is a 'performative practice connected to 'presence' instead of the storing of memories for eternity' (2013: 106). To a younger generation, a paper print which can be handled already has an archaic feel.

Everyday photography – taking and circulating photographic images – is an activity now more widely engaged in than ever before. One reason for this significant social shift, is that the camera, the basic tool of all photographers, carefully designed to create pleasing images, is being displaced by technologies which have multiple functions, to which images are incidental. At the time of writing the most influential and frequently used of these for personal photography are smart phones and online social networks, such as Facebook, both designed to promote conversation and communication. Together they

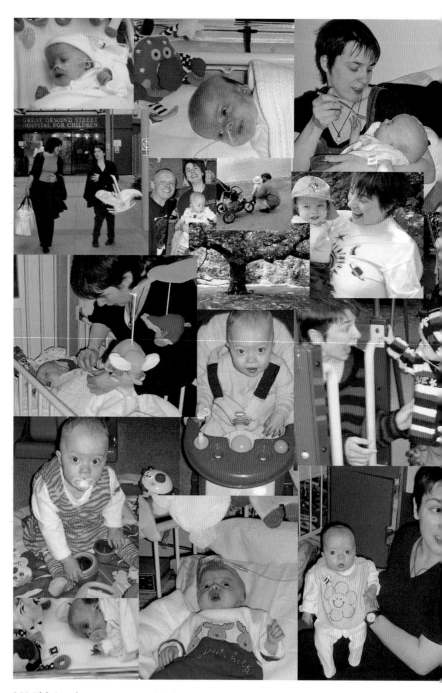

3.20 Nick Saunders, *Eve, Karen and Nick*, 2003

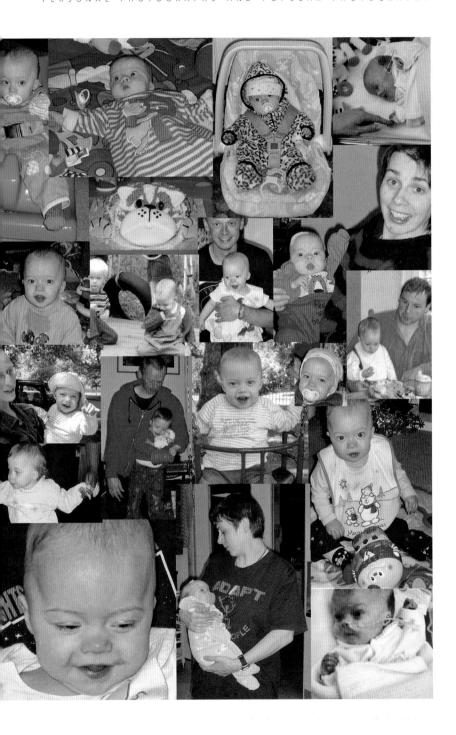

enable photographic images to become part of multi-media communications, which may be one-to-one and private, but may also be publicly circulated in the 'domain of networked intimacy'. Consequently, for everyday photography, not only are cameras losing their central role, but the image itself carries less significance as it becomes part of a wider communicative act.

The user-generated content of what is known as Web 2.0, has promoted photographic imagery through well-used photo-sharing sites, such as Flickr and Instagram, where many family and personal pictures are up-loaded and viewed. But, more significantly, it has facilitated informal networks of friendship and personal contact. The appeal of the 'absent faces' of friends, described by M.C. Duncan in the last decade of the nineteenth century, has taken on a new meaning in the second decade of the twenty-first. Today, 'friends', especially amongst younger people, may well be Facebook 'friends' who have never met in person. A Facebook page will combine a variety of modes of friendly communication: still photographs are embedded in the conversational flow, sharing the space with video clips and informal text. And here the public/ private distinction breaks down yet again, as a conversational exchange of images may be an intimate one-to-one, and, at the same time, something closer to a broadcast: a wide scattering of information to 'friends' who may not be personally known to the sender. This material itself becomes available to friends of friends who may pick it up and re-use it.

These changes have brought some wide-ranging claims about the nature of social interaction. 'We have come to experience the world differently' wrote researcher Nathan Jugenson on *The Atlantic* website:

> We are increasingly aware of how our lives will look as a Facebook photo, status update or check-in . . . Today, we are in danger of developing a 'Facebook Eye': our brains always looking for moments where the ephemeral blur of lived experience might best be translated into a Facebook post; one that will draw the most comments and 'likes'.[18]

Through personal photography the everyday world is perceived on screens which increasingly replace, interpret, and even, it is claimed, screen out, the material world. Journalist Michael Bywater described the scene at US President Obama's inauguration:

> A woman appeared to watch the inauguration on the screen of her camera. She was there. It was real. But perhaps it wasn't really real unless seen on that great tyrant of our culture: the screen. Doesn't matter what screen. Doesn't matter how big or how bright or what resolution. If it's not on-screen, it's not happening.
>
> (*The Independent*, 11 February 2009)[19]

18 www.theatlantic.com/ technology/archive/2012/ 01/the-facebook-eye/ 251377/ (Thanks to George Barker for drawing my attention to this and other relevant websites. All the websites referred to here were accessed on 20 December 2013.)

19 www.independent.co. uk/life-style/gadgets-and-tech/features/digital-photography-has-it-become-an-obsession-1606148.html

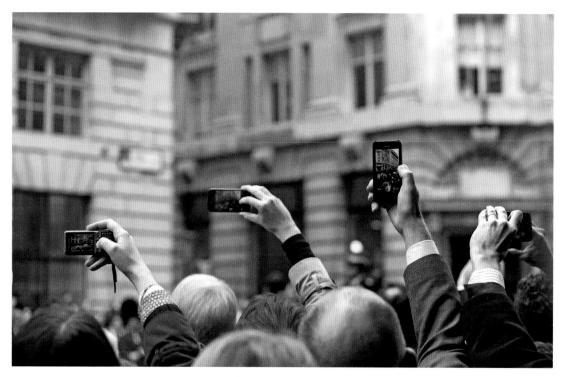

3.21 Members of the public recording events at Baroness Thatcher's funeral, London 2013.

Yet scholars are not in agreement. Some see an ontological change, arguing that technological developments 'strike at the very heart of what the photographic image is becoming', while others point to continuities (Lister 2012: 137). In particular, as this chapter has pointed out, many of the tendencies which were always present in personal photography – towards informality, dependence on context, playfulness, questions of performance – have become more widespread within photographic practice. And the *continuities* within the context of personal photography remain striking.

Continuities

In an important study of mothers of young children carried out between 2000 and 2009, Gillian Rose documented the move the digital age (**Rose 2010**, 2013). The mothers whose activities she investigated continued to record stages of life, explore family histories, and mark the sort of significant family events which have long held pride of place in family albums. Her interviewees valued their pictures: sometimes they were framed, sometimes kept in boxes, sometimes 'dotted around the house', even in the toilet, and sometimes whole walls were given over to generational pictures. 'Looking at pictures is central

GILLIAN ROSE (2010) **Doing Family Photography: The Domestic, the Public and the Politics of Sentiment** Farnham: Ashgate.

to the togetherness that they articulate.' (2013: 76). She observed that the arrival of digital photography did not alter but enhanced the practice.

At Christmas 2013 the computer giant Apple also drew attention to continuities in family images. A website advertising iPhoto print products, echoed the spirit of Kodak when it declared 'It's easy to make memories even more memorable'.[20] Customers were invited to use up-to-the-minute technology to create albums and photobooks with a strongly traditional feel. The illustration shows the familiar image of an 'ideal' four person nuclear family – two parents, two children – grouped together against holiday scenery (Holland 2004: ch. 2). The technology may have changed but the image has a long history. Here traditional family values can be preserved in a book we can hold in our hands – defying the immateriality and screen base of the digital era.

But, as we have seen, personal photography has always been fluid, adapted to different uses. Its history is interwoven with questions about the nature of visual communication and what sort of intimate social relationships are appropriate and significant. We would argue that the most important form of continuity is not in the image itself, but in the constant re-configuration of photographic imagery for different social uses. Personal photography remains highly differentiated, with different practices appropriate for different social groupings. Rose studied the practices of middle class British mothers with young children. This was utterly different from that of the soldiers on active service discussed by Struk (2013). And generational differences have come to characterise the digital age, as teen culture is heavily dependent on social media. Garde-Hansen quotes research with young people, aged 15–18yrs (2013: 96) who used their camera phones chiefly to connect with their friends. Recording family rituals was left to their parents.

Finally we can trace these changes and continuities through each of the moments we identified earlier (the moments of taking, organising, viewing and sharing an image, as well as searching and re-viewing individual images or collections of images (see p. 137):

Moment of taking

Over the history of personal photography technological developments have been driven by the desire to simplify the all important moments of taking the picture. At the end of the nineteenth century Kodak promoted its 'point and shoot simplicity' to produce its square, black and white snapshot. At the beginning of the twenty-first, the 'intelligent' technology of the digital age has enabled anyone to create, refine and manipulate sophisticated images which in the analogue years would have involved specialised skills. As the ability to take an image is no longer dependent on the ownership of a camera, the range of individuals who now take personal pictures has widened – including children. The 2013 Review by the UK broadcasting regulator Ofcom, found that 18% of children aged 8–11 and 62% of children aged 18–15 now owned a smart phone (Ofcom 2013: 4).

20 www.apple.com/uk/ ilife/print-products.html? cid=CDM-EU-34471&cp= em-P0011107–181007 &sr=em

However, in the digital era the moment of taking is no longer privileged. It is no longer confined to the family ceremony, or even the family holiday, promoted by the Apple iPhoto advertisement, but is represented by a continuous flow of images from smart phones and social media. They record the minutiae of daily experience – often characterised by the 'selfie', the personal image which says 'Here I am, and I'm feeling happy/sad/lonely depending on the expression I adopt'.[21] The continuing desire to 'make all your memories happy ones' has been replaced a low-key form of visual conversation (Van House 2011).

Public events have also become part of the flow of personal pictures. Passers by with camera phones have been witness to a disaster, as in the London bombings of 2005 and the Japanese earthquake of 2011, or they may simply grab a picture of a celebrity spotted on the underground. Television news reader Huw Edwards wrote:

On the Tube the other morning a young woman came and stood two feet away from me, pointed her mobile at my face and took several photos – with flash to boot – then walked away. Not a word. Not a flicker of communication.

(*Evening Standard* 16 December 2013)

A screen had once more displaced personal contact. In these ways concepts of privacy and publicness are increasingly blurred.

Moment of viewing and sharing

Viewing and sharing have always been central to the meaning and use of personal pictures – whether with family, immediate friends or an extended network. But the experience has changed in relation to both time and space. Viewing is simultaneous with taking, and sharing need no longer draw viewers together in a single space. Photographs may be part of a conversational exchange carried on in real time, as one picture responds to another. The sense of immediacy, of liveness, is central to the experience.

In this context a photograph may be less like a visual statement packed full of information, and more like a word, one element in a flow of images which makes up a sentence. Discussing the online 'album site' Picasa, where a single event may be represented by many hundreds of pictures, Sandbye writes 'it would make no sense to emphasise only one image' or to seek out a specific 'poetic' composition (2013: 114). Social media have created different types of relationships between family, professional contacts and peer groups – such as contacting lost family members. As soon as they set up Facebook accounts two British teenagers were contacted by their Swedish half-sisters, whom they had not seen since their parents split up when they were four.[22]

And social media have created a recognised space for imagery which had previously been kept hidden and pushed to the margins of the acceptable.

21 'Selfie' was named as the 'word of the year' by the Oxford Dictionaries in 2013 (http://blog.oxford dictionaries.com/2013/11/word-of-the-year-2013-winner/)

22 We wanted to illustrate this point with a screen shot taken from a Facebook page, but, although the owners of the pictures gave their permission, Facebook refused.

Especially amongst young people, online flirting may include provocative imagery. 'Sexting', the exchange of sexual images – an activity which is both risky and unacceptable face to face – is sufficiently common amongst teenagers – for the child abuse charity Childline to run a service advising young people on what to do if they receive images they feel uncomfortable with or feel that 'everyone else is doing it and want to fit in with friends'.[23]

Moment of organising

Many writers express acute anxiety – which sometimes verges on panic – over the sheer volume of pictures created with digital technology. 'We have too much stuff!' writes Lister (Lister 2013: 15–16). How can we deal with this 'tsunami of images' when, in 2011, Flickr announced that they had reached their six billionth image, and Facebook claimed 100 million pictures uploaded daily. [24] 'Accretion is easier than sorting or ordering (and a source of anxiety to those accustomed to traditional photo albuming)' states Katerina Sluis (Sluis 2011). Pictures are almost impossible to find and selection has been replaced by passive accumulation.

Garde-Hansen observed that younger phone users delete more freely. For the 15–18 year olds she spoke with, deletion was part of everyday practice. They gave a range of reasons: 'it's out of date; I've forgotten the incident; it's boring; not relevant; it's old; a rubbish photo; I don't look good' (2013: 98–100). She concluded that deletion is a more important practice than preservation. These young people 'understand the politics of the archive' she writes (2013: 98–100). And deletion has become automatic in the increasingly popular photo-messaging application Snapchat (launched July 2011), where images remove themselves from the recipient's screen within seconds.

But, paradoxically, personal pictures have moved beyond personal archives. There is a new interest in found images which deliberately eschews evaluation, quality and aesthetic judgements.

Reviewing and use: the role of the archive

Image sharing sites have many uses – equally eroding the boundary between the public and the private as personal and family pictures are more widely circulated. A personal picture may be entered for one of the many online competitions or it may be sold for commercial use. In addition there is a new fascination with found pictures, and collecting other people's private images. The 'Look at me' project started with a few photos picked up by Frederic Bonn and Zoe Deleu in a Paris street in 1998. It invites 'found pictures' to be submitted to its website. These must be completely unknown to the person submitting, at least 25 years old, not cropped or treated in any way and must abide by the codes of personal photography with at least one person looking at the camera.[25]

To conclude, personal photography is dissolving into a circuit of communication of which a camera is only a part, and the photograph is not itself the

23 Childline: www.childline.org.uk/explore/onlinesafety/pages/sexting.aspx?utm_source=google&utm_medium=cpc&utm_campaign=NSPCC_Sexting&utm_term=sexting_examples&gclid=CMrj7vb62rsCFa3KtAodQH8APg

24 http://latimesblogs.latimes.com/technology/2011/08/flickr-reaches-6-billion-photos-uploaded.html

25 The LOOK AT ME project: http://look-at-me.tumblr.com/

most important element. Personal photography is both more and less private: the family context is, on the one hand, reinforced by greater access both to cameras and camera phones to record the present and, on the other, to archives which preserve the past. The networks of intimacy have expanded well beyond family limits. Control over what is recorded and preserved is no longer in the hands of adults alone. The technologies are available to all members of relatively prosperous families, and very frequently the younger members are more adept. This is, in any case, part of wider cultural changes in which pressures from teenagers, changing family structures and other disruptions are common. And the imagery is less formal, drawing on a culture of disrespect and cynicism. When faced with a camera it may be more appropriate to pull a face or make a gesture rather than to put on the once obligatory smile.

And in the galleries . . .

As we have seen, since the 1970s, a fascination with the personal and everyday life, together with influence from the feminist movement brought private photography into the galleries in new ways. Some photographers took the world of inner experience as their subject-matter, incorporating snapshots or imitating their style (Williams 1994). Some, including Christian Boltanski, exploited the public and political dimension of personal photography (Brittain 1999: 213; van Alphen 1999). Others developed a form of domestic hyper-realism, seeking out the squalor of everyday life, peeling off the conventions of the family snapshot. Notable are Richard Billingham's painful yet hilarious images which relentlessly record, in huge and garishly coloured panels, the chaos of his parents' home, and Nan Goldin's intense yet casual pictures of the New York drug culture of which she was part.

Now, digital photography has brought ever wider possibilities. Women photographers in particular have developed intimate, personal themes. Marjolaine Ryley and Rosie Martin draw on snapshots and personal imagery to explore their own childhood, and relations with their parents. Others have taken up topics previously taboo in public galleries, including pregnancy, childbirth – and, in the case of Finnish photographer Elina Brotherus – the emotional pain of infertility and IVF treatment (Bright 2013; Matthews and Wexler 2000).

Sally Mann, Nancy Honey and Tierney Gearon photographed their children with an intimacy which questions easy judgements about childhood sensuality. Art historian Anne Higonnet comments that 'mothers know more than they used to' and argues that a *maternal* view of children and domestic life is for the first time validated both in art and in private photography (Higonnet 1998: 197; Mann 1992; Honey 1992; Hirsch 1997: ch. 5).

But these remain the public works by acknowledged artists, produced and distributed within a context which is very different from that of the mundane family snapshot. However strongly they challenge the boundaries between the public and the private, they are designed to be *read* by the world at large.

187

Personal photography itself remains a minor discourse, a knowledge without authority, apart from that of its creator, designed to be *used* rather than read.[26] It is precisely because of this special quality, this everyday unimportance, that we would do well to attend to what it has to tell us.

26 French sociologist Pierre Bourdieu, in his classic 1965 study, described photography as a 'middle-brow art'.

CHAPTER 4

The subject as object

Photography and the human body

MICHELLE HENNING

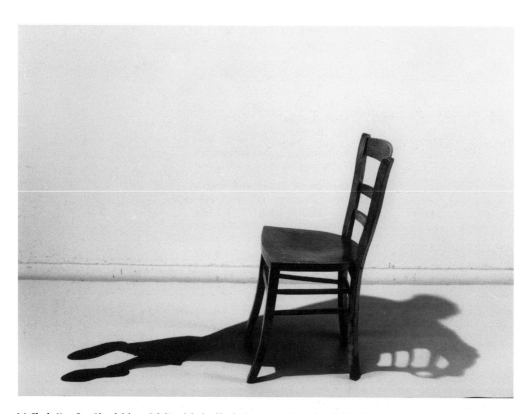

4.1 Floris Neusüss, *Bin gleich zurück (Be right back)*, photogram and wooden chair, 1984/87

The subject as object
Photography and the human body

INTRODUCTION

The photographic body in crisis

It is hard to imagine photography without images of people: we dominate our own visual culture. Not all images of people are *about* the body, in the sense of constructing the body as a central concern, or reflecting on human physicality. In different periods and cultures, ways of understanding and imaging the human body differ: as this chapter will show, in times of war or in famines and epidemics, there are competing discourses of the human body (as vulnerable, 'armoured', contaminating for instance) and bodies are differentiated according to such ideas. New medical disciplines and technologies change the way in which the body is imagined. For example, since the eighteenth century, the principle discipline of the body was anatomy, which described bodies in terms of skeletal and muscular structure, organs and tissues. Yet now, fields such as endocrinology, immunology and genetics construe the body as an informational, communicative ensemble (van der Ploeg 2003: 64–66). This informational model of the body – the body as data – informs contemporary visual practices, in particular the collection of image-based biometrics such as fingerprints and iris-scans. In vernacular (amateur, everyday) photography, people regularly translate their own bodies into data by sharing digital images on online networks.

Nevertheless, today 'the body' does not seem to be the hot topic that it was for many photographic artists and critics at the end of the twentieth century.

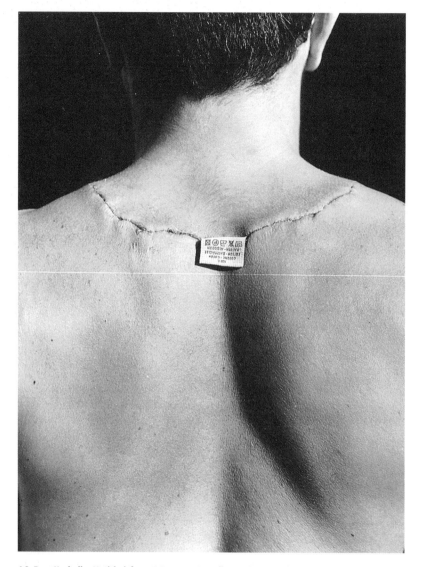

4.2 Fran Herbello, *Untitled*, from A Imaxe e Semellanza, 2000
Herbello's images represent the body as a kind of attire, and deal with the transformation of identity in the digital era, and the changes this may produce in our relationship with our bodies.

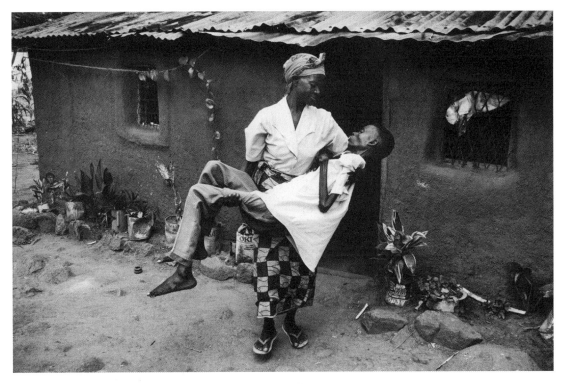

4.3 Gideon Mendel, *Tanzanian mother carrying her son*, 2000.
Dorika Gabriel carries her ill 30-year-old son Joseph to sit in the shade. Though this photograph depicts Joseph's physical frailty and dependence, photographers including Mendel have also responded to AIDS activists' calls to represent people with HIV and AIDS living active lives.

As one art critic wrote in 2004, 'the body itself, following two decades as a fashionable object of academic and critical theorising, is no longer the tense, thrilling battleground it once was' (Morton 2004). In the late 1980s and 1990s an extraordinary number of photographic practices and critical texts took the human body as their central subject. For instance, artists as diverse as Jo Spence, Cindy Sherman, Annette Messager, Mona Hatoum and Adrian Piper all used photography to address perceptions of gender, ageing and of racial difference. Other photographers such as Fran Herbello and Inez Van Lamsweerde used digital and analogue techniques to produce unlikely and illusionistic images, drawing analogies between image manipulation and actual body-altering practices and producing unsettling composite bodies (Figure 4.2). These and many other photographers were concerned not simply with how to represent bodies, or what kinds of bodies should be represented, but with the emergence of specifically photographic ways of seeing the body, and with the role of photography in the production of desire.[1]

1 The work of many of the artists and photographers discussed in this chapter is reproduced in widely available monographs and exhibition catalogues. It has not been possible to include full publication references for all of them.

In the 1990s, photography historians and theorists suggested that the new interest in the body in photography was linked to the emergence of new critical theories and 'body politics' (Pultz 1995b: 7–10; Foster 1996: 122–3). Social crises politicised these photographic practices – notably the AIDS epidemic, which became highly politicised because of its association with stigmatised or marginalised populations – gay urban communities in the West and impoverished populations in Africa. Official representations of the AIDS crisis were opposed by agitational graphics groups such as Gran Fury, and in 1989 the photographer Nan Goldin curated *Witnesses: Against our Vanishing* an exhibition of New York artists responding to the AIDS crisis. While photo-journalists including David Goldblatt, Pep Bonnart, Tom Stoddart and Gideon Mendel (Figure 4.3) documented the impact of the epidemic in Africa, artists such as Goldin in New York and Mark Leslie in Montreal depicted how AIDS had affected themselves and their friends (Dubin 1992: 197–225; Crimp and Rolston 1990; Kotz 1998; Squiers 2005: 170).

In this period, photography was a means by which minority communities could make themselves visible. According to **Deborah Bright**, in the United States, the right wing responded to this new-found visibility by attacking state funding of photography exhibitions which dealt with issues related to minorities, and especially to homosexuality. In particular they questioned the funding by the National Endowment for the Arts (NEA) of exhibitions of photographs which they saw as undermining norms of decency; this usually meant photographic representations of bodies, body parts, bodily fluids or sexual practices. Most notorious were the 1989 attacks on exhibitions of the photographs of Robert Mapplethorpe and Andres Serrano, both funded by the NEA, leading to (self-) censorship of this work by museums and galleries and to legislation restricting the NEA's grant-giving powers (Bright 1998: 6–7; Dubin 1992).[2] The notion of the body as a site of conflict was also highlighted by feminist campaigns of the period around pornography and abortion: the slogan "Your Body Is a Battleground" was used in a 1989 march for women's reproductive rights in Washington, and immortalised in conceptual artist Barbara Kruger's famous artwork that was originally produced for that campaign.

Carole S. Vance, writing on photography and censorship in the USA, showed how ideas about bodies and ideas about the meanings and uses of photographs are deeply interconnected (Vance 1990). Instances of censorship bring to light the way that conflict between different interest groups is played out through conflicting interpretations of photography. Ways of reading photographs are used to challenge the legitimacy of different sexual practices and identities. Vance demonstrated how photographs of human bodies are caught up in social struggles, and how different views about the meanings and uses of photographs have political implications. These struggles are as old as photography, but they became particularly vivid in the late twentieth century with the rise of both sexual politics and religious fundamentalism and with

DEBORAH BRIGHT (1998) **The Passionate Camera: Photography and Bodies of Desire**, London and New York: Routledge.

2 This was vividly demonstrated in the reactions to Robert Mapplethorpe's touring photographic exhibition *The Perfect Moment* (1989) and to Andres Serrano's 1987 photograph *Piss Christ*. See Dubin 1992.

CAROLE S. VANCE (1990) 'The Pleasures of Looking: The Attorney General's Commission on Pornography versus Visual Images' in Carol Squiers (ed.) **The Critical Image: Essays on Contemporary Photography**, Seattle: Bay Press.

the globalisation and diversification of media that made the range of photo-graphic representations of the body more visible than ever.

This heightened atmosphere in which the body and its photographic representations were being fought over during the late 1980s and 1990s no longer exists in the same form. In the early twenty-first century, the new crisis of the body appears to be obesity, especially amongst the poor in developed nations. This doesn't mean the end of famine – rather it is connected to starvation in other parts of the world, via the uneven distribution of global wealth and the world trades in food and fuel. While documentary and reportage depicts both extremes, advertising and fashion photography have been criticised for promoting evidently anorexic models as 'ideal' female bodies. Photographic mass media is now both more explicit in its representations of the body (more bloodied corpses in news imagery, for example) and more withheld or eviscerated, as in magazine images that depict women in particular as blandly styled and 'photoshopped' to the point of dehumanizing them.

The body remains an object of anxious media attention: developments in genetics and medicine that appear to offer the possibility of radically trans-formed bodies, and media controversies have centred on fears about 'designer babies', stem cell research, cloning, and the possible effects on our bodies of genetically modified food. In the early 1990s, many cultural theorists and writers had viewed the prospect of a technologically altered 'posthuman' or cyborg body as exciting, even liberating. A decade later, as this seemed an ever more plausible reality, it was increasingly viewed in dystopian, rather than utopian terms (on the 'posthuman' see Deitch 1992; Hayles 1999; Badmington 2000).

Today, the technological transformation of bodies, and the role of photography in that transformation, needs to be understood as both the physical manipulation of human and animal bodies and also the translation of the body into data, which accelerated in proportion to the perceived security risks and tightened border controls of the so-called 'war on terror'. The smartphone has accelerated the processes of photographic production, circula-tion and consumption: they happen instantly, at the touch of a finger on a handheld screen. Photography appears at once less material and more close to the body (the image that circulates never leaves your hand). It has become an instant and transient form of communication – for instance, in apps such as 'Snapchat' where images disappear after a period of 1 to 10 seconds. While current artistic and curatorial practice seems less focused on the body as a theme, there is renewed interest in the materiality of the photograph, in response to changes in our embodied experience of photography.

This chapter is organised thematically to allow discussion of a number of current and historical photographic practices and debates. The ideas and theories introduced here may be applied to a wider range of examples than those specifically considered here. The first section looks at how photography has been used historically as part of a broader attempt to 'read' people's bodies, especially in relation to racial and ethnic classifications and social deviancy. It discusses the relationship between this history and newer attempts to translate bodies into digital data in the name of nation-state security. The next section considers how gender and sexuality are visually coded in certain photographs. Here photographs of celebrities and pornographic photographs are discussed and some key concepts from psychoanalysis are introduced. The third section attends to the ways in which the camera as a technology intervenes in the body, and also how it represents the body's relationship with technology, through a consideration of medical imaging, early avant-garde photography and contemporary advertising images. It also addresses how digital manipulation participates in new ways of seeing and conceptualising the human body. A case study looks at materialist practices in art photography to suggest how photographic practices can evoke the human body and the experience of embodiment without directly or straightforwardly representing human figures. The final section explores the view that photography is a practice deeply associated with death, and considers photographs relating to both birth and death.

EMBODYING SOCIAL DIFFERENCE

Photography and identification

By the end of the nineteenth century, photography was being used to classify people into 'types', illustrating and extending the Victorian sciences of **phrenology** and **physiognomy**. These popular sciences were part of a 'vast attempt at deciphering the body' in which the desire to classify bodies according to visual appearance is justified by the belief that the surface reveals hidden depths; in other words, that the outer surfaces of the body could be read as a series of signs or codes revealing or expressing inner character (Magli 1989: 124). Both phrenology and physiognomy appealed to an enthusiasm for classification according to 'type', and both became popular in the 1840s and 1850s at the same time as photography. 'Typological' classification was reassuring to the urban middle classes because its convenient generalisations helped make the mass of strangers in the city seem more familiar. As the sociologist Georg Simmel noted, visual appearances were particularly important in a period when new means of public transport meant that many social encounters were primarily visual encounters:

> Before the development of buses, railroads and trams in the nineteenth century, people had never been in a position of having to look at one another for long minutes or even hours without speaking to one another.
>
> (Simmel quoted in Benjamin 1938: 38)

phrenology was developed at the end of the eighteenth century by Franz Josef Gall. It was based on the idea that the contours of the skull could give clues to the mental functioning of the brain.

physiognomy was an ancient science, systematised in the 1770s by Johann Caspar Lavater, which claimed to read the character of a person through the classification of the features of head and face. Lavater saw a 'correspondence between the external and the internal man, the visible superficies and invisible contents' (Lavater 1789 quoted in Lalvani 1996: 48).

Simplified, popularised versions of physiognomy and phrenology could be used to counteract the anonymity of urban life, and provided 'a method of quickly assessing the characters of strangers in the dangerous and congested spaces of the nineteenth century city' (Sekula 1989: 348). These 'sciences' are not, however, as harmless as they first appear. Whilst they may have reassured the dominant class, physiognomy and phrenology were also deployed as a means of social control via photography. Because it shows us only surfaces, photography is ideally suited to physiognomic and phrenological interpretation, and it became part of an increasingly professionalised and systematic police force.

Photographer and theorist **Allan Sekula** argues that the photographs taken for police and prison records should be seen alongside the portrait photographs that flourished at the same time. People were encouraged to read portraits using physiognomy, so the portrait of the respectable citizen emphasised facial characteristics associated in physiognomy with moral character and citizenship. The photographic police archives also relied on a physiognomic norm: the 'average man' was the physical and social ideal against which the criminal body was measured (Sekula 1989: 347, 354–6).

ALLAN SEKULA (1989) 'The Body and the Archive' in Richard Bolton (ed.) **The Contest of Meaning: Critical Histories of Photography**, Cambridge, MA: MIT Press.

Photography historian **John Tagg** has also discussed photographs of criminals, using the work of the French social historian Michel Foucault (see also margin note p. 67) to understand how photography is used to 'discipline' people. Discipline in Foucault's sense refers to processes of surveillance, identification, classification, labelling, analysis and correction – as opposed to older regimes of punishment which did not seek to understand the deviant/ deviation but rather to eliminate it. According to Foucault, in modern society, power is dispersed through social institutions (such as schools, asylums, prisons) and exists in insidious ways in everyday practices. The construction of archives is crucial to the everyday ways in which disciplinary power is exercised. Tagg quotes texts from the 1850s through to the 1970s which lay down strictures for photographing social deviants for the purpose of police, prison, asylum and legal archives. At first the photographic archive was a vast accumulation of unclassified and often unrecognisable photographic portraits, but in the 1880s a French bureaucrat, Alphonse Bertillon, developed techniques to standardise police records and enable identification of repeat offenders. He used photography as a means to train police in the classification and recognition of different facial features. His filing card system involved detailed measurements of the criminal, description of identifying marks, and use of two photos – front view and profile – which were taken using standardised focal length and lighting (Lalvani 1996: 109; Sekula 1989: 357–63; Kemp and Wallace 2000: 144–7).

JOHN TAGG (1988) **Burden of Representation: Essays on Photographies and Histories**, London: Macmillan.

To study the disciplinary uses of photography means considering the ways in which people are represented, arranged for the camera, made available to be gazed at, and placed in a system of signification which codes and classifies them. As Tagg notes, we can see

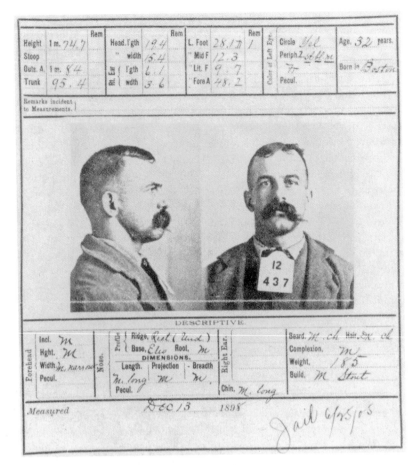

4.4 Filing card using Bertillon's 'anthropometric' system, 1898
The standardised police records initiated by Bertillon produce 'a portrait of the product of the disciplinary method: the body made object' (Tagg 1988: 76)

a repetitive pattern, the body isolated; the narrow space; the subjection to an unreturnable gaze; the scrutiny of gestures, faces and features; the clarity of illumination and sharpness of focus; the names and number boards. These are the traces of power, repeated countless times, whenever the photographer prepared an exposure, in police cell, prison, consultation room, home or school.

(Tagg 1988: 85)

One significant legacy of the nineteenth-century disciplinary uses of photography is in contemporary biometric data systems that deploy digital photographs, iris scans and, most commonly, fingerprinting. All are techniques of visualisation used to sort and classify people, and assumed to directly encode the physical body. While photography criticism has devoted itself to challenging this notion of indexical photographic truth, biometrics devotes itself to perfecting techniques for making bodies yield up the truth of their identity. In 2007, the British government's visa website publicised its plans to collect fingerscans and digital photographs (mugshots) from all visa applicants, presenting biometrics as a 'natural step' and describing fingerscans as 'identifiers' applicable to everyone (www.ukvisas.gov.uk/). In practice, biometric security systems struggle with 'illegible bodies', that is, bodies which the systems cannot adequately depict or identify (Murray 2007: 348). It has been argued that in the USA and the UK these bodies belong to those groups historically marginalised (women, the elderly, manual workers, people with dark skin and dark eyes), because the technologies are calibrated to bodies assumed to be 'normal', i.e. young, white, male, white-collar workers, just as photographic film was historically calibrated for light-coloured skin (Murray 2007: 351–2; Dyer 1997: 90). This inability to capture all bodies might seem a positive thing in the context of a Foucauldian analysis of disciplinary power, but when establishing one's identity becomes a condition of access to citizenship and to rights, to be illegible or invisible and outside the archive is to be at risk.

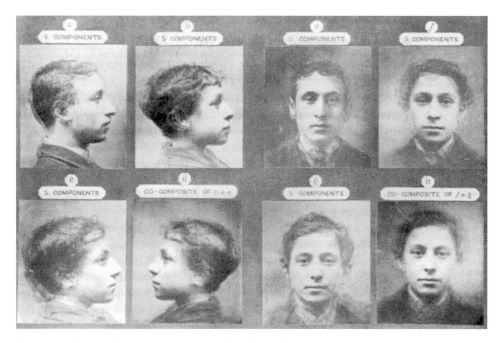

4.5 Francis Galton, *The Jewish Type*, composite photographs, 1883
Joseph Jacobs, the Jewish man who commissioned these images, saw them as validating Jewish identity, but they also reinforced Galton's own anti-Semitic views.

199

One of the early pioneers of fingerprinting for identification was Francis Galton, who also developed the photographic technique of composite portraiture in the 1880s. Galton superimposed the photographed faces of people with shared characteristics or circumstances. The composite image produced in this way supposedly revealed hereditary physical characteristics, the surface 'symptoms' of innate biology. At first he presented his technique as useful in the diagnosis of disease, but he also attempted to use composite portraiture to reveal the characteristic physiognomy of different 'types': the faces superimposed may all have committed the same crimes, or belong to the same ethnic groups. Galton's method naturalised social differences by describing social 'types' in terms of biology, that is, along the lines of race. In his work, different cultural groups or social classes appear as separate races with definite and visible physical characteristics.

The popular sciences of phrenology and physiognomy, combined with new photographic techniques, produced a new and fundamentally racist vision of society. It was Galton, the pioneer of composite photography, who introduced the 'science' of eugenics, understood as 'the self-direction of human evolution'. Eugenics proposed that intellectual and moral qualities were hereditary and that the 'human stock' could be improved through selective breeding. Eugenics was embraced by both the political left and right, and was used as justification for European colonialism, for the class structure, and later for Nazism. These photographic practices are not confined to the nineteenth century. For instance, Sekula compares Galton's work to the use of composite (digital) photography by the American artist Nancy Burson, suggesting that the shared faith in surface appearances undermines the intended liberal content of Burson's practice (Sekula 1989: 377).

Computer-generated composites have also now become a form of entertainment (as in 'Foto Morphosis', photo-booths that combine the faces of two individuals to produce their 'virtual reality' child), and a means to identify criminals by classifying facial features according to type.[3] The photographer Gerhard Lang also used Galton's techniques, but with closer attention to their social and historical significance and in more precise ways than Burson (Kemp and Wallace 2000: 190–9). Japanese photographer Ken Kitano uses a similar process in his 'metaportraits' of social groups in which a face seems to emerge from a sketchy mass, perhaps suggesting the impossibility, rather than the necessity, of classifying people.

One of the main ways in which data about individuals is generated today is through their own submissions of images and information to online databases and social networks. In this context, self-portraiture has become much more common, in the form of the digital 'selfie'. While self-portraiture is a familiar topic in fine art photography, until recently it was relatively uncommon in vernacular photography (Jones 2002; Bright 2010; Schwarz 2010: 163). Researching the use of 'selfies' in one social network, Ori Schwarz considered how self-portraits became a means to gain celebrity status. By using marketing

3 'I had Bill Clinton's Baby', **Marie Claire** 104, April 1997, p. 92. Even this mechanised composite uses racial typology – as well as programming in the preferred sex of your child you can choose your child's racial characteristics from 'Asian, Afro-Caribbean, Hispanic or Caucasian'. Chapter 5 gives a contemporary example of the way this works: some of Benetton's ads, while ostensibly about global harmony, use visual signifiers of racial and ethnic identity which reproduce ideas of absolute racial difference.

strategies to increase 'likes' or 'hits', participants work hard to gain what Schwarz terms 'corporeal capital' (Schwarz 2010: 171). Schwarz sees the 'selfie' as currency in fragile social interactions, a means of overcoming the absence of any other kind of social or cultural capital. Participants are subject to public scrutiny and possibly stigmatisation instead of celebrity — as Schwarz puts it 'extracting value from your body is a risky game' (Schwarz 2010: 180).

OBJECTS OF DESIRE AND DISGUST

Objectification, fetishism, voyeurism

Even erotic imagery depended on the classification of social types, though not primarily through physiognomy. Clothing and props act as signifiers of class and occupation in Victorian pornography. These images represented social types considered to be sexually available: for example, the laundress. The art historian Eunice Lipton has shown how, in Paris, the laundresses' low pay, visibility (the laundries were open on to the street), and tendency to drink wine to counteract the heat of the laundry, led to their reputation as sexually 'loose' women (Lipton 1980). Other Victorian pornographic images showed women and couples in clearly middle-class domestic surroundings.[4]

See Figure 3.4 which hints at this reputation, though more explicitly sexualised images of laundresses were also common.

Today, erotica also works through classifying its subjects into recognisable types – in this way it makes different women appear sexually available to a presumed heterosexual male viewer. And, just as the criminal photograph reduces the depicted person to a series of signifiers, so mainstream pornographic images offer women as available for sexual fantasy by attaching certain meanings to a narrow set of signifiers. In the 1970s and 1980s, such representations of women became a focus of feminist criticism. Feminists questioned the existing distinctions between legitimate and illegitimate images (such as 'hardcore' pornography) which were based on degrees of explicitness of nudity and/or sexual activity.[5] They criticised advertising and publicity images as well as erotica for eroticising the female body in a way which turned women into mere objects for a male gaze, a process usually termed **objectification**.[6]

4 Detailed discussion of Victorian erotic and pornographic photography can be found in Solomon-Godeau (1991c); Kendrick (1987) and Williams (1995).

5 The argument against the traditional 'hard'/'soft' distinction is put by Brown (1981).

The concept of objectification has special relevance to photography. In one sense photography inadvertently objectifies people by turning them into things to be looked at (Solomon-Godeau 1991c: 221–2). But it has also been suggested that in everyday life women are already constituted as objects to be looked at and men as 'possessing the **gaze**'. According to this argument, women internalise the male gaze to the point that they survey themselves. This relationship has been expressed by the critic John Berger:

6 Solomon-Godeau concludes that 'it may well be that the most insidious and instrumental forms of domination, subjugation and objectification are produced by mainstream images of women rather than by juridically criminal or obscene ones' (Solomon-Godeau 1991c: 237).

Men look at women. Women watch themselves being looked at. This determines not only most relations between men and women but also the relation of women to themselves. The surveyor of woman in herself

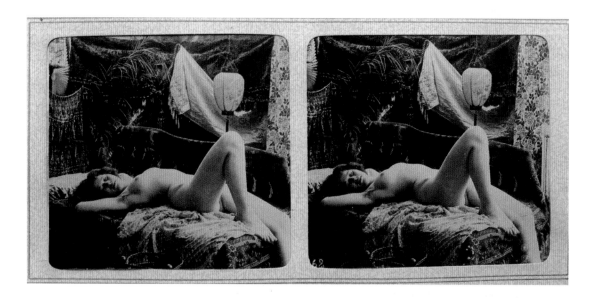

4.6 Anonymous stereoscope photograph from around 1895
The plants, fabrics and lamp in this image are used to suggest an exotic interior associated with the Orient and with the harem.

is male: the surveyed female. Thus she turns herself into an object – and most particularly an object of vision: a sight.

(Berger 1972a: 47)

If women are already objectified by the male gaze, and if objectification is in any case what photography does, then photographic images of women are doubly 'objectifying' (see Solomon-Godeau 1991: 221–2). Feminist writers have drawn on psychoanalysis to understand how the pleasures of looking at photographic images are implicated in the exercise of power. In particular the concepts of **voyeurism** and **fetishism** have been influential. These concepts were most famously formulated by Sigmund Freud, and have been developed by psychoanalysts such as Jacques Lacan, Melanie Klein and Luce Irigaray (see Gamman and Makinen 1994: ch. 3). However, we will focus here on the terms as they were initially developed by Freud (Freud 1905, 1927). (See also note, p. 39.)

A Freudian approach considers the spectator's experience of visual pleasure in terms of his or her subjectivity which is shaped from early childhood. This visual pleasure or **'scopophilia'** is usually understood as an erotic pleasure gained in looking at another person or at images of other bodies. This pleasure is voyeuristic when it is dependent on the object of this gaze being unaware, not looking back. Voyeurism is a form of objectification which Freud saw as originating in childhood curiosity. At its extreme, it becomes an obsessive sexual practice. Voyeurism describes a mode of looking related to the exercise of power in which a body becomes a spectacle for someone else's pleasure, a world divided into the active 'lookers' and the passive 'looked at'. To some

202

extent photography, by the very nature of the medium, invites voyeuristic looking, although some photographs, such as those which depict a normally private or taboo activity and a subject apparently unaware that they are being photographed, are more explicitly voyeuristic (Sontag 1979: 11–14). The concept of voyeurism is applicable not only to sexualised or erotic images, but also in relation to the depiction of colonised peoples and of disability as spectacle.

Another concept central to Freudian analyses of photography is fetishism (see Burgin 1982: 177ff). In Freudian theory an important moment in the shaping of the self is the point at which the child becomes aware of sexual difference and moves away from its early close relationship with its mother: this process of entry into sexuality is what produces, in some people, sexual fetishism. Freud's definition of fetishism is derived from older anthropological definitions, in which an inanimate object takes on special powers such as warding off danger and misfortune and is the centre of religious rituals. In Freud's interpretation, an object becomes a fetish when it becomes the focus of (usually male) sexual desire. The male child develops an unconscious fear of castration at the sight of a woman's body, and fetishism is one means of allaying this anxiety. Fetishism, in Freud's interpretation, involves freezing a moment (the moment before the trauma of recognition) and fixating on a fragment.

The use of Freud's concept of fetishism to explain visual pleasure is controversial because it relies on the theory of male castration anxiety which implies that the fetishist is by definition male (Gamman and Makinen 1994: chs 3 and 6). Nevertheless, it provides a useful corrective to those literal interpretations in which a pornographic image which does not include a woman's head has 'decapitated her', or flattening lighting made for a 'one-dimensional' representation. The concept of fetishism suggests that flattening and fragmentation are part of the process by which the pleasure of looking at (or imagining touching) a body is transferred into the pleasures of looking at or handling a photograph or magazine page. The film theorist **Christian Metz** argued that a photograph works like a fetish because it freezes a fragment of reality, 'cutting off a piece of space and time . . . keeping it unchanged while the world around continues to change' (Metz 1985: 85). Most of all, the photograph can be a fetish because of its physicality – we can touch and hold a photograph: 'The familiar photographs that many people carry with them always obviously belong to the order of fetishes in the ordinary sense of the word' (Metz 1985: 87).

CHRISTIAN METZ (1985) 'Photography and Fetish', **October** 34, Autumn.

The celebrity body

The theory of fetishism has been important in analysing film and photography because it helps to account for the ways in which visual images objectify and fragment women's bodies using techniques that are not common in representations of the male body.

LAURA MULVEY (1975) 'Visual Pleasure and Narrative Cinema' Reprinted 1989 in **Visual and Other Pleasures**, London: Macmillan.

7 In 1957 Roland Barthes observed similar qualities in the cinematic representation of the face of Greta Garbo (Barthes 1986: 56–7).

8 However, an advertisement such as this is clearly intended for a female readership. Even taking into account Berger's argument that women internalise the male gaze, the Freudian theory of fetishism is inadequate in explaining the fetishistic qualities of these advertisements (Gamman and Makinen 1994: 37–44, 95–105).

Freud's definition of fetishism can be understood in relation to the Marxist explanation of commodity fetishism: in which goods exchanged in a market appear to have value independent of the human labour that produced them, and independent of their usefulness. What a commodity is worth comes to seem 'natural' or inherent, comparable to the value of other commodities in the same way that their weight or size might be compared. It is this mystification of commodity value which Marx refers to as fetishism.

9 'Are such things likely to increase sexual immorality among young people? I find it hard to imagine much connexion between them and heterosexual activity. They may encourage masturbation: in their symbolic way they may promote that kind of sealed-off sexual response' (Hoggart 1957: 191–2).

The film theorist and filmmaker **Laura Mulvey** used the theory of fetishism to explain ways in which certain films objectify the female star. She suggested that the female figure on screen is potentially troubling to male spectators: 'the woman as icon, displayed for the gaze and enjoyment of men, the active controllers of the look, always threatens to evoke the anxiety it originally signified' (Mulvey 1989: 21). Mulvey contended that the male spectator is unconsciously reminded of the traumatic moment when he recognised sexual difference. One way he can deal with this is by disavowing it through fetishism. Mulvey suggests that certain films turn the represented figure of a female star (such as Marlene Dietrich, Figure 4.7) into a fetish by bringing together the beauty of the film as spectacle, the play of light and shadows, with the beauty of the woman as object. Close-ups, lighting and make-up fragment, flatten and render the female face one-dimensional (Mulvey 1989: 21–3).[7] The formal qualities of the projected image are the reassuring substitute object which distracts the male spectator from the threat that the woman poses. Similar qualities can be seen in the representation of the female face in current cosmetic advertisements in women's magazines where a blank space in the image stands in for flesh. Faces are flattened with no shadows visible, reduced to a set of facial features arranged on a smooth and atonal expanse of skin. In this way the medium and image are conflated, the glossy, smooth feel of the magazine page stands in for the woman's skin (see Burgin 1986: 19).[8]

In most accounts of fetishism (not just psychoanalytic accounts), the desirability of objects is related to a conflation of the human and the object world, so that things appear to be inherently desirable or valuable, even animated (Leslie 2002: 6–8). Reciprocally, human beings become perceived and represented as objects. The rise of fetishistic representations of women in both pornography and advertising photographs is connected to the development of a capitalist economy, and to the fetishising of commodities.

As early as 1957, the writer Richard Hoggart noted the resemblance of women's bodies in softcore and glamour photography to commodities. He commented on the new 'technicolour cheesecake' magazines:

Everything has been stripped to a limited range of visual suggestions – can one imagine a musky body-smell, un-artificially disordered hair, an uneven texture to the skin, hair on the arms and legs, beads of perspiration on the upper-lip, on one of these neatly-packaged creatures?
(Hoggart 1957: 191)

Hoggart saw this as part of the Americanisation and de-politicisation of British working-class culture and as a lack of realism that might encourage 'sexual immorality'.[9] For more recent theorists, fetishism describes not just a sexual preference of a minority (classified by Freud as one of the 'perversions') but a culturally dominant way of seeing both the object world and ourselves.

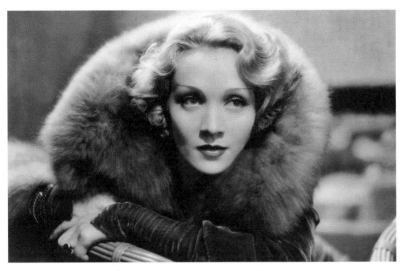

4.7 Marlene Dietrich in *Shanghai Express*, dir. Josef von Sternberg, 1932
Sternberg and Dietrich's films exemplify the fetishism of classical Hollywood cinema, but this is complicated by the way Dietrich's face is used to signify her character's sexual and ethnic identity in this particular film.

While Hoggart was concerned with male viewers, 'neatly-packaged' images also affect how women view themselves. Aligning themselves with women's own possible frustrations at this lack of realism certain (British) magazines use paparazzi photographs to pass judgement on the bodies of (mostly female) celebrities. Text and graphic additions repeatedly reflect on the capacity of digital manipulation and bodily manipulations (such as plastic surgery) to deceive and conceal 'flaws'. Through graphic devices like the 'circle of shame', *Heat*, the *Daily Mirror*'s 'Celebs on Sunday' magazine and the *News of the World*'s 'Sunday' magazine, for instance, poke fun at celebrity bodies for having hairy lips, large ears, lumpy chins and 'turkey necks'; stretch marks, cellulite and bulging tummies; bad skin, sunburn and badly applied fake tans; wrinkles and evidence of cosmetic surgery; too large, marked or hairy hands and bitten nails; sweaty, hairy or 'ugly' armpits. In this way, the 'crisis of photography', the loss of faith in its capacity to truthfully represent the world, is resolved by paparazzi photos that appear to show us the 'truth' behind staged celebrity portraits, and the 'crisis of the body' and its imperfections is assuaged by these pictures demonstrating that there *are* no perfect bodies. However, while these photos seemingly reassure readers about their own bodies, they also encourage them to view them critically by finding potential flaws in every anatomical part.

The practice of critiquing celebrity bodies also takes place in relation to celebrities' use of cosmetic surgery, which is understood in terms of 'optimising' or 'customising' the body (Ugrina 2014: 37). Celebrity gossip magazines and blogs invite readers to judge the quality of surgery in 'before and after' photographs, often accompanied by commentary by cosmetic surgeons, distinguishing 'botched' from successful procedures. Luciana Ugrina compares this to biometrics: as with biometric surveillance systems, these magazines and websites tend to assume that that the body – and photography – can be 'easily read and thoroughly known' (Ugrina 2014: 28, 35).

Pornography and sexual imagery

In soft porn and advertising, everyday cultural objects, domestic settings and familiar poses are commonly used to give a sense of realism (a notable exception is the collaboration between Riccardo Schicchi and La Cicciolina whose anti-naturalistic, overtly kitsch photo-spreads broke with pornographic conventions in the 1980s). As feminist theorist Beverley Brown has argued, this limited visual vocabulary operates as a 'short-cut' to sexual fantasy and in turn, leaves everyday life with a 'certain afterglow' (Brown 1981: 138–40). In advertising, this process is part of the attempt to eroticise commodities (see ch. 5). If such an 'afterglow' is an effect, it is a much more subtle one than the harmful effects often attributed to pornography. For example, American radical feminist Robin Morgan argued that 'Pornography is the theory – rape is the practice' and Andrea Dworkin famously stated: 'Pornography is violence against women' (Rodgerson and Wilson 1991: 26; Dworkin 1981).

Anti-pornography feminism found allies in right wing religious groups which were usually opposed to feminism, and shared their evangelical style.[10] Radical feminism differed from previous forms of feminism in seeing texts (both visual and written) rather than social discrimination, as central to male dominance. However, it depended on a very narrow interpretive approach to photographs, and offers little evidence for the view that a photograph can be a cause of violence against women (Kendrick 1996: 231). One reason that the anti-pornography campaigns, with their focus on harm, paid most attention to still and moving images over written pornography, is that photography and video have a strong claim to realism. In many pornographic images, this realism is heavily emphasised: bright lighting, careful positioning of bodies and choice of camera angles emphasise that the sexual act depicted really happened. In other words, much visual pornography goes out of its way to invite a literal reading. Another reason for the focus on visual erotica is that most imagery seemed to be of women for viewing by men, while written erotica more frequently addressed a female audience. The Kinsey report research of the 1940s suggested that women are less sexually aroused by images than by literature, and this view is still commonly held. Walter Kendrick points out that attitudes to pornography in America (and Britain) have now shifted so much that '"Pornography" now means pictures, preferably, moving pictures' (Kendrick 1996: 243). The visual pornography industry remains oriented to male desire and male fantasy, with pornography specifically for women remaining highly marginal.

10 The feminist lawyer Catherine MacKinnon drafted anti-pornography legislation in Minneapolis which was then adopted by right-wing legislators in Indianapolis and New York (legislation subsequently declared unconstitutional).

Today the feminist debates about pornography have been overtaken by the larger scandal of child pornography, where vulnerability and lack of consent are much more clear cut. For art photographers who have photographed nude children, the defence of art and freedom of expression is difficult when photographs circulate so easily. As art historian Anne Higonnet wrote 'No subject is as publicly dangerous now as the subject of the child's body' (Higonnet 1998: 133). For instance, Sally Mann's book *Immediate Family* had elicited outraged responses when it was published in 1992 because it represented the children as too knowing, too adult, and (it was argued) implicitly sexual. Although she was not prosecuted, the book was subject to book-burning campaigns and some exhibitions were cancelled. The images have, perhaps inevitably, been shared online amongst paedophile groups (Parsons 2008: 132). Though some photographers have been accused of exploiting their child subjects, the main accusations refer to the illicit pleasures the image might give an imagined paedophile viewer. Such accusations are of course very difficult to refute or answer since they are based on the potential for desires to be projected onto photographs, rather than any content or meaning intended or controlled by the photographer.

In the UK, at least, paeodophilia has remained a public concern. Celebrity court cases and media coverage often point, as the radical feminists did, to a direct connection between the use of pornographic images as part of sexual fantasy and the subsequent perpetration of acts of sexual violence against children. Today, anxieties about paedophile networks mean increased censorship (and self-censorship) of images of unclothed children. In many cases a visit by police is enough to close an exhibition – artists censored or threatened with censorship include Tierney Gearon (2002), Betsy Schneider (2004), Nan Goldin (2007) and Bill Henson (2008). Images of 'full-frontal' adult male nudity have long been subject to censorship, but in Anglophone countries today museums and galleries are more likely to be wary of images of child nudity.

In this context, it is interesting that the confrontational hardcore photographs by Leigh Ledare, of his mother having sex with a series of younger men, have been shown in several fairly high-profile public exhibitions (Bright 2013). The Oedipal relationship that Ledare's photographs suggest between mother and son is extreme and disturbing, yet the son in question is an adult and the photographer, and the depicted individuals are consenting heterosexual adults.

Arguably, hardcore pornographic images have become more acceptable in the broader culture as well as in the sphere of fine art. Recent media and academic writing has claimed that there has been a 'pornification' of culture, with pornography readily available, even unavoidable, especially via the internet, and with popular or mass culture generally becoming more sexualised (see, for example, Paasonen *et al.* 2007). However Clarissa Smith has argued that the debates about pornography and pornification ignore the specific ways in which pornography is regulated, produced, consumed and circulated; and how producers and consumers of sexually explicit materials talk about these things themselves (Smith 2007: 13–27). Others have argued that the umbrella term 'pornography' includes a broad range of images, which have widely differing meanings and uses for their audiences, often giving visibility to minority desires and communities. As the critic Katherine Enos puts it:

> For conservative feminists and the religious right, pornography is the theory, the rape and murder of women the practice. For queer culture, the production of their own pornographies can be a self-affirming form of representation in a straight culture where a 'lesbian kiss' on TV is so unheard of as to be a matter of public debate.
>
> (Enos 1997/1998)

Conservatives tended to idealise an earlier America, of the 1950s, believing that images appealing to supposedly deviant desires were a more recent phenomenon. While it is true that in the 1950s gay men and lesbians had little access to images or media representations which represented homosexuality, and those which were available usually portrayed it in a negative light, some writers have argued that homoerotic desire was addressed, but in highly coded ways to avoid censorship. The art historian **Emmanuel Cooper** explains how the American 'physique' magazines of the 1950s, which were primarily photographic magazines depicting toned and muscular male bodies for a male readership, legitimated their male readership's interest through the use of visual references to classical antiquity (Cooper 1990: 100–1). These classical references work in a dual way: legitimating the images by emphasising their aesthetic (rather than erotic) nature; and simultaneously working as coded references for the readership, drawing on the homoerotic associations of ancient Greek art and culture. However, Gavin Butt argues that the repressive culture of 1950s America meant that readings were fragile, based in connotations and associations dependent on the viewer's own homoerotic desire. The heavily coded nature of the image is evidence of the illegitimate and unspoken nature of such desire at the time, rather than of a thriving 'gay' identity (Butt 1998: 280).

In the 1980s, a new sexual politics, partly developed in response to government policies regarding HIV and AIDS, rejected older gay and lesbian attempts to be accepted within the status quo and instead challenged the dominant construction of 'normal' versus 'deviant' through a revival and reinflection of the category 'queer'. Queer activists demanded public visibility for people and practices deemed 'abnormal' or 'unnatural' in the face of a history of social invisibility and repression. Part of this new sexual politics was a re-evaluation of the cross-dressing which was an important part of working-class 'butch/femme' lesbian culture in the early twentieth century. Previously, this had been dismissed by lesbian feminists as a sign of repression, and as reinforcing old 'inversion' theories of homosexuality (in which lesbians are 'mannish' women). Queer politics shed a different light on this history, celebrating cross-dressing as undermining fixed gender roles. Queer photographers such as Del LaGrace

EMMANUEL COOPER (1990)
Fully Exposed: The Male Nude in Photography,
London: Unwin Hyman.

208

Volcano challenged anti-pornography feminism by producing queer erotica, including SM images, which emphasised role-playing and cross-dressing, and questioned the stability and naturalness of gender. Photographic practices that play with gender roles and emphasise the constructedness of sexual identities might act as ripostes to the tendency of anti-pornography campaigners to read photographs literally.

This is one reason that anti-censorship writers have tended to focus on photographs that involve role-play or are evidently constructed. The problem with this, as Smith points out, is that it creates a two-tier structure which separates out politically acceptable images (often from art or 'alternative' contexts) from ordinary, mass-market pictures (Smith 2007: 48). It does not help us to understand the vast majority of pornographic images.

Class and representations of the body

The long-established tendency to distinguish between 'good' sexual imagery ('erotica') and bad ('pornography') is related to distinctions of social class (with mass-market pornography associated with lower social classes). Furthermore, the connections between sexual fetishism and commodity fetishism link modern sexual pleasures with the economic structure of capitalism.

The historian Norbert Elias has shown how ideas about the body are connected with social class and the development of capitalism, describing the change in attitudes that occurred as part of a shift from feudal society to a capitalist system in Europe. He suggested that, as a new class becomes dominant, it transforms the dominant ideas about the body and bodily decorum that had prevailed in the old social order (Elias 1994). Medieval, feudal society was rigidly hierarchical, and control of bodies was a central part of social control of the population. But, as the Russian literary theorist **Mikhail Bakhtin** pointed out, in the medieval carnival these hierarchies were disrupted, and ideas of bodily decorum ridiculed or ignored. Carnival was the legitimate space where bodily excess was celebrated, where the lower body, orifices, reproduction, eating, defecation and copulation, pregnancy, birth and death were openly represented (Stallybrass and White 1986: 13; Dentith 1995: ch. 3).

Bakhtin referred to this carnivalesque body as the 'grotesque' body. In the grotesque conception of the world, birth and death are cyclically related, and bodies are understood in collective terms, linked to one another and the world and continually growing and changing. Gradually, the grotesque body of the carnival was displaced by the dominant representation of the body, epitomised by the classical nude. The classical body is a smooth, orifice-less and self-sufficient body. While the grotesque tradition represents the body as ever-changing, from birth to death, and connected to the earth and to other bodies, 'classical' representations of the body omit these aspects: 'The ever unfinished nature of the body was hidden, kept secret; conception, pregnancy, childbirth, death throes, were almost never shown' (Bakhtin 1984: 29).

MIKHAIL MIKHAILOVICH BAKHTIN (1895–1975)
Bakhtin was a Soviet literary theorist. In 1929 he was arrested by Stalin's regime and until his death in 1975 worked in internal exile in the Soviet Union. His work focused on culture as a reciprocal process, and especially on the relationship between representation and social conflict, in which subordinate groups modify and reinterpret the representations produced by the dominant social class. His work was controversial and subject to censorship, since it defended the idea of multiple and conflicting perspectives ('heteroglossia') at a time when the Stalinist government was attempting to impose one ideological worldview. Bakhtin's most famous writings include the essays written in the 1930s and early 1940s, published in *The Dialogic Imagination* (trans. Caryl Emerson and Michael Holquist, University of Texas, 1981).

Bakhtin wrote about carnival and the grotesque in relation to the work of Rabelais and Dostoevsky in books eventually published in the mid-1960s: *Rabelais and his World* (trans. Hèiène Iswolsky, Indiana University Press, 1984) and *Problems of Dostoevsky's Poetics* (trans. Caryl Emerson, University of Manchester Press, 1984).

LAURA KIPNIS (1992) '(Male) Desire and (Female) Disgust: Reading Hustler' in Lawrence Grossberg *et al.* (eds) **Cultural Studies**, London and New York: Routledge.

11 *Hustler* had been used by Andrea Dworkin to demonstrate the misogyny she believed to be central to pornography (Dworkin 1981: 29–30). Kipnis' argument is a critique of approaches such as Dworkin's, which focus exclusively on gender in their discussions of pornography.

LINDA WILLIAMS (1995) 'Corporealized Observers: Visual Pornographies and the Carnal Density of Vision' in Patrice Petro **Fugitive Images**, Bloomington: Indiana University Press.

One way the merchant classes in the sixteenth century and the industrial bourgeoisie in the eighteenth century maintained their political **hegemony** was through strictures about bodily control and decorum. Capitalist society places enormous emphasis on individualism, constructing a strict separation between the 'private' and the 'public'. Increasingly, the classical body became the publicly acceptable representation of the body in modern society, while those aspects associated with the lower body and the body's connection with the world were banished to the realm of the private, seen as disgusting and shameful, displaced into illicit and secret representations which were unmentionable and invisible in 'polite society' (Stallybrass and White 1986: 188). However, the advent of photography as mass reproduction made this division increasingly hard to control and the representation of the disgusting, the base, the distasteful became a means of challenging social hierarchies.

The cultural theorist **Laura Kipnis** uses the example of the pornographic magazine *Hustler*.[11] Kipnis argues that *Hustler* needs to be understood in terms of class as well as gender, since it sets out primarily to provoke and disgust the 'establishment' (Kipnis 1992: 373–91). She contrasts *Hustler*'s use of photography with the more 'tasteful' images of *Playboy* and *Penthouse*:

> The Hustler body is an unromanticized body – no vaselined lens or soft focus: this is neither the airbrushed top-heavy fantasy body of Playboy, nor the ersatz opulence, the lingeried and sensitive crotch shots of Penthouse, transforming female genitals into *objets d'art*. It's a body, not a surface or a suntan: insistently material, defiantly vulgar, corporeal.
>
> (Kipnis 1992: 375)

But being insistently 'grotesque' does not necessarily make an image politically radical. The targets of carnivalesque ridicule and attack were just as often social outsiders or those considered inferior, such as women. To understand a reaction of shock or disgust at a photograph may mean paying attention to complicated intersections of categories such as class and gender. Middle-class women's disgust at the explicit representation of women's bodies for a male audience is inseparable from their own relationship to images of women's bodies and to their own bodies. Attempts to legally restrict the distribution of explicit photographs of women's bodies or of sexual activity were made to protect 'ladies' against seeing such representations, though it is likely that they saw them nevertheless (**Williams 1995**: 25). This was part of a wider ideology which incited in middle-class women a disgust at their own bodies. 'Ladies' were encouraged to develop a delicate 'feminine' sensibility premised on the repression and unmentionability of bodily experiences such as menstruation, excretion, and even childbirth (Stallybrass and White 1986: 188–9).

The fantasy bodies of both 'hard' and 'soft' pornography resemble classical bodies insofar as they are smooth and hairless and flawless. Like the classical nude, female bodies in contemporary pornography often lack pubic hair:

something which could be associated with the fetishistic disavowal of sexual difference discussed earlier and that arguably makes the body more like a commodity. However, smoothness and hairlessness (of both male and female bodies) is part of the explicitness of the pornographic image. Explicitness is a sort of realism, a guarantee that 'this really happened', and explicit photographs prioritise visibility over any other formal or aesthetic considerations, rather than fetishistically conflating body and medium in the way discussed earlier.

Responses of disgust and distaste are often reactions to the fact of visibility, the transgression of the boundary of private and public, which is why censorship has historically been concerned with degrees of explicitness, not just the perceived immorality of the acts depicted. One example of this can be found in the United States government's response to the publication of photographs of prisoners being tortured at Abu Ghraib in 2006. As Susan Sontag noted, the Bush administration pronounced its 'disgust' while privately seeking to censor the flow of further photos, not end the torture. The fact of torture, itself sufficient cause for disgust, was made more politically difficult by the fact that these photographs, taken by soldier-participants, seemed to represent it as a sexualised entertainment (Sontag 2004).[12]

As the controversies around explicit images suggest, disgust and desire are not necessarily mutually exclusive: 'disgust always bears the imprint of desire. These low domains, apparently expelled as "Other", return as the object of nostalgia, longing and fascination' (Stallybrass and White 1986: 191). Photographs of bodies arouse these responses because, as psychoanalytic photography theory implies, there is a similarity between looking at other bodies and looking at photographs of bodies, and our visceral responses to such photographs are connected to the notion that photographs have a special connection to reality, even while we may recognise that they are not always truthful.

12 Sontag speculated that the forms of torture shown seemed designed to be photographed, and that the photos might be an example of the adaptation of the vocabulary of SM pornography circulated on the internet: 'Most of the photographs seem part of a larger confluence of torture and photography; a young woman leading a naked man around on a leash is classic dominatrix imagery' (Sontag 2004).

TECHNOLOGICAL BODIES

The camera as mechanical eye

Recent writers have considered photography in terms both of the bodies depicted and of its relationship to the bodies of the viewer and of the photographer (Crary 1993; Jay 1993). They suggest that photographs should not be thought of in terms of a single, centred and disembodied 'gaze' but as part of a new visual practice which presumes an embodied observer. **Jonathan Crary** places photography in the context of a range of popular nineteenth-century toys and devices which produce illusions of movement or depth. Devices such as **mutoscopes** and **stereoscopes** were enjoyed precisely because they 'tricked the eye' and, as Linda Williams has suggested, because of the tactile bodily sensations they provided since the observer engaged with them by holding the eyepiece of the machine or cranking a handle (Williams 1995: 14).[13]

JONATHAN CRARY (1993) **Techniques of the Observer: On Vision and Modernity in the Nineteenth Century**, Cambridge, MA: The MIT Press.

13 Williams argues that understanding photography in relation to the body is particularly crucial for erotic images since the observer engages with them by touching their own body as well as the machine through which they are viewing or the paper of the image (Williams 1995: 14).

The **mutoscope** was one of many entertainment devices developed as a result of the Victorian fascination with the phenomenon of persistence of vision, in which the human brain retains an image for a fraction of a second longer than the eye actually sees it. The mutoscope was an arcade machine invented in 1895 by Thomas Edison. It was basically a mechanised version of a flipbook, in which a person looked through a viewer and cranked a handle to flip the photographs inside, which gave the images the illusion of continuous movement.

The **stereoscope** was a form of entertainment popular from the 1850s. It consisted of either a hand-held or a cabinet-style viewer and pairs of photographs on cards. The pictures were taken from different viewpoints corresponding to the spacing of the eyes. The stereoscope was constructed so that each eye only sees one photograph, giving the impression of a three-dimensional image. Sometimes tinted tissue paper was used as a backing, adding colour to the image when seen through a backlit viewer; or pinpricks included to simulate sparkling jewels or streetlamps; or objects painted on the tissues so that they would suddenly appear when held to the light.

See ch. 3, pp. 129–30 for more mention of stereoscopes.

MARTA BRAUN (1992)
Picturing Time: The Work of Etienne-Jules Marey (1830–1904), Chicago: University of Chicago Press.

Early scientific uses of photography give us an idea of its significance for understanding the human body. In the 1880s, the French scientist Etienne-Jules Marey used photography to explore human and animal physiology. As the photography theorist **Marta Braun** explains, Marey developed special cameras and photographic techniques to study human and animal locomotion (Braun 1992: ch. 3). His contemporary, the American artist Eadweard Muybridge, performed similar experiments. His images of a horse in motion, published in 1878, were sensational because they showed for the first time that horses ran in a different way than was usually pictured.

Through their photography, Marey and Muybridge opened up to vision things that the human eye could not perceive. This ability of photographic technology to expand the capabilities of the eye was noted by writers, photographers and filmmakers in the early part of the twentieth century. In the 1920s and 1930s, the camera (both the still and the motion camera) was understood as a kind of mechanical eye. As the Soviet filmmaker Dziga Vertov expressed it:

> I'm an eye. A mechanical eye. I, the machine, show you a world the way only I can see it. I free myself for today and forever from human immobility. . . . My way leads towards the creation of a fresh perception of the world. Thus I explain in a new way the world unknown to you.
>
> (Vertov 1923 quoted in Berger 1972a: 7)

The literary critic and philosopher Walter Benjamin also commented on the ability of photography and film to expand perception. For Benjamin, this was part of their utopian, liberatory potential: in enabling people to see the world in new ways, it offered them the possibility of questioning and ultimately changing their everyday lives (Benjamin 1936: 229–30). A number of theorists have argued that cinema produced an expanded gaze at the cost of an increasing immobility of the body (Manovich 2001: 107–9; Friedberg 1993: 28). Early photography required its subjects to be static, even using an apparatus to clamp the 'sitter' still for the duration of the exposure. However, photography quickly became a relatively mobile practice, and now the incorporation of cameras into mobile phones (cellphones) that can also be used to transmit and view images, gives photography a different relation to the body. If film let our vision go wandering while rendering our physical bodies increasingly immobile, now 'mobile' technologies travel with us: the expanded gaze locks our bodies to the technology, we move, but 'hooked up', 'plugged in', 'online' (Manovich 2001: 114). Thus, the technology which gives us this bigger perceptual world also changes the ways we inhabit the physical world which surrounds us. The camera is one of a number of machines (including telephones and computers) which appear to be like prosthetics in that we treat them as extensions of our own bodies but which change the ways we physically engage with the world. The very presence of the camera transforms the

212

scene, it *intervenes* in reality. The camera threatens to take over and displace the eye: it gets between the viewer and the viewed and 'shapes reality according to *its* terms' (Krauss 1986: 116). The experience of looking through the camera, and the conventions surrounding photographic practice, affect the way we see. Seeing through the camera is different from seeing without it and, since photography, seeing is a changed practice.

The camera and other technologies for seeing also affect the way we value our own sense of sight. The cultural theorist **Lisa Cartwright** has argued that in medicine, photography and cinematography 'supplanted or replaced sensory perception', since the data produced via these techniques came to be

LISA CARTWRIGHT (1995)
**Screening the Body:
Tracing Medicine's Visual
Culture**, Minneapolis and
London: University of Minnesota
Press.

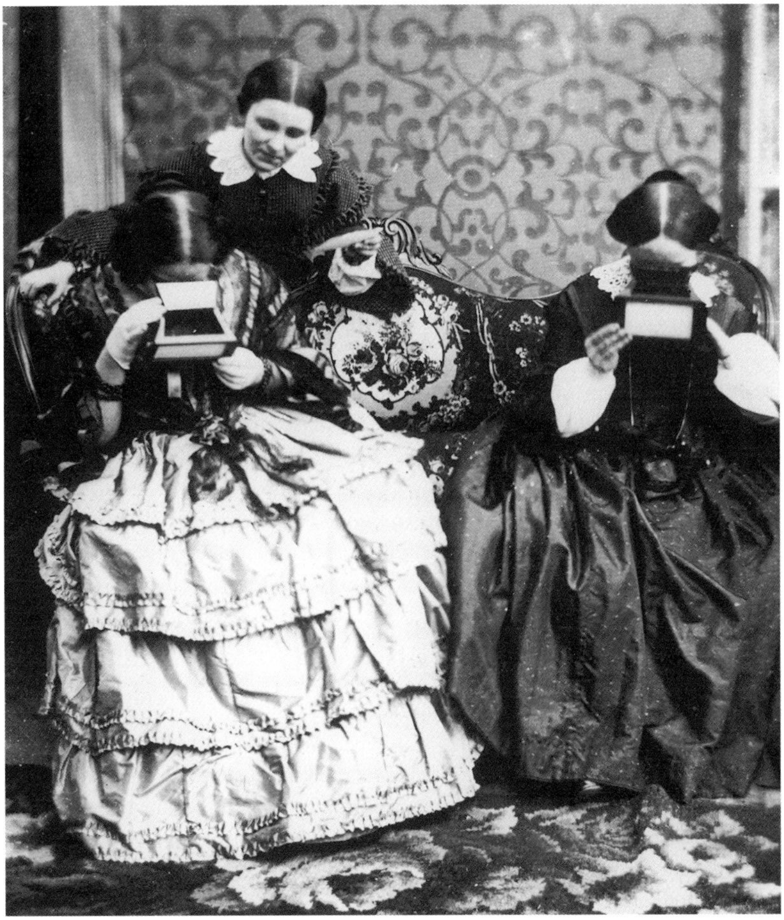

4.8 L.L. Roger-Viollet, *Women Using Stereoscopes, c.* Second Empire
This photograph is a reminder that women, as well as men, enjoyed optical toys and the pleasures of spectatorship.

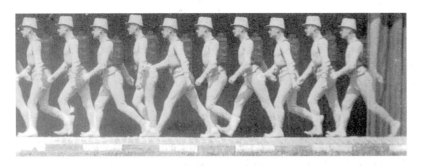

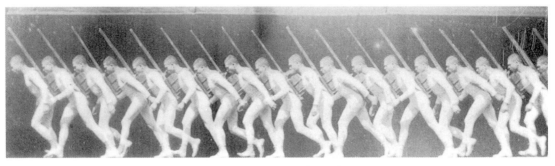

4.9 Etienne-Jules Marey
Marey's 'chronophotographic' studies can be understood as part of the drive to increase the efficiency of human
motion in the military, in industry and in sport

seen as having more authority than the doctor's or technician's own observations (Cartwright 1995: 34). Indeed, these images not only affect our understanding of our own vision, but also fit with understandings of what counts as authoritative forms of knowledge. In the case of foetal ultrasound scans, the images allow obstetricians to depend less on the pregnant woman's account of her own pregnancy. Yet while doctors may view sonograms as a source of information and means of diagnosis, these images are popularly understood (like early X-rays were) as a kind of photograph, a portrait of the unborn child. They shape our perception of life before birth, and seem to support the view that the foetus is a person, hence the use of such images in anti-abortion campaigns (Taylor 2000).

Non-photographic media such as X-rays (radiography), ultrasound (sono-grams) and magnetic resonance imaging, techniques such as tomography (which allows cross-sections or slices through the body to be imaged) together with microscopic photography (micrography), enable us to see aspects of the body not visible to the naked eye (Ewing 1996). Yet these photographic and non-photographic imaging techniques actively transform the body in the process of representing it. Nineteenth-century surgical experiments combined photography and cinematography with vivisection, as in the 1898 film of a dog's beating heart (Cartwright 1995: 20). Other medical imaging techniques had inadvertent and unexpected effects on bodies, producing tumours and cancers (notably radiography; see Cartwright 1995: chs 5 and 6).

Interventions and scientific images

Many techniques for visualising the interior of bodies are intended to prevent extreme forms of intervention. Intervention is associated with loss of objectivity. By surgically entering the body, the scientist disturbs its natural order or normal functions. Yet even Marey's techniques for picturing motion, which developed out of his rejection of animal vivisection, produced a selective representation of the body. Marey attempted to remove from the picture all features of the body not connected to its motion, all the 'readable' signs which the physiognomist is anxious to record. Through his photographic technique, 'Marey effectively reorganised the body to make it embody its own status as an object subject to laws of temporality and duration' (Cartwright 1995: 36).

Marey was involved in the 'science of work', the European equivalent of the 'scientific management' techniques of the American Frederick Winslow Taylor. From 1911, Frank Gilbreth, a follower of Taylor, used Marey's chronophotographic techniques to break down, analyse and reorganise the movements of a person at work (Braun 1992: 340–8; Lalvani 1996: 139–68). The shift from the analysis and classification of bodies, as in physiognomy, towards their corrective transformation is described by Michel Foucault as part of a general shift in the exercise of power in the modern period.

The Visible Human Project demonstrates the relationship between the exercise of power and the project of making the body the subject of knowledge. This project, commissioned in 1993 by the United States government, involved making images of two human cadavers (one male, one female) using computed axial tomography (CAT) and magnetic resonance imaging (MRI), then dissecting them into thousands of slices, and photographing each slice to produce a detailed 'atlas' of the body – a complete digital/photographic anatomy (Waldby 2000). The images are used by companies and institutions for research purposes and in the production of, for instance, crash test dummies and prosthetic body parts. This project is similar in intention to Bertillon's development of a police archiving system, only here the filing cards are replaced by the electronic database. As with Bertillon, the project aims to make bodies intelligible. In doing so, it represses the singularity of the bodies used and the diversity of human bodies. The male body is presented to us as 'complete', 'normal' and 'representative', yet it is also the body of a 39-year-old man called Joseph Jernigan, who was convicted of murder and donated his body to science before being executed by lethal injection in Texas. This is the cadaver of a criminal killed by the State, dissected and turned into a representation by the Federal Government. The particular history of this singular corpse points to the violence and policing involved in the production of rational scientific knowledge via photography. The representation that circulates as the Visible Human Male is not Joseph Jernigan but a body as object, isolated from its social and physical context and its sensory entanglement with the world.

The Visible Human Project necessarily omits the ways in which the body is already culturally inscribed, meaningful and historical, as it turns it into the object of rational, scientific knowledge (Curtis 1999: 263). The project shares something with the human genome project and with biometric security systems, which have very different social aims, but also involve a translation of physical bodies into information stored in a digital database.

The body as machine

The reduction of a human being to a 'data set' is a new development in an historical tradition of thinking and representing the body in mechanistic and

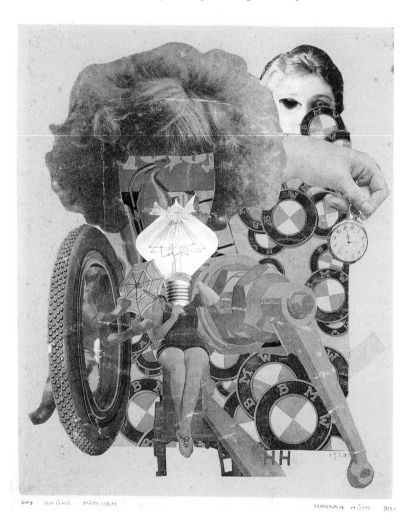

4.10 Hannah Höch, *Das schöne Mädchen* (*The Beautiful Girl*), photomontage, c. 1920
The photomontages of the Dada artist Hannah Höch celebrate the 'New Woman', playfully juxtaposing magazine images of women with photographs of machine parts, but also seem critical of the uniform, idealised and machine-like mannequins depicted in the same magazines.

technological terms. Almost a century before the Visible Human Project, the photographs and films of Marey and Gilbreth were among a large number (including industrial, commercial, medical and art photographs) which contributed to the perception of the human body as a machine. This perception depended on a highly idealised and utopian concept of the efficient, smooth-running machine, which ignored the ways in which certain kinds of machines mutilate bodies (for example, in factories and war). In popular culture, an

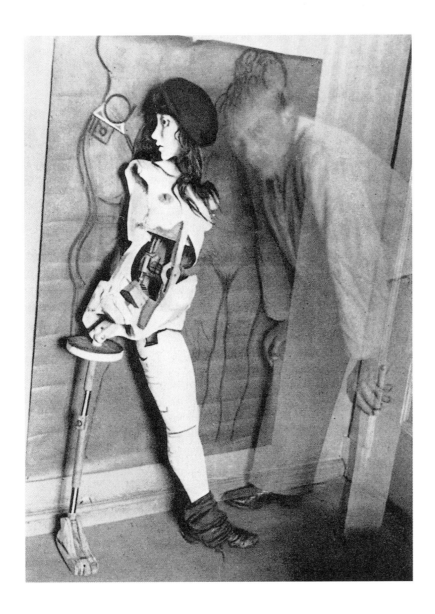

4.11 Hans Bellmer, *Hans Bellmer with First Doll*, 1934

uneasy mixture of traditional ideas of femininity and the new image of the disciplined, machine-like body informed the representation of women. In 1920s Germany, women's magazines enthusiastically showed female aviators and female celebrities beside their cars, while advertising photographs depicted women as automaton-like mannequins (Lavin 1993: 3, 59 and 132).

Avant-garde artists used new photographic techniques both to celebrate technology and to critique it.[14] The political stakes of this became clear in the late 1930s, as Nazi ideology embraced a version of the machine body. This combined ideas of classical perfection from ancient Greek art with the racial classifications of nineteenth-century physiognomy, and Fordist/Taylorist ideas of the ideally machine-like, efficient and uniform worker. The ideal male body was a self-contained, muscular, armoured machine. Some avant-garde photography challenged the image of the body as machine favoured by Taylorism and the Nazi emphasis on the male body as a disciplined fighting machine. The art historian **Hal Foster** shows how Hans Bellmer's Surrealist photographs of dismembered and mutilated dolls, which can be read as deeply misogynistic and paedophiliac, have different connotations in this historical context. Bellmer's photographs of distorted bodies, complete with prosthetic limbs, are simultaneously a rebuke to the militaristic ambitions of Fascism and Fascist ideas of bodily (and racial) purity, and a reminder of the real mutilations produced by technological warfare (Foster 1993: 114–20).

In the early twenty-first century, amputees have become more visible through news coverage of war in Afghanistan. When photographer Giles Duley lost one arm and both legs from a land-mine, he made a studio self-portrait to show his injuries without presenting himself as a victim.[15] In 2012 the Summer Paralympics, held in London, made use of an advertising campaign entitled 'Meet the Superhumans' that represented disabled athletes as heroes who had overcome adversity (Figure 4.12). The posters showed a confrontational group photograph of the British team in an 'edgy' urban space, suggesting the team's competitiveness and their challenge to conventional images of the disabled. Athletes with aerodynamic wheelchairs or hi-tech artificial limbs gave the impression of technologically enhanced, cyborg bodies. David Howe argues that it is these technological enhancements, which have increased the profile and commercial success of the Paralympic games, that continue to marginalise individuals with more severe impairments, whose bodies are less co-ordinated, less 'media-friendly' or whose impairments are not visible (Howe 2013).

The 2012 Paralympics imagery was effective in increasing the visibility and social acceptability of certain kinds of disabled bodies, and could also be said to have helped normalise the technologically transformed body. In the Channel 4 'Meet the Superhumans' television advertisements, technology appears as both a cause of disability (the car crash, the bomb) and as the means by which disabled bodies become 'superhuman'. Such representations of technology as enhancing or improving bodies have to carefully navigate the sense that

14 Maud Lavin notes that 'the Berlin Dadaists prided themselves on both affirming and negating their principal themes. While they were applauding the newly rationalized man – associated in their minds with the machine, the engineer, and the Soviet artist Vladimir Tatlin – they were also satirizing man-as-machine idealism, particularly as it had been played out in the carnage of World War I' (Lavin 1993: 16).

HAL FOSTER (1993)
Compulsive Beauty,
Cambridge, MA, and London:
The MIT Press, chs 4 and 5.

15 The portrait can be viewed at http://gilesduley.com/#/galleries/becoming-the-story-self-portrait-london-2011.

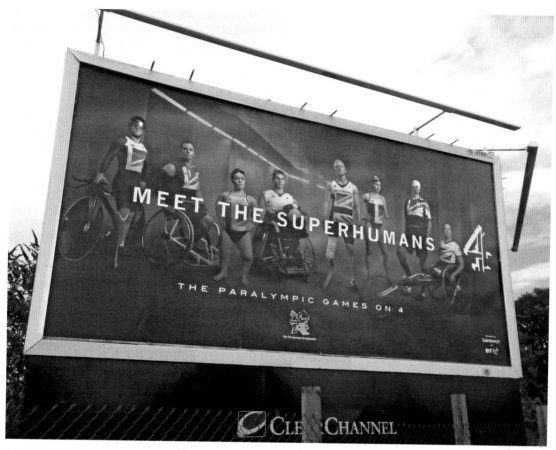

4.12 'Meet the Superhumans', Channel 4 advertisement for the Paralympics, 2012.

technology is threatening to humanness and destructive to bodies and the potential for violence in the intersection of human and machine.

In a 1998 advertisement for the Saab 9-3 car (see Figure 4.13), the photographic/digital montage blending car seat and human torso recalls the avant-garde use of **photomontage**. However, avant-garde montage depended on the incongruous and violent juxtaposition of bodies and machine parts. Here, the seamless blend of chair and torso suggests a painless transition from human to technological. The seat seems more human than the torso, its headrest becomes a kind of head, and it has wrinkles, while the torso has no hairs or irregularities, its flesh a polite shade of beige, smooth as a mannequin. The head is missing but not severed; instead, the neck discreetly fades into shadow. Thus the advertisement humanises technology, presenting the merging of technology and the body as desirable but also as inherently safe. The text

photomontage The use of two or more originals, perhaps also including written text, to make a combined image. A montaged image may be imaginative, artistic, comic or deliberately satirical.

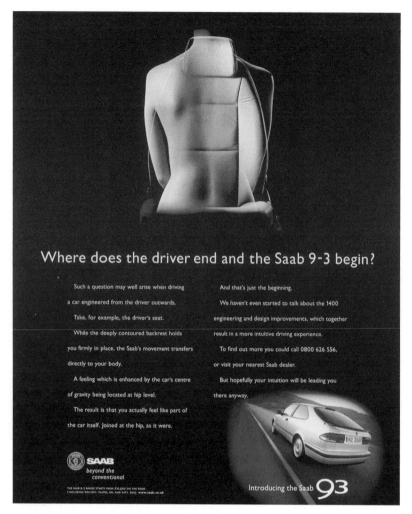

4.13 Advertisement for Saab, 1998 (original in colour)
One of the themes central to current representations of the body is the merging of the corporeal and the technological, and the potential displacement of the body by the machine. By presenting a seamless merging of human and machine, this advertisement reassures us of the harmlessness of the car, and conceals the fact that technology can pierce and shatter bodies.

confirms this: 'you actually feel like part of the car itself. Joined at the hip, as it were.' The ad has the task of picturing the intermingling of body and machine without reminding us of the violent collision of flesh and metal which happens in a car crash. To tread over this line would undermine the ideology of the harmlessness of technology which it is promoting, and make the image disturbingly suggestive of death.

Digital imaging and the malleable body

The Saab ad is a good example of digital compositing. As the new media theorist Lev Manovich says,

> Compositing in the 1990s supports a different aesthetic characterized by smoothness and continuity. Elements are now blended together, and boundaries erased rather than emphasised . . . where old media relied on montage, new media substitutes the aesthetics of continuity.
>
> (Manovich 2001: 142)

More recently, advertising has gone further, manipulating human bodies in illusionistic ways, to give flesh and skin a plasticity beyond that of actual human flesh. A simple, and relatively restrained example can be found in advertisements for the confectionary Toblerone, which show people's faces with one cheek implausibly stretched to reveal Toblerone's 'trademark' triangular shape. Distorted bodies are not new to photography: the photographers André Kertész and Bill Brandt are well known for their optically distorted nudes. In their work, the distortions are achieved using lenses and mirrors. However, the distortions produced using digital image manipulation software (such as Adobe Photoshop) are not optical but painterly, made by retouching the image. In this respect, they have more in common with drawn and painted animated cartoons than the photographs of Kertész and Brandt. Animation uses techniques of distortion, including 'squash and stretch' to give an illusion of realistic motion. This was at its height in Disney animations of the 1920s and 1930s. The filmmaker Sergei Eisenstein gave the term 'plasmatic' to that elastic quality of animation that allows bodies in cartoons to metamorph into other bodies, objects to come alive. Eisenstein saw this in Utopian terms, as expressing the potential of humans to change themselves and their world, rejecting the idea of static form in favour of a return to 'primal protoplasm' (Leslie 2002: 231–7). By the late 1930s, though, other writers were noting the loss of this playful shapeshifting in favour of more sanitised cartoons in which, in the view of the theorists, the physical violence meted out on the pliable cartoon bodies disciplined the audience and encouraged a submissive masochism (Leslie 2002: 171–7). This raises the interesting question of how to read the digitally 'morphed' bodies of contemporary culture. Digital manipulation of photographs gives the body a photo-real malleability related to the fluidity given by film special effects, most famously the liquid metal body of the T-1000 in the film *Terminator 2* (dir. James Cameron, 1991). As with the plasmatic character of animation, this can be understood in utopian terms, as enabling us to imagine a new and liberating cyborg, 'posthuman' body; or in dystopian terms, as part of the continued objectification of the human body, in a culture where body parts are increasingly understood as commodities (as in the trading of human organs for medical use).

The everyday use of digital manipulation to 'enhance' (slim and smooth) images of women, particularly in women's magazines has been countered by campaigns such as Dove's 'Campaign for Real Beauty'. However, their emphasis on 'photoshopping' tends to overlook the extent to which studio photography already constructs the body through lighting, lenses, cosmetics and styling. Nor is 'real beauty' the issue: such images of women are not damaging because they are not accurate depictions of actual women, but because of the underlying implication that women ought to be plastic, malleable, manipulable. As with the 1930s cartoons, there is a thin line between playful shapeshifting and masochistic submission.

CASE STUDY: MATERIALISM AND EMBODIMENT

Sometimes the material substance of the photograph can allude to an absent body without bodies being directly figured in the image. The African-American artist Lorna Simpson became known for photo-text works such as *You're Fine* (1988), and *Necklines* (1988) that explore black women's experience through anonymous figures with their backs to the camera or fragments of bodies such as details of skin and hair. When, from 1994, she began screen-printing photographs of buildings and public spaces onto felt panels, critics read it as 'a shift from political content to aesthetic form' despite the references to sexual encounters in the accompanying text and the connection between the textures of felt and hair (Belisle 2011: 158, 168–70).

Other images of bodies without figures include Helen Chadwick's *Viral Landscapes* (1988–9) and Joan Fontcuberta's *Hemograms* (1998), made using blood samples as negatives. Recalling **Julia Kristeva**'s psychoanalytic concept of the **abject** as well as Bakhtin's notion of the grotesque aspects of the body, these visceral practices evoke anxieties about bodily contamination and the horror of the uncontained, fluid body that appears in epidemics (particularly evident in responses to AIDS).

More recently, an interest in embodiment has been part of a larger turn towards an increased attention to the physicality of photography and the relationship of the viewer to the photograph. Since the early 2000s, cultural theorists have started to consider nature, technology and matter as animate or active, emphasising the tactile or 'haptic' qualities of visual culture, and the ways in which the human body itself can become a medium for images (Marks 2002; Mitchell 2004; Latour 2005; Bennett 2010; Belting 2011). These theories have influenced 'new materialist' approaches in the arts, which view materials as active and dynamic, resisting or lending themselves to certain uses (Bolt and Barrett 2014). After all, a photograph is never simply an image, but always a material object (even if on a screen) which comes with its own sensual properties (Edwards and Hart 2004: 1). Materialist photographic practices invite the viewer

abject In Julia Kristeva's *Powers of Horror* the abject is associated with material that produces a reaction of horror because it threatens the distinction between subject and object or the boundary between self and other. Abject material can include bodily fluids, wounds, or corpses, and the horrified or repulsed responses these can produce in the viewer is not because of what they *mean*, since abjection is not to do with symbolic meaning, but to do with deep, primal and unconscious drives.

KRISTEVA, JULIA (1982), **Powers of Horror: An Essay on Abjection**, New York: Columbia University Press.

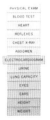 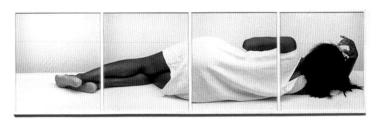

to address not just what the picture represents, but what kind of a physical object it is.

4.14 Lorna Simpson,
You're Fine, **1988**

Some photographic processes produce a strong impression of the direct and unique imprint of a human body at a given moment. In Floris Neusüss' whole-body photograms (cameraless photographs) first exhibited in the 1960s, the image hovers between a sense of direct presence of a body and its absence and inaccessibility – in the photogram the body is only ever a silhouette or a shadow, a shape that we have to imaginatively 'fill in' and it becomes not an object, but an event or performance (Figure 4.1). In practices that emphasise the physicality of the photograph itself, embodiment is still present, not as a depicted figure, but in the body of the viewer and the relationship between the viewer's own bodily experience and the physical material of the photograph. Liz Deschenes' photographic installation *Tilt/Swing* (2009) references early twentieth century avant-garde exhibition design and experiments with perception. Deschenes' photograms are empty, and face the viewer like dull or fogged mirrors, so that the subject of the installation becomes the viewer or visitor as they move around the space. The interest in the photograph as object is also evidenced in many exhibitions, including *The Photographic Object*; *The Object of Photography* (Photographers' Gallery, London, 2009), *The Unphotographable* (Fraenkel Gallery, San Francisco, 2013) and *What Is a Photograph?* (International Center for Photography, New York, 2014; Squiers 2013).

The concern with the materiality of the image is a response to the apparent 'dematerializing' tendencies of digital culture, and the impact of digital photography. Photography has been transformed into a 'dry' computer-mediated process rather than a 'wet' chemical process. For professional photographers and artists, the experience of making photographs has become a less visceral, messy experience. Some photographers have responded by turning to old processes such as the daguerrotype, finding in it a kind of physicality and intimacy that suits an exploration of the human body: for example, Chuck Close and Jerry Spagnoli's series of finely detailed nudes from the early 2000s, or Mark Kessell's close-up daguerrotypes of faces and hands, that parallel the chemical process with the chemistry of the body through scratches, blotches and solarization (Rexer 2002: 30–43). News photographer Michael O'Brien began producing

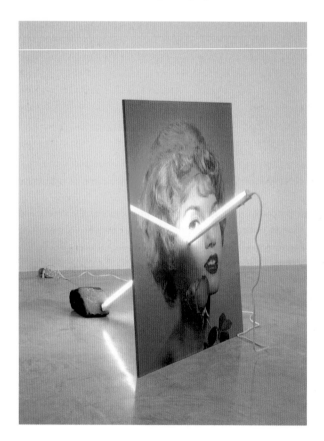

4.15 Marlo Pascual,
***Untitled*, 2010**

224

portraits of homeless people in Austin Texas as 'a way to stay busy' when digitisation and online publication made him increasingly unemployed. He used an old view camera with Type 55 Polaroid film that produces both negative and print instantly so the print can be given to the subject immediately. This enabled him to establish a reciprocal relationship with the vulnerable people he photographed and to give them 'something tangible' while the camera with its slow exposures and black focussing cloth covering the photographer meant a more lingering, gentle experience (O'Brien and Waits 2011).

As with Simpson's felt pictures, in such practices the materiality of the photograph can stand in for the materiality of the body. In 2000, Heather Ackroyd and Daniel Harvey's *Mother and Child* used photosynthesis to expose a negative on grass: the resulting object is, like the family-snap moment it represents and the human body itself, growing, transient and impossible to preserve unchanged. Other artists use found photographs and objects to produce a more material, visceral experience for viewers in an age of screens: Marlo Pascual, for example, uses found photographs of actors and folds them or applies lit candles, rocks, pieces of furniture and other objects to break apart the surface (Squiers 2013: 43; Figure 4.15).

Artists using photography have often linked the photograph as object to the physicality of the human bodies it represents or evokes, or emphasised its status as a fetish, but in the twenty-first century and in the context of increasingly computer-based labour, such parallels take on new significance. Photography is understood as more than just a process of making visual images, but a means of constructing physical objects that produce certain kinds of embodied experiences for an audience.

THE BODY IN TRANSITION

Photography, birth and death

Photography's particular ability to objectify the body associates it with death – this is expressed by **Susan Sontag**: 'All photographs are memento mori. To take a photograph is to participate in another person's (or thing's) mortality, vulnerability, mutability. Precisely by slicing out this moment and freezing it, all photographs testify to time's relentless melt' (Sontag 1979: 15).

The qualities that make a photograph work as a fetish – its immobility and silence, its ability to freeze a past moment – are deathly qualities (Metz 1985: 83–4). Roland Barthes has argued that our horror at photographs of corpses is related to our faith in photographic realism. Since, according to Barthes, we tend to conflate the real and the live, a photograph of a corpse seems to attest 'that the corpse is alive, as corpse: it is the living image of a dead thing'; in other words, the corpse appears to have been live at the moment of its encounter with the camera (Barthes 1984: 78). Photography renders the living

SUSAN SONTAG (1979)
On Photography,
Harmondsworth: Penguin.

ROLAND BARTHES (1984)
Camera Lucida, London: Fontana.

immobile, frozen: the living person photographed may subsequently die, but remains preserved in the photograph, while the dead body photographed is 'horrible' since it is given the same 'immortality'. According to Barthes, photography 'produces Death while trying to preserve life' (Barthes 1981/1984: 92; Jay 1993: 450–6).

Current attitudes to post-mortem photography are related to the tendency to accept photographs as reflections of the real as well as to contemporary attitudes towards death (Rosler 1991; Linkman 2011). Everyday (as opposed to sensational or exceptional) death is among those aspects openly represented in medieval carnival but was increasingly relegated to the private realm in the modern era.

The practice of photographing dead relatives or friends was a publicly acceptable practice until about 1880, with photographs of corpses displayed openly in American homes, and professional photography studios advertising the services. It is usually assumed that the practice stopped, particularly in English-speaking countries. Anthropologist Jay Ruby has challenged this perception, showing that it continues in present-day North America, but has come to be seen as shameful, or highly private, and is seldom discussed, and the photographs are seldom displayed publicly (Ruby 1995: 161). Helen Ennis has noted a re-emergence of vernacular postmortem photography in Australia as digital cameras have taken hold (Ennis 2011).

Originally, the significance of corpse photography was to preserve a likeness. For many bereaved people, photographs still privately served this function, but

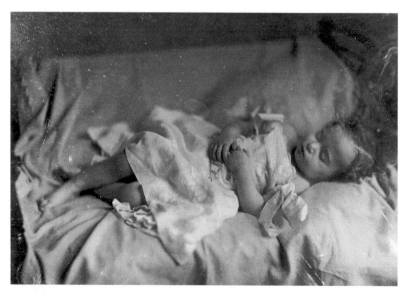

4.16 Post-mortem daguerreotype of unidentified child, Boston, c. 1850s
An example of the mid-nineteenth-century tendency to photograph the dead as if they were asleep.

a new public unease grew around photographing the dead. Ruby suggests that the fact that nineteenth-century photographers were frequently commissioned to produce post-mortem photographs does not necessarily mean that theirs was a culture much more comfortable with death than our own. Great effort was made in early postmortem photography to present the corpse as merely asleep, in keeping with funerary practices and cultural representations which depicted death as a deep sleep (a notion still present in the modern 'chapel of rest') (Ruby 1995: 63–72; Figure 4.16). However, this representation of death as sleep derives from the Christian belief in the afterlife of the soul: the image complies with the notion that the soul of the person continues to live after bodily death (see Linkman 2011: 21–62 for a detailed discussion of this).

The beauty of the Victorian post-mortem photograph was intended to suggest a soul at peace. In fashion photography in the early twenty-first century, the 'beautiful corpse' reappears in staged, sexualised and aestheticised images of violent death, as in a series of photographs commissioned as part of the reality TV show *America's Next Top Model* in March 2007 that involved the women contestants posing as corpses in 'crime scenes'. Media critic and activist Jennifer L. Pozner pointed to this as an example of extreme, misogynistic objectification (Pozner 2007).

Though nowadays commercial photography studios do not photograph corpses, a number of art photographers have done so. The early 1990s saw a growth in the number of exhibitions and photography projects including *Photodeath* (Australian National Gallery, 1991) and *The Dead* (National Media

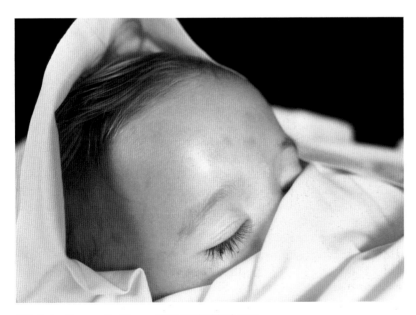

4.17 Andres Serrano, *The Morgue (Fatal Meningitis II)*, 1992

Museum, UK, 1995). Audrey Linkman (2011) lists projects from the 1970s to the early 2000s by Jeffrey Silverthorne, Hans Danuser, Rudolf Schäfer, Louis Jammes, Clare Strand, and Walter Schels (Linkman 2011: 161–2). To these we can add Sally Mann's collection *What Remains* (2003), Andres Serrano's *The Morgue (Cause of Death)* (1992) and Sue Fox's *Post-Mortem* (1997).

Some mortuary photographs such as Sue Fox's perhaps seem more 'horrific' because their documentary-style composition has the effect that Barthes noted: of making the dead seem alive.[16] Yet Fox also depicts the corpse dissected, as meat, stripped of personality. However, Serrano's photographs continue the Victorian religious tradition of making the dead appear asleep. In some of the Morgue series, the wounds and marks on the flesh operate also as references to Christian religious iconography (in one entitled *Rat Poison Suicide II* a wound on a foot recalls the stigmata, the crucifixion wounds of Christ which appear miraculously on believers). Serrano's Morgue series, like his series depicting body fluids, including the (in)famous *Piss Christ,* draws on a Roman Catholic tradition of representing the bloodied bodies of martyrs and the dead Christ. Transposed to photography and expanded to include the representation of bodily fluids such as urine and semen, and deaths by suicide and illness, this becomes a very heretical version of Catholicism.

Serrano's photographs are lush, large scale, and highly staged (using studio lighting techniques). The combination of this high artifice and the Catholic references gives the images a kitsch quality. As with the kitsch of Cicciolina or the camp aesthetic of the 1950s Physique photos, the bodies here have much in common with Bakhtin's characterisation of the classical body. The composition and sumptuous colour conflict with the horror of the subject-matter. Serrano's photographs hint at a social world through small but poignant details such as the mark left on a child's flesh by the elastic of its sock.

The Dutch photographer Rineke Dijkstra also uses the body to speak of a world of experience beyond that depicted in the photograph. She too makes monumental photographs of people, shot with a large-format camera and exhibited in an art gallery context. A set of three naturalistic photographs of mothers depict them naked, or almost naked, in front of a plain white wall, clutching their tiny newborn babies. In one photograph a woman named Julie stands before the camera wearing only the disposable underpants commonly used after childbirth, her hand protecting the baby's face from the camera flash (Figure 4.18). What she has been through only an hour before seems to show in her eyes and her ambiguous expression. In common with many of Dijkstra's subjects, she has a dazed look. This may be the result of the physiological changes associated with natural childbirth (the surge of adrenalin and hormones), since the baby was born at home. Dijkstra paired this series with another series of photographs of male bullfighters just out of the ring, and they also look in a state of shock, pupils dilated, seemingly unaware of their blood-spattered and dishevelled appearance. The subjects of both series have

16 For reproductions and discussion of Sue Fox's photographs see Townsend 1998.

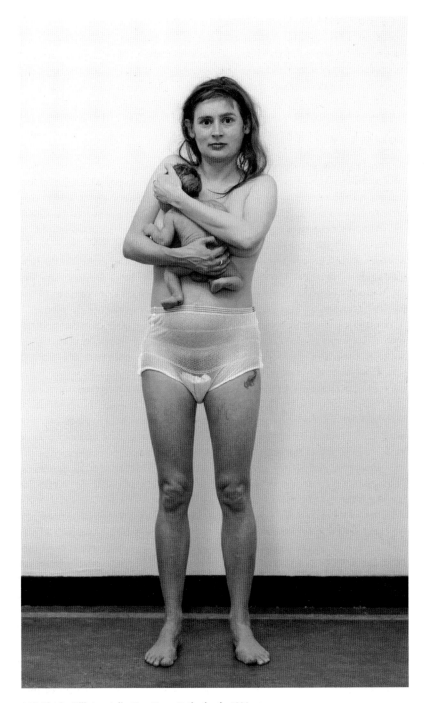

4.18 Rineka Dijkstra, *Julie, Den Haag, Netherlands*, 1994

been transformed through experience. In *Julie*, the act of birth is still present, traced on the bodies of both mother and child. Dijkstra's photographs point to the animal aspect of the body at the same time as they depict bodies as social and changeable, transformed by experience. Although they are displayed to us, these bodies are not frozen, not easily objectified. They are bodies in transition.

SUMMARY

As the examples in this chapter demonstrate, campaigns and conflicts over photographs of the body hinge on the relationship between photography and reality and the extent to which the photograph is understood as a reflection of reality. Yet it is also clear that photography is one of the means by which individuals are constructed as social subjects: the use of photographs in medicine, policing and in scientific studies of work shows how photography participates in the disciplining of the body. In disciplining the body, these photographic practices also exclude (or attempt to exclude) those sensory and social aspects of bodies and bodily experience which do not conform to the particular understanding of the body on which the practice is premised. A photograph constructs different meanings for human bodies through the way it represents them, and through the circumstances in which it circulates. Some photographs may conform to and reproduce dominant ideas about sex, about race, about what it is to be human, male or female, whilst other photographs challenge these ideas. However, these meanings are not firmly attached to particular methods, techniques or styles; instead, the significance of particular ways of photographing bodies changes with its context. For instance, the muscled male body and the classical aesthetic could be associated with either a coded homoeroticism (in American physique magazines of the 1950s) or the deeply homophobic culture of Fascism. In all instances, photographs do not simply speak of 'the body' but of particular bodies, of social groups and the relationships of power between them.

Photographs also speak to the body, in that they are sensual physical presences experienced by an embodied visitor. The haptic and tactile qualities of the photograph and of the processes of taking or making photographs suggest that the human body is not only a subject in photography, it is the basis of the subjective experience of photography. Even, or especially, in the age of screen media, looking is a sensual, embodied practice.

230

CHAPTER 5

Spectacles and illusions

Photography and commodity culture

ANANDI RAMAMURTHY

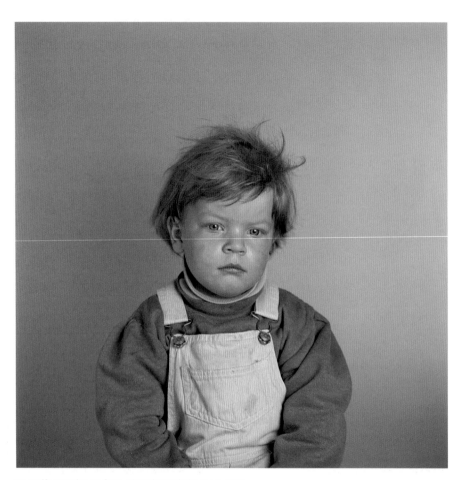

5.1 Wolfram Hahn, #1 from *Disenchanted Playroom*, 2006

Spectacles and illusions
Photography and commodity culture

INTRODUCTION: THE SOCIETY OF THE SPECTACLE

> In societies dominated by modern conditions of production, life is presented as an immense accumulation of spectacles. Everything that was directly lived has receded into a representation.
>
> (Debord 1967: section 1)

In the twenty-first century, commodity relations rule our lives to such an extent that we are often unaware of them as a specific set of historical, social and economic relations which human beings have constructed. Like any cultural and technical development, the development of photography has been influenced by its social and economic context. The photograph is both a cultural tool which has been commodified as well as a tool that has been used to express **commodity culture** through advertisements and other marketing material. Capitalism's exploitation of the mass media and visual imagery to create an array of spectacles and illusions that promote commodity culture can be explored by considering some of the ideas that the French Situationist Guy Debord discussed in his book *Society of the Spectacle* (Debord 1967).[1]

In this book Debord outlines the way in which modern industrial capitalist society has created a world in which the majority of people are increasingly passive and depoliticised as a society of spectacles, both media and otherwise, absorbs us into a world of illusions and false consciousness. He describes these spectacles as 'a permanent opium war' and discusses the way in which 'the

1 Debord was a leading member of the Situationist International who was influenced both by Marxist and anarchist thought. Their main aim was to encourage ordinary workers to become involved in the transformation of everyday life immediately and not wait for a distant revolution. They were involved in the French student protests of 1968. Through Debord's writings, the ideas of the Situationists gained longevity.

spectacle presents itself as a vast inaccessible reality that can never be questioned. Its sole message is: "what appears is good; what is good appears"'. Debord's concern is with the endless proliferation of media messages – frequently visual and usually photographic – that saturate our existence both inside and outside our homes, through billboards, television, films, magazines, newspapers, the internet, commodity packaging and ephemera. These media messages are predominantly focused on a world of glamour and entertainment where labour relations and issues of conflict (when addressed) are usually packaged around an array of feel-good factor articles and presentations to remove the sting from conflict and contradiction and to present these as a distant 'other' world. Debord's key argument is that ordinary people as spectators of spectacle remain passive, uncreative and therefore powerless in the running of society. Wolfram Hahn draws our attention to the passive stupor that even children are induced into through televised spectacles (Figure 5.1). Baudriallard and other postmodernists have also recognised the impact of spectacles and media messages in the late twentieth and twenty-first century. They have described the world of spectacle as a *hyperreality*, as a form of representation in which mediated images appears more real than reality itself. Baudriallard argued that we live in a world of simulations where images of reality circulate through the media and impact on our understanding of the world more than lived experience. In such a world mediated messages circulate to reference other mediated messages gaining their value through their intertextuality (Baudriallard 1983; Eco 1987). Debord however highlights how the spectacle does not simply impact on our reality but is part and parcel of the entire political economy that Marx describes which creates a 'false consciousness' from which he believes we can free ourselves. Baudriallard denies this possibility. Douglas Kellner has recently applied Debord's ideas to discuss media spectacles in the late twentieth century (Kellner 2003). Kellner discusses the way in which global mega-spectacles such as celebrity murder trials like that of Oscar Pistorius in South Africa are given so much space and time on television and in the rest of the mass media that these events are elevated in the minds of media consumers in the Global North to positions of greater or parallel importance to those of wars or other atrocities.[2] Photographic images – both still and moving – are crucial in supporting the society of spectacle.

> Cameras define reality in two ways essential to the workings of an advanced industrial society: as a spectacle (for masses) and as an object of surveillance (for rulers). The production of images also furnishes a ruling ideology. Social change is replaced by a change in images. The freedom to consume a plurality of images and goods is equated with freedom itself.
>
> (Sontag 1979: 178–9)

Margaret Bourke White touched on these ideas as early as 1937 in her documentary photograph, 'The American Way' (Figure 5.2). The image

[2] The global north refers to those countries that have high socio-economic status and are listed above 0.8 on the UN's Human Development Index. Most of these countries are in the northern hemisphere. These countries are primarily those that benefited from the Transatlantic slave trade and colonised nations in the Global South during the eighteenth and nineteenth centuries

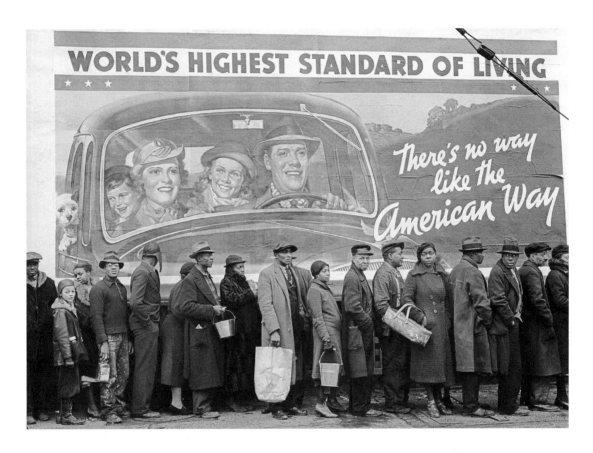

suggests the possibility of challenging false consciousness by highlighting the contradiction of lived experience.

This chapter will consider examples of the photograph as a commodity and its role in promoting and representing commodity culture. It will explore the way in which capitalist ideology has impacted on forms and styles of photography which we see today and the way in which photographic use and practice is organised. This first section on the society of the spectacle concentrates on exploring examples of commercial photography which are outside of the field of advertising and marketing, the kind of photography which needs to be understood commercially but is not created to sell commodities, but to sell itself.

Photographic portraiture and commodity culture

John Tagg has described the development of photography as 'a model of capitalist growth in the nineteenth century' (**Tagg 1988: 37**). The rise of commodity culture in the nineteenth century was a key influence on the way in which this technology was developed and used. The way in which

5.2 Margaret Bourke White, *The American Way*, 1937

JOHN TAGG (1988) 'A Democracy of the Image: Photographic Portraiture and Commodity Production' in **The Burden of Representation: Essays on Photographies and Histories**, London: Macmillan.

daguerreotype Photographic image made by the process launched by Louis-Jacques-Mandé Daguerre in France in 1839. It is a positive image on a metal plate with a mirror-like silvered surface, characterised by very fine detail. Each one is unique and fragile and needs to be protected by a padded case. It became the dominant portrait mode for the first decades of photography, especially in the United States. See also p. 130.

carte-de-visite A small paper print (2½–4⅛") mounted on a card with the photographer's details on the reverse. This way of producing photographs for sale was developed by André-Adolphe Disdéri in France in 1854. Eight or more images were made on the same glass negative by a special camera with several lenses and a moving plate-holder. The prints were then cut up to size. Such prints could be produced in very large numbers. See also p. 132.

ELIZABETH ANNE McCAULEY (1994) **Industrial Madness: Commercial Photography in Paris 1848–1871**, New Haven, CT, and London: Yale University Press.

SUREN LALVANI (1996) **Photography, Vision, and the Production of Modern Bodies**, Albany, NY: SUNY Press.

photographic genres were affected by capitalism is illustrated in Tagg's essay by the demand for photographic portraits in the nineteenth century by the rising middle and lower-middle classes, keen for objects symbolic of high social status. The photographic portraits were affordable in price, yet were reminiscent of aristocratic social ascendancy signified by 'having one's portrait done'. Tagg describes how the **daguerreotype** and later the **carte–de–visite** established an industry that had a vast clientele and was ruled by this clientele's 'taste and acceptance of the conventional devices and genres of official art' (Tagg 1988: 50). The commodification of the photograph dulled the possible creativity of the new technology, by the desire to reproduce a set of conventions already established within painted portraiture. It was not, however, simply the perspectives and desires of the clients visiting photographic studios that encouraged the adherence to convention, but also the attempt, as McCauley has highlighted in her study of mid-nineteenth-century commercial photography in Paris, of the small business owners of these photographic studios both to establish themselves as part of a bourgeois class, as well as to assert the claim of photography as a highbrow art (**McCauley 1994**).

Suren Lalvani has also highlighted the way in which nineteenth-century photographic portraiture was a powerful expression of bourgeois culture through the conventions of display in both dress and the arrangement of the body. Lalvani gives examples of the way in which these portraits upheld capitalist values about the nation–state, the family and the individual. 'In bourgeois portraiture, it is especially the arrangement of heads, shoulders and hands – as if those parts of our body were our "truth"' that act to furnish evidence of the individual as though 'the world may be civilized by the domestication of the hand by the head' (**Lalvani 1996**: 52). Photography was not acting independently in the development of the bourgeois ideal, but borrowed from and was influenced by other disciplines such as physiognomy and phrenology (see ch. 4, pp. 173–7). Lalvani also points out the way in which these images, frequently produced for public consumption as the craze for *cartes-de-visite* developed, represent the development of a spectacular economy of images. He notes how political leaders of the time as well as royalty exploited the craze for collecting and exchanging the cartes-de-visite to promote their own popularity (see ch. 3, p. 132). President Lincoln, for example, is said to have believed that the *carte* which Brady produced of him helped him to win the presidency. Photographic portraiture in the nineteenth century therefore acts as an example of the influence of bourgeois thought both on the form and style of portraiture as well as an example of the development of 'a regime of the spectacle' (Lalvani 1996: 82). Today Facebook and Instagram photography continue the conventions of display that express the capitalist promotion of the individual most acutely witnessed through the development of the selfie.

The regime of the spectacle developed in the early days of photography consolidated both racial and class-based hierarchies as they produced new forms of commodities. The *cartes-de-visite* acted to affirm the status of Europe's bourgeois class through named and individual portraiture. At the same time the picture postcard marked out a colonial spectacle that consolidated a racialised regime of representation, where Africans and Asians were measured and recorded for their difference, rarely named but marked instead as exotic and subjugated types to enhance the European bourgeois' belief in their own superiority.

Just as photographic genres have been affected by commerce, so has the development of photographic technology. The 'Instamatic', for instance, was clearly developed in order to expand camera use and camera ownership. In turn, this technology limited the kind of photographs people could take (**Slater 1983**). The camera capabilities of the mobile phone with filters to create images that adhere to established conventions of photographic practice perform a similar function.

DON SLATER (1983) 'Marketing Mass Photography' in H. Davis and P. Walton (eds) **Language, Image, Media**, Oxford: Blackwell.

Photojournalism, glamour and the paparazzi

Another area in which we can observe the operations of spectacle is that of photojournalism. Although a documentary form of photography which has been used to highlight atrocities and deliver information and news, the photojournalist is keenly aware of the need for spectacular images that will draw attention on the news stand and encourage sales above those of rival newspapers. In Britain and America in the 1930s, the establishment of publications such as *Life* and *Picture Post* saw the photographic image begin to command what was considered newsworthy. Dramatic and sensational images meant newsworthiness. In wars and situations of conflict photojournalists have frequently intervened to create more dramatic images. In 1937 for example, H.S. Wong placed a baby on to the railway line of the bombed-out Shanghai railway station to create an image which could captivate the despair and devastation of the Japanese bombing. More recently in 2003 Brian Walksi a photographer for the *Los Angeles Times* montaged two photographs, taken seconds apart, of a British soldier with a civilian crowd in Basra to create a 'better' image. The altered image that ran on the front cover of the Los Angeles Times, along with the two original photographs used to create it, can be viewed at http://sree.net/teaching/lateditors.html. Walski was instantly fired by the LA Times upon the discovery that he had photo-shopped the image. His actions were seen as inexcusable in a world which maintains a belief in journalism as capturing raw reality as opposed to 'acknowledging news as a subjective cultural practice shaped by naturalized conventions' (**Carlson 2009**) The pressure put on journalists to feed back dramatic images can be seen as a key reason for Walski's action. Such drama does not always exist in life. Stories without it are ignored by the papers. On some occasions, people have used their knowledge of the newspapers' need for photographs of high drama to get their perspective heard. With the publication in 1988 of the *Satanic Verses* by Salman Rushdie, quiet protests by Muslim organisations against the book

MATT CARLSON (2009): 'The Reality of a Fake Image: News norms, photojournalistic craft, and Brian Walski's fabricated photograph', **Journalism Practice**, 3(2): 125–139.

did not make the news. It was only when one group in Bradford, UK, provided the cameras with a dramatic image of book-burning that their voice and position was heard. Such an image of people acting as extremists is a recognised strategy for selling papers.

Although individuals have sometimes intervened in the production of the spectacle, it has been primarily produced by those with the financial clout to do so. The first Gulf War saw a major PR company, Hill & Knowlton, promote the need for war after being hired for the princely sum of $5.64 million by an organisation of 13 members (Citizens for a Free Kuwait). Their PR strategies included Kuwait Student Information days, countless press conferences and the production of documentary images that they distributed of Iraq's invasion of Kuwait and of human rights abuses there. As Mark Miller writes, 'indeed, throughout these crucial months [September to December] there was, on TV, no other footage of or about Kuwait: every single documentary image that was telecast had been prepared by Hill & Knowlton' (Miller 1994: 64). In the recent invasion of Iraq, Freimut Duve, the expert on media freedom for the Organisation of Security and Cooperation in Europe argued: 'We are entering a historic phase where war is turned into a spectacle. A high percentage of people are watching without realising that it is a war' (AFP 2003). During the first days of the war, it was presented as a real media spectacle to be followed around the clock. Viewers were led to believe that they were 'very close' to the action, 'but it was in fact a form of reportage, especially on US television, that avoided the reality of war. It was extremely far away from the realities in the cities, in the region' (Rahir 2003). In the light of such promotional practices, Walski's montage is an inevitable practice which acknowledges the constructed and ideological nature of news discourses.

The development of the spectacle has also spawned a journalism of the sensational. The tabloid newspapers such as the *Sun*, *Daily Star*, *Daily Mirror* and *News of the World* in Britain, and the *Globe*, *Star* and *Enquirer* in the USA focus entirely on the production of a journalism of the spectacle which promotes and destroys stars and celebrities to provide a treadmill of stories of sex and scandal. Photographs play a major role in these stories. Two styles and forms of photography dominate this journalism: the official photographs provided by the stars and their media machines, and the 'stolen' paparazzi photographs that often tell a different story. Carol Squiers has discussed the photography of stars, the origins of paparazzi photography and the exploitation of the image of Princess Diana by the tabloid press. In her essay she outlines how the posed images of stars taken for editorial and advertising purposes place a high value on the stars' ability to control and manipulate every aspect of the image – lighting, makeup, costume, hairstyle, facial expression, posture, and gesture. 'Big stars usually demand and receive blanket control over who takes the pictures, how they will be constructed, where in a publication they will be used, and which images will be reproduced' (**Squiers 2003**: 274). The effect is to construct the stars as individuals in a spectacularly perfect world,

CAROL SQUIERS (2003) **Over Exposed: Essays on Contemporary Photograph**, New York: The New Press.

238

with perfect clothes, perfect hair, perfect bodies, perfect lips and perfect lives. These, usually high gloss photographs are akin to the photographic world of advertising by their creation of technically perfect images of dreams and images of desire. By contrast, the paparazzi photographs are the opposite of this. They are images of individuals caught unaware – stripped of their luxury and dazzle.

> Rather than molding a celebrity as a uniquely magical creature the way posed pictures do, paparazzi images show celebrities as more mundane figures who sometimes inhabit the same space (a city sidewalk, a parking lot), perform similar tasks (shopping, jogging) and wear same clothing (blue jeans, sloppy sweaters) that the non celebrity does.
>
> (Squiers 2003: 274)

These images are sometimes blurred and of poor quality, but this simply adds a mark of their authenticity – their 'truth'. These photographs however, while seemingly reporting on the 'real' star and therefore apparently concerning itself with issues of the 'truth', channel the tabloid into focusing on the truth about stars as opposed to issues of the truth about how society operates. Paparazzi photography is also often a play between the celebrity and the photographer, with celebrities using photographers at particular moments to construct their image. Witness Diana's use of photographers on an official visit to India when her marriage with Charles was failing. She visited the Taj Mahal by herself and allowed herself to be photographed alone, against a backdrop of one of the most ornate monuments to love (Squiers 2003: 300). Her image captivated the journalists and she upstaged her husband in the news coverage.

More recently Beyonce posted photographs of herself drinking a glass of wine and relaxing with her daughter to prove that she was not pregnant again. The snapshot style of photography in these posts is important in producing an image of constructed authenticity that encourages interest and belief in their 'truth' value. This journalism of the spectacle has no moral conscious-ness and is not intended to encourage the viewer/consumer to reflect on the deeper conflicts in society. It is a journalism which feeds off personalities and stars created through former media coverage – both official and paparazzi. The image of stars is carefully managed. Too plastic, sensational and consumer focused an image can also have a detrimental effect and damage public opinion. This media game is acknowledged in popular cinema. *The Hunger Games* trilogy is set around an understanding of media propaganda. In the second film *Catching Fire,* mentor Haymitch Abernathy asserts to Catniss and Peeta 'you two are mentors now, from now on your job is to be a distraction so people forget what the real problems are', articulating Debord's state-ment 'What is good appears, what appears is good'. The need to control the celebrity image to ensure it appears real is also commented on when Plutarch Heavensbee promises Snow that punishing ordinary citizens while putting Katniss' wedding planning on display will serve to make her look shallow and disengaged. 'What's the dress going to look like? Floggings,' Plutarch suggests. 'What's the cake going to be? Executions . . . They're going to hate her so much, they might kill her for you.'

Celebrities and stars take care to project themselves as rounded personalities and photographic imagery is central in this orchestration. While Beyonce has signed one of the highest endorsement deals with Pepsi for $50 million which includes using her face on limited edition cans of drink and appearances in television commercials, she is also careful to keep involved in charity work to maintain her 'A' list status. These charity appearances are most importantly photographed to add to her carefully managed brand profile. The branding of her image has developed so extensively in 2013 that Beyonce's charity work is no longer found on her website under www.beyonce.com/charity but instead under 'beygood' to match the 'beyhive' section of her website that acts as a more traditional celebrity blog promoting people and companies that she offers association with. The centrality of the photographic image in communicating the Beyonce brand in music, fashion and good causes can be seen by the almost complete absence of any textual discussion of issues or experience. The images are left to resonate, to mean whatever the viewer invests in them. In #Beygood, the only verbal communication is of Beyonce's own compassion: 'Everything I am, with everything I do I have to give back, I have to reach out, we are all in this together'. It highlights the charity appearances, their photographic documentation and the totality of the site as a space to consolidate the Beyonce brand.

The management of appearance is an endless balance as Anthea Turner, a British television presenter, was to learn to her cost in August 2000 when she sold her wedding photographs to *OK* magazine. The story adds another dimension to the whole notion of the stolen image in commercial photography. On negotiating exclusive rights for her marriage photographs with *OK* magazine, Anthea claims that she was duped when asked to eat a new chocolate bar that Cadbury's were launching. As part of the agreement with *OK*, Anthea had agreed to supply one picture of her wedding to the press in general. She left *OK* to choose the image. *OK* magazine chose to sell a photograph of Anthea and her husband eating the new chocolate to all the tabloid newspapers, requesting them to mention the chocolate by name in the caption. An image of Anthea in her wedding dress was also displayed on the cover of *OK* magazine with a free Snowflake chocolate on the left-hand side. Inside were images of Anthea, her new husband Grant and celebrity guests eating the chocolate bar. The wedding appeared to be sponsored by Cadbury's, and with the free chocolate on the magazine cover, all readers could join in the celebrity wedding. The tabloids used the opportunity to condemn Anthea for what they do every day – exploit all opportunities for profit. They themselves obviously secured profit by condemning Anthea Turner. As Kevin O'Sullivan, the showbiz editor of the *Daily Mirror*, said, '[Anthea] certainly became the whipping girl, but you know, I think we all felt it was selling papers' (*Tabloid Tales*, 3 June 2003, BBC1). The photograph in this incident was pivotal, and what was on one level an official wedding photograph turned into a stolen, almost paparazzi-style image which destroyed her celebrity status. It took her six years to develop her public status and become reestablished as a television personality. The incident indicates the multiple levels of exploitation in the field of tabloid journalism – where the exploitation of commercial profit feeds a journalism of the spectacle.

Stock photography, image banks and corporate media

> The spectacle is the stage at which the commodity has succeeded in totally colonizing social life. Commodification is not only visible, we no longer see anything else; the world we see is the world of the commodity.
>
> (Debord 1967: Section 42)

In the glossy world of magazine culture and the proliferation of lifestyle blogs and sites on the web, there is another vast area of photography, which does not mark the existence of an event and does not constitute advertising – creative stock photography. These images fill increasingly vast digital image banks, where they can be bought and sold across the world. Generally, as David Machin writes, they can be spotted easily: they are those bright, airy images showing attractive models, flat, rich colour, and a blank background. And they are recognisably less than realistic (**Machin 2004**). The main reason for this is that the more multi-purpose and generic they are the more reusable they are, and therefore the more they will sell. The blank or reduced background, by de-contextualising the subject, enables the images to act as generic types. The settings that do exist are generic – a window, the sea, the mountains, an ocean or a nondescript city street. Where attributes or props do exist, they are symbolic – a computer to signify office, or a hard hat to highlight construction. The models too adhere to the mood of the generic image: 'the models are clearly attractive, but they are not remarkable, because a striking face, an easily recognisable face, will be less easy to re-use' (Machin 2004: 323). Machin argues that these images are changing the way in which we use and understand photography. The photograph is no longer witness here, its use is symbolic. What is interesting about these images is that they speak very little. The context provides meaning, just as the context in advertising provides meaning to those images (see 'The grammar of the ad', p. 253). The balance between denotation and connotation which Barthes discussed is no longer apparent (Barthes 1977b). This is a photography in which there is only connotation. As Frosh argues, the catalogues and archives act as 'a *concentrated representational space* through which images are materialized: made to emerge as physically discrete and at least minimally communicative resources' (Frosh 2003: 118).

DAVID MACHIN (2004) 'Building the World's Visual Language: The Increasing Global Importance of Image Banks in Corporate Media' **Journal of Visual Communication** 3(3).

This stock photography industry is dominated today by four firms: Getty Images, Corbis, Shuttershock and Fotolia who account for approximately $1.4 billion (50%) of the gross revenue of the industry. Corbis, established in 1989, is owned by Bill Gates and was set up because Gates believed that people would someday decorate their homes with a revolving display of digital artwork (Hafner 2007). It dominates the digital distribution of artworks from across the world. In 1994 the company shifted direction with the acquisition of significant photographic collections such as the Bettmann archive which holds some of the US's most iconic photographs, such as that of Rosa Parks riding on a bus in 1956 or of Marilyn Monroe on a New York subway grate. The aim was to build the most comprehensive digital photographic archive in the world. Getty Images established in 1997 always described their photographic collections as creative stock as well as editorial photography (news and documentary) for commercial use, although they have also acquired significant historical collections such as the Hulton Picture Archive and those of Time and Life magazine. With Corbis holding approximately 100 million images and Getty 80 million it is clear that these companies have immense control over the visualisation of human history. The nature of stock imagery has also impacted on our own production of imagery whether on Facebook, Flickr, Photobucket or Instagram.

Geoffrey Batchen has highlighted the impact of image banks such as Corbis on our understanding of traditional photography and the role of photography in the recording of history (Batchen 2003).

Today colour supplements cannot afford to pay photographers to shoot appropriate images for all their articles, so these stock images are a cheap way of brightening up a page. Getty inform photographers of the kinds of images that they are looking for and are clearly interested in being 'a leading force in building the world's visual language' as their promotional material asserts. John Morrish has highlighted how these stock images must be 'striking, technically superb yet meaningless' so that they will 'never conflict with the client's message' (Morrish 2001). Machin argues that while these images may appear to be meaningless, in the sense that they are able to absorb radically different meanings from their context, it is not helpful to see them in this way, since what these images are doing is reasserting the concepts of branding in a non-branding context.

Let us look at an example of a mundane stock image. It depicts a woman floating in the sea in tranquillity (Figure 5.3). In searching for this image in the Getty archive, in 2003 there were 94 pages of images that depicted a woman floating in the sea connoting tranquillity or relaxation. In 2008 there were over 1,600 images in the Getty Archive depicting women floating and relaxing. In 2014 there are 2,923, many of the images are extremely similar. This image was used on a supplement to the *Independent* magazine for 14–20 June 2003. The image acts to highlight a feature about the best beaches in Europe. The image, however, is typical of generic images that can be used in a variety of contexts. It could just as easily have been used to illustrate an article which asked whether our seas were polluted or not or to talk about dealing with stress. This woman floats in a sea that may not even be European. In fact this same image has been used in a 2003 travel brochure by British Airways for *tropical* beaches. Here she visualises a section on 'well-being', as the copy beside the image indicates: 'Ever imagined lazing around in your own pavilion on an isolated patch of white-sand beach, listening to the sound of waves on the turquoise sea, as the warm breeze and the touch of healing hands pass quietly by.' She is an indistinctive model, wearing an indistinct bikini in an indistinctive sea. The photograph is striking because of the slightly peculiar angle, which emphasises her forearm and the fairly bold swathes of colour in the blue sky and what appears to be a digitally retouched green sea. The image acts perfectly to represent concepts important to the process of branding, such as contemplation, enjoyment, well-being and relaxation. In fact, just in case you are in need of other similar images, when you do click on to such an image which interests you, Getty lists subjects and concepts which you may wish to explore to find similar images. The concepts are the descriptive labels, the moods that Getty perceives that the image contains. For this image they list 'contemplation, enjoyment, getting away from it all, heat, leisure activity, relaxation, serene people, vacations and well-being'. The list of concepts to indicate various types of enjoyment and calm is detailed.

The terms and concepts around which Getty archives can be searched privilege consumer relations. If we wished to search the archive for images that comment of the class-based nature of society it is virtually impossible to make effective searches. 'Class conflict' brings up images of classes in war zones or of students protesting about changes in education but not ones that consider wider questions about class relations in our current age of austerity, for example. The search facilities for images are extremely important given the millions of images in Getty's archive. Some will become practically inaccessible. This raises an important point about images, their commercial value and how profits are made.

One of the key factors which has made Getty and Corbis such profitable companies lies not simply in their ownership of images but in their ability to distribute them. Like all commodities they must circulate effectively. Getty and Corbis have corporate buyers who subscribe to their image banks, and receive feeds of new images that may be of value to them. This provides their customers with images that are relatively cheap per image but Getty makes their money through subscription, which maintains a large turnover. Their service in organising image access and the thousands of customers that turn to Getty and Corbis have meant that they pay photographers, whose labour and commodities they sell, only 20 per cent of the payout (which they have already reduced through their emphasis on increased circulation) and reap 80 per cent for themselves (Pickerell 2012). This system mirrors the increasing lack of profitability in the production of commodities world-wide where

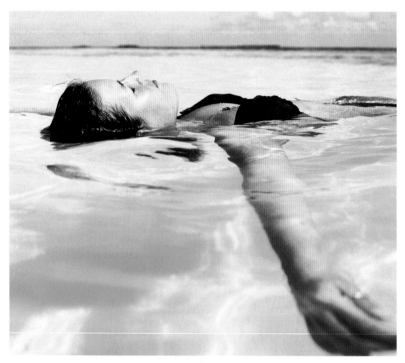

5.3 Stock image of a woman floating

trainers cost a few pence to make through the exploitation of workers in the Global South and the profits rest in the construction of global brands where exchange value is inflated through brand identities to reap profit from unknown workers' labour.

In 2011 the stock photography industry was worth $2.88 billion (Glückler and Panitz 2013: 7). Having transformed the world's media, however, it has now in turn been forced to re-invent itself. The increased participation of citizens across the world in photographic production has impacted on the work and profits of the large corporate image banks. At the end of 2012 there were 250 million photos uploaded to Facebook every day; 40 million daily uploads to Instagram; 10 billion photos on Photobucket from 100 million registered members; and there were 2.98 billion photos on Flickr available for public viewing (Pickerell 2013b). In 2003 and 2005 Shuttershock and Fotolia were established by young entrepreneurs as royalty-free archives that were more affordable for large and small corporations working in both print and digital media. The idea of Shuttershock enabled greater participation in the stock photo business. Anyone could upload photos without great investment and expense and create in particular those anodine, multi-purpose, generic shots of landscapes or human activity (that focuses on consumption rather than work) that are easily reusable in the world of commercial media. The rise of Shuttershock and Fotolia has not challenged photographic practice but it has undermined the profits of organisations such as Getty Images in a capitalist structure where circulation is essential for expansion and growth. In the light of these changes Getty has been forced to rethink their marketing practices as their profits on premium stock creative images began to fall from $561 million in 2012 to $300 million in 2013 (Pickerell 2013a). In 2007 Getty bought the pre-existing royalty-free stock photography company i-stockphoto to develop a midstock collection. However, while Getty had 25 million downloads from i-stock in 2010, by 2013 it was in the region of 10 million. As a result Getty images have established Thinkstock which describes itself as 'premium art-directed and user-generated royalty-free photos, vectors and illustrations' that are organised with budget users in mind. While a stock photograph in 2003 could command hundreds of pounds, in 2013 the figure is nearer £30 (Pickerell 2013c).

The drive to control the flow of images in both creative imagery and editorial has demanded access to images and footage of all major news events as quickly as possible and put pressure on agency staff to get access to strong images of events of global impact to maintain the reputation of the organisation as a key image source. This has at times led to unethical practices in image acqusition. In November 2013 freelance photojournalist Daniel Morel was awarded $1.22m in damages when Agence France-Press (AFP) and Getty images willfully infringed his copyright by sourcing his images from Twitter and distributing the images of the 2010 Haitian earthquake (Laurent 2013). Morel, a native of Haiti and a professional photojournalist who had previously worked for Associated Press, was in Haiti at the time and took photographs within minutes of the earthquake happening, including an image used by hundreds of newspapers and news sites worldwide of a woman being pulled from the rubble. It was first sold by AFP and Getty as belonging to Lisandro Suero. The extent of the damages awarded to Morel were because of what was described by his lawyers as the 'lackadaisical, dismissive and inexcusably ineffective' response by Getty and AFP to repeated requests on behalf of Mr Morel to 'set the record straight, get the pictures down from the websites of their paying customers and stop licensing his works under their names' (Official Transcripts 2013, *Morel vs. AFP and Getty*: 35).

While Getty and AFP acted in this manner, their copyright policy suggests their determination to uphold copyright infringement in the interests of both photographers and the archives and highlights their reserve right to charge five times the cost of an image that is used with copyright infringement. AFP and Getty sold 1,000 downloads of Morel's photographs, for some of which they were paid over $1,000. While Morel was paid over $1 million in damages, the subject of the image, the woman pulled from the rubble, has no rights over its use or over the commercial value of her own image.

The tension between corporations and photographers and the imbalance of power has led to photographers trying to establish their own image banks. Stocksy is one of the most recent, which one photographer describes as a sort of 'photographer-owned coop' that pays photographers 50% of payouts. The tension between photographers and corporations has a long history. It led to the establishment of Magnum photography cooperative in 1947 to enable photographers to maintain control over their own photographs in a world where circulation has become more critical than production in the drive for profit (Hawk 2013).

Commodity spectacles in advertising photography

While photographs are commodities in themselves, photography has also supported the buying and selling of every conceivable product and service, to the point where we are almost unaware of the medium of photography. Photographs for commerce appear on everything from the glossy, high-quality billboard and magazine advertisements to small, cheap flyers on estate agents' blurbs. Between these two areas there is a breadth of usage, including the mundane images in mail-order information and catalogues, the seemingly matter-of-fact but high-quality documentary-style images of company annual reports, the varied quality of commodity packaging, and of course the photography on marketing materials such as calendars, produced by companies to enhance their status. Within the traditional histories of photography, advertising photography has largely been ignored, despite the fact that photography produced for advertising and marketing constitutes the largest quantity of photographic production. One possible reason for the lack of documentation and history-writing in this area is that commercial photography, for the most part, has not sought to stretch the medium of photography, since one of the key characteristics of all commercial photography is its parasitism. Advertising photography cannot be seen to constitute any kind of photographic genre; rather, it borrows from and mimics every existing genre of photographic and cultural practice to enhance and alter the meaning of lifeless objects – commodities.

By reading the opinions of advertising photographers for the students of commercial advertising, we can explore the way in which this photography has developed the commodity spectacle. One of the first instances suggesting the power of photography for advertisers dates back to the mid-nineteenth century, when the photographer Disdéri wrote an article offering 'indispensable advice' to exhibitors in the 1855 *Exposition Universelle* in Paris, emphasising the speed, exactitude and economy of photographic reproductions and suggesting 'wouldn't the propagation of a model of furniture appreciated by all the visitors to the exposition attract numerous orders to the manufacturer?' (McCauley 1994: 196). It is clear that as forms of mass production began to develop, the photograph, which constituted one of these forms, was also seen as a medium through which these commodities could be popularised and marketed. In this sense, from the very beginning photographs were employed to induce desire and promote the spectacle of commodities. Thomas Richards discusses the display of commodities at the Great Exhibition of 1851 as a spectacle of goods, a spectacle which was soon taken up by advertisers as they moved from advertising products to brands (Richards 1990).

By the inter-war period, photographs began to be used more regularly within advertisements. This was partly due to the increased production of illustrated papers during the period, but also due to the development of a visually literate British public during the 1930s, the result of the dissemination of photography through the illustrated newspaper. Two comments by those working in the industry highlight the shifting concerns for photographers during this period:

> The advertisement photographer visualises his work . . . holding its own . . . where it will not be looked at deliberately unless it has the power to arrest and intrigue the casual eye of the reader.
>
> (Stapely and Sharpe 1937)

> now, the leading London dailies devote whole pages to photography, while the Sunday and Provincial press freely scatter photographs throughout their editorial columns. Photographic news brought photographic advertising and a public that had been educated to visualise the world's events soon began to visualise its own needs.
>
> (George Mewes of Photographic Advertising Limited 1926–60 quoted in Wilkinson 1997: 28)

It is clear that while the simple use of arresting photography was enough in the early period, as the century progressed and the regime of spectacle developed, advertising photography has sought to develop dreams and desires in the images that they create. The period of the 1930s was one of flux; while some simply interpreted the role of the advertising photographer as one who would create a striking and arresting image, George Mewes of Photographic Advertising Limited understood the role of the photographer as one who would create needs and desires. In doing this, they did not create new forms of photography, but borrowed forms of photography popularised through the new illustrated papers and through the developing film industry.

Helen Wilkinson notes how advertising photography began to appropriate, first, journalistic methods of a seemingly 'realistic' style as well as the conveyance of narrative through a combination of image and text; and second, commercial cinematic conventions. For example, deep shadows to convey emotions were employed along with the close-up for a more naturalistic style of portraiture, which still retained an element of glamour. Some of the cinematic conventions of photography can be seen in stock photography sheets belonging to Photographic Advertising Limited. One sheet represents head-and-shoulder portraits of women (Figure 5.4). All the women have been shot in dramatic studio lighting and wear makeup, conventions which adhere to an image of cinematic glamour. All are photographed in a relatively relaxed manner and seem to reflect moments within a narrative. Some of the women are even involved in mundane activities like eating and drinking, actions which would not have been recorded in conventional portraiture. Thus they all appear to have a degree of naturalism which could be misconstrued as 'realism' despite their obvious glamour. The relationship between glamour and naturalism is a key aspect of 1930s advertising photography, as Wilkinson describes in relation to a 1930s Horlicks advertisement which depicts a close-up shot of a glamorous and attractive woman in a relaxed image of Horlicks-induced sleep. The degree of naturalism allowed the ordinary consumer to identify with the model and combined with an image of glamour, provided a route to encourage desire that was transmuted to the product through the advertisement.

Glamorising mundane activities and commodities is part of the process through which photography has helped to imbue products with meanings and characteristics to which the commodity has no relationship. As Karl Marx noted, commodities are objects – usually inert – that have been imbued with all kinds of social characteristics in the marketplace. Marx called this process the fetishism of commodities, since in the marketplace (which means every place where things have been bought and sold) the social character of people's labour was no longer apparent, and it was the products of their labour instead that interacted and were prominent. Photography is pivotal in acting to fetishise commodities in the world of advertising by investing products with what Marxists have described as false meanings (see Williams 1980; Richards 1990). Advertising photography aims to turn something which is ostensibly mundane into an exciting and arresting image. In selling dreams and aspirations commercial photography has painstakingly created elaborate yet intimate images that invite the viewer to almost imagine a story rather than just see the objects in the shot (Ward 1990).

By the late twentieth century promotional culture had developed further to not simply suggest the ability of the commodity to fulfill aspirations but to centre the commodity as a personification of desires such as happiness and love. Robert Goldman remarked in a study of 1980s advertising imagery: 'ads offer a unique window for observing how commodity interests conceptualise social relations' (**Goldman 1992**: 2). Commodities in the late twentieth and twenty-first century are no longer inanimate objects but are invested with human qualities with which we build relationships. Perfumes, for example, literally morph into being emotions and feelings that only humans and animals can feel. They have been given names such as 'obsession', 'passion', 'happy', 'freedom', 'dazzling'. And where they are not attributed with such emotions, narratives, tag lines and images suggest that we can have fulfilling relationships with products. Omega's campaign with Cindy Crawford titled 'Cindy's choice' presents her with a larger than life watch that, through the power of

ROBERT GOLDMAN (1992)
Reading Ads Socially,
London: Routledge.

248

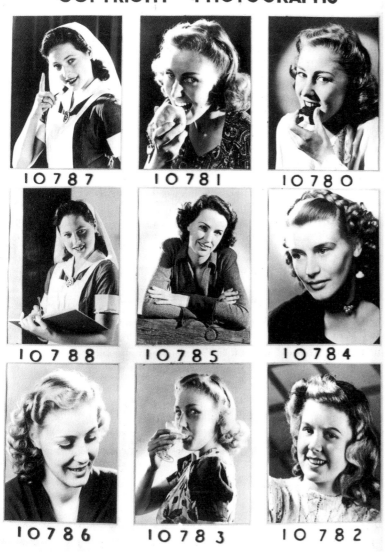

5.4 Advertising stock sheet W1910783 from the Photographic Advertising Agency, London, 1940s

photomontage, literally encircles her protectively, replacing her husband as her partner. Photographs play a crucial role in bringing commodities alive. In another Omega advertisement Cindy looks seductively out at the viewer and the watch – enlarged to the size of a human – is photographed next to her with the tagline of 'Omega and Cindy – time together', constructing Cindy through text and image as in a relationship with the watch. As Joachim Giebelhausen wrote in 1963, 'The camera has long been the favourite medium of the advertiser. It convinces with its realism even as it fascinates with the magic of a dream so that even the people of our time are cajoled into worshipping the idols it creates' (Giebelhausen 1963). As the language of advertising has become ever more sophisticated, images have increasingly been left to speak without anchorage (Barthes 1977) and the tag line 'Cindy's choice' becomes too uni-directional. The 2003 advertisement for Omega depicts a photographic image of Cindy Crawford sitting in the driving seat of an open topped car, with wind-swept hair deep in thought (The image can be viewed at: www.omegawatches.com/press/press-kit-text/364). The words 'Cindy Crawford' and 'Choices' in slightly different fonts are placed discretely over the image to the lower left divided by the photograph of a larger than life Omega Constellation watch (the only object to be enlarged in the ad) which is literally suspended between the words. Given the incompleteness of the phrase 'Cindy Crawford . . . choices' and the watch's positioning within the phrase, the watch through its size and solidity is left to resonate as a resolution to the predicament of choices; it literally fills the gap in the phrase. The use of the photograph enables the advertisement to resonate with possibilities. The advertisement does not tell us that the watch is a solution to her choices, but we are encouraged to construct this meaning as its presence forecloses the possibility of other choices. What is visualised is a world in which commodities become central to the story of ourselves. As Jhally asserts, advertising tells us that the way to happiness and satisfaction is through the consumption of objects: 'things . . . will make us happy' (Jhally 2006: 13). While advertising traditionally placed the commodity at the centre of visual messages, such as that above, and photographs have been used to enhance the appearance of things, there are times when photographic styles of realism and documentary have been employed to challenge a world of glamour.

All photographs will be viewed by different people in different ways, whether in commercial contexts or not. The same photograph can also mean different things in different contexts, even different styles of photography will carry different messages. Let us look at an advertisement which does not use a style of photography normally associated with advertising. Because advertisers have traditionally been concerned with creating glamorous, fantasy worlds of desire for their products, they have tended to shy away from the stark, grainy, black and white imagery traditionally associated with documentary images and photojournalism. They have gone instead for glossy, high-colour photography to enhance their images of desire. Yet, at times of company crisis, or when companies have wanted to deliberately foster an image of no-nonsense frankness, they have used black and white imagery. In 1990, a short while after Nelson Mandela was released from jail by the South African authorities, the Anglo-American Corporation of South Africa brought out an advertisement entitled 'Do we sometimes wish we had not fought to have Black trade unions recognised?' Underneath this title was a documentary photograph of a Black South African miner, in a show of victory. At a moment when Anglo-American foresaw massive economic and political change, they attempted to distance themselves from the apartheid regime. Yet Anglo-American was by far the largest company in South Africa, 'with a near total grip over large sectors of the apartheid economy'.[3] While presenting this advertisement to the public, De Beers – Anglo's sister company, in which they had a 35 per cent stake – also cancelled their recognition agreement with the NUM at the Premier Diamond Mines, despite 90 per cent of workers belonging to the union. The frank and honest style of address which black and white photography provided hid the reality for black workers in South Africa. The miner depicted was in fact celebrating his victory against Anglo-American in 1987. Here, at another moment of crisis, Anglo-American appropriated this image of resistance. The parasitic nature of advertising enables it to use and discard any style and content for its own ends. Anglo-American are no longer interested in fostering this image (they declined permission to have the advertisement reproduced here). There is an added irony in Anglo-American's use of this image, since it is not strictly speaking a documentary image at all, but a montage of two images used to capture the mood of the strike as the *Independent* saw it.

Black and white imagery has been used in other company contexts at moments of crisis. Carol Squiers has discussed the way in which they have been used in annual reports. Black and white, she notes, 'looks more modest and costs less to print'. As Arnold Saks, a corporate designer, said: 'There's an honesty about black and white, a reality. . . . Black and white is the only reality' (**Squiers 1992**: 208). In severe cases of company crisis, even the black and white photograph could seem to be extravagant. Northern Rock's Annual Report for 2007 following the nationalisation of the bank in order to prevent its collapse used no images.

In the world of consumer advertising, black and white documentary photography has also been used to try to encourage the idea of rational consumer choice creating a kind of factual illustrative photography, which suggests an attention to scientific detail. An advertisement for Halfords children's bikes uses this kind of image to emphasise the inappropriateness of other manufacturers' children's handlebars. It is an interesting advertisement since the photograph does not actually represent their product, but a design fault in their rivals'. The advertisement also highlights the way in which the text of advertisements is crucial in anchoring their meaning. Angela Goddard and Guy Cook both discuss the way in which texts anchor meaning (Cook 1992; Goddard 1998).

3 As stated in anti-apartheid campaign literature of the time.

CAROL SQUIERS (1992) 'The Corporate Year in Pictures' in R. Bolton (ed.) **The Contest of Meaning: Critical Histories of Photography**, Cambridge, MA: The MIT Press.

The symbolic value of using or not using a photograph has also been discussed by Kathy Myers in her exploration of Green advertising. At times advertisers have chosen to use and not use photographic images in an attempt to find symbols of ecological awareness (**Myers 1990**).

Today photographs are primarily used to visualise concepts and situations. In marketing today branding is central. While brands have existed since the 1880s and first acted as an assurance of quality for particular commodities, as brands developed they began to create personalities, suggesting 'lifestyles' and with the aid of photographic imagery, fully fetishising commodities by privileging the social interactions of the market place and hiding the social characteristics of labour, as in the Omega watch ad above where we learn nothing about how the watch was made. Today, however, brands transcend beyond the material commodity to communicate not just a product but a human experience. Brands, for example, have associated themselves with emotions and qualities that belong to human beings such as inspiration, determination, fearlessness, impatience and happiness. Nike are no longer in the business of selling trainers but aim to 'enhance people's lives through sports and fitness', IBM don't sell computers but 'solutions' (Klein 1999). In this context photographs often act to resonate with our own experiences, triggering associations and feelings in us that latch on to memories and meanings in our own personal lives, hence the millions of 'creative' photographs that fill both corporate and small scale image banks constructed to symbolise concepts. In moving beyond the marketing of material goods to the marketing of ideas and feelings, in the twenty-first century brands are no longer advised to even sell to consumers but to situations (Tenno 2009).

Helge Tenno's arguments are integrally linked to the changes taking place in methods of communication as a result of the rise of digital technologies. These changes have been hailed as groundbreaking in terms of the possibilities for consumer interaction and involvement in communication processes. Such ideas increase the centrality of viewers/consumers as creating not simply the meaning of texts but the texts themselves, shifting processes which we have seen in the production of photographic imagery. While this suggests the possibility of increased agency (groups can represent themselves), the vast accumulation of messages, visual and textual, both outside and inside digital spheres are frequently mediated through corporate communications.

How can we analyse the way these messages are structured? Do the semiotic approaches of Roland Barthes, Judith Williamson and others continue to offer ways to interrogate these texts and their role in the making and maintenance of ideologies and the hegemony of commodity culture (**Barthes 1973, 1977b; Hall 1993, Williamson 1978**)? The next section, 'The grammar of the ad', will use some of the ideas of scholars writing about advertising and mass culture to explore in detail how we may be able to read the commercial messages on new media platforms.

KATHY MYERS (1990) 'Selling Green' in C. Squiers (ed.) **The Critical Image: Essays on Contemporary Photography**, Seattle: Bay Press.

ROLAND BARTHES (1973) *Mythologies*, London: Granada; (1977b) 'The Rhetoric of the Image' in S. Heath (ed.) **Image, Music, Text**, London: Fontana.

STUART HALL (1993) 'Encoding/Decoding' in S. During (ed.) **The Cultural Studies Reader**, London: Routledge (first published 1980).

JUDITH WILLIAMSON (1978) **Decoding Advertisements: Ideology and Meaning in Advertising**, London: Marion Boyars.

THE GRAMMAR OF THE AD

CASE STUDY: THE COMMODIFICATION OF HUMAN EXPERIENCE – COCA COLA'S OPEN HAPPINESS CAMPAIGN

In unravelling the meanings of images, Roland Barthes, Judith Williamson, Robert Goldman and **Paul Messaris** have all explored the structure of advertisements and have tried to find systems which could be applied to help decode any commercial message. In his essay 'The Photographic Message', Barthes described photographs as containing both a denoted and a connoted message (**Barthes 1977a**). By the denoted message Barthes meant the literal reality which the photograph portrayed. The connoted message is the message that makes use of social and cultural references. It is an inferred message. It is symbolic. It is a message with a code.

In his essay 'The Rhetoric of the Image', Barthes explored the way advertising messages privilege symbolic and connoted meanings (Barthes 1977b). In fact Barthes argues that it is impossible to distinguish between literal and connoted messages in advertisements. If we consider the structure of signs, and the changing nature of branding where the meanings encoded encourage an identification with brands as bigger than the world of commodities, we can see these inferred messages are increasingly understood in less precise ways than is sometimes anticipated, as signs battle for attention and meaning with other signs and are constructed in the commercial world to stretch in meaning in order to accommodate an often complex global and shifting consumer base (Klein 1999). Today an advertisement rarely works independently of other media; there may be a television campaign, radio commercials, as well as other PR 'happenings' that all interact with each other to inflate connoted/symbolic meanings of advertising messages. In a world in which the still and moving image can be captured on cameras, phones and tablets, it also does not make sense to explore still photographic imagery in a sphere wholly separated from the moving image.

To explore the way marketing messages are constructed to transcend material goods within branded communication today and to consider the role of photographic imagery within this process, I will explore viral videos from Coke's Open Happiness campaign.

In 2009, Coke launched their Open Happiness campaign with a music video on the television show American Idol and throughout 2009 the campaign was rolled out globally in East Asia, China, Brazil, the Middle East, New Zealand and Australia. While the initial message focused on a fantasy, psychedelic Wizard of Oz /Willy Wonka dream world of magic, surrealism and the unexpected, providing moving image compatibility with the phantasmagoria of fashion spreads by Annie Liebowitz and David La Chapelle, the campaign has expanded through installing interactive Coke dispensing machines where Coke records 'live

PAUL MESSARIS (1996)
Visual Persuasion: The Role of Images in Advertising, Thousand Oaks, CA: Sage.

ROLAND BARTHES (1977a)
'The Photographic Message' in S. Heath (ed.) **Image, Music, Text**, London: Fontana.

happiness' in cities across the world, which are then uploaded on the internet to create 'viral swish(es) of happiness' (Shayon 2012). As they have sought to penetrate and develop new markets in the Global South, Coke has moved into producing 5 minute documentaries that capture the corporation granting happiness like the feudal lords of past ages. One video follows Coke's sponsorship of Filipino migrants' trips home to see their families, another documents Coke's creation of a space for communication between Indians and Pakistanis. These stories have been videoed, managed and produced to create messages that Coke hopes will travel virally and touch on real human experiences that one cannot fail to be moved by. The videos provide a compelling example of what Barthes meant by advertisements failing to have denoted messages that are independent of connotation, for here despite the documentary/reality TV style narrative of workers' dreams turned to reality, which we watch before our eyes, the real tears of joy and pain are created through and endorsed by a world of branded philanthropy. Coke employs these stories to construct itself as benign. This image of Coke as a leveller and bringer of harmony is a theme that Coke used as early as the 1970s with the song 'I'd like to buy a world a Coke', of which the non-commercial version 'I'd like to teach the world to sing' by the New Seekers became a global hit single.

The 2013 project entitled 'Bringing India and Pakistan together', which launched the 'Open Happiness' campaign in India and Pakistan, provides an example where the photographic image plays a central role in the construction of meaning in such a context. The partition of the Punjab and Bengal between India and Pakistan, led to the forced migration of 14 million people in 1947. Thousands died as a result of communal violence but amongst tales of trauma are also those of support and the memory of ancestral villages and lost friendships are still in living memory. Many families have stories of Hindu-Muslim unity which are often recalled as an innocent pre-partition world. For Punjab the fracture has never healed and the longing to build links remains amongst many, despite three wars between India and Pakistan and the intense propaganda on both sides of constructing the other nation as their enemy. The almost complete lack of communication can be seen by the level of psychological distance apparent from a question I was once asked in Amritsar by a young girl when I was about to cross the border to Pakistan. 'What is the weather like in Lahore?' she asked me, although the city is only 30 miles away. Coke's project capitalises on this history of rupture and the feelings of grief and loss that still resonate today. Coke India and Coke Pakistan liased over this project which involved establishing 'small world machines' in Delhi and Lahore – two historic cities that both once belonged to the province of Punjab under the British Raj. The staged interactive performance was created by Coke in order to produce a 5 minute viral video for circulation, which can be viewed in full at www.coca-colacompany.com/stories/happiness-without-borders, and has received nearly 2.4 million views. There are two texts here, the performance and the viral video. The video records the interactions between residents of these two historic cities through live communication portals that look like Coke machines. Placed in shopping centres in both cities, people could see each other and communicate using powerful gestures such as touching palms, drawing peace signs or smilies, dancing, as well as, of course, drinking Coke together and waving goodbye. By following directions on screen and completing the actions, the participants are then rewarded with a free Coke that they can share together. The gesture of the open palm is also particularly significant in India, since Abhayamudra is a gesture that signifies safety and reassurance. The machines – as life-size webcams – place the camera at the centre of the experience. The machines hold an intimacy and a power that transcends the experience of Skype video because in these 'small world machines' we are captured through the same screen that we see the participants on the other side. The screens are not separated as they are on a computer. Indians and Pakistanis appear to inhabit spaces that are literally opposite each other. These screens are also life size – they are like the glass that separates prisoners from their families which are physically touched in ways that one imagines are similar to the prison context – the placing of palms together, or tracing movements to try at all costs to share a moment and to minimise the actual physical separation that exists. The feeling of an enforced separation is also enhanced in the video text (rather than the text of the performance), which starts with shots emphasising wire fences and barbed wire through which we see scenes of daily life from both sides with voices that speak of separation and the desire for communication that are not attributed to individuals in either country so they act to suggest the desire of both sides for the same thing. Most importantly the photographic image in these 'small world machines' are used in a way in which photographs have been used most powerfully – as witness and as evidence. The people on both sides *witness* real people on the other side participating in the sharing of moments to give *evidence* of the desire for change.

In *Decoding Advertisements*, Williamson explores the structure of the sign that contains what she describes as manifest and latent meanings in advertising messages to consider the way in which we carry out 'advertising work' (Williamson 1978). Our involvement in transferring meanings from one sign in an ad to another involves us in the production of ideologies that support consumerism. In these performed events, consumers do not simply work to produce meaning from advertisements but actively work to enact the events that imbue value for the commodity and are used to create the video text. In these performance and video texts we can see the way in which the commodity is no longer central. Coke here 'markets to situations': the longing for greater contact between India and Pakistan. People participate, accepting the staged perform-ance of which they become the actors for the recording of an event that will witness the production of a Coke-sponsored 'moment of happiness'. 'A moment of happiness' is the first textual message that we see in the video too, presented in red writing on a white background – the colours of Coke. The final message in the video text is also reserved to reaffirm Coke as a source through which we may 'open happiness'. The quality of the photographic image as witness and evidence is crucial in impacting on the meaning-making process in both the video text and that of the performance in this example.

The transfer and contestation of meaning

In his essay 'Encoding/Decoding', Stuart Hall considered our involvement in the production of meaning (Hall 1993). He discusses how images are first 'encoded' by the producer, and then 'decoded' by the viewer. The transfer of meaning in this process only works if there are compatible systems of signs and symbols which the encoder and decoder use within their cultural life. Our background – i.e. our gender, class, ethnic origin, sexuality, religion, etc. – all affect our interpretation of signs and symbols. Our relationship and understanding of various forms of photography are part of those signs and symbols. Hall points to the fact that messages are not always read as they were intended, because our various cultural, social and political backgrounds lead to different interpretations. Hall suggests that there are three possible readings of an image: a dominant or preferred reading, a negotiated reading, and an oppositional reading. The dominant reading would comply with the meaning intended by the producer of the image. The importance of readers interpreting images as they were intended is obviously crucial for commercial messages, and is one of the reasons why advertisers use text and montage to anchor meanings and restrict the ways in which we may interpret their images.

While Coke may endeavor to create 'situations' in India to develop the brand as a signifier of happiness and peace, the meaning of the brand is complicated by others that have challenged Coke's production practices, which have caused the depletion of ground water resources to meet the needs of bottling plants in the Mehdiganj area of Utter Pradesh. Communities have held the corporation responsible for water shortages through over-extraction and pollution. Campaigns against the company have continued since 2003 and in March 2013, as Coke set up their small world machine in Delhi, community councils in Mehdiganj appealed to the authorities to reject Coca-Cola's application for expansion and to shut down the current operations immediately to ease the water problems in the area (Figure 5.5). By April, 15 local village councils close to Mehdiganj had called upon the government to reject the corporation's planning application. The India Resource Centre has highlighted how groundwater resources in Mehdiganj have fallen precipitously since Coca-Cola began bottling operations in the area, dropping 7.9 meters (26 feet) in the 11 years that Coca-Cola started its bottling operations (India Resource Centre 2013). The 'open happiness' events cloak the injustices of a corporate giant that has created devastating unhappiness in India, Columbia and many other parts of the world through production and employment practices that are solely driven by the profit motive (www.cokejustice.org; killercoke.org).

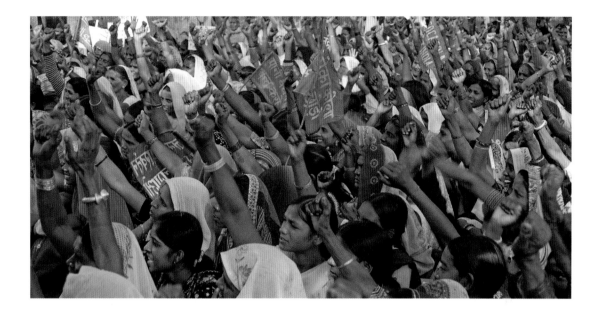

Coke is set to invest $3 billion to expand its market in India through to 2020, in order to double its profits in the country through this decade (cocacola. co.uk). As corporations globalise their marketing campaign, campaigners globalise the resistance (Figure 5.6). The circulation of photographic imagery that promotes 'situations and experiences' remains a battleground between the hegemonic and the counter-hegemonic.

5.5 Protest at Mehdiganj to shut down Coca-Cola

HEGEMONY IN PHOTOGRAPHIC REPRESENTATION

Commercial photography constantly borrows ideas and images from the wider cultural domain. It is clear that when we point the camera we frame it in a thousand and one ways through our own cultural conditioning. Photographs, like other cultural products, have therefore tended to perpetuate ideas which are dominant in society. Commercial photographs, because of their profuse nature and because they have never sought to challenge the status quo within society (since they are only produced to sell products or promote commodity culture) have also aided in the construction and perpetuation of stereotypes, to the point at which they have appeared natural and eternal (see Barthes 1977b; Williamson 1978: part 2). Through commercial photography we can therefore explore hegemonic constructs of, for example, race, gender and class. Below, I consider examples from advertisements. It is just as possible to use examples from the wider gambit of commercial photography as has been highlighted above in discussing stock photography and as raised below in discussing fashion photography.

257

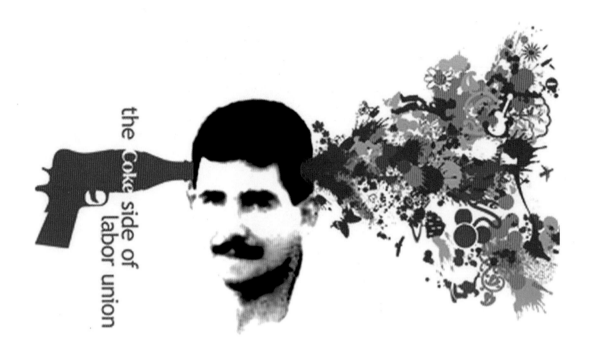

5.6 'The Coke Side of Labor Union' by Julien Torres from KillerCoke.org.
Featuring Columbian Union leader Isidro Gil.

4 John Heartfield was a German artist who used his talent to further both the anti-Nazi and socialist cause. His most celebrated work was produced for the Communist Party's illustrated newspaper *Arbeiter Illustrierte Zeitung* which included montages that exposed the rhetoric of Hitler's speeches, his sources of funding and the tragic impotence of organisations such as the League of Nations.

SALLY STEIN (1981) 'The Composite Photographic Image and the Composition of Consumer Ideology', **Art Journal**, Spring.

Photomontage: concealing social relations

One of the key ways in which commercial photography has sought to determine particular readings of images and products has been through **photomontage**. Advertisements are in fact simple photomontages produced for commercial purposes, although most books on the technique seem to ignore this expansive area. While socialist photographers like John Heartfield use photomontage to make invisible social relations visible (Figure 5.6),[4] advertisers have used montage to conceal those very social relations. One of the peculiar advantages of photomontage, as John Berger wrote in his essay 'The Political Uses of Photomontage', is the fact that 'everything which has been cut out keeps its familiar photographic appearance. We are still looking first at things and only afterwards at symbols' (Berger 1972b: 185). This creates a sense of naturalness about an image or message which is in fact constructed. An early example of the photomontage naturalising social relations has been discussed by Sally Stein, who considers 'the reception of photography within the larger matrix of socially organised communication', and looks at the rise of Taylor's ideas of 'scientific management' in the factory, and the way these ideas were also applied to domestic work (**Stein 1981**: 42–4). She also notes how expensive it was to have photomechanical reproductions within a book in the early part of the century.

Yet in Mrs Christine Frederick's 1913 tract, *The New Housekeeping*, there were eight pages of glossy photographic images. This must have impressed the average reader. In her chapter on the new efficiency as applied to cooking, an image was provided which affirmed this ideology as the answer to women's work. The image consisted of a line drawing of an open card file, organised into types of dishes, and an example of a recipe card with a photograph of an elaborate lamb dish (Figure 5.7). Despite Frederick's interest in precision, the card, which would logically be delineated by a black rectangular frame, does not match the dimensions of the file, nor does it contain practical information such as cost, number of servings, etc. which Frederick suggests in her text. As Stein points out, however, most readers must have overlooked this point when confronted with this luscious photographic image, which they would have accepted at face value.

> Because the page is not clearly divided between the file in one half and the recipe card in the other but instead flows uninterruptedly between drawing below, text of recipe, and photograph of the final dish, the meticulous organisation of the file alone seems responsible for the full flowering of the dish. As a symbolic representation of modern house work, what you have in short order is a strict hierarchy, with an emblem of the family feast at its pinnacle.
>
> (Stein 1981: 43)

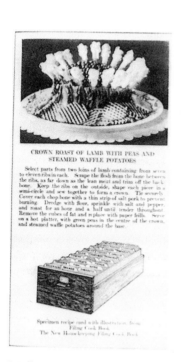

5.7 Illustration from Mrs Christine Frederick's *The New Housekeeping*, 1913

259

The more down-to-earth questions of time and money are ignored and almost banished. In response to those who believed that her reading was too contrived, Stein wrote: 'If it seems that I am reading too much into this composite image, one need only note the title of Frederick's subsequent publication – *Meals that Cook Themselves*' (Stein 1992).

There are two key issues we can draw from Stein's analysis. First, the example highlights the power of the photographic image to foster desire. While a rather ordinary photograph of a cake or a roast may have impressed an early twentieth-century audience, in the twenty-first century we are also seduced by the use of the latest technology and luscious photography. The photography of food continues to produce tantalising images through the play of colour and texture. Dishes are often painted or glazed to highlight colours and textures in order to produce more mouth-watering images. Roland Barthes also discussed food advertising in his essay 'The Rhetoric of the Image' (Barthes 1977b). Using an advertisement for Panzani pasta he highlights the sense of natural abundance that is often focused on in commercial food photography, to encourage the association of naturalness with the prepacked produce. The constant juxtaposition of uncooked fruit or vegetables with prepared food also conceals and thereby in effect dismisses the labour process. The total metamorphosis of a coconut into Carte D'Or's coconut ice cream (Figure 5.8) is a classic example of the ability of the latest technology to deny the labour of production. The concealing of social and economic relations in advertising led Victor Burgin to create the montage 'What does Possession mean to you?, 7% of our population own 84% of our wealth', with a stereotypical image often found in perfume advertising of a couple embracing. Such spoof ads have become the hallmark of organisations such as Adbusters in the twenty-first century, an organisation whose challenge to the authority of corporate power encouraged the formation of Occupy Wall Street (www.adbusters.org).

The fetishisation of labour relations

Photography and photomontage have not only acted to conceal social and labour relations, but have also acted to fetishise and romanticise the labour process. Judith Williamson has also discussed this with regard to a Lancia car advertisement from around 1978. The image depicts the Lancia Beta in an Italian vineyard. It shows a man who appears to be the owner, standing on the far side of the car with his back towards us, looking over a vineyard in which a number of peasants are working happily. In the distance, on a hill, is an old castle (this image is illustrated in **Williamson 1979**). Williamson asks a series of questions:

JUDITH WILLIAMSON (1979) 'Great History that Photographs Mislaid' in P. Holland, J. Spence and S. Watney (eds) **Photography/Politics: One**, London: Comedia.

Who made this car? Has it just emerged new and gleaming from the soil, its finished form as much a product of nature as the grapes on the vine? . . . Who are these peasants? Have they made the car out in this most Italian field? . . . How can a car even exist in these feudal relations, how can such a contradiction be carried off? . . . What is this, if not a complete slipping over of the capitalist mode of production, as we survey a set of feudal class relations represented by the surveying gaze of possession, the look of the landlord with his back to us?

(Williamson 1979: 53)

Williamson also notes how the feudal Italian owner's gaze does not encompass both car (the product of industrial capitalism) and the owner's field of vision (the relations of Italian feudalism). She discusses the structure of the advertisement in order to understand why we don't question the contradictions of the image. The ad uses the traditional grammar of car advertisements with the showroom-effect camera angle, which intersects with the representation of 'Italianness'. The positioning of the car seems so casual that the man leaning against it could have just stopped to have a break and look at this Italian view. Maybe he is not Italian? Perhaps he will drive on and leave the 'most Italian' scene behind. The narrative of chance on the horizontal axis of the photograph naturalises the vertical axis of Italian castle, feudal relations and commodity ownership.

Many contemporary advertisements adopt a romanticised and non-industrial working environment to give their products an image of quality and historicity. Whiskey distillers have used this image to represent their brand as one which has been produced with special attention and one that has the experience of time behind it. Jack Daniel's whiskey has produced advertisements since the 1990s which present a labour environment that could not possibly exist today. One worker is often highlighted, and their work is represented as skilled and individualised (the opposite of factory production). The photographs are either black and white or exude a feeling of tradition with natural light and yellow and brown tints creating a feeling of a pre-electric world. There is a reassuring sense of stability. The photograph, because of its relationship to realism, seems to delude us into believing that this is a 'real' world. Hovis and other wholemeal bread producers have often used the image of the family bakery. McCain Chips used this image to launch their new website in 2010 'McCain It's All Good', which constructed the idea of a family farm/kitchen garden as the environment for their website. In this process, the representation of industrial labour has been domesticated (Macleod 2010).

One area of advertising photography that has made consistent use of a frequently gendered and domesticated image of workers are the images for the 'ethical consumption' market, a market that affirms the structural in-equalities between the Global North and Global South, by establishing consumerism as an activity for only part of the world. Here, we usually see individualised workers from the Global South, whose labour affords our living standards. The smile on the faces of these photographed workers estab-lishes an affective bond while at the same time representing them as consenting and happy (**Ramamurthy 2012**). However as Marilyn Frye has identified:

ANANDI RAMAMURTHY (2012) 'Absences and Silences: The Representation of the Tea Picker in Colonial and Fair Trade Advertising', **Visual Culture in Britain**, 13(3): 367–81.

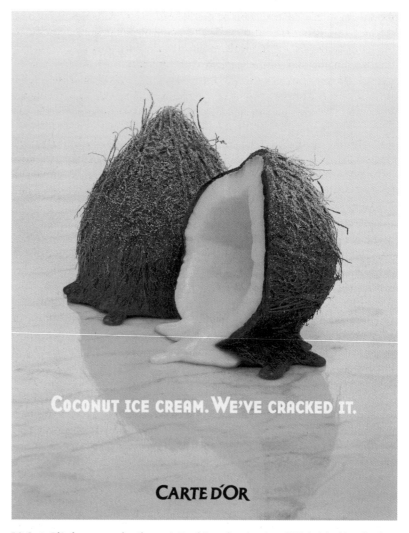

5.8 Carte D'Or ice cream advertisement, *Good Housekeeping*, June 1998 (original in colour)

'it is often a requirement upon oppressed people that we smile and be cheerful. ... We acquiesce in being made invisible, in our occupying no space. We participate in our own erasure.' (Frye 1983). The images deny the structural inequalities that persist both in relation to gender as well as north/south relations, naturalising racialised hierarchies in a similar way to colonial imagery in advertising and more widely in photography.

The gaze and gendered representations

While the concealing of class relations and the representation of commodity culture as natural and eternal is the most overwhelming construct of advertising, racialised and gendered regimes of representation are also widely exploited (Hinrichsen 2013; Ramamurthy 2003; **Hall 2013**; **Pieterse 1992**). This section will discuss gendered representations. (For explorations of 'race' and racism in commercial photography, see the case studies on pp. 272–80 and 284–8.)

As Jean Baudriallard has highlighted, the body as 'the finest consumer object' is represented as both capital and fetish in commercial culture and the body is primarily naturalised as feminine (Baudriallard 1998: 129). The stereotypical and highly coded representations of women in popular culture have been given attention by many critics (**Berger 1972a; Winship 1987a**, 1987b; Williamson 1978). One of the key criticisms has been the way in which ads always represent women as objects to be surveyed. This has tended to increase the representation of women as both passive and objects of sexual desire. In his book *Gender Advertisements*, Erving Goffman has explored the way in which men's and women's body language has been photographed to perpetuate gender roles (Goffman 1979). It is important to remember that the photographer always surveys his or her subject and personally selects what is believed to be worth photographing. The photographic process can also, therefore, exacerbate the voyeuristic gaze. Analyses of popular film and the **scopophilic** nature of mainstream film products is also useful in reading and interpreting advertising (see Mulvey 1975). In understanding the role of photographs in representing stereotypical images of women, Janice Winship has explored the contrasting ways in which men's and women's hands have been photographed in advertisements (see Winship 1987a). While male hands are usually photographed as active and controlling, female hands are invariably represented as decorative and caressing.

Winship's essay also draws attention to the increasing fragmentation of the body within recent commercial photography. It makes the body more easily commodified and packaged. In a content analysis of lipstick advertisements, Robert Goldman has pointed out that while most lipstick ads in 1946 depicted the whole body of a woman, by 1977 most ads only showed a part of the body. There continues to be countless examples of women's makeup ads that present women's bodies as fragments that can be worn or discarded at will. As Griselda Pollock indicates, it was only 'after Picasso had visually hacked up the body, [that] we have been gradually accustomed to the cutting up of specifically feminine bodies: indeed, their cut-up-ness has come to be seen as a sign of that femininity'. Significantly, Pollock adds that this 'came to be naturalised by photographic representation in film, advertising, and pornography, all of which are discourses about desire that utilise the dialectic of fantasy and reality effects associated with the hegemonic modes of photographic representation' (**Pollock 1977**; 1990: 218). One of the most famous examples

STUART HALL (2013) **Cultural Representations and Signifying Practice**, London: Sage.

JOHN BERGER (1972a) **Ways of Seeing**, Harmondsworth: Penguin.

JANICE WINSHIP (1987a) 'Handling Sex' in R. Betterton (ed.) **Looking On: Images of Femininity in the Visual Arts and Media**, London: Pandora.

GRISELDA POLLOCK (1977) 'What's Wrong with "Images of Women"', reprinted in R. Parker and G. Pollock (eds) **Framing Feminism**, London: Pandora Press.

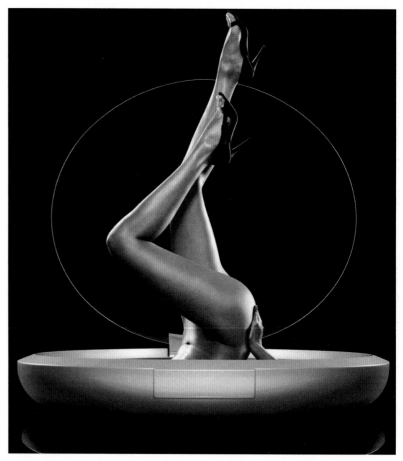

5.9 Pretty Polly 'Love Legs' cosmetics advertisement, 2008

of the fragmentation of women's bodies was a billboard advertisement for
Pretty Polly tights in the 1970s, that depicted a woman's legs emerging from
an egg. This objectification and fragmentation received criticism at the time.
Oppositional graffiti sprayed on to the advert included 'born kicking'. In 2014,
it is often asserted that we are in a post-feminist age, suggesting that we live
in a world of equality, yet as women we continue to earn less than men,
continue to suffer domestic violence and to be bombarded with messages that
encourage us to perceive ourselves as objects to be looked at. In 2008, Pretty
Polly appear to have thought nothing of reusing their image of disembodied
legs appearing from an egg. Their advertisement in *Elle* (June 2008) presents
two disembodied, naked legs wearing stiletto-heeled shoes rising out of an
egg-shaped cosmetic case (Figure 5.9). The increasing depiction of women's
bodies as not simply hacked up but violated and sometimes even represented

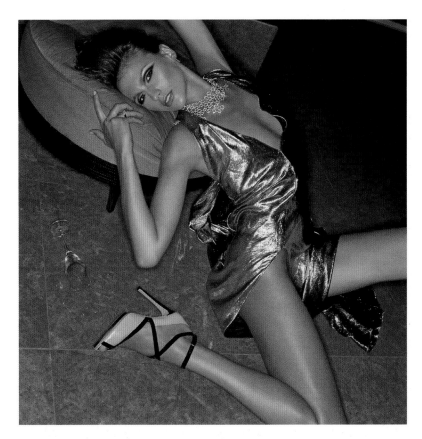

5.10 'Night Diva', *Marie Claire*, July 2003

as dead has provoked response from web organisations such as about–face (www.about–face.org).

Recent commercial photography has undoubtedly objectified both male and female bodies in the constant drive for commodification (Nixon in Hall 2013). Yet women's bodies continue to be the more powerful object of the gaze. New technology such as digital imaging has been used repeatedly to heighten the display of women's sexual availability. Women's bodies can now be contorted into impossible positions. *Marie Claire's* fashion spread 'Night Diva' from March 2003 shows such a manipulation (Figure 5.10). Her body is twisted and stretched in order to increase its display for the viewer. Digital imaging enables legs to be lengthened, bodies thinned, breasts enlarged, depending on the image that is flavour of the month. Such photography sets impossible ideals for both ordinary women and models, encouraging eating disorders such as anorexia, which led to the deaths of three models between 2006 and 2007. In September 2007, the fashion label Nolita used their advertising to highlight the problem of anorexia by photographing the French actress Isabelle Caro naked, weighing just 31 kilos. Posed as an object of display, her emaciated body looks ugly and the opposite of an image of desire. Produced by Oliviero Toscani, of Benetton fame, the image was welcomed by the fashion industry as raising awareness of an issue that was deeply affecting the industry. Others questioned its effectiveness however, with health organisations fearing that those suffering from this mental illness could even compete with Caro over her thinness. Riccardo Dalle Grave, head of an Italian association dealing with eating disorders, said: 'You can die from this disease. If they really want to prevent it, it would be better to help young women accept a variety of body measurements and understand that beauty comes in all sizes.' Nolita have not yet chosen this course of action, following the banning of the advertisement by Italy's Publicity Control Institute. The dominant ideals of beauty continue to benefit the fashion industry and its partners in cosmetics and plastic surgery. For non-white women desirability and beauty is often wrapped up in images of whiteness. In the commercial media even black super stars such as Beyonce are lightened through photographic manipulation and *Vogue Africa* and *Vogue India*, while designed for local elites, primarily hire models with fairer skin privileging whiteness as an image of beauty.

FASHION PHOTOGRAPHY

ROSETTA BROOKES (1992) 'Fashion Photography' in J. Ash and E. Wilson (eds) **Chic Thrills: A Fashion Reader**, London: Pandora.

CAROLINE EVANS AND MINNA THORNTON (1989) **Women and Fashion: A New Look**, London: Quartet.

The display of gender and sexuality has been one of the most all-pervading themes in fashion photography. It is a subject that many early commentators on the fashion image focused on. Femininity, as Jennifer Craik notes, 'became co-extensive with the fashion photograph' by the 1930s. By the 1970s and 1980s fashion photographers such as Helmut Newton and Guy Bourdin were exploring sexuality and eroticism through the fashion image (**Brookes 1992**: 17–24). The way in which women read fashion images of women has also been explored (see **Evans and Thornton 1989**: ch. 5). As Berger commented: 'Men look at women. Women watch themselves being looked at' (Berger 1972a: 47). 'Contemporary fashion photography's various plays with sex and gender, race and difference, are among its most significant elements', writes Abigail Solomon-Godeau (see case study 'Tourism, fashion and "the Other"' on p. 271). Solomon-Godeau also notes that

> another significant aspect of the genre is its ideological address, its complex orchestrations of spectatorial desire, projection, identification, fetishism, voyeurism, and all the other psychic mechanisms that account for the power, the influence, and indeed the pleasure such pictures produce.

Paul Jobling has highlighted how fashion spreads today have ceased to be simply about clothes but 'beckon us into a world of unbridled fantasies', which it would be 'myopic to argue . . . is innocent or without deeper ideological signification' (Jobling 1999: 2). We are presented with spectacles of beauty (usually conventional), sensuality, eroticism and pleasure. These images, however, do not constitute a genre as Shinkle emphasises (Shinkle 2008: 2). As with all commercial photography, fashion photography draws parasitically on every available idea, style and image to promote and fetishise commodities. Early portrait photography and the *carte-de-visite*, for example, had already established ways of photographing people in fashionable or dramatic clothing, which were adopted by early fashion photographers (Ewing 1991: 6–10). Fashion photographers such as André Barre, Irving Penn and Erwin Blumenfield borrowed ideas and styles from art movements such as Surrealism. Bruce Weber's photographs for Calvin Klein were influenced by the work of Leni Riefenstahl. The power of photojournalism and documentary photography in the 1930s also affected fashion images, especially as photographers moved between the genres. Filmatic conventions have also influenced fashion photography, both in terms of the creation of looks and styles, as well as the way in which we as viewers read what would otherwise appear as fragmentary and disjointed image sequences in the fashion spread. More recently the snapshot style of photography has been used as a convention within the fashion image. The range of influences indicates the impossibility of considering various commercial image-making forms in isolation. The conventions of the fashion image are 'neither fixed nor purposeful' as Craik highlights in *The Face of Fashion* (**Craik 1994**: 114).

While fashion photography has been identified as too wide to be a genre, there are certain features of the fashion image which can be highlighted, although these features are often contradictory. First, the transitory nature of fashion has impacted on the fashion image. Evans and Thornton have discussed this in terms of the ability of the fashion image to take 'extraordinary liberties' and get away with images which are unduly violent, pornographic or outrageous. Polly Devlin has pointed out the contradictory nature of the fashion image's transitoriness, since it aims to be both timely and timeless: 'Its subject is a product with built-in obsolescence, and the result may be an amusing, ephemeral picture or a monumental statement' (Devlin 1979: 113). This contradiction has continued with photographers who work across the genre of fashion and the slightly removed world of art photography, using the space of the fashion magazine to comment on the social attitudes of a period. Steven Meisel and Cindy Sherman are two examples that will be discussed below.

The relationship of the fashion spread to magazines rather than the manufacturers also emphasises the importance of the images' ability to comment on society and its conventions and norms (Evans and Thornton 1989: 82). Val Williams' *Look at Me: Fashion and Photography in Britain* highlights the crucial role that particular magazines such as *Nova* in the 1960s and later *I-D* and

JENNIFER CRAIK (1994) 'Soft Focus: Techniques of Fashion Photography', in **The Face of Fashion**, London: Routledge, ch. 5.

The Face in the 1980s have played in developing conventions of challenge within certain areas of fashion photography (Williams 1998). She notes how the photography encompassed discussions of race, sexuality and class within fashion and style. The possibilities of commenting on social attitudes and exploring not just an idealised beauty but a chronicle of contemporary life have absorbed fashion photographers since the 1990s in particular (Cotton 2000). Yet despite providing 'conventions of challenge', these magazines and the photographs within them are still subsumed within a culture of commodification in which identities, whether traditional or not, form part of a vast reservoir of appearances that can be packaged and sold. As Steve Edwards wrote with regard to the *Next Directory* in the late 1980s:

> As we flip the pages multiple identities whizz past our eyes. Distance and depth collapse into the intricate and exquisite surface of the image. What is there now to prevent us switching back and forth between these marvellous identities? She: now sipping tea on the lawn of the country seat, bathed in golden light, 'well-dressed, well-bred', in that 'endless summer'. Now the belle of the southern states, young and raw, perhaps with an illicit negro lover. Now the cultured woman, on her travels through Europe in search of adventure. He: from the big city gentleman, to the rugged biker, to the fictions of Havana. These are the worlds that the photograph has to offer . . . . Our only choice is between its choices, we have no choice but to consume . . . or so the argument goes.
>
> (Edwards 1989: 5)

Other contradictions are apparent within the fashion image. Rosetta Brookes has suggested that in fashion photography 'we see the typical instead of the unique moment or event' (Brookes 1992: 17). Yet, at the same time as producing the typical, fashion photographers have aimed to construct a sense of what is original and unique within a particular fashion. They have also tried to produce images which stand their ground beyond the transitory space of the magazine and the transitory nature of fashion, and, for example, enter the gallery or the coffee-table book.

Two examples are the exhibitions and catalogues *Imperfect Beauty* for the V&A (Cotton), and *Fashioning Fiction* for MOMA (Kismark and Respini). Both texts and exhibitions testify to the relationship as well as the tension between fashion and art photography. In these catalogues, the colour plates remove the photographs from the mundane context of the magazine with its juxtaposed texts including prices and brand names that unabashedly fix the relationship of the image to its commercial context. In repositioning these images outside of the magazine space we are encouraged to explore the photographs as individual works of art – rather than cultural products, since there is no reference to, for example, stylists involved in the production of the photo shoots or others who may have collaborated on these editorial expressions. As **Solomon-Godeau** points out,

> the act of decontextualizing these photographs by isolating, framing, and mounting them on walls effectively flattens their specificity, their instrumentality, and their original mode of address, and thus the consumer or audience targeted by the photographic work is obscured (there is, of course, no universal spectator).
>
> (Solomon-Godeau 2004)

Despite the blurring of contexts, there is no doubt that the photographs in both exhibitions reflect and comment on society including commodity culture. Since the 1990s fashion images have been particularly powerful in creating narratives that refer to the world outside of fashion as both catalogues highlight. For example, Steven Meisel, in constructing obviously contrived images of an idealised family with over-saturated colours and apparently perfect family members for his spread 'The Good Life' in *Vogue Italia* (October 1997), encourages us not only to ponder the artifice of commodity culture that fails to provide us with the love and friendship bonds we all yearn for, but also to question the way we memorialise our family life, through the family album which only records the successes of our lives and 'the family'. Yet in the context of a fashion magazine, these ironic images are contained as a nostalgic comical reflection on contrived 1950s advertising imagery.

Cindy Sherman's fashion spreads that play with her own image and identity also suggest a blurring of boundaries between fashion and art photography. Her photographs for Harpers Bazaar (1993), Comme des Garcons (1994) and Balenciaga all emphasise the constructed nature of the images and identities, an issue she has explored throughout her artistic work, especially in her Untitled Film Stills. These images attempt to critique the fashion industry from within by deliberately creating images that challenge the usual idealised representations (Figure 5.11). Yet, if we accept that context impacts on meaning, does the scopophilic gaze that Sherman interrogates in order to comment on women's oppression and female sexuality lose some of its critical power when entwined within the context of fashion promotion, where it continues to furnish the spectacle?

The title of Craik's text, *The Face of Fashion*, emphasises the focus that many scholars writing about fashion photography have concentrated on – the face of fashion. This face, this mask, this external image, invariably although not exclusively about beauty, sexuality and pleasure, hides the relations of production to which the whole industry is so inextricably linked. Like all commercial photography fashion images fetishise commodities and hide the relations of production. The images of sensuous beauty and desire created in fashion photography are ones that we all engage with in both serious and playful ways. As with all commercial photography, the conventions of these

ABIGAIL SOLOMON-GODEAU (2004) 'Modern Style: Dressing Down (Issues Raised by Museum of Modern Art's "Fashioning Fiction")' **Artforum International**, 42(9): 192.

5.11 Cindy Sherman,
***Untitled**, 2007/2008*

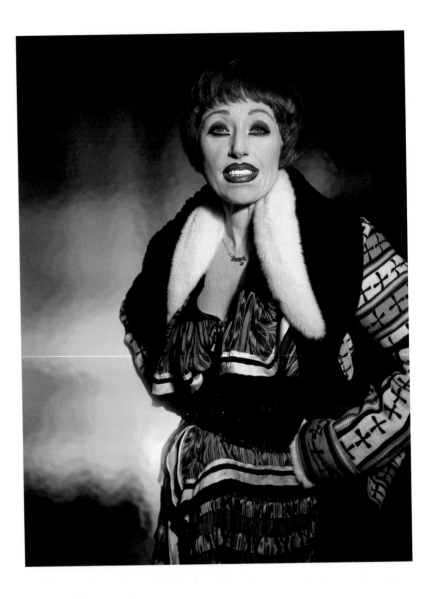

images shift according to the needs of the market. Yet, as Angela McRobbie has emphasised, the relationship between our experiences of pleasure in consumption and our experiences of exploitation in the labour force, ironically, can be linked ones. McRobbie has identified how all the black and Asian fashion students in particular whom she interviewed in her research on the fashion industry talk about fashion in terms of pleasure and enjoyment, yet they come from families where mothers were invariably homeworkers making garments for low wages and where they often made their own clothes because they could not afford to consume the fashions in the shops (McRobbie 1997: 82). Within the area of retail, many individuals who work in fashion outlets 'identify strongly with fashion and less with retail', as McRobbie points out, yet

> they are now employed on short-term, part-time contracts, often they are working largely for commission. Their self-image as working in the glamorous fashion industry must surely be undercut by the reality of knowing that in a few years time possibly with children to support it is unlikely that they would hold onto the job of decorating the shopfloor at Donna Karan
>
> (McRobbie 1997: 87)

McRobbie's research emphasises the importance of recognising the multiple meanings – dominant, negotiated and oppositional – in the fashion image. The vast majority of fashion students never visit a factory throughout their degree. As one fashion academic intimated to McRobbie, 'It would take all the romance out of it for them' (McRobbie 1997: 86). Such a perspective works to increase the fetishisation of fashion and deliberately hides the relations of production that other scholars have consistently tried to expose (see Klein 2000; **Jhally 2006a**). For women this is especially important since, as she notes, the fashion industry is 'an almost wholly feminized industry. Apart from a few men at the top, including manufacturers and retailers, celebrity designers and magazine publishers, it is and has been a female sphere of production and consumption' (McRobbie 1997: 84).

SUT JHALLY (2006) 'Advertising, Cultural Criticism and pedagogy' in **The Spectacle of Accumulation: Essays in Media Culture and Politics**, New York: Peter Lang.

CASE STUDY: TOURISM, FASHION AND 'THE OTHER'

Abigail Solomon-Godeau's observation that 'contemporary fashion photography's various plays with sex and gender, race and difference, are among its most significant elements' provides the rationale for this next case study which will explore a hegemonic construction consolidated in the nineteenth century – that of the exotic/primitive **'Other'** – and consider the way in which it has been exploited in the commercial world. Some of the most dominant ideological and photographic constructs were developed during the nineteenth century, a period of European imperial expansion. This history has affected the representation of the Global South in all forms of photographic practice (see Gupta 1986; **Bailey 1988**; *Ten/8* 16; *Ten/8* 2(3)). During the nineteenth century, the camera joined the gun in the process of colonisation. The camera was used to record and define those who were colonised according to the interests of the West. This unequal relationship of power between the white photographer and the colonised subject has been discussed by many (Freedman 1990; **Prochaska 1991**; Schildkrout 1991; Edwards 1992; Bate 1993; Eileraas 2007). These early

DAVID A BAILEY (1988) 'Rethinking Black Representations' **Ten/8**, 31.

DAVID PROCHASKA (1991) 'Fantasia of the Phototheque: French Postcard views of Senegal', **African Arts**, October.

anthropological and geographical photographers were sometimes paid employees of companies who organised campaigns to explore new markets. Emile Torday, for example – an anthropologist who used photography as a research aid – was paid by the Belgian Kasai Company to explore the Congo.

This history of photography is integrally linked to colonial and economic exploitation. A sense of submission, exoticism and the 'primitive' were key feelings, which these photographers documented and catalogued. Through these images, the European photographer and viewer could perceive their own superiority. Europe was defined as 'the norm' upon which all other cultures should be judged. That which was different was disempowered by its very 'Otherness'.

During this period, the sense of 'Otherness' and exoticism was not only captured 'in the field' but was also exploited by photographers working in commercial enterprises. Malek Alloula has documented the genre of exotic/ erotic colonial postcards which were sent back to France by French colonists. In his book *The Colonial Harem* he discusses images of Algerian women taken by French studio photographers in Algeria (**Alloula 1987**). In the confines of the studio, French photographers constructed visions of exoticism which suited their own colonial fantasies and those of the European consumers of these images. The paid Algerian models could only remain silent to the colonisers' abuse of their bodies (Figure 5.13). These images encapsulate Edward Said's description of Flaubert's Egyptian courtesan:

MALEK ALLOULA (1987) **The Colonial Harem**, Manchester: Manchester University Press.

> She never spoke of herself, she never represented her emotions, her presence or history. He spoke for and represented her. He was foreign, comparatively wealthy, male, and these were historical facts of domination that allowed him not only to possess Kuchuk Hanem physically but to speak for her and tell his readers in what way she was typically oriental.
>
> (Said 1985: 6)

The dominance of photographs of women in these commercial images is not by chance. Colonial power could be more emphatically represented through gendered relations – the white, wealthy male photographer versus the non-white, poor female subject. These images, bought and sold in their thousands, reflect the commodification of women's bodies generally in society. They were part of the development of postcard culture which enabled the consumption of photographs by millions. The production of exotic postcards also brought photographs of the 'Empire' and the non-European world into every European home. It was not only the photographs of non-European women which were sold: landscape photographs, which constructed Europe as developed and the non-European world as underdeveloped, were also popular (Prochaska 1991). Gen Doy has developed this discussion of Algerian postcards arguing that those produced in the European studio and those produced in Algeria sometimes present conflicting images of this stereotype, because the sitters in Algeria were not always aware nor did they always adhere to the constructed codes with which the European artist wished to frame them (**Doy 1996**: 30–1).

Rebecca Deroo has also noted how these postcards were sent and consumed by European women as well as men, giving evidence of a racialised regime of representation in female consumption (Deroo 2002). In exploring contemporary tourist and fashion photography, colonialist discourses of 'otherness' which construct the non-European as primitive and/or exotic are still apparent. The fashion image privileges what is exotic, dramatic, glamorous and different. It is easy to see how some photographers have moved between areas of anthropological and fashion photography, since in classifying the non-western world, anthropologists searched for what was different and exotic.

Irving Penn's *Worlds in a Small Room* documents a series of constructed images of peoples from around the world, whom Penn photographed while on assignments for *Vogue* (Penn 1974). In these images the genres of fashion and visual anthropology seem to collapse. The images tell us little about the people, but say a lot about Penn's construction of these people as primitive and exotic. As with the fashion shoot, these images are contrived and stylised, and Penn is at pains to find what is extraordinary and to create the dramatic. The isolated space of the studio removes the subjects from their own time and space, in a similar way to the French colonial postcards discussed above (Figure 5.12), and gives the photographer free rein to create every aspect of the image. Interestingly, Penn described this studio space as 'a sort of neutral area' (Penn 1974: 9). Yet, as we look through his book and peruse the photographs of Penn constructing his shots, the unequal relationship of power makes a mockery of the notion of neutrality.

The latent relationship between fashion and popular anthropological photography explains why the fashion magazine *Marie Claire* could include ethnographic articles when it was first established, without losing the tone of the fashion magazine. In their first issue, the article 'Arabia Behind the Veil' represented the jewellery and makeup of Arab women in a series of plates, like fashion ideas. If we look closely at the images it is clear that the photographer has used just two or three models and dressed them differently to represent a series of styles, just like a fashion shoot.

Marie Claire UK, was first published in 1988, during the rise of multiculturalism in Europe. The early anthropological shoots featured in the magazine were part of a constructed identity of liberalism in which whiteness still remained the privileged identity. The ethnographic language of social and cultural 'types' that situate the non-European as permanently othered has been celebrated in contemporary fashion photography in Paolo Roversi's 'multi-ethnic gallery' for *Vogue Italia* in 2013, where models from various countries are dressed and photographed to enact cultural difference (Figure 5.13).

Primitivism and exoticism have both played a role in developing images of otherness that also act as a site of desire. The harem as a site of a European constructed fantasy has been one of the most persistent representations of 'the

GEN DOY (1996) 'Out of Africa: Orientalism, Race and the Female Body' **Body and Society**, 2(4): 17–44.

5.12 French Colonial postcard c. 1910
During the nineteenth century and today, the harem has remained a site for colonial fantasy and a space which ensures the representation of the 'Orient' as the opposite of the 'West'.

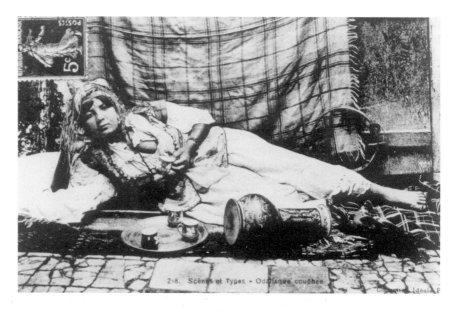

other' in contemporary fashion photography, and like the earlier postcards described by Deroo, these images perpetuate a racialised regime of representation in female consumption. In the late 1980s as multiculturalism as a social and civic policy developed in the US and UK, orientalist/harem narratives repeated themselves in a variety of fashion magazines. Slavoj Žižek has described multiculturalism as 'a disavowed, inverted, self-referential form of racism, a "racism with a distance" – it "respects" the Other's identity, conceiving the Other as a self-enclosed "authentic" community towards which he, the multiculturalist, maintains a distance rendered possible by his privileged universal position (Žižek 1997: 44). Roversi's image maintains these subject–viewer positions. In the 1980s and 1990s, fashion spreads featuring the harem projected it as a site of fantasy and an exotic world of desire while maintaining the white female reader of the fashion magazine as the 'privileged' universalist. The November 1988 issue of *Company* magazine provides an example. A fashion spread titled 'Arabesque: Rock the Casbah – This is Evening Wear to Smoulder in' features non-white women in brocaded clothes, sitting and lying indoors on heavily ornamented fabrics, while pining over black and white photographs of men. The photographs of the women are bathed in an orangey, rich light. By contrasting colour and black and white photography, the men seem to appear more distant and further unobtainable. The representation of sexuality here is of an unhealthy obsession. In contrast, the fashion spread following it, 'Cold Comfort', features a white couple together, in a relationship of relative equality. Blue and brown predominate, in contrast to the previous spread, and the much more standard photographic lighting contrasts with the previous yellow haze, to present images which seem much more matter-of-fact, like the denim clothing advertised. Here,

274

however, matter-of-factness acts to represent Europe as rational in opposition to the irrational East.

In *Marie Claire*'s June 1994 issue, another pair of fashion spreads also provides a similar comparison. In 'Indian Summer', the image of an exotic woman in physical and sexual abandon predominates the pages (Figure 5.14), as in the previous spread and the colonial postcard already discussed (Figure 5.12). The pages of this photo-story are almost like a film sequence with rapid cuts. As in the Company magazine's last 'Orientalist' sequence, this woman is alone, but the themes of physical and sexual desire are paramount – her isolation invites the viewer in for their own sexual pleasure. Many of the shots use wide angles to enhance their depth and, along with rich oranges and blues, it gives the sequence a heightened sense of physicality. The spread which follows this, entitled 'The Golden Age of Hollywood', contrasts by representing white men and women together, in relative harmony (Figure 5.15). This sequence is much more about glamour than 'Cold Comfort', yet here again the notion of rationality is also encouraged by the style of clothing as well as the standard photographic lens

5.13 Paolo Roversi, *Multi Ethnic Gallery*, 2013

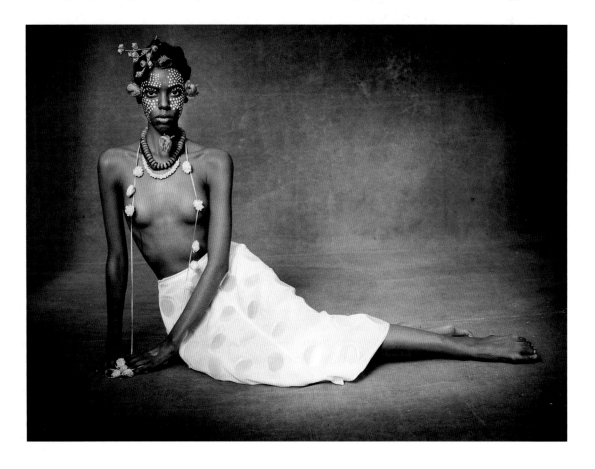

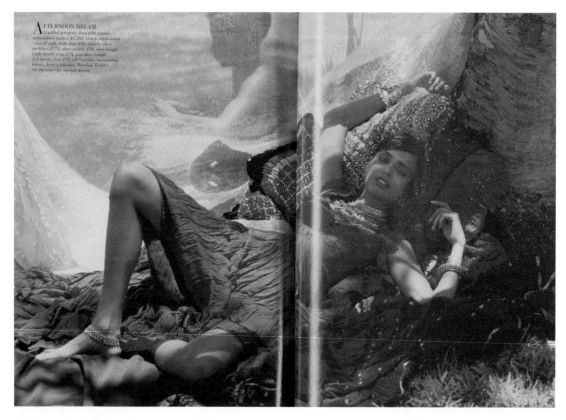

AFTERNOON DREAM
A crinkled georgette dress with sequin-embroidered bodice, £1,282. Ochre, white metal 'chased' cuffs, both from £89. Silvery silver necklace, £275, silver anklet, £76, silver bangle (right hand), from £75, and silver bangle left hand), from £75, all Frontiers, surrounding fabrics, from a selection, Rainbow Textiles. See Directory for stockist details.

5.14 *Afternoon Dream* **from 'Indian Summer',** *Marie Claire,* **June 1994**
Rich reds and oranges dominate this scene in which the mood of sexual abandon that is created is more important than the display of clothes.

SANJAY SHARMA AND
ASHWANI SHARMA (2003)
'White Paranoia: Orientalism in
the Age of Empire', **Fashion
Theory** 7(3/4): 1–18.

used. There is also an almost colonial feel to this fashion spread, through the sepia tones of the photographs and the 1930s styling. The context of these images within the fashion magazine leaves the white woman not only as the surveyor of 'Other' women, but in the privileged position of winning her man while the non-white woman acts simply as an object of titillating fantasy.

Since 2000/1, the image of the Orientalist harem has been less of a focus in fashion magazines. The rise of Islamophobia has complicated the use of images of Arab women and Arab culture as a subject of desire. This has been difficult to sustain in a climate in which the image of Islam has increasingly become framed within a discourse on violence and terrorism. Fashion photography as a commercial form of image-making steers clear of creating meanings that could rock hegemonic discourses. As **Sanjay and Ashwani Sharma** have highlighted:

The white subject's apparent enjoyment of the multicultural spectacle of ethnicized Asian culture is structured by the exclusion of the unknowable,

276

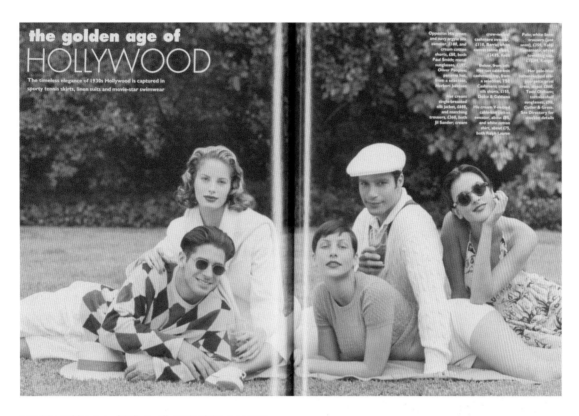

5.15 'The Golden Age of Hollywood', *Marie Claire,* **June 1994**
In contrast to the 'East', the 'West' is represented as more rational and restrained.

undesirable radical Other – exemplified at present by the figure of the
"Muslim" – who shatters the myth of liberal white universality and racial
harmony.'

(Sharma and Sharma 2003:11)

This exclusion was discernible in the response to a Dunkin Doughnuts advertisement in May 2008, which featured a white woman wearing a paisley patterned
tassled scarf. The Zionist lobby branded this fairly innocuous image as pandering
to Islamic terrorism, since they argued that the scarf was similar to the Keffiyeh,
a form of dress which, while traditional in many Arab cultures, they described
as associated with terrorist sympathisers. Dunkin Doughnuts bowed under Zionist
pressure and eventually pulled the ad.

The contemporary impossibility of representing the Arab world as a site of
fantasy is discernible in the *Vogue* archives, where references to the Middle East
only appear in news related features such as an article about the American

277

journalist Lara Logan, which runs with a documentary photograph of Logan wrapped in a shawl with her head uncovered 'in the field' and contrasted to the veiled woman to her right. She is constructed as the liberal 'priviledged universalist'. In *Vogue* the only other recent representation of the Middle East is through an exhibition of art that removes the need to represent people.

The representations of colonial fantasies, however, are not erased, but simply shift and continue to maintain a difference between whiteness and a constructed other. In 2000, for example, the actress Julianne Moore, was posed after Ingres' *La Grande Odalisque* by Nigel Thompson for *Vanity Fair*. In 2008 Naomi Cambell was modelled holding the fan of Ingres' *Grande Odalisque*, but she is turned towards us with one breast exposed to remind us of another painting: Manet's *Olympia*, a painting which was described as representing a prostitute because of her direct gaze. Campbell stares out at us in the strident fashion that had caused outrage when Manet's painting was first shown and lies on a bed strewn with food. Her sexuality is constructed through historical reference as deviant, but representable in this current Islamaphobic age.

In tourist brochures of the Arab world the removal of people is also apparent, with a world focused heavily on a display of exotic architecture and lavish hotels, creating a depopulated world ready for the tourist to inhabit. The non-European world is frequently represented as a playground for the West, denying the reality of resourcefulness and intense physical work which actually constitutes most people's lives in the Global South. In many tourist advertisements, the image of work, if represented at all, is so glamorised that we cannot perceive the reality.

The dominant photographic language of the tourist brochure has also affected how tourists construct their own photographs. These snapshots tend to reinforce the constructed and commodified experience of travel: what is photographed is that which is different and out of the ordinary. Most tourist snapshots also use a vocabulary of photographic practice that is embedded in power relations. Let us look at the photographs by Western tourists in the non-Western world. Tourism within Europe produces a slightly different set of relations. In the non-Western world, the majority of tourists who travel abroad are Western. Automatically a relationship of economic power is established, both generally and in terms of camera ownership.

While Don Slater has discussed the contradictory way in which the expansion of camera ownership has not led to new or challenging photographic practices (Slater 1983), in the non-Western world this contradiction between ownership and practice is less evident. Tourists, having already consumed an array of exotic and glamorised photographs of the place before arrival, search out these very images and sites to visit and photograph in order to feel that their trip is complete. While many of the experiences revolve around architectural monuments, the desire to consume exotic/anthropological images of people has found a new trade, which has its parallel in the earlier studio-anthropological photography. In many tourist locations – in India, Morocco and Algeria, for example – men and women sit in elaborate garb that the tourist can recognise

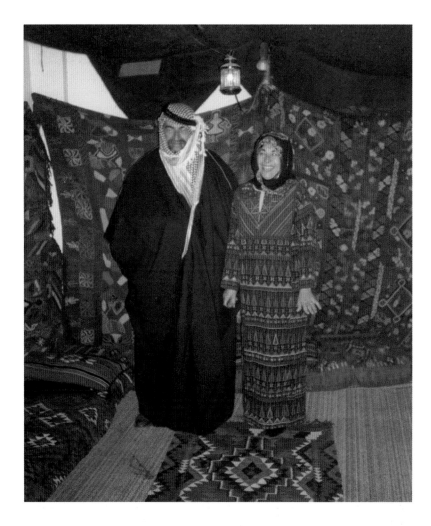

5.16 Tourist photograph
This photograph was taken in a carpet shop where tourists could dress up and role-play in a mock bedouin tent.

as traditional and, more importantly, exotic. These people wait for those willing to pay to have their photograph taken with them. Tourism creates its own culture for consumption. Just like the model in the studio, they are also paid by the photographer to conform to an image which has already been constructed. Alternatively, at other sites, tourists can dress up as part of the exotic experience, and photograph themselves (Figure 5.16). The trade in these new 'anthropological' images may have expanded to include the unknown snapshooter, but their purpose is not to encourage an understanding of a culture, but rather to commodify and consume yet another aspect of a place through the photographic image – the people.

It is important to recognise that there are a growing number of tourists and travellers that have acted more sensitively. Ambilavent at first about using her camera in Kolkota, Ariadne van de Ven has argued that the visual hierarchies created by photography are not always clear cut and that the camera can create a stage around itself in which photographers and subjects participate and collaborate (Van de Ven 2011). Yet the uneven relationship between the well-heeled travellers from the Global North and their encounters with peoples in the Global South, less able to make those cosmopolitan journeys, is impossible to deny.

THE CONTEXT OF THE IMAGE

Don Slater has criticised the semiotic critique of advertisements (characterised by writers such as Roland Barthes and Judith Williamson) for taking as assumed precisely what needs to be explained – 'the relations and practices within which discourses are formed and operated' (Slater 1983: 258). Barthes' and Williamson's readings of advertisements have provided a very limited social and historical context. Often even simple pieces of information, such as the magazine from which the images have been extracted and the date of advertisements, have not been mentioned. Liz Wells has commented on some of the limitations of *Decoding Advertisements*, especially Williamson's lack of consideration of multiple readings (Wells 1992).

While scholars have devoted some space to the understanding of a broad cultural context, the exploration of political and economic contexts is more rare. The vast array of commercial messages has also made their contextualisation increasingly difficult. It would be impossible to contextualise them all. Information about processes of production is not always easily available, and this increases the reality of consumption over that of production:

> What commodities fail to communicate to consumers is information about the process of production. Unlike goods in earlier societies, they do not bear the signature of their makers, whose motives and actions we might access because we knew who they were. . . . The real and full meaning of production is hidden beneath the empty appearance in exchange. Only once the real meaning has been systematically emptied out of commodities does advertising then refill this void with its own symbols. Production empties. Advertising fills. The real is hidden by the imaginary.
>
> (Jhally 1990: 50)

To decode photographs and advertising images more effectively, it is essential for us to understand their context. Let us take, for example, Williamson's reading of the Lancia car advertisement (1979) (see pp. 261–2). Would a discussion of Lancia manufacturing and car production in the late 1970s reveal more about the image?

Since the founding of the Lancia firm in 1907, Lancia had been known for their production of quality cars for gentlemen, as one writer described it. With increasing conglomeration in all industries throughout the twentieth century, Lancia, as a family firm, ran into trouble and was eventually taken over by Fiat in 1969 (Weernink 1979). The Beta saloon was the first car to be produced by Lancia after the merger. Fiat, which was known for producing smaller, cheaper cars, needed to distinguish the Beta from its own cars. Style and quality needed to be suggested, and 'Lancia – the Most Italian Car' was the slogan used to enhance the sense of stylishness of the Lancia range generally. It is this slogan which has been visualised in the 1979 advertisement discussed by Williamson.

Apart from asserting a sense of style and quality, why has Lancia chosen to represent any form of labour relations in the advertisement? Most car advertisements of this period tended to talk about the car itself and its features – for example, its economical use of petrol or the size of its boot. This advertisement does not discuss the car's actual features at all. In the late 1970s strikes took place in many major industries in Britain and Europe. In September 1978, for example, the Ford car workers at Dagenham went on strike for nine weeks. Car manufacturers generally must have wanted to maintain an image of good industrial relations. The illusion of the contented happy peasant worker in the vineyards depicted by the ad discussed earlier (see pp. 261–2) glosses over the general unrest that was present during this period. Finally, the image of the peasant worker could carry another function. During the mid-1970s, the car industry began to introduce micro-processors into production for increased automation. The peasant workers depicted in the ad, outside of industrial production, also acted to represent Lancia as a quality hand-crafted, gentleman's car. A growing number of scholars have researched into the context of production for marketing photography. Below we discuss David Nye's account of General Electric photography. Another example of the value of research into the context of photographic production can be seen in Brian Osborne's essay on the Canadian state and the Canadian National Railways' use of photography to promote the export of Canadian goods and to attract potential immigrants (Osborne 2003).

Image worlds

Let us look at an example of marketing photography, where an understanding of the context within which images are produced helps us to perceive the extent to which commercial interests affect photographic practice. In *Image Worlds*, David Nye gives us a detailed exploration of the context of production, dissemination and historical setting of General Electric's photographs between 1900 and 1930 (**Nye 1985**). David Nye notes how commercial photographers do not strive for uniqueness (as does the artist photographer), but rather for a solidity of a predictable character. In spite of their documentary appearance, Nye notes the contrast between the images produced by a socially concerned

DAVID NYE (1985) **Image Worlds: Corporate Identities at General Electric 1890–1930**, Cambridge, MA: The MIT Press.

documentary photographer and a commercial photographer, even when the subject is the same. He compares two photographs of Southern textile mills, one by Lewis Hine, the other by a photographer working for General Electric. While Hine emphasises the people and children in the mills who work in potentially dangerous environments, the commercial photographer's image stresses machinery, electrification and technical progress (Nye 1985: 55–6).

Nye notes how, by the beginning of the twentieth century, the management of General Electric discovered the need to address four distinct groups – engineers, blue collar workers, managers and consumers. Their desire to say different things to different groups affected the production of images for the company's various publications. While the *General Electric Review* (a company-sponsored scientific journal) used photographs which emphasised the machines, the publications for workers employed images which concentrated on the idea of the corporation as community.

Nye not only notes the varying sorts of photographs for different publications, but also the changing production of images over time. While images from 1880 to 1910 expressed a sense of relationship between workers and managers (they were often photographed together), images after this date present a picture of a workforce which was much more highly controlled by management. Nye details how by the 1920s General Electric had 82,000 workers in their employment, in contrast to 6,000 in 1885. The burgeoning workforce made management's role more important, and the artisanal skills of the previous era had also all but disappeared. Labour unrest began to increase during the 1910s. In 1917, partly in response to these conflicts, General Electric began to publish a magazine called *Works News* which was distributed to all blue collar workers twice a month. The paper did not address the general workforce, but was tailored to each site. The covers of the magazine produced a new kind of photographic image not previously used by the company. They featured individual skilled workers photographed from head to toe and engrossed in a piece of interesting work. This kind of image was repeated on the cover of nearly every issue of *Works News*, and did not represent the reality for most of General Electric's employees; but, since these workers were individualised and isolated, the generalisation was only implicit. These kinds of images hardly existed inside the magazine, which concentrated instead on the workers – as a community which went on holiday, played in sports teams and participated in other forms of recreation. The style of the cover photographs had a history in Lewis Hine's work a decade earlier. He had aimed to represent and give dignity to 'real men' in difficult work. In adopting this style, the General Electric photographers were simply using it as a representational strategy to define the image world of the General Electric plant. It is only through an appreciation of the context of the image that we can understand the intent in the production of images by Hine and the General Electric photographer as different, and can therefore appreciate the different meanings of the image. The production of meaning is a process. As Marx noted in *Grundrisse*:

> It is not only the object that production creates for consumption . . .
> [It] also gives consumption its precise nature, its character, its finish.
> . . . Hunger is hunger, but the hunger that is satisfied by cooked meat
> eaten with a knife and fork is a different hunger from that which bolts
> down raw meat with the aid of hand, nail and tooth. Production thus
> produces not only the object but also the manner of consumption, not
> only objectively but also subjectively.
>
> (Marx quoted in Slater 1983: 247)

For General Electric the process of production and conditions of production changed in 1917, with the success of the Bolshevik Party in Russia and the ensuing Russian Revolution in October 1917, an event which shook the world. New images of dignified workers emerged as a result. General Electric borrowed and absorbed this new language to control and mollify their own workforce.

CASE STUDY: BENETTON, TOSCANI AND THE LIMITS OF ADVERTISING

The case of Toscani's Benetton advertising enables us to draw together a number of strategies for considering commercial photography that have been suggested in this chapter. We can recognise the way in which spectacle works, the value of giving due importance to economic and social contexts, the value of exploring the language of particular advertisements and their reception, as well as the limits of advertising photography and advertising in general to highlight social issues and strategies for change. Toscani's relationship with Benetton is also a rare example of an advertising photographer who gained an almost celebrity status and became named in the art world through his imagery for Benetton.[5] Yet his attempt to use advertising as a means to speak beyond the limits of the spectacle also brought an end to his relationship with the clothing firm.

In 1984, when Toscani joined Benetton, the United Colors campaign was initiated. The image of young people from around the world wearing Benetton clothing suited the newly international interests of the clothing firm. In 1978, Benetton's export market was 26 per cent of its total sales, but by 1981 its export share had increased to 40 per cent of its total output. By 1983, export sales exceeded domestic sales. In 1986 the Benetton Group was finally launched on the stock exchange. During the mid-1980s, therefore, the company changed from being an Italian (and family) company, to becoming an international player for world markets (Belussi 1987: 12–22). Toscani's imagery provided the company with an image of global consumption that can be described as a form of multicultural multinationalism that ignored the realities of globalisation which can be characterised by the exploitation of workers in the Global South for the benefit

5 Benetton imagery was shown in *The Globe* exhibition which toured the UK in 1989. The image of the new-born baby was also shown in an exhibition of images of motherhood at Boymans-van-Beunigen Museum, Rotterdam, Holland.

HENRY GIROUX (1993)
'Consuming Social Change:
The "United Colors of
Benetton"', **Cultural Critique**
26: 5–32.

L. BACK AND V. QUAADE
(1993) 'Dream Utopias,
Nightmare Realities: Imagining
Race and Culture within the
World of Benetton', **Third
Text** 22.

of increased consumption in the Global North and the elites of nations worldwide. Henry Giroux defines these images as containing violence at their core through 'constituting principles that accentuate individualism and difference as central elements of the market' where racial differences are accentuated but 'linked primarily to the dynamics of consumption and largely subordinated to the logic of the marketplace' (**Giroux 1993**). Back and Quaade have highlighted how these images of international harmony were constructed within a 'grammar of race' (**Back and Quaade 1993**: 65). These images, carefully constructed within the confines of the studio, acted as a visual affirmation of the ideology of capitalism and individualism at the very moment when the Soviet Union was collapsing. In March 1987, for example, an advertisement made up of two double-page spreads depicted a Russian boy, dressed in red Benetton clothing and sporting Soviet regalia, and a young American girl called Stacey Reynolds in denim clothing (*The Face*, March 1987). 'Stacey' was obviously a mythic character since two different American girls are given this name in Benetton advertisements. Toscani says different things about America and the USSR through the models' poses and regalia. The Soviet boy stands straight, and salutes us with a stern expression on his face. In his left hand, he carries a paper rocket in army camouflage colours – perhaps a reference to the arms race. In contrast, the American girl smiles at us gently and carries a model of the Statue of Liberty. Symbolically, we have America represented as the upholder of liberty, which is contrasted with the stern and uncompromising USSR that is presented as responsible for the buildup of arms. In another image from 1988, a Chinese boy, dressed in blue, carries a copy of Chairman Mao's 'Little Red Book'. The book is upside down. Other Benetton advertisements from this period also indicate support for imperialist ideologies (Ramamurthy 2003: 219–20). The advertisements represent the ideological and economic interests of the company: 'Our international image and the substance of our company are the same – a global group open to the world's influences and engaged in a continuing quest for new frontiers' (Benetton 1993).

The contradiction in Benetton's images of global harmony can be seen by exploring their context of production. Benetton's business success has rested on their 'flexibility in manufacturing', which allows the company to respond quickly to changes in fashion trends. Benetton was one of the first companies to construct a computerised network that linked retailers with the company's headquarters, so that the company could be made aware immediately of fast-selling items, which could then be reproduced according to demand. This process has increased subcontracting, a system that encourages unskilled 'shell making' in the Global South where labour is cheap and in small workshops with non-unionised labour, and homeworking, which is notorious for being badly paid (Mitter 1986: 112–15; Phizacklea 1990: 14–16). Much of Benetton's success in world markets has also been linked to the establishment of the multifibre agreement, which limits clothing imports from the Global South for the benefit of European manufacturers.

Shock advertising: ahistoricism and ambiguity

In 1989, Toscani, aware that his images were being read ambiguously, discarded the slightly sugary image of children smiling sweetly for a series of bold images which played on contrasts, particularly that of skin colour. Before 1989, Benetton's images still seemed to relate to the genre of studio fashion photography. Benetton clothes and other accoutrements of fashion were worn by the models, who were positioned in a shallow space. After 1989, this relationship collapsed and the clothes ceased to be represented at all. Back and Quaade (1993) have described the 1989 to 1991 phase as that of 'racialisation and ambiguity'. The notion of racial essences continued; but beyond this, racist imagery and history were evoked. This series included the image of a black woman nursing a white child. It created uproar in America, as well as discontent in Britain. The image clearly echoed slave relations, where black slave mothers nursed white children. The image also dehumanised the black woman through the way it was cropped – she is a headless unidentifiable 'Other'. This image has visual references to the photograph of a torso of a Dahomey woman by Irving Penn. Her headless body is totally **objectified** and dehumanised, and is presented for consumption to the predominantly white viewer – she cannot even look back (see Penn 1974: 39).

Images, like everything else, are historically based and although they change in meaning according to their context, they cannot avoid the meanings and symbolisms from the past. This is part of their context. Historical interpretation, however, was dismissed as individual interpretation by Benetton. Following the storm over this and other advertisements in the United States, Benetton's sales figures fell in America, but only for a short while. Controversy eventually seemed to increase sales. As Vittoria Rava, Benetton's advertising manager, of the time commented: 'we believe our advertising needs to shock – otherwise people will not remember it' (Graham 1989).

Pseudo-documentary and the courting of controversy

The controversy of Benetton images increased (as did their sales) as Benetton discarded the constructed fantasy image of advertising for the seeming realism of photodocumentary. They were one of the first companies to reconstruct their identity as 'a corporate force for social responsibility' (Giroux 1993: 12; Ramamurthy and Wilson 2013). The new campaign included a photograph of David Kirby dying from AIDS, an African soldier holding a human femur behind his back, a burning car in an Italian street, an albino Zulu girl being shunned by others and an image of poor black people scrambling into a waste lorry. In using these images, Toscani defied the boundaries of photographic genres, in which the 'reality' of the documentary image stands in stark contrast to the fantasy world of advertising. The collapsing of these genres, however, caused outrage.

The photograph of the man dying from AIDS, the Zulu girl and the fire-bombed car had all been published earlier in documentary contexts, but as has been noted above, the production of meaning is a process, and that process is affected by the photograph's context. This third phase of advertising has been described as experimentation with 'pseudo-documentary' whose overriding theme is 'a fetishisation of images of abject catastrophe'' (Back and Quaade 1993: 74). In using controversy to increase consumer awareness the company sometimes exploited the quandaries of magazine editors. *Elle* magazine, for example, accused Benetton of deliberately sending advertisements to magazines just before printing deadlines. On one occasion *Elle* was forced to leave a double page of the magazine blank. The page however explained why, giving Benetton more publicity. On another occasion, Benetton refused to substitute the advertisement of an albino Zulu girl being shunned by other girls for the *New Yorker*. The paper was running a piece about Malcolm X and racial tension in the same issue. They did not want viewers to think they were mixing advertising and editorial. Benetton argued that pulling the ad would set up 'a dangerous precedent' (Savan 1990: 47). Yet during the LA riots of 1992, Benetton withdrew their billboards of a burning fire-bombed car from the streets of LA of their own accord. Suddenly Benetton seemed to care about the new meanings which their images could create. They replaced this image with one of people of various ethnic backgrounds smiling broadly. Benetton exploited the free publicity of the news cameras again. CNN sent a camera crew to document the event. Fred Bacher commented on Benetton's approach: 'What I find offensive about the ads is not their extreme violence; it's their trendy ambiguity. Benetton's ads are not constructed to help their consumers form ideas about social issues' (Bacher 1992: 45–6). Toscani revelled in the 'trendy ambiguity' as interviews with him make clear (*Blood on the Carpet*, 9 January 2001, BBC2). Lorella Pagnucco Salvemini has discussed Benetton's shock strategies in her book *United Colors: The Benetton Campaigns* (Salvemini 2002).

In reading these 'pseudo-documentary' images, we must remember that Benetton did not just add their green logo. These photos were cropped and touched up, in a similar way to which a commercial photographer might enhance the image of a cake to give it greater visual appeal. The original black and white photo of Kirby was hand-coloured by Benetton. One interesting fact about Benetton's use of documentary images is that until 1995 they were always in fantastic colours, despite the rich black and white documentary tradition. Benetton's shock tactics have been explored by Pasi Falk who describes them as the Benetton-Toscani effect (**Falk 1997**).

Toscani, the spectacle and the market

In the mid-1990s, Toscani seemed invincible in his constant innovation and use of shock tactics for Benetton campaigns. His use of this strategy can be traced back to the influence from his father, a journalist who taught Toscani the

PASI FALK (1997) 'The Benetton-Toscani Effect – Testing the Limits of Conventional Advertising' in Mica Nava *et al.* (eds) **Buy This Book**, London: Routledge.

power of shock and scandal to sell photographs. Toscani applied this to the fashion image and influenced a whole genre of commercial photography that now exploits shock imagery as well as social issues. See, for example, Diesel's Brand O campaign and Cordaid's 'People in Need' campaign. In his last year at Benetton, Toscani photographed an issue that was too close to his heart. He could not adopt the 'trendy ambiguity' of his previous campaigns in photographing men on death row in America. He found himself unable to twist this issue into the spectacle and drama of 'the permanent opium war'. Toscani tried to use his images to voice his abhorrence of the death penalty and to raise concerns about miscarriages of justice. The reaction and consequent campaign by those in support of execution, which included one family whose son had been murdered, was to lose Benetton a contract with Sears department store for 100 Benetton stores. On this occasion, when ambiguity was removed and when Toscani tried to attack the conservative ideologies of America, Benetton lost revenue and enormous potential revenue. The campaign ended, as did the relationship between Benetton and Toscani a few months later. The experience highlights beautifully the limitations of advertising and its inevitable ideological position of upholding hegemonic ideas and ideals. Issues can be used to enhance and decorate the spectacle but cannot be seriously discussed. The key interest of advertising is profit (*Blood on the Carpet*, 9 January 2001 BBC2). As Luciano Benetton articulated after the incident: 'Campaigning is not my subject, I am an entrepreneur'.

Benetton has continued to employ its photographic promotional culture to create controversy and boost editorial coverage of its campaigns and develop its brand identity. In line with the shift in brands to represent ideas rather than products and 'situations' rather than people, the Benetton group like other multinationals has developed corporate social responsibility projects that enhance their branded concepts. In 2007, the Benetton group established the Unhate foundation which describes itself as seeking 'to contribute to the creation of a new culture against hate'. Developed by the PR company 72andSunny, which describes itself as an organisation that 'creates cultural impact on behalf of brands', the group created 'Unhate', adopting the style of Toscani's previous advertising to depict various leaders kissing, including US president Obama and the Chinese premier Hu Jintao, the Pope and an Egyptian immam, the Palestinian and Israeli leaders, as well as German and French presidents Merkel and Sarkozy. Just as in previous campaigns, there is little attempt to understand the root of problems. Nothing is done to address concerns over Benetton's use of cheap ununionised labour or its poor environmental record; instead, controversy was evoked with the Vatican declaring the foundation's image of the Pope to be a 'grave' act of disrespect. Promoted in the year following a fall in Benetton profits by 33 per cent, the editorial coverage undoubtedly acted to promote brand awareness amongst a global metropolitan youth audience.

Photographic imagery plays a key role in the marketing of commodities, brands, ideas and ideologies in the twenty-first century. The way we use the camera, the way in which images circulate, the ideas of beauty that we construct through photography and our understanding of what is significant, are all impacted by the wider values of a society based on profit, consumerism and commodity exchange. Such values, the use and abuse of photographic imagery, and the development of photographic practices within it do not go unchallenged as individuals and groups attempt to use photography to evidence counter hegemonic ways of living and creating in our media-saturated world.

CHAPTER 6

On and beyond the white walls

Photography as art

LIZ WELLS

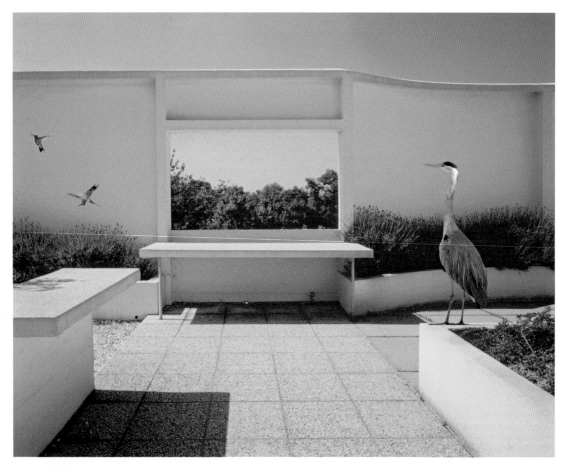

6.1 Karen Knorr, 'The Rooftop', from the series *Villa Savoye*, 2008

On and beyond the white walls

Photography as art

INTRODUCTION

Photography is ubiquitous as a means of visual communication. But the history of photography as art has focused not so much on photographic communication as upon photographs as objects, reified for their aesthetic qualities. It follows that such histories typically focus on pictures, and on the works of specific practitioners. Thus, until recently the story of photography as art tended to be presented as a history of 'great', or 'master' (*sic*), photographers. Such accounts not only divorce photography as fine art from the larger history of photography with its ubiquity of practices, but also rarely engage with broader political issues and social contexts.

In this chapter we use 'Art' to refer to the web of practices relating to the Arts establishment (galleries, museums, public and private sponsorship, auction houses . . .) by contrast with more general understandings of photography as an 'art' or expressive skill.[1] The position of photography in relation to the gallery is complex; on the one hand, photographic media (chemical or digital prints, lightbox imagery, video projection . . .) may be used by artists, possibly in conjunction with other media, as a means of expression; here photographic pictures or series may be made primarily for gallery viewing. Photography is thus contextualised as art through being shown in galleries, museums, and artists' publications. Photomedia are also used by artists in contexts beyond the

1 The term 'Art' is used to indicate focus upon Arts institutions and gallery exhibition. This follows Raymond Williams' distinction between 'art' as creative skill and 'Art', used in Britain since the early nineteenth century to refer to the Art establishment, a network of galleries, museums, funding organisations, publishing and festivals (Williams 1976). The notion of Art as a specialised field of practice has been criticised variously, for instance, in Soviet Constructivism, or, more recently, through practices such as publishing imagery on the internet, exhibiting on (advertising) hoardings, or organising community-based arts projects.

2 Community arts as a
movement (for instance, in
Britain in the 1970s/1980s)
challenged what was
perceived by some as elitism
in the arts establishment
through taking art to people
– on housing estates, in
schools, at public fairs, and
so on – and through
encouraging wider
participation in arts events
and practices. Recently,
certainly in northern
Europe and North America,
there has been a resurgence
of interest in social
engagement and in site-
specific practices.

MIKE WEAVER (1989a) **The
Art of Photography**,
London: Royal Academy of Arts.

3 The title references a
description (attributed to
Lincoln Kirstein, poet, critic,
curator and founder of the
New York City Ballet) of
Walker Evans' work as
'tender cruelty' linking
photography within the
gallery to social
documentary. Documentary
uses of photography were
emphasised in this
exhibition which, in
common with many shows,
brought work originally
made for other purposes
into the gallery.

gallery, for instance, as billboard art, or within community arts.[2] On the other hand, imagery made in other contexts, such as documentary or fashion, may later be taken up by galleries or museums. Collections at major institutions such as MOMA, New York or the Victoria and Albert Museum in London clearly illustrate this.

This chapter considers debates relating to photography, the art gallery, arts institutions and the market for photography as art. The first section focuses on nineteenth-century debates and practices, noting that from its very inception photography was conceptualised in terms of both its apparent ability to accurately transcribe from reality and its expressive potential. This acts as historical context for discussion of twentieth-century photography considered as related to Western modern, and postmodern art movements. In **modernism**, the emphasis was upon photography as a specific medium with particular qualities or attributes. Postmodern theory loosened the focus on the formal, viewing the photographic as a particular language or sign system. Finally, the chapter reviews current debates, practices and gallery systems, and comments on the internationalism of contemporary art within which photographic media are now ubiquitous. As with any overview, a word of caution is appropriate: this discussion should be taken as a starting point for fuller exploration of sets of debates, not as a comprehensive compendium. The chapter includes three case studies: on Soviet constructivism, Surrealism as an art movement, and Landscape. Each directly illustrates points made; they were also chosen in part as examples of the interrelation of history, politics, intellectual debate and art, and in part to offer summary introduction to materials not necessarily easily accessible. Photographs relating to land, landscape and environment are used as illustration throughout. This focus allows more immediate comparison of form, content and subject-matter than would be the case with a random compilation of images. Landscape was selected to contrast with the emphasis on people (in personal albums, on the streets, or as 'body') in previous chapters.

Photography as art

In 1989, 150 years after Fox Talbot's announcement of 'photogenic drawing' (the calotype), the Royal Academy, London, mounted its first ever photography exhibition, *The Art of Photography*. Arguably this represented the acknowledgement by the Arts establishment in Britain that had been sought, variously, throughout photography's history. The first major photography show at the Tate (Tate Modern, London), titled *Cruel and Tender*, was not until 2003.[3] Photography has fared better elsewhere with, for instance, active development of the photography collection and gallery at the Victoria and Albert Museum, London (V&A) in the final decades of the twentieth century and the long-established collection at the Museum of Modern Art, New York.

Historically, tension between the photograph as document and artistic interpretation has been at the heart of debates as to the status of the photograph as art. Photographs have been exhibited right from the inception of photography. In Britain they were included in the Great Exhibition of 1851, and the Royal Society of Arts organised its first show of photography in 1852.[4] The Société Française de Photographie (formed 1854) mounted gallery shows in Paris in 1855 and 1857 (Frizot 1998: 93–5). In the nineteenth century, there were no mass media of the sort taken for granted now, so exhibition was one of the prime ways of communicating information about artistic, scientific and technological innovations. But, from very early days, critics and practitioners disagreed as to the status of photography as art.

This debate begs the question as to what is meant by 'art'. Definitions here have been variously contested. For aesthetic philosophers post-Renaissance art relates to the sensual, the beautiful and the refined; thus, questions of taste are centrally related to expressive practices. Here, the artist is characterised as a special sort of 'seer', or visionary of 'truth', poetically expressed. In the case of photography, the artist is viewed as transcending 'mere recording' of events, as offering a unique perspective on or insight into people, places, objects, relationships, circumstances. But taste involves judgement, and judgement may be exercised by few – albeit, in certain political scenarios, ostensibly on behalf of the many. For example, in Britain – as elsewhere in Europe – traditionally it had been the aristocracy and the upper classes who exercised hegemonic influence through their power of patronage although, particularly since the mid-nineteenth century, city museums and galleries were opened thereby founding publicly available collections. Now, increasingly, influence and judgement falls to curators, critics, arts educators, and the world of the media, as well as private buyers whose investment in work by a particular artist may be instrumental in supporting the possibility of the artist pursuing further projects. In the USA the arts establishment greeted and promoted modern art from Europe (and, indeed, immigrant artists from Europe) especially in the period before and during the Second World War, thus influencing debates about art including critical criteria for the appreciation of formalism or of abstract expressionism.

Many critics, including the influential American curator and historian Beaumont Newhall, have based claims for photography on formal and expressive qualities which accord with the Western, post-Renaissance tradition. Such claims stem from connoisseurship; that is, valuation of the sensitive and the precious. They are not necessarily intended to assert parity of status with older media such as painting or sculpture, but they do reinforce the notion of the photograph potentially offering a special mode of perception both through its ability to capture and freeze a moment in time and through artistic sensibilities. In the nineteenth century, when photography was first announced and developed, art and technology – the expressive and the mechanical – were viewed as distinct. This distinction influenced the reception of photography and attitudes towards it as many people categorised cameras and photography as mechanical. But photography also conformed to aesthetic

4 The 1851 exhibition, a celebration of British achievements, was held at the purpose-built Crystal Palace, London. The Royal Society of Arts is also London-based.

See also ch. 1, pp. 58–60 for a discussion of Beaumont and Nancy Newhall's *The History of Photography*.

conventions in terms of composition and subject-matter, highlighting particular features in order to stress their significance. For serious photographers, it was creative potential along with its apparent accuracy of transcription that was the source of fascination with the medium.

However, they did not necessarily see themselves as artists. For instance, British photographers such as Julia Margaret Cameron or Lady Clementina Hawarden, whose work might now be viewed as art, and who certainly hold a central place within museum collections, did not themselves make this claim. As historian Margaret Harker notes, combination printing, using two or more 'negatives' (glass plates) in order to achieve particular pre-visualised results, was common from the 1850s. This could be viewed as an artist's approach to using the medium. Yet she affirms that the first attempt to promote photography as *fine art* was not made until a Camera Club exhibition in Vienna in 1881 (Harker 1979). By contrast, Aaron Scharf, in relation to the Paris photography exhibition of 1855, describes photographers including Durieu, Nadar and Bayard as '"immigrants" to the Fine Arts' (Scharf 1974: 140). As we see, historians disagree as to when photography was first viewed as an art; this not only reflects debates about art versus technology but is also influenced by differing national contexts and attitudes.

Thus, we should distinguish between claims made by photographers for themselves, or for particular movements, and claims made at a later stage by historians, critics and curators. For instance, Soviet revolutionary artists aimed to take work out from the gallery into everyday social life, viewing art as both an essential tool in the re-education of the mass of the Russian people and as 'art for the people'. Nowadays, retrospectives of their work are curated for galleries, spaces which the Soviet artists would surely have viewed as bourgeois and elitist! Likewise, as already noted, early twentieth-century documentary, originally destined for publications in social surveys, magazines or books, now takes pride of place within the gallery and the archive. Peter Galassi, curator of an exhibition selected from the photography archive at the Museum of Modern Art in New York, distinguishes between photography intended as art and 'vernacular' photography, noting the differing lineages of work now included within the same collection (Galassi 1995). Such a binary distinction over-simplifies a complex history. It may be useful as a means of classification for museums and archives that, since the late twentieth century, have become increasingly prominent in both the conservation of images and their interpretation. However, precisely because of the influence of museum archivists and curators in constructing what are inevitably selective histories of the medium, any tendency towards over-simplified categorisation has become a source of concern for academic researchers.

Noting a number of moments of transition in the late nineteenth and early twentieth centuries in which photography was central to art movements, critic **Peter Wollen** argued that:

PETER WOLLEN (1978) 'Photography and Aesthetics', **Screen 19(4)**, Winter, reprinted in *Readings and Writings*, London: Verso and New Left Books, 1982.

For photography to be an art involves reformulating notions of art, rejecting both material and formal purism and also the separation of art from commerce as distinct semiotic practices that never interlock.

(Wollen 1982: 188)

Writing in the 1930s, Walter Benjamin likewise argued that the 'aura' associated with the uniqueness of the work of fine art, such as a painting, should wither in favour of the photograph, which he welcomed as a more democratic – or less exclusive – medium because of possibilities for mass reproduction (Benjamin 1936). Here it is the anti-elitist potential of (chemical) photography, by contrast with the singularity of each individual painting, that was being stressed. We can assume that Benjamin would have welcomed the reproducibility of the digital and the openness of the internet.

EARLY DEBATES AND PRACTICES

The complex relations between photography and art

Understanding the relationship between photography and painting in the nineteenth century involves a number of interconnected considerations. Photography, first announced in Britain and in France in 1839, was initially heralded for its technical recording abilities. With few exceptions, the emphasis was upon *picture-taking* rather than *picture-making* – to echo a distinction made by Margaret Harker (Harker 1979). She suggests that the development of the art of photography in the late 1850s can partly be accounted for through the increasing involvement of people trained as artists. They brought with them a concern for form and composition and, in particular, the use of light. She notes that the use of photographs as illustrations for poetry or literature, or as pictoral narrative and allegory, also dates from the late 1850s. **Mary Warner Marien** argues that what she terms 'High Art Photography':

MARY WARNER MARIEN (1997) 'Art, Photography and Society', ch. 3 of **Photography and its Critics, A Cultural History, 1839–1900**, Cambridge and New York: Cambridge University Press.

orchestrated separate media. High Art photographs blended theater, printmaking, and painting with photography. Actors or other players were posed singly or in a *tableau vivant*. Interestingly, specific paintings were only occasionally replicated in High Art Photography. For the most part, these images rendered original conceptions, illustrating religious or moral precepts often in the manner of maudlin genre painting and popular Victorian prints. By partaking in the established didactic function of the fine arts, High Art photographers attempted to skirt objections to the medium's inartistic verisimilitude.

(Warner Marien 1997: 87)

In this section we consider, first, the influence of the transcriptive qualities of photography within changing nineteenth-century fine art practices; second, photography democratising art; and third, photography, aesthetics and western art. In the following section we discuss pictorialism, and claims for the photograph as a fine art made by photographers at the turn of the century. Writing on *Art and Photography* **Aaron Scharf** (1974) emphasises uses of photographs by artists; for example, as reference notes. Only in the later chapters on twentieth-century art movements does he acknowledge the photograph as art in its own right. As both **Van Deren Coke** and Scharf have indicated, a number of artists used photographs as study devices, eliminating the need to pay for models or to spend long periods of time sketching. For some, these photographic 'sketches' ultimately took over as works in their own right. For example, the French caricaturist, Nadar, first used photography as the basis for satirical portraiture, later acknowledging the photographs themselves.[5] Photography also allowed painters to extend their range of references, as photographic notes supported paintings later made in the studio. Photographs could be used as research, or directly as models for painting. For instance, Scharf observes that Edouard Manet used photographs of the Mexican emperor, and of soldiers, when working on his paintings of the emperor's execution. Scharf also includes two examples, a riverscape and a seascape, by the French realist painter Gustave Courbet, which seem to be based directly upon contemporary photographs (Scharf 1974: 127).

Realism and systems of representation

Courbet and Manet were prominent among artists associated with nineteenth-century Realism within which photography was implicated as an aid to painting. Discussing the implications of Realism as a historical movement in painting and in literature, in France and elsewhere, Linda Nochlin has suggested that the degree of social change experienced in Britain during the Industrial Revolution from the late eighteenth century onwards, and the political revolutions in France, induced artists to explore everyday social experience (Nochlin 1978). Noting the dominance of Realism as a radical movement from about 1840 until 1870/80, she suggests that there are a number of associated ambiguities including, crucially, the issue of the relation between **representation** and 'reality', itself a problematic concept. She argues that:

> The commonplace notion that Realism is a 'styleless' or transparent style, a mere simulacrum or mirror image of visual reality, is another barrier to its understanding as an historical and stylistic phenomenon. . . . Realism was no more a mere mirror of reality than any other style and its relation *qua* style to phenomenal data . . . is as complex and difficult as that of Romanticism, the Baroque or Mannerism. So far as Realism is concerned, however, the issue is greatly confused by the assertions of both its supporters and opponents, that Realists were doing

AARON SCHARF (1974)
Art and Photography,
Harmondsworth: Pelican Books, revised edition.

VAN DEREN COKE (1972)
The Painter and the Photograph, New Mexico: University of New Mexico Press.

5 This was clearly indicated in sketches, photographs and tear sheets from the collection at the Paris Bibliothèque Nationale exhibited at the Maison de Balzac as part of *Mois de la Photo*, 1990.

no more than mirroring everyday reality. . . . These statements derived from the belief that perception could be 'pure' and unconditioned by time or place.

(Nochlin 1978: 14)

Central to her approach is the contention that perception is culturally conditioned.

Paris underwent massive architectural and cultural change in the first half of the nineteenth century, becoming, in effect, the first modern city. Modes of vision, and subject-matter appropriate for artists, were up for debate. Writing at that time, French poet and philosopher Baudelaire argued that the painter of 'modern life' should focus on the contemporary, upon flux and changes that had revolutionised everyday experience. He was among the first critics to support Realism's challenge to previous aesthetic convention through the introduction of everyday subjects and ordinary people into pictures, and through the use of less 'finished' styles of painting than those previously expected or in keeping with the conventions of the French Academy of Art. Yet he made no particular connection between Realism and photography, dismissing the latter as an inferior form of artistic expression due to its mechanical nature. Thus his view of the potential and limitations of the camera seems in line with that, for instance, of critics who dismissed Courbet's series of large-scale pictures of the rural community in Ornans on a number of grounds, including not only the everyday content of the image but also, as one critic put it, its appearance as 'a faulty **daguerreotype**'. Arguably, photography influenced changing ways of seeing, albeit inheriting rather than subverting formal codes of picture-making.

Aesthetic conventions reflect broader sets of ideas. For instance, from the Renaissance to the early twentieth century, Western art used perspective as the principal system of visual organisation. Perspective involves a single, central viewing point. As film theorist Bill Nichols has suggested, 'Renaissance painters fabricated textual systems approximating the cues relating to normal perception better than any other strategy until the emergence of photography' (Nichols 1981: 52).

Some critics have argued that, in prioritising a single central viewing position, this system reaffirms individualism; in other words, it reflects the emphasis on individual actions and responsibilities that emerged within entrepreneurial capitalism. This contrasts with, for instance, political philosophies that foreground community and affirm collectivity. In this respect image-making conventions reaffirm a way of seeing that emphasises humans as individuals.

Focus, which refers to the use of the camera lens to give a 'sharp' image of objects in a particular area of the picture, interacts with perspective to support ways of seeing founded on geometric mapping of space. That camera optics conform with the rules of perspective meant that photographs could support

daguerreotype Photographic image made by the process launched by Louis-Jacques-Mandé Daguerre in France in 1839. It is a positive image on a metal plate with a mirror-like silvered surface, characterised by very fine detail. Each one is unique and fragile and needs to be protected by a padded case. It became the dominant portrait mode for the first decades of photography, especially in the United States. See also p. 130.

composition in painting. Indeed, since one of the claims made was that photographs had the technical ability to reproduce from actuality more definitively than any other form of re-presentation, they could be referenced to enhance accuracy of representation. Arguably photography, itself a product of scientific and technological development, fitted within the spirit of modernity, as well as offering realist possibilities for depicting aspects of modern life.

Photography extending art

Photography provoked artists to re-examine the nature and potential of paint as a particular medium. Artists used cameras as a method of note-taking, in effect, a substitute for the sketchbook; but also as a means of exploring the physical and social world. Photography appeared to be more successful than painting in capturing likenesses. It also had a sense of instantaneity which painting lacked. It has been suggested that photography encouraged the Impressionist painters to experiment with manners of painting which could also capture a sense of moment, and of the passage of light. It is a truism that photography 'released' painting from its responsibility for literal depiction, allowing it to become more experimental. The developing relationship between the two media was considerably more symbiotic.

Photography encroached very directly upon genres of painting such as portraiture, not only taking over some of the work of painters, but extending the compass of the work. For instance, few could afford the time and cost of sitting for a painted portrait, but the professional studio photographer could offer a similar service much more cheaply. As such, portraiture became more generally available. Both high street studios and touring 'jobbing' photographers were common from the mid-nineteenth century (see ch. 3, pp. 153–8). This did not prevent a continuing hierarchy; the painted portrait was still commissioned by the wealthy and the aristocracy. But photographs did allow a greater number of people the status of seeing themselves pictured.

Another respect in which photography extended fine art was in its role as the re-presenter of art objects. It was no longer necessary to travel to Florence to see paintings commissioned by the Medicis, or to Egypt to contemplate classical architecture and artefacts; you could attend slide talks, or visit an exhibition, and view reproductions. Virtual reality, with its ability to seemingly travel around a painting or sculpture, viewing it from every possible angle, now makes the 2D black and white photograph appear highly limited as a means of showing an object. But, at the time, the possibility of seeing photographs of art was highly radical. Among the first illustrated art histories was an 1847 limited edition book of Spanish Art which included 66 **calotypes** by Fox Talbot (Scharf 1974: 160).

Photographs also mirrored drawing and painting as pictures were made in accordance with established formal conventions. *Before Photography*, **Peter Galassi**'s comparative study of photographs and paintings within the same genres, draws our attention to continuities in aesthetic convention including

DOROTHY KOSINSKI (1999) **The Artist and the Camera, Degas to Picasso**, New Haven, CT: Yale University Press.

calotype Photographic print made by the process launched by William Henry Fox Talbot in England in 1840. It involved the exposure of sensitised paper in the camera from which, after processing, positive paper prints could be made. Not much used in England in the early days, because it was protected by Fox Talbot's own patents, but its use was developed in Scotland, especially by David Octavius Hill and Robert Adamson.

PETER GALASSI (1981) **Before Photography**, New York: MOMA.

compositional similarities. Likewise, in a more detailed manner, **Mark Haworth-Booth** examined the construction of *River Scene, France* by Camille Silvy, which was a combination print involving staging people within the rural setting (Figure 6.2). Not only does its composition echo traditional aesthetics, but the image replicates the romantic pastoral familiar within eighteenth- and early nineteenth-century landscape painting.

Indeed, staged photographs depicting idealised or mythical scenes became common from the 1850s onwards. Among earlier examples is the work of Julia Margaret Cameron (**Ford 2003**). She invited friends, family and servants to pose for her, either for portraits or as actors within her dramatic scenarios. She moved in Victorian middle-class circles, so this legacy includes portraits of well-known artists, writers and intellectuals, including Alfred Lord Tennyson and Charles Darwin, many of whom visited her at her home, Dimbola Lodge at Freshwater on the Isle of Wight, where Tennyson also kept a house. Her tableaux, staged using friends, servants and local people as actors or characters,

MARK HAWORTH-BOOTH (1992) **River Scene, France**, Los Angeles, CA: J. Paul Getty Museum.

COLIN FORD (2003) **Julia Margaret Cameron: 19th Century Photographer of Genius**, London: National Portrait Gallery.

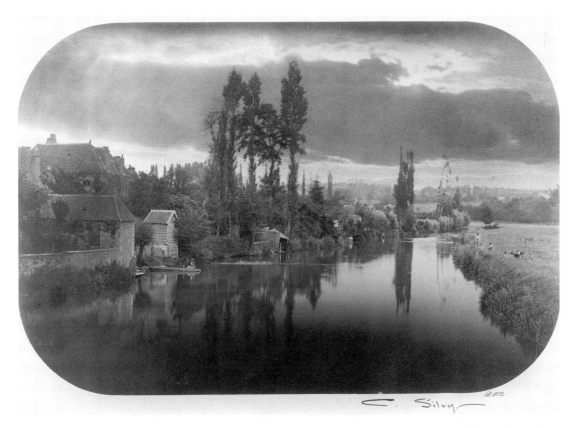

6.2 Camille Silvy, *River Scene, France*, 1858
Two exposures combined to create the idealised rural scenario.

6 The Pre-Raphaelites were a group of British artists of whom Dante Gabriel Rossetti (the son of an Italian refugee), William Holman Hunt and John Everett Millais were the most famous. Taking nature as their primary subject, they sought to retrieve what they viewed as a simplicity and sincerity in art which had been lost in the Renaissance. Examples of their work may be found in many English municipal galleries (the most extensive collection is in Birmingham City Art Gallery).

MIKE WEAVER (ed.) (1989b)
British Photography in the Nineteenth Century: The Fine Art Tradition, Cambridge: Cambridge University Press. A collection of essays on major photographers of the Victorian era.

have particular significance. Cameron's photography coincided with, and in some respects echoes, Pre-Raphaelite Art in Britain.[6] Arguably, through mythologising the past, the Pre-Raphaelites offered a conservative response to modernity. Cameron likewise staged mythical scenes, referencing the seasonal and the cyclical, using costumes and titles to emphasise the poetic. Continuity rather than change was emphasised, and there is no hint of the modern metropolis in her work.

Julia Margaret Cameron was one of a number of serious 'amateurs' who figure prominently in the history of photography in Britain. Others were professional in that photography was their source of income. For instance, Swedish painter-photographer Oscar Rejlander set up a commercial studio in Victoria, London. But he became known for his allegorical compositions, in some cases on a scale equivalent to paintings. For example, 'The Two Ways of Life', involving a number of models playing roles that contrasted the religious (charity) with the debauched (gambling), was nearly three feet (one metre) wide. It was made from 30 separate photographs, entailing pre-visualisation on a grand scale. Such work reflected Victorian preoccupations, including religion, class and morality. This particular picture must have accorded with social concerns acceptable to the Establishment – it was purchased by Queen Victoria in 1857.

As these examples indicate, pictures made by Victorian photographers reflected conventions and tensions in other areas of Victorian Art. Indeed, photography itself impacted on such tensions and aesthetic developments. There was an emerging schism between those preoccupied with the realist representation particularly of the effects of nineteenth-century industrialisation and those with more expressive aspirations.

Photography claiming a place in the gallery

In 1892 a number of photographers seceded from the Photographic Society of Great Britain – which in the 1870s and 1880s had emphasised the science and technology of photography, offering no support for the progress of photography as art. Led by Henry Peach Robinson, they formed the Linked Ring Brotherhood (which did include a few women). Robinson suggested:

MARGARET HARKER (1979)
The Linked Ring: The Secession Movement in Photography in Britain, 1892–1910, London: Heinemann.

NAOMI ROSENBLUM (2007)
A World History of Photography, London, New York and Paris: Abbeville Press, ch. 7 on Pictorialism.

It must be admitted by the most determined opponent of photography as a fine art that the same object represented by different photographers will produce different pictorial results and this invariably not only because the one man uses different lenses and chemicals than the other but because there is something different in each man's mind which somehow gets communicated to his fingers' ends and thence to his pictures.

(Harker 1988: 46)

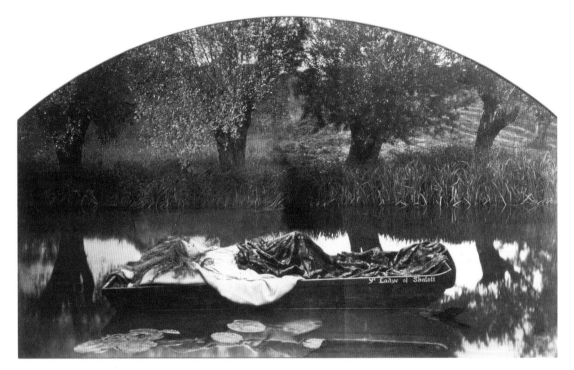

6.3 Henry Peach Robinson, *The Lady of Shalott*, 1860–1
A medieval tale interpreted allegorically.

Retrospectively labelled 'pictorialist', typically their imagery was soft focus, with metaphoric connotations, often drawing upon traditional fable and allegory (Figure 6.3). Again, the Pre-Raphaelites may have been one source of influence. Defining pictorial photography, Mike Weaver notes the aim:

> to make a picture in which the sensuous beauty of the fine print is consonant with the moral beauty of the fine image, without particular reference to documentary or design values, and without specific regard to personal or topographical identity.
>
> (Weaver 1986: Preface)

Membership of the Linked Ring was international, with photographers in other secessionist movements in Europe and the USA joining by invitation. In France the first exhibition of the newly formed Photo-Club of Paris was held in 1894; in Germany Hamburg became the centre for art photography. The Photo-Secession in New York, which was founded by Alfred Stieglitz (a member of the Linked Ring), was not established until 1902. Its objectives echoed the emphasis on the expressive potential of the medium which characterised the European movements. However, membership was restricted

7 The Impressionists, mid-
to late nineteenth century,
include Monet, Cezanne,
Pisarro, Bonnard, Morisot,
Renoir, Van Gogh and
Sisley. Relatively informal
technique seemed to offer a
vision of the world which
was both instantaneous and
subjective. Their concern to
find ways of painting which
reflected light, movement
and speed echoed the
emphasis on modernity and
immediacy by critics such
as Baudelaire, although the
subject-matter treated by
many of the artists was rural
or natural rather than urban.
The most extensive
collection is in the Musée
D'Orsay, Paris, but most
major art collections
(including the Metropolitan
Museum of Art, New York
and the National Gallery,
London) offer examples.

to Americans. Margaret Harker suggests that this was to facilitate the raising
of standards within American photography to exceed those in Europe. Indeed,
Europe was a source of influence on American art (the Armory show, 1913,
a major exhibition of new work from America and Europe, particularly France,
included work by over 300 artists). Stieglitz organised a number of exhibitions of work by European painters, introducing the Impressionists to New
York and bringing what he considered to be the best in European art to
America.[7] He also founded and edited *Camera Work*, published from 1903 to
1917, described by Scharf as 'undoubtedly one of the most influential journals
ever published to be concerned equally with art and photography' (Scharf
1974: 240).

Given the complexity of the relation between photography and painting,
and the extent to which photographers since the mid-century had sought
'artistic results', why was there such emphasis on photography as art at the
end of the century? One factor is that secessionism coincided with the
development of technologies such as roll film and the box camera, which
allowed the casual amateur to take photographs. In claiming artistic status,
serious amateurs were also marking a distinction between themselves and the
newly emerging mass market in photography.

Furthermore, dissent within photography, represented by the various
secessionist groups, echoed dissent more generally within the arts. The end of

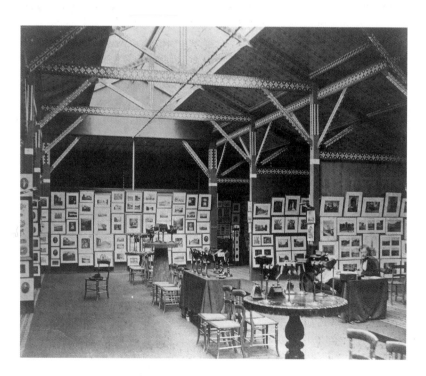

6.4 Thurston Thompson,
Exhibition Installation,
1858
Installation shot of the fifth
exhibition of the Photographic
Society of London, 1858.
Photographs were framed and
matted but crowded in blocks,
some so high or low as to
render them difficult to see.

302

the nineteenth century witnessed the challenge posed by the Impressionists in painting, naturalism in theatre and, indeed, the birth of cinema.[8] It also witnessed the development of lithographic techniques necessary for the mass reproduction of photographs in print. It was an era of considerable change, characterised by tension, debate and dissent. The pictorialists claimed the photograph as fine art, but this claim coincided with more radical challenges to dominant aesthetics. Pictorialism appears conservative now; to many people then it probably already seemed overly traditional.

English photographer Peter Henry Emerson became known for picturing life in East Anglia. Emerson's emphasis was upon what he termed 'Naturalistic Photography', which was the title of his book published in 1889. He advocated realism and 'truth-to-nature' as opposed to the impressionist or the idealistic. For this reason he has been viewed by some critics as a forerunner of modern photography, although others see his work as too picturesque.[9] Indeed, his concern with composition and differential focusing, including soft focus where appropriate, would have allowed him a place within Pictorialist circles had he so desired. Well-documented disputes with H.P. Robinson were probably the main cause of his exclusion.[10]

Aside from illustrated talks, the exhibition was the principal space for public display for all photographs.[11] Claiming photography as high art did not mean seeking different forms of display so much as claiming different cultural significance. Also it should not be assumed that the Victorian gallery operated like the contemporary gallery. Display conventions emphasised quantity of work, rather than the singularity of the specific image. Paintings, prints and photographs were hung floor to ceiling, with little regard to size or frames (Figure 6.4). Since it would be almost impossible to view those hung at floor or ceiling level, certain parts of the wall were, in effect, pride of place. An example of this may be found in the Round Room at Birmingham Museum and Art Gallery, England, which has been hung to demonstrate the style of the gallery in 1885 (although with only about 50 paintings rather than nearly 90, as originally). The legacy – and difficulties – of this style of hanging may also be seen annually, particularly in the print sections, at the British Royal Academy Summer Show. Galleries were not painted white, and lighting was limited, in contrast to the visibility standards of today. Just seeing monochrome images must have been difficult, let alone discerning the detail of resolution and tonal contrast for which the Pictorialists strived. Indeed, the Pictorialists were instrumental in introducing changes to the gallery, emphasising the presentation of the picture. British photographer, Frederick Evans, is credited with the introduction of mounts in more muted colours in order not to distract from the delicacy of detail and imagery achieved through the various photographic printing and toning processes. Photographs were framed more uniformly and less heavily than previously; more wall space was allocated to each picture, and the hanging space restricted to the central area of the wall, not too high or too low. Although the concentration of photographs would

8 Naturalism in painting now refers to close observation and detailed study of external appearances. Naturalism in late nineteenth-century theatre referred to drama in which social environment was depicted as the primary influence on characters, actions and events. Key dramatists include the Scandinavians Henry Ibsen and August Strindberg.

9 Defining 'picturesque', Harker notes 'emphasis on acute observation and appreciation of scenery; an understanding of proportion and perspective in landscape; and the conception of architecture at one with its natural environment (not to be considered in isolation)' (Harker 1979: 27).

10 Emerson remained in the Photographic Society and is credited with responsibility for Royal acclaim, hence the change of title to the Royal Photographic Society (RPS). Paradoxically, perhaps, the RPS became the major archive for nineteenth-century British Pictorialism, holding work by many of those who led the secessionist challenge to the Photographic Society. The collection is now housed at the National Media Museum (NMM) Bradford, Yorkshire, UK.

11 Books of photographs date from the very early days with Henry Fox Talbot's *The Pencil of Nature* or Anna Atkins' use of photographic illustrations in her studies of flora. Each image had to be separately hand printed, so books could only be produced in limited editions.

See www.bmag.org.uk/
birmingham-museum for a
virtual tour of the round room
(accessed 10 December 2013)
in which we can see the
paintings hung three high.

surprise viewers accustomed to late twentieth-century gallery conventions, this represented new standards of display at the time.

THE MODERN ERA

Modernism and Modern Art

> The Modern Movement in the twentieth century has often involved painters and sculptors in an exploration of the idea that art has a purely formal language in which meaning is conveyed by shape, texture, colour and size. This exploration has been in a shifting dialogue with the traditional subjects of art, such as landscape, the figure and still life.
>
> (Tate Gallery, St Ives, Cornwall, 1995)

Key galleries/collections:
in Britain, Tate Modern, Tate
Britain, London; Tate Liverpool.
The Tate, St Ives, holds a
collection of English Modernism.
In North America collections
include MOMA, New York; San
Francisco Museum of Modern
Art. Check international city art
museum and gallery websites
such as MACBA (Barcelona) or
Pompidou Centre (Paris) for
information on their collections.

In his essay 'When Was Modernism', cultural critic Raymond Williams noted that the idea of the modern began to take on what he terms 'a favourable and progressive ring' in the mid-nineteenth century (Williams 1989). He adds that, in its more specific use, 'modern' soon developed into a categorisation of a number of art movements broadly located between the 1890s and the 1940s, so that by 1950 it was possible to contrast 'modern art' with 'contemporary art'. 'Modernism' increasingly came to refer to avant-garde art movements within which the emphasis was on the specific medium (paint, marble, bronze, photography . . .) and on experiments in forms of expression. Williams cited a number of factors which contributed to making the early twentieth century a key era of artistic change. These included the growth of publishing: he noted that the Futurists, Surrealists, Cubists, Constructivists and others announced the birth of their new art movement through manifestos published in magazines or journals. There were also sociopolitical factors: the dislocation of artists caused by war and revolution contributed a sense of the internationalism of art movements as artists migrated within Europe or to North America, spreading ideas and making work which suggested new ways of seeing. This was not new; since the Renaissance it had been common for artists to travel to work and study in major centres such as Rome, Florence, Paris, Berlin. Arguably travel or study abroad induces a more particular perspective on 'home'. Of course this is not exclusive to artists, but it further enhances the fetishisation of artistic sensibilities, including the notion of the artist as somehow outside of modern society and therefore in a position to offer a particular perspective on it. There is some truth in this. For instance, Bill Brandt was born and brought up in Hamburg (although he later claimed to have been born in London). He studied in Paris (1929–31) with Man Ray, who himself was American. On his return from Paris Brandt made a number of studies which collectively investigated Englishness, including his well-known contrast between lifestyles 'upstairs' and 'downstairs' and pictures of stately

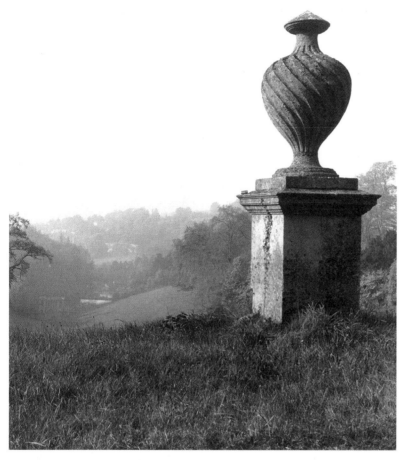

6.5 Bill Brandt, *Prior Park, near Bath*, 1942
Straight photography used with attention to depth of field and compositional effect to describe the contours of the park, whilst emphasising the presence of the sculptural urn in the foreground.

homes and parks (Figure 6.5). Likewise, some decades later, Robert Frank, who was Swiss-born and an immigrant to the United States, produced his famous study of *The Americans* (Frank 2008).

The influential American critic Clement Greenberg wrote extensively on the subject of Modernism, taking the position that art is autonomous from its social context of production. In 1939, Greenberg had distinguished between avant-garde art, and 'kitsch', by which he meant the popular and the commercial 'product of the industrial revolution which urbanised the masses of Western Europe and America and established what is called universal literacy' (Greenberg 1939: 533). For him the avant-garde was the historical agency which functioned to keep culture alive in the face of capitalism.

At this point in his development as a critic, Greenberg acknowledged the social and historical contexts in which the experience of art occurs, asserting that the avant-garde was a type of political engagement. He particularly emphasised medium and method of expression, arguing that:

> the essence of Modernism lies . . . in the use of the characteristic methods of a discipline to criticise the discipline itself, not in order to subvert it but in order to entrench it more firmly in its area of competence.
>
> (Greenberg 1961: 308)

Greenberg's unequivocal support for abstract art contributed to the international respect accorded to American Abstract Expressionism (including painters such as Mark Rothko and Jackson Pollock). He condemned the literal in painting. By contrast, he welcomed it in photography:

> The art in photography is literary art before it is anything else: its triumphs and monuments are historical, anecdotal, reportorial, observational before they are purely pictorial. . . . The photograph has to tell a story if it is to work as art.
>
> (Greenberg 1964: 131)

In his view the photograph was transparent, documentary, and marked by speed and ease (relative to painting): 'All visible reality, unposed, unaltered, unrehearsed, is open to instantaneous photography' (Greenberg 1964). This view clearly prioritised **straight photography**, by then well established in American documentary, over American photographic **formalism** which, as we shall see, in its mid-century heyday, was experimental and more gallery oriented.

Modern Art came to occupy a relatively autonomous, arguably elitist position which remained unchallenged until the 1960s (see **Arnason and Kalb 2004; Arnason 1988**). The internationalism of Modern Art rests on this notion of autonomy. If art is viewed as *not* context-specific it can be assumed that it communicates regardless of national and cultural differences. Artist-critic Victor Burgin has commented sardonically on such assumptions:

> *Art* is an activity characteristic of humanity since the dawn of civilisation. In any epoch the *Artist*, by virtue of special gifts, expresses that which is finest in humanity. . . . The visual artist achieves this through modes of understanding and expression which are 'purely visual' – radically distinct from, for example, verbalisation. This special characteristic of art necessarily makes it an autonomous sphere of activity, completely separate from the everyday world of social and political life. The autonomous nature of visual art means that questions asked of it may

H.H. ARNASON AND P. KALB (2004) **History of Modern Art**, Upper Saddle River, NJ: Pearson Education, 5th edition. Also see H.H. ARNASON (1988) **A History of Modern Art**, London: Thames and Hudson. This revised and updated third edition includes photography.

only be properly put, and answered, in its own terms – all other forms of interrogation are irrelevant. In the modern world the function of art is to preserve and enhance its own special sphere of civilising human values in an increasingly dehumanising technological environment.

If these beliefs sound familiar – perhaps even self-evident – it is because they long-ago became part of the received common-sense we in the West learn at our mother's knee.

(Burgin 1986: 30)

Modern photography

Nowadays modern photography is central to the archive. Historical connoisseurship has created a canon of photographers whose imagery is now highly regarded. This was not always the case. As is suggested elsewhere in this book, the main impetus in photography for most of the twentieth century was in documentary and photojournalism, studio portraiture and commercial art. From about 1905 (towards the end of Pictorialism) photography had little visibility in the art gallery in Britain. The work of British photographers – such as Bill Brandt and George Rodgers, whom we now celebrate – was not made initially for gallery exhibition, nor was it necessarily widely known. Bill Brandt's now famous collection *Perspective of Nudes* was not published until 1961. Photography fared better elsewhere in Europe and in the USA; as we shall see, it was central to Surrealism, and also to American formalism.

Broadly speaking, modern photography sought to offer new perceptions, literally and metaphorically, using light, form, composition and tonal contrast as the central vocabulary of the image. As Wollen noted:

During the 1910s the pictorialist paradigm began to crack. It moved, however, not towards greater intervention, but towards less. The straight print triumphed, shedding at the same time its *fin-de-siècle* aesthetic pretensions and overcoming its resistance to photography of record. Not only was the gum process rejected but also softness, darkness, blurriness and *flou* altogether. Following the crucial innovations of Strand and Sheeler, ambitious photography accepted illumination and sharpness. The way was cleared by the new machine aesthetic of modernism, which gave fresh confidence to the photographer and validated clarity and precision . . . pictorialism transmuted into a new modernist photography of geometrical compositions, machine forms, hard-edge design and clear delineation of detail.

(Wollen 1982: 180–1)

Wollen also observed that this was the era when the pictorial and documentary came together under the influence of new principles of composition. Photographers such as Florence Henri (France) or Paul Strand (USA) seem to have echoed the Cubists in their concern with form. In the case of many of

Key collections include: The Print Room, Victoria and Albert Museum, London; George Eastman House, Rochester, USA; Center for Creative Photography, University of Arizona, Tucson; MOMA, New York. Use online search engines to locate archives in order to explore work from the period.

307

Strand's more famous photographs, people are depersonalised to the extent that they become anonymous figures in the cityscape (see, for instance, 'Wall Street', or 'Central Park', both 1915/1916). Wollen engages with the aesthetic implications of this new photography, arguing that the camera as machine does not in itself make the photograph more objective (and therefore less amenable to the expression of particular perceptions), 'it simply substitutes discovery for invention in the traditional categories of classical aesthetics' (Wollen 1982: 182). Here it is the process of realisation of the image which is at stake. Put more bluntly: creativity resides in the artist, not in the technology.

Photographers move geographically and aesthetically over a lifetime, changing their style and subject-matter, their work reflecting differing political contexts. Photography figured extensively within European avant-garde movements of the 1910s to 1930s, but in ways which did not necessarily pose images as art or lead to gallery exhibition. Reconstruction in Europe, subsequent to both the First World War and the Russian Revolution, offered obvious social and political context and a sense of immediacy. Photomontage was commonly used as a means of direct political comment or more general reflection on social change. For instance, Herbert Bayer's montage of hands and eyes within an urban setting might be interpreted in terms of supplication, or of constant surveillance, as well as referencing the hand and eye, observation and crafting, central to art (see the frontispiece to this book, p. xxii).

Discussing photography and architecture in Europe between the wars, Ian Jeffrey describes 1920s photographic modernism in Europe as engaged with social totalities and worthy of respect, 'premised on selflessness, transcending local and even national affiliations' (Jeffrey 1991: 60). By contrast, he notes more archaic subject-matter in the 1930s, with more romantic focus on secret worlds and marginalised people within the city. The imagery of Krull, Atget, Brassai can be viewed as more conversational, in a classic documentary manner, less experimental and less inclined to celebrate the promise of a new social order so eagerly supported in the first half of the 1920s. In effect, reminding us of the changing European political circumstances, Jeffrey proposes that optimism in the 1920s was superseded by a retreat into romanticism in the 1930s and, crucially, that this can be discerned in the shifting subject-matter and style of the image. Furthermore, work was made for publication in the then popular picture press (see ch. 2, p. 80), not for the gallery. The formal concerns and documentary subject-matter of the period were only later taken up by museums and art galleries.

Photo-eye: new ways of seeing

Shifting political circumstances were specifically reflected in the fortunes of the German Bauhaus (1919–33), which was founded in Weimar under the leadership of Walter Gropius. It moved to Dessau in 1925, by which time

Herbert Bayer, photographer and typographer, was a key influence; and to Berlin in 1932, before disbanding in consequence of the election of Hitler's National Socialists.[12] The Bauhaus was a clear response to the destruction and dereliction witnessed during the First World War. 'Bauhaus' literally means 'house for building'. Although multi-disciplinary, and concerned to integrate art, design and social purpose, architecture came to be the central concern. Taking the notion of reconstruction as the central tenet, Bauhaus theorists emphasised the relation between form and function, and stressed what they saw as a potential unity of art, design and the everyday (see Rowland 1990; **Willett 1978**). László and Lucia Moholy-Nagy were perhaps the best-known photographers associated with the Bauhaus. They stressed ways in which use of light, mechanical reproduction and the possibility of sensitive printing expressed the machine aesthetic of the Modern Age. In parallel with the Soviet emphasis upon photo-eye as the modern method of communication, Moholy-Nagy emphasised the relation between the mechanical nature of the camera, form, angle of vision, the use of light and visual perception, arguing that photography enhances sight in relation to time and space. Their radical approach was not uncontroversial. For instance, Frankfurt School theorist Walter Benjamin expressed impatience with such experimentation, accusing the 'new objectivity' photographers of the Bauhaus of making the world artistic rather than making art mundane.[13] As already noted, Benjamin was interested in photography as a democratic means of mass communication; he opposed formalism and abstraction because, he argued, experimentation in visual languages tends to be exclusive, and therefore elitist. The Bauhaus theorists viewed radicalism in photography in different terms. Like Benjamin, they opposed the reification of the individual artist. Unlike Benjamin, they stressed aesthetic experimentation, viewing this as central to new (and contemporary) modes of expression.

The following case study briefly considers the example of Soviet Constructivism in which art was seen as playing a role in building a new post-revolutionary society.

CASE STUDY: ART, DESIGN, POLITICS: SOVIET CONSTRUCTIVISM

A brief background

Discussing experimentation in Russian art from the 1860s to the early 1920s, Camilla Gray traces a number of strands within Russian Modern Art, ranging from spiritual interest in medieval icon painting to a realism which mirrored developments in other parts of Europe (Gray 1962). In the mid-nineteenth

12 Many Bauhaus theorists were exiled to the United States where they formed The Chicago Art Institute.

JOHN WILLETT (1978)
The New Sobriety, Art and Politics in the Weimar Period, London: Thames and Hudson.

13 The Frankfurt School of Social Research included philosophers, aestheticians, and social scientists, variously concerned with politics and culture, and influenced by the writings of Marx and Hegel. Theodore Adorno, Walter Benjamin, Erich Fromm, Jürgen Habermas, Max Horkheimer, Herbert Marcuse were all associated. Many members ended up in exile in the USA, having escaped the Nazis. Benjamin committed suicide in 1940 whilst waiting to cross from occupied France to Spain (his companions made the journey the next day).

century, 'The Wanderers' – a group of Russian painters who, like their contemporaries in France, had broken from the Russian Art Academy – committed themselves to developing art which was about the everyday. Links with Paris, Munich and Vienna, especially immediately after the failure of the 1905 Revolution, led to a number of major exhibitions in Moscow and St Petersburg wherein Russian artists showed alongside their Western European contemporaries. By the time of the 1917 Revolution there was an identifiable avant-garde which, in the paintings of Kasimir Malevich, Livbov Sergeyevna Popova, El Lissitzky, paralleled Cubism in France in exploring the surface of the canvas and the nature of artistic language.

Experiments in the social role of art

The success of the 1917 Revolution led to a new political context, one in which the nature and social role of art was hotly debated. A number of artists, led by Malevich, stressed the formal and spiritual supremacy of art in itself. A Russian form of Modernism! Others emphasised proletarian culture advocating a social role for artist-workers in the vanguard of Revolutionary change (see **Phillips 1989**; **Solomon-Godeau 1991**). The new situation encouraged a radical aesthetic. Painter-photographer Alexander Rodchenko asserted that:

> Art has no place in modern life. It will continue to exist as long as there is a mania for the romantic and so long as there are people who love beautiful lies and deception. . . . Every modern cultured man must wage war against art, as against opium. . . . Photograph and be photographed.
>
> (Rodchenko 1928)

For Rodchenko and the other Constructivists, new art involved, first, the depersonalisation of practice, that is, taking art out of the realm of individual artistic expression; second, logical laboratory study of form and composition; and third, analysis of rules governing the nature of artistic communication. Photography as a technological medium seemed particularly appropriate. Art set out to renegotiate itself as a type of practice which was utilitarian in foregrounding design and function, and selfless from the point of view of the artist. As such it represented the socialist ideals of the Revolution. Soviet Constructivism flourished for about a decade, before being superseded by Socialist Realism with its focus on glorification of the worker, the peasant and 'heroes' of the Revolution.

Constructivist photography

The Constructivists saw photography as a popular form which, through its usage in posters, magazines and publishing, could be at the forefront of taking new ideas to the people. Emphasising art's post-Revolutionary responsibilities, Rodchenko stated that he was fed up with 'belly button' shots, by which he meant photographs composed conventionally, shot from waist level through

CHRISTOPHER PHILLIPS (ed.) (1989) **Photography in the Modern Era: European Documents and Critical Writings 1913–1940**, New York: MOMA.

ABIGAIL SOLOMON-GODEAU (1991) 'The Armed Vision Disarmed: Radical Formalism from Weapon to Style' in **Photography at the Dock: Essays on Photographic History, Institutions and Practices**, Minneapolis: University of Minnesota Press.

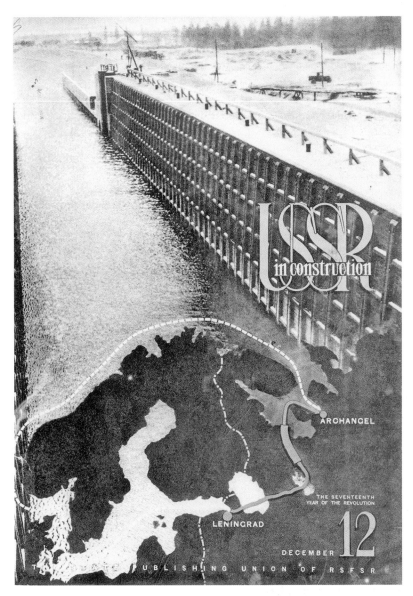

6.6 Alexander Rodchenko, *White Sea Canal*, from *USSR in Construction* 12, 1933
One example of the geometric style and the commitment to a new angle of vision, literally and metaphorically, that characterised Constructivism.

14 Cameras were very
different then to the phones
and light digital cameras of
today, made to fit in pockets
or handbags, although the
legacy can be seen in the
design of medium and large
format cameras still in use.
They were commonly
designed with a viewfinder
on top so the photographer
looked down; the camera
would be steadied at waist –
or 'belly button' – level.
Examples can be viewed in
most museums of the
history of photography.

cameras with their viewfinder on top.[14] He argued for full exploration of the geometry of the image which would, literally and metaphorically, engineer a new angle of vision (see Figure 6.6). Indeed, for Rodchenko photography was the true modern art. He argued that, unlike painting and sculpture, which he viewed as outdated, photography could express the reality of post-Revolutionary society. Thus, in Soviet Constructivism, the issue was not one of photography attempting to claim status as Art, but rather of a democratisation of artistic practices in the service of social and cultural revolution within which photography, by its enquiring nature and its ubiquity, could play a leading role.

Emphasis on form

The above case study offers an example of links between aesthetics and politics. Other links emerged, for instance, photography was implicated within Surrealism as an art movement (see case study, pp. 315–19). The modern emphasis on photo-eye, and on exploring the potential of camera vision, was also characterised by emphasis on form, in Europe through '*New Objectivity*' particularly – although by no means exclusively – associated with German photography in the 1920s and 1930s. Here, as with Soviet Constructivism, photographers were exploring what could be revealed about objects, people and places, through new angles of vision and through experimenting with the possibilities afforded by film chemistry, camera and darkroom technologies (exploring the effects of aperture, or double exposure or direct print methods such as photograms, and so on). Through different uses of lenses and lighting (whether natural or studio set-ups) and also exploring fragmentation, photomontage, or *trompe l'oeil* (wherein an image tricks the eye) they sought to extend image-making potential. Within this, some artists specifically experimented with the qualities of natural and artificial light, testing effects and affects. Hungarian artist, Laszlo Moholy-Nagy, emphasised photography as a means not only of reproduction but also of discovery through detailed observation. He viewed light sensitivity, rather than pictorial representation, as the key characteristic of photography – literally 'writing with light' (Moholy-Nagy 1967). He invented **photograms** made by direct contact between objects and chemically sensitised paper that was exposed to light (Figure 6.7). Such imagery may be seen within a lineage dating from the early Victorian era wherein English photographer Anna Atkins first used contact photography for illustrating flora and fauna, and, as we shall see, contemporary cameraless photography. Moholy-Nagy was working at the Bauhaus in Germany at the same time as American photographer Man Ray, then living in Paris, developed 'Rayograms', using solarisation as a key element within the process. This simultaneity testifies to the experimental approach to photographic media, still images and moving imagery, that typified the European avant-garde of the era.

312

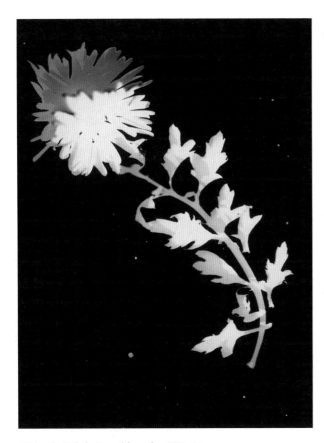

6.7 Laszlo Moholy-Nagy, 'Flower', c. 1925–7

American formalism

Concern with form and precision can be seen at its extreme in what became characterised as American formalism, for example, in the work of the West Coast f/64 Group, founded in 1932 by a number of American photographers, including Edward Weston, Imogen Cunningham and Ansel Adams, which was so-titled precisely to stress visual clarity. Their approach emphasised photography as a specific type of medium with its own optical, chemical and consequent aesthetic properties.[15] This approach became – and remains – highly influential: it was mirrored in the work of East Coast photographers such as Harry Callahan and Minor White. Here European influences are also relevant; for instance, in 1946 Callahan went to teach for Moholy-Nagy at the 'New Bauhaus' in Chicago.[16]

The specificity of photographic seeing was commented upon by curator John Szarkowski in his discussion of the properties of photography wherein he

15 f/64 references smallness of aperture and thus symbolises intent to maximise depth of field.

16 The work of these photographers, and other American photographers of the era, has been extensively published in histories of photography as well as in monographs or biographic essays on individual photographers.

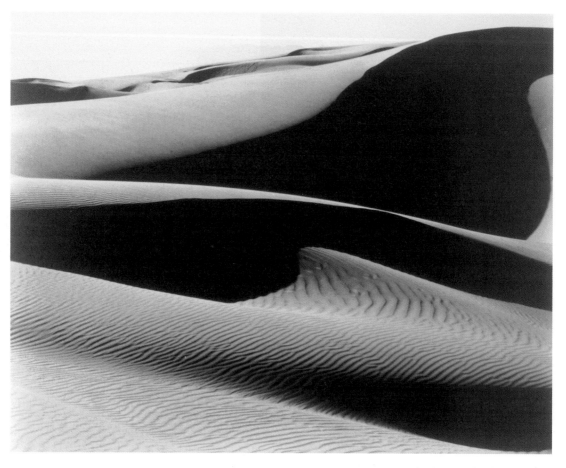

6.8 Edward Weston,
Dunes, Oceano

Photographic seeing with
emphasis on visual form and
rhythm.

suggested that the facticity of photographs, detail, framing, exposure time and vantage point (literally, point of view) come together in the image (Szarkowski 1966). Ansel Adams, who himself had studied music, famously drew an analogy between music and photography wherein he likened the negative to the score, or composition, and the print to performance, that is, interpretation. For Edward Weston, the trademark of photography lay in precision of definition, the fine detail that can be recorded, in the continuity of tonal gradings (black to white), and in the qualities of the surface of the paper used for the print. He defined his approach as both abstract and realist, emphasising the observational basis of the photograph and the aim of the photographer to reveal the nature of the world inhabited. Edward Weston's visual poetics emerged from concentration on tone and shape, although he claimed concern with the subject of the image. Beaumont Newhall stressed the interdependence of the technological and the aesthetic in Weston's work, noting his insistence upon pre-visualisation of the image. Weston sought clarity of form and extolled the

314

camera for its depth of focus and its ability to see more than the human eye. The formalists were not exclusively concerned with a more abstract aesthetic; for example, Weston made portraits of family and friends throughout his life. Tina Modotti, acclaimed for her studies of natural forms and craft objects, for instance, 'Roses', 1925, or 'Hammer and Sickle', 1927, is also remembered for her documentation of the 1926–9 Mexican Revolution.

Unlike other photographic movements of the time, formalism sought gallery exhibition. Indeed, work by these photographers is now highly prized (and priced) and is included in all major photography archives as examples of one of the most significant photography movements of the twentieth century.[17]

Formalism could be defined as a tendency in American art, one that was taken up by the Art establishment. It was not announced as an art movement; rather the label is retrospective. The following case study considers photography in relation to a specific art movement, one which was constituted through manifestos – namely Surrealism. Intellectual currencies which informed Surrealism, its multidisciplinary nature, and subsequent comments and reappraisals, are noted. The case study offers an example of ways in which photography within specific broader movements may be analysed and contextualised. It also draws attention to the emphasis on aesthetic radicalism which typified Modern movements.

17 Curiously, the influential photographer and curator Alfred Stieglitz never showed Edward Weston's work in New York in his Madison Avenue gallery, named An American Place, which he ran from 1929 to 1946. However, in the second half of the twentieth century almost all major historical surveys or gallery overview exhibitions give prominence to the work of the American Formalists. The individual photographers are featured in a number of monographs so their work is easily found in bookshops and libraries.

CASE STUDY: ART MOVEMENTS AND INTELLECTUAL CURRENCIES: SURREALISM

What was Surrealism?

In pursuing academic analysis it is always relevant and interesting to trace links between the general intellectual climate of any era and aesthetic developments. Surrealism took the idea of the individual psyche as its theoretical starting point, thus particularly reflecting the psychoanalytic work of Sigmund Freud. Surrealism emphasised artistic processes whereby the imaginary can be recorded through automatic writing or drawing which would thus offer insights into the world of 'thought' and therefore disrupt taken-for-granted perceptions and frames of reference. For the surrealists, the artist was the starting point or material source of what was to be expressed. Freud had distinguished between the Id, the **unconscious** instinctual self, and the Ego, the largely conscious socialised self. Likewise, surrealists distinguished between 'thought' and 'reason', and aimed to bypass what they saw as the **repressive** nature of reason in order to express natural desires.[18]

Surrealism has been regarded as attempting to replicate the world of dreams. This is premised directly on Freud's dream theory wherein he argued that analysis of the manifest content of dreams offers perception on subjective responses to experience. However, this is to oversimplify, as the aims of Surrealism were

18 Surrealists included André Breton (founder), Antonin Artaud, Luis Bunuel, Claude Cahun, Jean Cocteau, Salvadore Dali (later expelled from the movement because of his support for General Franco and the Spanish Right), Max Ernst, René Magritte (in Belgium where there was a separate Surrealist group), Lee Miller, and painter-photographer Man Ray. Surrealism was championed in Britain by Roland Penrose.

complex and, to some extent, changed over time. They included a direct attack on the nature of art; many of the early surrealists had also been involved in the First World War anti-art movement, Dada (Ades 1974). Both Dada and Surrealism were interventionist in challenging what was happening in the gallery. For instance, Marcel Duchamp placed a urinal in the gallery claiming that the location made it 'Art'.

French poet André Breton described 'A desire to deepen the foundations of the real; to bring about an ever clearer and at the same time ever more passionate consciousness of the world perceived by the senses' (Breton 1978: 115). In the late 1920s, surrealists, led by Breton, called for adherence to Marxist dialectical materialism and to the ideal of revolution. This caused splits in the Paris-based group. But fundamentally, Surrealism was premised on challenging philosophical distinctions between interior experience and exterior realities. The radicalism of Surrealism lay in its aims: to disorient the spectator; to push towards the destruction of conventional ways of seeing; and to challenge rationalist frameworks. Surrealist aesthetics were not based on intention to shock, as has occasionally been suggested, although this was sometimes the effect.

Fine art movements transcend national boundaries, albeit reflecting particular national features. It is necessary to take into account the interplay between that which characterises specific social and political circumstances, and more general international contexts. For instance, the first Surrealist Manifesto was published in Paris in 1924, but the first International Surrealist Exhibition in Britain did not take place until 1936, by which time, arguably, the movement had lost its more experimental edge.[19] Furthermore, a number of the original Paris-based group became members of the Communist Party. In Britain, with Roland Penrose as the key surrealist artist and exponent, the emphasis was more on visual form and psychoanalytic references than on political revolution.

Surrealist photography

How does lens-based imagery, including photography, fit within Surrealism? For Dali, the mechanical nature of the camera was liberating: 'photography sets imagination free', he claimed. Breton stated:

> The invention of photography has dealt a mortal blow to the old modes of expression, in painting as well as in poetry, where automatic writing, which appeared at the end of the nineteenth century, is a true photography of thought.
>
> (Breton 1978: 7)

He also noted approvingly that 'belief in an absolute time and space seems to be vanishing', a reference to the photograph's ability to picture the past, or the geographically distant, and welcomed the fact that 'today, thanks to the cinema, we know how to make a locomotive *arrive* in a picture' (1978: 7). Despite

19 Held in London at the New Burlington Galleries in Burlington Gardens; that is, in a modern gallery, as opposed to an established institution such as the Royal Academy of Arts.

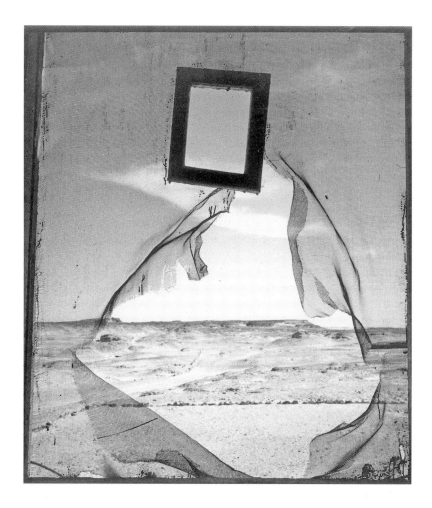

6.9 Lee Miller, *Portrait of Space*, near Siwa, Egypt, 1937
An example of a Surreal juxtaposition of interior/exterior to achieve a dreamlike effect. Mirrors frequently feature, referencing reflection and also the self as source of angst, trauma and artistic creativity.

the involvement of artists such as Herbert Bayer, previously associated with the Bauhaus, where the emphasis was on observation, rather than on interiority, Surrealist photography clearly differed both in principle and in vision from the formalist 'new objectivity' of the Bauhaus or of Soviet Constructivism. Stressing the imagination as the source of insight on experience, the surrealists used **photomontage**, double exposure, **rayographs**, or **solarisation**, in order to produce disorienting imagery. Key surrealist artist-photographer, Man Ray, remarked that he painted that which cannot be photographed and photographed that which cannot be painted. The realism associated with the photograph was utilised, more-or-less playfully, as a tactic to contribute to the Surrealist provocation of new insight as objects, persons or locations were rendered in unexpected conjunctions or distortions or particular motifs doubled within the image.

photomontage The use of two or more originals, perhaps also including written text, to make a combined image. A montaged image may be imaginative, artistic, comic or deliberately satirical.

rayographs, solarisation Aesthetic techniques associated in particular with the work of Man Ray and Lee Miller. Solarisation involves brief exposure to light during printing thereby altering tonal contrast. Rayographs or photograms are cameraless photographs, made by placing objects on photographic paper then exposing to light.

Critical reappraisals

Debates relating to (photographic) representation of the real, distortions, and emergent surreal effects, have figured within critical reappraisals of the movement. Asking 'What is a surrealist photograph?' **David Bate** argues that the 'surreal' refers not to a type of picture but to a type of meaning, an enigma (Bate 2004: ch. 1). This usefully reminds us that the surrealists were concerned to explore new ways of looking at the world that could draw attention to disturbing tensions or contradictions. In line with their interest in the everyday, their work was published in popular forms such as pamphlets or films as well as through exhibitions; indeed, as Bate notes, it was only in the 1930s, with several international surrealist exhibitions, that a perception of surrealism as primarily an art movement was consolidated (Bate 2004: 240). Nowadays installations of surrealist work commonly include displays of more ephemeral materials alongside paintings and larger-scale photography, making the point that Surrealism aimed to be a total revolution. Some critics, including **Rosalind Krauss**, focused on taken-for-granted realism of the photographic as the source of the *coup d'oeuil* effect which often operated to disorient the spectator. Krauss notes metaphoric effects: 'we see with a shock of recognition the simultaneous effect of displacement and condensation, the very operations of symbol formation, hard at work on the flesh of the real' (Krauss and Livingston 1986: 19). In this formulation the shock emanates from the refusal of the transcriptive realism expected of photography. Ian Walker has argued that this position is problematic as it rests on a distrust of 'straight' photography, with its claims to authenticity as source of authority, and reflects a binary opposition between art and documentary still current in North America in the 1980s (Walker 2002). He suggests that in Europe documentary has never been polarised from other areas of practice such as Surrealism and argues that critical focus on a surrealist realism concerned with photography of the city (in their case, Paris) can contribute to more comprehensive evaluation of the import of Surrealist photography. This is further pursued for example in a collection of essays on Czechoslovakian surrealism (**Fijalkowski *et al.* 2013**).

Feminism also contributed to reappraisal of Surrealism, drawing both on debates about patriarchal attitudes in psychoanalysis and, more specifically, through new art history. Women figured in Surrealism as artists but, until recently, their position and contribution has been largely ignored (see Chadwick 1985, 1998). Reinstatement has focused attention on the work of many women surrealists, including photographers Lee Miller and Claude Cahun. Indeed, allegedly Lee Miller 'discovered' solarisation by opening a darkroom door, not realising that Man Ray was printing.

The feminist critique drew attention to the role of woman as muse. Considered from a feminist perspective, the expression of unconscious desires, central to surrealist imagery, seems merely an excuse for male heterosexual fantasy. 'Woman' is objectified. The distorted or fragmented female figure is a common motif. Hans Bellmer's female dolls most obviously degrade and violate woman

DAVID BATE (2004) **Photography and Surrealism**, London: I.B. Tauris.

ROSALIND KRAUSS AND JANE LIVINGSTON (1986) **L'Amour Fou**, London: Arts Council of Great Britain.

IAN WALKER (2002) **City Gorged with Dreams**, Manchester: Manchester University Press.

KRZYSZTOF FIJALKOWSKI, MICHAEL RICHARDSON AND IAN WALKER (eds) (2013) **Surrealism and Photography in Czechoslovakia**. London: Ashgate.

through her disfiguration or dismembering. Surrealists viewed such imagery as an expression of innate but repressed desire, but also used this to challenge bourgeois boundaries of permissibility and draw attention to the violence of war (ch. 4, p. 219 and Figure 4.11). Such images were thus simultaneously revolutionary and, in the light of feminist analysis, misogynistic.

RUDOLF E. KUENZLI (1991) 'Surrealism and Misogyny' in Mary Ann Caws, Rudolf Kuenzli and Owen Raaberg **Surrealism and Women**, Cambridge, MA: The MIT Press.

LATE TWENTIETH-CENTURY PERSPECTIVES

The American and European Avant-garde art movements of the 1960s emphasised idea and process over the conventions of painting and sculpture. The war in Vietnam, the civil rights movement in America, the development of feminist politics and theory, and the student protests of 1968, were reflected in works that were challenging to the status quo, to ideas about the artist as apolitical and working alone, and to art institutions.

(*Comment and Commitment: Art and Society 1975–1990*, Tate Gallery, London 1995)

A number of shifts occurred in the second half of the twentieth century which had ramifications for gallery practices. From the 1960s onwards the image world of the media became increasingly influential within art practices. Second, as art retreated from modernist preoccupations with form and medium, it once again engaged with social and political landscapes so that national and international developments such as civil rights movements, feminism, war, first world/third world relations figured as themes. Third, postmodern theory became a source of influence upon conceptual and interpretative processes, that is, the making and the reading of pictures.

Conceptual art and the photographic

Photography in the 1960s was centrally implicated in the expansion of the mass media, including fashion shots, album covers for long-playing (33⅓) records, photojournalism (the British *Sunday Times* colour supplement was launched in 1962). Two parallel developments in the 1960s and 1970s contributed to shifting the position of photography in the gallery. First, pop artists such as Andy Warhol (USA), Roy Lichtenstein (USA), David Hockney and Richard Hamilton (both British) started to use the photographic in order to reference and comment on lifestyles and consumerism.[20] But, unlike now, with photomedia (chemical or digital, still or time-based) taken for granted as media of artistic expression, photography then was still seen as inherently different (commercial, popular, documentary) from more established art forms such as painting and sculpture. This was no doubt in part because, to echo Roland Barthes, many elements within their pictures were *déjà-lu* ('already

20 Pop Art in the 1960s essentially commented upon evidence of transformation into a consumerist society. Artist Richard Hamilton described Pop Art as popular, transient, expendable, low cost, mass produced, young, witty, sexy, gimmicky, glamorous and big business.

read'). But this was the whole point. Raymond Williams suggested that the two dimensions of the modern, radical aesthetics and technological change, came together in the pictures of artists whose work engaged with the 1960s revolution in mass culture that was consequent upon developments in technology and communications such as broadcast television (Williams 1989). Arguably photography had contributed to creating a more visually sophisticated audience than had previously obtained: 'that painters have used photographs does not legitimise photography; on the contrary, such cross-pollination has primarily helped *painting* remain a vital and effective medium' (Coleman 1979: 121). Through Pop Art the photographic gained a presence in the gallery (see Alloway (1966) for an account of British Pop Art).

Second, in Conceptual Art the photographic became accepted as a valid medium of artistic expression. It was in the 1970s that American Art magazines, including *Artforum* and *Art in America*, took photography into their remit. As phototheorist John Roberts has argued:

> Photography was the means by which conceptual art's exit from Modernist closure was made realisable as *practice*. Yet photography itself was of little interest to most conceptual artists, producing a situation in which critical agency is given to the photographic image without photography becoming theoretically self-conscious as a medium. Photography, then, had an indirect function: it allowed conceptual art to reconnect itself to the world of social appearances without endorsing a *pre*-Modernist defence of the pictorial.
>
> (Roberts 1997: 9)

Modernist theory had focused on the medium. By contrast, Conceptual Art stressed ideas. Artists were concerned to draw attention to the manner or vocabulary of expression; also, to contexts of interpretation, that is, the influence of the situation within which the spectator responds to the image or art object. Indeed, in a number of instances artists placed a statement about an art object in the gallery, thereby focusing attention on the idea, rather than the object (which might never have been actually made). From recent theoretical perspectives the notion of explicitly requiring spectator interpretation comes as no surprise. But, at the time, Conceptual Art, especially in its more critical or political forms, constituted a challenge to the art establishment (see Harrison and Wood 1993; also **Green 1984**). In conceptual photography the characteristics of the medium could be used as a part of the means of expression of an idea. Thus, for instance, Keith Arnatt's sequence of digging himself into a hole in the ground (Figure 6.10) is obviously, at one level, a metaphoric reference to the well-known phrase. But the documentary idiom secures a sense that this event literally did take place.

Conceptualism challenged the dominance of abstract formalism. It was not that it denied the significance of form. Rather, form was brought into play

JONATHAN GREEN (1984) 'The Painter as Photographer' in **American Photography**, ch. 9, New York: Harry N. Abrams.

320

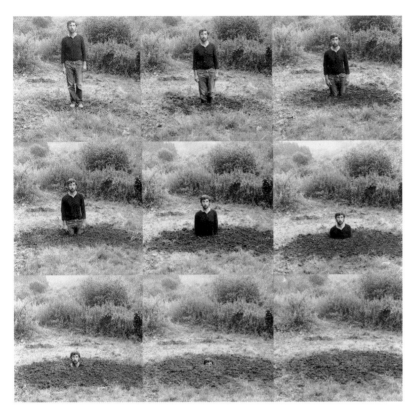

6.10 Keith Arnatt, *Self Burial*, TV Interference Project, 1969
Photograph on paper, 467 × 467cm. The humour of the piece of work emanates from the realism attributed to photography. One way of testing the implication of choice of specific medium, and therefore the implied comment on the nature of the medium, is to imagine what interpretational shift might occur if the sequence had been, say, painted.

differently with a view to social, political, metaphysical, or simply humorous, comment. However, as photography became accepted within Conceptual Art, so attention came to be paid to photographs (pictorialist, formalist and documentary) and to photography history. In effect, Conceptual Art offered photography a bridge into the gallery.

This era featured other challenges that, although incorporating some of the aesthetic characteristics of formalism, took for their starting point ideas that were anchored socially (rather than aesthetically). For instance, the 'new topographics' photographers, including Lewis Baltz (USA) and Bernd and Hilla Becher (Germany), explored the act of looking, as well as topographic features, through the detailed mapping of industrial edifices, or of locations.[21] In the Bechers' work similar images are blocked next to one another, thereby bringing to attention differences between examples within a particular type. Clearly

21 The term 'new topographics', used in the 1970s, refers back to nineteenth-century topographical work, especially the photographic charting of the American West.

321

this work drew on the emphasis upon detailed seeing typical of, for instance, the f/64 group and, as Susanne Lange argues, the Bechers did pay attention to aesthetics, but the new topographics, in charting the industrial landscape, implied a social and environmental questioning which did not figure in American formalism (Lange 2006). Land art also dates from this period. Here, the photograph is the record, and the final product, of an engagement with or intervention within the rural. Work by British artists, including Hamish Fulton, Richard Long and Andy Goldsworthy, became well known not through direct experience of the results of their investigations and interventions, but through their photographs. The artist's journey takes place in specific time. A sculptural intervention ameliorates, deteriorates, and becomes reabsorbed within the environment. Ultimately only the picture remains.

Photography and the postmodern

From the 1970s onwards there were significant developments in art practices founded in a new centrality of critical ideas to the visual arts, and in what was often referred to as a 'return to the figurative'. Of course the figurative had never entirely disappeared. The 'return' was more a question of a re-generation of interest in the representational on the part of curators and critics, now moving beyond modernist preoccupations with the specificity of each medium. New art also posited questions of representation. By the 1980s art had ceased to be self-obsessed, was looking outward beyond the boundaries of the gallery, taking on contemporary issues and making a range of references that ruptured modernist assertions of the autonomy of art.

Critical theorist, Douglas Crimp, suggested that photography contributed centrally within this challenge to the museum and gallery:

> From the parochial perspective of the late-1970s art world, photography appeared as a watershed. Radically reevaluated, photography took up residence in the museum on a par with the visual arts' traditional mediums and according to the very same art-historical tenets. New principles of photographic connoisseurship were devised; the canon of master photographers was vastly expanded; prices on the photography market skyrocketed. Counterposed against this reevaluation were two coincident developments: a materialist history of photography and dissident photographic practices . . . taken together and brought into relation, they could tell us something about Postmodernism, a term coming into wide use at just that time.
>
> (Crimp 1995: 2)

Thus, from the 1970s on, emphasis upon conceptual ideas and critical practices contributed to creating a place for the photographic within the gallery. Furthermore, photography contributed to the regeneration of art practices. The sources of this shift are complex. First, the radicalism of 1968 in Europe heralded a Left cultural agenda in the 1970s. This underpinned critical interrogation of dominant cultural practices. Examples may be found in the art of Victor Burgin and Mary Kelly, both of whom, notably, wrote about photographic practices as well as using photography as a medium. Second, and as a part of this, modern theory had begun to be questioned across many realms of academic enterprise, from the scientific to the aesthetic. In art theory this questioning took off earlier in North America than it did in Europe. Thus a further influence was new American art, including photographically based work by artists such as Cindy Sherman and Barbara Kruger. (See Nairne 1987: ch. 4; Kruger 1983, 1990; Sherman 1997.) Fourth, developments including community arts, performance art and 'happenings' signified a broadening of art practices. In addition, particularly in Britain, there were energetic claims from within the documentary movement for the artistic integrity of the medium, and such claims were further fuelled by the commercial success of leading British 1960s photographers (such as David Bailey and Cecil Beaton).

David Campany's *Art and Photography* (2003) focuses on photography within art practice from the late 1960s onwards and brings together images, sources and documents in order to interrogate and reflect upon late twentieth-century histories and developments. The book offers a very useful compendium of materials and images marking the diversity of issues, styles, methods and content that characterised the era; over 160 artists are included, almost all of whom are based in Western cultures, and work is situated through reference to then contemporary documents and debates. For instance, documentation includes an interview from 1989 by photography historian and critic Steve Edwards with Martha Rosler, originally published in *Ten/8* magazine. The book opens with discussion of the contradiction between deploying popular media – film, video, photography, postcards – in order to effect political intervention yet showing work in the (privileged) space of the art gallery. Campany suggests that 'every significant moment in art since the 1960s has asked, implicitly or explicitly: "What is the relation of art to everyday life?"' (Campany 2003: 11) and that photography as an everyday medium has lent itself to such explorations. As a compendium it is useful for his introductory historical and critical overview, although there is no sustained address to issues of aesthetics, to the social role of the artist, or to the changing status accorded to photography as contemporary art – a point to which we shall return.

Developments in art education also reflected an era of change. For instance, in England in the 1970s, incorporation of art schools within the polytechnic (later university) sector involved changing the erstwhile 'liberal studies' agenda to a more purposeful critical appraisal of art history. Art school graduates, who subsequently formed the new generation of gallery curators, were increasingly well informed and interested in exhibiting a greater range of ideas-based work. A number of new degrees in photography became established wherein 'theory' meant thinking about photography semiotically, and in relation to questions of

DAVID CAMPANY (2003)
Art and Photography,
London: Phaidon.

22 The most prominent
example in the UK was in
the 1980s at the Polytechnic
of Central London (now
University of Westminster)
where tutors included art
theorist Victor Burgin.

identity, gender and representation.[22] Not only had photography moved into the art gallery but critical ideas had moved onto the agenda in photography education; an agenda that was increasingly influenced by then radical feminist and post-colonial perspectives and critiques that linked to everyday themes and concerns. By the 1990s the implications of the digital were also central.

Discussing pluralism in American art in the 1970s, critic Corinne Robins comments on the increasing eclecticism of photography, noting:

> Photographers concentrated on making up or creating scenes for the camera in terms of their own inner vision. To them, reportage as such had become the job of the video artist, who had the heritage of *cinéma vérité* behind him [*sic*]. To the 1970s camera people, realism belonged to the earlier history of photography and, as seventies artists, they were embarked on a different kind of aesthetic quest. It was not, however, the romantic symbolism of photography of the 1920s and 1930s, with its emphasis on the abstract beauty of the object, that had caught their attention, but rather a new kind of concentration on narrative drama, on the depiction of time changes in the camera's fictional moment. The photograph, instead of being presented as a depiction of reality, was now something created to show us things that were felt rather than necessarily seen.

(Robins 1984: 213)

fabrication The crafting of images which have been **staged** or appropriated and adjusted for the camera. The term is more common within American photography than European, referencing the craft base of the medium. It stands by contrast with 'constructed' imagery, which inflects the directorial approach in more political terms through referencing both Soviet Constructivism and theories of deconstruction.

staged images Described by American critic A.D. Coleman as 'falsified documents', this refers to the creating of a scene for the camera (as in staging within theatre).

image-text Pictures within which visual imagery and written text are juxtaposed in order to effect a play of meaning between them.

Central to these developments was an emphasis on **construction**, the forging, **staging** or **fabrication** of images. Such pictures are preconceived by the artist. Constructed photography included photomontage, **staged imagery**, **image-text** works, slide-tape installations, photographs derived from land art; indeed, any photographic imagery wherein the conceptual engineering of the artist is clearly evident. Artists as divergent in concerns as Bernard Faucon, Andreas Gursky, Mary Kelly, Peter Kennard, Barbara Kruger, Richard Long, Mari Mahr, Cindy Sherman, Susan Trangmar, Jeff Wall and Joel-Peter Witkin all fall within this broad category. The notion of construction derived from two sources: first, the idea that art can intervene politically, as in the example of the Soviet Constructivists or of the German *monteurs*. Second, in postmodern terms, 'construction' directly related to **deconstruction** theory and practices. Both approaches refuse to take the world at face value. Constructed imagery in effect *critiques* what critic Andy Grundberg defined as 'concentration on the literal surfaces of things and on subject matter that seems to speak for itself' (Grundberg 1990a: 82).

For instance, in the example of Karen Knorr's series *Villa Savoye*, which forms part of a larger collection of *Fables,* the artist explores bourgeois lifestyles (Figure 6.1, p. 290). This is obviously a carefully planned image (we would not just come across this scene, with these particular lighting conditions, and capture it photojournalistically – although, of course, the birds in flight must have been opportunistic). It represents something of the architecturally constructed atmosphere of the Villa, and the bird, looking out of the photograph, stands in metanymically for humans enjoying the view. This is underscored by the pictorial effect of the framing of the trees through the rooftop wall. The image uses the **indexical** qualities of the photographic – that is, the way in which the photograph draws upon actuality – as part of its vocabulary of expression, but only a part of it. It invites the spectator to actively *read* the image and implicates questions of ownership, locality and **identity** through its reference to the mansion and the landscape. The title merely indicates location, leaving the reader to respond to the picture within the picture.

There are a number of methods whereby the interpretive latitude of an image may be contained. These include photomontage, sequencing and image-text techniques. We also have to take account of factors beyond the image itself. The mounting and framing of pictures – whether single images, or series, or sequences – is not neutral. Framing contributes to the rhetoric of the image through delineating the edge of the picture, that which is put into the frame. It also acts as a margin between the work and the wall on which it hangs. The established convention in post–Renaissance Art of framing paintings means that the frame also signifies the special status of a picture. However, the meaning of the frame is ambiguous: from the point of view of the gallery wall it is a part of the picture, but from the point of view of the picture it dissolves into the wall. In relation to the single image, this ambiguity is relatively clearly comprehended. Within sequences, or blocks of images, the play of the frame is more complex: the frame not only plays between the setting and the image, but also interacts with other frames within the grouping of pictures.

Written text commonly accompanies both single pictures, and series, groups or sequences. Written text includes titles, captions, artists' statements, poetry, or forewords which accompany an exhibition or book publication. Titling, and the signature of the artist, contribute to the claim for the status of the image as art. Titles may be cryptic, or metaphoric, operating to extend resonances, or they may be primarily descriptive. For instance, a title such as *Rome, 1975* or *Waiting Room* specifies place or type of location. However, the caption does not simply anchor; writing constitutes a further signifier within the complex interaction of discourses with which the spectator engages. For instance, the title *Rome* at the very minimum means something different to an Italian than to someone of another nationality. Titles, or captions, simul-taneously anchor, and become implicated in, play of meaning. The refusal of a title, as in *Untitled*, is likewise not neutral. This implies that the image is to 'speak for itself'.

Writing operates complexly. This is often particularly so in constructed imagery within which text is montaged as an integral element. Here the verbal is articulated not only as a poetic reference but also as a visual element. Colour, handwritten or typographic style, placing, scale, prominence – all contribute to how we read the overall piece. Likewise, artists' statements do not simply contextualise, or determine a position from which the work is to be read, although, of course, they do offer this. If an artist is viewed as a special sort of seer, offering particular insights into the world of experience, then his or her statement contributes to this claim for authority.

Developments do not proceed in an orderly and coherent fashion. Whilst digitally produced work takes its place alongside the straight photograph and constructed imagery, the relative lack of photographs in a number of major museum collections indicates that photography is still seen by some as a lesser art. The corollary of the new emphasis upon ideas and critiques was that, from the mid-1980s onwards, *straight* photography found itself positioned ambiguously. On the one hand, museums established photography sections.[23] On the other hand, it became more difficult to maintain independent specialist spaces and organisation; the foothold established in the 1970s had come to seem precarious. This was expressed partly in the practical issue of scale. Photography galleries had been designed to accommodate the standard-format image. A number of the newer photo-media galleries, which were larger scale (often converted from disused industrial buildings), became key institutions within the new debates. The standard photograph became harder to show, smaller pictures being dwarfed within cavernous warehouse – now, gallery – spaces (many of which subsequently embraced video installation and digital experimentation).

Women's photography

> The mere mention of the phrase 'women's art' sends shivers down the art establishment spine – more radical feminists on the war-path! Feminism, advocacy of women's rights on the ground of equality, is usually misinterpreted to mean exclusively female, probably radical and, more than likely, shaven-headedly lesbian. It's curious how this misconception perpetuates!
>
> (Libby Anson, *Untitled #7*, Winter 1994/1995)

The resurgence of feminism in the 1970s challenged the patriarchal establishment. This challenge included a set of questions about women, representation and art, which led to critical work on three key fronts. First, examination of ways in which women have been represented in Western art. Within patriarchy, active looking has been accorded to the male spectator. 'Woman' becomes the object of his **gaze**. Although this does not only concern 'the nude', the representation of naked women for visual consumption formed one obvious focus for accusations of sexism in visual culture. It was argued that the term 'nude', central to the visual arts tradition, lent a guise of respectability to the practice of naked women being objectified for **fantasy** libidinous gratification. Second, feminist art historians pursued the archaeological project of rediscovering and drawing attention to the work of women artists, previously ignored or marginalised. Third, women in art schools, galleries and publishing

23 For instance, the Museum of Modern Art, New York, has a number of galleries permanently dedicated to photography; the V&A, London, opened a permanent space for photography exhibition in 1998. Some museums are entirely dedicated to audio-visual media, including photography; these include the National Museum of Media, Bradford, Yorkshire, England. See list of archives for further information (pp. 369–72).

asserted a right for space devoted to contemporary *women* artists. The revolution took several forms. In art education the art history curriculum was brought under scrutiny, and various guises whereby sexism figured in studio relations and practices were challenged. Alongside this, the demand was made that galleries and publishers should examine their record in exposing the work of women artists – and set out to rectify it. Protests were mounted against exhibitions showing work deemed offensive to women.

Question: **Do women have to be naked to get into the Metropolitan Museum of Art?**

Answer: **Less than 5% of the artists in the Modern Art sections are women, but 85% of the nudes are female**

(Guerilla Girls)

This revolution obviously influenced photography, itself forging space in the gallery. Three projects stand as key examples. They relate, respectively, to the diverse history of photography, modern aesthetics and postmodern gallery-based practices. First, in *Women Photographers: The Other Observers 1900 to the Present*, writer-curator **Val Williams** traced and surveyed a range of British work, from high street studio portraiture to fashion photography, from the documentary and photojournalistic to the snapshot, and to contemporary feminist practices. The purpose was to expose the names and work of women photographers, previously hidden from history, and to demonstrate the diversity of practices within which they had been active. The exhibition, with its broad remit, opened in 1986 at the National Museum of Photography, Film and Television (now the NMM); significantly, a media organisation (as opposed to an art gallery). It contrasts with the second example, **Constance Sullivan**'s selection, also entitled *Women Photographers*, which took an international approach (albeit with some emphasis on North American artists) and more specifically recuperated women as artists in terms of the precepts and principles of *modern* photography. From the point of view of considering photography and the art gallery in the context of contemporary, postmodern practices, the third example, *Shifting Focus*, curated by **Susan Butler**, was of central import for both its focus upon contemporary work made for the gallery and its internationalism. Most significantly, *Shifting Focus* posited the question: What happens when women look? If, traditionally, women have been the object of the gaze, the viewed rather than the viewer, the represented rather than the author of representation, what happens when she takes a more active role? Butler was concerned to explore ways in which, in exercising the right to look, women alter the terms of visual culture which, as feminist art historians have argued, was premised upon unequal viewing relations.

It has become commonplace for exhibitions to include work by women artists. But perhaps the strength and confidence of women's work was

Key resources: IRIS International Centre for Women in Photography, www.irisphoto.org/live/index.asp; Women in Photography International, www.womeninphotography.org.

VAL WILLIAMS (1986) **Women Photographers: The Other Observers 1900 to the Present**, London: Virago (second edition published as *The Other Observers: Women Photographers 1900 to the Present*). This was researched and curated for the National Museum of Media, Bradford, Yorkshire as a touring show with accompanying book, although it is the text which has become the classic introduction to the recuperation of a range of types of work by women.

CONSTANCE SULLIVAN (ed.) (1990) **Women Photographers**, London: Virago. This book concentrates on high-quality reproduction of photographs by women historically, with a view to reclaiming their work for the canon.

SUSAN BUTLER (1989) **Shifting Focus**, Bristol/London: Arnolfini/Serpentine. The catalogue comments internationally on contemporary work by women.

Also DIANE NEUMAIER (ed.) (1996) **Reframings, New American Feminist Photographies**, Philadelphia: Temple University Press.

most evident in a shift to more specifically themed exhibitions, for example, self-portraiture, war, the family, lesbian identity. The presence of women photographers in the gallery is now taken for granted. Furthermore, the shift in focus influenced new themes within the work of male photographers.[24]

The influence of women's photography thus went beyond simply securing a rightful place for work by women. Feminist theory posed a more fundamental critique of aesthetic conventions and practices. This led to determined retrieval of the terms of visualisation. As American artist Barbara Kruger asserted in one of her renowned photomontages, 'we will not play nature to your culture'. Women's photography moved beyond critiques of representation to exploration of relations of looking and questions of identity.

Questions of identity

Poststructuralist thinking opposes the notion that a person is born with a fixed identity. . . . It suggests instead that identities are floating, that meaning is not fixed and universally true at all times for all people, and that the subject is constructed through the unconscious in desire, fantasy and memory.

(Bailey and Hall 1992: 20)

One of the functions of art is to explore and comment upon individual and social worlds of experience. Historically art has been understood as contributing to the myths and discourses which inform ways of making sense of and responding to cultural phenomena. From medieval church frescos to academic history paintings artists have told stories which help us to interpret our world of experience. Stories – such as the religious or the historical – help us to locate ourselves within sociopolitical hierarchies.

Psychoanalytic theory suggests that images, through offering points of identification, offer fantasy resolutions for subjective angst. Identification, in this context, refers to processes whereby the individual subject assimilates an aspect, property or attribute of that which is seen, and is transformed, wholly or partially, after the model which the other – in this instance the image – provides. Personality is constituted through such imaginary identifications. Thus art may be seen as feeding our need for a clear sense of identity and of cultural belonging. This is most evident in portraits that show us to ourselves as well as to a wider social world. As a genre, historically portraiture also testified to the status of the person(s) depicted, since only those of relative wealth could afford to employ an artist for the several days required for making a painting, In the formal portrait the skill lies in representing something of the looks and character of the portraitee(s). As David Bate has remarked,

If the photographic portrait is a shorthand description of a person, then portraiture is more than 'just a picture', it is a place of work: a semiotic

24 Examples include John Coplan's imaging of the male body (Tate collection), Paul Reas' exploration of his relationship with his father (included in *Who's Looking at the Family*, Barbican Gallery, London, 1994) and David Lewis' appraisal of the black body within anthropology (*The Impossible Science of Being*, The Photographers' Gallery, 1995).

DAVID A. BAILEY and STUART HALL (eds) (1992) **Ten/8** 2(3), **Critical Decade**.

event for social identity. Portraits fix our identity in what is essentially an art of description.

(Bate, 2009: 67)

How someone is depicted influences their sense of self. Likewise, the contexts within which people are represented suggest something of social place and hierarchies. Identity is neither uniform nor fixed; rather it is subject to challenge and shift leading to desire for reassurance within a continuous flow of apprehension, uncertainty and (temporary) reassurance of social role, status, location and belonging.

The emphasis on the body in 1990s gallery art seemed also linked to issues of identity in a changing world wherein communications are increasingly virtual and global. Cyberculture, with its related dislocation of place and location, seemingly enhanced curiosity about actual physical space and presence. For example, Boris Mikaihlov's lifesize pictures of people caught in the effluent of the post-Soviet economy attracted international attention not only because of their photographic realism but also because of a type of exoticism of degradation. Rineke Djikstra's photographs of bullfighters stained with blood or of naked women who have just given birth, with their babies (Figure 4.18, p. 230) tell of real physical exertion in an era of prosthetics. Cindy Sherman's more recent masquerades, perfomances which take the body as a starting point for construction of the image, arguably link to similar concerns.

Identity and the multi-cultural

Issues of identity are of double relevance to people who see themselves as outside of dominant culture, if not marginalised by it. For instance, in Britain, in the early 1980s context of Thatcherism, and inner-city racial tension, key exhibitions and initiatives included *Reflections of the Black Experience* (curator, Monika Baker, Brixton Art Gallery, 1986); as a primarily documentary show, it offered evidence not only of the diversity of black experience in Britain but also of the presence of good black photographers. The Association of Black Photographers, later Autograph, was formed soon after this to promote the work of black photographers across a range of fields. Meanwhile, *D-Max* (curator, **Eddie Chambers**) showed work by British Afro-Caribbean photographers made for the gallery.

EDDIE CHAMBERS (1999) 'D-Max: An Introduction' in **Run Through the Jungle**, Annotations 5, London: INIVA.

Racism, the post-colonial context and the desire to explore ethnic difference, meant that questions of identity figured centrally in Black art – and continues to do so. Obvious avenues of exploration include the dislocated family, diaspora, internationalism, and media representation of '**the Other**'. Exhibitions which explored such themes included *Disrupted Borders*, which connected work from widespread parts of the world – including Finland, India, North America – all of which in some way engaged questions of cultural integration or marginality (**Gupta 1993**); and *Mirage*, which included work, in a range of media, by black artists from Europe and North America (Bailey, ICA, 1995). A number

SUNIL GUPTA (ed.) (1993) **Disrupted Borders**, London: Rivers Oram Press.

of British-based photographers became prominent within new Black art practices. These include Ingrid Pollard, whose work posed questions of history and heritage (see p. 308), and David A. Bailey, now senior curator at Autograph, whose 1987 series on the family album was the subject of the following evocative description:

> Against the background of a 'Made in England' clock and a montage of snapshots, a family album is displaced by a Black magazine which in turn is displaced by the screaming headlines of a tabloid newspaper. As the clock ticks on, marking the shifting historical context, the changing assemblages of images address the contradictions between private and public representations of race.
>
> (Tawadros in Haworth-Booth 1988: 41)

British explorations of post-colonial identity typically interlinked the political and personal. Two themes predominated: first, the legacy of colonialism; and second, what it is to be British, regardless of ethnic identity, given 'New Europe'.

Post-colonial preoccupations are clearly marked in Black art, but likewise figure within Scottish and Irish art. To take an example: black artist David Lewis pictured the map of Africa as a chessboard for a game played by European players (*D-Max*). Scottish artist Ron O'Donnell depicted a map of Scotland with a noose round the Highlands (*I-D Nationale*, Portfolio Gallery, Edinburgh, 1993). The point is similar. Likewise in North America, Afro-American photographers have been concerned to trace particular heritage(s) exploring visual iconography as well as personal and political histories. For example, Stephen Marc's project, 'Awakened in Buffalo', traces escape routes for slaves seeking freedom by reaching the northern states or Canada; his related series, 'Soul Searching', which is digitally montaged, acknowledges his African American heritage and identity by including himself somewhere in each picture. The story is told; the aesthetic allows the particular personal resonance to be incorporated.

Given current global tensions and mobility, there is now increased interest in work by – sometimes exiled – artists from Asia and the Middle East, as well as from former Soviet bloc nations. In North America, the end of the twentieth century also witnessed developing interest in Latin American photography. This partially reflects increasing Hispanic population and influences, especially in the southern states of the USA. But the interest in what the *New York Times*, in reviewing *Image and Memory* by **Watriss and Zamora**, described as 'vast national subconscious made visible and waiting to be fathomed', begs more complex explanation. Arguably it also reflects neo-colonial concerns with identity; Latin America geographically is both the closest threat to the USA's political supremacy and also offers the nearest exotic from the point of view of commerce, travel and fascination with other cultures.

Key resources in Britain: Institute of International Visual Arts (INIVA), London, an umbrella organisation coordinating multi-cultural initiatives now working in tandem with Autograph. The Stuart Hall Library at Rivington Place, London, offers a specialist library and archive.

WENDY WATRISS and LOIS ZAMORA (eds) (1998) **Image and Memory: Photographs from Latin America 1866–1994**, Austin: University of Texas Press. Drawing from the more than 1,000 images exhibited at Houston's FotoFest in 1992, this book documents the work of 50 photographers from 10 countries. The photographs range from the opening of the Brazilian frontier in the 1880s to documentary images from El Salvador's recent civil war to works of specifically aesthetic and experimental nature.

Research, exhibition and publishing of historical and contemporary photography from Central and South America feeds this fascination in the USA.

CASE STUDY: LANDSCAPE AS GENRE

> I make landscapes, or cityscapes as the case may be, to study the process of settlement as well as to work out for myself what the kind of picture (or photograph) we call 'landscape' is. This permits me also to recognize the other kinds of picture with which it has necessary connections, or the other genres that a landscape might conceal within itself.
>
> (Wall 1995, in Morris 2002: 2)

In offering a brief overview of one genre of practice, we not only trace historical developments but also draw attention to ways in which clusters of themes and concerns, none of which are exclusive to any specific genre, come together to characterise a particular genre.

Genre

Developed within film studies to reference groups of movies of a similar sort (such as the Western, melodrama, film noir), the term 'genre' refers to types of cultural product. But genre is not simply a classification. Genres carry with them specific sets of histories, practices, ideological assumptions and expectations, that shift over time to take account of changing cultural formations. We have chosen the example of landscape, but the principal point about change and continuity can be examined in relation to any genre.

Landscape as genre

There is a key distinction between 'land' and 'landscape'. In principle, land is a natural phenomenon, although most land, especially in Europe, has been subjected to extensive human intervention (creating fields, planting crops, shoring up the coastline, and so on). 'Landscape' is a cultural construct. It dates from seventeenth-century Dutch painterly practices, but became central to English painting and also became a method for artists and topographical draughtsmen to explore territories elsewhere. Eighteenth-century English landscape painting did not simply echo the Dutch, but re-articulated the genre to incorporate the increasing emphasis in Britain on technological achievement (Bright 1990) – a clear example of accommodation to particular cultural circumstances!

Landscape can be defined as vistas which encompass both nature and the changes that humans have effected in the natural. Broadly interpreted, this includes sea, fields, rivers, gardens, buildings, canals, and so on. It thus encompasses emblems of property ownership (such as fences), or of industrialisation (such as mines or factories). Landscape pictures rarely depict work or, if they do

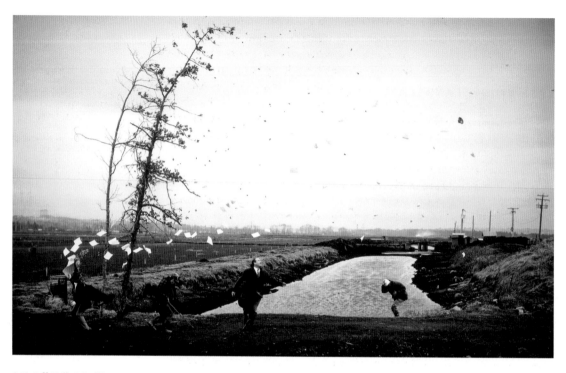

6.11 Jeff Wall, *A Sudden Gust of Wind (after Hokusai)*, 1993

so, they romanticise the rural labourer. For the English aristocracy, landed gentry and nineteenth-century industrialist, land ownership symbolised hereditary status or entrepreneurial success. As John Berger has argued, landscape paintings operated to reassure this status (Berger 1972a).

Jeff Wall's landscapes (Figure 6.11) are staged images, usually shown as large lightboxes, which reflect upon landscape as a genre within fine art. His digitally assembled pictures are meticulously staged in accordance with standard conventions of perspective and the 'golden rule' (strictly applied this refers to the one-third/two-thirds horizontal division of the canvas between sky and land/water, designed to induce a sense of harmony). Often they reference other traditions in landscape imagery, for instance, the woodcuts of Japanese artist, Hokusai. But Wall's images always include the unexpected; in *A Sudden Gust of Wind* it is the uncontrollable effect of the wind as papers are thrown into the air. The gesture interrupts the serenity otherwise implied.

Landscape photography

In considering landscape as an example of a genre within photography, we are concerned first to identify typical aesthetic and sociopolitical characteristics of landscape imagery; and second to explore ways in which the genre has accommodated change, reinvented and reinvigorated itself over time. Landscape photography has largely inherited the compositional conventions of landscape painting. Typically, landscape photographs are a lateral rectangle – it is no accident that 'landscape format' has come to describe photographs in which the width is greater than the height. Compositionally, the 'golden rule' of one-third/two-third horizontal proportions is usually obeyed, as are the rules of perspective.[25]

Landscape photography is founded as much in the documentary endeavours of travelling photographers, at home and abroad, as in the gallery. Thus there are two key lines of inheritance within the genre: on the one hand, straight photographs, topographical in intent, on the whole echoing the composition of the classic landscape painting, and, on the other hand, more pictorial images constructed in accordance with a preconceived idea, be it poetic, mythological or critical in import. As with all genres, landscape also reflects new aesthetic ideas; for instance, surrealist dreamlike states (Figure 6.9, p. 317) or the Constructivist compositional radicalism based on the ideal of a new angle of vision (Figure 6.6, p. 311).

Historical development and change

By the nineteenth century, especially in Europe, 'landscape' also stood as an antidote for the visual and social consequences of industrialisation, offering a view of nature as therapeutic, a pastoral release from commerce and industry. Art movements such as Romanticism and Pictorialism reflected such changing attitudes, ignoring ways in which the industrial actually impacted on the visual environment. Romanticism in painting reified the rural idyll, albeit emphasising the spiritual and the metaphysical. This reification is reflected in photographs of the time, for instance, early mountainscapes. On a less **sublime** scale, pastoral imagery such as Camille Silvy's *River Scene, France* (Figure 6.2, p. 299) made from two separate exposures and using people as models, offers a carefully staged myth about the calm, leisure and pleasure of the countryside. There are several examples of seascapes, for instance, by Gustave le Grey (also French) wherein combination printing has, similarly, been used to effect pleasing scenes; for instance, clouds above serene waters. Both examples invite the viewer to reflect upon the rural or seascape and both reflect idealist notions of harmony.[26]

As we have seen, such stagings are taken further in Pictorialism, within which people were frequently depicted in close relation to what was perceived as 'natural' environment, with no stated documentary or topographic location. Thus, for instance, *The Lady of Shalott* is re-presented by Henry Peach Robinson as a picturesque tale (Figure 6.3, p. 301). Here landscape becomes the background against which a story is staged.

Unlike most of Europe, the American West is characterised by vast open spaces. Nineteenth-century pioneers, such as Carleton Watkins, whose work is now central to the photography archive, were employed to chart land prior to its opening up by, in this case, the laying of the Pacific Railroad. Mary Warner Marien notes the differing cultural contexts within which European and American landscape photography developed:

25 As with all genres, there are exceptions. Aside from constructivist experiments, exceptions might include more metaphoric imagery, dealing, for instance, in landscape and memory, or pictures shot close-up which draw upon the conventions of still life as well as landscape.

26 In idealist philosophy, dating from Plato, emphasis is on measured behaviour, on civilisation as an imposition of order. The term 'measure' is useful here as it implies caution or restraint, whilst also implying mathematical principles. In classical, i.e. Renaissance art, this is expressed through the principles of composition, perspective and proportion (including relations between the vertical and the horizontal).

Where English and European amateurs might craft an antimodern, picturesque photograph that lamented the decline of an agriculturally based society, Watkins synthesized a soaring sublime based on wilderness. . . . The viewer of his photographs is often flung out over and above dizzying, deep chasms. The immediate sensation is one of transcendence and invincibility, a feeling profoundly different from the quiet reflection and nostalgic passivity evoked by much European amateur landscape photography. Indeed, a sense of the sublime, vested in natural wonders like Niagara Falls and Yosemite but transferable to human works like the railroad, is characteristic of nineteenth-century American cultural life.

(Warner Marien 1997: 95–6)

New aesthetics

Modern landscape photography remains particularly associated with American photographers, including Ansel Adams, Imogen Cunningham, Minor White and Edward Weston, who subscribed to the notion of pure photographic seeing. Modern photographers stressed the aesthetic and spiritual dimensions of landscape, producing elegant and elegiac abstract imagery. Edward Weston's images, in which the sharpness of the realisation of the photograph is tempered with the rhythm of form, offer prototypical examples (Figure 6.8, p. 314).

Genres typically are characterised by continuity through change, by an ability to re-form in order to incorporate new aesthetics and circumstances. Landscape is no exception. Now fences, the railway, brick walls, motorways, pylons, signs and hoardings have all, variously, become rendered as a part of traditional imagery and myth. Of course, 'translations' are involved: landscape photographs are often monochrome, the countryside represented in terms of shape and tonal gradings. The fundamental point is that the photograph re-inflects subject-matter in terms which reflect current cultural currencies. In this sense, the modernist landscape, with its emphasis on aesthetics, was one moment in the regeneration of the genre. The focus upon more obviously intrusive cultural elements, or industrial legacies, for instance, in the work of British photographers Ray Moore or John Davies offers another.[27]

The modern and the postmodern

Analysis of aesthetic and ideological change involves engagement with broad socioeconomic and political circumstances as well as with aesthetics. But genre analysis is always best pursued through comparison of specific examples. For instance, in this chapter there are two photographs, by **Bill Brandt** (Figure 6.5, p. 305) and Karen Knorr (Figure 6.1, p. 290). Both use photographic techniques and conventions to effect a sense of harmony. Yet they are different in import. Brandt's image is a documentary statement, the location is given. Knorr's, through the presence of the bird and the framed view of treetops, offers a conceptual comment upon French culture with its formal gardens, one which provokes

27 Work by most of the photographers mentioned in this section can be found in monographs published under their name, or in exhibition catalogues published variously.

The Land: 20th Century Landscape Photographs, also by **Bill Brandt**, was exhibited at the Victoria and Albert Museum in 1975.

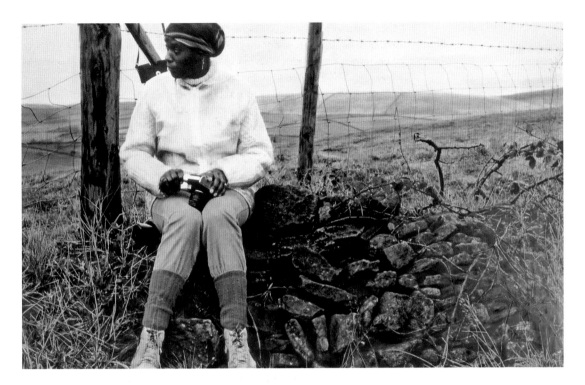

6.12 Ingrid Pollard, from
***Pastoral Interludes*, 1987**

critical interpretation. Difference between the modern aesthetic and the post-modern critique is evident, albeit subtle. It is not the image in itself so much as its broader context that adjusts our response.

Landscape and heritage

A number of contemporary photographers in Britain, including John Davies, John Kippin, Ingrid Pollard and Jem Southam, engage in critical terms with notions of landscape, commenting, for example, on the legacy of industrialisation whether it be rural industry such as tin-mining (Southam) or the Northern industrial landscape (Davies), or on the implicit racialisation of pastoral imagery (Pollard). Fay Godwin's work on land, access and property rights offered a further significant example. Landscape imagery reflects and reinforces particular ideas about class, gender, race and heritage in relation to property rights, accumulation and control (see Taylor 1994; **Wells** 1994, **2011**). Several contemporary photographers have made it their business to question this. The contrast between this type of contemporary emphasis and the nineteenth-century idyllic image is obvious from a comparison of the work of Pollard (Figure 6.12), with that of Silvy or Peach Robinson. Such critical engagements offer an example of ways in which genres may renew themselves hegemonically; where photographs of decayed rural areas or abandoned industrial sites once seemed radical (Kippin 1995), as we shall see, they may now appear highly aestheticised as 'industrial sublime'.

LIZ WELLS (2011) **Lands Matters: Landscape, Photography, Culture and Identity**, London: I.B. Tauris.

Such concerns are culturally specific in a range of respects. For instance, Norwegian landscape photography tends to dramatise the mountains and fjords of the north. Nineteenth- and early twentieth-century Norwegian landscape painting and photography is clearly influenced by the Kantian sublime (best typified by German painter Casper David Friedrich). The Norwegian mountain became a national icon – especially prominent at the turn of the twentieth century when Norway was seeking independence from Swedish rule. In effect the mountain for Norwegians became an equivalent to the Wordsworth country of the Lake District for Englishness. Thus when contemporary Norwegian photographers focus upon a more ordinary, everyday landscape such as lands used for recreation close to urban and suburban spaces, there is an implicit questioning of myths of Norwegianness. The iconic is culturally specific; it follows that art which challenges established attitudes to some extent relies upon audience familiarity with particular national themes and aesthetic histories.

Many artists working with land and landscape are less concerned with the overtly sociopolitical, working in terms which echo earlier formalist preoccupations but which may also reflect current ecological curiosities and concerns. Within a few years of the foundation of photography in the nineteenth century, Anna Atkins was using the **cyanotype** process to make detailed images of flora and fauna. Artists continue to use photograms and other contact printing methods to register nature. For example, using natural and artificial light, Susan Derges places sensitised paper below the surface of water to register the effects of reflection of plants and trees and the movement of, for instance, grains of earth or sand in rivers or waves breaking on the seashore (Figure 6.13). Others have critically explored issues of perception, subjectivity and the gaze, employing a range of tactics to dis-locate our sense of ourselves in relation to space depicted.[28]

Recent decades have witnessed particular concern with environmental change and with the politics of environment. Prominent twentieth-century examples of work questioning uses of land included Richard Misrach's *Desert Cantos* (1979–99) in which he investigated (mis-)uses of the Nevada desert. Some decades ago, the American photographer and critic Deborah Bright argued that 'whatever its aesthetic merits, every representation of landscape is also a record of human values and actions imposed on the land over time' (Bright 1989: 126). Her point was that much of the so-called natural landscape has been organised and re-shaped in ways that remain visually marked. For example, the hedgerows that characterise much of the English landscape result from property owners demarcating their territory (whether agricultural or domestic). Bright also pointed to the commoditisation of landscape as an antidote to politics and as tourist destination, both of which operate in part through ways in which pictorial composition aestheticises the rural, often distracting us from environmental realities.

cyanotype (blueprint), ferric ammonium citrate and potassium ferricyanide are applied to a surface and dried. An object or negative is placed on the treated surface, then exposed to the sun.

28 It has not been possible to include full publication references for all the artists named in this chapter. Most university library catalogues offer search facilities by keyword, in this instance, the name of the artist. Many dealers, galleries and museums have websites offering information on artists and their work, sometimes including book and magazine references.

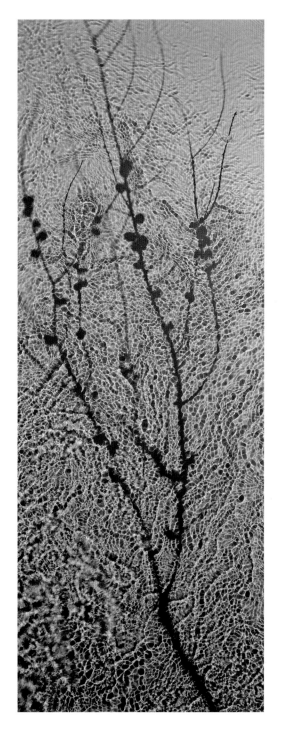

**6.13 Susan Derges, 'Larch',
from *The Streens*, 2002**

Fay Godwin's extensive explorations of *Land* (1985) and *Our Forbidden Land* (1990) invite us to pause to reflect on the British landscape. Her pictures often work through incongruous juxtapositions, for example, a sheep pictured through metal fencing below the barbed wire that indicates that this land belongs to the Ministry of Defence, or a sign stating 'private' on apparently open undulating hillsides that, as she indicates in the picture title, are part of the British Duke of Westminster's estates. In exploring the countryside she had an eye for the improbable. Through her photography (and her association with the Ramblers organisation in the UK) she campaigned for public recreational access to rural areas. Other photographers have focused on edgelands, over-looked spaces such as areas bordering rivers, canals, roads, motorways and parking lots, drawing attention both to detritus and to ways in which little areas of wasteland function as natural oases of vegetation encouraging animal and insect habitat.

In parallel with this more overt questioning are many examples of artists exploring particular sites in relation to specific social and personal histories, for instance, returning to explore, remember and revisualise places familiar from childhood (Figure 6.14). For example, in her series *Between Dog and* Wolf, Chrystel Lebas explored the forest area in her home region, focussing in particular on ways in which the light and atmosphere of the woods changes at dawn and dusk (Figure 6.14). Her interest is in the relation of humankind to nature, in our attitudes to nature, and in ways in which the natural is managed for our benefit. She has also pursued residencies in places such as the Risjnak National Park, northeast of Rijeka, Croatia, and at Bel-Val in the Ardennes, France. Like Susan Derges, she pays detailed attention to specific effects of light and season, reminding us of complex and subtle ways in which our environment affects us.

6.14 Chrystal Lebas, 'Blue Hour', untitled no. 4, 2005, from *Between Dog and Wolf*

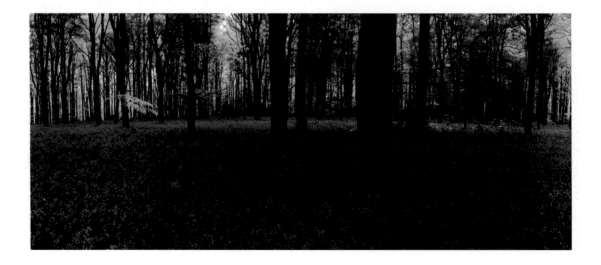

Reflections on the Contemporary Sublime

In considering landscape as genre and in characterising landscape photography from the first decade of the twenty-first century we see many strands of development. Environmental issues have been particularly addressed, including ways in which they relate to shifts in centres of industrial production (from Europe and North America, to Asia and South America). For instance, British photographer, John Kippin has long been concerned with the impact of industrial decline and the shift to a service sector economy in the northeast of England, formerly a region particularly known for coal mining and ship yards. In recent decades, container shipping and mechanisation has replaced dockland labour. The West has become a net importer of goods produced more cheaply in new industrial centres elsewhere. Industrial edifices, now redundant, symbolise a regional economic structure that no longer obtains (Kippin 1995) (Figure 6.15).

Kippin's focus is on the region where he is based, but the issues resonate globally as the impact is not only in the former industrial centres in the UK, the

6.15 John Kippin, 'Monument' from *Futureland Now*, 2012.

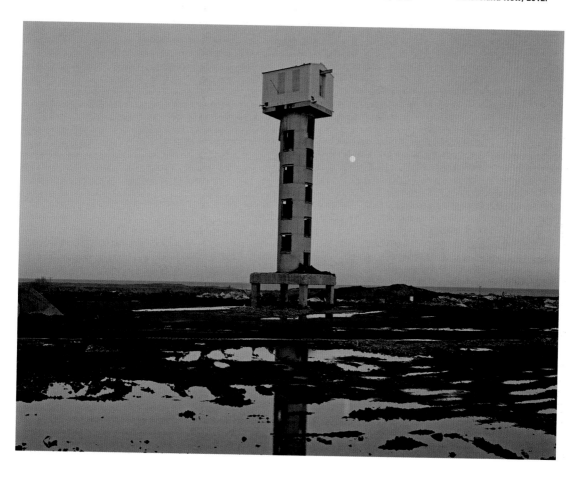

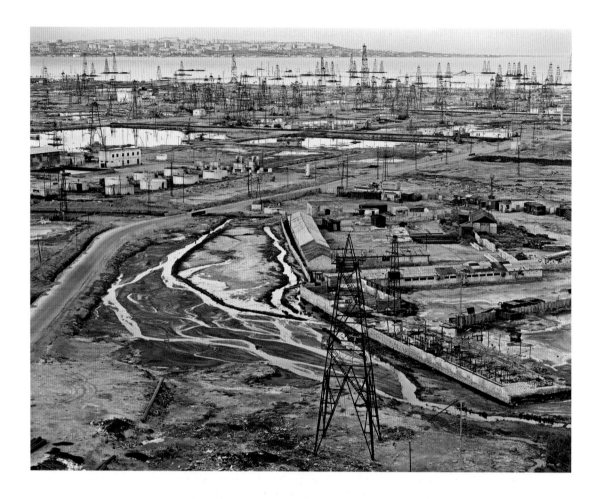

6.16 Edward Burtynsky,
SOCAR Oil Fields #9 Baku,
***Azerbaijan,* 2006.**

USA, and elsewhere, but also on the regional economy and work conditions of those employed in factories in current boom areas, particularly the new Asian economies. Canadian photographer Edward Burtynsky has contributed significantly to debates about shifting economic centres, industrial working conditions and uses of natural resources. For instance, in his series *Oil* (2009) he travelled to North America and Asia exploring global chains of production, use and disposal characteristic of contemporary industrial capitalism, particularly the motor industry with its dependence on oil as a primary energy resource involving drilling for oil, piping it to oil refineries and then on via pipes, ships or land transportation to points of consumption. Each picture is carefully composed, often from a high vantage point offering an overview of a scene or situation, for example, the patterns of intersecting highways in Los Angeles. Several of the individual pictures are sublimely memorable, for example, a sea-based oil rig in Socar set against a cool pink sky or great mounds of discarded tyres in California

340

(www.edwardburtynsky.com/site_contents/Photographs/Oil.html). Others are more topographic in idiom (Figure 6.16). In both examples, Kippin's monument to the past and Burtynsky's contemporary scenario, the geometric construction is orderly, with a horizon and a central line (the coal tower pointing upwards, or the road taking the eye through the centre before sweeping off on a diagonal), the aesthetic form contributing to constructing an apparent harmony of human artefacts and the natural environment

There has been much debate in recent years relating to the notion of industrial sublime. This debate draws on eighteenth-century concepts of the sublime wherein philosophers including **Edmund Burke** and **Immanuel Kant** related the notion to that which is awesome or frightening yet, because we are experiencing it through a picture (or a poetic description), perversely pleasurable, since there is no danger of pain or death as would be the case were we to encounter the actual circumstances depicted. In the Kantian model the sublime relates more to comprehensibility, that which cannot be understood through rational measurement or debate. For Burke, the key emotion is astonishment. In exploring the visual import and environmental consequences of industrialisation, Burtynsky offers us a series of pictures that we may find astonishing in terms of the implications of the content of the image, yet, at the same time, poetically appealing.

There has been extensive debate as to the political impact and import of such photographic projects. Deborah Bright (1989) also remarked on the ease with which single images from series intended as investigative nonetheless could be seen as testaments to transcendent notions of 'Nature'. In other words, individual photographs may seem celebratory even when an overall series conveys more critical perspectives. We are reminded that meaning does not reside in images themselves, but rather derives from situations in which they are viewed, how they are contextualised through associated images, texts or other related information, and the interests and experiences influencing the viewer. Three decades later this last point remains salient. For example, Burtynsky's *Oil*, when seen in exhibitions or publications, has a cumulative impact as photograph after photograph come together to suggest dysfunctional effects of global dependence on oil in terms of the cultural impact of industrialisation, the visual changes wrought through extensive roadways and other modes of transportation, and the human and environmental costs of industrial waste. Taken overall, his work can be interpreted as questioning the consequences of Capitalism and globalisation. However, paradoxically, pictures viewed in isolation risk being construed as an ode to industrial success.

Similar questions apply to investigations of remaining wilderness landscapes. Photographers are often interested not only in exploring and documenting places but also in questioning consequences of human presence for erstwhile remote environments that may previously have been uninhabited or sparsely occupied (by regionally based groups such as Inuit or Sami peoples). Take, for example, the fact that there is now a space observatory at the South Pole, until only very

EDMUND BURKE (1729–1797) Irish political writer and philosopher, author of **A Philosophical Enquiry into the Origin of our Ideas of the Sublime and Beautiful**, first published in 1757.

IMMANUEL KANT (1724–1804) German philosopher, author of **Critique of Judgement**, 1790; Part I is concerned with aesthetics.

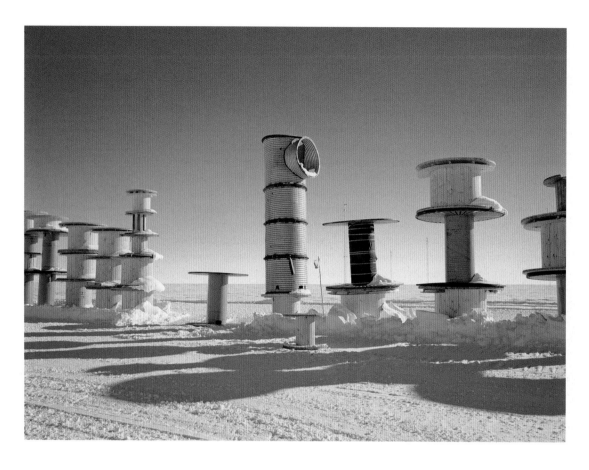

6.17 Anne Noble,
'Spoolhenge' no.3, South
Pole, Antarctica, 2008

recently viewed as a wilderness area (Figure 6.17). There are several telescopes,
people live there, planes fly in and out, provisions arrive, waste has to be
removed, the Americans have built a roadway across the Antarctic ice which can
be re-opened each Southern summer for transporting provisions and equipment,
and laying power lines. The purpose of the Hubble telescope is to investigate
and document outer space – arguably, the landscape frontier of our time. As
with the opening of the American West in the nineteenth century – in which
landscape photography was centrally implicated as one means of documenting
the nature of new-found lands – picturing significantly contributes to coming to
terms with regions new to us. Digital data facilitates visualisation, but information generated may be used for a range of purposes, not only exploring and
mapping the unknown, but also surveillance, security or inter-planetary expansion. For instance, in *The Other Night Sky*, California-based photographer Trevor
Paglen tracks satellites, debris and other objects identified within the orbit of
planet Earth, thereby reminding us that outer space is the geographic frontier
of the twenty-first century (Figure 6.18).

342

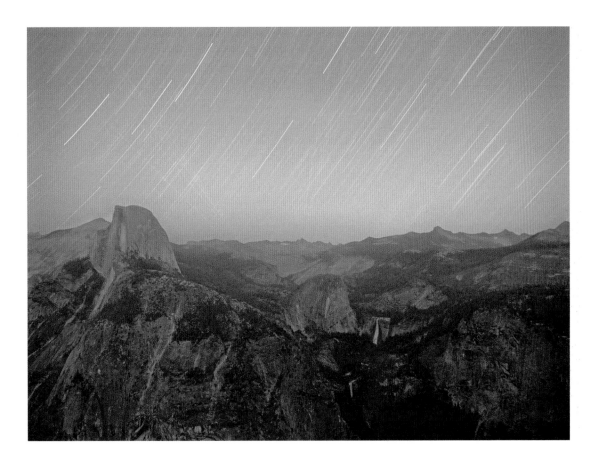

Several photographers have visited Antarctica, remoter parts of the Arctic, and equatorial forests such as that of the Amazon region, documenting human impact as well as natural phenomena. Their reflections on extreme places invite us to reformulate notions of the sublime. We continue to wonder at the immensity of mountain ranges, tropical forests and the polar regions. But we might also ask whether our awe at natural phenomena can be uncoupled from the association of the sublime with (male) figures from the so-called heroic era of expeditions, whether seeking a North-West Passage, racing to the South Pole, or exploring rivers to sources in the jungle.

As this case study has demonstrated, landscape is not just somehow 'there' waiting to be observed. Rather, photographers travel to places intending to explore particular histories and issues, hoping that their work can reveal something that might otherwise be overlooked, or that they can contribute to understanding our environment and our impact on it. Unlike portraiture, landscapes are generally not staged, and unlike photojournalism, there is rarely a sense of 'decisive moment' (Cartier-Bresson 1952) when content and aesthetics

6.18 Trevor Paglen, 'Keyhole Improved Crystal' from Glacier Point (Optical Reconnaissance Satellite; USA 224) from *The Other Night Sky*, 2011

come together to create a telling image. Landscape photographers are not simply observers of the world around us; rather they interrogate it, drawing upon their experience as photographers to enhance the manner of seeing. As photo historian, Roger Taylor, remarked when discussing Fay Godwin's work,

> An experienced photographer knows intuitively where to place the camera and which lens to use for the best effect, much in the same way a pianist arrives at the proper pitch and touch through daily rehearsal. It is all a matter of fluency and assurance.
>
> (Taylor 2001: 13)

Of course this is not simply a matter of professional experience, but also one of personal 'voice'. Discussing 'Truth in Landscape', American landscape photographer Robert Adams suggested that the best landscape pictures involve geography (the actual topography of place), autobiography (the photographer with particular interests, experiences, ways of seeing and methods of working) and metaphor (the aesthetics of the image, and also cultural resonances) (Adams 1996: 14). Whilst not all critics would agree that these are the key components – or the only components – of imagery relating to land, landscape, place and circumstance, this trinity of engagement offers a useful starting point for thinking critically about landscape practices and how they operate to engage attention, provoke reflection or alert us to environmental change.

Genres are defined not by uniformity, but by clusters of characteristic themes, formal and aesthetic concerns, and ideological preoccupations. They are revitalised through aesthetic experimentation and through new issues, often typifying attitudes and discourses characteristic of particular eras. As can be seen from the various examples of landscape included in this chapter, a range of factors and questions are in play when discussing specific fields of practice. It is productive to analyse genres in terms of both specific historical traditions within visual culture and contemporary issues and aesthetics.

PHOTOGRAPHY WITHIN THE INSTITUTION

Since the 1970s lens-based media, including photography, video, slide projection and installation have been absorbed within broader fine art practices. It is no accident that a key exhibition of contemporary British photography at the Victoria and Albert Museum in 1988 was titled *Towards a Bigger Picture*. The double meaning of the title referred in particular to the extension of photography within art practices and to diversity of subject-matter. But it also referenced conceptual understanding of ways in which scale contributes to the claim for place within the gallery. For example, very small-scale work, carefully mounted and framed, inherits the sense of the precious associated with miniature painting. It demands close-up and detailed looking. Preciousness is emphasised if individual works are hung with space between them. By contrast, large-scale photographic works claim the status traditionally accorded to academic painting and other art made for public spaces. They assert their presence and, therefore, the significance of their theme or subject-matter. Such pictures engage with contemporary myth in ways that echo the ideological and political involvements typical of classical painting.

Questions of national identity are not only reflected in art practices but also in the centrality of the gallery and museum within many nations and cultures. In most nations funding for arts, both for the contemporary gallery and for heritage institutions such as museums, is a mixed economy drawing upon private, commercial and public resources – in some cases, including regional or national lottery funding as well as state subsidy.[29] (Even in major national institutions exhibition organisers often rely on private or commercial sponsorship as well as revenue from admission tickets and sales such as postcards and catalogues.) In Britain the 1970s and 1980s were characterised not only by the extension of provision for photography collections and exhibitions, but also by an increase in major institutions located away from London.[30] By the mid-1980s there were over 2,000 museums and galleries in the United Kingdom, with new ones opening at the rate of one a fortnight. Discussing *The Heritage Industry*, Robert Hewison argued that 'in the twentieth century museums have taken over the function once exercised by church and ruler, they provide the symbols through which a nation and a culture understands itself' (Hewison 1987: 84). Museums have become key patrons of art, influencing priorities and pricing within the art market. Given the monumental dimensions of some late twentieth-century centres, for instance, the Pompidou Centre, Paris, or the Tate Modern in London, not to mention MOMA, New York, or the San Francisco Museum of Modern Art, galleries also influence the conceptual scale of imagery. The photograph has been used extensively within the expanding museum to both document and celebrate the history. It has also been implicated in critiquing this 'heritage industry' (Taylor 1994: 240ff.).

Simultaneous with this extension of roles for photographic media within museums and other heritage sites, the advent of digital technologies facilitated the online expansion of the remit and accessibility of museum collections. In addition, museums have become increasingly inter-active in terms of audience engagement, making extensive use of photography within this. In terms of photography as art the impact of this particularly relates to the development of web-based resources by art museums, public and commercial galleries, dealers, and, indeed, photographers themselves, whereby online access to reproductions of works, statements of provenance, and critical socio-historical or biographical appraisals of the *oeuvre* of artists are made easily accessible – at any rate, for those with regular online access.

In addition, the web has become a site of online artworks by individual artists or collaborations involving networks of artists regionally, nationally or globally, as well as offering a resource for materials appropriated and re-purposed by artists.

29 Funding arrangements and the relative balance of the various sources of income differ according to national fiscal and cultural policies. It is not possible to offer a full overview here.

30 Historically, developments in Britain included the opening of The Photographers' Gallery in London, 1971, and of Impressions Gallery, York, in 1972 (relocated to Bradford in 2007). Stills Gallery, Edinburgh, was set up in 1977, and the Association of Welsh Photographers, later Ffotogallery, Cardiff, in 1978. Plans to establish the National Museum of Photography, Film and Television (NMPFT) in Bradford, as a branch of the Science Museum, were announced in 1980. (This is now the National Media Museum.) Also in 1980 the Royal Photographic Society (RPS) moved its library and archive from London to Bath; later to NMPFT, Bradford. The Scottish Photography Archive, part of the National Galleries of Scotland, was established in 1984 and, by 1995, included over 20,000 photographs. In 1998 the V&A opened the Canon Photography Gallery dedicated to exhibitions of the art of photography.

Appraising the contemporary

Photography, then, is situated both within the gallery system and beyond it. In addition, previous distinctions between photography galleries, and those that include photographically produced work within their collection seem increasingly unclear as all galleries now host photography, photo-video and digital installation, and have an online presence. Remaining photography galleries may have a narrower remit in terms of focus upon the photographic, but a much broader cultural remit in, potentially, displaying and interrogating all aspects of photography as visual communication, historically and now. It follows from this ubiquity that the task of researching and mapping contemporary developments in photo-based art is daunting.

Charlotte Cotton notes that although photography historically has made varying claims for status as art, it was only in the 1990s that it achieved a confident presence within contemporary art circuits (Cotton 2004: 20). She accounts for this primarily in terms of, first, the influence of conceptual art from the 1970s onwards within which the photographic often figured, and second, the emergence of colour photography within art practice. Although this can be traced to the 1970s (for instance, the work of William Eggleston and Stephen Shore) its more general acceptance only dates from the 1990s. This is important as it contributed to blurring boundaries between art photography, with its emphasis on monochromic virtuosity, and photographic practices as critical engagement since colour, within what otherwise appeared as 'straight' photography, along with experiments in the grammar of scale in photography, interrupted seemingly established distinctions. In 1994, in her introduction to *Documentary Dilemmas*, **Brett Rogers** observed:

> Ignored by the art world which favours big pictures and high prices, and outstripped by technology that gives the edge to television and digital developments, documentary photography has also come under harsh scrutiny from post-modern critics, who question its tendency to separate and exploit certain groups of people, serving up the poor as exotic fare for voyeuristic consumers.
>
> (Rogers 1994: 5)

She went on to suggest that this has led to the ignoring of new rhetorical strategies in use within documentary, including fill-in flash, colour, scale, captioning, sequencing, and the use of text within the image. Twenty years later this has clearly changed. As Cotton comments, art practices such as the creation of large-scale staged photographic tableaux (Collins, Blees Luxemburg, Wall), or the deadpan, anti-dramatic scenarios associated in particular with the younger generation of Frankfurt School artists (Gursky, Höfer, Struth) presuppose the validity of a colour aesthetic. It follows from this ubiquity that the task of researching and mapping contemporary developments in photo-based art is daunting.

CHARLOTTE COTTON (2004; revised ed., 2014) **The Photograph as Contemporary Art**, London: Thames and Hudson. A very useful view of developments towards the end of the twentieth century.

BRETT ROGERS (ed.) (1994) **Documentary Dilemmas: Aspects of British Documentary Photography 1983–1993**, London: British Council. This exhibition was curated for an international tour and included work by John Davies, Anna Fox, Julian Germain, Paul Graham, Anthony Haughey, Chris Killip, John Kippin, Karen Knorr, Martin Parr, Ingrid Pollard, Paul Reas, Paul Seawright and Jem Southam.

Lucy Soutter poses questions from a slightly different point of view asking *Why Art Photography?* as a starting point for interrogating ways in which photography within the gallery context matters to us in terms of aesthetic and social values. She opens with a more historical discussion pursued through reference to portraiture and the nude as genres that, she suggests, have become increasingly hybrid. Then, in common with Cotton, she addresses 'deadpan', raising questions of realism, objectivity and authenticity. She later returns to reflect on authenticity in relation to subjectivity and on photography as a performative process, often related to everyday experiences (for instance, in the work of Nan Goldin or Wolfgang Tillmans). She also suggests that in recent years there has been a shift from the centrality of critics and art historians, as mediators of images as texts from which meaning is to be deciphered, towards an interest on the part of artists in the direct experience of viewers.

In terms of critical methods, this shift also reflects a transition from the poststructuralist thinking that characterised debates towards the end of the twentieth century, certainly within Western art historical culture, towards more **phenomenological** models. This development was not simply in response to perceived limits of the legacies of the structuralist emphasis on image as text, albeit one understood as 'read' in specific socio-historical contexts, but also reflected the import of online viewing spaces and social media within photographic practices. Over the last decade photographs have been increasingly experienced as images that are not prints; rather they shimmer on laptops and circulate as numerically based composites rather than existing as tactile objects for which scale, surface and luminosity are contributory components. For artists these characteristics are important considerations, yet, when viewed on screen, works acquire a degree of conformity. This has contributed to a renewed interest in the constitution of photographs as physical phenomena occupying a place within the gallery and also, in the 'dialogue' with other artworks that occurs in exhibitions. The physicality of the encounter with the photographic object, that may be larger than us or miniature, characterised by hyper-saturated colour or by muted tones, forms part of the experience of viewing thereby influencing the way in which we respond to and are affected by art.

This relatively recent emphasis on the tactile qualities of photographs as objects is echoed in a resurgence of interest in photobooks. Photographs in folios, sold as collectors' items, date from the very beginnings of photography. Fox Talbot's *Sun Pictures in Scotland* dates from 1844, although it is not strictly a book, rather a portfolio with no text other than picture captions, is perhaps the first major example of a photographically illustrated publication.[31] Badger and Parr cite Anna Atkin's three portfolio volumes (1843–53) of cyanotypes of *Photographs of British Algae* as the first significant example, followed by Talbot's *The Pencil of Nature*, published in 5 parts (1844–46). Such collections were hand-made in that each print had to be separately developed. Indeed, arguably some of the most interesting developments in the uses and circulation

LUCY SOUTTER (2013) **Why Art Photography?** London and New York: Routledge. Soutter situates ideas about contemporary art internationally within the context of recent debates about art photography and the gallery context.

31 Published in an edition of 1,000, and financed through pre-subscription, it involved printing 23,000 handmade salted paper prints from calotype negatives, each pasted in by hand! See Graham Smith in di Bello *et al.* (2012) for a detailed discussion of the images and Talbot's journey following in the footsteps of Sir Walter Scott.

347

32 See Richard Benson
(2008) *The Printed Picture*
for a detailed historical
discussion of developments
in print processes.

MARTIN PARR AND GERRY
BADGER (2004) **The
Photobook:
A History**. Vol. 1 (2006),
Vol. 2 (2014), Vol. 3, London:
Phaidon.

Also see ANDREW BOOTH (ed.)
(2004) **The Open Book**
(based on The Hasselblad
Center collection, and
publications cataloguing a
range of examples from various
regions (including Latin-
America, Japan, The
Netherlands, Switzerland).

33 For a fuller discussion
see Wells (2012) 'Beyond
the Exhibition – from
Catalogue to Photobook' in
Di Bello, Wilson and Zamir
(2012) *The Photobook*.

34 In viewing exhibitions,
you should take into
account particular relations
set up between the work
of different photographers
and consider how this
contributes to
interpretation. One obvious
question is: What work is
hung at the entrance point?
Does this indicate a central
theme or preoccupation?

of photographs occurred with the expansion of possibilities for the printed page at the beginning of the twentieth century. This facilitated photojournalism (see ch. 2) and also the presentation of photographs as books, since possibilities for mechanical reproduction allowed for less labour intensive production processes and larger editions of each book printed.[32]

What is a photobook? **Parr and Badger** define it as:

a book – with or without text – where the work's primary message is carried by photographs. It is a book authored by a photographer or by someone editing and sequencing the work of a photographer, or even a number of photographers. It has a specific character, distinct from the photographic print, be it the simply functional 'work' print, or the fine-art 'exhibition' print.

(Parr and Badger 2004: 6)

Parr and Badger also comment that 'the sum is greater than the parts, and the greater the parts, the greater the potential of the sum' adding that photobooks have 'a particular subject – a specific theme' (Parr and Badger 2004: 7).

Di Bello, Wilson and Zamir question the notion that the 'primary message' is necessarily carried through photographs, arguing that the relegation of text as subsidiary fails to account for publications such as James Agee and Walker Evans (1941) *Let Us Now Praise Famous Men*, wherein there are 31 photographs and hundreds of pages of text by Agee (di Bello *et al.* 2012). It also doesn't account for hybrid photobook publications, often including poetry or interviews with portraitees, wherein meaning and resonance are clearly intended to emanate from the inter-relation of images and texts.

Whilst the history of the production and development of photobooks transcends that of art photography, there has been a long-standing relationship between exhibitions and publications, with catalogues listing pictures in exhibitions dating from the late nineteenth century.[33] Indeed, as Mary Kelly has argued, there is a sense in which the gallery itself, although of central symbolic significance, is less important in the history of artistic production than catalogues, books, reviews, and other accompanying, more permanent, forms of reproduction of work (Kelly 1981). Exhibitions are ephemeral. Critical evaluation of contemporary exhibition practices is limited by the fact that it is not possible to visit and view all shows; websites and catalogues often say little about the impact of how each show was hung within particular gallery spaces.[34] It is published materials, rather than the shows themselves, that reach the wider audience. Increasingly, catalogues have given way to photography books, possibly published in association with a particular exhibition, but intended as a free-standing artist's monograph or edited collection conceived as a publication in its own right (perhaps as part of more general interests in media arts and media education on the part of publishers). Along with monographs and critical texts, several recent publications that collate examples of work by contemporary photographers indicate the extent to which the photobook has become part of an expanding market for objects and publications sold at gallery, museum and city-centre shops, as well as, of course, online. In other words, publishing has responded to audience demand for gallery mementoes (and to the need on the part of galleries and museums for additional income streams). Thus, in order to consider changing thematic or aesthetic concerns in recent years, we need not only to trace histories of exhibitions via catalogues, exhibition reviews, and museum and gallery websites, but also to consider publishers' lists. More particularly, photography journals and magazines (including contemporary art journals and online blogs) trace debates and developments, through featuring the work of particular photographers, discussing contemporary issues, and reviewing shows and books, thereby marking and contributing to shaping our sense of histories of debates and practices.

Curators, collectors and festivals

Major museums not only maintain archives but also purchase contemporary work, thereby, in effect, supporting photographers. Curators may commission new work for particular shows as part of their responsibility for conceiving and organising photography exhibitions which tour nationally and internationally – and commonly feature as websites as well as physical entities. Museum and gallery exhibitions are 'hired' by or co-produced with other galleries; it is not uncommon for shows to be 'on the road' for two years or longer. Normally they are curated by one or more people, whose role includes researching the exhibition concept, the selection (or commissioning) of work, planning how the work will be hung within the exhibition space, and writing a significant part of any accompanying book or catalogue. The power of the curator, operating regionally, nationally or internationally, has been questioned. Of course, curators take initiatives which contribute to the exposure of work. But they may also regularly favour certain artists, or types of work, at the expense of others. Furthermore, it has been suggested that curators often act more as 'creators', putting together themed exhibitions which, however relevant and interesting, serve as much to advance themselves as to showcase the work of artists. Indeed, all exhibitions and collections reflect the particular interests of their curators and archivists as well as the mission statement, priorities and terms of reference of particular organisations (Sekula 2003).

Since the 1980s international photography festivals have burgeoned. The purpose of festivals is to offer a focus, meeting place and showcase for work. As such they contribute to raising the profile of photography nationally and internationally; indeed, many have markedly commercial dimensions. But, along with gallery exhibitions, photography magazines and books, they do indicate contemporary trends as well as foregrounding the work of particular photographers.

The first such international festival was established as an annual meeting place and showcase for photography at Arles, France, in 1970. Others, such as Fotofest, Houston (biennial since 1986), have been loosely based upon the same model involving some thematic focus, a number of lectures and events, opportunities for less-experienced or less-established photographers to show their portfolio to known photographers, critics and curators and, in certain instances, some form of schools- and community-based spin-off. Another major European festival is the biennial Paris *Mois de la Photo* which, since 1980, has taken place throughout the city and is now twinned with festivals in Vienna, Berlin and elsewhere as part of a European Month of Photography. Photographic work has also increasingly featured in major international art events such as Venice Biennale or *Documenta*, Germany.

Curators, critics, archives, exhibitions, art magazines and festivals all interact with the market for both contemporary and historical photographic work. International auction houses, such as Christie's or Sotheby's, note the influence of exhibitions (and events, such as the death of an artist) on auction prices.[35] Commercial art dealers scrutinise trends in order to maintain their position in a competitive market. In Britain, the market for both old and contemporary photography is a late twentieth century phenomenon; a response, perhaps, to both the renewal of interest in the photograph in the 1970s and 1980s and the increasing emphasis upon private commercial practices which characterised 1980s Thatcherism. But 'collection' as a commitment on the part of particular individuals or businesses is not new. Indeed, royal patronage for artists, since the Renaissance, has taken precisely this form. The key purchasers may now be media stars and entrepreneurs rather than European aristocrats, but patronage through payment for ownership of the art object persists.

Photobooks have also become collectors' items, and it is not uncommon for a book to be published in two versions, one of which is a short run, numbered, collectors edition often also including a separate print (that can be mounted and framed). As Walter Benjamin suggested in 1931, 'The most profound enchantment for the collector is the locking of individual items within a magic circle in which they are fixed as the final thrill, the thrill of acquisition, passes over them' (Benjamin 1931b: 62).

The gallery as context

Charlotte Cotton remarks that 'to identify "art" as the preferred territory for their images is now the aspiration of many photographers' (Cotton 2004: 7). Photography now sits alongside painting and sculpture within contemporary art institutions. Commitment to working as an artist has become an accepted career objective for photography students and the gallery has become a destination for photographic imagery. But what might this mean in terms of artists engaging in the circulation of ideas? Arguably, the gallery network not only offers visual pleasures but also operates to reassure a certain sense of

35 For example, in 1995, prior to auction, a collection of paintings and photographs by Man Ray was exhibited at the Serpentine, one of London's higher profile public galleries for contemporary art.

intellectual and cultural elitism. Part of the pleasure of looking at pictures lies in discussing images, in sharing responses. This assumes and reaffirms biographical and cultural similarities in terms of class, gender, ethnicity, education and interest or involvement in the arts. Sociologist Terry Lovell suggested that 'the discerning of aesthetic form itself must be seen as a major source of pleasure in the text – the identification of the "rules of the game", and pleasure in seeing them obeyed, varied and even flouted' (Lovell 1980: 95). Galleries have specific profiles in relation to this, sometimes operating overtly as a site of political engagement or as a regional centre.

Indeed photography has been used in a range of contexts to challenge dominant aesthetics, usually with some commitment to political empowerment. Central to the politics of representation is the question of whose experience is validated. As we have seen, this motivated the work of many contemporary women and black artists, particularly in the 1980s and early 1990s. The political role and significance of the contemporary gallery is complex. There is a sense in which curator, critic, audience and artist are all complicit in perpetuating an exclusive system which functions hegemonically in ways that seem relatively detached from economic imperatives. On the other hand, the private collector, and the public museum and gallery, along with commercial sponsorship and public subsidy, exercise a significant degree of economic influence on developments within the arts.[36]

Blurring the boundaries

Art photography is now global in terms of collections and connoisseurship, with auction houses, museums and exhibition curators operating internationally in response to market economics. However, in terms of meaning, shifts in cultural context influence interpretation and perceptions of significance in terms of both theme and aesthetics. What may appear exotic to those in one region may seem familiar in other areas. Of course this is not new; there has been a long-standing interest on the part of collectors and institutions in the West in, for example, photography from regions with which there were trade links in the nineteenth century. But in the twenty-first century this has become an increasingly multi-directional process, with, for example, American dealers as likely to be selling at fairs in the Middle East or China as at Paris-Photo in Paris or Los Angeles.[37] Reflecting on the apparently enhanced internationalism of photography and, indeed, the art market, David Bate has suggested that contemporary art photography has been assimilated within 'a primarily photographic global economy of images', arguing that within the global art industry 'the legibility of local traditions suffer the easily read image of the "universal" language of pictorial realism' (Bate 2009: 145). In other words, aesthetic and cultural differences, once manifest through pictorial form and theme, that might have fascinated viewers interested in the unfamiliar, have become subsumed within the international art market where photography now has an established presence.

36 See, for instance, Stuart Alexander, 'Photographic Institutions and Practices' (1998) in Michel Frizot, *A New History of Photography*, Cologne: Könemann.

37 For information on dealers present at the various fairs see websites for event organisers and also individual gallery websites. (Although galleries are listed, it is not possible to determine and comment on sales and turnover as this is commercially sensitive data.)

There has also been a convergence, a blurring of boundaries, within art practices. As has been suggested, the inter-relation of art and photography historically was complex in terms of definitions, debates and practices. Likewise, there is a close historical relation between photography and film. Film also implicates light and atmosphere as well as an ontological relation to the external world of objects and events. Indeed, early film was based on the photographic, although, of course, soon developed as a narrative, story-telling mode drawing on theatre and music – played to accompany silent 'movies'. In recent decades, as (digital) video has in many respects substituted for film, there has been increasing interest on the part of artists in the qualities of film as a projected medium with particular effects and affects. The installation of 'FILM' (2011–12, 35mm, 11 mins) by artist Tacita Dean in the Turbine Hall at Tate Modern, London, is but one of many such examples. Alongside this, given possibilities afforded by developments in digital camera technology (now usually including still and video shooting options) or in editing software, a number of photographers have turned to working in 'moving image' as well as still imagery. This is not a return to 'movies' as a narrative form so much as animation drawing on the depictive characteristics of photography. As gallery viewers, moving image has more in common with projected slide installations than with narrative cinema.[38] In terms of convergence, moving image is now as likely to be constituted through an editing of still shots as originally made as video, and often programmed in short film screenings or festivals and made available on online video sites as well as encountered in art exhibitions.

Indeed, in tandem with such developments there has been an extension of online resources. The majority of artists, also commercial galleries, maintain websites as information points, profiling work, news, and projects in development. It is also common for museums, public galleries and archives to run websites intended as a first port of call detailing exhibitions or collections as well as offering starting points for research on particular artists and projects. Many profile key historical and contemporary figures. For instance, through their website the V & A Museum in London offers information about their holdings (the contents of their collection) along with selected biographical profiles and discussions of work by contemporary photographers as well as that of Victorian photographers such as William Fox Talbot or Lady Constance Hawarden; likewise George Eastman House, Rochester, USA. Indeed, our ease of access to archives has been massively enhanced through the advent of the world wide web (www.) and through digital reproduction of images from collections allowing for online viewing. In effect there has been a democratisation of access to such materials, as anyone, anywhere can now view material online (assuming access to electricity and online search facilities), whereas previously access was restricted to those who could afford to travel to print collections. Of course, what we experience is image content rather than the visual and tactile qualities of an historic or contemporary print, or a paper publication. In addition, although collections may also offer contextual

38 Slide installations used (Kodak) projectors, transparency film and slide carousels, technology commonly available in the second half of the twentieth century but now obsolete, replaced by video projection. In terms of the visceral, slides changed with a memorable clunking noise, whereas video is silent.

information, the histories on offer are sometimes orthodox in that they deal in historical consensus and avoid controversy. This reminds us that information does not substitute for critical thinking. A description of what a photographer has achieved is not the same as an interrogation of the significance of his or her achievement; it is a starting point but does not substitute for analysis of work in relation to the aesthetic and technical modes of an era, socio-political contexts, and subsequent ways in which work has been viewed, reclaimed or re-positioned within historical and contemporary debates.

As we saw in the case study of photography and landscape, art practices shift over time, responding to changing social concerns, priorities and circumstances. Likewise theoretical and critical debates develop and mutate, taking into account shifts in aesthetics and technologies, and also new contexts. Where once photography had to argue for acknowledgement as an art form, now art photography plays a significant economic role within the international art market and is extensively profiled online as well as in festivals, auction houses, galleries and art museums.

Afterword

Photography is ubiquitous. There is almost no aspect of our lives that is untouched by photographic imaging in some form or another, whether online or in the physical world. In this respect, the idea of a critical introduction to photography is impossible! No publication can encompass, discuss and evaluate all aspects of the medium, its social effects and psychological affects. However, as has been seen in the various chapters in this book, there are many questions that can be asked in relation to meaning-producing processes. We raise them through theorising ways in which photographs tell stories or set out scenarios that reference, reflect, represent and influence people, places, events and experiences locally and globally.

Suggesting questions that we might ask and methods by which we can engage critically with images is the remit of this book that, now, in its fifth edition, has itself gone through a series of shifts in emphasis. Changes and updates are particularly evident in relation to contemporary developments in photography. They also reflect ways in which new theoretical and political emphases contribute to re-positioning and re-evaluating the medium and its practices. This is so whether we are concerned with ontological questions pertaining to photographic media or engaging questions framed through the pre-occupations of political theory, media and cultural studies, psychoanalytic models or new modes of historical and anthropological engagement.

A generation has passed since we first started researching this publication (in 1994). Over this time, various shifts in historical, political, and theoretical preoccupations have occurred. There has been a welcome increase in research and publication on histories of photography and on the work of individual photographers or movements. Some themes dispersed, only to reappear in modified forms. For example, in the 1970s and 1980s, questions of representation relating to class, gender and ethnicity, were extensively discussed. Indeed, for those of us involved with this publication this was a formative era. When we embarked on this textbook, questions of subjectivity, identity (socio-political and postcolonial) and democratic agency were still centrally debated, although student engagement with women's issues had become less marked, certainly in the British context that centrally informed the first edition of this book. Recently there has been a resurgence of feminist debate, particularly in university and political contexts, perhaps partly in response to the social effects of economic crisis in the West, and certainly issues of representation continue to trouble us, as do inter-related questions of gender equality. By contrast, reflections on notions of the 'postmodern' in art that rumbled on from debates of the 1970s and 1980s now seem resolved, with legacies of critiques that fuelled post-modern positions within the arts integrated within new perspectives heralded by the virtual and the digital.

Indeed, the most significant developments over the following twenty years have been in the field of what was initially termed 'new media', in other words, areas of practice and of viewing experience that were transformed through digital experimentation and innovation and the expansion of virtual space. Terms such as 'hybrid', 'convergent', 'telematic' and 'networked' acquired meaning in relation to spheres of practice that had previously seemed separate in terms of technology, even if they were already convergent in terms of pictorial form and subject matter. That mobile phones or watches might develop as cameras was difficult to imagine – except within the frame of spy fiction. That the family album might migrate online, and, with 'selfies', become a central strand of social media was not anticipated. This is not simply a question of new interests replacing older ones so much as re-inflections of political and theoretical concerns to take into account new developments. For instance, questions of identity and subjectivity became implicated in debates about the inter-relation of our online presence and offline existence.

We now take everyday photographic surveillance for granted. That our movements are traced on video footage seems normal; indeed, this may be a source of reassurance in terms of personal security as well as being useful for military or criminal investigations. But the socio-political implications of such tracking, including ever more sophisticated face recognition software, are troubling, and raise questions about democratic freedom of movement and privacy. Satellite imaging, including mapping systems such a Google Earth, likewise has become integrated into everyday experience. Again, this has influenced modes of behaviour, for example, using a picture called up on a smart phone to define a meeting place at short notice rather than pre-planning, or never needing to learn to read maps as 'satnav' does it for us. There is a deskilling – or, at any rate, a shift of skills – associated with our increased reliance on 'apps'.

Meanwhile questions of authenticity and realism in photojournalism and documentary have resurfaced. Having got past the 'crisis' of authenticity of the 1990s, when there were extensive debates relating to our faith in news and documentary images, there is renewed focus on questions of representation and communication that relates to globalisation not because international networks are new, but because of the increased speed of communication and flow of imagery. There are also questions of (government) regulation as online distribution and citizen photojournalism facilitate multiple viewpoints and sources (including photos used within charity, pressure group and activist campaigning).

In academic terms, there has been renewed interrogation of the formal qualities and significance of the indexical characteristics of photographs along with increased interest in tactile aspects of the photographic print and of photo books as designed objects. This has been fuelled in part through anthropological and museological concerns associated with the digitalisation of collections (forming virtual archives whether for museums or for commercial image banks) that involves selection and prioritisation of images with an associated risk of the loss of – or restricted access to – source photographs as historical documents. In addition, pictures are now collated not as tactile objects but as electronic files located in a virtual space for which the metaphor of 'cloud' seems increasingly appropriate since clouds dissolve and reform; we have limited understanding of the security and potential longevity of virtual picture archive systems yet we place increasing reliance on online resources.

In summary, new technologies have transformed the scope of the photographic in ways previously unimaginable. Whilst it is not clear what the long-term implications are and where further developments may lead, it is clear that they have been transformative not only in terms of some of the social shifts summarised above but also in terms of visual consciousness. The circumstances within which we engage and discriminate between visual stimuli have changed. Given the immersive flow of photographic imagery, arguably the status and import of individual pictures have shifted. Yes, but in what respects and how might we discuss this? In musicology, linguistics and oral studies, being trained to discriminate aurally between sounds and tonal inflection or becoming familiar with the particular timbre of the various types of musical instrument is a matter of being trained to listen. Likewise, although sight is one of our primary senses, learning to *see* and to pause to look with attention are central to visual literacy. Given the increased complexity of visual communications, not to mention media hybridity, it is only through enhanced ability to engage critically within visual culture that we work out ways of intervening socially as image-makers aiming to offer alternative ways of seeing and also as sceptics, trained in 'disbelief', always questioning content and contexts implicated. More theoretically, we might ask in what ways does this immersion influence *what* we see and *how* we remember. Does the ubiquity of photography shift the psychological nature or capacity of visual memory?

In what ways might we now re-evaluate visual communication systems in terms of the social and the political and also reflect on the very nature of visual sensibilities? What questions demand attention?

Liz Wells
May 2014

Glossary

KEY TERMS

abject In Julia Kristeva's *Powers of Horror* the abject is associated with material that produces a reaction of horror because it threatens the distinction between subject and object or the boundary between self and other. Abject material can include bodily fluids, wounds, or corpses, and the horrified or repulsed responses these can produce in the viewer is not because of what they *mean*, since abjection is not to do with symbolic meaning, but to do with deep, primal and unconscious drives.

aesthetic Pertaining to perception by the senses, and, by extension, to the appreciation or criticism of beauty, or of art. Thus 'aesthetics' references the criteria whereby we judge a work of art. Such criteria primarily include formal conventions (composition, tonal balance, and so on). Aesthetic philosophy is concerned with principles for the appreciation of the beautiful, including the beautiful in art.

analogue A form of representation, such as a painting, a chemical photograph or video tape, in which the image is composed of a continuous variation of tone, light or some other signal. Similarly, a gramophone record is an analogue medium for reproducing sound or music. Analogue representation is based upon an unsegmented code while a digital medium is based upon a segmented one in which information is divided into discrete elements. The hands of a traditional (analogue) clock which continuously sweep its face, in contrast to a digital clock which announces each second in isolation, is a common example of the difference.

art Imagery created principally for exhibition in galleries, museums, or related contexts. In this book we use 'Art', to refer to 'high art' and related gallery and funding systems and institutions.

autographic A generic term applied to all of those processes – drawing and painting being the main ones – in which images are made by the action and coordination of the eye and hand, and without mechanical or electronic intervention. Autographic images are authored wholly by physical and intellectual skill, or as a general field of (artistic) practices.

carnivalesque A concept developed by the Russian theorist Bakhtin to describe the taste for crude laughter, bad taste, excessiveness (particularly of bodily functions) and offensiveness. It celebrates a temporary liberation from recognised rules and hierarchies and is tolerated because, once people have been allowed to let off steam, those norms can be re-established.

code Used here in the **semiotic** sense to refer to the way in which signs are systematically organised to create meaning – the Morse code is one simple example. Cultural codes determine the meanings conveyed by various cultural practices, say, the way people dress or eat their meals; photographic codes control the way meanings are conveyed in a photograph – for example, the details that give a news photograph its sense of authenticity, or a wedding photograph the right sort of dignity. Cultural codes are centrally examined in chapter 5.
See **semiotics**

commodity Something which is bought and sold. The most commonly understood forms of commodity are goods which have been manufactured for the marketplace, but within capitalism other things have also been commodified. Natural resources and human labour have also been metamorphosed into commodities.

commodity culture A term used to describe the culture of industrial capitalism. Within today's culture everything, even the water we drink, has become a product to be bought and sold in the marketplace. Commodity *culture* also infers the naturalisation of this system to the extent that we cannot imagine another way of living.

construction The creating or forging of images and artefacts. In photography this particularly references the deliberate building of an image, rather than its taking from actuality, through staging, fabrication, montage and image-text. The term also reminds us of Soviet Constructivism in which the role of art in the building of a new social order was emphasised and industrial elements were often used as a basis for art. Through inversion, it also references theories of **deconstruction**.

deconstruction A radical poststructuralist theory, centred upon the work of French literary theorist Jacques Derrida, which investigates the complexity and, ultimately indeterminable, play of meaning in texts. Derrida's focus is literary, but the analysis may be extended to the visual.

dialectics A method of enquiry premised on a logical mode of argument whereby a position is stated, it's anti-thesis is also stated, and, through discussion, a synthesis is reached. It is important in art history as a means of accounting absorption of avant-garde movements and their influence on art practices.

discourse Circulation of an idea or set of ideas through imagery, speech or writing. Photography is one of the many media – including newspapers, books, conversation, television programmes, and so on – which constitute contemporary discourses.
See **ideology**

epistemology A branch of philosophy concerned to establish by what means knowledge is derived. It is concerned with questions such as what it is possible to know and asks how reliable knowledge can be. In the present context, questions can be asked about what kinds of knowledge images provide, and how they do it.

fantasies The term 'fantasy' usually refers to stories, daydreams and other fictions. It is sometimes distinguished from 'phantasy', which is a more technical term from **psychoanalysis** referring to **unconscious** processes. This book draws on both meanings, especially when discussing writers and photographers influenced by psychoanalytic thought.
See **unconscious**

fetishism The substitution of a part for the whole; or use of a thing to stand in for powerful but repressed forces. In Freudian theory fetishism refers to the displacement and disavowal of sexuality. Fascination or desire are simultaneously denied, and indulged through looking at an object or image which stands in for that which is forbidden. Thus a photographic image of a fragment of a woman's body may stand in for woman as the object of sexual desire.
See **objectification, psychoanalysis, voyeurism**

formalism Prioritisation of concern with form rather than content. Focus on composition and on the material nature of any specific medium.

gaze This has become a familiar term to describe a particular way of looking at, perceiving and understanding the world. It was brought into currency by writers on cinema, concerned to analyse the response of the audience as voyeurs of the action on the screen. The voyeuristic gaze is used to describe the way in which men often look at women, as well as the way in which Western tourists look at the non-Western world. More recently, discussions have focused on the implications of a 'female gaze'.

hegemony Dominance maintained through the continuous negotiation of consent by those in power in respect of their right to rule. Such consent is underpinned by the possibility of coercion.
See **ideology**

heuristic An educational strategy in which students (or researchers) are trained to find things out for themselves.

historicisation The process by which events or other phenomena are given a place in an historical narrative. Photography may be defined by the position that it occupies in a larger historical schema or an unfolding over time of technologies and practices.

identity A person's identity is his or her sense of self and the different contexts within which that selfhood is constructed. It is never simple or coherent, nor is it stable as people, attitudes and understandings change over time in response to events and experiences. For example, the national identity into which one is born may well clash with the cultural identity of the community in which one chooses to live; or a gay identity, based on sexuality, may clash with a religious identity based on strict rules governing sexual behaviour.

ideology This term is commonly used in two differing but interconnected ways. In this book it is used primarily to refer to bodies of ideas which may be abstract, but which arise from a particular set of class interests. The term is also commonly used to refer to ideas which are illusory, whose purpose it is to mask social and economic relations which actually obtain. For instance, the idea that children need their mother at home (which was common in the 1950s) masked the economic relations of patriarchy whereby married women were rendered financially dependent upon their husbands.

index One of three kinds of sign defined by American semiotician, C.S. Peirce. The indexical sign is based in cause and effect; for example, a footprint in wet sand indicates or traces a recent presence. The other two types of sign are the *iconic* (that which is based in resemblance), and the *symbolic*, or sign proper (that which is entirely conventional).

indexicality This term refers to a cluster of qualities and ideas about photographs which are associated with their indexical nature (see **index** above), that is, with the manner in which a photograph can be understood to be a chemical trace or imprint, via the passage of light, of an existing (or once existing) physical object. By extension this links with ideas that photographs are closely related to memory, the past, presence and absence, and death. Also, that they are tangible evidence of a thing's existence. A further meaning is that the 'taking' of a photograph can be thought of as 'pointing' to something in the world.
See **semiotics**

mimetic representation Based upon imitation, upon showing rather than telling, a concept central to traditional post-Renaissance art theory.
See **representation**

modernism In everyday terms 'modern' is often used to refer to contemporary design, media or forms of social organisation (as in 'the modern family'). But 'modern' also frequently refers to the emphasis upon modernisation from the mid-nineteenth century onwards, and, more particularly, to Modern movements in art and design from the turn of the twentieth century. It is essentially a relative concept (modern by contrast with . . .); its precise usage depends upon particular contexts. In this book we distinguish between two terms: *modernism*, sets of progressive ideas in which the modern is emphasised and welcomed; and *modernity*, social, technological and cultural developments. The term '*Modernism*' is used (in chapter 6) to refer to particular emphasis on form and materiality in modern art. Throughout the book a distinction is made between the modern, and the postmodern or contemporary.
See **postmodern**

objectification It is often argued that photography objectifies people by turning them into things or objects to be looked at, thereby disempowering them.
See **voyeurism**

ontological Ontology is a branch of philosophy. It concerns the study of how things exist and the nature of various kinds of existence. It involves the logical investigation of the different ways in which things of different types (physical objects, numbers, abstract concepts, etc.) are thought to exist.

the Other A concept used within **psychoanalysis** and **identity** theory, and within post-colonial theory, to signify ways in which members of dominant groups derive a sense of self-location and identity partly through defining other groups as different or 'Other'. Thus, within patriarchy, the male is taken as the norm, and woman as 'Other'; that is, not male. Similarly, in racist ideologies, whiteness is taken for granted, therefore blackness is seen as Other.
See **identity, psychoanalysis**

phenomenology A philosophical movement founded by Edmund Husserl in the early twentieth century in which the focus is on perception and consciousness, upon what the senses and the mind notice.

polysemic A property of signs is that they can have many meanings: their context and the interests of their readers. Hence captions, or words within the image, are frequently used to help anchor meaning.

positivism As is implied in the roots of the term itself, positivism stresses that which is definite or positive, i.e. factually based. Positivism, with its associated emphasis upon logical deduction and empirical research methods, including the social survey, is associated with the Victorian period in Britain, although its roots lie in earlier, eighteenth-century philosophy.

postmodern Literally 'after the modern', the postmodern represents a critique of the limitations of modernism with its emphasis upon progress and, in the case of the arts, upon the materiality of the medium of communication. Philosophically, postmodernism has been defined as marking the collapse of certainty, a loss of faith in explanatory systems, and a sense of dislocation consequent on the global nature of communication systems and the loss of a clear relation between signs and their referents.

poststructuralist At its most simple, this means 'after Structuralism', also implying critical thinking that contests and goes beyond Structuralist theory and method, rejecting the idea that all meaning is fundamentally systematic. In this book it is used to refer to a group of theories which stress the way that the human 'self' and the meaning made of the world is constructed through the languages (including visual languages) which we use. Poststructuralist thinking challenges the idea that there is a fixed and stable human subject or that knowledge can be certain.
See **identity, structuralism**

private and public spheres We lead our lives within two relatively distinct modes, a 'private' sphere, which is made up of personal and kinship relations and domestic life, and a 'public' sphere, made up of economic relations, work, money-making and politics. The 'private' sphere tends to be controlled by moral and emotional constraints, the 'public' sphere by public laws and regulations. This distinction, although contested by feminist writers, and more recently by those interested to analyse the extensive media penetration within the domestic, underlies the way the terms 'private' and 'public' are used in this book (especially in chapter 3).

psychoanalysis The therapeutic method established by Sigmund Freud, which involves seeking access to traumatic experiences held in the **unconscious** mind.
See **repression, unconscious**

representation This refers to ways in which individuals, groups or ideas are depicted. Use of the term usually signals acknowledgement that images are never 'innocent', but always have their own history, cultural contexts and specificity, and therefore carry **ideological** implications.

repression Unpleasant or unwelcome thoughts, emotions, sensations are 'repressed' when they are forced into the **unconscious**. The phrase 'the return of the repressed' means that such emotions surface into the conscious world in different forms.
See **psychoanalysis, unconscious**

reproduction The production (by machine) of many identical copies. The process of mass production when applied, through photography, print technology, and electronic recording to the copying of visual images or music. As this process has become increasingly sophisticated, the reproduction of original works of art has reached a stage where the reproduction is, for almost all intents and purposes, as good as the original. Where it does not, and cannot, replace the original autographic work is in bearing the traces and marks of its maker. Such originals have been spoken of as having an 'aura' (Benjamin 1936) due to our sense of their being unique and of having a history. There are, broadly, two schools of thought about the impact of reproduction on original images. One deplores the 'cheapening' of unique originals through reproduction; the other celebrates the process as a way of democratising visual and aural culture. Whatever the case, photography is a technology which has reproducibility built in. A negative is produced precisely so as to be able to make infinite numbers of prints, each, in principle, being identical, and digital technologies are inherently reproduceable. The continuing phenomenon of the 'artist' photographer's proof, or 'original' print, is therefore an ironic twist and an example of the political economy triumphing over technological determinations. In principle digital technology now renders distinctions between 'original' and 'reproduction' irrelevant.

scopophilia The human drive to look or observe; in Freudian theory the fundamental instinct leading to **voyeurism**.
See **fetishism, voyeurism**

semiology See **semiotics**

semiotics The science of signs, first proposed in 1916 by linguist Ferdinand de Saussure, but developed in particular in the work of Roland Barthes (France) and C.S. Peirce (USA). Semiotics – also referred to as semiology – is premised upon the contention that all human communication is founded in an assemblage of signs – verbal, aural and visual – which is essentially systematic. Such sign systems are viewed as largely – or entirely – conventional; that is, consequent not upon 'natural' relations between words or images and that to which they refer, but upon arbitrary relations established through cultural convention. The sign proper has two aspects, signifier and signified. The signifier is the material manifestation, the word, or pictorial elements. The signified is a mental concept that is conventionally associated with the specific signifier. While separable for analytic purposes, in practice the signifier and the signified always go together.
See **code**.

social and economic history History may be written in many ways. Economic history deals with changes in work patterns and the ways in which human societies have sustained themselves. Social history deals with the organisation of societies – marriage, education, child-rearing and the like. A history of photography is normally seen as part of art history or, more broadly, of the history of visual culture. In chapter 3 it is suggested that we can understand personal photography better if we consider it within a social and economic context. Chapter 5 takes the social and the economic as the primary context for understanding commercial uses of photography.

straight photography Emphasis upon direct documentary typical of the Modern period in American photography.

structuralism Twentieth-century theoretical movement within which stress is laid upon analysis of objects, cultural artefacts and communication processes in terms of systems of relations rather than as entities in themselves.

sublime That which is grand, noble or outstanding. In art the sublime is associated with awe, deep emotional response, and even pain. In landscape, the sublime relates to places where things run beyond human control, where nature is untameable. In his essay, 'A Philosophical Enquiry into the Origin of our Ideas of the Sublime and the Beautiful' (1757), the English philosopher Edmund Burke (1729–97) placed discussion of the sublime ahead of that of the beautiful, suggesting that pain is a stronger emotional force than pleasure. Burke wanted to explore human fascination with the sublime, noting that if pain or danger are too imminent they are simply terrible, but if held at some distance, for instance, through photographic representation, they are pleasurable. This apparent paradox has excited much subsequent debate in relation to imagery, not the least within psychoanalysis.

technological determinism The proposition that technological invention alone determines new cultural formations. The notion has been criticised primarily on the grounds that new technologies arise from research enterprises driven largely by economic imperatives and perceived social or political needs. Technological developments may be seen as an effect of cultural desires as well as a major influence within cultural change.

teleology Arguments and explanations in which the nature of something is explained by the purpose or 'end' which it appears to have. In this view photography, and then cinema, may be understood as being caused by a human desire to achieve ever more comprehensive illusions of reality, and are assumed to be striving towards further future achievements.

unconscious In **psychoanalysis**, that which is **repressed** from the individual's conscious awareness yet gives rise to impulses which influence our behaviour. Freud insisted that human action always derives from mental processes of which we cannot be aware.
See **repression, psychoanalysis**

voyeurism Sexual stimulation obtained through looking. In photography voyeurism refers to the image as spectacle used for the gratification of the (hitherto construed as male, heterosexual) spectator.
See **fetishism, objectification, psychoanalysis**

For a comprehensive definition and discussion of *technical* terms in chemical photography see:

GORDON BALDWIN AND JÜRGENS, MARTIN (1991) **Looking at Photographs: A Guide to Technical Terms**, Los Angeles, Getty Publications. Revised edition.

For fuller discussion of various contributions to twentieth-century debates, including Barthes, Benjamin, Foucault and Freud see:

JOHN LECHTE (1994) **Fifty Key Contemporary Thinkers**, London: Routledge.

FROM ANALOGUE TO DIGITAL

Illustrations used by Professor Martin Lister, author of the final chapter in earlier editions of this publication, to detail the implications of digital photography.

ANALOGUE AND DIGITAL

Traditionally, images were analogue in nature. That is, they consisted of physical marks and signs of some kind (whether brush marks, ink rubbed into scored lines, or the silver salts of the photographic print) carried by material surfaces. The marks and signs are virtually inseparable from these surfaces. They are also continuously related to some perceivable features of the object which they represent. The light, for instance, cast across a rough wooden table top becomes an analogous set of tonal differences in the emulsion of the photograph. A digital medium, on the other hand, is not a transcription but a conversion of information. In short, information is lodged as numbers in electronic circuits. It is this feature of digitisation which has meant that images can now exist as electronic data and not as tangible, physical stuff. Some of the key differences can be set out as follows:

Analogue	Digital
transcription: the transfer of one set of physical properties into another, analogous, set	*conversion*: physical properties symbolised by an arbitrary numerical code
continuous: representation occurs through variations in a continuous field of tone, sound, etc.	*unitised*: qualities divided into discrete, measurable and exactly reproducible elements
material inscription: signs inseparable from the surface that carries them	*abstract signals*: numbers or electronic pulses detachable from material source
medium specific: each analogue medium bounded by its materials and its specific techniques	*generic*: one binary code for all media, enabling convergence and conversion between them

Digitisation is also the effective precondition for the entry of photographic images into the flow of information which circulates within the contemporary global communications network. It is their translation into a numerical code that now enables them to be electronically transmitted. For the above reasons, questions have arisen about the place of images in time and space, where they can be said to actually exist, about how and where they are stored when in electronic form, how and by whom they can be accessed, used, owned and controlled.

For a full discussion of the analogue/digital distinction see:

TIMOTHY BINKLEY (1993) 'Refiguring Culture' in P. Hayward and
T. Wollen (eds) **Future Visions: New Technologies of the Screen**,
London: BFI.
A-M. WILLIS (1990) 'Digitisation and The Living Death of Photography' in
P. Hayward (ed.) **Culture, Technology and Creativity in the Late Twentieth
Century**, London: John Libbey and Co Ltd.

DIGITISING PHOTOGRAPHS: THE INITIAL IMPLICATIONS

- A shift in the location of photographic production: from the chemical darkroom to the 'electronic darkroom' of the computer.
- The outputting of single photographic originals in an expanded range of ways, from 'hard copy' through transparencies and varying forms of print, to the computer and TV screen, and websites.
- An unprecedented ease, sophistication and invisibility of enhancing and manipulating photographic images.
- The entry of photographic images into a global information and communications system as they become instantaneously transmissible in the form of electronic pulses passing along telephone lines and via satellite links.
- The high-speed transmission of news images which are no longer containable within territorial and political boundaries.
- The conversion of existing photographs and historical archives into digital storage banks which can be accessed at the screens of remote computer terminals.
- The potential of the new information and image networks for greatly extending the practices of military and civil surveillance.
- The unprecedented convergence of the still photographic image with previously distinct media: digital audio, video, graphics, animation and other kinds of data in new forms of interactive multimedia.

Photography archives

Work by many photographers, historical and contemporary, is kept under proper conservation conditions in specific archives (or collections). Researching images – perhaps for an extended essay or dissertation – may mean that you want to look at original prints. Here we list some key archives that may be of help to you. However, you should always phone or e-mail in advance to check that the work that interests you is available and to make a viewing appointment. Most archives have some materials reproduced on their website (NB website addresses below correct May 2014).

KEY PUBLIC ARCHIVES IN BRITAIN (Tel: +44)

National Media Museum, Pictureville, Bradford, West Yorkshire BD1 1NQ Tel: (0)844 856 3797, www.nationalmediamuseum.org.uk/photography/ Includes the collection of the Royal Photographic Society

National Portrait Gallery, St Martin's Place, London WC2H 0HE Tel: (0)207 306 0055, www.npg.org.uk For photographic portraiture archives and exhibitions

Scottish National Portrait Gallery, 1 Queen Street, Edinburgh EH2 1JD Tel: (0)131 624 6200, www.nationalgalleries.org Portraiture archives

Victoria and Albert Museum, South Kensington, London SW7 2RL Tel: (0)207 942 2000, www.vam.ac.uk Holds the National Collection of the Art of Photography

Also see www.24hourmuseum.org.uk

OTHER ARCHIVES

Autograph-Association of Black Photographers, Rivington Place, London EC2A 3BA Tel: (0)20 7729 9200, www.autograph-abp.co.uk/

Barnardo's Photographic and Film Archive, Tanners Lane, Barkingside, Ilford, Essex 1G6 1QG Tel: (0)208 550 0429, www.barnardos.org.uk/resources/photo_archive.htm

The Documentary Photography Archive, 56 Marshall Street, Manchester N4 5FU Tel: (0)161 832 5284, www.manchester.gov.uk/info/448/archives_and_local_studies/4689/documentary_photography_archive

Jo Spence Memorial Archive, 152 Upper Street, London N1 1RA

National Sound Archive, British Library, 96 Euston Road, London NW1 2DB Tel: (0)207 412 7676, www.bl.uk/soundarchive (search by name of photographer) Interviews with contemporary photographers

The Women's Library, LSE Library, 10 Portugal Street, London, WC2A 2HD Tel: (0)207 955 7229, www.lse.ac.uk/library/collections/featuredCollections/womensLibraryLSE.aspx Includes the Fawcett Library (women's rights)

Many organisations, including newspapers and commercial companies, maintain their own archives. However, access to these may be limited, by appointment only or based on payment of search fees. Among the foremost such collections are:

Hulton Getty Picture Collection, www.gettyimages.com/archival See website for worldwide offices and locations. Archives include *Picture Post, Express, Evening Standard*

Mary Evans Picture Library, 59 Tranquil Vale, London SE3 0BS Tel: (0)208 318 0034, www.maryevans.com

Most city libraries include photography in their local history collections. Sometimes this covers major bodies of work; for example, Edinburgh City Libraries house a large collection of calotypes by Hill and Adamson. Birmingham City Library holds a significant collection of historical work from central England.

ARCHIVES IN THE USA (Tel: +1)

International Museum of Photography and Film, George Eastman House, 900 East Avenue, Rochester, New York 14607–2298 Tel: (585) 271 3361, www.eastmanhouse.org/collections/photography.php Work by over 10,000 photographers; more than 400,000 photographs and negatives

New York Public Library Photography Collection, Fifth Avenue and 42nd Street, New York, NY 10018–2788 Tel: (212) 930 0837, http://wallachprintsandphotos.nypl.org/ Work by over 2,000 photographers, nearly 400,000 photographic prints

Collections with holdings of over 1,000 photographers

Art Institute of Chicago, 111 South Michigan Avenue at Adams Street, Chicago, IL 60603–6404 Tel: (312) 443 3600, www.artic.edu/aic/collections/photo

Center for Creative Photography, University of Arizona, Tucson, AZ 85721 Tel: (520) 6217968, www.creativephotography.org/collections

Colorado Historical Society, 1300 Broadway, Denver, Colorado 80203 Tel: (303) 866 3395, www.historycolorado.org/researchers/photographs Holds 750,000 photographic images and 250,000 negatives

Getty Center for the History of Art and the Humanities, 1200 Getty Center Drive, Los Angeles, CA 90049–1688 Tel: (310) 440 7335, www.getty.edu/research/tools/photo/ Archive of 1.5 million images

Harry Ransom Humanities Research Center, University of Texas at Austin, 300 West 21st Street, Austin, TX 78712 Tel: (512) 471 8944, www.hrc.utexas.edu/collections/photography Houses over five million photographs

The Library of Congress, Prints and Photographs Division, 101 Independence Avenue, SE, Washington DC 20540–4730 Tel: (202) 707 6394, ww.loc.gov/pictures/ Over 13.7 million prints and photographs including early daguerreotypes

J. Willard Marriott Library, University of Utah, Salt Lake City, UT 84112–0860 Tel: (801) 581 6273, www.lib.utah.edu/collections/multimedia-archives/index.php

Metropolitan Museum of Art, New York (Department of Photographs), 1000 Fifth Avenue at 82nd Street, New York, NY 10028 Tel: (212) 535 7710, www.metmuseum.org/about-the-museum/museum-departments/curatorial-departments/photographs

Museum of Fine Arts, 1001 Bissonnet Street, Houston, Texas TX 77005 Tel: (713) 639 7300, www.mfah.org/art/departments/photography/

Museum of Modern Art, 11 West 53rd Street, New York, NY 10019–5497 Tel: (212) 708 9400, www.moma.org/collection/depts/photography Has been collecting photographs since 1930 and holds over 25,000 works from 1840 to now. A large gallery is devoted to permanent collections where vintage prints of the great photographers are housed. Contemporary photographs are also held

Museum of New Mexico (photographic archives), Palace of the Governors, 120 Washington Avenue, P.O. Box 2087, Santa Fé, NM 87504–2087 Tel: (505) 476 1200, www.palaceofthegovernors.org/photoarchives.html

National Museum of American History, Smithsonian Institute, 14th Street and Constitution Ave, NW, Washington DC 20013 Tel: (202) 633 1000, http://american history.si.edu/collections/subjects/photography

New Orleans Museum of Art, 1 Collins Diboll Circle, City Park, New Orleans, LA 70124 Tel: (504) 658 4100, www.noma.org/collection/category/131/

San Francisco Museum of Modern Art, 151 Third Street, San Francisco, CA 94103 Tel: (415) 357 4000, www.sfmoma.org/explore/collection/photography

University of New Mexico, Albuquerque, NM 87131 Tel: (505) 277 9100, http://econtent.unm.edu/ 80,000 images dating from the 1850s to the recent past, focussing on histories of New Mexico, the Southwest and Latin America

Visual Studies Workshop, 31 Prince Street, Rochester, New York 14607 Tel: (585) 442 8676, http://vsw.org/rc.php

Women in Photography International Archive, Beinecke Rare Book and Manuscript Library, Yale University, P.O. Box 208240, New Haven, Connecticut 06520-8240 Tel: (203) 432 2972, www.cla.purdue.edu/waaw/palmquist/index.htm

For smaller archives, and for listings of photographers included in the collections listed above, see Andrew H. Eskind (ed.) (1995) *Index to American Photographic Collections*, compiled at the International Museum of Photography at George Eastman House, Rochester, revised edn, New York: G.K. Hall & Co.

See also *USA Photography Guide* (1998 3rd edn, Tucson/Munich: Nazraeli Press) for details of galleries, publishers, associations, museums and collections, and courses.

ARCHIVES ELSEWHERE (ENGLISH-LANGUAGE BASED)

Australia (Tel: +61)
Collections of photography are held at:

Art Gallery of New South Wales, The Domain, Sydney, NSW 2000 Tel: (2) 9225 1700, www.artgallery.nsw.gov.au/collection/photography/

LaTrobe Library, State Library of Victoria, 328 Swanston Street, Melbourne, Victoria 3000 Tel: (3) 8664 7000, www.slv.vic.gov.au/our-collections/what-we-collect/pictures

Mitchell Library, State Library of New South Wales (major photography collection), Macquarie Street, Sydney, NSW 2000 Tel: (2) 9273 1414, www.sl.nsw.gov.au/discover_collections/society_art/photography/index.html

National Gallery of Australia, Parkes Place, Canberra, ACT 2601 Tel: (2) 6240 6511, www.nga.gov.au/Photography/Index.cfm (Art collection including photography)

National Gallery of Victoria, 180 St Kilda Road, Melbourne, Victoria 8004 Tel: 9208 0222, www.ngv.vic.gov.au/collection

National Library of Australia, Parkes Place, Canberra. ACT 2600 Tel: (02) 6262 1111, www.nla.gov.au/pict

Queensland Art Gallery, Stanley Place, South Bank/PO Box 3696, South Brisbane, Queensland 4101 Tel: (7) 3840 7303, www.qagoma.qld.gov.au/collection

Canada (Tel: +1)

Library and Archives Canada, 395 Wellington Street, Ottawa, ON K1A0N4 Tel: (613) 996 5115, www.collectionscanada.gc.ca/02/020115_e.html

National Gallery of Canada, 380 Sussex Drive, PO Box 427, Station A, Ottawa, Ontario K1N 9N4 Tel: (613) 990 1985, www.gallery.ca/en/see/collections/category_index.php (click on Photography) An international collection of almost 20,000 photographs ranging from early photography to the contemporary

New Zealand (Tel: +64)

Alexander Turnbull Library, POB 12349, Wellington 6144 Tel: (4) 474 3120, www.natlib.govt.nz/collections/a-z-of-all-collections/photographic-archive Some 846,000 photographs

Auckland Museum, Private Bag 92018, Parnell, Auckland 1 Tel: (9) 309 0443, www.aucklandmuseum.com/collections-and-library/library-info-centres/pictorial-collections

National Archives, 10 Mulgrave Street, PO Box 12–050, Thorndon, Wellington Tel: (4) 499 5595, www.archives.govt.nz Over 200,000 photographs

For listings of all major and regional photograph collections in New Zealand see *Directory of New Zealand Photograph Collections*, 1992.

South Africa (Tel: +27)

Bensusan Museum of Film and Photography, in MuseumAfrica, at 121 Bree Street, Newtown, Johannesburg 2001. Tel: (11) 833 5624 Historical collection, with particular reference to South Africa.

Note: for other European archives see H. Evans and M. Evans (compilers) *Picture Researcher's Handbook: An International Guide to Picture Sources and How to Use Them*, London: Chapman and Hall. See also *European Photography Guide 8*, Göttingen: European Photography 2003 which includes information for over 3,000 individuals and institutions in 33 European countries and also information on magazines and journals, grants, awards, festivals and fairs, auctions and bookstores.

KEY BRITISH MAGAZINES AND JOURNALS

It is difficult to keep track of all serious photography magazines and journals that include historical, political and theoretical essays and critical responses to artists' works or to new developments especially as in recent years the number of new magazines and serious photoblogs has expanded. The following list represents some of those that are well-established.

British Journal of Photography, London (founded 1854), weekly. Focus on commercial photography. www.bjp-online.com

Camerawork, London (until 1985). Concerned with social and political issues

Creative Camera, London (until 2001) published six times a year. Contemporary gallery-based photography

History of Photography (academic journal, founded 1977), quarterly. www.tandfonline.com/toc/thph20/current

Philosophy of Photography, Vol 1, issue 1, March 2010, twice-yearly. www.intellectbooks.co.uk/journals/view-journal,id=186/

Photographies, Vol 1, Issue 1, Spring 2008, twice-yearly. www.tandfonline.com/toc/rpho20/current

Photography and Culture, 3 times a year, first issue, July 2008. www.bloomsbury.com/uk/journal/photography-and-culture

Photoworks, previously published twice a year; annual since 2013, Brighton, http://photoworks.org.uk

Portfolio, Edinburgh, (until 2010) biannual. www.portfoliocatalogue.com

Source, Belfast, quarterly. www.source.ie/index.php

Ten/8, Birmingham (until 1992; titled *Ten.8* in the two final issues)

KEY NORTH AMERICAN MAGAZINES AND JOURNALS

Afterimage, Visual Studies Workshop, Rochester, NY. Issues in photography and video. http://vsw.org/afterimage

Aperture New York/San Francisco, quarterly since 1952. Themed issues and portfolios. (Also for photography books.) www.aperture.org/magazine

Blackflash, The Photographers Gallery, Saskatoon, Saskatchewan, Canada. Three yearly. Journal of photo-based and electronic-art production. www.blackflash.ca/the-magazine/about

Border Crossings; Winnipeg, Manitoba, quarterly. An interdisciplinary arts review featuring articles, book reviews, artist profiles, and interviews covering the full range of the contemporary arts in Canada and internationally. http://bordercrossingsmag.com

Canadian Art, Toronto, Ontario, quarterly. Visual arts in Canada. Includes critical profiles of new artists and established art world figures. www.canadianart.ca/

October, The MIT Press, Cambridge, MA, quarterly since 1976. Academic journal: art, criticism, theory and history. www.mitpressjournals.org/loi/octo

Visual Anthropology Review, published by the American Anthropological Association. Debates on documentary and anthropology. http://onlinelibrary.wiley.com/journal/10.1111/(ISSN)1548-7458

OTHER MAGAZINES AND JOURNALS

Published in English or with translation

Camera Austria, contemporary photography. Quarterly. www.camera-austria.at

European Photography, Göttingen, Germany, founded 1980. Twice yearly. www.european-photography.com

Flash Art International, European Art magazine, firt published as *Flash*, 1996. Quarterly. www.flashartonline.com

NZ Journal of Photography, New Zealand Centre for Photography, PO Box 27–344, Wellington, articles about NZ photography and portfolios of images. Quarterly (until 2008). www.nzcp.com/Publications/tabid/473/Default.aspx

Photofile, Australian Centre for Photography, Sydney, founded 1983. Thrice yearly. www.acp.org.au/photofile

WEBSITES

Dealing with photography and digital media. These are just a few of what is now a huge range of sites. You should also use keyword searches, to ensure you find the most up-to-date sites.

CTHEORY   www.ctheory.net
Ctheory is an international journal of theory, technology and culture. Articles, interviews and key book reviews in contemporary discourse are published weekly as well as theorisations of major 'event-scenes' in the mediascape.

INTUTE   www.intute.ac.uk/artsandhumanities/
A searchable catalogue of internet resources internationally selected and catalogued by professional librarians in UK higher education (archived in 2011 but still accessible).

LEONARDO – Electronic Almanac   http://leonardo.info/leoinfo.html
An electronic journal dedicated to providing a forum for those who are interested in the convergence of art, science and technology. Includes: profiles of media arts facilities and projects; profiles of artists using new media; feature articles comprised of theoretical and technical perspectives; an on-line gallery exhibiting new media art.

PHOTOMONITOR   www.photomonitor.co.uk
An online magazine focused on artists using lens-based media in the UK and Ireland.

SCREENING THE PAST   www.screeningthepast.com
An international electronic journal of visual media and history. Covers photography, film, television and multimedia.

STILL SEARCHING   http://blog.fotomuseum.ch/
A blog written by guest critics commissioned by Fotomuseum, Winterthur, Switzerland.

ZONEZERO   www.zonezero.com/
ZoneZero is dedicated to photography and its journey from the analogue to digital world. It aims to carry an ongoing debate on all the issues surrounding the 'representation of reality' and other subjects relevant to the transition from analogue to digital image-making. It aims to promote an understanding of where, in the context of the digital age, the tradition of the 'still image' is headed. Carries extensive on-line exhibitions of photography. Has a special interest in Latin American work.

Bibliography

Adams, Robert (1996) *Beauty in Photography*, New York: Aperture

Ades, Dawn (1974) *Dada and Surrealism*, London: Thames and Hudson

Addison, Graeme (1984) 'Drum Beat: An examination of Drum', *Creative Camera*: 235/236, July/August: 1465

AFP (2003) 'Pan-European Security Body Slams TV for Turning War into Entertainment', 1 April, www.spacedaily.com/2003/030401163856.i0695hif.html

Agee, J. and Evans, W. (1941) *Let Us Now Praise Famous Men*, New York: Random House

Aitken, Ian (1990) *Film and Reform*, London: Routledge

Alexander, S. (1998) 'Photographic Institutions and Practices' in Michel Frizot *A New History of Photography*, Cologne: Könemann

Allan, Stuart (2006) *Online News: Journalism and the Internet,* Buckingham: Open University Press

Allen, M. (1998) 'From Bwana Devil to Batman Forever: Technology in Contemporary Hollywood Cinema' in Steve Neale and Murray Smith (eds) *Contemporary Hollywood Cinema*, London: Routledge

Alloula, Malek (1987) *The Colonial Harem*, Manchester: Manchester University Press

Alloway, Lawrence (1966) 'The Development of British Pop' in Lucy R. Lippart (ed.) *Pop Art*, London: Thames and Hudson

Arnason, H.H. (1988) *A History of Modern Art*, London: Thames and Hudson, third edition (updated and revised to include photography)

Arnason, H.H. And Kalb, P. (2004) *History of Modern Art*, Upper Saddle River, NJ: Pearson Education. Fifth edition

Arts Council (1972) *From Today Painting is Dead*, London: Arts Council

—— (1975) *The Real Thing, An Anthology of British Photographers 1840–1950*, London: Arts Council

—— (1979) *Three Perspectives on Photography*, London: Arts Council

—— (1987) *Independent Photography and Photography in Education*, London: Arts Council

—— (1991) *Shocks to the System*, London: The South Bank Centre

Ascott, R. (1996) 'Photography at the Interface' in T. Druckery (ed.) *Electronic Culture: Technology and Visual Representation*, New York: Aperture

Axelmunden, V.H., Iglhaut, Stefan and Roetzer, Florian (eds) in collaboration with Alexis Cassel and Nikolaus G. Schneider (1996) 'Photography after Photography: Memory and Representation in the Digital Age', Amsterdam: OP17 and Munich: Siemens Kulturprogramm

Bacher, Fred (1992) 'The Popular Condition: Fear and Clothing in LA', *The Humanist*, September/October

Back, L. and Quaade, V. (1993) 'Dream Utopias, Nightmare Realities: Imagining Race and Culture within the World of Benetton', *Third Text* 22

Badger, Gerry (2007) *The Genius of Photography – How Photography has Changed our Lives*, London: Quadrille

Badger, Gerry and Benton-Harris, John (eds) (1989) *Through the Looking Glass,* London: Barbican Art Gallery

Badmington, Neil (2000) *Posthumanism*, New York: Palgrave

Bailey, David (1988) 'Re-thinking Black Representations', *Ten/8* 31

—— (1989) 'People of the World' in P. Wombell (ed.) *The Globe: Representing the World*, York: Impressions Gallery

Bailey, David and Hall, Stuart (eds) (1992) *Ten/8* 2(3), *Critical Decade*

Baker, Lindsay (1991) 'Taking Advertising to its Limit', *The Times*, 22 July, p. 29

Bakhtin, Mikhail (1984) *Rabelais and His World*, Bloomington, IN: Indiana University Press

Baldwin, Gordon and Jürgens, Martin (2009) *Looking at Photographs: A Guide to Technical Terms*, Los Angeles: Getty Publications. Revised edition

Barrett, M. and McIntosh, M. (1982) *The Anti-social Family*, London: Verso

Barthes, Roland (1973 [1957]) *Mythologies*, London: Granada. Republished in London by Grafton Books, 1986

—— (1977a) 'The Photographic Message' in S. Heath (ed.) *Image, Music, Text*, London: Fontana

—— (1977b) 'The Rhetoric of the Image' in S. Heath (ed.) op. cit.

—— (1977c) 'The Third Meaning' in S. Heath (ed.) op. cit.

—— (1984 [1980]) *Camera Lucida*, London: Fontana. Previous English publication 1981, New York: Hill and Wang

Batchen, Geoffrey (1990) 'Burning with Desire: The Birth and Death of Photography', *Afterimage*, January

—— (1997) *Burning With Desire*, Cambridge, MA: The MIT Press

—— (1998) 'Spectres of Cyberspace' in Nicholas Mirzeoff (ed.) *The Visual Culture Reader*, London and New York: Routledge

—— (2001) 'Ectoplasm' in *Each Wild Idea: Writing: Photography: History*, Cambridge, MA and London: The MIT Press

—— (2003 [1998]) 'Photogenics' in L. Wells (ed.) *The Photography Reader*, London and New York: Routledge.

—— (2004) *Forget Me Not – Photography and Remembrance*, Amsterdam: Van Gogh Museum, and New York: Princeton Architectural Press

—— (2007) 'Dividing History', *Source* 52, Autumn

—— (2008) 'Snapshots, Art History and the Ethnographic Turn', *photographies* 1(2), Autumn

—— (ed.) (2009) *Photography Degree Zero: Reflections on Roland Barthes's Camera Lucida*, Cambridge, MA: The MIT Press

—— (2012) 'Looking Askance' in Geoffrey Batchen, Mick Gidley, Nancy K. Millar and Jay Prosser (eds) *Picturing Atrocity: Photography in Crisis*, London: Reaktion Books

Bate, David (1993) 'Photography and the Colonial Vision', *Third Text* 22
—— (2001) 'Blowing it: Digital Images and the Real', DPICT 7, April/May
—— (2004) *Photography and Surrealism*, London: I.B.Tauris
—— (2009) *Photography, The Key Concepts*. Oxford and New York: Berg
Baudelaire, Charles (1859) 'The Salon of 1859', reprinted in P.E. Charvet (ed.) (1992) *Baudelaire, Selected Writings on Art and Artists*, Harmondsworth: Penguin
Baudrillard, Jean (1983) 'The Ecstasy of Communication' in H. Foster (ed.) *The Anti-aesthetic*, Washington, DC: Bay Press
—— (1995) *The Gulf War Did Not Take Place*, Bloomington, IN: Indiana University Press
—— (1998) 'The Finest Consumer Object' in *The Consumer Society: Myths and Structures*, London: Sage
Bazin, André (1967) 'The Ontology of the Photograph' in *What is Cinema?* Vol. 1, Berkeley, Los Angeles and London: University of California Press
Becker, K. (1991) 'To Control our Image: Photojournalists Meeting New Technology' in P. Wombell (ed.) *PhotoVideo: Photography in the Age of the Computer*, London: Rivers Oram Press
Bede, Cuthbert (1855) *Photographic Pleasures*, London
Behdad, Ali and Gartlan, Luke (eds) (2013) *Photography's Orientalism: New Essays on Colonial Representation*, Los Angeles: Getty Research Institute
Belisle, Brooke (2011) 'Felt Surface, Visible Image: Lorna Simpson's Photography and the Embodiment of Appearance', *Photography and Culture* 4(2): 157–78
Beloff, Halla (1985) *Camera Culture*, Oxford: Blackwell
Belting, Hans (2011) *An Anthropology of Images*, Princeton: Princeton University Press
Belussi, Fiorenza (1987) *Benetton: Information Technology in Production and Distribution: A Case Study of the Innovative Potential of Traditional Sectors*, Brighton: SPRU, University of Sussex
Benetton (1993) *Global Vision: United Colors of Benetton*, Tokyo: Robundo
Benjamin, Walter (1931a) 'A Short History of Photography' in *One Way Street* (1979), London: New Left Books. Also published (1972) as 'A Short History of Photography', *Screen* 13(1)
—— (1931b) 'Unpacking My Library' in *Illuminations*, London: Jonathan Cape, 1970; Fontana, 1973/1992. Originally published in *Literarische Welt*, 1931
—— (1934) 'The Author as Producer' in V. Burgin (ed.) (1982) *Thinking Photography*, London and Basingstoke: Macmillan
—— (1936) 'The Work of Art in an Age of Mechanical Reproduction' in Hannah Arendt (ed.) *Illuminations*, London: Fontana. Revised edition 1992. Originally published in *Zeitschrift für Sozialforschung* 5(1), 1936
—— (1938) 'The Paris of the Second Empire in Baudelaire' in *Charles Baudelaire: A Lyric Poet in the Era of High Capitalism*, London: Verso, 1985
—— (1939) 'Some Motifs in Baudelaire' in Hannah Arendt (ed.) *Illuminations*, London: Fontana
Bennett, Jane (2010) *Vibrant Matter: A Political Ecology of Things*, Durham, NC: Duke University Press
Benson, Richard (2008) *The Printed Picture*, New York: Museum of Modern Art
Benson, S.H. (n.d.) *Some Examples of Benson Advertising*, S.H. Benson Firm
Berger, John (1972a) *Ways of Seeing*, Harmondsworth: Penguin
—— (1972b) 'The Political Uses of Photomontage' in *Selected Essays and Articles, The Look of Things*, Harmondsworth: Penguin
Berger, J. and Mohr, J. (2002) *Another Way of Telling*, London and New York: Writers Publishing Cooperative Society Ltd
Bernstein, B. (1971) *Class, Codes and Control*, Vol. 1, *Theoretical Studies Towards a Sociology of Language*, London: Routledge & Kegan Paul

Best, S. and Keller, D. (1991) *Postmodern Theory: Critical Interrogations*, London: Macmillan

Bezencenet, Stevie (1982a) 'What is a History of Photography?', *Creative Camera* 208, April

—— (1982b) 'Thinking Photography', *Creative Camera* 215, November

Bhabha, H. (1990) 'Novel Metropolis', *New Statesman and Society*, 9 February

Binkley, T. (1993) 'Refiguring Culture' in P. Hayward and T. Wollen (eds) *Future Visions: New Technologies of the Screen*, London: BFI

Bishton, D. and Rearden, J. (eds) (1984) 'Black Image – Staying On', *Ten/8* 16

Blood on the Carpet (2001) *Blood, Sweaters and Sears*, BBC2, 9 January

Boddy, W. (1994) 'Archaeologies of Electronic Vision and the Gendered Spectator', *Screen* 35(2): 105–22

Bode, S. and Wombell, P. (1991) 'Introduction: In a New Light' in P. Wombell (ed.) *PhotoVideo: Photography in the Age of the Computer*, London: Rivers Oram Press

Boffin, T. and Fraser, J. (1991) *Stolen Glances: Lesbians Take Photographs*, London: Pandora Press

Bolt, Barbara and Barrett, Estelle (2014) *Carnal Knowledges*, London: Routledge

Bolter, Jay David and Grusin, Richard (1999) 'Digital Photography' in *Remediation: Understanding New Media*, Cambridge, MA, and London: The MIT Press

Bolton, Richard (ed.) (1989) *The Contest of Meaning*, Cambridge, MA: The MIT Press

Bourdieu, P. (1990 [1965]) *Photography: A Middle Brow Art*, London: Polity Press

Braden, Su (1978) *Artists and People*, London: Routledge & Kegan Paul

Brandt, Bill (1961) *Perspective of Nudes*, London: The Bodley Head

Braun, Marta (1992) *Picturing Time: The Work of Etienne-Jules Marey (1830–1904)*, Chicago, IL: University of Chicago Press

Breton, André (1978) *What is Surrealism? Selected Writings* in F. Rosement (ed. and introduction), London: Pluto Press

Bright, Deborah (1989) 'Of Mother Nature and Marlboro Men: An Inquiry into the Cultural Meanings of Landscape Photography' in Richard Boston (ed.) *The Contest of Meaning*, Cambridge, MA: The MIT Press

—— (ed.) (1998) *The Passionate Camera: Photography and Bodies of Desire*, London and New York: Routledge

Bright, Susan (2010) *Auto Focus: The Self-Portrait in Contemporary Photography*, London: Thames and Hudson

—— (2013) *Home Truths: Photography and Motherhood*, London: Art/Books

Brittain, D. (ed.) (1999) *Creative Camera: 30 Years of Writing*, Manchester: Manchester University Press

Brookes, Rosetta (1992) 'Fashion Photography' in J. Ash and E. Wilson (eds) *Chic Thrills: A Fashion Reader*, London: Pandora

Broomberg, Adam and Chanarin, Oliver (2008) 'Unconcerned but not Indifferent', *Foto 8*. Reprinted in Julian Stallabrass (ed.) *Documentary*, Whitechapel Gallery and MIT Press, 2013, p. 99

Brown, Beverley (1981) 'A Feminist Interest in Pornography: Some Modest Proposals' in Parveen Adams and Elizabeth Cowie (1990) *The Woman in Question*, London and New York: Verso

Buck-Morse, S. (1991) *The Dialectics of Seeing: Walter Benjamin and the Arcades Project*, Cambridge, MA: The MIT Press

Burgess, N. (2001) 'From Golden Age to Digital Age', DPICT 7, April/May

Burgin, Victor (ed.) (1982) *Thinking Photography*, London: Macmillan

—— (1986) 'Re-Reading Camera Lucida' in *The End of Art Theory: Criticism and Postmodernity*, London: Macmillan

—— (1991) 'Realising the Reverie', *Ten/8* 2(2), *Digital Dialogues*

Bush, Kate and Sladen, Mark (eds) (2006) *In the Face of History: European Photographers in the 20th Century*, London: Black Dog Publishing

Butler, Susan (1985) 'From Today Black and White is Dead' in D. Brittain (ed.) (1999) *Creative Camera*, Manchester: Manchester University Press

—— (1989) *Shifting Focus*, Bristol: Arnolfini, and London: Serpentine

Butt, Gavin (1998) *Men on the Threshold: The Making and Unmaking of the Sexual Subject in American Art 1948–1965*, unpublished Ph.D. thesis, University of Leeds

Cameron, Fiona and Kenderdine, Sarah (eds) (2007) *Theorizing Digital Cultural Heritage*, Massachusetts: The MIT Press

Campany, David (2003) *Art and Photography*, London: Phaidon

Carlebach, M.L. (1992) *The Origins of Photojournalism in America*, Washington, DC: Smithsonian Institute

Carlson, Matt (2009) 'The Reality of a Fake Image: News Norms, Photojournalistic Craft, and Brian Walski's Fabricated Photograph', *Journalism Practice* 3(2): 125–39

Carr, E.H. (1964) *What is History?*, Harmondsworth: Penguin

Cartier-Bresson, H. (1952) *The Decisive Moment*, New York: Simon and Schuster

Cartwright, Lisa (1995) *Screening the Body: Tracing Medicine's Visual Culture*, Minneapolis and London: University of Minnesota Press

Castells, M. (2000) *The Rise of the Network Society*, Oxford and USA: Blackwell

Chadwick, Whitney (1985) *Women Artists and the Surrealist Movement*, London: Thames and Hudson

—— (1998) *Mirror Images: Women, Surrealism and Self-representation*, Cambridge, MA: The MIT Press

Chambers, Eddie (1999) 'D-Max: An Introduction' in *Run Through the Jungle*, Annotations 5, London: INIVA

Chanan, M. (1996) *The Dream That Kicks*, London: Routledge

Chandra, Mohini (2001) *Album Pacifica*, London: Autograph

Chester, Gail and Dickey, Julienne (eds) (1988) *Feminism and Censorship: The Current Debate*, Bridport, Dorset: Prism Press

Christian, J. (1990) 'Paul Sandby and the Military Survey of Scotland' in N. Alfrey and J. Daniels (eds) *Mapping the Landscape*, Nottingham: University of Nottingham

Clark, Kenneth (1956) *The Nude*, Harmondsworth: Penguin

Clarke, Graham (1997) *The Photograph*, Oxford: Oxford University Press

Coe, B. (1989) 'Roll Film Revolution' in C. Ford (ed.) *The Story of Popular Photography*, Bradford: Century Hutchinson Ltd/National Museum of Photography, Film and Television

Coe, B. and Gates, P. (1977) *The Snapshot Photograph: The Rise of Popular Photography 1888–1939*, London: Ash and Grant

Coke, Van Deren (1972) *The Painter and the Photograph*, New Mexico: University of New Mexico Press

Coleman, A.D. (1979) *Light Readings*, New York: Oxford University Press

Connarty, Jane and Lanyon, Josephine (2006) *Ghosting: The Role of the Archive Within Contemporary Artists' Film and Video*, Bristol: Picture This

Cook, Guy (1992) *The Discourse of Advertising*, Oxford: Oxford University Press

Cooper, Emmanuel (1990) *Fully Exposed: The Male Nude in Photography*, London: Unwin Hyman

Corner, John and Harvey, Sylvia (1990) 'Heritage in Britain', *Ten/8* 36

—— (eds) (1991) *Enterprise and Heritage*, London: Routledge

Cotton, Charlotte (2000) *Imperfect Beauty: The Making of Contemporary Fashion Photographs*, London: Victoria and Albert Museum

—— (2004) *The Photograph as Contemporary Art*, London: Thames and Hudson (revised edition 2014).

Craik, Jennifer (1994) 'Soft Focus: Techniques of Fashion Photography' in *The Face of Fashion*, London: Routledge

Crary, Jonathan (1993) *Techniques of the Observer: On Vision and Modernity in the Nineteenth Century*, Cambridge, MA: The MIT Press

—— (1999) *Suspensions of Perception: Attention, Spectacle and Modern Culture*, Cambridge, MA: The MIT Press

Crawley, G. (1989) 'Colour Comes to All' in C. Ford (ed.) *The Story of Popular Photography*, Bradford: Century Hutchinson Ltd/National Museum of Photography, Film and Television

Crimp, Douglas (1995) *On the Museum's Ruins*, Cambridge, MA: The MIT Press

Crimp, Douglas and Rolston, Adam (1990) *AIDS Demo/Graphics*, Seattle: Bay Press

Csikszentmihalyi, M. and Rochberg-Halton, E. (1992) *The Meaning of Things: Domestic Symbols and the Self*, Cambridge: Cambridge University Press

Curtis, Neal (1999) 'The Body as Outlaw: Lyotard, Kafka and the Visible Human Project', *Body and Society* 5(2–3): 249–66

Darley, A. (1990) 'From Abstraction to Simulation: Notes on the History of Computer Imaging' in P. Hayward (ed.) *Culture, Technology, and Creativity in the Late Twentieth Century*, London: John Libbey and Co. Ltd

—— (1991) 'Big Screen, Little Screen: The Archaeology of Technology', *Ten/8* 2(2), *Digital Dialogues*

Davidoff, L. and Hall, C. (1976) 'The Charmed Circle of Home' in J. Mitchell and A. Oakley (eds) *The Rights and Wrongs of Women*, Harmondsworth: Penguin

Davis, S. (1995) 'Welcome Home Big Brother', *Wired* Magazine, May

Debord, Guy (1970 [1967]) *The Society of the Spectacle*, Detroit: Black and Red

Deitch, Jeffrey (1992) *Post Human*, Amsterdam: Idea Books

Delpire, Robert and Frizot, Michel (1989) *Histoire de Voir*, Paris: Photo Poche

Dennett, Terry and Spence, Jo (1979) *Photography/Politics: One*, London: Photography Workshop

Dentith, Simon (1995) *Bakhtinian Thought: An Introductory Reader*, London: Routledge

Deroo, Rebecca (2002) 'Colonial Collecting: French Women and Algerian Cartes Postales' in Eleanor M. Hight, Gary D. Sampson (eds) *Colonialist Photography: Imag(in)ing Race and Place*, London and New York: Routledge

Devlin, Polly (1979) *Vogue Book of Fashion Photography*, London: Condé Nast

Dewdney, A. (1991) 'More Than Black and White: The Extended and Shared Family Album' in J. Spence and P. Holland (eds) *Family Snaps: The Meanings of Domestic Photography*, London: Virago

Dewdney, A. and Boyd, F. (1995) 'Television, Computers, Technology and Cultural Form' in M. Lister (ed.) *The Photographic Image in Digital Culture*, London and New York: Routledge

di Bello, Patrizia (2007) *Women's Albums and Photography in Victorian England: Ladies, Mothers and Flirts*, London and Burlington, VT: Ashgate

di Bello, Patrizia, Wilson, Colette and Zamir, Shamoon (eds) (2012) *The Photo Book*, London: I B Tauris

Doherty, Robert J., Hurley, Jack F., Kloner, Jay M. and Ryant, Carl G. (1972) 'Roy Stryker on FSA, SONJ, J&L' in Peninah R. Petruck (ed.) *The Camera Viewed: Writings on Twentieth-century Photography*, New York: E.P. Dutton

Doy, Gen (1996) 'Out of Africa: Orientalism, Race and the Female Body', *Body and Society* 2(4): 17–44

Drake, M. and Finnegan, R. (eds) (1994) *Studying Family and Community History: 19th and 20th Centuries*, Vol. 4, *Sources and Methods: A Handbook*, Cambridge: Cambridge University Press and the Open University Press

Druckery, T. (1991) 'Deadly Representations or Apocalypse Now', *Ten/8* 2(2): 16–27, *Digital Dialogues*

Dubin, Steven C. (1992) *Arresting Images: Impolitic Art and Uncivil Actions*, London and New York: Routledge

Duganne, E. (2007) 'Photography After the Fact' in M. Reinhardt, H. Edwards and E. Duganne (eds) *Beautiful Suffering: Photography and the Traffic in Pain*, Chicago, IL: University of Chicago Press

Durand, R. (1999) 'The Document, or the Lost Paradise of Authenticity', *Art Press* 251

Durden, Mark (2006 [2001]) *Dorothea Lange*, London: Phaidon Press

Dworkin, Andrea (1981) *Pornography: Men Possessing Women*, London: The Women's Press

Dyer, Geoff (2005) *The Ongoing Moment*, London: Little, Brown

Dyer, Richard (1997) *White*, London and New York: Routledge

Eastlake, Lady Elizabeth (1857) 'Photography', *Quarterly Review*, April. Reprinted in Beaumont Newhall (ed.) (1980) *Photography: Essays and Images*, London: Secker and Warburg

Eco, Umberto (1979) *The Role of the Reader: Explorations in the Semiotics of Texts*, London: Hutchinson

—— (1987) *Travels in Hyperreality*, London: Picador

Edwards, Elizabeth (ed.) (1992) *Photography and Anthropology 1860–1920*, New Haven, CT: Yale University Press

—— (2008) 'Photographs, Orality and History' in Elizabeth Edwards and Kaushik Bhaumik (eds) *Visual Sense*, Oxford and New York: Berg

Edwards, Elizabeth and Hart, Janice (2004) *Photographs Objects Histories: On the Materiality of Images*, London and New York: Routledge

Edwards, Steve (1989) 'The Snapshooters of History', *Ten/8* 32

—— (2006) *Photography, A Very Short Introduction*, Oxford: Oxford University Press

Eileraas, Karina (2007) *Between Image and Identity: Transnational Fantasy, Symbolic Violence and Feminist Misrecognition*, Lanham, MD: Lexington Books

Elias, Norbert (1994) *The Civilising Process: Vol. 1, History of Manners*, Oxford: Blackwell

Elkins, James (2007) *Photography Theory*, London: Routledge

Ellis, J. (1991) *Visible Fictions: Cinema, Television, Video*, London and New York: Routledge

Emerling, Jae (2012) *Photography, History and Theory*, London and New York: Routledge

Ennis, Helen (2011) 'Death and Digital Photography', *Cultural Studies Review* 17(1): 125–45

Enos, Katherine (1997/1998) 'Crash & Pornography Culture', www.pomegranates.com

Evans, C. and Thornton, M. (1989) *Women and Fashion: A New Look*, London: Quartet

Evans, Jessica (ed.) (1997) *The Camerawork Essays*, London: Rivers Oram Press

Ewing, William (1991) 'Perfect Surface' in *The Idealising Vision: The Art of Fashion Photography*, New York: Aperture

—— (1994) *The Body*, London: Thames and Hudson

—— (1996) *Inside Information: Imaging the Human Body*, London: Thames and Hudson

Falconer, J. (2001) *India: Pioneering Photographs 1850–1900*, London: The British Library

Falk, Pasi (1997) 'The Benetton-Toscani Effect – Testing the Limits of Conventional Advertising' in Mica Nava, Andrew Blake, Iain MacRury and Barry Richards (eds) *Buy this Book*, London: Routledge

Felman, S. and Laub, D. (1992) *Testimony: Crises of Witnessing in Literature, Psychoanalysis and History*, London: Routledge

Ferguson, Russell (1992) 'A Box of Tools: Theory and Practice' in R. Ferguson, K. Fiss and W. Olander (eds) *Discourses: Conversations in Postmodernism, Art and Culture*, Cambridge, MA: The MIT Press

Fernandez, H. (2012) *The Latin American Photobook*, New York: Aperture

Fijalkowski, Krzysztof, Richardson, Michael and Walker, Ian (eds) (2013) *Surrealism and Photography in Czechoslovakia*, London: Ashgate

Fisher, Andrea (1987) *Let Us Now Praise Famous Women*, London: Pandora

Flusser, Vilém (2000) *Towards a Philosophy of Photography*, London: Reaktion Books

Ford, C. (1989) *The Story of Popular Photography*, Bradford: Century Hutchinson Ltd/National Museum of Photography, Film and Television

—— (2003) *Julia Margaret Cameron: 19th Century Photographer of Genius*, London: National Portrait Gallery

Foster, Hal (1993) *Compulsive Beauty*, Cambridge, MA, and London: The MIT Press

—— (1996) 'Obscene, Abject, Traumatic', *October* 78, Autumn

Frank, R. (2008 [1958/1959]) *The Americans*, Göttingen: Steidl & Washington/National Gallery of Fine Art

Freedman, Jim (1990) 'Bringing it all Back Home: A Commentary on *Into the Heart of Africa*', *Museum Quarterly*, February

Freud, Sigmund (1905) 'Three Essays on Sexuality' in Vol. 7 of *Sigmund Freud (1953–1964) Standard Edition of the Complete Works*, trans. James Strachey, London: Hogarth Press

—— (1927) 'Fetishism' in Vol. 7 of *Sigmund Freud (1953–1964)* op. cit.

Freund, Gisele (1980) *Photography and Society*, London: Gordon Fraser

Friedberg, Anne (1993) *Window Shopping: Cinema and the Postmodern*, Berkeley: University of California Press

Frizot, Michel (ed.) (1998 [1994]) *A New History of Photography*, Cologne: Könemann

Frosh, Paul (2003) *The Image Factory: Consumer Culture, Photography and the Visual Content Industry,* Oxford and New York: Berg

Frye, Marilyn (1983) 'Oppression and the Use of Definition' in *The Politics of Reality: Essays in Feminist Theory*, Trumansburg, NY: The Crossing Press

Gabriel, T. (1995) 'The Intolerable Gift', unpublished conference paper, London: BFI

Galassi, Peter (1981) *Before Photography*, New York: MOMA

—— (1995) *American Photography 1890–1965*, New York: MOMA

Gamman, Lorraine and Makinen, Merja (1994) *Female Fetishism: A New Look*, London: Lawrence and Wishart

Garde-Hansen, J. (2013) 'Friendship Photography: Memory, Mobility and Social Net-working' in Larsen, J. and Sandbye, M. *Digital Snaps: The New Face of Photography* London: I.B.Tauris

Gasser, Martin (1992) 'Histories of Photography 1839–1939', *History of Photography* 16(1), Spring

Gates, Kelly A. (2005) 'Biometrics and Post-9/11 Technostalgia', *Social Text* 83, 23(2), Summer

—— (2004) 'The Past Perfect Promise Facial Recognition Technology', Reseach of the Program in Arms Control Disarmament, and International Security University of Illinois at Urbana-Champaign, www.ideals.uiuc.edu/handle/2142/38

Geraghty, C. (1991) *Women and Soap Opera: A Study of Prime Time Soaps*, Cambridge: Polity Press

Gernsheim, Alison (1981 [1963]) *Victorian and Edwardian Fashion, A Photographic Survey*, New York: Dover. Revised edition

Gernsheim, Helmut and Gernsheim, Alison (1965) *A Concise History of Photography*, London: Thames and Hudson

—— (1969 [1955]) *The History of Photography from the Earliest Use of the Camera Obscura in the Eleventh Century up to 1914,* 2 vols, London and New York: McGraw-Hill

Gidal, T.N. (1973) *Modern Photojournalism*, New York: Macmillan

Giebelhausen, Joachim (1963) *Techniques of Advertising Photography,* Munich: Nicolaus Karpf

Gierstberg, F. and Suermondt, R. (2012) *The Dutch Photobook*, New York: Aperture

Gillis, J. (1997) *A World of Their Own Making: A History of Myth and Ritual in Family Life*, Oxford: Oxford University Press

Gilroy, Paul (2007) *Black Britain: A Photographic History,* London: Saqi Books

Giroux, Henry (1993) 'Consuming Social Change: The "United Colors of Benetton"', *Cultural Critique*, 26: 5–32

Glückler, J. and Panitz, R. (2013) *Survey of the Global Stock Image Market 2012, Part I: Players, Products, Business*, Heidelberg: GSIM Research Group

Goddard, Angela (1998) *The Language of Advertising: Written Texts*, London: Routledge

Godfrey, Tony (1998) *Conceptual Art*, London: Phaidon

Goffman, Erving (1979) *Gender Advertisements*, London: Macmillan

Goldberg, Vicki (ed.) (1981) *Photography in Print*, Albuquerque: University of New Mexico

Goldman, Robert (1992) *Reading Ads Socially*, London: Routledge

Goldman, Robert and Papson, Stephen (1996) *Sign Wars: The Cluttered Landscape of Advertising*, New York: Guilford Press

—— (1999) *Nike Culture: The Sign of the Swoosh,* Thousand Oaks, CA, and London: Sage

Graham, B. (1995) 'The Panic Button (in which our Heroine Goes Back to the Future of Pornography)' in M. Lister (ed.) *The Photographic Image in Digital Culture*, London and New York: Routledge

Graham, Judith (1989) 'Benetton "Colors" the Race Issue', *Advertising Age*

Graham-Brown, Sarah (1988) *Images of Women: The Portrayal of Women in Photography of the Middle East 1860–1950*, London: Quartet Books

Gray, Camilla (1962) *The Russian Experiment in Art*, London: Thames and Hudson

Green, D. (1994) 'Classified Subjects', *Ten/8* 14: 30–7

—— (ed.) (2003) *Where is the Photograph?* Brighton: Photoforum, and Maidstone: Photoworks

Green, Jonathan (1984) 'The Painter as Photographer' in *American Photography*, New York: Harry N. Abrams

Greenberg, Clement (1939) 'Avant-garde and Kitsch' in *Art and Culture*, Boston, MA: Beacon Press, 1961. Reprinted in C. Harrison and P. Wood (eds) (1992) *Art in Theory 1900–1990*, Oxford: Blackwell

—— (1961) 'Modernist Painting'. Reprinted in F. Frascina and J. Harris (eds) (1992) *Art in Modern Culture*, London: Phaidon

—— (1964) 'Four Photographers'. Reprinted in *History of Photography* 15(2), Summer 1991

Green-Lewis, Jennifer (1996) *Framing the Victorians, Photography and the Culture of Realism*, Ithaca, NY and London: Cornell University Press

Grey, C. (1991) 'Theories of Relativity' in J. Spence and P. Holland (eds) *Family Snaps: The Meanings of Domestic Photography*, London: Virago

Griffin, Michael (1999) 'The Great War Photographs: Constructing Myths of History and Photojournalism', in B. Brennan and H. Hardt (eds) *Picturing the Past: Media, History and Photography*, Urbana, University of Illinois Press

Griffiths, P.J. (1971) *Vietnam Inc.*, New York: Macmillan

Grundberg, Andy (1986) 'Veins of Resemblance' in P. Holland, J. Spence and S. Watney (eds) *Photography/Politics: Two*, London: Comedia

—— (1990a) 'On the Dissecting Table' in Carol Squiers *The Critical Image*, London: Lawrence and Wishart

—— (1990b) 'Photography in the Age of Electronic Simulation' in *Crisis of the Real*, New York: Aperture

—— (2005) 'Point and Shoot: How the Abu Ghraib Images Redefine Photography', *American Scholar* 74(1), Winter: 108

Gunning, Tom (1991) 'Heard over the phone: the lonely villa and the De Lorde tradition of the terrors of technology', *Screen* 32(2): 184–96

Gunthert, André (2008) 'Digital Imaging Goes to War: The Abu Ghraib Photographs' in *photographies*, 1(1), Spring: 103–12. Originally published in *Etudes photographiques* 15 (2004)

Gupta, Sunil (1986) 'Northern Media, Southern Lives' in P. Holland, J. Spence and S. Watney (eds) *Photography/Politics: Two*, London: Comedia

—— (1990) 'Photography, Sexuality and Cultural Difference', *Camerawork Quarterly* 17(3)

—— (ed.) (1993) *Disrupted Borders: An Intervention in Definitions of Boundaries*, London: Rivers Oram Press

Haddon, L. (1993) 'Interactive Games' in P. Hayward and T. Wollen (eds) *Future Visions: New Technologies of the Screen*, London: BFI

Hafner, Katie (2007) 'A Photo Trove, a Mounting Challenge', *New York Times*, 10 April

Hall, C. (1979) 'Early Formation of Victorian Domestic Ideology' in S. Burman (ed.) *Fit Work for Women*, London: Croom Helm

Hall, Stuart (1988) 'The Work of Art in The Electronic Age', *Block* 14

—— (1991) 'Reconstruction Work: Images of Post-war Black Settlement' in J. Spence and P. Holland (eds) *Family Snaps: The Meanings of Domestic Photography*, London: Virago

—— (1993 [1980]) 'Encoding/Decoding' in S. Durring (ed.) *The Cultural Studies Reader*, London: Routledge

—— (ed.) (1997) *Representation: Cultural Representations and Signifying Practices*, London: Sage/Open University

—— (2013) *Cultural Representations and Signifying Practice*, London: Sage

Hamilton, P. and Hargreaves, R. (2001) *The Beautiful and the Damned: The Creation of Identity in Nineteenth Century Photography*, London: Lund Humphries in association with The National Portrait Gallery

Hanley, L. (2007) *Estates: an Intimate History*, London: Granta

Hannavy, J. (1975) *Roger Fenton of Crimble Hall*, London: Gordon Fraser

Hardy, B. (1977) 'Bert Hardy', *Camerawork* 8

Hariman, Robert and Lucaites, John Louis (2007) *No Caption Needed, Iconic Photographs, Public Culture, and Liberal Democracy*, Chicago, IL: University of Chicago Press

Harker, Margaret F. (1979) *The Linked Ring: The Secession Movement in Photography in Britain 1892–1910*, London: Heinemann

—— (1988) *Henry Peach Robinson*, Oxford and New York: Blackwell

Harrison, Charles and Wood, Paul (1993) 'Modernity and Modernism Reconsidered', ch. 3 of Paul Wood, Francis Frascina, Jonathan Harris and Charles Harrison *Modernism in Dispute*, London: Yale University Press and the Open University Press

Harrison, Martin (1991) *Appearances: Fashion Photography Since 1945*, London: Jonathan Cape

Harvey, D. (1989) *The Condition of Postmodernity*, Cambridge, MA: Blackwell

Harvie, C., Martin, G. and Scharf, A. (1970) *Industrialisation and Culture 1830–1914*, London: Macmillan and the Open University Press

Hawk, Thomas (2013) 'Why I Quit Getty Images and Why I am Moving My Stock Photography Sales to Stocksy', http://thomashawk.com/2013/03/why-i-quit-getty-images-and-why-im-moving-my-stock-photography-sales-to-stocksy.html

Haworth-Booth, Mark (ed.) (1975) *The Land: Twentieth Century Landscape Photographs*, selected by Bill Brandt, London: Gordon Fraser Gallery

—— (ed.) (1988) *British Photography: Towards a Bigger Picture*, New York: Aperture

—— (1992) *River Scene, France*, Los Angeles, CA: J. Paul Getty Museum

—— (1997) *Photography: An Independent Art*, London: V&A Publications

Hayles, N. Katherine (1999) *How We Became Posthuman: Virtual Bodies in Cybernetics, Literature, and Informatics*, Chicago, IL, and London: University of Chicago Press

Hayward, P. (1993) 'Situating Cyberspace: The Popularisation of Virtual Reality' in P. Hayward and T. Walker (eds) *Future Visions: New Technologies of the Screen*, London: BFI

Heiferman, Marvin (1989) 'Everywhere, All the Time, for Everybody' in Marvin Heiferman and Lisa Phillips (eds) *Image World*, New York: Whitney Museum of Art

Heim, M. (1995) 'The Design of Virtual Reality' in Mike Featherstone and Roger Burrows (eds) *Cyberspace, Cyberbodies, Cyberpunk: Cultures of Technological Embodiment*, London, California and New Delhi: Sage

Heron, Liz and Williams, Val (1996) *Illuminations: Women Writing on Photography from the 1850s to the Present*, London and New York: I.B. Tauris

Hershkowitz, R. (1980) *The British Photographer Abroad: The First Thirty Years*, London: Robert Hershkowitz Ltd

Hewison, Robert (1987) *The Heritage Industry*, London: Methuen

Higonnet, A. (1998) *Pictures of Innocence: The History and Crisis of Ideal Childhood*, London: Thames and Hudson

Hiley, M. (1983) *Seeing Through Photographs*, London: Gordon Frazer

Hill, Paul and Cooper, Thomas (1992) *Dialogue with Photography*, Manchester: Cornerhouse Publications

Hinrichsen, Malte (2013) *Racist Trademarks: Slavery, Orient, Colonialism and Commodity Culture*, Berlin: LIT Verlag

Hirsch, J. (1981) *Family Photography: Context, Meaning and Effect*, New York: Oxford University Press

Hirsch, M. (1997) *Family Frames: Photography, Narrative and Postmemory*, Cambridge, MA: Harvard University Press

Hoelscher, Steven (ed.) (2013) *Reading Magnum: A Visual Archive of the Modern World*, Austin: University of Texas Press

Hoggart, Richard (1957) *The Uses of Literacy*, Harmondsworth: Penguin

Holland, P. (1991) 'The Old Order of Things Changed' in J. Spence and P. Holland (eds) *Family Snaps: The Meanings of Domestic Photography*, London: Virago

—— (1992) *What is a Child?*, London: Virago

—— (1997) 'Press Photography' in A. Briggs and P. Cobley (eds) *Introduction to Media*, London: Longman

—— (2004) *Picturing Childhood: The Myth of the Child in Popular Imagery*, London: I.B.Tauris

Holland, P. and Dewdney, A. (eds) (1992) *The Child, Seen but Not Heard?*, Bristol: Watershed Media Centre. Exhibition catalogue

Holland, Patricia and Sandon, Emma (2006) 'Can Whiskey come too? Re-viewing Cultural Identity at the End of Empire' in Anandi Ramamurthy and Simon Faulkner (eds) *Visual Culture and Decolonisation in Britain*, Aldershot: Ashgate, pp. 153–88

Holmes, Oliver Wendell (1859) 'The Stereoscope and the Stereograph', *Atlantic Monthly* 3. Reprinted in B. Newhall (ed.) (1980) *Photography: Essays and Images*, London: Secker and Warburg

Honey, N. (1992) *Entering the Masquerade: Girls from Eleven to Fourteen*, Bradford: National Museum of Photography, Film and Television

Hopkinson, T. (1962) *In the Fiery Continent*, London: Victor Gollancz

Horne, Donald (1984) *The Great Museum: The Re-presentation of History*, London: Verso

Howard, F. (1853) 'Photography Applied to Fine Art', *Journal of the Photographic Society*, London

Howarth, S. and McLaren, S. (2010) *Street Photography*, London: Thames and Hudson

Howe, P. David (2013) 'Sport, the Body and the Technologies of Disability' in David L. Andrews and Ben Carrington (eds) *A Companion to Sport* (Blackwell Companions to Cultural Studies), Oxford: Wiley-Blackwell

Hudson, D. (1972) *Munby, Man of Two Worlds*, London: John Murray

Huhtamo, Erkki (1996) 'From Kaleidoscope to Cybernerd: Notes Toward an Archeology of Media' in T. Druckery (ed.) *Electronic Culture: Technology and Visual Representation*, New York: Aperture

Hurley, Jack (1972) *Portrait of a Decade: Roy Stryker and the Development of Documentary Photography in the Thirties*, Baton Rouge: Louisiana State University Press

Hutchison, Robert (1982) *The Politics of the Arts Council*, London: Sinclair Browne

Iles, Chrissie and Roberts, Russell (eds) (1997) *In Visible Light*, Oxford: Museum of Modern Art

India Resource Centre (2013) '15 Village Councils Reject Coca-Cola Plans', 18 April, www.indiaresource.org/news/2013/1008.html

Isherwood, C. (1939) *Goodbye to Berlin*, Harmondsworth: Penguin

Isherwood, S. (1988) *The Family Album*, London: Broadcasting Support Services

James, Sarah (2013) 'Making an Ugly World Beautiful? Morality and Aesthetics in the Aftermath' in J. Stallabrass (ed.) *Memory of Fire: Images of War and the War of Images*, Brighton: Photoworks

Jameson, Fredric (1984) 'Postmodernism or the Cultural Logic of Late Capitalism', *New Left Review* 146, July/August

—— (1991) *Postmodernism, Or, the Cultural Logic of Late Capitalism*, London: Verso

—— (1993) 'Postmodernism and Consumer Society' in A. Gray and J. McGuigan (eds) *Studying Culture*, London, New York, Melbourne and Auckland: Edward Arnold

Jay, Martin (1992) 'Scopic Regimes of Modernity' in S. Lash and J. Friedman (eds) *Modernity and Identity*, Oxford: Blackwell

—— (1993) *Downcast Eyes: The Denigration of Vision in Twentieth Century French Thought*, San Francisco: University of California Press

Jeffrey, Ian (2001) 'Revisiting the histories of photography' in Joan Fontcuberta *Photography: Crisis of History*, Barcelona: ACTAR

—— (1981) *Photography, A Concise History*, London: Thames and Hudson

—— (1982) 'Some Sacred Sites', *Creative Camera* 215, November

—— (1991) 'Morality, Darkness and Light: The Metropolis in Pictures' in Martin Caiger-Smith *Site Work*, London: The Photographers' Gallery

Jhally, Sut (1990) *Codes of Advertising*, London: Routledge

—— (2006a) *The Spectacle of Accumulation: Essays in Media, Culture and Politics*, New York: Peter Lang

—— (2006b) 'Advertising, Cultural Criticism and Pedagogy' in *The Spectacle of Accumulation: Essays in Media Culture and Politics*, New York: Peter Lang

Jobling, Paul (1999) *Fashion Spreads: Word and Image in Fashion Photography*, Oxford: Berg

Johannesson, Lena and Knape, Gunnilla (eds) (2003) *Women Photographers – European Experience*, Gothenburg: Acta Universitatis Gothoburgensis

Jones, Amelia (2002) 'The "Eternal Return": Self-Portrait Photography as a Technology of Embodiment', *Signs: Journal of Women in Culture and Society* 27: 4

Jukes, P. (1992) 'The Work of Art in the Domain of Digital Production', *New Statesman and Society*, 17 July: 40–1

Kalogeraki, K. (1991) 'My Father's Land' in J. Spence and P. Holland (eds) *Family Snaps: The Meanings of Domestic Photography*, London: Virago

Kaneko, R. and Vartanian, I. (2009) *Japanese Photobooks of the 1960s and '70s*, New York: Aperture

Kellner, Douglas (2003) *Media Spectacle*, London: Routledge

Kelly, A. (1979) 'Feminism and Photography' in P. Hill, A. Kelly and J. Tagg *Three Perspectives on Photography*, London: ACGB

Kelly, Mary (1981) 'Reviewing Modernist Criticism', *Screen* 22(3)

Kember, S. (1995a) 'Medicine's New Vision' in M. Lister (ed.) *The Photographic Image in Digital Culture*, London and New York: Routledge

—— (1995b) 'Surveillance, Technology and Crime: The James Bulger Case' in M. Lister (ed.) *The Photographic Image in Digital Culture*, London: Routledge

—— (1998) *Virtual Anxiety: Photography, New Technologies and Subjectivity*, Manchester and New York: Manchester University Press.

—— (2003) 'The Shadow of the Object: Photography and Realism' in Liz Wells (ed.) *The Photography Reader*, London and New York: Routledge. Originally published in 1996 in *Textual Practice* 10(1): 145–63

Kemp, Martin and Wallace, Marina (2000) *Spectacular Bodies: The Art and Science of the Human Body from Leonardo to Now*, London: Hayward Gallery Publishing

Kendrick, Walter (1987) *The Secret Museum: Pornography in Modern Culture*, New York: Viking. Republished in 1996 by University of California Press

Kenyon, D. (1992) *Inside Amateur Photography*, London: Batsford

Kern, Stephen (1983) *The Culture of Time and Space 1800–1918*, Cambridge, MA: The MIT Press

Kilbourne, Jean (2000) *Can't Buy My Love: How Advertising Changes the Way We Think and Feel*, New York: Touchstone

Kipnis, Laura (1992) '(Male) Desire and (Female) Disgust: Reading Hustler' in Lawrence Grossberg, Cary Nelson and Paula Treichler (eds) *Cultural Studies*, London and New York: Routledge

Kippin, John (1995) *Nostagia for the Future*, London: The Photographers' Gallery

Kismaric, Susan and Respini, Eva (2004) *Fashioning Fiction in Photography since 1990*, New York: MOMA.

Klein, Naomi (2000) *No Logo: Taking Aim at the Brand Bullies*, Toronto: Knopf

Kosinski, Dorothy (1999) *The Artist and the Camera, Degas to Picasso*, New Haven, CT: Yale University Press

Kotz, Liz (1998) 'Aesthetics of Intimacy' in Deborah Bright (ed.) *The Passionate Camera: Photography and Bodies of Desire*, London and New York: Routledge

Kozloff, Max (1979) *Photography and Fascination*, New Hampshire: Addison House

—— (1987) *The Privileged Eye*, Albuquerque: University of New Mexico Press

Kracauer, Siegfried (1960) 'Photography', ch. 1 of *Theory of Film*, Oxford: Museum of Modern Art

Krauss, Rosalind (1981) 'A Note on Photography and the Simulacral', *October*, Winter. Reprinted in Carol Squiers (ed.) (1991) *The Critical Image*, Seattle: Bay Press, and London: Lawrence and Wishart

—— (1986) *The Originality of the Avant-garde and Other Modernist Myths*, Cambridge, MA: The MIT Press

Krauss, Rosalind and Livingston, Jane (1986) *L'Amour Fou*, London: Arts Council of Great Britain

Kristeva, Julia (1982) *Powers of Horror: An Essay on Abjection*, New York: Columbia University Press

Kruger, Barbara (1983) *We Won't Play Nature to your Culture*, London: Institute of Contemporary Arts

—— (1990) *Love for Sale: The Words and Pictures of Barbara Kruger*, New York: Harry N. Abrams, Inc.

Kuenzli, Rudolf E. (1991) 'Surrealism and Misogyny' in Mary Ann Caws, Rudolf Kuenzli and Owen Raaberg *Surrealism and Women,* Cambridge, MA: The MIT Press

Kuhn, A. (1991) 'Remembrance' in J. Spence and P. Holland (eds) *Family Snaps: The Meanings of Domestic Photography*, London: Virago

—— (2002) *Family Secrets: Acts of Memory and Imagination*, London: Verso

Lager Vestberg, Nina (2008) 'Archival Value: On Photography, Materiality and Indexicality', *photographies* 1(1), March: 49–65

Lalvani, Suren (1996) *Photography, Vision, and the Production of Modern Bodies*, Albany, NY: State University of New York Press

Landau, P.S. and Kaspin, D. (eds) (2002) *Images and Empires: Visuality in Colonial and Post-colonial Africa*, Berkeley, CA: University of California Press.

Lange, Dorothea (1960) 'The Assignment I'll Never Forget' in Beaumont Newhall (ed.) (1980) *Photography: Essays and Images*, London: Secker and Warburg

Lange, Susanne (2006) *Bernd and Hilla Becher: Life And Work*, Cambridge, MA, and London: The MIT Press

Langford, M. (2001) *Suspended Conversations, the Afterlife of Memory in Photographic Albums*, Montreal: McGill-Queens University Press

Larsen, Jonas and Sandbye, Mette (eds) (2013) *Digital Snaps: The New Face of Photography*, London: I.B. Tauris

Latour, Bruno (2005) *Reassembling the Social: An Introduction to Actor Network Theory*, Oxford: Oxford University Press

Laurent, Olivier (2013) 'Jury finds Agence France-Presse, Getty Images Guilty of Wilful Copyright Infringement, Awards $1.22m to Photojournalist', *British Journal of Photography*, 23 November, www.bjp-online.com/2013/11/jury-finds-agence-france-presse-getty-images-guilty-of-wilful-copyright-infringement-awards-1-22m-to-photojournalist/

Lavin, Maud (1993) *Cut with the Kitchen Knife: The Weimar Photomontages of Hannah Höch*, New Haven, CT: Yale University Press

Lawrence, Francis (dir.) (2013) *The Hunger Games: Catching Fire* [film]

Lechte, John (1994) *Fifty Key Contemporary Thinkers*, London: Routledge

Leiss, W., Kline, S. and Jhally, S. (1986) *Social Communication in Advertising*, Toronto: Methuen

Lemagny, Jean-Claude and Rouille, André (1987) *A History of Photography*, Cambridge: Cambridge University Press

Leslie, Esther (2002) *Hollywood Flatlands; Animation, Critical Theory and the Avant-garde*, London: Verso

Lewinski, J. (1978) *The Camera at War*, London: W.H. Allen

Lewis, B. and Harding, D. (eds) (1992) *Kept in a Shoebox: The Experience of Popular Photography*, Bradford: Yorkshire Art Circus/National Museum of Photography, Film and Television

Linfield, Susie (2010) *The Cruel Radiance: Photography and Political Violence*, Chicago: University of Chicago Press

Linkman, Audrey (1993) *The Victorians: Photographic Portraits*, London: Tauris Parke Books

—— (2011) *Photography and Death*, London: Reaktion Books

Linkman, A. and Warhurst, C. (1982) *Family Albums*, Manchester: Manchester Polytechnic

Lipton, Eunice (1980) 'The Laundress in Nineteenth Century French Culture', *Art History* 3(3): 215–313. Abridged version in Francis Frascina and Charles Harrison (1983) *Modern Art and Modernism: A Critical Anthology*, HarperCollins

Lister, M. (ed.) (1995) 'Introductory Essay' in M. Lister (ed.) *The Photographic Image in Digital Culture*, London and New York: Routledge

—— (2012) *The Photographic Image in Digital Culture*, London and New York: Routledge. Revised edition

—— (2013) 'Overlooking, rarely looking and not looking' in Larsen, J. and Sandbye, M. *Digital Snaps: The New Face of Photography*, London: I.B.Tauris

Lister, M., Dovey, J., Giddings, S., Grant, I. and Kelly, K. (2008) *New Media: A Critical Introduction*, London and New York: Routledge

Lloyd, J. (1985) 'Old Photographs, Vanished Peoples and Stolen Potatoes', *Art Monthly* 83, February

Lovell, Terry (1980) 'Is Art a Form of Knowledge?' in *Pictures of Reality*, ch. 5.3, London: BFI

Lury, Celia (1992) 'Popular Culture and the Mass Media' in R. Bocock and K. Thompson (eds) *Social and Cultural Forms of Modernity*, Cambridge: Polity Press

—— (1998) *Prosthetic Culture: Photography, Memory and Identity*, London and New York: Routledge.

Lyons, Nathan (1966) *Photographers on Photography*, Englewood Cliffs, NJ: Prentice Hall

Lyotard, Jean-François (1985) 'Argument', *Camerawork 32*, Summer

McCauley, Elizabeth Anne (1994) *Industrial Madness: Commercial Photography in Paris 1848–1871*, New Haven, CT, and London: Yale University Press

Macleod, Duncan (2010) 'McCain Pride Its All Good', 25 September, http://theinspiration room.com/daily/2010/mccain-pride-its-all-good/

McClintock, A. (1995) *Imperial Leather: Race, Gender and Sexuality in the Colonial Conquest*, London: Routledge

McCullin, Don (2003) *Don McCullin*, London: Jonathan Cape

Macdonald, G. (1979) *Camera: A Victorian Eyewitness*, London: Batsford. Based on a Granada television series

McGrath, R. (1984) 'Medical Police', *Ten/8* 14: 13–18

McRobbie, Angela (1997) 'Bridging the Gap: Feminism, Fashion and Consumption', *Feminist Review* 55, Spring: 73–89

Machin, David (2004) 'Building the World's Visual Language: The Increasing Global Importance of Image Banks in Corporate Media', *Journal of Visual Communication* 3(3): 316–36

Magli, Patrizia (1989) 'The Face and the Soul' in M. Feher *et al.* (eds) *Zone 4: Fragments for a History of the Human Body, Part Two*, Cambridge, MA: Zone and The MIT Press

Makela, Tapio (1997) 'Photography, Post-photography', *Creative Camera*, April/May

Malina, R.F. (1990) 'Digital Image – Digital Cinema: The Work of Art in the Age of Post-mechanical Reproduction', *Leonardo*, Supplemental Issue: 33–8

Mann, S. (1992) *Immediate Family*, London: Phaidon

Manovich, L. (1996) 'The Automation of Sight: From Photography to Computer Vision', in T. Druckery (ed.) *Electronic Culture: Technology and Visual Representation*, New York: Aperture.

—— (2001) 'The Synthetic Image and its Subject' in *The Language of New Media*, Cambridge, MA, and London: The MIT Press

—— (2003) [1995] 'The Paradoxes of Digital Photography' in L. Wells (ed.) *The Photography Reader*, London and New York: Routledge.

Marks, Laura (2002) *Touch: Sensuous Theory and Multisensory Media*, Minneapolis: University of Minnesota Press

Martin, R. (1991) 'Unwind the Ties That Bind' in J. Spence and P. Holland (eds) *Family Snaps: The Meanings of Domestic Photography*, London: Virago

Martin, Rosy and Spence, Jo (2003) 'Photo-therapy: Psychic Realism as a Healing Art?' in Liz Wells (ed.) *The Photography Reader*, London: Routledge. Reprinted from *Ten.8* 30, 1988

Marvin, C. (1988) *When Old Technologies Were New*, New York: Oxford University Press

Matthews, S. and Wexler, L. (2000) *Pregnant Pictures*, London: Routledge

Mavor, C. (1996) *Pleasures Taken: Performances of Sexuality and Loss in Victorian Photographs*, London: I.B. Taurus

Mayer, Paul A. (1999) *Computer Media and Communication*, Oxford and New York: Oxford University Press

Mayhew, H. (1967 [1861]) *London Labour and the London Poor*, London: Frank Cass

Mayle, Peter (1983) *Thirsty Work: Ten Years of Heineken Advertising*, London: Macmillan

Maynard, P. (2000) [1997] *The Engine of Visualization: Thinking Through Photographs*, Ithaca, NY: Cornell University Press

Mayne, R. (1986) *The Street Photographs of Roger Mayne*, London: V&A Museum

Mellencamp, Patricia (1992) *High Anxiety: Catastrophe, Scandal, Age and Comedy*, Bloomington: Indiana University Press

Messaris, Paul (1996) *Visual Persuasion: The Role of Images in Advertising*, Thousand Oaks, CA: Sage.

Metz, Christian (1985) 'Photography and Fetish', *October* 34, Autumn

Meyer, Moe (ed.) (1994) *The Politics and Poetics of Camp*, London: Routledge

Miller, Mark (1994) *Spectacle: Operation Desert Storm and the Triumph of Illusion*, New York: Poseidon Press

Minto, C.S. (1970) *Victorian and Edwardian Scotland from Old Photographs*, London: Batsford

Mitchell, W.J. (1992) *The Reconfigured Eye: Visual Truth in the Post-photographic Era*, Cambridge, MA: The MIT Press

Mitchell, W.J.T. (2004) *What do Images Want? The Lives and Loves of Images*, Chicago: University of Chicago Press

Mitter, Swasti (1986) 'Flexibility and Control: The Case of Benetton' in *Common Fate Common Bond; Women in the Global Economy*, London: Pluto

Moholy-Nagy, László (1967) *Painting, Photography, Film*, London: Lund Humphries

Montoussamy-Ashe, Jeanne (1985) *Viewfinders: Black Women Photographers*, New York: Dodd, Mead

Morris, Roderick C. (1992) 'The Best Possible Taste', *Spectator*, 15 February

Morrish, John (2001) 'Getty's New Digital Empire', *Business 2.0*, April edition, Bizjournals, Seattle

Morton, Tom (2004) 'Helen Chadwick' (review), *Frieze* 86, October

Mulvey, Laura (1975) 'Visual Pleasure and Narrative Cinema', *Screen* 16(3): 6–18

—— (1981) 'Visual Pleasure and Narrative Cinema' in T. Bennett, S. Boyd-Bowman, C. Mercer and J. Woollacott (eds) *Popular Television and Film*, London: BFI and the Open University. Also in Mulvey, L. (1989) *Visual and Other Pleasures*, London: Macmillan

Murray, Heather (2007) 'Monstrous Play in Negative Spaces: Illegible Bodies and the Cultural Construction of Biometric Technology', *The Communication Review* 10: 347–65

Musello, C. (1979) 'Family Photography' in J. Wagner (ed.) *Images of Information*, London: Sage

Myers, Kathy (1986) *Understains: Sense and Seduction in Advertising*, London: Comedia

—— (1990) 'Selling Green' in Carol Squiers (ed.) *The Critical Image: Essays on Contemporary Photography*, Seattle: Bay Press

Nead, L. (1992) *The Female Nude: Art, Obscenity and Sexuality*, London and New York: Routledge

Neale, S. (1985) *Cinema and Technology: Images, Sound, Colour*, London: Macmillan

Neumaier, Diane (ed.) (1996) *Reframings, New American Feminist Photographics*, Philadelphia, PA: Temple University Press

Newhall, Beaumont (1982 [1937]) *The History of Photography*, New York: MOMA, fifth edition, revised and enlarged

Nichols, Bill (1981) *Image and Ideology*, Bloomington: University of Indiana Press

—— (1988) 'The Work of Culture in the Age of Cybernetic Systems', *Screen* 29(1), Winter

Nochlin, Linda (1978) *Realism*, Harmondsworth: Penguin

Nunberg, G. (1996) 'Farewell to the Information Age', in G. Nunberg (ed.) *The Future of the Book*, Berkeley: University of California Press

Nye, David (1985) *Image Worlds: Corporate Identities at General Electric 1890–1930*, Cambridge, MA: The MIT Press

Nye, David E. and Gidley, Mick (eds) (1994) *American Photographs in Europe*, Amsterdam: VU University Press

O'Brien, Michael and Waits, Tom (2011) *Hard Ground*, Austin: University of Texas Press

Ofcom (2013) *Children and Parents: Media Use and Attitudes Report* London: Office of Communication Research Report

Official Transcripts (2013) *Morel vs. AFP and Getty*, November, http://photomorel.com/?page_id=2049

Ohrn, Karen Becker (1980) *Dorothea Lange and the Documentary Tradition*, Baton Rouge: Louisiana State University Press

Okabe, Daisuke (2004) 'Emergent Social Practices, Situations and Relations through Everyday Camera Phone Use', Keio University, www.itofisher.com/mito/archives/okabe_seoul.pdf

Olalquiaga, Celeste (1992) *Megalopolis: Contemporary Cultural Sensibilities*, Minneapolis: University of Minnesota Press

Olin, Margaret (2009) 'Touching Photographs: Roland Barthes's "Mistaken" Identification' in Geoffrey Batchen (ed.) *Photography Degree Zero: Reflections on Roland Barthes's Camera Lucida*, Cambridge, MA: The MIT Press

O'Reilly, John (1998) 'Death is Probably the Last Pornographic Issue Left', *Guardian*, 2 February

Orvell, Miles (2003) *American Photography*, Oxford: Oxford University Press

Osborne, Brian S. (2003) 'Constructing the State, Managing the Corporation, Transforming the Individual: Photography, Immigration and the Canadian National Railways, 1925–30' in J. Schwartz and J. Ryan (eds) *Picturing Place: Photography and the Geographical Imagination*, London: I.B. Tauris

Paasonen, Susanna, Nikunen, Kaarina and Saarenmaa, Laura (2007) *Pornification: Sex and Sexuality in Media Culture*, Oxford: Berg

Parr, M. (1986) *The Last Resort: Photographs of New Brighton*, Stockport: Dewi Lewis Publishing

—— (1995) *Small World: A Global Photographic Project, 1987–1994,* Stockport: Dewi Lewis Publishing

Parr, Martin and Badger, Gerry (2004) *The Photobook: A History*, Vol. 1, London: Phaidon Press

—— (2006) *The Photobook: A History*, Vol. 2, London: Phaidon Press

—— (2014) *The Photobook: A History*, Vol. 3, London: Phaidon Press

Parr, M. and Stasiak, J. (1986) *'The Actual Boot': The Photographic Post-card Boom 1900–1920*, Bradford: A.H. Jolly (Editorial) Ltd/National Museum of Photography, Film and Television. Exhibition catalogue

Parsons, Sarah (2008) 'Public/Private Tensions in the Photography of Sally Mann', *History of Photography* 32(2)

Penlake, R. (1899) *Home Portraits for Amateur Photographers*, London: Upcott Gill

Penn, Irving (1974) *Worlds in a Small Room*, London: Studio Vista

Petro, Patrice (ed.) (1995) *Fugitive Images*, Bloomington: Indiana University Press

Pfrunder, P. (2011) *Swiss Photobooks from 1927 to the Present: A Different History of Photography*. Zurich: Lars Muller Publishers

Phaidon (1997) *The Photography Book*, London: Phaidon

Phillips, Christopher (ed.) (1989) *Photography in the Modern Era: European Documents and Critical Writings 1913–1940*, New York: MOMA

Phizacklea, Annie (1990) 'The Benetton Model' in *Unpackaging the Fashion Industry: Gender, Racism and Class in Production*, London: Routledge

Pickerell, Jim (2012) 'Stock Photo Market Statistics', *Selling Stock: Inside the Stock Image Industry*, 29 March, www.selling-stock.com/Article/stock-photo-market-statistics

—— (2013a) 'Can Getty Take Market Share From Shutterstock?', *Selling Stock: Inside the Stock Image Industry*, 4 September, www.selling-stock.com/Article/can-getty-take-market-share-from-shutterstock

—— (2013b) 'A Litany of Woes for Career Photographers', Black Star Rising, 15 April, http://rising.blackstar.com/a-litany-of-woes-for-career-photographers.html

—— (2013c) 'Decline in Return-per-image', *Selling Stock: Inside the Stock Image Industry*, 16 September, www.selling-stock.com/article/decline-in-return-per-image

Pinney, C. (1997) *Camera Indica: The Social Life of Indian Photographs*, London: Reaktion Books

Piper, K. (1991) 'Fortress Europe: Tagging the Other' in P. Wombell (ed.) *PhotoVideo: Photography in the Age of the Computer*, London: Rivers Oram Press

Pollock, Griselda (1977) 'What's Wrong with "Images of Women"?'. Reprinted in R. Parker and G. Pollock (eds) (1987) *Framing Feminism*, London: Pandora Press

—— (1990) 'Missing Women – Re-thinking Early Thoughts on Images of Women' in Carol Squiers (ed.) *The Critical Image: Essays on Contemporary Photography*, Seattle: Bay Press

Posner, Jill (1982) *Spray it Loud*, London: Routledge

Pozner, Jennifer L. (2007) 'Top Model's Beautiful Corpses: The Nexus of Reality TV's Misogyny and Ad Industry Ideology', www.wimnonline.org/WIMNsVoicesBlog, accessed 1 July 2008

Price, D. (1983) 'Photographing the Poor and the Working Class', *Framework* 22(22), Autumn

Price, Mary (1994) *The Photograph: A Strange, Confined Space*, Stanford, CA: Stanford University Press

Prochaska, David (1991) 'Fantasia of the Phototheque: French Postcard Views of Senegal', *African Arts*, October

Pryce, W.T.R. (1994) 'Photographs and Picture Postcards' in M. Drake and R. Finnegan (eds) *Studying Family and Community History: 19th and 20th Centuries*, Cambridge: Cambridge University Press and the Open University Press

Puglia, Stephen (2003) 'Preservation Reformatting: Digital Technology vs. Analog Technology', 18th Annual Preservation Conference, US National Archives and Records Administration, www.archives.gov/preservation/conferences/papers-2003/puglia.html

Pultz, John (1995a) *The Body and the Lens: Photography 1839 to the Present*, New York: Harry N. Abrams, Inc

—— (1995b) *Photography and the Body*, London: Weidenfeld & Nicolson

Punt, Michael (1995) 'The Elephant, the Spaceship and the White Cockatoo: An Archaeology of Digital Photography' in M. Lister (ed.) *The Photographic Image in Digital Culture*, London and New York: Routledge

Quartermaine, P. (1992) 'Johannes Lindt: Photographer of Australia and New Guinea' in M. Gidley (ed.) *Representing Others: White Views of Indigenous Peoples*, Exeter: University of Exeter Press

Rabinowitz, Paula (1994) *They Must be Represented: The Politics of Documentary*, London: Verso

Rahir, Patrick (2003) 'Pan-European security body slams TV for turning war into entertainment', *Agence France Presse*, 1 April

Ramamurthy, A. (2003) *Imperial Persuaders: Images of Africa and Asia in British Advertising*, Manchester: Manchester University Press

—— (2012) 'Absences and Silences: The Representation of the Tea Picker in Colonial and Fair Trade Advertising', *Visual Culture in Britain* 13(3): 367–81

Ramamurthy, A. and Wilson, K. (2013) '"Come and Join the Freedom Lovers!": Racism, Appropriation and Resistance in Advertising' in *Colonial Advertising and Commodity Racism*, Münster: Lit Verlag

Ray-Jones, T. (1974) *A Day Off: An English Journal*, London: Thames and Hudson

Rexer, Lyle (2002) *Photography's Antiquarian Avant-Garde: The New Wave in Old Processes*, New York: Harry N. Abrams

Richards, Thomas (1990) *Commodity Culture in Victorian Britain*, London: Verso

—— (1993) *The Imperial Archive: Knowledge and the Fantasy of Empire*, London: Verso

Ride, P. (1997) 'Photography and Digital Art', *Creative Camera*, April/May

Riis, J.A. (1918) *The Making of an American*, New York: Macmillan

Ritchin, F. (1990a) *In Our Own Image: The Coming Revolution in Photography*, New York: Aperture

—— (1990b) 'Photojournalism in the Age of Computers' in Carol Squiers (ed.) *The Critical Image*, Seattle: Bay Press

—— (2013) *Bending the Frame: Photojournalism, Documentary and the Citizen*, New York: Aperture

Roberts, John (1993) *Renegotiations: Class, Modernity and Photography*, Norwich: Norwich Gallery, Norfolk Institute of Art and Design

—— (ed.) (1997) *The Impossible Document: Photography and Conceptual Art in Britain 1966–1976*, London: Camerawords

—— (1998) *The Art of Interruption: Realism, Photography and the Everyday*, Manchester: Manchester University Press

Robertson, G., Mash, M., Tickner, L., Bird, J., Curtis, B. and Putnam, T. (eds) (1994) *Travellers' Tales: Narratives of Home and Displacement*, London: Routledge

Robins, Corinne (1984) *The Pluralist Era: American Art 1968–1981*, New York: Harper & Row

Robins, K. (1991) 'Into the Image: Visual Technologies and Vision Cultures' in P. Wombell (ed.) *PhotoVideo: Photography in the Age of the Computer*, London: Rivers Oram Press

—— (1995) 'Will Images Move Us Still?' in M. Lister (ed.) *The Photographic Image in Digital Culture*, London and New York: Routledge

Rodchenko, Alexander (1928) 'Against the Synthetic Portrait, for the Snapshot', *Novy LEF: New Left Front of the Arts*. Reprinted in C. Phillips (ed.) (1989) *Photography in the Modern Era: European Documents and Critical Writings 1913–1940*, New York: MOMA

Rodgerson, Gillian and Wilson, Elizabeth (eds) (1991) *Pornography and Feminism: The Case Against Censorship*, London: Lawrence and Wishart

Rogers, Brett (ed.) (1994) *Documentary Dilemmas: Aspects of British Documentary Photography 1983–1993*, London: British Council

Rose, Gillian (2010) *Doing Family Photography: The Domestic, the Public and the Politics of Sentiment*, Farnham: Ashgate

—— (2013) 'How Digital Technologies do Family Snaps, Only Better' in *Digital Snaps: The New Face of Photography*, London: I.B.Tauris

Rosenblum, Naomi (2010 [1994]) *A History of Women Photographers*, New York, London and Paris: Abbeville Press

—— (2007) *A World History of Photography*, New York, London and Paris: Abbeville Press (previous editions 1984, 1989, 1997)

Rosler, Martha (1989) 'In, Around and Afterthoughts (on Documentary Photography)' in Richard Bolton (ed.) *The Contest of Meaning: Critical Histories of Photography*, Cambridge, MA: The MIT Press

—— (1991) 'Image Simulations, Computer Manipulations, Some Considerations', *Ten-8* 2(2), *Digital Dialogues*

Roth, Andrew (ed.) (2004) *The Open Book*, Gothenburg: The Hasselblad Center

Rowland, Anna (1990) *The Bauhaus Source Book*, ch. 6, 'Graphics', Oxford: Phaidon

Royal Photographic Society (1977) *Directory of British Photographic Collections*, London: Heinemann

Rubinstein, Daniel and Sluis, Katrina (2008) 'A Life More Photographic', *photographies* 1(1), Spring: 9–28

Ruby, Jay (1995) *Secure the Shadow: Photography and Death in America*, Cambridge, MA, and London: The MIT Press

Ryan, James R. (1997) *Picturing Empire: Photography and the Visualisation of the British Empire*, London: Reaktion Books

Said, Edward (1985 [1978]) *Orientalism*, London: Penguin

Salvemini, Lorella Pagnucco (2002) *United Colours: The Benetton Campaigns*, London: Scriptum Editions

Sampson, A. (1983) *Drum: An African Adventure and Afterwards*, London: Hodder and Stoughton

Sandbye, M. (2013) 'The Family Photo Album as Transformed Social Space in the Age of Web 2.0' in Ulrick Ekman (ed) *Throughout: Art and Culture Engaging with Ubiquitous Computing*, Boston: MIT

Sarvas, Risto and Frohlich, David (2011) *From Snapshots to Social Media: The Changing Picture of Domestic Photography*, London: Springer

Sassoon, Joanne (2004) 'Photographic Materiality in the Age of Digital Reproduction' in Elizabeth Edwards and Janice Hart (eds) *Photographs Objects Histories*, London and New York: Routledge.

Savan, Leslie (1990) 'Logo-rrhea', *Voice*, 24 November, New York

Scharf, Aaron (1974) *Art and Photography*, Harmondsworth: Pelican, revised edition

Schildkrout, Enid (1991) 'The Spectacle of Africa Through the Lens of Herbert Lang', *African Arts*, October

Schwarz, Ori (2010) 'On Friendship, Boobs and the Logic of the Catalogue: Online Self-Portraits as a Means for the Exchange of Capital', *Convergence* 16(2): 163–83

Scott, Clive (2007) *Street Photography from Atget to Cartier-Bresson*, London: I.B. Tauris

Segal, Lynne and Macintosh, Mary (eds) (1992) *Sex Exposed: Sexuality and the Pornography Debate*, London: Virago

Sekula, Allan (1978) 'Dismantling Modernism, Reinventing Documentary (Notes on the Politics of Representation)' in J. Liebling (ed.) *Photography: Current Perspectives*, Rochester, NY: Light Impressions Co.

—— (1986) 'The Body and the Archive', *October* 39 (16). Reprinted in Richard Bolton (ed.) (1989) *The Contest of Meaning: Critical Histories of Photography*, Cambridge, MA: The MIT Press

—— (2003) 'Reading an Archive: Photography Between Labour and Capital' in Patricia Holland, Jo Spence and Simon Watney (eds) *Photography/Politics Two*, London: Comedia, 1986. Reprinted in Liz Wells (ed.) (2003) *The Photography Reader*, London: Routledge

Sharma, Sanjay and Sharma, Ashwani (2003) 'White Paranoia: Orientalism in the Age of Empire', *Fashion Theory: The Journal of Dress, Body and Culture* 7(3/4): 1–18

Shayon, Sheila (2012) 'Coca-Cola Continues to Open Happiness, From Coke Machine to Truck to Table', *Brandchannel*, 19 September, www.brandchannel.com/home/post/Coca-Cola-Open-Happiness-091912.aspx

Sherman, Cindy (1991) 'Reading an Archive' in Brian Wallis and Marcia Tucker (eds) *Blasted Allegories*, Cambridge, MA: The MIT Press

—— (1997) *Retrospective*, London: Thames and Hudson

Shields, Rob (2003) *The Virtual*, London and New York: Routledge

Shinkle, Eugenie (ed.) (2008) *Fashion as Photograph: Viewing and Reviewing Images of Fashion*, London: I.B. Tauris

Slater, D.R. (1983) 'Marketing Mass Photography' in H. Davis and P. Walton (eds) *Language, Image, Media*, Oxford: Blackwell

—— (1991) 'Consuming Kodak' in J. Spence and P. Holland (eds) *Family Snaps: The Meanings of Domestic Photography*, London: Virago

—— (1995a) 'Photography and Modern Vision: The Spectacle of "Natural Magic"' in C. Jenks (ed.) *Visual Culture*, London: Routledge

—— (1995b) 'Domestic Photography and Digital Culture' in M. Lister (ed.) *The Photographic Image in Digital Culture*, London and New York: Routledge

—— (1997) *Consumer Culture and Modernity*, Cambridge, MA: Blackwell

Sluis, K. (2011) Talk at Roehampton University

Smith, Clarissa (2007) *One for the Girls: The Pleasures and Practices of Reading Women's Porn*, Bristol: Intellect Press

Smith, L. (1998) *The Politics of Focus: Women, Children and Nineteenth Century Photography*, Manchester: Manchester University Press

Snyder, Joel (1980) 'Picturing Vision', *Critical Enquiry* 6, Spring: 499–526

—— (1994) 'Territorial Photography' in W.J.T. Mitchell (ed.) *Landscape and Power*, London: University of Chicago Press

Snyder, J. and Allen, N.W. (1975) 'Photography, Vision, and Representation', *Critical Enquiry* 2, Autumn: 143–69

Solanke, A. (1991) 'Complex Not Confused' in J. Spence and P. Holland (eds) *Family Snaps: The Meanings of Domestic Photography*, London: Virago

Soloman, J. (1995) 'Interrogating the Holiday Snap' in J. Spence and J. Soloman *What Can a Woman do with a Camera?*, London: Scarlet Press

Solomon-Godeau, Abigail (1991a) *Photography at the Dock: Essays on Photographic History, Institutions and Practices*, Minneapolis: University of Minnesota Press

—— (1991b) 'Who is Speaking Thus?' in A. Solomon-Godeau op. cit.

—— (1991c) 'Reconsidering Erotic Photography: Notes for a Project of Historical Salvage' in A. Solomon-Godeau op. cit.

—— (2004) 'Modern Style: Dressing Down', *ArtForum International* 42(9): 192(5)

Sontag, Susan (1979) *On Photography*, Harmondsworth: Penguin

—— (2002) *On Photography*, Harmondsworth: Penguin. A new edition with an introduction by John Berger.

—— (2003) *Regarding the Pain of Others*, London: Hamish Hamilton

—— (2004) 'Regarding the Torture of Others', *New York Times Magazine*

Soutter, Lucy (2013) *Why Art Photography?* London and New York: Routledge

Spence, J. (1987) *Putting Myself in the Picture*, London: Camden Press

—— (1991) 'Soap, Family Album Work . . . and Hope' in J. Spence and P. Holland (eds) *Family Snaps: The Meanings of Domestic Photography*, London: Virago

—— (1995) *Cultural Sniping*, London: Routledge

Spence, J. and Holland, P. (eds) (1991) *Family Snaps: The Meanings of Domestic Photography*, London: Virago

Spence, J. and Soloman, J. (eds) (1995) *What Can a Woman do with a Camera?*, London: Scarlet Press

Spender, H. (1978) 'Humphrey Spender: M.O. Photographer', *Camerawork* 11

Spiegel, Lynn (1992) *Make Room for TV: Television and the Family Ideal in Postwar America*, Chicago, IL: University of Chicago Press

Squiers, Carol (ed.) (1990) *The Critical Image*, London: Lawrence and Wishart

—— (1992) 'The Corporate Year in Pictures' in R. Bolton (ed.) *The Contest of Meaning: Critical Histories of Photography*, Cambridge, MA: The MIT Press

—— (2003) 'Class Struggle: The Invention of Paparazzi Photography and the Death of Diana, Princess of Wales' in Carol Squiers (ed.) *Over Exposed: Essays on Contemporary Photography*, New York: The New Press

—— (2005) *The Body at Risk: Photography of Disorder, Illness and Healing*, Berkeley: University of California Press

—— (2013) *What is A Photograph?* New York: International Center of Photography and DelMonico Books

Stafford, B.M. (1991) *Body Criticism, Imaging the Unseen in Enlightenment, Art and Medicine*, Cambridge, MA: The MIT Press

Stallabrass, J. (1997) 'Sebastiao Salgado and Fine Art Photojournalism', *New Left Review* 223

Stallabrass, J. (ed) (2013) *Memory of Fire: Images of War and the War of Images*, Brighton: Photoworks

Stallybrass, Peter and White, Allon (1986) *The Politics and Poetics of Transgression*, Ithaca, NY: Cornell University Press

Stanley, J. (1991) 'Well, Who'd Want an Old Picture of me at Work?' in J. Spence and P. Holland (eds) *Family Snaps: The Meanings of Domestic Photography*, London: Virago

Stapely, G. and Sharpe, L. (1937) *Photography in the Modern Advertisement,* London: Chapman and Hall

Steele-Perkins, Chris (ed.) (1980) *About 70 Photographs*, London: Arts Council of Great Britain

Stein, S. (1981) 'The Composite Photographic Image and the Composition of Consumer Ideology', *Art Journal*, Spring

—— (1983) 'Making Connections with the Camera: Photography and Social Mobility in the Career of Jacob Riis', *Afterimage* 10(10)

—— (1992) 'The Graphic Ordering of Desire: Modernisation of a Middle-class Women's Magazine 1919–1939' in R. Bolton (ed.) *The Contest of Meaning: Critical Histories of Photography*, Cambridge, MA: The MIT Press

Stokes, Philip (1992) 'The Family Photograph Album: So Great a Cloud of Witnesses' in Graham Clarke (ed.) *The Portrait in Photography*, London: Reaktion Books

Stott, W. (1973) *Documentary Expression and Thirties America*, London: Oxford University Press

Strand, Paul (1917) 'Photography', *Camera Work* 49/50, reprinted in B. Newhall (1982) *The History of Photography*, New York: MOMA

—— (1980) *Photography: Essays and Images*, London: Secker and Warburg

Strauss, D.L. (2003) *Between the Eyes: Essays on Photography and Politics,* New York: Aperture Books

Struck, J. (2011) *Private Pictures: Soldiers' Inside View of War*, London: I.B.Tauris

Struk, Janina (2003) *Photographing the Holocaust: Interpretations of the Evidence*, London: I.B.Tauris

Sullivan, Constance (ed.) (1990) *Women Photographers*, London: Virago

Swingler, S. (2000) 'Victorian/Edwardian Women as Photographers and Keepers of the Family Album' in Liz Wells, Kate Newton and Catherine Fehily (eds) *Shifting Horizons*, London: I.B. Tauris

Szarkowski, John (1966) 'Introduction' in *The Photographer's Eye,* New York: MOMA

—— (1989) *Photography Until Now*, New York: MOMA

Tabloid Tales (2003) *Anthea Turner* BBC1, 3 June

Tagg, John (1988) *The Burden of Representation: Essays on Photographies and Histories*, London: Macmillan

Taylor, Janelle S. (2000) 'Of Sonograms And Baby Prams: Prenatal Diagnosis, Pregnancy, and Consumption', *Feminist Studies*, Summer

Taylor, John (1994) *A Dream of England: Landscape, Photography and the Tourist's Imagination*, Manchester: Manchester University Press

Taylor, Mark C. (1997) *Hiding*, Chicago, IL, and London: University of Chicago Press

Taylor, Roger (2001) 'Topographer with Attitude' in Fay Godwin *Landmarks*, Stockport: Dewi Lewis Publishing

Tenno, Helge (2009) 'A Bigger Idea – Branded Context and Brand Situations', *Slideshare*, 31 January, www.slideshare.net/helgetenno/a-bigger-idea-branded-context-and-brand-situations

Thomas, Alan (1978) *The Expanding Eye*: *Photography and the Nineteenth Century Mind*, London: Croom Helm

Thomas, Deborah Willis (1985) *Black Photographers 1840–1940: An Illustrated Bio-bibliography*, New York: Garland

Thompson, F.M.L. (ed.) (1990) *The Cambridge Social History of Britain 1750–1850*, Vol. 2, *People and Their Environment*, Cambridge: Cambridge University Press

Thomson, J. (1877) *Street Life in London*, n.p.n.

Tietjen, Friedrich (2003) 'Experience to See – Jeff Wall's Photo Works: Modes of Production and Reception' in *Jeff Wall. Photographs,* Vienna: Museum Moderner Kunst Stiftung Ludwig

Townsend, Chris (1998) *Vile Bodies: Photography and the Crisis of Looking*, Munich and New York: Prestel-Verlag and Channel Four Television Corporation

Trachtenberg, A. (1982) *The Incorporation of America*, New York: Hill and Wang

—— (1989) *Reading American Photographs*, New York: Hill and Wang

Tucker, Anne (1973) *The Woman's Eye*, New York: Knopf

—— (1984) 'Photographic Facts and Thirties America' in David Featherstone (ed.) *Observations: Essays on Documentary Photography*, Carmel, CA: Friends of Photography

Tucker, Jennifer (2013) 'Eye on the Street: Photography in Urban Public Spaces', *Radical History Review* 114, Fall: 7–18

Turner, Peter (1987) *History of Photography*, London: Hamlyn

Ugrina, Luciana (2014) 'Celebrity Biometrics: Norms, New Materialism and the Agentic Body in Cosmetic Surgery Photography', *Fashion Theory* 18(1): 27–44

Urry, J. (1990) *The Tourist Gaze: Leisure and Travel in Contemporary Societies*, London: Sage

Urry, J. and Larsen, J. (2011) *The Tourists' Gaze 3.0*, London: Sage

van Alphen, E. (1999) 'Nazism in the Family Album: Christian Boltanski's *Sans Souci*' in Marianne Hirsch (ed.) *The Familial Gaze,* Hanover, NH: Dartmouth College

Van Gelder, Hilde and Westgeest, Helen (2011) *Photography Theory in Historical Perspective*, Oxford: Wiley-Blackwell

Van House, Nancy A. 'Personal Photography, Digital Technologies and the Uses of the Visual', *Visual Studies* (Special Issue: 'New Visual Technologies: Shifting Boundaries, Shared Moments'), Volume 26, Issue 2, 2011, pp.125–34

Van Schendel, W. (2002) 'A Politics of Nudity: Photographs of the "Naked Mru" of Bangladesh', *Modern Asian Studies* 36(2)

Vance, Carole S. (1990) 'The Pleasures of Looking: The Attorney General's Commission on Pornography versus Visual Images' in Carol Squiers (ed.) *The Critical Image: Essays on Contemporary Photography*, Seattle: Bay Press

van der Ploeg, Irma (2003) 'Biometrics and the Body as Information: Normative Issues of the Socio-Technical Coding of the Body' in David Lyon (ed.) *Surveillance as Social Sorting: Privacy, Risk, and Digital Discrimination*, New York: Routledge

Van de Ven, Ariadne (2011) 'The Eyes of the Street Look Back: In Kolkata with a Camera around my Neck', *Photographies* 4(2): 139–55

Vanhaelen, A. (2002) 'Street Life in London and the Organization of Labour', *History of Photography*, Autumn.

Veltman, K.H. (1996) 'Electronic Media: The Rebirth of Perspective and the Fragmentation of Illusion' in T. Druckery (ed.) *Electronic Culture: Technology and Visual Representation*, New York: Aperture

Virilio, P. (1989) *War and Cinema*, London: Verso

Virilio, P., Baudrillard, J. and Hall, S. (1988) 'The Work of Art in the Electronic Age', *Block* 14

Waldby, Catherine (2000) *The Visible Human Project; Informatic Bodies and Posthuman Medicine*, London and New York: Routledge

Walker, Ian (1995) 'Desert Stones or Faith in Facts' in M. Lister (ed.) *The Photographic Image in Digital Culture*, London and New York: Routledge

—— (2002) *City Gorged with Dreams*, Manchester: Manchester University Press

—— (2007) *So Exotic, So Homemade: Surrealism, Englishness and Documentary Photography*, Manchester: Manchester University Press

Walkerdine, V. (1991) 'Behind the Painted Smile' in J. Spence and P. Holland (eds) *Family Snaps: The Meanings of Domestic Photography*, London: Virago

Wall, Jeff (1995) 'About Making Landscapes' in Lynda Morris (ed.) (2002) *Jeff Wall*, Norwich: Norwich Gallery and Birmingham: Article Press

Ward, Dick (1990) *Photography for Advertising*, London: Macdonald Illustrated

Warner, Marina (1990) 'Parlour Made' in David Brittain (ed.) *Creative Camera: 30 Years of Writing*, Manchester: Manchester University Press

Warner Marien, Mary (1988) 'Another History of Photography', *Afterimage*, October: 4–5

—— (1991) 'Toward a New Prehistory of Photography' in Daniel P. Younger (ed.) *Multiple Views*, Albuquerque: University of New Mexico Press

—— (1997) *Photography and its Critics, a Cultural History, 1839–1900*, Cambridge and New York: Cambridge University Press

—— (2014 [2002]) *Photography, a Cultural History*, London: Laurence King Publishing Ltd. Fourth edition

Watney, S. (1991) 'Ordinary Boys' in J. Spence and P. Holland (eds) *Family Snaps: The Meanings of Domestic Photography*, London: Virago

Watriss, Wendy and Zamora, Lois (eds) (1998) *Image and Memory: Photographs from Latin America 1866–1994*, Austin: University of Texas Press

Weaver, Mike (1982) *Photography as Fine Art*, London: Thames and Hudson

—— (1986) *The Photographic Art*, London: Herbert

—— (1989a) *The Art of Photography*, London: Royal Academy of Arts/New Haven, CT: Yale University Press

—— (1989b) *British Photography in the Nineteenth Century: The Fine Art Tradition*, Cambridge: Cambridge University Press

Weernink, Wim (1979) *La Lancia: 70 Years of Excellence*, London: Motor Racing Publications

Weibel, Peter (1996) 'The World as Interface' in Timothy Druckery (ed.) *Electronic Culture*, New York: Aperture

Wells, Liz (1992) 'Judith Williamson, Decoding Advertisements' in M. Barker and A. Beezer (eds) *Reading into Cultural Studies*, London: Routledge

—— (ed.) (1994) *Viewfindings, Women Photographers: 'Landscape' and Environment*, Tiverton, Devon: Available Light

___ (ed.) (2009) *Photography: A Critical Introduction*. Fourth edition. London and New York: Routledge

—— (2011) *Land Matters: Landscape Photography, Culture and Identity*, London: I.B. Tauris

Werge, J. (1890) *The Evolution of Photography*, London

Weski, T. (2003) 'Cruel and Tender' in E. Dexter and T. Weski (eds) *Cruel and Tender*, London: Tate Publishing

West, Nancy Martha (2000) *Kodak and the Lens of Nostalgia*, Virginia: University of Virginia Press

Westerbeck, Colin and Meyerowitz, Joel (1994) *Bystander: A History of Street Photography*, London: Thames and Hudson

Wilkinson, Helen (1997) '"The New Heraldry": Stock Photography, Visual Literacy and Advertising in 1930s Britain', *Journal of Design History* 10(1)

Willett, John (1978) *The New Sobriety, Art and Politics in the Weimar Period*, London: Thames and Hudson

Williams, Linda (1995) 'Corporealized Observers: Visual Pornographies and the Carnal Density of Vision' in Patrice Petro *Fugitive Images*, Bloomington: Indiana University Press

Williams, Raymond (1974) *Television, Technology and Cultural Form*, London: Fontana

—— (1976) *Keywords*, London: Fontana

—— (1979) 'The Arts Council', *Political Quarterly*, Spring

—— (1980) 'Advertising the Magic System' in *Problems in Materialism and Culture*, London: Verso

—— (1989) 'When Was Modernism' in *The Politics of Modernism*, London: Verso

Williams, Val (1986) *Women Photographers. The Other Observers, 1900 to the Present*, London: Virago. Revised edition 1991, *The Other Observers. Women Photographers from 1900 to the Present*

—— (1994) *Who's Looking at the Family?*, London: Barbican Art Gallery. Exhibition catalogue and introduction

—— (1998) *Look at Me: Fashion and Photography in Britain, 1960 to the Present*, London: British Council

Williamson, Judith (1978) *Decoding Advertisements: Ideology and Meaning in Advertising*, London: Marion Boyars

—— (1979) 'Great History that Photographs Mislaid' in P. Holland, J. Spence and S. Watney (eds) *Photography/Politics: One*, London: Comedia

Willis, A-M. (1990) 'Digitisation and the Living Death of Photography' in P. Hayward (ed.) *Culture, Technology, and Creativity in the Late Twentieth Century*, London: John Libbey and Co. Ltd

Winship, Janice (1987a) 'Handling Sex' in R. Betterton (ed.) *Looking On: Images of Femininity in the Visual Arts and Media*, London: Pandora

—— (1987b) *Inside Women's Magazines*, London: Pandora

Wollen, Peter (1982 [1978]) 'Photography and Aesthetics', *Screen* 19(4) Winter. Reprinted in *Readings and Writings*, London: Verso and New Left Books

Wombell, P. (1991) *PhotoVideo: Photography in the Age of the Computer*, London: Rivers Oram Press

Ziff, T. (1991) 'Taking New Ideas Back to the Old World' in P. Wombell (ed.) *PhotoVideo: Photography in the Age of the Computer*, London: Rivers Oram Press

Žižek, Slavoj (1997) 'Multiculturalism, or the Cultural Logic of Multinational Capitalism', *New Left Review* I/225, September–October

Index

Note: Page numbers in **bold** indicate illustrations. Page numbers followed by 'm' refer to marginal text.